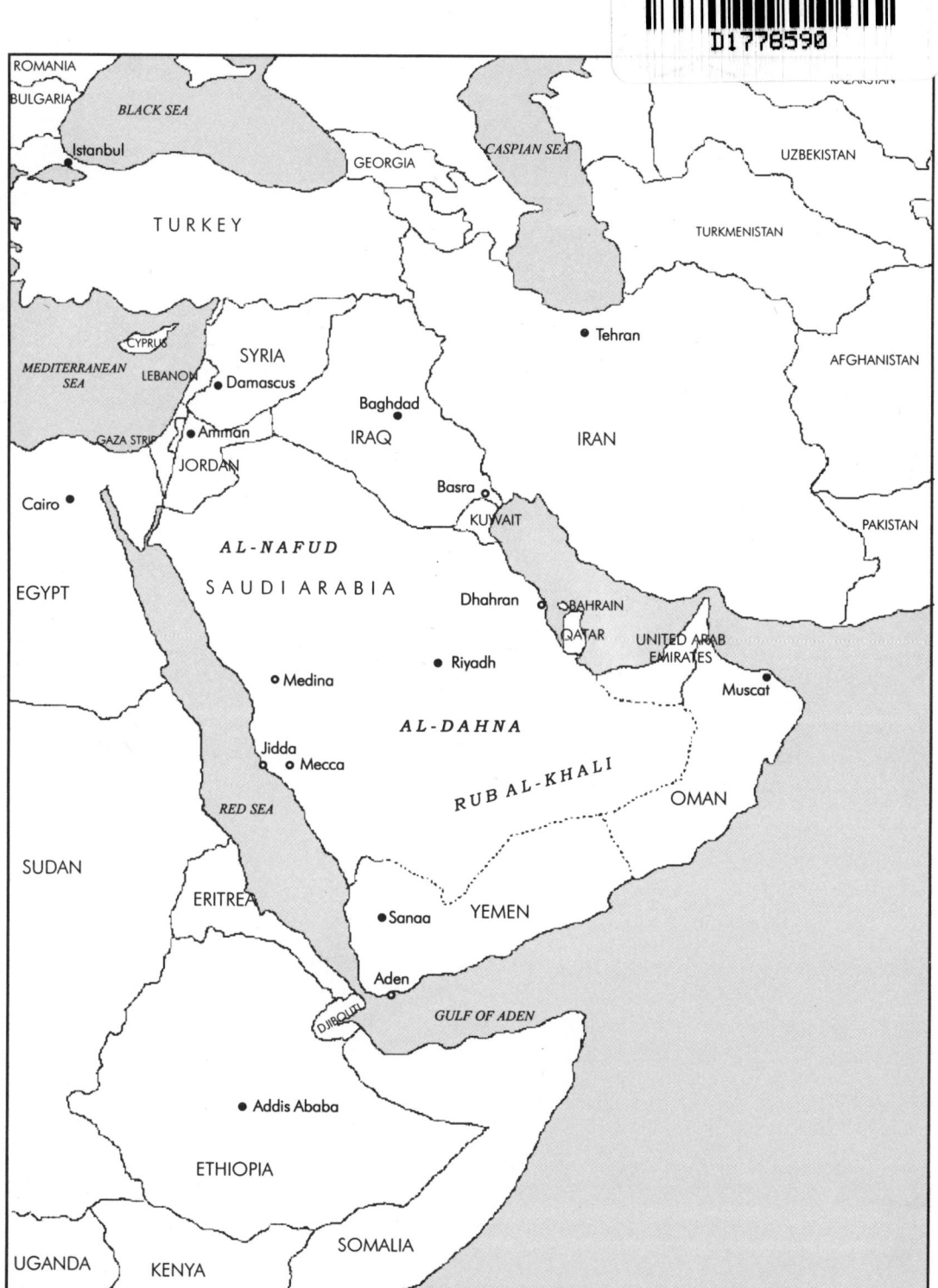

The Arabian Peninsula

THE HISTORY OF SAUDI ARABIA

Alexei Vassiliev

THE HISTORY OF SAUDI ARABIA

Saqi Books

British Library Cataloguing-in-Publication Data
A catalogue record for this book is available from the
British Library

ISBN 0 86356 935 8 (hb)

©Alexei Vassiliev, 1998
This edition first published 1998
In-house editor: Jana Gough

Saqi Books
26 Westbourne Grove
London W2 5RH

Contents

A Note on the Spelling and Transliteration System 7
List of Abbreviations and Acronyms 8
Simplified Genealogy of the House of Saud 10

Preface 11

Part One
1. Arabia on the Eve of the Emergence of Wahhabism: Economy, Society, Politics 29
2. Muhammad ibn Abd al-Wahhab and his Teaching 64
3. The Rise of the First Saudi State (1745–1811) 83
4. The Social and Political System of the Emirate of al-Diriya 112
5. The Wahhabis Routed by the Egyptians (1811–1818) 140
6. From the Fall of al-Diriya to the Egyptian Evacuation of Arabia (1818–1840) 158
7. The Second Saudi State (1843–1865) 174
8. The Disintegration of the Emirate of Riyadh and the Rise of Jabal Shammar 192
9. The Renaissance of the Emirate of Riyadh in the Early Twentieth Century (1902–1914) 210
10. Najd and Hijaz during the First World War (1914–1918) 235

Contents

Part Two

11.	The Consolidation of the Arabian Territories around Najd (1918–1926)	253
12.	Increased Centralization and the Ikhwan Movement (1926–1934)	268
13.	The Socio-political Structure of Saudi Arabia after its Creation	287
14.	The Oil Concessions	312
15.	Saudi Arabia and the Second World War (1939–1945)	321
16.	Domestic and Foreign Policy (1945–1958)	328
17.	The Struggle for Power and its Outcome (1958–1973)	354
18.	Domestic and Foreign Policy (the 1970s and the early 1980s)	393
19.	The Socio-economic Structure of Saudi Arabia in the Oil Era (the 1950s to the early 1980s)	401
20.	The Political Regime (the 1950s to the early 1980s)	436
21.	Economy, Society, Politics (the 1980s and the 1990s)	452

Conclusion   474

Notes   483
Bibliography   538
Glossary   558
Index   565

A Note on the Spelling and Transliteration System

Since the text contains an abundance of Arabic names, it was decided to avoid a fully transliterated system; thus no diacritical marks are used. They would have made the text unnecessarily complicated for the reader who has no knowledge of Arabic, whereas the Arabist will easily deduce the true Arabic form.

In the Arabic words, *dh* stands for emphatic *d*, the fifteenth letter of the Arabic alphabet. *Gh* represents deep velar *g*, the nineteenth letter. *H* is used to denote both the equivalent of the English *h* and the guttural *h*, respectively the twenty-seventh and sixth letters. *Q* is pronounced as a deep velar *k* (the twenty-first letter). *S* may mean the simple or the emphatic consonant (respectively the twelfth and fourteenth letters). Similarly, *t* may be simple or emphatic (the third and sixteenth letters). *Th* is pronounced as in 'through'. *Z* represents three consonants: simple, interdental (*th* in 'this') and emphatic (respectively the eleventh, ninth and seventeenth letters). *Ain* (the eighteenth letter) and *hamza* (guttural explosive) are ignored. No distinction is made between long and short vowels.

Although we have aimed at uniformity, some exceptions were unavoidable. Well-established spellings that contradict our system, such as Gamal Abdel Nasser (rather than Jamal Abd al-Nasir) and Cairo (rather than al-Qahira) have been retained. The original spelling has been retained in quotations from English-language works, but the variants employed by the authors (such as Kassem for Qasim) are not included in the indexes.

Abbreviations and Acronyms

AD	air defence
ALCO	Arabian-Italian Engineering Contractors
Aramco	Arabian-American Oil Company
AWACS	Airborne Warning and Control System
b/d	barrel(s) per day
bn	billion(s)
CENTO	Central Treaty Organization
CIA	(US) Central Intelligence Agency
cu. m	cubic metre(s)
EEC	European Economic Community
FAO	Food and Agriculture Organization
FLOSY	Front for the Liberation of Occupied Southern Yemen
g	gram(s)
GCC	Gulf Cooperation Council
GDP	gross domestic product
GNP	gross national product
IBRD	International Bank for Reconstruction and Development
IDA	International Development Association
IMF	International Monetary Fund
IPC	Iraq Petroleum Company
ITT	International Telephone and Telegraph Corporation
JV	joint venture
kg	kilogram(s)
km	kilometre(s)

Abbreviations and Acronyms

lb	pound(s) [weight]
m	million(s); metre(s)
mb/d	million barrel(s) per day
NATO	North Atlantic Treaty Organization
NCO	non-commissioned officer
OAPEC	Organization of Arab Petroleum Exporting Countries
OPEC	Organization of Petroleum Exporting Countries
PDRSY	People's Democratic Republic of South Yemen
PDRY	People's Democratic Republic of Yemen (South Yemen)
Petromin	General Petroleum and Mineral Organization
PLO	Palestine Liberation Organization
RDF	Rapid Deployment Force
SAMA	Saudi Arabian Monetary Agency
SOCAL	Standard Oil of California
sq. km	square kilometre(s)
Tapline	Trans-Arabian pipeline
TASS	[the Soviet news agency]
TBD	torpedo-boat destroyer
UAE	United Arab Emirates
UAR	United Arab Republic
UN	United Nations
US	United States
USSR	Union of Soviet Socialist Republics
YAR	Yemen Arab Republic (North Yemen)

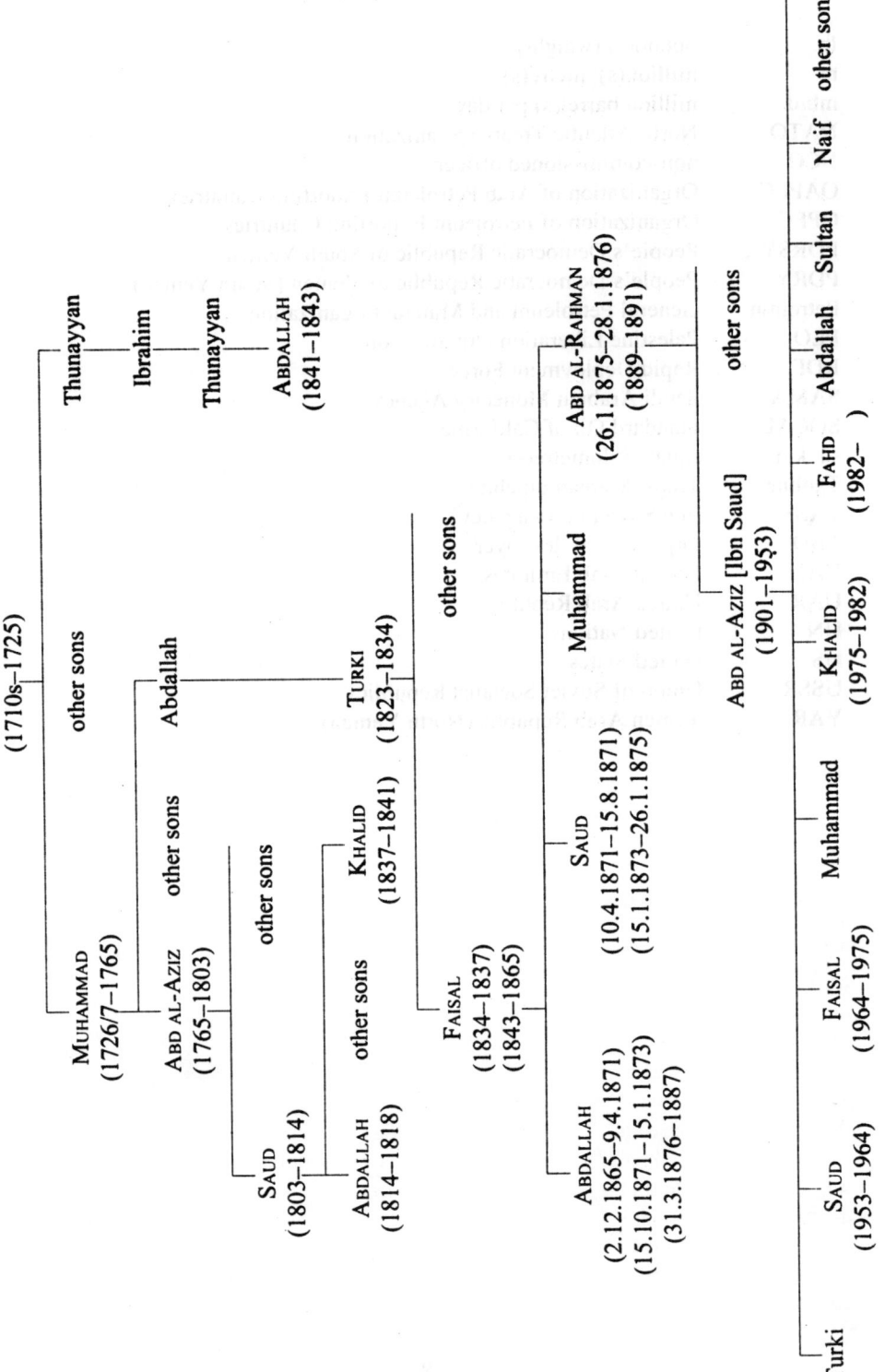

Preface

This is a history of the Saudi Arabian state from its emergence in 1745 to the early 1990s. The main issues under consideration are the evolution of the social and political structures of Saudi society, the Wahhabi movement for a reform of Islam, Saudi Arabia's place in the modern world, the impact of oil on its society, the emergence of new social groups, and the contradictions within Saudi society and the ways in which they are resolved.

~※~

Saudi Arabia, which had a population of some 12 million indigenous citizens in the early 1990s, has acquired far greater influence in the contemporary world than might initially be thought. Accounting for almost one third of the world's explored oil resources outside Russia, Central Asia and China, Saudi Arabia has become the single largest oil producer and exporter. Incapable of using all the proceeds from its exports of that valuable raw material (measured in astronomical figures) within the country, Saudi Arabia has also become one of the world's largest exporters of capital. In absolute terms, the wealth of the royal house of the Al Saud exceeds that of the richest financial magnates of the US, Japan and Europe.

The decisions taken in Riyadh are not always independent – some of them are even imposed by outside forces. They nevertheless influence, whether directly or indirectly, the balance of payments, the rate of economic development and the inflation rate in the United States and other countries; the future of the dollar; the course and outcome of the Arab-Israeli conflict; and the stability of regimes in a number of developing countries. The most serious armed conflict after the Cold War – the 1990–91 Gulf war

Preface

– was caused not only by Iraq's seizure of Kuwait but also by the threatened occupation and dismemberment of Saudi Arabia.

Saudi Arabia's unique financial and economic situation is given added weight by its role as the birthplace of Islam. The two holiest cities of Islam are on Saudi territory: Mecca with the Kaaba, towards which believers turn during prayers and where they perform the *hajj* (pilgrimage), as prescribed by Islamic canons; and Medina, the resting-place of the body of Muhammad, the founder of Islam. The increasing tension between Islam and the West, combined with growing religious sentiment in the Muslim world, means that many socio-political conflicts (including those between states and ethnic groups in the Islamic world itself) have religious overtones.

The socio-economic structure of Saudi Arabia has undergone fundamental changes within the lifespan of literally one or two generations. A market economy was introduced from the outside into a feudal-tribal society that was not prepared for such a transformation and lacked the necessary personnel, state and public institutions and legal system. This resulted in a painful disintegration of the traditional economy, society and mores. At the time that oil was discovered in Saudi Arabia in the early 1930s, the country was ruled by one of the world's most archaic regimes: a new society is now being built, one whose characteristics defy the usual definitions.

The growing interest in Saudi Arabia has naturally been accompanied by an increase in the number of publications on its problems. Numerous books and articles were published in Russia (then a part of the USSR) in the 1970s and 1980s. They are listed in the first edition of the present author's *Bibliography of Saudi Arabia* and in its second edition (to be published shortly). Since the publication of the first Russian edition of the present book in 1982, no new works on the kingdom's history or economic and socio-political evolution from its creation in the mid-eighteenth century to the present day have appeared in Russian.

The chronology of the events described here goes up to the early 1990s, when Saudi Arabia regained its stability after the Gulf war crisis. Subsequent events are too recent for an unbiased historical analysis and are therefore outside the scope of the present work.

The sources for the history of Saudi Arabia may be divided into several groups. First are the Arab chronicles, written both by supporters and opponents of the Al Saud dynasty and the Wahhabi teaching and by neutral observers. It should be noted at the outset that we apply the term 'Wahhabism', adopted in the Western literature, to the religious-political teaching that arose in Arabia in the eighteenth century, in spite of the fact that it has no coinage in Saudi Arabia itself. Another important group of sources are works by Muhammad ibn Abd al-Wahhab and his followers and by prominent Arabian *ulama* (theologians).

Then there are descriptions by European travellers, diplomats, scholars and intelligence officers who visited Arabia and the neighbouring countries between the eighteenth and the twentieth century. The gazetteers of the British administration in

Preface

India throw light on several issues relating to the nineteenth and early twentieth centuries. Information on Saudi Arabia's economy, social relations and legal system is available in government publications. Some US handbooks with detailed data on Saudi Arabia may be treated as primary sources. We have also used relevant documents from the Russian archives.

Arab chronicles

To our knowledge, there is only one Arab chronicle written by someone who observed the development of the Wahhabi movement and the Saudi state from its very beginning. It is *The History of Najd, Called the Garden of Ideas and Concepts* by Husain ibn Ghannam (d. 1811), an *alim* (theologian; sing. of *ulama*) from al-Hasa. The first part reproduces several works by Muhammad ibn Abd al-Wahhab while the second gives the history of the Wahhabis' wars from 1746 to 1796/97.[1] Ibn Ghannam was a follower of Ibn Abd al-Wahhab's teaching. In his opinion, Allah Himself inspired the Wahhabis, whereas their enemies were led by the devil. Although searching for data on the socio-political structure of the first Saudi state in his work is like looking for a needle in a haystack, Ibn Ghannam's annals are nevertheless a uniquely important source. They reflect the author's personal observations and provide first-hand information.

Another chronicle, *The Symbol of Glory in the History of Najd*, is by Uthman ibn Abdallah ibn Bishr (d. 1871/72), a prominent Najdi religious scholar from the oasis of Shaqra in Washm province. He was a contemporary witness to many of the events in Arabia covered by Ibn Ghannam's chronicle. Ibn Bishr also supported the Wahhabi teaching, but his views were less narrow than those of his predecessor. He recorded valuable facts concerning the structure of the first Saudi state and social life in Arabia. His chronicle opens with the events of 1745, with digressions into earlier Arabian history. The last year covered is 1854.

The chronicles of Ibn Bishr and Ibn Ghannam agree on many matters. Ibn Bishr quotes in full his predecessor's elegy for Ibn Abd al-Wahhab, for example, which is also available in *The History of Najd*. However, their descriptions of numerous facts, their interpretation of events and their dates and figures differ on many occasions. Perhaps Ibn Bishr never saw Ibn Ghannam's work. He mentions Ibn Ghannam's death in the preface and speaks of his merits as an *alim* and poet, but is silent on his historical works and does not mention him among the other chroniclers. A cross-checking of Ibn Ghannam's and Ibn Bishr's data with reports by Europeans confirms their authenticity. Arab and European historians have only discovered these two sources in the twentieth century.

The chronicle of the Al Saud annexed by the French historian Félix Mengin to his *Histoire de l'Egypte sous le Gouvernement de Mohammed-Aly* has escaped the attention of orientalists for some reason. Mengin compiled his chronicle on the basis of information from Ibn Abd al-Wahhab's grandson, who was exiled to Egypt after the seizure of al-Diriya in 1818, and perhaps from other Wahhabis. It seems strange that scholars who know of the existence of Mengin's book have not used that excellent source. Mengin also quotes valuable data on Arabian society from the reports of the Egyptian administration in Najd in the 1810s.

In recent decades, orientalists and some Arab historians have begun to pay attention to *The Brilliance of the Meteor in the Life of Muhammad ibn Abd al-Wahhab* [*Lam al-Shihab* . . .], a chronicle whose original is preserved in the British Museum. Most authors consider the work to be anonymous. The 764-page manuscript covers the period of Arabian history from the 1730s to December 1817, when the description suddenly ends. Although the author treats Ibn Abd al-Wahhab with respect, he considers his teaching as *ibtida* (heresy), basing his views on the opinions of 'shaikhs from Basra and al-Zubair'.

The Brilliance of the Meteor is a series of sketches, based on accounts by participants in the events in question, together with rumours and legends. This does not deprive the chronicle of its unquestionable merits, which rank it with the three other Arab sources of that era – the annals of Ibn Ghannam and Ibn Bishr and Mengin's account of the Wahhabi chronicle. Compiled by an author who disagreed with the Wahhabi teaching, *The Brilliance of the Meteor* is nevertheless objective and valuable precisely because of its independent and unofficial character. It is an additional source of information on the character of feudal-tribal relations in Arabia, trade and handicrafts in Najd, forms of law among the nomadic tribes, the organization of power, taxation, the judicial system and the armed forces in the first Saudi state.

Ibn Abd al-Wahhab's works quoted in the manuscript are undoubtedly the oldest versions to have come down to us. Two of them – *The Book of Monotheism* and *The Book of Detection of Doubts in Monotheism* – agree with recent publications in their main points. At the same time, they indicate that the texts of Ibn Abd al-Wahhab's works published in the twentieth century either underwent modification and cuts or were based on other versions.

Additional information on the Wahhabi movement and the first Saudi state, and materials allowing established facts to be cross-checked, can be found in the works by Ahmad ibn Zaini Dahlan from Hijaz, Muhammad ibn Ali al-Shawkani from Yemen, Salil-ibn-Razik from Oman, Abd al-Rahman al-Jabarti, the renowned Egyptian historian, Muhammad al-Nabhani from Bahrain, Uthman ibn Sanad al-Basri from Basra and Ibrahim al-Haidari al-Baghdadi from Baghdad.

Ibn Bishr's chronicle of developments in Najd was continued by Ibrahim ibn Isa (b. 1853/54 in Shaqra). His *The Pearl Necklace of the Developments that Occurred in Najd* ends with the events of 1885/86, but it was written or concluded during the rule of Abd al-Aziz (Ibn Saud), the founder of modern Saudi Arabia, who is extolled in the introduction. The book was unavailable to the present writer, who relied instead on its version, *The History of Some Events that Occurred in Najd*.

A later manuscript, *The Symbol of Happiness and Glory in the Good Thoughts about the History of Hijaz and Najd*, by Abd al-Rahman ibn Nasir, covers events up to the mid-1930s. The present writer relied on its narration by the British orientalist H. St John Philby and several Arab historians.

Another important source is a chronicle by Dhari ibn Fuhaid ibn Rashid, which gives the Shammari viewpoint of events in Najd in the second half of the nineteenth and the early twentieth centuries. *The History of the Saudi Kings* by Saud ibn Hizlul deals with the late-nineteenth and early twentieth centuries. Its author belonged to the Al Thunayyan, a collateral branch of the Al Saud.

In recent years, further manuscript chronicles have been discovered and quoted in scholarly works. That by Abdallah al-Bassam has been used by the present author as a source of information on the creation of Saudi Arabia in the first third of the twentieth century.

Works by Muhammad ibn Abd al-Wahhab and his followers are essential in the study of Wahhabi ideology. There are numerous manuscript versions, some of which are found in European libraries and museums. The works that express the credo of Wahhabism – *The Book of Monotheism* (the earliest of all, written in the 1730s), *The Book of Detection of Doubts in Monotheism, The Questions of Jahiliya Debated between Allah's Messenger and the People of Jahiliya* and *A Brief Description of the Messenger's Life* – are mentioned as early as in Ibn Ghannam's and/or Ibn Bishr's annals. Ibn Abd al-Wahhab's other works, including *Edification for One Who Derives Benefit from the Unbelief of One Who Deviates from Monotheism, The Principles of the Faith, The Dignity of Islam, Advice to the Muslims, Based on the Hadith and on the Seal of the Prophets, Three Principles and Their Evidence* and numerous *Messages* appear in the bibliography to *The History of the Islamic Peoples* by C. Brockelman.

Ibn Abd al-Wahhab's published works follow the early copies of the late eighteenth and the first half of the nineteenth centuries, which seem to have been modified later. The data collected by European orientalists on the Wahhabi teaching largely correspond to the dogma stated in them.

Ibn Abd al-Wahhab's son Abdallah was also the author of several theological works. One of them, *The Message*, was translated into English from an Arabic manuscript in *The Journal of the Asiatic Society of Bengal* (1874, vol. 43, part 1, pp. 68–82), where the author is erroneously mentioned as the religious leader's grandson, and then in *The Sunni Gift and the Wahhabi Masterwork from Najd*, a Wahhabi miscellany (1923/24). It is valuable because of its lack of excessive quotations from the traditions and comments and its clear expression of some of the principles of Wahhabism.

Ibn Abd al-Wahhab's grandson, Abd al-Rahman ibn Hasan, was a prolific writer on theological issues. His *Discovery of the Glorious* is a detailed commentary on *The Book of Monotheism*. Ahmad ibn Nasir ibn Uthman al-Muammari's *Message* also follows the general principles of Wahhabism. Its author, a Najdi religious scholar, was a descendant of the noble family of Al Muammar.

It is far more difficult nowadays to find anti-Wahhabi writings. Besides the above-mentioned works by Ahmad ibn Zaini Dahlan and Salil-ibn-Razik, two manuscripts on questions of dogma, preserved in the library of Tübingen (Germany), are worth mentioning: *A Message of Objection to Ibn Abd al-Wahhab* by Muhammad ibn Afaliq al-Hanbali and *Old Questions in Reply to the Wahhabis* by Ibn al-Suwaidi.

Preface

Accounts by Europeans who visited Arabia and the neighbouring countries in the eighteenth and early nineteenth centuries

The Danish traveller Carsten Niebuhr was the first to bring reports about the Wahhabis to Europe more than 200 years ago. Although Comte Constantin François de Volney, a French Encyclopaedist and traveller, did not go to Arabia, he visited Syria and Palestine in the 1770s. His notes about the Arab bedouin, based on his observation of the tribe of Wahidat, who roamed near Gaza, and on accounts of the tribes of inner Arabia, are characterized by acute observations and judgement. Badia-y-Leblich, a Spaniard and Napoleon's agent, visited Hijaz and Mecca in 1807 under the name of Ali bey.

John Lewis Burckhardt occupies a prominent place among the European travellers. A British subject of Swiss origin, he was an indomitable traveller. Hijaz, where he stayed in 1814–15, was just one stage in his wanderings. He collected a wealth of information on Arabia and the Arabs' way of life from his talks with people from Hijaz and Najd. Burckhardt studied not only the Wahhabis' history and ideology and the structure of the first Saudi state, but also social relations among both the bedouin and the settled people, and the law. He also took an interest in the family, the various forms of ownership and the taxation system. His erudition and his broad outlook, combined with a rare intellectual honesty, enabled him to write works which have immeasurably enriched our knowledge of Arabia in the eighteenth and nineteenth centuries. Burckhardt's numerous merits also include his captivating style, a great contrast to the weary boredom of many Europeans' travel notes.

In 1819 Captain George F. Sadlier, a British officer, crossed the Arabian peninsula from al-Qatif to Yanbu. Europeans who visited the neighbouring countries also reported on Arabia. First place among the works of this kind belongs to the *Histoire des Wahabis* [The History of the Wahabis] (1810) by Louis Alexandre Olivier de Corancez, the French consul in Aleppo. His work contains much information on the political history, structure and ideology of the Saudi state, but is not free from errors and superficial judgements. J. Raymond, a French artilleryman in the service of the pasha of Baghdad, collected information in Iraq and submitted it to the French ministry of foreign affairs. Sir H. Jones Brydges, the East India Company's political agent in Basra (from 1784) and subsequently in Baghdad, published his recollections several decades after his return from the Arab world.

The Russian press mainly derived information on the Wahhabis from West European channels. The earliest report (after Volney's *Voyage* was translated into Russian) seems to have appeared in *Vestnik Evropy* in 1803: 'Arabia is destined to be the cradle of the Asian revolutions. Its new prophet Abd al-Wahhab has gathered numerous troops and is approaching Mecca.' The next articles on developments in Arabia are to be found in *Zhurnal Razlichnykh Predmetov Slovesnosti* (1805) and *Vestnik Evropy* (1819).

Sadlier and other European travellers who visited the Arabian peninsula in the nineteenth century collected an impressive array of materials on its socio-political life. Whether expanding, confirming or disproving the works by Burckhardt, Volney,

Preface

Niebuhr and the Arab chroniclers, they broadened the study of Arabian society of the eighteenth, nineteenth and early twentieth centuries.

James R. Wellsted, a British officer, visited Oman and travelled along the Arabian coast in the 1830s. At the same time, the Frenchman Maurice Tamisier visited Hijaz and Asir. Professor George A. Wallin, a Finnish scholar, travelled in Hijaz and northern Arabia in the 1840s, and the British traveller Richard Burton visited Hijaz and the Syrian desert in the 1850s. Charles Didier of France came to Mecca in 1854. William Palgrave, a member of the Society of Jesus and a French agent, infiltrated into central Najd and visited Riyadh (the capital of the restored Wahhabi state), Qasim (a province of Najd) and al-Hasa in the 1860s. Whether Palgrave actually undertook such a journey was repeatedly questioned because of numerous errors in his descriptions, but it has now been established beyond any doubt. Colonel Lewis Pelly, the British resident in Bushire, went to Riyadh in 1864. The Italian Carlo Guarmani visited northern Najd at almost the same period. Charles M. Doughty, the British archaeologist and writer, travelled in northern Najd and Hijaz between 1876 and 1878. His work is considered a masterpiece of travel literature and is full of interesting information.

Among other travellers one should also mention Charles Huber of France, who went to northern Najd and Hijaz in 1878 and 1883–84 and was killed there; Wilfred and Lady Anne Blunt, who visited the Syrian desert and Jabal Shammar in 1878–79 and 1881; the Russian stud-owners S. A. Stroganov and A. G. Shcherbatov, who travelled in the Syrian desert in 1888 and 1890; and Davletshin, a Russian officer, who was in Hijaz in the late 1890s.

Important works on the Arabian bedouin include those by M. von Oppenheim, a German Arabist and intelligence officer, who travelled in the Syrian desert in the 1890s and published his three-volume study some decades later.

The golden period of the European exploration of Arabia continued into the first half of the twentieth century. Two names are especially prominent – those of H. St John Philby and H. R. P. Dickson. Both spent the greater part of their lives in Arabia, studying its geography, ethnography and social relations. Philby, a British army officer in India, had been with the British expeditionary corps in Iraq since 1917 and soon became the British political agent at Ibn Saud's court. In the early 1920s he was appointed British political commissioner to Transjordan. In 1925 he retired from government service and settled in Riyadh, embracing Islam some years later. He had the agency for Ford cars in Arabia for several years. Philby was among the mediators who concluded the agreement with and granted the concession to Standard Oil of California, thus laying the foundations of Aramco, the world's largest oil producer. Philby surveyed several areas of Saudi Arabia, including the Rub al-Khali desert, and left numerous descriptions of his travels.

Dickson travelled less widely. As British political agent in Bahrain (*c.* 1920) and then in Kuwait (1929–36), he visited the central areas of the peninsula. His *The Arab of the Desert* and *Kuwait and Her Neighbours* contain important and sometimes unique descriptions of the life, economic activities and social structure of the bedouin tribes as well as providing invaluable information on the history of Saudi Arabia and Kuwait.

T. E. Lawrence deserves special mention. He was a British liaison officer at the sharif of Mecca's office during the anti-Turkish revolt of the Arabs of Hijaz. After the First World War, the British propaganda machine needed heroes and Lawrence was the ideal candidate. His works, written with undoubted literary talent, increased his glory. But they deal with his role in the anti-Turkish revolt rather than with the revolt itself or Arabia, describing events through the prism of his own false pride. His works are of scant scientific significance.

Alois Musil, a Czech scholar, travelled in northern Arabia and the neighbouring countries from the late 1890s to 1917. During the First World War, he carried out assignments for the Austro-Hungarian General Staff in Jabal Shammar. He was the author of numerous works, including several on ethnography. A. Jaussen's study of the bedouin of northern Arabia and R. Montagne's works are also worth mentioning.

Records in various forms have been left by A. D. M. Carruthers, a British naturalist, who worked in north-western Arabia and al-Nafud; B. Raunkiaer of Denmark, who visited Najd in 1912; the German C. R. Raswan, who worked in the Syrian desert from 1911 to 1914 and in the early 1920s; and the Britons S. S. Butler, G. E. Leachman and R. E. Cheesman. Gertrude Bell, a British intelligence officer and prominent Arabist, was the author of several works. Bertram Thomas described his travels in central Arabia in the 1920s and published surveys of central and southern Arabia.

Works by other authors of the same period, such as William B. Seabrook, an American traveller, D. van der Meulen, the Dutch consul in Jidda, and John Bagot Glubb, the future commander of the Arab Legion in Transjordan and a prolific writer on the Arab world, provide some understanding of the socio-economic and political situation of Arabia in the 1930s and 1940s.

A number of books by Europeans and Americans who visited Arabia from the 1930s to the 1950s – C. A. Nallino, G. de Gaury, A. Zischka, G. Kheirallah, F. Balsan, H. Armstrong, D. A. Howarth, E. Rutter, F. J. Tomiché, K. S. Twitchell, A. Falk, M. S. Cheney, R. H. Sanger and P. Harrison – provide illuminating and frequently unique data on Arabian society, enabling the reader to follow the transformations in social institutions that had persisted there for centuries. Information on the European explorers of Arabia is available in works by A. Zehme, A. Ralli, S. M. Zwemer, D. G. Hogarth, V. V. Barthold, R. H. Kiernan and J. Pirenne.

Documents and publications of the British administration in India form another major group of sources. The most important of them is a collection of treaties between India and the neighbouring countries, compiled by C. U. Aitchison and published in Calcutta in 1892. Its second expanded edition appeared in Delhi in 1933.

J. G. Lorimer, an official of the Indian Civil Service, prepared the *Gazetteer of the Persian Gulf, Oman and Central Arabia* (1908–15) for official use. Consisting of several thousand large-format pages, it became available to foreign scholars only after the Second World War. The *Gazetteer* gives an indication of the views of the administration of British India on the situation in the Gulf and reveals the information it possessed about the region from the eighteenth to the early twentieth century. Lorimer's work has a drawback, however: there are few references to the sources and it is often unclear whether he derived his information from the works by Burckhardt, Corancez, Mengin, Bridges and others or from reports by British agents.

Preface

In this sense, J. A. Saldana's publications are of great value. They deal with events in the Gulf in the nineteenth and early twentieth centuries and are based on the archives of the government of British India. The present writer unfortunately failed to gain access to them and had to rely on the abundant references in R. B. Winder's *Saudi Arabia in the Nineteenth Century*.

Official publications

Important data, including those on the composition of Saudi society, are available in the *Statistical Annual* of the Saudi ministry of economy and finance. Collections of Saudi documents and statements are also of interest.

The Saudi-British conflict over the al-Buraimi oases in the late 1940s and early 1950s gave rise to a three-volume *Memorial of the Government of Saudi Arabia* and a two-volume memorial by the British government. Although the Saudi publication is aimed at proving Riyadh's rights to the disputed territory, it includes some new data on tribes and taxation.

Among twentieth-century Arabic sources by participants in the events described in the present book, one is comparable in importance with *The Brilliance of the Meteor* and Ibn Bishr's *The Symbol of Glory*. It is the four-volume *The Arabian Peninsula in the Era of King Abd al-Aziz* by Khair al-Din al-Zirikli. While it is an unashamed apologia for the founder of Saudi Arabia, the Al Saud and the Saudi regime as a whole, it nevertheless contains much valuable information on many aspects of the country's life – from its history to the organization of the army, from the legal and judicial system to ethnography, from the economy to anecdotes concerning everyday life at the royal court. Having had long experience in the ministry of foreign affairs, al-Zirikli includes several important documents from the Saudi diplomatic service in his book. The main defect in his work is the lack of references to sources. (Al-Zirikli is also the author of several other works.)

Other Arabic sources

Hafiz Wahba, an Egyptian who spent half a century in the service of King Ibn Saud, left several works that increase our understanding of the evolution of Saudi society. He represented Ibn Saud at diplomatic negotiations, held important administrative posts in Hijaz after its conquest and was minister of education before being appointed Saudi ambassador to London. His books describe the economic activities of the settled people and the bedouin of central Arabia before the emergence of the oil industry, and the religious-political movement of the Ikhwan. Books by the Syrian Fuad Hamza, who also served the Saudi monarch, provide, among other topics, information on the socio-political and economic situation in Saudi Arabia before the 'oil era'.

A few works are available by Saudi opposition leaders, including extreme leftists such as Nasir al-Said. They are valuable in describing the programmes of those organizations that opposed the Saudi regime.

Preface

In addition to the hundreds of superficial publications in Arabic of no scholarly importance, some more serious studies have appeared since the 1930s. One example is the study of socio-economic change in Qasim in the mid-1960s by Abd al-Rahman al-Sharif. The Arab League published a collection of materials on the bedouin, including those in Saudi Arabia, in 1965. Abd al-Rahman Nazzar al-Qiyali has written a detailed commentary on labour legislation in Saudi Arabia. Muhammad Sadiq (apparently an Egyptian) has studied the evolution of the Saudi administrative machinery.

Works in Arabic on the history of Saudi Arabia are based mainly on the Arab chronicles and seldom rely on European sources. The authors usually confine themselves to a narration of historical events without analysing their political content, still less their social implications. This criticism applies even to the best Arab historians – Mahmud Shukri al-Alusi, Amin Rihani, Ahmad Ali, Amin Said, Salah al-Din al-Mukhtar, Ahmad Abd al-Ghafur Attar, Muhammad Abdallah Madhi, Rajab Harraz and Munir al-Ajlani.

The following authors devote particular attention to the Wahhabi teaching: Abdallah al-Qasimi, Ahmad Amin, Muhammad Hamid al-Faqi, Abbas Mahmud al-Aqqad and Muhammad Rashid Ridha, a leader of the Muslim reformation movement in Egypt. Muhammad al-Ahsai has concentrated his studies on eastern Arabia. The works by Muhammad al-Madani and Husain Nasif are helpful in understanding the creation of Saudi Arabia.

A more solid work is *The Just Imam* by Abd al-Hamid al-Khatib from Hijaz. The book concentrates on the time of Ibn Saud. Written by a former opponent of the Al Saud and one of the founders of the Liberal Party of Hijaz, it includes a series of unknown or lesser known historical facts. After the party was defeated, its leaders were pardoned and co-opted to Ibn Saud's side. The works by Abdallah Abd al-Jabbar and Fahd al-Mariq deal with the ideology and literature of Saudi Arabia in the twentieth century.

Subhi al-Muhammasani, an Arab jurist, gives a detailed analysis of the legal system of Saudi Arabia. The works by Abd al-Rahim Abd al-Rahman Abd al-Rahim on the first Saudi state, and by Abd al-Fattah Abu Aliya on the second, rely on new material from the Egyptian and other archives. Sulaiman ibn Sahman's polemical works in defence of Wahhabism include, besides the Wahhabi belief-system, quotations from its opponents.

More recent Western sources

The number of European and American works on Saudi Arabia increased dramatically during the 'oil era', and especially after the Second World War. Many of these authors touch on the socio-political and economic changes in the country in their works, some of which deserve particular mention.

In the early 1950s F. Vidal conducted a field study of al-Hasa at Aramco's request and collected new materials on the economic and social life of the inhabitants of its

Preface

oases. M. Katakura, a Japanese scholar, conducted a field survey of the ethnographic and socio-economic situation in the villages of Wadi Fatima between Mecca and Jidda (Hijaz) in the late 1960s. Her work is valuable for its description of settlements, the relations between the settled people and the bedouin, the traditional social connections and the penetration of commodity–money relations. W. Rugh, head of the information service of the US embassy in Riyadh, analysed the education system in the country and its impact on society. He collected much interesting data, though his attempt to divide people into 'classes' on the basis of their educational level is a serious methodological drawback.

There are other works by American authors which, although they cannot be treated formally as sources on the history of Saudi Arabia, actually are so: *The Arabia of Ibn Saud* by R. Lebkicher, G. Rentz and M. Steineke, all Aramco employees (1952); *Saudi Arabia: Its People, its Society, its Culture* by G. A. Lipsky et al. (1959); *Labor Law and Practice in the Kingdom of Saudi Arabia* (US Bureau of Labor Statistics); and the *Area Handbook for Saudi Arabia*, a confidential reference book by the US government, which has run into several regularly updated editions.

These books are based on materials collected in Saudi Arabia itself, including the results of ethnographic, anthropological, sociological and economic field surveys. The *Area Handbook*, for example, quotes reports and analyses by US intelligence, the US embassy and Aramco. Its authors obtained access to several original statistical reports produced by Saudi agencies. These books are not intended for the general public, but for experts and those directly connected with Saudi Arabia – business people, engineers, diplomats and journalists. They are full of facts and figures and provide some objective judgements. Together with the entire US literature on Saudi Arabia, however, they have a fundamental weakness: an apologetic approach to US policy and the activities of Aramco. Their evaluations of the Saudi regime are extremely cautious and are closer to compliments than to scholarly analysis. Yet they provide a vast array of information on the nature of agrarian relations and land tenure, changes in agriculture, the growth of a bourgeoisie, changes within Saudi society, the restructuring of the power mechanism and the development of the legal system. R. Knauerhase's valuable work on the Saudi economy of the mid-1970s provides a wealth of facts and figures taken directly from Saudi sources.

Among works of a somewhat political or even journalistic character, but which nonetheless contain important information on the situation in Saudi Arabia, one should mention *Arabia Without Sultans* by F. Halliday, two books by J.-L. Soulié and L. Champenois, and articles by P. Bonnenfant, all fairly serious works. Authors of later works on the Saudi economy rely on a wide range of factual material and use modern techniques of economic and statistical analysis. Examples are the books by C. R. Crane, R. Loony and F. al-Farsy.

The most notable Western authors who have written on the question of oil in the Middle East are S. Longrigg, B. Shwadran, S. Klebanoff, F. Rouhani, J. M. Chevalier, S. R. Ali and the authors of the *Aramco Handbook* and special OPEC and OAPEC directories.

Among several interesting studies dealing with the contemporary socio-economic problems of Saudi Arabia are the work by J. Birks and C. Sinclair on population migration, books by J. Carter and Saad Eddin Ibrahim and the collective work *State, Society and Economy in Saudi Arabia*, edited by T. Niblock.

G. M. Baroody has analysed the legal system of Saudi Arabia. P. Hobday, A. R. Kelidar, D. E. Long and the contributors to the collection of articles in *The Kingdom of Saudi Arabia* (edited by R. Dunipace) pay detailed attention to socio-political problems, including the structure of power and legal issues.

Numerous articles on Saudi Arabia have appeared recently in both Western and Arab periodicals. Western and US interest in Saudi Arabia increased essentially in the 1980s and 1990s. It is impossible to encompass even the most important works in this brief preface. We shall therefore confine ourselves to mentioning the works by the American scholar N. Safran and the British scholar S. K. Aburish, to which Riyadh reacted adversely.

European and Russian literature on Arabian history

This includes many works characterized by a preponderance of descriptive material, a neglect of the social significance of events and superficial observations on political motives. Most European orientalists are reluctant to admit that there was any sign of development within Arabian society before the twentieth century. A. Krymski's works are no exception.

Until recently, the only European work to provide a comprehensive picture of Saudi history was Philby's *Saudi Arabia* (1955), an expanded version of his *Arabia* (1930). Philby was the first European to describe developments by relying only on the Arab chronicles from Ibn Ghannam to Ibn Hizlul. However, he avoided European sources on Arabian history and paid minimal attention to the evolution of the economy and the socio-political structure. It is impossible to credit Philby with an objective, unbiased account of historical facts. He was fascinated by Ibn Saud and idealized the Al Saud. Yet the historian who studies the problems of Saudi Arabia should not ignore Philby's travel books and historical works. His intimate, first-hand knowledge of life in Arabia enabled him to note nuances in the Arab chronicles that might well be ignored by academic scholars. Musil, the Czech orientalist, also used Arab chronicles.

Several works by American Arabists deal with specific periods in Arabian history. Two of them are worthy of note: *Saudi Arabia in the Nineteenth Century* by R. B. Winder and *The Birth of Saudi Arabia* by G. Troeller. The latter covers the first two decades of the twentieth century. Both are confined mainly to a description of political events.

European orientalists, such as the Hungarian scholar I. Goldziher, have provided an accurate description of the dogmatic and theological aspects of Wahhabism and noted specific characteristics of the Wahhabi cult. A detailed account of the Wahhabi belief-system is found in D. S. Margoliouth's article in the first edition of *L'Encyclopédie de l'Islam*. The French orientalist H. Laoust wrote several important works on Ibn Taimiya, the Wahhabis' predecessor, and the impact of his teaching on

Preface

the ideology of the Saudi regime. His article on Muhammad ibn Abd al-Wahhab is included in the new edition of the *Encyclopaedia of Islam*.

Since the late 1970s many works have been published on the activities of religious movements in the East, paying particular attention to Islam in Saudi Arabia. They include E. Mortimer's works, monographs on Islam in foreign policy, and numerous publications in various periodicals.

Russian and other sources

In Russia, M. Tomara was the first to examine the history of Wahhabism and the Saudi state and to raise the question of the social roots of Wahhabism. However, his conclusions are now outdated.

A. I. Pershits produced a series of works on Arabia and its socio-political and ethnographic composition. He summed up the results of his many long years of study in *The Economy and the Socio-political Situation in Northern Arabia in the 19th and the First Third of the 20th Century*, an excellent volume that was the basic source for the first chapter of the present work. Pershits analyses Arabian society, relying on numerous facts taken from books by European travellers. His work provides a valuable introduction to European narrative sources. However, some of his conclusions are open to dispute and his views have undergone a certain evolution.

M. V. Churakov's work is an exposition of Amin al-Rihani's *The History of Modern Najd*, which, in its turn, relies on Ibn Bishr in describing events prior to the mid-nineteenth century. The author has selected the passages that are relevant for a study of ethnography and social relations in central Arabia. *The Arabs, Islam and the Arab Caliphate in the Early Middle Ages* by E. A. Belyaev provides a historical background for studies of the history of Arabian society and its ideology throughout the centuries.

Important materials for comparative studies of Arabia are found in N. A. Ivanov's works on the Arab tribes of North Africa and the history of Morocco and Arab-Ottoman society; and in those by I. M. Smilyanskaya on western Asia in the eighteenth and nineteenth centuries.

N. I. Proshin's *Saudi Arabia* is interesting for its detailed description of the Ikhwan revolt of the 1920s and of developments in the 1940s, 1950s and early 1960s.

V. V. Ozoling's scholarly works on Saudi Arabia, focusing mainly on the economy, also contain reliable material on Saudi society and the evolution of socio-economic institutions and organizations. Ozoling's economic analysis was used in the present work in the chapter on the socio-political structure of Saudi Arabia in the oil era.

L. V. Valkova has written on Saudi Arabia's foreign policy, mainly that in the 1960s and 1970s. Her other work is *Saudi Arabia: Oil, Islam, Politics*.

A. I. Yakovlev has studied the socio-economic development of Saudi Arabia and its relations with the West. He and V. V. Mashin have published a book on the role of the Gulf in the foreign policy of the US and Western Europe. Other scholars who have studied Saudi Arabia's foreign policy include R. V. Borisov, L. l. Medvedko, E. M.

Preface

Primakov, R. M. Tursunov and the authors of the monograph on *The Foreign Policy of the Middle Eastern Countries*.

Saudi Arabia, a reference book, published in 1980, is a rich source of facts and figures.

G. L. Bondarevski's work on the situation in the Gulf in the late nineteenth and early twentieth centuries throws light on some issues concerning the history of Arabia during that period. The course of the First World War in Arabia may by traced from *The Collapse of Turkish Dominance in the Arab East* by M. S. Lazarev.

Several legal questions become clearer from the collection of Russian translations of the constitutions and other fundamental laws of Middle Eastern countries. S. A. Kaminski's works deal with the institution of monarchy in the Arab world. L. R. Syukiyainen has studied the problems of *fiqh* (jurisprudence) and Shariat in the Saudi legal system in his articles and monograph on Muslim law.

Many works on Islam, touching on the contemporary problems of Islam in Saudi Arabia, appeared in Russia in the 1980s and early 1990s. Examples are *Islam in the Contemporary Politics of the Countries of the East*, *The Islamic Factor in International Relations in Asia*, a reference book on Islam, and books by A. V. Kudryavtsev, D. V. Malysheva, G. V. Miloslavski and R. M. Sharipova.

Others who have written on the problems of Saudi Arabia are I. P. Belyaev, V. L. Bodyanski, M. S. Lazarev and O. G. Gerasimov. Articles on various problems of Saudi Arabia's social life and politics have also appeared in Russian periodicals.

The problems of the oil industry and its impact on Saudi society, as well as on the societies of other Middle Eastern countries, have received particular attention in the works of R. N. Andreasyan, B. V. Rachkov, A. A. Maksimov, I. L. Piotrovskaya, A. E. Primakov, I. A. Seifulmulukov and other Russian authors. V. I. Shestopalov's research deals with the problems of the delimitation of the continental shelf in the Gulf.

Bibliographical works

Lastly, some bibliographical works on Arabia should be mentioned: those by E. Macro, J. Heyworth-Dunne, J. H. Stevens and R. King, and Abdallah Salim al-Qahtani and Yahya Mahmud Saati, an annotated list published in Washington in 1951, the list of works on the Arabian peninsula preserved in the National Library of Cairo and the *Selected Bibliography on King Faisal*. Fahd al-Sammari, a scholar from Riyadh, has published a detailed list of works on the time of Ibn Saud. *The Bibliography of Saudi Arabia* by the present author includes more than 4,000 titles in Arabic, Russian and various European languages. *The Bibliography of the Countries of Southern and Eastern Arabia* by A. V. Shvakov supplements it to some degree. One of the most complete bibliographies, that by H.-J. Philipp, was published in 1984; the second volume appeared in 1989. Unfortunately, it does not include publications in Russian, East European and oriental languages. The total number of bibliographies concerning Saudi Arabia is far in excess of 100.

Preface

The author cannot but express his deep gratitude to A. I. Yakovlev, who assisted him in writing the nineteenth, twenty-first and a part of the twentieth chapters; P. A. Seslavin, who translated the book into English; and D. R. Zhentiev, lecturer at Moscow University, and S. A. Eliseeva, B. G. Petruk, N. P. Podgornova and S. M. Shlenskaya, researchers at the Institute for African Studies at the Russian Academy of Sciences, who helped in compiling the bibliography and the index and checked the names and dates. It is to their dedicated work that the book owes its merits, while the responsibility for its shortcomings lies entirely with the author. The academic quality of the book, as well as the quality of the English translation, have been greatly enhanced by Jana Gough: without her tireless efforts, the work would hardly have appeared in English at all. Finally, Professor Tim Niblock's comments were invaluable in achieving a correlation between the author's own social and historical analysis and the intellectual framework of contemporary Anglo-Saxon Middle Eastern studies.

Moscow
April 1998

Part One

Part One

CHAPTER 1

Arabia on the Eve of the Emergence of Wahhabism: Economy, Society, Politics

The Saudi state arose in Arabia in the eighteenth century on the basis of Wahhabism, a Muslim reform movement. The key to understanding the Wahhabi ideology – and the causes of the emergence, development, downfall and renaissance of the state that is today known as Saudi Arabia – lies first and foremost in a study of Arabian society. It should be stated at the outset that this book concentrates on the central, northern and eastern regions of the peninsula: Najd and al-Hasa (the Eastern Province). Yemen and Oman are outside the scope of the present study (except insofar as events there had a direct connection with Saudi Arabia), not only because they have remained independent of Saudi Arabia, but above all because of their pronounced peculiarities: geographic, historical, economic, ethnic and religious. These provide sufficient grounds for treating their inhabitants as separate peoples with their own socio-political structures and destinies.

Mecca and Medina, the holy places of Islam, were too tempting a booty for any Middle Eastern empire to permit Hijaz, where they are located, to preserve its independence. Although the socio-political and economic situation of Hijaz differed very little from that of Najd, the latter practically never experienced foreign domination. The status of Hijaz as a province first of the Umayyad and Abbasid caliphates, and then of Egypt and the Ottoman empire, as well as the *hajj* (pilgrimage) and related trade and other economic activities, made it different from its neighbours. Thus when we refer to 'Arabian society', we mean principally that of Najd, the cradle of Wahhabism and the Saudi state, together with the adjacent regions in the north and south.

Two 'sand seas' – the Great al-Nafud in the north and the Rub al-Khali in the south – determine the approximate northern and southern boundaries of Najd. In the west,

Najd is bounded by the Hijaz mountains and in the east by the coastal strip of the Gulf.*
Overall, the territory slopes gradually from west to east. The climate is characterized by regular fluctuations of temperature – an intense dry heat in summer and a pronounced cold in winter. Almost all the area is arid and years without any rains are frequent. But rain is only a partial blessing. *Sayls* (stormy mud streams) sweep the wadis (valleys), frequently with catastrophic consequences.

The most famous valley is Wadi al-Rum, which begins in Hijaz, to the north-east of Khaibar, continues some 360 km to the east, vanishes in the sands and then reappears under the new name of al-Batina, to end near Basra (Iraq) some 1,000 km from its starting-point. Other major valleys are wadis Hanifa, al-Dawasir and Najran. Subsoil waters are closest to the surface in wadis, making life possible. It was in Wadi Hanifa that several large oases emerged and became the cradle of Wahhabism and the Saudi dynasty (the Al Saud).

Buraida and Anaiza, the main towns of the province of Qasim, are located in Wadi al-Rum. Najd is divided into regions none of which has clear boundaries. Historically, however, these regions had a kind of geographic unity. The most important of them are the central regions, al-Arid (crossed by Wadi Hanifa), Mahmal, Sudair and Washm. The capital Riyadh is located in al-Arid. The main southern regions are al-Kharj, famous for its deep wells and basins; al-Aflaj, where ancient underground irrigation canals have survived; al-Dawasir; and, lastly, Najran. The northern regions of Qasim and Jabal Shammar have always had an important role. The rival towns of Buraida and Anaiza are located on the route from Basra to Medina, and so have always been major trading centres. Jabal Shammar lies to the south of al-Nafud and is the northernmost area of Najd.

Artefacts and documents from the eighteenth century reveal isolated fragments of Arabia's social life and later information allows us to reconstruct at least a general outline. The slow development of the economy and the stable, age-old social structures allow us to assume that life in the nineteenth and early twentieth centuries in Arabia had not changed greatly since medieval times. For the overwhelming majority of people in Najd, al-Hasa and Hijaz, life was connected chiefly with two kinds of economic activity – irrigated farming in the oases and nomadic animal husbandry.

Irrigated farming

The arid, subtropical climate in most of the peninsula means that artificial irrigation is necessary for farming. More or less abundant subterranean waters reach the surface only in the eastern regions of Arabia. In other regions, the sources of irrigation are wells. Collected rainwater and *sayl* streams are used less frequently. Water sources are sometimes dozens or even hundreds of kilometres apart. But in Najd (where water-

---

* For events on the Arabian side of the Gulf, the author prefers to use 'the Arabian Gulf', or simply 'the Gulf', rather than 'the Persian Gulf'.

bearing layers are close to the surface of the soil) and al-Hasa a fairly dense concentration of oases can be observed.

Well-building demanded considerable labour and resources; primitive water-raising mechanisms used camels, mules and asses. Naturally, this restricted the area of irrigated farming and the volume of agricultural production. A 10-m-deep well with a water-raising device was enough to irrigate 1 feddan (approx. 1 acre).[1]

Dates were the main crop in the northern and central regions of Arabia. They were consumed in various forms and were the only agricultural product of vital importance that met the needs of the settled and nomadic population in favourable years. Date palms required constant attention and only began fruiting fully some fifteen years after planting. Second to dates were cereals – barley, millet, wheat and oats. It is known that cereals were exported from Najd to Hijaz in certain years. Rice and cotton were grown in some areas. Vegetables and fruit were grown where water was abundant: al-Taif, for example, was famous for its gardens.

Irrigated plots yielded relatively good crops, but the total volume of production was insignificant because of the limited area of arable land, the shortage of fertilizers and the primitive agricultural methods. Repeated droughts, whose catastrophic consequences were reported both by the Arabian chroniclers and by European travellers, meant that there was no guarantee of stable crops even on irrigated land. Some wells dried up completely during prolonged droughts. The crops perished, the cultivated areas decreased, even the date palms ran wild and then withered, and the inhabitants starved, died or left long-occupied settlements. When the rains came again, wells and reservoirs filled with water and the peasants resumed their sowing and took care of the surviving date palms. But oases could be swallowed by the desert and disappear for ever.

Both droughts and the rare, drenching rains could prove the peasants' enemies. Strong *sayls* might carry away the upper layer of soil from the fields together with the crop, sweep away houses and destroy the fruits of many long years of labour. Locusts often devoured all the plants and left people with no means of subsistence. Food shortages on the eve of the new crop were not infrequent. Wallin reports, for example, that the inhabitants of Tabuk appeased their hunger in the spring almost exclusively by consuming wild grass, 'eaten raw, or merely boiled in water, without anything more substantial in addition'.[2] Frequent epidemics (cholera and plague) depopulated whole villages.

The narrow economic base, the hostile forces of nature (the social factors will be discussed later), the primitive agricultural technology and the isolation of the oases all resulted in a very slow rate of economic development. Oasis farming was characterized by a fragmentation of effort and was undertaken by small peasant groups and individual families. There were no large-scale irrigation facilities or huge tracts of irrigated and cultivated land in medieval Arabia. Combined with the isolation of the oases, this meant that there was no need for a centralized government.

Nomadic and semi-nomadic animal husbandry

There were two main types of animal husbandry among the Arabian nomads: camel-breeding and sheep- or goat-breeding. The nomads who mainly or exclusively bred camels, 'almost the most universal of all animals',[3] were considered the 'genuine bedouin'. Camel milk (fresh or sour), cheese and butter were often their only food for many weeks. On special occasions, animals were slaughtered and their meat and fat were eaten. Camel wool was used for clothes, their skin for various articles, manure for fuel, and urine for washing and for medical purposes. The hardy, undemanding camel was irreplaceable when crossing arid areas. 'The camel is such an important animal in the desert that had it perished, the whole population would follow it,'[4] notes Volney.

However, the widely quoted saying by the Austrian orientalist Sprenger, 'The bedouin is a parasite of the camel,' is nothing more than a witticism. The camel-breeding nomads' labour was hard and required well-tested skills. They had to know how to exploit their pastures, drive camels from one grazing area to another, treat the animals when they were sick, milk the female camels, cut the wool and so on. Younger camels were trained to perform various tasks and to walk saddled and loaded. The bedouin dug and maintained wells in the desert.

The life of the bedouin was full of privations. In the rare snowy winters, young camels perished, female camels stopped giving milk and the livestock starved. A dry summer, too, spelled hardship and danger. Even the scarce reserves of dates and grain came to an end and poor bedouin ate wild tubers and fruit; many of them died of malnutrition. Their summer pastures usually lie close to cemeteries.[5]

The famous Arab horses – a source of pride for those who owned them and of envy among those who did not – were used only for military purposes and for show. In their long roamings, horses needed either a water reserve or camel milk. To support that noble animal, a poor bedouin would partly deprive his family of water and milk.

Those who mainly or exclusively bred sheep and goats were usually known as *shawiya*. Since their ability to cross arid areas was limited, they roamed over a radius of several hundred kilometres to pastures that were close to water sources. Travelling over relatively short distances in areas with permanent water sources, sheep-breeders could engage in farming. They ceased migrating in the agricultural seasons to look for date-palm groves and cereal fields. Farming became the main occupation of a substantial number of sheep-breeders.

This combination of farming and nomadic animal husbandry in northern Najd is described by Wallin:

> In consequence of the close and intimate relations, before adverted to, which connect the two classes of the Shammar, we find the villagers, to a certain degree, still clinging to the customs and manners of nomadic life, while the Bedawies, on the other hand, apply themselves to avocations, which are generally regarded as not becoming. A great many of the former wander during the spring with their horses and their herds of camels and sheep to the desert, where they live, for a longer or

shorter time, under tents as nomads, and most of the Bedawy families possess palm-plantations and corn-fields . . . which they cultivate on their own account.[6]

Burckhardt reports that a subdivision of the Harb tribe in Hijaz:

> possess some watering-places, situated in fertile spots, where they sow corn and barley; but continue to live under tents, and pass the greater part of the year in the desert.[7]

There were, as a rule, no rigid boundaries in the sense of economic activities between nomadic camel-breeders, semi-nomadic sheep-breeders and settled people. Many camel-breeding bedouin started sheep-breeding; and a part of the nomads settled. Simultaneously, the opposite process of nomadization occurred. The sliding balance between the nomads and the settled people was determined by the natural geographic conditions of Arabia and could not exceed a certain framework. The excess nomadic population migrated to the north. If they settled there, they tended to give up their bedouin past. Not for nothing was it said that 'Yaman is the womb or cradle of the Arabs, as the proverb has it, and Iraq is their grave.'[8] To a certain extent, this held true for Syria too. In this way, sedentarization and nomadization balanced each other within the boundaries of Arabia itself.

The division into camel-breeding bedouin and sheep-breeding semi-nomads might coincide with the tribal division. However, sometimes a part of the tribe bred camels, another part bred sheep and goats and yet another part engaged in farming and became settled.

The nomadic economy depended on precipitation even more than farming did. After heavy rains, the steppes and deserts were covered with juicy grass, the animals grew stout and the nomads flourished. Droughts, the winter cold and regular outbreaks of disease among the livestock led to murrain, famine and a reduction in the numbers of bedouin.

Handicrafts and trade

The settled peasants' domestic handicrafts satisfied their very limited needs. Baskets, sacks and mats were made of palm leaves, and ropes and harnesses of palm fibre; tree trunks were used to produce agricultural implements and to build houses. Primitive pottery, woollen cloth and cotton fabrics were manufactured. At the same time, a sizeable part of the produce of the less developed bedouin handicrafts (rough woollen cloth and leather articles) was marketed.

In the large oases, professional handicrafts developed to some extent. Among the *sunnaa* (craftsmen), there were gunsmiths, coppersmiths, tinsmiths, jewellers, joiners, carpenters, builders, plasterers, wheel-makers (producing wheels for water-raising devices), shoemakers, tailors, gold embroiderers, mat-makers and masters who made marble mortars for grinding coffee.[9] Metalworkers and gunsmiths formed the most numerous stratum of the craftsmen – it was they to whom the word *sunnaa* referred in the narrow sense. However, the gunsmiths repaired more imported weapons than they produced. A certain regional specialization of handicrafts developed, but it is difficult to determine its characteristics in the period prior to the eighteenth century. It is known, for example, that 'cotton fabrics were manufactured in Najd, of which clothes were made and which were exchanged for wool and livestock with the tribes'.[10] Woollen cloth was woven and the woollen cloaks known as *abas* (for which al-Hasa was famed) and tent pieces were sewn in some regions.

There were no large workshops in Arabia and it was only on rare occasions that the artisans set up something like guilds. Some craftsmen migrated together with the bedouin tribes. They shoed horses and repaired arms and utensils, and some of them treated the animals. The nomadic *sunnaa* also engaged in animal husbandry.

Arabia had virtually no towns in the strict sense, in other words where the greater part of the population subsisted on means other than agriculture.[11] Mecca was an outstanding exception. The notions of 'town' and 'large oasis' mostly coincided. Al-Diriya, the capital of the future state of the Al Saud, was formed from several neighbouring villages. Handicrafts did not determine the economic life of the Arabian 'town-oases'. Their important role in Arabian society was connected with the intense commercial exchange generated by the division of labour between the peasant farmers and the nomads.

The nomads' economy was far less self-sufficient than that of the peasant farmers. Although some bedouin subsisted mainly on camel milk for long periods, they could not do without agricultural products such as dates and grain; they needed the handicrafts too. Burckhardt describes a rich nomad's expenses as follows: 4 camel loads of wheat, 200 piastres; barley for a horse, 100 piastres; garments, 200 piastres; coffee, tobacco, sweets and mutton, 200 piastres. These amounted to some £35–40.[12] The lack of dates in the list may be explained by the fact that well-off bedouin might receive them from subject peasant farmers as tribute rather than through exchange. Ordinary bedouin might also buy many of the goods on Burckhardt's list, though in smaller amounts.

In summer, the bedouin gathered in the large oases and trading centres, bringing livestock, wool, butter and cheese to exchange for dates, grain, cloth and items of clothing, mats, horseshoes, arms, gunpowder, bullets, medicines, coffee and tobacco. Trade was conducted partly in the form of barter, but the numerous mentions of the prices of various goods in the Arabian chronicles testify to a well-developed system of monetary circulation. The nomads' summer migrations (*musabilas*) to the trading centres were considered the 'greatest event of the year'[13] both by them and by the settled people. The greatest volume of exchanges of products occurred at the summer fairs.

The bedouin's trade was not confined to the adjacent oases. The scope of their commercial ties extended even outside the boundaries of the peninsula. Camels were then the main export and were in great demand. They served as a means of transportation not only throughout Arabia but also in other countries of the Middle East. Wool, butter, skins and thoroughbred horses were also exported from Arabia.

The items imported to northern and central Arabia, and particularly to Hijaz, were Egyptian and Indian rice, Egyptian and Yemeni wheat and barley, coffee from Yemen, spices from India, dried fruits from Syria and sugar from Egypt, together with arms, iron, copper, lead for bullets and sulphur for gunpowder.[14] Arabian handicrafts suffered from competition with the more developed handicraft centres in the Middle East. According to *The Brilliance of the Meteor* [*Lam al-Shihab* . . .], a medieval Arabian chronicle:

> *Kufiyas* are brought to Najd from Iraq, al-Hasa and al-Qatif, *abas* from al-Hasa and Iraq. Rich women wear Indian silk, one frock costs 20 rials or more. Silk is of various colours – red, yellow and green. The Najdi women are excessively fond of jewels; even the poor buy gold adornments and the men decorate sabres, guns and lances with silver . . .[15]

> Trade is a special occupation of the Najdi people [the chronicler continues]. Many of them are traders and travel to the lands of Rum [western Asia and Anatolia] and different parts of the Arabian peninsula. They do not come to the Rum's lands with their own Najdi goods; they come with money and bring silk, copper, iron or lead from Aleppo and Damascus, depending on the conditions. They sell thoroughbred horses, which are in great demand in the Rum lands. Besides, they sell many camels in Aleppo and Damascus. Some people told me that they had seen merchants from Najd, particularly from Qasim, who sold dates from their regions in Damascus; perhaps they went even to Egypt. They buy only arms and coral. They trade with other Arab lands too. They go there with money. They bring much coffee, storax and incense from Yemen . . . I know that the Najdi merchants have no special warehouses for the purchased and sold goods but keep them in their houses. Those who sell little have shops . . . They have no covered and crowded bazaars, unlike the Iranians. Their market is open, without a roof. The road that crosses the market is very broad; loaded caravans can pass through it. I know also that some goods from India, like sugar, cardamom, cloves, cinnamon, pepper and curcuma, are in demand in Najd. Most of them are brought from Yemeni ports. Some goods come from the ports of the Omani littoral. Many goods are brought there from the al-Qatif and Bahrain ports. The Najdis' customs allow them to leave their motherland for twenty years or more, even for China. Many Najdi merchants live in Aleppo and Damascus, as well as Egypt . . .

> The settled peasants of Najd till many fields, plant palms and other trees and look after them. They have sheep, goats, cows and camels. They use their livestock, though little perhaps, as the source of milk and meat and as a means of transportation.

> As for the Najdi bedouin, they live in tents of goats' wool. They have nothing but livestock. Some of them engage in trade only when a drought occurs. They come to the towns and villages with their families. Some nomadic Arabs travel with their wives, sisters, mothers or daughters wherever they go in search of food and to

sell fat, wool and animals since, as they say, a woman's sight is stronger in that matter. They [the men] do not like doing the housework unless their women want them to.[16]

The bedouin supplied livestock and drivers for commercial transportation in Arabia and participated in the caravans sent abroad. In northern Arabia there were associations of camel traders and camel drovers who considered themselves to be members of the Uqail tribe. They settled in various parts of Najd, although some of them lived in Iraq. In the late eighteenth century they enjoyed a monopoly over the right to form, guide and guard the caravans that crossed the Syrian desert.[17]

The traders made large fortunes, though the Najdi trading houses were by no means as rich as the Hijazi wholesalers. The capital accumulated by traders in coffee and Indian goods in Jidda could amount to hundreds of thousands of pounds. But the central Arabian merchants, too, made handsome profits from exporting camels and horses and importing food and handicrafts.

The *hajj*, or yearly pilgrimage to Mecca and Medina, was of major importance to Arabia as a whole and especially to Hijaz. The main caravan routes of the Egyptian and Syrian pilgrims crossed northern Hijaz. Although less important, the route of pilgrims from Iraq and Iran ran across the northern regions of Najd with deviations northwards or southwards in different years. The fourth route began from the Gulf ports and Oman and crossed central Najd and Hijaz; the fifth joined Yemen with Mecca. The *hajj* was combined with trade, since the pilgrims brought various goods with them. The transportation of the pilgrims afforded many bedouin the means of subsistence.

The elements of patriarchal and tribal relations in the oases

Most of the settled population of Arabia were related to various kinship groups and were considered members of particular tribes. Settled and nomadic tribesmen maintained close relations, which might persist for many generations. Sometimes people from different tribes occupied separate areas within the same oasis. Hereditary *fellahin* (peasant farmers) and townsfolk traced their genealogy to ancient Arabian tribes. Several extended and nuclear families formed a community (*jamaa, hamula* or *jummaa*). According to Doughty:

> The jummaa is that natural association of households, born in affinity, that are reckoned to the same jid, or first-father, and are confederate under an elder, the head of their house, inheriting the old father's authority. In these bonds and divisions by kindreds, is the only corporate life and security in an anarchical infested country. In-coming strangers are reckoned to the alliance of their friends. Freed men are clients of the lord's household; . . . they are 'uncle's sons' together of the same jummaa . . . The jummaas in the oases are fraternities which inhabit several quarters. When townsmen fall out, that are not of the same fellowship, their elders seek to accord them friendly; but in considerable and self-ruling oases, as

Aneyza, the townsmen carry their quarrels to the emir sitting in the mejlis, as do the nomads to their great sheykh. Until the civil benefit of the Waháby government, the villagers were continually divided against each other, jummaa against jummaa, sûk [market] against sûk, in the most settlements of Upland Arabia.[18]

Anyone who lived outside such a community, a lone individual without kith or kin, had a difficult life for he had no group behind him to protect him from attempts on his life and property.

Kinship ties were particularly strong in the families of emirs and shaikhs and lent them considerable weight and influence. In addition, they were often united by common sources of income and ownership of land. The Russian ethnographer Pershits has noted:

The settled population, with the exception of those who had settled just recently and not yet severed the earlier ties, were absolutely unfamiliar with the kinship and tribal organization. What was really preserved was the extended family and a rather narrow group of relatives, a vestigial kinship cell, which is often described as patronymy in our ethnographic literature.[19]

We may accept this description, rejecting only the categoric 'absolutely unfamiliar'. Events in the last quarter of the twentieth century, not to mention earlier eras, show the continuing strength of kinship and tribal organization among the settled population of Arabia and the whole of western Asia. It would therefore be more correct to speak of a considerable weakening of, or rather a change in, the kinship and tribal organization among the peasants.

An extended family owned land and other property jointly and maintained a joint household under the guidance of the father. After his death, the property would be divided, with the eldest son enjoying preferential inheritance rights. Various forms of communal ownership of individual kin's land survived in some regions of Arabia. The peasant farmers owned and used the water jointly where there were substantial water resources. Some settled communities owned pastures. The oasis dwellers who had no pastures had to graze their livestock on lands owned by nomadic bedouin tribes.[20]

The custom of mutual assistance also existed to some extent among the settled people. Peasant farmers collectively maintained herdsmen and livestock guards and respected the custom of hospitality, though to a limited extent. The tradition of neighbours providing mutual assistance persisted. Some owners of fields did not collect the fallen ears of the crops, leaving them for the poor. The poor were sometimes allotted unreaped parts of fields or some palms with dates.[21] However, such bonds did not determine the social relations in the oases.

Social divisions in the oases

As a result of a long and complicated process in Arabia's agricultural society in the eighteenth century, a part of the land fell to the bedouin and the long-settled tribal nobility. For example, the ruler of the Uyaina oasis had properties in al-Hasa and derived an income from them in the first half of the century.[22] Palm plantations, gardens and fields might belong to religious scholars too, as is clear from the example of Muhammad ibn Abd al-Wahhab, the founder of Wahhabism.[23] However, neither the Arabian chroniclers nor European travellers mention a preponderance of large landowners in Najd, Hijaz or al-Hasa. Palgrave notes in the mid-nineteenth century that 'nor is it [i.e. land] often in the hands of large proprietors like the Zemindars of India and the wealthier farmers of England'.[24]

If they were deeply in debt, small landowners might lose their ownership of land and transfer it to rich money-lenders and merchants. Doughty writes about the peasants, 'They and their portions of the dust of this world are devoured (hardly less than in Egypt and Syria) by rich money-lenders: that is by the long rising over their heads of an insoluble usury.'[25] The phenomenon was probably widespread on the eve of the emergence of the Wahhabi movement and might explain the Wahhabis' vigorous denunciation of the charging of interest on loans.

Landowners rented plots to peasants under certain conditions. The main method of renting was through sharecropping, with the landowner's share determined by custom. The seizure of both large and small water sources by private individuals enabled the owners to sell the water, thus making a profit from the irrigated lands. Many peasants who had no draught animals could not use the communal wells, springs and land: they had to hire livestock.

Various levies imposed on the population brought substantial incomes for the nobility. It is known, for example, that emirs who enjoyed political power collected a tax from the local inhabitants in the mid-eighteenth century.[26] 'Duties' imposed on the trade caravans also enriched the ruling nobility. Strong settled rulers could replenish their exchequers by successful raids on the neighbouring oases and on the nomadic and semi-nomadic tribes. Indeed, this was the main source of many rulers' incomes.

The methods by which the nobility continued to amass wealth in the oases may be illustrated by the example of the sharif of Mecca. The bulk of his income came from custom duties in Jidda: he took part in the profitable transit trade via the town, owned a sea-going vessel and sold food to the pilgrims. He imposed a heavy poll tax on the Persian *hajjis* (pilgrims) and received gifts from rich Sunni pilgrims. He also seized part of the money sent from Istanbul to Mecca as the sultan's gift to the people of the holy city. The income from his lands in al-Taif and other oases, and from the houses he owned, went straight into his exchequer. In Burckhardt's opinion, the sharif of Mecca's annual income was close to £350,000.[27] Of course, the Meccan ruler enjoyed a special position in Arabia, but other emirs, too, derived an income from some of the above-mentioned sources, though in smaller amounts.

The direct attachment of the peasants to their land did not develop in Arabia.

Niebuhr notes, 'A peasant who is displeased with his seignior is free to leave him and settle in another place.'[28] But it was impossible to do without the protection of a powerful man or clan in such a climate of insecurity: this led to the peasants' personal, though weak, dependence on the ruler of the oasis.

Characterizing the pre-capitalist social relations which existed in the Arabian oases at this time as 'feudal' requires a substantial reservation, however. The social structure of the agricultural population of Arabia, which was in general a backward periphery of the Middle East, repeated the main elements of the social set-up in the more developed countries of the region in a primitive form. Therefore, by using hereafter the term 'feudalism' to characterize Arabian society, we imply the feudalism that was characteristic of Middle Eastern countries.

Relations within the nomadic tribes

The Brilliance of the Meteor includes a list of the nomadic confederations of central, eastern, northern and western Arabia in the eighteenth and early nineteenth centuries[29] which is not found in the Wahhabi annals of the same period. According to the author of the chronicle, the largest Arabian tribe (we should describe it as a confederation of tribes) was the Anaza, which was divided into 3 groups, each some 60,000 men strong – the anonymous chronicler means by that figure the number of bedouin capable of carrying arms. (Mengin mentions the ratio of fighting personnel to women, children, old people and the infirm as 1:3,[30] which allows one to calculate the total number of the Anaza as almost half a million people.) The Anaza were famous as skilled riders. The traditions of mutual assistance and solidarity were stronger among them than in other tribes. When some Anaza subdivisions roamed from Najd to the Syrian semi-desert, they were helped by members of their tribe who lived there. The chronicler reports that the greater part of the Anaza had submitted to the Saudis (the Al Saud) without a war. This is a significant fact, probably indicating that attempts by the emirs of al-Diriya to achieve centralization and unity accorded with the interests of the tribe that had spread throughout a sizeable part of Arabia.

The Shammar, who had settled in northern Najd and considered the Qahtan from the Tai confederation their ancestors, could mobilize 20,000 men. The Harb tribe from Hijaz had 30,000 armed bedouin and settled people. The Najdi tribe of Mutair, who were famous for their warriors and their fighting spirit, had 14,000 armed men; the tribe of Ataiba (of Qahtan descent), who roamed throughout Najd and Hijaz, had 40,000; the Baqum had 4,000; the Subai, who were particularly loyal to the Saudis, had 12,000; and the Suhul had 10,000.

The powerful Qahtan tribe in the south of Najd had 50,000 warriors and nobody dared to challenge them. The Qahtan joined the Saudis on condition that the latter supported their raids on Tihama, the Yemeni highlands and Hadhramawt. The Ajman could raise 5,000 armed men. The tribe seems to have grown in size and strength after moving from the Najran region to the north in the eighteenth century. In the last third of the nineteenth century they sent thousands of armed men to the battlefield in eastern Arabia. The Bani Murra or Al Murra, who lived on the edge of the Rub al-Khali, counted 2,000 bedouin 'or more', according to *The Brilliance of the Meteor*. Even the Arabian chronicler seems surprised at the harsh conditions under which they lived, noting that they could survive on camel milk and salty water. Lastly, the Bani Khalid, the masters of eastern Arabia in the mid-eighteenth century and the rivals of the emirate of al-Diriya during the period of its ascent, counted 30,000 men.

Needless to say, the above figures are all very approximate. The chronicler pays no attention to tribes who are not 'noble', slaves, freedmen and the *sunnaa*, who will be dealt with below. But his list of tribes gives a rough statistical picture of Arabian nomadic society (excluding Yemen and Oman) at that time. The total number of bedouin who were capable of carrying arms reached almost 400,000; thus the numerical strength of the Arabian nomads must have been between 1.2 and 1.5 million.

Since the general features of the social structure of the Arabian nomads have been comprehensively studied elsewhere, we shall confine ourselves here to a brief description. The smallest unit of the tribe was the family. Sometimes a group of three or four families, bound by close kinship ties, owned 'more or less undivided properties',[31] but this was rare. The specific demands of the nomadic economy, and the care and pasturing of the livestock, did not necessitate the joint labour of large groups.

Several families of relatives (both close and distant) who remembered or recognized a common ancestor formed a small kinship group. A broader kinship group – usually known as *ashira* – embraced those families who were united by a remote kinship link. Its members were bound by the strict obligations and rights of mutual assistance and responsibility. The *ashira* was headed by an elder, or shaikh, or sometimes by an *aqid* (military leader). It usually had an *arif* (expert in and interpreter of *urf*, or customary law). Each had its own name, *damgha* (seal), war-cry and often cemetery. An *ashira* might adopt strangers.

The next level was the sub-tribe – a group of kin bound by imaginary genealogical ties or by real blood ties, as well as by a political or military alliance. Above this came the tribe, usually referred to as *qabila*. It had its own territory, seal and war-cry and, to some extent, a common dialect, lifestyle, culture and system of beliefs. The tribesmen saw themselves as all descended from a common ancestor. A tribe was headed by a shaikh and also had an *aqid* and several *arifs*. Tribal groupings formed along ethnic (kinship) lines as well as on the basis of political considerations. Relations between the kindred tribes were regulated by the canons of *urf*.[32]

The phenomena peculiar to tribal society survived within the bedouin tribes. They include, first and foremost, the tribes' collective ownership of the *dira* (pasturelands). The boundaries of the lands belonging to a tribe were strictly determined. According to Volney:

Each such tribe appropriates a territory that forms its possession. In that respect, they differ from the cultivating nations in the only matter that their lands must be vast enough to ensure their herds with fodder all the year round. Each of such tribes forms one or more camps, which are scattered throughout the locality. They gradually change the location of their camps in the territory as their herds consume the fodder around the camps.[33]

This information is corroborated by later travellers.

A large number of the desert wells and reservoirs also belonged to the bedouin tribes. Burckhardt reports that:

> most wells in the interior of the Desert, and especially in Nedjd, are [the] exclusive property, either of a whole tribe, or of individuals whose ancestors dug the wells . . . If a well be the property of a tribe, the tents are pitched near it, whenever rain-water becomes scarce in the Desert; and no other Arabs are then permitted to water their camels there.[34]

The kinship and tribal subdivisions might be the collective owners of cultivated lands in the oases.[35] The bedouin rented them to African freedmen or Arab *fellahin*, took the share of the crop that was due to them and distributed it among their families.[36] Most stud-horses were owned by tribal communities, but the mares were always considered private property.[37] There are reports of communal camel herds in some tribes. There were many examples of mutual assistance in economic activities among the bedouin. Shearing was one such occasion and it was accompanied by entertainment. Kinsmen helped each other during family events, too, such as weddings and circumcisions.

The bedouin were famed for their hospitality and to neglect their customs was considered a disgrace. According to Volney:

> If a stranger or even an enemy touches a bedouin's tent, his personality becomes untouchable, so to say. Even a just revenge to the detriment of hospitality would be a meanness, an indelible disgrace. If a bedouin agrees to share his bread and salt with a guest, nothing in the world can make him betray the guest.[38]

However, many people were unable to offer hospitality to a guest for a long period, in which case their kinsmen came to their aid: as they did when a guest lost part or all of his property and the host was obliged to reimburse him.

Material aid from kinsmen was of particular importance in instances of murrain, caused by drought or disease among the animals, and when property was lost during raids. The property was redeemed by gifts of livestock, money, utensils or camp appliances. Families who found themselves in difficult circumstances were helped by their kinsmen, and the kinship confederations sought the help of their tribesmen or allied tribes. Doughty comments that, irrespective of who was robbed, a:

> calamity as this is [considered] general, and to be borne by the tribe. None which had lost their cattle to-day would be left destitute; but the governing sheykh taxing all the tribesmen, the like would be rendered to them, out of the common contribution, in a day or two.[39]

It is worth noting, however, that it was usually impossible to cover the losses completely, even where tribal solidarity and kinship bonds were strong. If a tribe was deprived of a sizeable part of its livestock due to a crushing military defeat, for example, the custom of loss reparation became virtually inoperative. The poor were doomed to starvation in such cases. In instances of severe drought or epidemics among the livestock, all tribesmen were the losers and they were often unable to help those who had suffered most. The custom of loss reparations was thus not a fiction but was restricted by circumstances.

Relations between different kinship and tribal subdivisions were regulated above all by the important customary-law institution: the blood feud.[40] According to Volney:

> The interests of common security have long ago caused the introduction of a law among the Arabs that requires a victim's death to be avenged by shedding the killer's blood. They call it *sar*, or vengeance. The victim's closest relative is charged with it. His honour is so greatly wounded in all Arabs' eyes that he is disgraced for ever if he neglects the duty of revenge. So he waits for an opportunity to take revenge. If his enemy dies for any other reason, he feels no satisfaction and shifts his revenge to the killer's closest relative. That hatred is inherited by sons from fathers and ceases only with the extinction of one of the kin, unless the families agree to sacrifice the guilty or to pay the blood money (in cash or in livestock).[41]

As a rule, the blood feud among the bedouin embraced the relatives up to the fifth generation. Whole groups of kinsmen affected by a blood feud would leave their tribes and seek refuge with the powerful shaikh of an alien tribe. They would then try to arrange payment of the blood money. Unless the person killed was from the tribal nobility, his relatives were usually ready to accept the payment. Its amount differed from region to region and among the various tribes but it was always a substantial sum. All the killer's relatives contributed to the payment. But when the relative of a shaikh had been killed, his noble kinsmen would accept nothing less than a payment in blood.[42]

The entire kinship group helped to ransom its members from captivity.[43] The well-off bedouin helped their poorer kinsmen in an emergency, gave them food, clothes and livestock and arranged entertainments, thus gaining in popularity. A reputation for meanness was a disgrace to a representative of the tribal nobility. Generosity was counted among the highest virtues.[44]

The bedouin were unfamiliar with the payment of regular taxes. 'Tax payment is always a humiliation,'[45] they are reported to have said. The absence of taxes within a tribe was the most important proof of stable patriarchal and tribal relations. Nonetheless, even observers who admired the bedouin's tradition of solidarity and mutual assistance found some phenomena among the tribes that were far from the supposed idyll.

Arabia on the Eve of the Emergence of Wahhabism

Elements of inequality within the nomadic tribes

Towards the end of 1784, Volney called on the shaikh of a tribe that roamed in the Gaza region. It is revealing to compare the standard of living of that representative of the tribal nobility (though not rich by European standards) with the income of an ordinary bedouin. The shaikh was:

> considered the most powerful in the whole locality, but it seemed to me that his expenses did not exceed those of a rich tax-farmer. His movables, which consisted of garments, carpets, arms, horses and camels, might be estimated at no more than 50,000 *livres*. It should be noted that the said sum included 4 full blood mares, each worth 6,000 *livres*, and camels, each worth 10 *louis d'or*. Therefore, our usual notions of a sovereign or a seignior cannot be applied to the bedouin. It would be more correct to compare them with well-off tax-farmers from the mountain regions whom they resemble in their simple clothes, domestic life and habits. A shaikh who commands a detachment of 50 horsemen does not disdain saddling and bridling his horse, giving it barley and chopped straw. His wife makes coffee, kneads dough and boils meat in the tent by her own hands. His daughters and female relatives wash the linen and go to the well with jugs on their veiled heads to draw water. It looks exactly as it was described by Homer or in the story of Abraham in Genesis.
>
> The bedouin's simplicity or, if you like, poverty is commensurable with the conditions of their chieftain's life. A family's entire property consists of the items whose almost full list is given below: some male and female camels, some hens, a mare with harness, a tent, a 13-foot-long [4 m] spear, a curved sabre, a rusty gun, a pipe, a portable mill, a cauldron, a coffee-frying pan, a mat, some clothes, a coat of black wool, and lastly, instead of all jewels, some silver or glass rings worn by the women on their feet or hands. A family that has all this is rich. A mare is something the poor have not but wish to have more than anything else.[46]

Although Volney idealizes the simple life of a bedouin shaikh, the shaikh had far more possessions than a simple bedouin who owned a horse. The condition of the poor nomads was incomparably worse. According to Volney:

> I noted that the shaikhs, i.e. the rich people, and their servants were generally taller and stouter than the common people. It may be explained only by their nutrition, more abundant in the first group than in the second. One may even say that a common bedouin lives always in poverty and starves permanently ... The food most of them consume within a day does not weigh more than 6 ounces [170 g]; moderation in eating reaches the extreme in the Najdi and Hijazi tribes. Six or seven dates, moistened in melted oil, and a little fresh or soured milk form a bedouin's daily ration. He feels happy if he can add to it some pinches of rough meal or some rice. Meat is eaten only on the most important festivals. A kid is slaughtered only for a wedding or funeral. Only rich shaikhs and military commanders may slaughter young camels and eat rice cooked with meat. Due to the unceasing want, the

ordinary people are always hungry and do not disdain even the most wretched food – locust, rats, lizards, snakes . . .[47]

While it is true that locusts were the greatest delicacy for the bedouin, rats, lizards and snakes may well be a figment of Volney's imagination.

Inequalities among the nomads were most evident in the ownership of livestock. While the poor in the Anaza tribe owned barely a dozen camels each, the herds of the more well-off numbered up to fifty beasts and the shaikhs' and their relatives' families owned hundreds of camels.[48] The most powerful shaikhs might own several thousand camels.

Through regulating the seasonal migrations and taking part in the distribution of pastures, the tribal nobility acquired preferential rights to dispose of the land, though their rule was restricted by tribal custom (*urf*). The shaikhs' herds received the best pastures. The reserved pastures (*hima*) for the shaikhs' livestock had existed since ancient times. Part of the water sources also became the property of the tribal nobility, who received a payment for their use from the common bedouin.

The exploitation derived, paradoxically, from the tribal tradition of mutual assistance during the seasonal transfers of livestock to new pastures. At such times, a poorer kinsman would receive a temporary loan in the form of animals.[49] This enabled the large livestock-owners to preserve and increase their herds. Livestock might also be leased to poor bedouin; in return, the owners received some of the young animals and a part of the products of animal husbandry.[50] The transfer of sheep for pasturing was even more widespread than that of camels. Camel-breeders could not take the young animals with them during their prolonged migrations and so left them with sheep-breeders of other kinship groups or tribes. The families of the tribal nobility who were unable to look after their camel herds used the labour of slaves or of people from other tribes, but seldom of their own tribesmen.

The levies that covered the expenses of providing hospitality became another means by which the nobility grew rich at the expense of the bedouin. Burckhardt reports that:

> in case strangers arrive for whom a lamb is to be killed, then the Arabs usually bring one for that purpose to the sheikh's tent. In some encampments, the Arabs will not permit their sheikh to slaughter a lamb on any occasion, but furnish by turns the meat for his tent.[51]

Since the shaikh 'has to receive guests very often, he takes a camel or a sheep here and there and is given readily, because the giver often eats in the shaikh's tent after the guests'. That is how the mechanics of the 'guest levy' were explained to Musil even as late as the beginning of the twentieth century.[52] The tribe helped the shaikh in buying a horse; and if his herd was depleted by a raid, his tribesmen would try to cover his loss. In similar circumstances, an ordinary bedouin could only partly rebuild his herd, according to Burckhardt.[53]

The shaikhs and *arifs* received remuneration for court proceedings. Some ordinary bedouin found themselves in a situation of personal dependence on the tribal nobility as a result of the well-established institution of seeking the protection (*dakhila*) of a powerful shaikh of one's own or another tribe. Some 'small families that were not strong enough for an independent life and needed protection and alliances'[54] would group themselves around such a shaikh.

A more developed form of dependence was trusteeship (*wisaya*), under which the poor asked for the shaikh's protection in return for payment. Whole groups often sought such protection. For example, those who feared a blood feud after a murder might seek the protection of the nobility in an alien tribe. This imposed certain duties, including economic ones, on the bedouin and thus their personal freedom was somewhat restricted.[55] The weakening of tribal bonds is also clear from the fact that a debtor was not entitled to any aid in repaying a creditor who was his tribesman, unlike the practice of mutual assistance in repaying creditors who were strangers.

Social relations within the nomadic tribes should not be considered in isolation from Arabian society as a whole: such an approach would distort the true picture. The bedouin, the semi-nomads and the settled people of Arabia were a united and interconnected social organism. The interrelations between different groups of the Arabian population, as well as many specific features of Arabian life, are of particular interest in determining the characteristics both of a bedouin tribe and of the society as a whole.[56]

Raids

Taking advantage of the lack of a strong centralized power, the bedouin regularly raided their neighbours. Their most frequent target was livestock, but they did not disdain camp equipment, utensils, arms and slaves, and carried off goods from merchants and agricultural produce and utensils from settled people. There was a distinction between a *ghazu* (raid) and a genuine war for pastures and wells, but both kinds of hostilities were regularly interwoven. According to Burckhardt:

> The Arab tribes are in a state of almost perpetual war against each other; it seldom happens that a tribe enjoys a moment of general peace with all its neighbours, yet the war between two tribes is scarcely ever of long duration; peace is easily made, but again broken upon the slightest pretence. The Arab warfare is that of partisans; general battles are rarely fought: to surprise the enemy by a sudden attack, and to plunder a camp, are chief objects of both parties. This is the reason why their wars are bloodless; the enemy is generally attacked by superior numbers, and he gives way without fighting, in hopes of retaliating on a weak encampment of the other party. The dreaded effects of 'blood-revenge', which shall be hereafter noticed, prevent many sanguinary conflicts.[57]

Volney also wrote about the bedouin raids:

> Being a plunderer rather than a fighter, an Arab does not strive for bloodshed: he attacks just to plunder and when resistance is offered, he considers that a scanty plunder is not worth the risk of being killed. To embitter him, one needs to shed his blood, but then he becomes as much stubborn in revenge as cautious in evading dangers. The Arabs were often reproached for their inclination to plunder, but, without any intention to justify it, I'd like to call attention to the overlooked fact that their striving for plunder is spearheaded only against a stranger whom they consider an enemy. Therefore such a striving is based on the public law of most nations.[58]

Raiding was considered the most noble occupation, and the dream of plunder constantly excited the bedouin's imagination. Participation in the *ghazu* was voluntary, but in practice, the bedouin, especially the young men, could not decline an invitation. A man who evaded taking part in a raid would be branded a coward, one who did not deserve the respect of his relatives and tribesmen. According to Niebuhr, 'I heard that a young man is not permitted to marry before he accomplishes some feats.'[59] The names of successful raiders were on everyone's lips and were celebrated by poets. Even twentieth-century writers sing of these glorious heroes with their bedouin daring (*furusiya*).

A poor bedouin could improve his situation or even become well-off after one successful raid. The *ghazu* was undoubtedly one cause of the persistence of a stratum of independent nomads. The raids enriched the tribal nobility, who seized most or the best part of the plunder.[60] The raids were led either by shaikhs or by *aqids* (military commanders). The shaikh received his share even when he did not take part in the raid. Plunder invariably appears among the main sources of income of the tribal nobility.

Naturally, the permanent raiding inflicted damage on the Arabian economy. Some raids involved bloodshed and led to cruel and destructive wars. Whole kinship groups and tribes could perish, either in battle or from starvation as a result of defeat. 'Sometimes a weak tribe rises and spreads its influence, while another tribe, once powerful, falls into decay or is even destroyed,'[61] writes Volney. Jaussen's observations, more than a century later, are similar:

> A tribe may disappear from the region in many ways. One of them is an exodus caused by big quarrels or a permanent famine in the region . . . A more frequent cause of annihilation of the tribes should be sought in permanent wars and raids . . . One unhappy day is enough to destroy the whole tribe; men remain in the battlefield and women scatter in the neighbouring tribes or . . . die of starvation.[62]

Tribes that had once been strong might decline, lose people, livestock and pastures, then submit to other tribes and sometimes even merge with them. The military strength of the various tribes and their subdivisions depended not only on the bravery of the fighters and the leaders' talent and courage but on the character of the bedouin's economic activities. It was camel-breeders, the 'genuine' nomads, who possessed the greatest military might. Camels carried them quickly over long distances through arid deserts and enabled them to concentrate their forces and deliver sudden blows. If defeated, the bedouin retreated to the desert – an asylum that was inaccessible to the enemy. The camel-breeders were usually successful in raids, won major battles and had no rivals but other camel-breeders. Overall, the balance of gains and losses resulting from raids was favourable to the nomads and unfavourable to the semi-nomadic sheep-breeders. The settled people, too, usually avoided confronting the 'genuine' bedouin in the open field. The security of their trade, their livestock in the desert and semi-desert pastures, their fields and palm groves all depended on their relations with the bedouin.

The stronger bedouin camel-breeding tribes imposed tribute on the weaker tribes, chiefly those engaged in sheep-breeding, and on the settled population. The *ghazu* served as a way to coerce others into tributary and sometimes even vassal dependence.

Tribute

The payment of *khuwa* (tribute) to the bedouin by the semi-nomadic and settled people had been understood as a system of remuneration in return for protection since ancient times. That is why the tribute was referred to as 'brotherhood' (the literal meaning of *khuwa*). Burckhardt writes:

> The tribute is generally paid to the sheikh or some respectable man of the tribe. When this is first agreed upon between a village and an Arab, the latter requires that part of the stipulated annual sum should be paid down immediately; out of this he purchases some eatables, which he divides among his friends, that they may be witnesses of the compact, as having eaten part of the khoue [*khuwa*].[63]

It was not only the payer's protector who received the tribute. Wallin reports that 'generally the tribute consists in presents of clothing, given not only to the principal shaikh of the tribe, but also to almost every influential person of the different clans'.[64] A sizeable part of the *khuwa* remained with the elite of the tribe, but the rank-and-file kinsmen also received a share. The settled and semi-nomadic people might make payments to more than one tribe simultaneously and the latter collected the tribute from the many oases and the sheep-breeding tribes.[65] Sometimes the *khuwa*-paying semi-nomads, in their turn, imposed a tribute on the weaker tribes or oases. Sophisticated forms of dependence were thus created. The *khuwa* brought substantial returns to the tribal nobility and to all the bedouin. The bedouin tribes fought for the right to collect the tribute, killing the tributaries too. The yoke of 'adopted brothers' might be discarded only in the event of armed resistance, which was seldom victorious.[66]

The tributary relations frequently turned into vassalage, in which case the subdued tribes took part in their suzerain's raids, or in other words, they paid the 'blood tribute'. A vassal shaikh demonstrated his respect for the suzerain shaikh. Some tribes were so highly dependent that Dickson describes the Rashaid tribe as 'serfs' of the Mutair, and the Awazim tribe as 'servants' of the Ajman.[67] While both these accounts relate to the twentieth century, similar relations seem to have existed earlier too.

The bedouin imposed duties – also referred to as *khuwa* – on the merchants' and pilgrims' caravans. Ibn Bishr uses the cognate word *ikhawat*[68] to denote the levy, a word used as early as the works of Ibn Khaldun. In the eighteenth and nineteenth centuries, the Sublime Porte had to pay large sums to the bedouin to ensure the safe passage of the Ottoman pilgrims' caravans to Mecca. Burckhardt estimated these dues at between £50,000 and £60,000 a year in the early nineteenth century.[69] In 1756 the pasha of Damascus delayed making the payment and even had the shaikhs executed when they came to collect the dues. Two years later, however, the united bedouin tribes annihilated the pilgrims' guards, looted the caravan and compelled the Turkish authorities to resume the payments.[70] The tribal nobility also received a payment that was stipulated by custom as for the 'protection' of vagrant craftsmen and traders.[71]

The 'lower' tribes

The powerful bedouin tribes also collected tribute from the so-called 'lower' tribes – the Sulubba, Hitaim, Shararat and their branches. The peculiarities of their historical development had resulted in their splitting into several kinship subdivisions, which seldom had a territory of their own and were scattered throughout the peninsula in small groups: this explains their weakness. According to Burckhardt:

> Of the innumerable tribes who people the deserts of Arabia, none is more dispersed, nor more frequently seen in all parts of that country, than the Heteym [Hitaim]. In Syria, in Lower and Upper Egypt, along the whole coast of the Red Sea down to Yemen, in Nedjd [Najd] and Mesopotamia, encampments of the Heteym are always to be found. Perhaps it is from this wandering disposition that they are much less respected than any other tribe ... They are, besides, obliged almost everywhere, to pay tribute to the neighbouring Bedouins for permission to pasture their cattle.[72]

The Sulubba's main means of transportation was the ass rather than the camel. As a rule, animal husbandry could not support these pariahs; they engaged in occupations that were despised by Arabian society – such as specific crafts, music, dancing and quackery.[73] They might also forecast the weather and indicate the best pastures in return for payment.[74]

The members of the 'lower' tribes were subjected to the bedouin's ruthless extortions. Doughty gives an example:

> Some Annezy [Anaza] men came one day haling a naked wretch, with a cord about his neck, through the village street: it was an Heteymy [Hitaimi]; and the Beduins cried furiously against him, that he had withheld the khûwa, ten reals! and

Arabia on the Eve of the Emergence of Wahhabism

they brought him to see if any man in Kheybar [al-Khobar], as he professed to them, would pay for him; and if no, they would draw him out of the town and kill him.[75]

This incident alone is sufficient to illustrate the wide gap between a free bedouin and a member of a 'lower' tribe.

Slaves and freedmen

Slavery persisted in Arabia for many centuries.[76] Most slaves were brought to the peninsula from East and Central Africa. They were seized and purchased by special expeditions of slave-traders or brought to be sold by pilgrims who wanted to cover their *hajj* expenses. The slave trade was concentrated chiefly in Mecca but was conducted in other towns, too, such as Hufuf and Muscat. Several thousand slaves probably came every year to Arabia. Arabs were only very rarely enslaved. The children of slaves (known as *muwalids*) sometimes inherited their parents' social status.

Most slaves were found around the centre of the slave trade, in Hijaz, where every relatively well-off family would expect to buy a slave. Outside Hijaz, only rich families owned them. Palgrave writes, 'Throughout Arabia we had frequently met with negroes – in Djowf [Jawf], Shomer [Shammar], Kassem [Qasim], and Sedeyr [Sudair]. But we had only met with them in the condition of slaves, and rarely in other than in the wealthier households.'[77] Travellers reported that the number of Africans and mulattos increased in southern Najd and they formed a majority in some oases. 'Riad abounds with them, Manfoohah and Selemee'yah yet more, while they swarm in the Hareek, Wadi Dowasir, and their vicinity.'[78] The tribal nobility also owned slaves. Burckhardt writes about the Anaza, 'Every powerful sheikh procures annually five or six male slaves, and some females.'[79] The situation in other bedouin tribes was similar.

Slaves performed the hardest and dirtiest work. They pastured the nomads' livestock, brought water, pitched and struck tents and gathered the firewood. Slave labour was used in agriculture and handicrafts too, but to a very limited extent. It was mainly used in the household, where slaves acted as servants, guards and housekeepers.

Certain characteristics of the conditions of slaves in Arabia deserve special mention. Slavery was patriarchal in character, which explains the generally kind treatment of slaves, who, particularly if they were *muwalids*, were treated as if they were subordinate members of their master's family. Sometimes they even inherited their master's property. Female slaves became concubines, mainly of the urban nobility. They and their children were usually manumitted after their master's death. Although oppressed and humiliated socially, the slaves might enjoy a better standard of living than the half-starving nomads or peasants.

Large numbers of slaves were freed in Arabia: it was not the exclusive lot of concubines and their children. The number of 'hereditary' slaves was insignificant. The process of manumission was more widespread among the bedouin tribes than among the settled people. Once a certain period had elapsed, the bedouin always freed their slaves and would marry them to women with the same skin colour. According to Burckhardt, 'The Aenezes [Anaza] always abstain from cohabitation with their female slaves, but, after a service of some years, give them their freedom, and marry them to their male slaves, or the descendants of slaves, established in the tribe.'[80] The freedmen, known as *abds*, engaged in small-scale trade and handicrafts or entered service with rich houses.

The liberation of slaves had another meaning, too, in Arabian conditions. For example, a shaikh of the Anaza had:

> above fifty tents belonging to persons who were once his slaves and owe their good fortune wholly to the liberality of that sheikh. He cannot now exact from them any yearly tribute, as they are reckoned free Arabs; but he demands their daughters in marriage for his newly-purchased and emancipated slaves; and if in time of war those black men should acquire considerable booty, the sheikh may ask from them a fine camel, which they never refuse to give.[81]

Some freedmen united in formal kinship lines, but such kin were considered lower than those of pure Arabs. The freedmen remained dependent, both economically and personally, on the bedouin rulers.

The bulk of freedmen engaged in agriculture. Since they had no land, they were obliged to rent it, chiefly from the settled or nomadic nobility (sometimes from whole nomadic tribes). The sharecroppers were subjected to ruthless exploitation and, according to Wallin, very few of them were well-off.[82] Their dependence on their former masters was considerable. Besides, in some cases, a freedman who intended to leave his ex-master's house was required to return the property that the master had given him when he was freed,[83] which was often impossible. The returns from the lands cultivated by freedmen were among the bedouin rulers' most important sources of external (i.e. extra-tribal) income.

The role of external income sources in a nomadic tribe

While non-class relations prevailed between the tribal nobility and the ordinary bedouin, the nomadic nobility appeared as a sort of feudal class outside the tribe. The share in the *ghazu* plunder, the tribute paid by the settled people and by the semi-nomadic and 'lower' tribes, and the rent for irrigated lands formed the lion's share of their income.[84] As noted above, the bedouin nobility could receive only an insignificant income from their tribesmen's labour. But agriculture ensured higher productivity and permitted a more intense exploitation of the peasant farmers. Besides, the nobility might impose a heavy tribute on strangers, which condemned the tributaries to deprivation and starvation. Raids may also be considered a predatory, barbaric method of exploitation which sometimes caused the death of the victims.

A tribe's external income enriched its elite and increased economic stratification.

But a part of the income fell to the ordinary nomads – this was conducive to the preservation of the stratum of independent bedouin and helped to even out inequalities. The dual character of the tribal nobility – as richer and more noble tribesmen and as exploiters of strangers – determined the nature of political power among the nomads and in Arabian society as a whole.

The organization and nature of power in a nomadic tribe

Within a tribe, the shaikh was first and foremost the patriarchal elder and the manager of economic activities. He guided the tribes' migrations, allocated pastures and wells and chose the time and place to pitch camp. The shaikh might act as judge or arbiter in the disputes and misunderstandings that arose within the tribe concerning family and everyday life; he supervised the observance of tribal customs, especially those related to incest; and he kept watch over the return of stolen property. He represented the tribe in its relations with the outside world and received distinguished guests on its behalf. The shaikh might also be the *aqid* and he could declare war and conclude peace.[85]

The shaikh took the major decisions after consultations with the tribal nobility or the *majlis* (tribal council),[86] which preserved the features of a democratic tribal organization. As Doughty reports, 'let him speak here who will, the voice of the least is heard among them; he is a tribesman'.[87] According to Burckhardt, 'The sheikh cannot declare war or conclude terms of peace, without consulting the chief men of his tribe; if he wish to break up the camp, he must previously ask the opinions of his people.'[88] The *majlis* was also:

> the council of the elders and the public tribunal: hither the tribesmen bring their causes at all times . . . The sheykh meanwhile takes counsel with the sheukh, elder men and more considerable persons; and judgment is given commonly without partiality and always without bribes. This sentence is final.[89]

It was the *arifs* (experts in *urf*) who conducted trials before a court. If a tribesman was sentenced to a fine and disagreed with the court's decision, he had to leave the tribe.

The military-democratic character of the tribal organization was revealed in the division of power into 'civil' (that of the shaikh) and 'military' (that of the *aqid*). According to Burckhardt:

> Every tribe has, besides the sheikh, an agyd [*aqid*]; and it rarely happens that the offices of both are united in one person, at least no instance of such a case is known to me; although some Arabs mentioned, that they had seen a sheikh acting as agyd among the Basrah Arabs . . . If the sheikh join the troops, he is for the time commanded by the agyd, whose office ceases whenever the soldiers return home: the sheikh then resumes his own authority.[90]

Reports by the Arabian chroniclers, together with the latest information, however, make it clear that the cumulation of the shaikh's and the *aqid*'s power was a far more frequent event than Burckhardt believed it to be. The shaikh's son or some other relative might become the *aqid*, and the families of the shaikh and the *aqid* were frequently related.

The head of the tribe had, as a rule, no outer attributes of power and did not observe any special ceremonial in his relations with the tribesmen. Ordinary bedouin associated with him as equals. When the shaikh died or became infirm, a new one was elected in his place. The qualities that the head of a tribe was supposed to possess included generosity, courage, wisdom, prudence and wealth (in both livestock and land). He was expected to have numerous supporters, both relatives and servants.[91] Volney reports:

> Actually, it is the chief shaikh of every tribe who must maintain those who come and go; it is he who receives the allies and everybody who comes for business purposes. A big marquee is pitched near his tent to accommodate all strangers and guests. Assemblies of shaikhs and noble persons are often held in it on the questions of pitching and striking the camp, of war, peace, disputes with Turkish governors or peasants, settlement of conflicts between private persons. These people, who come in turns, need to be served coffee, bread that is baked in ashes, rice and sometimes fried camel's or goat's meat – in brief, the shaikh must be hospitable. Generosity is the more important as the most essential articles are concerned. His influence and might depend on it: a hungry Arab puts the generosity that provides him with food above all other virtues. This prejudice is not unfounded, since experience has shown that mean shaikhs have never been magnanimous.[92]

In principle, any bedouin might become a shaikh, but from the necessary qualifications listed above it is clear that the route to power in the tribe was closed to the poor. In most tribes, the title of shaikh remained with members of the same noble family for decades or even centuries. As Doughty claims, 'No commoner, nor any of strange blood, even though he surpassed all men in wealth and sufficiency, can come to be the head of a nomad *ashîra*.'[93] Noble descent was an important qualification when contesting the title of shaikh.

Power was often transferred from father to son, but when the heir lacked the necessary qualities, another representative of the tribal nobility was elected instead. The same rule held for the *aqid*. Shaikhs and *aqids* were rivals within the same tribe, and some *aqids* seized civil power too. The *arifs* also belonged to the nobility.[94] A ruthless power struggle was often waged within the ruling group of a tribe, accompanied by intrigue, murder and internal divisions. The claimant's personal virtues were an ideal: they did not always determine the outcome of the struggle.

The concentration of important administrative posts in the hands of the tribal nobility proved that authority was losing its patriarchal features. But did the shaikhs also enjoy the embryonic attributes of a primitive state? In other words, were not their apparently patriarchal functions endowed with a different content? To a certain degree, they were. A shaikh undoubtedly served first and foremost the interests of the bedouin nobility. He allotted the nobles the best pastures and watering-places and the greater part of the plunder. To impose his will, a shaikh not only used generosity and his personal authority, but also relied on his numerous relatives and supporters and on his armed detachments, which consisted of slaves and freedmen. However, it seems to the present writer that, notwithstanding an obvious trend in the transformation of the power of the shaikhs and their entourages within the tribes into power of a feudal type, that transformation had not yet occurred in the period under discussion.[95] To clarify this problem, we need to establish whether the nomadic nobility had a special apparatus that stood above society and could be used to realize its will. According to Volney:

> The mode of rule in that society is simultaneously republican, aristocratic and even despotic, without being exactly any of them. It is republican, because in that society the people enjoy the main influence in all matters and nothing is done without the majority's consent. It is aristocratic, because the shaikhs' families enjoy certain privileges, which originate from might everywhere. Lastly, it is despotic, because the chief shaikh's power is boundless and almost absolute. When the shaikh is a man with a strong character, he may use and even misuse his power, but even such misuse is rigidly limited. Indeed, if a shaikh commits a great injustice, for example the murder of an Arab, he is almost unable to evade punishment. The injured person's anger would not reckon even a little with his title; he will be subject to revenge and inevitably perish unless he pays for the bloodshed. It is easy to do so due to his simple private life in the camp.
>
> If he burdens his subjects with his severity, they leave him and join other tribes. His relatives use his mistakes to overthrow him and occupy his place. He cannot use foreign troops against them. The intercourse among his subjects is so easy that he cannot divide them and create a sizeable group of his own. Besides, how can he bribe such a group when he collects no taxes in the tribe, when most of his subjects have to content themselves with the necessary minimum, when his properties are rather insignificant and his present expenses are huge?[96]

According to Burckhardt's observations:

> the sheikh has no actual authority over the individuals of his tribe; he may, however, by his personal qualities obtain considerable influence. His commands would be treated with contempt; but deference is paid to his advice . . . Should a dispute happen between two individuals, the sheikh will endeavour to settle the matter; but if either party be dissatisfied with his advice, he cannot insist upon obedience . . . and in fact, the most powerful Aeneze chief dares not inflict a trifling punishment on the poorest man of his tribe, without incurring the risk of mortal vengeance from the individual and his relatives.[97]

Other European explorers of Arabia at that time give similar accounts.

Under the then structure of Arabian society, the tribal nobility as a whole was not interested in the destruction of the tribal organization and its replacement by a state machinery. It was only by relying on the tribe's military might that the nobility could dominate the non-tribal groupings.[98]

The feudal character of power in the oases

The English traveller Lady Anne Blunt noted the dual character of the power of the bedouin nobility:

> The towns put themselves each under the protection of the principal Bedouin Sheykh of its district, who, on the consideration of a yearly tribute, guarantees the citizens' safety outside the city walls, enabling them to travel unmolested as far as his jurisdiction extends, and this, in the case of a powerful tribe, may be many hundred miles and embrace many cities. The towns are then said to 'belong to such and such a tribe', and the Bedouin Sheykh becomes their suzerain, or Lord Protector . . .
>
> A farther development then ensues. The Bedouin Sheykh, grown rich with the tribute of a score of towns, builds himself a castle close to one of them and lives there during the summer months. Then with the prestige of his rank (for Bedouin blood is still accounted the purest), and backed by his power in the desert, he speedily becomes the practical ruler of the town, and from protector of the citizens becomes their sovereign. He is now dignified by them with the title of Emir or prince, and *though still their Sheykh to the Bedouins, becomes king of all the towns which pay him tribute* [author's emphasis].
>
> In the town, on the other hand, the Bedouin prince, despotic though he may be, is still under close restraint from public opinion . . . The Emir, irresponsible as he is in individual acts, knows well that he cannot transgress the traditional unwritten law of Arabia with impunity.[99]

The transformation of the nomadic nobility into a dominant group occurred gradually and took various forms. The powerful shaikhs of tribes and tribal confederations might establish their control over an oasis or a group of oases, but some of them continued the bedouin way of life and remained nomadic shaikhs *par excellence*. For example, the noble clan of Al Humaid of the Bani Khalid tribe controlled al-Hasa, a rich agricultural province, in the seventeenth and eighteenth centuries but, like the first Umayyads, preferred not to leave their bedouin camp. This did not prevent them from stationing their garrisons in the key oases. The noble family of Al Shaalan, the chieftains of the Rwala tribe, who roamed to the south of Syria, behaved likewise in the nineteenth century.

Those members of the nomadic nobility who seized power in oases cut themselves off from their tribes and became settled feudal rulers. Their attempts to exploit the agricultural population clashed with the interests of the bedouin as tribute-collectors. The former bedouin shaikhs who had become part of the settled nobility protected their estates and incomes from the nomads' encroachments. This was the origin both of the Saudis (the Al Saud, the emirs of al-Diriya) and of the Rashidis (the Al Rashid, the rulers of Hail).

Lastly, a powerful settled ruler would raid, rob and sometimes impose tribute on the neighbouring nomads either on his own or in an alliance with other tribes. Among the rulers who did so were the Saudis and the Rashidis in the period when they were strong, the Saudis' vassals the al-Madaifi, the ruler of al-Taif and some bedouin chieftains of Hijaz, as well as Abu Nuqta, the emir of Asir. The same was true in principle of the sharifs of Mecca.

In the Arabian oases, power was not always concentrated in the hands of a single ruler. Some peasants from different tribes fought among themselves, had no single ruler and were governed by their own shaikhs or emirs. The rulers of the oases were referred to in different ways. The most frequent title was emir or shaikh, but the terms *rais*, *sahib*, *wali*, *kabir* and *sayid* were also used. There is no clear distinction in the use of these titles in the writings of the Arabian chroniclers or the European travellers.

The power of a settled emir differed materially from that of a nomadic shaikh. The ruler of an oasis did not face a tribal military-political organization. Peasants, with their weakened tribal and kinship ties, were far more dependent on the nobility than the bedouin were. It is not surprising, therefore, that the Arabian chroniclers call the oasis-dwellers *raya*, meaning 'subjects', 'herd', 'human livestock'. An emir (a feudal ruler) relied, on the one hand, on the oasis nobility among whom he had many relatives and, on the other hand, on his own detachments, which consisted of slaves, freedmen and mercenaries. The judicial system was usually based on the *sharia*, containing the fundamentals of Muslim law. Justice was administered both by the ruler and by the *qadhi* (a judge who had studied jurisprudence and theology).

The organization of the settled emirs' feudal power may be exemplified by Mecca in the eighteenth century. It differed from the oasis-towns of the peninsula, however, especially from those in central Arabia: its unique status as a holy city for all Muslims, its large volume of trade via Jidda, the relatively high income of the sharif and the particularly noble status of his kin (supposed to be direct descendants of the Prophet) all contributed to its particular character.

The rulers of Mecca only came to power with the consent of the most influential sharifian families and with the formal sanction of the Ottoman sultan. The Meccan army consisted of several hundred *abds* and mercenaries. The sharif could increase its size in case of emergency thanks to his rich exchequer. His officials were usually slaves, from among whom he appointed a vicegerent to Jidda and a customs officer. The sharifs always tried to secure the favour of the neighbouring nomadic tribes and they sent their own children to the tribes to be brought up by the bedouin. The future warriors and rulers became strong, hardy and resourceful and, even more important, acquired friends and allies in the future struggle for power and influence.[100]

The political situation in Jabal Shammar, an emirate described by several travellers in the middle and second half of the nineteenth century, may have shared some of the features of the organization of power in the small oasis-states of central Arabia in the eighteenth century. In ruling the state, its emirs relied not only on their relatives but, above all, on their slaves and freedmen, who enjoyed the ruler's confidence to a greater extent. The Rashidis, as well as the sharifs of Mecca, relied on their guard composed of slaves and mercenaries. The top-ranking slaves, known as the *rajail al-shuyukh* (chief shaikh's men), occupied the most important posts in the palace and in the nascent state apparatus, and were appointed as vicegerents to oases. The most important criminal (and some civil) cases were examined by the emir's *majlis* in public with the participation of the nobility and the leading *ulama* (theologians). The ruler's guard also acted as a police force. There was a jail in Hail. Criminals were punished by the confiscation of their property, by caning or by their hand being amputated.[101] Statehood was less developed in other oases, however. When Doughty visited Anaiza, a large trading centre in Qasim, he found no jail there.[102]

The institution that supported feudal power in the oases was the slave guard, which was entirely dependent on the ruler and unrelated to the local population. The *abds* – soldiers, policemen and officials – occupied a privileged position, received large incomes and became virtually a part of the ruling group, although enjoying limited rights. Having acquired great weight and influence, these high-ranking slaves claimed and sometimes even seized power, as happened, for example, in Riyadh in the first half of the eighteenth century and in Mecca in the late 1780s.[103] The influence of the *abds'* military might could also reach the bedouin shaikhs. In Arabia, the *abds* might even have become the ruling class, as did the Turkic guard under the Abbasids and the Mamelukes in Egypt, but this possibility did not become a reality.

The elements of a caste system within Arabian society

The multifaceted structure of Arabian society was further complicated by the elements of caste division and the related customs and prejudices. Fundamentally, such elements were determined by the type of economic activity, tribal and kinship relations, social divisions and the psychological peculiarities of the population. As mentioned previously, camel-breeding bedouin were considered the noblest representatives of the human race. They themselves were convinced of their superiority over the settled and semi-settled people. Their 'noble blood' precluded any occupations but raiding, camel-breeding, caravan transportation and sometimes trade. In the 'blue-blood' bedouin tribes, sheep-breeders were despised and commanded no respect. If a camel-breeding nomad engaged in sheep-breeding or farming, he sullied his 'nobility' to such an extent that he could hardly return to the company of genuine bedouin.[104] The bedouin substantiated their claims to particularly noble blood by genealogical trees whose roots went back into the mists of time. Genealogists were kept busy in Arabia![105]

The next stage in the hierarchy was occupied by sheep-breeders, who in turn looked down on the settled people. The next lowest group were the peasant farmers, provided they could trace their origins back to noble ancestors. The inequalities between these groups were increased by the lack of regular intermarriage between them. Even a very poor bedouin seldom agreed to marry his daughter to a well-off peasant farmer.

The nobility, with its various degrees of 'blue blood', rose above the three strata of the Arabian population. The members of the nobility placed themselves as high above the common bedouin as the latter were 'superior' to the peasant farmers. Pershits has noted correctly:

> Unlike all other tribesmen, who traced their origin to a common ancestor, the families of chief tribal shaikhs often claimed a 'noble' genealogy, which differed from that of the tribe ... The blood of shaikhs and their relatives was either above any value (usually among the bedouin) or cost much more than that of a common tribesman (usually among the semi-nomads). Breaking the customary standards of kin and tribal endogamy, shaikhs married their daughters to the shaikhs of other tribes and took in marriage only shaikhs' daughters, in which case the bride price adopted in the shaikhs' milieu was much higher than usual.[106]

Doughty describes the tribal nobility as 'nobles of the blood, of a common ancestor'.[107] Volney's opinion is similar: 'The members of one or more families of the tribe are given the title shaikhs (seigniors). They are equivalent to the Roman patricians and the European noblemen.'[108] The settled nobility, too, stressed its origins in the bedouin nobility. On some occasions, its members strove to continue the bedouin way of life and they maintained blood ties with the nomadic nobility.

The 'lower' tribes, such as the Sulubba, the Ilitaim and the Shararat, were the pariahs of Arabian society. Applying their tribal names to others was a grave insult. The members of the 'lower' tribes had to demonstrate their esteem whenever they met 'noble' Arabs. Those with 'blue blood' in their veins never married people of the 'lower tribes',[109] about whose origins scandalous legends were spread. This did not prevent young men from the noble families from taking advantage of the rather loose morals of the 'lower' tribes in order to have love affairs with their girls. Such examples abound in the bedouin's oral poetry.[110] Some contemporary scholars maintain that certain 'lower' tribes, such as the Sulubba, are of a pre-Arab or even pre-Semitic descent.[111] Others believe that they came to the peninsula after the Arabs.[112]

Craftsmen were even more despised in Arabian society than were the 'lower' tribes. Professional handicrafts, especially weaving, were considered the worst occupation for an Arab. The word *sani* (craftsman; pl. *sunnaa*) was an insult. Even members of the 'lower' tribes tended to shun marriage with the *sunnaa*. Some craftsmen (particularly smiths) formed isolated castes of their own, scattered throughout the peninsula, and considered themselves members of a single tribe.[113] Craftsmen who were foreigners or freedmen did not enter their organization.

The lowest rung on the Arabian social scale was occupied by *abds* (slaves and freedmen). Only they intermarried with the 'lower' tribes and *sunnaa*, which may explain the distinct ethnic characteristics of both the craftsmen and the lower tribes.

It should be noted that each 'outcaste' group – the 'lower' tribes, the *sunnaa* and the *abds* – had its own 'elite'. Their wealth sometimes exceeded that of the ordinary bedouin and even of the nobility. As mentioned previously, some slaves rose to high office and their status was far above that of many of the settled or nomadic nobility. But even a very poor bedouin would look down upon an influential vicegerent of *abd* descent and would not marry his daughter to him under any circumstances.

Factors leading to decentralization or to unity

From the time of the Prophet Muhammad up to the emergence of Wahhabism in the eighteenth century, there was no all-Arabian power, and no peace or stability in the peninsula. For centuries, Arabia had been fragmented, mostly into small or tiny oasis-states or their associations, nomadic tribes or their confederations. The isolation of individual oases and tribes as independent economic entities, together with the vast size of the peninsula, where islands of human life were separated by the deserts (sometimes spreading over hundreds of kilometres), acted as factors for decentralization. Other obstacles to unity were tribal and local differences among the population, the various Arabic dialects, and the diversity and contradictory character of the religious beliefs and ideas.

The members of the tribal and oasis nobility were interested in expanding the boundaries of their territories to acquire new sources of wealth. However, the aspirations of each individual group of the nobility came into conflict with those of their neighbours. Their forces were exhausted in the mutual struggle. Sometimes, however, a noble group that relied on the military might of the bedouin or the settled people and was led by a talented leader managed to expand its territories and increase its dominance. As a result, relatively large states formed. The main motive force behind such mergers was the expansion of territory, which ensured military spoils. There were vast regions in Arabia – Hijaz, Najd, al-Hasa, Yemen and Oman – where the centrifugal forces of feudal-tribal anarchy were combined with the centripetal forces of unity.

The economy could develop at a somewhat faster rate in large territories under one ruler thanks to the sense of security and the influx of wealth from outside. But then the desire to conquer diminished, internal struggles and rivalries undermined the power of the authorities, the preconditions for internal discontent appeared, the centrifugal forces became dominant and the states broke up. Natural disasters and epidemics might drastically accelerate that process.

Two somewhat contradictory assertions may therefore be made. On the one hand, the potential forces for consolidation had existed for centuries in a fragmented Arabia. On the other, powerful forces for disintegration soon emerged in any new centralized state. The first Saudi state in Arabia was no exception. However, it attained a might and a size that had been unknown since the birth of Islam.

Arabia on the Eve of the Emergence of Wahhabism

The Ottoman empire and Arabia. The weakening of foreign influence in the peninsula by the mid-eighteenth century

The Muslim empires that had emerged and then disintegrated in the Middle East had all had an influence, whether direct or indirect, on Arabia. Since the sixteenth century, the Turks had become a permanent factor in Arabian politics. Soon after they seized Egypt, they conquered Hijaz, Yemen and other regions of Arabia. An Ottoman pasha was appointed to Jidda, the sea port of Mecca. Small Turkish garrisons were sometimes stationed in Mecca, Medina, Jidda and other towns, and officials were occasionally sent from Istanbul to Mecca and Medina. Nevertheless, Ottoman power in Hijaz was nominal and local rulers generally enjoyed a substantial degree of autonomy in local affairs.

Mecca was ruled by rival clans of sharifs, who sent money and costly gifts to the pasha of Egypt and the sultan. But Mecca was an unusual town since it lived at the expense of the pilgrims and on charitable donations from the Muslim world. Powerful sultans and pious Muslims donated money for the maintenance and repair of the Kaaba and mosques and for canal-building. A part of the donations remained in the town and was often credited to the exchequers of the sharifs. Mecca was an important but remote Ottoman province: the Turks could not keep it under their direct dominance and preferred it to be governed by local rulers. The sharifian families who lived in Istanbul were always kept in readiness for the Porte's political intrigues.[114] Central and eastern Arabia became virtually independent from the Turks at the beginning of the seventeenth century when riots and sedition spread throughout the Ottoman empire, although Ottoman vicegerents in Baghdad and Basra continued to influence developments in al-Hasa and Najd up to end of the century.

The Ottoman empire's decline began in the early eighteenth century, after the defeat at Vienna in 1683. Nor was the situation altered by the Turks' victories over the Persians in the first decades of the eighteenth century. The empire still possessed vast territories in Europe, Asia and Africa with huge natural and human resources. However, the basis of the Turks' might was crumbling. The janissaries' military strength decreased because of their involvement in family life, handicrafts and trade.[115] Dissolute behaviour and corruption replaced the earlier discipline of Ottoman soldiers and officials.

Military defeats removed the most important source of income for the ruling elite – the plunder seized from their defeated enemies. There was ruthless exploitation of the native people, particularly of the peasants, by the Turkish pashas and officials. Agriculture, the basis of the Ottoman economy, was rapidly being destroyed. Exorbitant levies and taxes undermined even the simple reproduction of the population. Villages became deserted and fallow lands now occupied a sizeable part of the empire's territory. The urban population, too, was ruined by plunder and extortion.

Neither life nor property was guaranteed in the Ottoman empire of the eighteenth century. Sultans, provincial and district rulers and officials often executed people just to confiscate their properties. Only the *ulama* enjoyed personal security and immunity for their property. To avoid confiscation, bankrupt landowners transferred their estates and houses to the *waqfs* (Muslim charitable foundations) and then leased them back.

As Ottoman provinces acquired increasing independence, they came under semi-independent rulers. It is not surprising that the Porte lost real control over the Arabian territories too. The sharifs of Mecca behaved with increasing independence and took less and less notice of the Turks. The Ottoman sultans conferred the title of 'pasha of Jidda' upon a series of individuals who seldom appeared in Hijaz. The sharifs of Mecca seized an increasing share of the taxes paid to the Jidda customs-house. The nomadic tribes dominated the pilgrimage routes. The Porte's stable outposts in Hijaz were then determined not by its military might but by the Hijaz nobility's interest in the income from the pilgrims (who came mainly from the Ottoman empire) and in valuable gifts from the Turkish sultans.[116] As for Yemen, in the first half of the seventeenth century it became independent, both formally and in practice, soon after the Turkish conquest.

In the east of the peninsula in the 1670s one Barrak, the shaikh of a subdivision of the Bani Khalid, united the whole tribe, expelled the small Turkish units from the al-Hasa oases and prevented even nominal Ottoman control of eastern Arabia.[117] The Bani Khalid then started periodic raids on Iraq.

The decrease in foreign interference in Arabian affairs showed itself also in the weakening of Portuguese positions on the Gulf coast. The Portuguese were driven out of Oman in the mid-seventeenth century after having seized it in the sixteenth. As for Britain and France, their attempts at colonial expansion in Arabia started mainly in the second half of the eighteenth century. The Persian invasions of the littoral towns of eastern Arabia in the early eighteenth century were only sporadic and did not lead to their gaining strength in that region of the peninsula. Thus around the time that Wahhabism emerged, Arabia had largely been left to itself for several decades.

Najd, Hijaz and al-Hasa in the first half of the eighteenth century

Central Arabia experienced invasions by its eastern and western neighbours in the seventeenth and the early eighteenth centuries. This did not preclude several successful raids by the Najdi tribes on the oases and tribes of Hijaz and al-Hasa. The Hijazis attacked almost all the provinces of Najd, starting with Qasim, and the central Arabian bedouin – the Anaza, Mutair and Zafir. Some central Arabian tribes and oases paid tribute to the sharifs of Mecca. Ibn Bishr describes some people from among the Hijaz nobility as Najdi sharifs.[118] According to Philby, this proves that the sharifs of Mecca were striving to substantiate their claims to the inner regions of Arabia.[119]

Economic conditions in Hijaz deteriorated in the early eighteenth century and Mecca became depopulated due to a devastating famine.[120] The struggle for power and the internal unrest increased to such a degree that it was impossible for the Hijazis to undertake raids into the inner regions of Arabia. The last large-scale campaigns against Najd were launched in the mid-1720s.[121] Hijaz's interference in central Arabian affairs then ceased for several decades.

Arabia on the Eve of the Emergence of Wahhabism

Barrak, the shaikh of the Bani Khalid, started raids on the bedouin who roamed between al-Hasa and Najd and then on Najd itself after establishing his power in eastern Arabia. His heirs continued the expansion. Al-Kharj, Sudair, Sadiq and al-Arid experienced inroads from al-Hasa. The Bani Khalid and the associated tribes of al-Hasa became powerful participants in the struggle for influence in Najd and competed for a share of the plunder. Sometimes they allied themselves with various central Arabian oases, towns and nomadic tribes. In 1722/23 Saadun ibn Arayar, the shaikh of the Bani Khalid, died.[122] An internecine struggle began among the tribal nobility; although it did not lead to a break-up of the confederation, it weakened it considerably.

There were no large confederations in Najd to play the role of dominant force, and some oases and bedouin tribes preserved their independence. Even the oasis-towns of Uyaina, al-Diriya and Riyadh, which were destined to play an important role in the struggle for hegemony in Najd, hardly stood out from the others. Their superiority was due to their location in al-Arid, the central province of Najd, on the crossroad of major trade routes. But their geographic position alone was not enough to see them as the only possible centre of an all-Najdi (still less, an all-Arabian) state. They had rivals in Qasim, al-Kharj and Jabal Shammar.

One can hardly agree with Philby, who saw al-Diriya as among the claimants to dominance in Najd, and even in the whole of Arabia, as early as the beginning of the eighteenth century.[123] *The Brilliance of the Meteor* reads:

> There was no strong leader [in Najd] who would curb the oppressors and help the oppressed. But every emir was an independent ruler in his village . . . The bedouin were scattered tribes then. Each tribe was ruled by a shaikh . . . There were petty shaikhs in some tribes who could oppose the bigger shaikhs . . . The inhabitants of the Najdi towns fought permanently with each other.[124]

In the first decades of the eighteenth century, conditions in the central area of Najd were characterized by a balance of forces between the main opponents. Al-Diriya was just coming to the end of a period of internal instability, with plots and power struggles among the ruling nobility. After a chain of murders and treacherous betrayals, Saud ibn Muhammad ibn Miqrin, the founder of the Saudi dynasty, became emir of the oasis in the 1710s. Some Saudis claim descent from the Bani Hanifa; others trace their genealogy to the Anaza, the most numerous and powerful tribe of central and northern Arabia.[125]

When Saud died in June 1725,[126] several bitter rivals competed for supremacy in the oasis. The struggle was accompanied by mutual acts of treachery and murder. Finally, Saud's cousin Zaid became emir.[127] At that time, the rulers of Uyaina were preoccupied with a war against their neighbours, the Manfuha and Sadiq, as well as against the bedouin. The hostilities were limited to local raids. A cholera epidemic devastated Uyaina in 1725/26;[128] as a result, it was unable to contest the domination over central Najd for many years. Taking advantage of Uyaina's weakened position, Zaid attacked the depopulated oasis in the following year. Muhammad ibn Muammar, the emir of

Uyaina, proclaimed his readiness to submit, but then enticed his enemies into his house and killed Zaid. Muhammad ibn Saud and a group of armed men managed to escape: it was he who became the emir of al-Diriya in 1726/27.[129]

In the late 1730s or early 1740s Dahham ibn Dawwas seized power in Riyadh – he was to be al-Diriya's most stubborn and merciless enemy for decades. Ibn Ghannam describes the story of his rise to power as follows:

> His father was the *rais* [ruler] of Manfuha. He took control of the oasis and then treacherously killed some peasants. He ruled the oasis for a period. After his death, his son Muhammad ruled. The latter's cousin Zamil ibn Faris and some Manfuha inhabitants rebelled against him, killed him and drove out his brothers. Dahham and his brothers were among those exiled and settled in Riyadh.
>
> The ruler of that oasis [Riyadh] was Zaid ibn Musa Abu Zura. His insane nephew killed him without any reason: he climbed to the roof where the emir was sleeping and stabbed him with a dagger. Then Khamis, one of Zaid's slaves, came and killed the emir's nephew. The said slave took possession of Riyadh. Since Zaid's children were still young, Khamis claimed that he would rule on their behalf until they became able to govern. Khamis ruled Riyadh for three years and then fled, fearing the people of the oasis on account of his deeds. Then he was murdered by a Manfuha inhabitant for having killed his father during his rule of Riyadh.
>
> Riyadh had no ruler for some time. When Khamis had taken Riyadh, Dahham ibn Dawwas had become his servant. When Riyadh had no ruler after Khamis' flight, Dahham became its *rais*. Zaid's son Abu Zu'a was Dahham's nephew, and Dahham promised to be the *naib* [regent] until the boy grew up and then to relinquish power. [However], Dahham later exiled Zaid's son from Riyadh.
>
> The Riyadh citizens hated Dahham and wanted to kill or dethrone him. They gathered, surrounded him and besieged his castle. They were a crowd of common people and had no leader. Dahham gave his brother Mishlab a horse and sent him to Muhammad ibn Saud, the emir of al-Diriya, with a request to help him in defeating his *raya* [subjects] ... [Muhammad] ibn Saud gave him help in the best manner: he sent his brother Mishari ibn Saud with armed men; they came close to the Riyadh castle, from where Dahham appeared with his men. Three or four Riyadh inhabitants were killed and the rest fled.
>
> Thereafter, [Dahham's] rule over the oasis strengthened and he became a *rais* and a *wali* [governor]. Mishari stayed with him for some months and did not expect him to demonstrate such meanness and malice ... His debauchery and unheard-of evil deeds grew, his spite at his subjects increased and they suffered a great deal from him. His terrible deeds resemble ... a Pharaoh's trial. Once he was angry with a woman and ordered [her] to sew up her mouth. Being angry with a man, he ordered [him] to cut off a piece of flesh from his thigh and said, 'You must eat it gradually.' The tortured man had no choice but to promise to fry and eat his own flesh. But Dahham did not agree with this and [the unfortunate man] had to eat his own flesh raw. Another example: [Dahham] was angry with a prisoner who was

said to have rescued himself from the chain with his teeth: [he was] ordered to knock out his teeth with an iron rod. Angry with another man, [Dahham] had his tongue cut out by his assistants [awan]. Examples of such deeds are plentiful.[130]

This excerpt from Ibn Ghannam's work concerning Dahham ibn Dawwas' rise to power, and the literature on developments in al-Diriya and Uyaina, describe the struggle for power, the merciless feuds, the devastating raids and the plunder which became normal events in the political life of Najd in the first half of the eighteenth century. The unclear system of succession led to great instability; a deceased ruler's brothers and nephews often rose against his sons. The oasis nobility's arbitrary rule and tyranny knew no bounds. Ibn Ghannam reports a rebellion by people who were outraged at the excesses of Dahham's rule. Muhammad ibn Saud demonstrated his solidarity with Dahham by sending his brother Mishari to help him, as mentioned above. The restoration of the old Muslim prohibition of interest on loans was, perhaps, the Wahhabis' reaction to the usurers' cruel oppression.

Economic conditions in the countries of the Middle East, particularly Arabia, deteriorated in the eighteenth century. The decay of the Ottoman empire, the destruction of the economy and the recession in commerce even led to a drop in sales of the main means of transportation – camels. The transit trade with India via Hijaz declined.[131] The internecine struggle within the Ottoman empire and the economic ruin of its population led to a fall in the numbers of pilgrims undertaking the *hajj*. All this was detrimental to the interests of the Arabian bedouin.

One may suppose that the devastating wars between Turkey and Persia in the early eighteenth century were ruinous to the *hajj* from Iraq and Iran and thus to the income of Najd. Under such circumstances, the bedouin might increase their raids on the local settled people and the rare caravans to compensate for the lost income from the pilgrims. The Wahhabis' later zeal for maintaining security on the roads was no accident.

Political stability, the ending of bedouin raids and the establishment of stable commercial ties could be achieved only under the conditions of a centralized state. Such a state could enlist popular support by reducing the oppression of the bulk of the population. But to protect the interests of the tribal nobility, new external sources of wealth, i.e. military spoils, were needed. In that period, a strong religious movement started in Najd and became the basis for the creation of a large centralized state.

CHAPTER 2

Muhammad ibn Abd al-Wahhab and his Teaching

The founder's life before the start of his political activities

An anonymous Russian journalist wrote in the early nineteenth century:

> Some half a century ago the [Wahhabi] sect was founded by an Arab shaikh whose name was Muhammad. According to the Wahhabis, he was descended from Abd al-Wahhab, the son of Sulaiman. According to their ancient legend, Sulaiman, a poor Arab from a small Najdi tribe, dreamed that a fire appeared from his body, spread far in the fields and destroyed camps in the desert and houses in towns. Frightened by his dream, Sulaiman asked the shaikhs of his tribe to interpret it: they found it to be a good omen. They told him that his son would found a new faith and the desert Arabs would embrace it. The dream was actually realized not by Sulaiman's son Abd al-Wahhab, but by his grandson Shaikh Muhammad.[1]

This legend perfectly conveys the 'feel' of the era.

The founder of the religious and socio-political movement known as Wahhabism was born in Uyaina in 1703/04 to the family of an *alim*.[2] His father Abd al-Wahhab ibn Sulaiman was a *qadhi* and his son's first teacher. His brother Sulaiman ibn Abd al-Wahhab told the Wahhabi historian Ibn Ghannam that the future founder of the new teaching in Islam had demonstrated outstanding ability as a child and learned the Quran by heart before he was 10. The boy studied *tafsir* (Quranic interpretation) and *hadith* (sayings attributed to the Prophet Muhammad). At the age of 12 his father arranged for him to be married. After the wedding, the future religious teacher undertook the pilgrimage to Mecca with his father's permission. Thereafter, he spent two months in

Muhammad ibn Abd al-Wahhab and his Teaching

Medina before returning home. He travelled widely in the neighbouring countries, made several visits to Hijaz and Basra and then settled in al-Hasa.[3]

His teacher in Medina was Abdallah ibn Ibrahim ibn Saif, a member of the nobility from the al-Majmaa oasis in Sudair. Ibn Abd al-Wahhab was later to report:

> The shaikh once asked me: 'Do you want to see the weapon I have prepared for it [al-Majmaa]?' 'Yes', I replied. He brought me to a house where many books were stored and said, 'This is the weapon I have prepared.'[4]

Ibn Abd al-Wahhab hinted thereby that his Medina teacher had prepared an 'ideological weapon' to combat the beliefs that were widespread in his oasis.

When Ibn Abd al-Wahhab was in Basra, he appealed to people to restore the standards of 'genuine monotheism' in Islam. He 'preached his teaching among the nobility and other people but was exiled'.[5] While travelling from Basra to al-Zubair, he nearly died of thirst but was saved by an inhabitant of al-Zubair.[6]

Ibn Abd al-Wahhab next spent some time in al-Hasa with Abdallah ibn Abd al-Latif, an *alim*. He had intended to go to Syria next, but not having enough money he went instead to Huraimala, an oasis in Najd. His father had moved there in 1726/27 after a quarrel with the new ruler of Uyaina, who had seized power after the death of the former emir (the latter had extended his protection to Abd al-Wahhab).[7] Ibn Abd al-Wahhab preached his ideas in Huraimala even more energetically than before, which led to a dispute with his father. He spent some years in the oasis, and it was then that he wrote *The Book of Monotheism* [*Kitab al-Tawhid*]. According to Ibn Ghannam, 'The shaikh's deed became famous throughout al-Arid – in Uyaina, al-Diriya, Manfuha. People were divided into his friends and foes.'[8]

In 1740/41 Abd al-Wahhab ibn Sulaiman died and Muhammad presumably replaced his father as *qadhi*. At that time, Huraimala was split between two subdivisions of the same tribe that were, perhaps, independent from each other. Ibn Abd al-Wahhab's preaching led to resentment among some of the people. 'Some inhabitants of Huraimala were *abds* who belonged to one of the clans. They were notorious for their debauchery. Ibn Abd al-Wahhab wanted to convert them to the true faith. Then the *abds* decided to kill the shaikh,'[9] according to Ibn Bishr. Ibn Abd al-Wahhab escaped by a lucky chance and fled to Uyaina.[10]

Ibn Abd al-Wahhab's trips to Baghdad and several Iranian towns, as well as to Damascus, are reported by European orientalists. These journeys are even mentioned in *The Encyclopaedia of Islam*: in 1933 the renowned orientalist Margoliouth reproduced this version in his entry on Wahhabism, following *The Brilliance of the Meteor*. Margoliouth claims that Ibn Abd al-Wahhab spent four years in Basra before living for five years in Baghdad, where he married a rich woman. She died, leaving him 2,000 dinars. After spending a year in Kurdistan and two years in Hamadan (Iran), Ibn Abd al-Wahhab left for Isfahan at the beginning of Nadir Shah's rule, i.e. in 1736. The future preacher spent four years there studying Aristotelian philosophy and Sufism and even teaching Sufism. He subsequently left for Qom, where he allegedly became an adherent of Ibn Hanbal's school. After visiting Qom he returned to Uyaina.[11] One of Ibn Abd al-Wahhab's descendants repeats Margoliouth's version in a book published in 1954.[12]

As reported in *The Brilliance of the Meteor*, Ibn Abd al-Wahhab was 37 (according to the lunar calendar) when he started his journey. He spent some six years in Basra, five years in Baghdad, one year in Kurdistan and two years in Hamadan. At the beginning of Nadir Shah's rule he moved to Isfahan, where he spent seven years. After that he lived in Qom and other towns, then spent six months in Aleppo, one year in Damascus, some time in Jerusalem and two years in Cairo. Next he visited Mecca before returning to Najd. He spent one and a half or two years in Yamama before settling in Uyaina in 1737/38 (AH 1150). He died, according to *The Brilliance of the Meteor*, in 1797/98 (AH 1212). The anonymous chronicler claims that Ibn Abd al-Wahhab changed his name many times: he was known as Abdallah in Basra, Ahmad in Baghdad, Muhammad in Kurdistan and Yusuf in Hamadan.[13] A simple arithmetic calculation shows that he must have spent at least eleven or twelve years in Isfahan, Qom, Aleppo, Damascus, Jerusalem and Cairo, if the chronicler's information is correct. In this case, he could only have returned to Najd in the late 1740s, which contradicts the date given in the chronicle two lines below. Thus Margoliouth has merely removed the numerous contradictions and errors in the chronicle.

The Wahhabi chroniclers and Mengin date Ibn Abd al-Wahhab's return to Najd to the 1730s. Ibn Zaini Dahlan, a nineteenth-century Hijazi historian, confirms their dating. According to Dahlan, Ibn Abd al-Wahhab started his preaching in Najd in 1730/31.[14] The Wahhabis' annals were discovered after the first edition of the *Encyclopaedia of Islam* had been published. Laoust's entry on the religious teacher in the new edition is based on the information provided by Ibn Ghannam and Ibn Bishr.[15]

The assertion that Ibn Abd al-Wahhab became a Hanbali during his travels, particularly in Qom, a centre of Shiism, is far from convincing – most *ulama* in the Najdi oases, including Ibn Abd al-Wahhab's ancestors, were Hanbalis. Besides, there are no traces of his acquaintance with Aristotelian teaching or Sufism in his works.

The author of *The Brilliance of the Meteor* was hostile to the Wahhabis. One may therefore assume that, even if he was Ibn Abd al-Wahhab's contemporary, he was never a member of the preacher's entourage and so gathered information about his life at second hand. The Najdi chroniclers provide very little information about the time that Ibn Abd al-Wahhab spent in southern Iraq and eastern Arabia. However, the energetic and inquisitive young *alim* may have joined caravans to reach Baghdad, Syria or the nearest towns in Iran – Munir al-Ajlani, the scrupulous historian of the first Saudi state, mentions this as a possibility.[16]

The Brilliance of the Meteor reports that Ibn Abd al-Wahhab, after his return to Najd, spent some time in Yamama, where his preaching aroused the hostility of the population. Since he was accompanied by seven or eight black slaves he had bought in Mecca and by four of his cousins, his enemies apparently preferred to send him into exile without engaging in an armed clash,[17] although other sources do not corroborate this report.

Muhammad ibn Abd al-Wahhab and his Teaching

Ibn Abd al-Wahhab's long journeys and years of theological study had a decisive influence on the formation of his world outlook. He had had an opportunity to become familiar with the cults and beliefs of Arabia and the neighbouring countries and decide his attitude to them. He had also studied theology, the interpretation of the Quran, the *hadiths* and the commentaries on them, and could derive arguments for his teaching from them.

The Sunna and bida *in the history of Islam*

Islam emerged in the society of Hijaz in the first third of the seventh century and reflected the rather primitive social conditions there. Expressed initially only in the Quran, the Arabs' religious system could not satisfy the requirements of the far more developed societies in the countries they conquered. It was necessary to give Islam a character that would correspond better to those societies. Numerous *hadiths* appeared concerning the Prophet's life and activities. Their code, the Sunna, determined the universal rules of conduct and acceptable views, allegedly on the basis of those of the Prophet. The compilation of the *hadiths* was completed approximately in the tenth century, some three centuries after the emergence of Islam.

The number of these *hadiths* was enormous. Even though collected and adopted by orthodox Islam, they included a large number of contradictions and unclear passages. Even the latter were interpreted differently in the interests of different groups and with regard to specific places and times. Later, every religious trend sought and found the *hadiths* that justified its principles. The Quran, too, was used in a similar manner. In the words of the Hungarian scholar Goldziher, 'The history of religion . . . is at the same time the history of the interpretation of the Scriptures.'[18]

The Sunna embodied an ossified tradition. But first customs and then the traditions had to change with the changing conditions of life. Islam adapts to the changing reality through the religious sanctification of new traditions and the demonstration of their correspondence with the Sunna. This operation is performed through *ijma* (consensus among *ùlama*) or *qiyas* (analogy).

An 'innovation' without any precedent in the approved *hadiths* is known as *bida*. Until an innovation is sanctified by *ijma*, it contradicts the Sunna. It implies an opinion, a thing or a mode of action that is unknown or has never been practised before. Thus the sanctification of a *bida* and its transformation into a *hadith* are a response by the Muslim religion to changes in socio-economic conditions and in spiritual life; it expresses Islam's reaction to reality, and its adaptation to the requirements of time and place.

Four orthodox schools (*mazhabs*) formed within Islam around the problem of the interpretation of the Sunna. Their main difference was the attitude to *bida*. The most flexible and tolerant school in that matter was Hanafism, while Hanbalism was the most rigid and rejected *bida* outright. In the Hanbalis' opinion, only what was prescribed by the Quran and the Sunna (and only in the form prescribed) was legitimate in matters of religious practice. Hanbalism encompasses a broad circle of problems in Islam; although it differs from other orthodox schools in various fields, the rejection of *bida* is its characteristic feature.

It is extremely difficult, however, to hold a position that implacably rejects any adaptation of Islam to the changing requirements of life. Wahhabism (which, as we shall see, is an extreme form of Hanbalism) was finally compelled to approve radio and television, the telephone, labour codes, national insurance and so on. Yet the negative attitude to *bida* made Hanbalism the most inflexible form of Islam, which largely restricted its expansion. The militant Hanbalis were a tiny group in comparison to the other schools just because they opposed their rivals from a position of 'ultra-orthodoxy'. At the same time, various sectarian teachings and heresies were the safety-valves through which discontent found an outlet: the sectarian ideology repeatedly became the banner of the oppressed people's movements.

One of the innovations in Islam was the cult of saints. The Romans merely included local gods in their pantheon to increase the ideological impact on believers in the newly seized territories, but Christianity introduced the cult of 'regional' saints. The worship of local deities was replaced by the worship of Christian saints, which absorbed the earlier cults after an appropriate process of transformation. Islam followed the same route. The cult of saints in the Muslim world is chiefly of local, pre-Islamic origin; but the earlier idols and Christian saints were replaced by Islamic preachers, the Prophet's Companions and prominent *ulama*. Absorbing these cults, Islam became a widespread religious movement, appealing to different social groups throughout various regions.

The spread of the cult of saints was closely related to the activities of Sufis, or Islamic mystics. To attract wide numbers of believers, they ascribed to their saints the ability to perform miracles. The Sufis claim that divine truth may be comprehended only through intuition; they bring themselves to a state of ecstasy by various methods and practise ascesis to reach a 'merger with the deity'. They initially demonstrated a disdain for social conventions and an indifference to canonical Muslim rites.

In the eleventh century al-Ghazali, the 'St Thomas Aquinas' of orthodox Islam, introduced some elements of Sufism, particularly the mystical love of God, into the orthodox religion. Simultaneously, he enriched Islam with certain rationalist ideas of al-Ashari, the tenth-century *alim*. Thus Sunni orthodoxy became an all-embracing ideological system which, besides religion and ritual, also included philosophy, law, political doctrine, rules governing everyday life, and ethics.

One of the representatives of the extreme trend of Hanbalism was the fourteenth-century Syrian *alim*, Taqi al-Din ibn Taimiya, among the most interesting and contradictory figures of Islamic theological and philosophical thought. In the field of theology, his preachings and works advocated changes in the current form of orthodox Islam, and he contrasted categorically the Sunna with *bida*. He fought against all 'innovations' that deviated from the original spirit of Islam in religious theory or practice. Ibn Taimiya also opposed the introduction of the Asharis' philosophical conceptions into Islam, the Sufis and the cult of saints and of the Prophet. He censured the pilgrimage to the Prophet's mausoleum in Medina as incongruous with Islam, although it had long been considered as supplementing the pilgrimage to Mecca.

Ibn Taimiya rejected the teaching of *ulama* who had legalized that kind of cult through *ijma*. He adopted the Sunna, and nothing else, as the basis. Al-Ghazali, the pillar of orthodox Islam, became a target for the 'new' Hanbalis, the followers of Ibn Taimiya. In his adoption of extreme positions, Ibn Taimiya differed even with the Hanbalis on some questions. He did not win recognition, however, was tried repeatedly by theological courts and finally died in prison in 1328, leaving some 500 works. A tiny group of his followers, of whom the most outstanding was Ibn al-Qayim, surrounded his name with an aura of holiness. According to Goldziher:

> His influence was felt subsequently and was exerted in a concealed form for four centuries. His works were studied carefully in Muslim circles and played the role of a tacit force, which now and then caused explosions of hostility to *bida*.[19]

Islam in the Ottoman empire

Under the Ottomans, Hanafism was the official *mazhab*, although other orthodox schools were also recognized. The establishment of the religious system was completed in the fifteenth and sixteenth centuries. The Ottoman sultan assumed the title of caliph, in other words the spiritual leader of all Muslims, and thus strengthened his authority.

The *ulama* were among the most influential social groups and the Porte relied on them not only in the religious and legal fields, but also in educational and intellectual matters. The head of the religious hierarchy was the mufti of Istanbul (the *sheikh-ul-islam*), who ranked equal with the grand vizier. Next came two *kadiaskers* (the highest judicial authorities in the empire after the *sheikh-ul-islam*) and various other officials. The Porte tried to control the *ulama* through the system of appointing local *qadhis*, who supervised legal and administrative matters, and *muhtasibs*, who kept watch on the morals of believers and controlled the activities of the guilds of artisans and merchants.

The general decay of the Ottoman empire did not spare the Muslim clergy, and the corruption, greed and injustice of the *ulama* were widely resented. In the eighteenth century, the orthodox Ottoman *ulama* shared influence and wealth with the shaikhs of the Sufi orders – the Islamic mystics who had by then renounced many anti-Sunni positions. A network of Sufi dervish orders (*tariqas*) spread throughout the empire. The number of dervishes grew considerably and many guilds, professional organizations and individuals were connected with them. It is known, for example, that the dervish order of the Bektashi was connected with the janissaries.[20] The Sufis spread ideas of fatalism and passivity, thus undermining people's ability to protest and take resolute action.

As mentioned earlier, the Sufis attached great importance to the worship of saints, who included, according to them, the prophets from Adam to Muhammad and many famous Sufis. There were living saints too. The Sunni *ulama* also supported the worship of saints; everybody who opposed this ran the risk of being assassinated. The

Sufis sang and played musical instruments, and some of them drank alcohol, smoked tobacco and hashish and earned their living by fortune-telling on the basis of astrology and magic.

Besides the economic and political ties, Arabia maintained wide contacts in the fields of ideology and culture with the more developed Middle Eastern countries. However, the isolation due to its huge geographic area and the unique features of its society led to many forms of spiritual life that were specific to Arabia.

The beliefs and cults of pre-Wahhabi Arabia

Hanbalism spread particularly in the Najdi oases, which was an extremely unusual situation in the Muslim world. When mentioning the deaths of outstanding individuals, the Wahhabi chroniclers never omit the names of Hanbali *ulama*. How did this Hanbali 'island' persist?

Social conditions in central Arabia – which was somewhat isolated from the other, more developed regions of the Middle East – did not differ greatly from the rather primitive conditions that persisted in Hijaz in the period of the nascence of Islam. The tenets of early Islam that had been elaborated in the first centuries of its existence included many elements that justified social relations in Hijaz at the time, and the *urf* of Mecca and Medina as sanctified in the *hadiths*. Since Hanbalism in principle recognized only early Islam, it conformed as a whole to the needs of central Arabian society in the eighteenth century.

Central and eastern Arabia had always been the 'stepsons' of the Muslim empires of the Middle East and had preserved their individuality and independence. That is why various 'heretical' movements found favourable conditions there: for example, the Kharijites and their subdivision, the Ibadhis. A strong Carmathian state, with its own particular social structure, existed for a long period in al-Hasa.

As for other regions of the peninsula, most of the population of Oman belonged to the Ibadhi sect while the Yemenis were Zaidis, a moderate Shia sect. Many Arabs professed Shiism in the eastern and north-eastern regions of the peninsula, which adjoined southern Iraq and Iran. Jews lived in some regions of Yemen and Najran[21] and Niebuhr met Sabaeans in al-Hasa.[22] Muslims belonging to the various orthodox branches of Islam were in the majority in the towns and oases of Hijaz. All shades of Islam coexisted peacefully with the cult of saints that was widespread throughout the peninsula and even with the survivals of idol worship. Ibn Ghannam has left a detailed description of the Arabians' beliefs.[23] 'Then [when Wahhabism emerged] most people wallowed in evil . . . They worshipped saints and pious people and abandoned monotheism and faith,' he reports. People came to the saints or their graves and asked them to perform a good deed or to save them from misfortune. They addressed their appeals to the living and the dead. Many people believed that such objects as stones and trees might benefit or harm them. The *shaitan* (the devil) played with their minds. In their unbelief, 'they outdid the people of the *jahiliya* [the pre-Islamic era]'.

'There were many such cases in the Najd oases, and everybody indulged' in the unholy practice, according to Ibn Ghannam. There was Zaid ibn al-Khattab's grave in Wadi Hanifa, for example, where people addressed the holy man and requested him to save them from trials and tribulations. Graves were worshipped in al-Jubail and al-Diriya, where some of the Prophet's Companions were said to have been buried. There was a palm tree in the township of Fida to which men and women came and asked for its blessing and then 'did the most infamous things'. Women who could not find husbands gathered there, came close to the tree and said, 'First of all, I want a husband.' People processed around the tree and hung decorations on it.

There was a holy cave near al-Diriya, called 'the cave of the emir's daughter', where people left offerings of bread and meat. According to legend, some licentious and godless men once wanted to ravish the emir's daughter. She called on Allah to help and a cave opened before her, later to become a place of worship. A famous 'saint' called Taj lived in al-Kharj near al-Diriya. People asked for his blessing and requested him to perform good deeds for them and avert their troubles. He was paid for this. Although the 'saint' was said to be blind, he walked without a guide. Even the local rulers were somewhat afraid of him.

In Mecca there were Abu Talib's mausoleum, and the graves of Maimuna bint al-Kharis Umm al-Muminin and Khadija, among others. Men and women shouted their requests out loud at the graves. The same shouts were heard near the grave of Abdallah ibn Abbas in al-Taif. Eve's grave was supposed to be in Jidda. The Awi mosque was built there and gave shelter to debtors, thieves and people who were bankrupt. Even the sharif could not touch them once they had been granted sanctuary. Once, a merchant who owed 70,000 rials took shelter in the mosque and thus forced his creditors to grant him a delay. Sacrifices were also made at saints' graves. In Yemen, people danced in procession and cut themselves with knives. (It was, perhaps, something like the Shia's *ashura*.)

Ibn Ghannam had heard about the cult of saints outside Arabia too. There were so many examples in Syria and Egypt that the chronicler does not even list them. He was indignant at the worship surrounding Ali's mausoleum in Iraq, writing that, in the Shia's opinion, a visit to that mosque is better than seventy pilgrimages to Mecca. Ibn Ghannam mentions numerous mausoleums and mosques at saints' graves around Basra, on the eastern coast of Arabia and in Bahrain.

Even soothsayers practised their craft at some places in Arabia, according to the available information. Ibn Abd al-Wahhab denounced them resolutely.[24] According to Ibn Bishr:

> The causes of the spread of polytheism in Najd were the men and women who came with the bedouin to pick fruit in the oases and treated their dwellers who were ill. The settled people came to the sorcerers from among the bedouin and asked for medicines that might cure their diseases. They were told, 'Make such-and-such a sacrifice at such-and-such a place, eat part of it and throw away such-and-such. Do not mention Allah's name. Maybe you will recover if it is Allah's will.' This

happened frequently and nobody could explain to the people that it was bad.[25]

The Arabs made sacrifices to jinns (spirits), asking to save them from disease, as reported by Ibn Abd al-Wahhab's grandson, Abd al-Rahman ibn Hasan. 'At a later period, like the inhabitants of Arabia in general, they [the people of Jawf] relapsed into semi-paganism and the worship of local genii.'[26] Even as late as a century after the emergence of Wahhabism, the people of Jawf, 'like the most of their brethren, had long since abandoned the very name of Mahometanism for a local fetichism and a semi-Sabaean worship, for prayers to the sun, and sacrifices to the dead.'[27]

The bedouin and Islam

All explorers of Arabia comment that Islam found it difficult to take root among the bedouin. Volney notes the bedouin's indifference to its prescriptions:

> The bedouin who live on the Turkish frontiers pretend to be Muslims for political reasons but they are so negligent of religion and their piety is so weak that they are usually considered infidels who have neither a law nor a prophet. They readily admit that Muhammad's religion was not created for them. They add, 'How can we perform ablutions without water? How can we give alms, being not rich? Why should we fast in Ramadhan after fasting all the year round? Why should we go to Mecca if God is everywhere?'[28]

Burckhardt reports that many bedouin were entirely unfamiliar with Islam before the emergence of Wahhabism.[28] Palgrave claims that:

> among the great mass of the nomadic population, Mahometanism during the course of twelve whole centuries has made little or no impression either for good or ill ... At the same time, surrounded by, and often more or less dependent on, sincere and even bigoted followers of Islam, they have occasionally deemed it prudent to assume a kindred name ... and bearing, and thus to style themselves Mahometans.[30]

Guided by heavenly bodies in their migrations, the bedouin developed a cult of the sun, the moon and the stars, according to Montagne.[31] On the basis of his observation of the bedouin of northern Arabia, Palgrave comes to the conclusion, 'God is for them a chief, residing mainly, it would seem, in the sun, with which indeed they in a manner identify him.'[32]

Wallin, a mid-nineteenth-century Finnish traveller, also focuses on this point:

> Like most of the tribes which were not forced to adopt the reformed doctrines of the Wahhâbiyé (Wahábiyeh) sect during the period of its ascendant power in Arabia, the Ma'âzé (Maazeh) [a tribe in western Arabia] are, in general, grossly ignorant in

the religion they profess, and I scarcely remember ever meeting with a single individual of the tribe who observed any of the rites of Islâm whatever, or possessed the last notion of its fundamental and leading dogmas; while the reverse might, to a certain degree, be said of those Bedooins who are, or formerly were, Wahhâbiyé (Wahábiyeh).[33]

Some decades later Davletshin, an officer of the Russian General Staff, commented, 'The nomadic Arabs are not at all notable for being religious and many of their peculiar rites and legends run counter to Islamic teaching.'[34]

The bedouin preserved the cult of ancestors. According to Jaussen, they made sacrifices to their ancestors or to Allah through their mediation. The Rwala never missed an opportunity to slaughter a camel at an ancestor's grave, saying, 'The gift and requital to the deceased.'[35] The cult of ancestors was also connected with the bedouin's 'banner' – the *markab*, a palanquin on the camel's back. The *markab* was considered the abode of the ancestor's spirit, and sacrifices were made to it. A driver (a slave or a boy) sat in it, and it was sometimes occupied by the most beautiful girl of the tribe or the shaikh's daughter who inspired warriors during battles.[36] One cannot help remembering the pre-Islamic priestesses who inspired fighting bedouin, sitting on the camels' backs. Clairvoyants and magicians often took part in raids and advised the commanders.[37]

Thus there was a wide gamut of shades of Islam in Arabia at the time that Wahhabism was emerging – from Hanbalis through the orthodox Sunnis of other schools to Zaidis, Shia and Ibadhis. The cult of saints was widespread. Pre-Muslim religious beliefs and cults – sorcery, idol worship, sun worship, animism, fetishism and the cult of ancestors – coexisted and became interwoven with Islam. It was within this spiritual milieu that Ibn Abd al-Wahhab lived, accepting or rejecting certain elements of that heritage as his views were formed.

Monotheism (tawhid) *and the denunciation of the cult of saints: the pivot of the Wahhabi belief-system*

Ibn Abd al-Wahhab's world outlook seems to have been formed on the basis of his careful study of Islamic theology since his early childhood and his attempts to 'remodel' the religion and alter public life to make it accord more closely with Islamic ideals. One may imagine his explanation of the disorders and distortions in the world that surrounded him: people had forgotten the genuine Islam, hence the general moral degradation, followed by political disorder, economic chaos, decay and destruction. To save the world from wallowing in sin, it was necessary to 'purify' religion and to restore its true character as during the first centuries of Islam.

The most important idea nurtured by Ibn Abd al-Wahhab during his travels and theological studies was monotheism, the main axis of Islam. In his opinion, monotheism was the conviction that Allah alone is the Creator of this world and its

Lord Who gives it His laws. None of His creations are equal to Him or are themselves able to create.[38] Allah does not need anybody's help, even from those who are closest to Him. Allah alone is able to do good or evil. Nobody is worthy of glorification or worship but Allah.[39]

In the Wahhabis' opinion, the Islamic world had deviated from these principles of monotheism. People indulged in *bida*, considered the worst sin.[40] They endowed Allah's creations with His abilities and attributes. For example, they went on pilgrimages to the mausoleums of Muslim saints, made vows to them, offered sacrifices and asked for their help, in the conviction that the saints could do good or evil.[41] Even plants and stones were endowed with Allah's attributes, which was incompatible with genuine monotheism.[42]

Since it was forbidden to 'give Allah a companion'[43] or endow His creations with divine attributes, the cult needed a set of rules that rejected all 'innovations'. Only Allah may be offered sacrifices, the Wahhabis asserted. Nobody but Allah should be asked for help or intercession.[44] Neither angels, prophets (Allah's messengers), pious people or saints can intercede for a Muslim before Allah.[45] Vows can only be made to Allah.[46] Pious people, the Prophet's Companions and saints should not be revered excessively and mosques should not be erected above their graves. Too much care should not be taken of the graves, and gravestones should not be idolized. Saints should be respected and honoured but not worshipped.[47]

The Wahhabis had a particular attitude to Muhammad, the Prophet and founder of Islam. They considered him an ordinary man whom Allah had selected for the prophetic mission. But he should not be deified, worshipped or asked for favours. His grave should not be worshipped although a Muslim might visit it without, however, making any requests. Muhammad should not be asked for help or to intercede in any way, though he might intercede with Allah for the Muslims on Doomsday. The places connected with the Prophet's life should not be objects of worship.[48] All kinds of worship and belief that contradicted the above rules were considered *shirk* (polytheism). Ibn Abd al-Wahhab appealed to people to combat magic, sorcery and fortune-telling,[49] although he never put a particular emphasis on this. He censured such vestiges of paganism as invocations, amulets and talismans.[50]

According to the Wahhabis, the only sources of Islam were the Quran and the Sunna. They recognized the four imams, the founders of the orthodox schools of Sunnism,[51] as well as the fourteenth-century religious scholars, Ibn Taimiya and Ibn al-Qayim, but rejected the theory and practice of virtually all subsequent generations. Some travellers and explorers believed that the Wahhabis also rejected the Sunna and recognized only the Quran, but this is erroneous.[52]

Wahhabism, the name given to the movement by its opponents or simply by non-Arabs, has taken root in the orientalist literature. Ibn Abd al-Wahhab's followers, however, called themselves monotheists or simply Muslims and never Wahhabis.

Muhammad ibn Abd al-Wahhab and his Teaching

The 'purification' of Islam

The Wahhabis borrowed their system of argumentation and their fierce attacks upon the cult of saints and *bida* from Ibn Taimiya and Ibn al-Qayim. Unlike these scholars, however, they did not delve deeply into sophisticated religious and philosophical problems. They admitted their differences with Ibn Taimiya over some minor questions concerning ritual and everyday life.[53] However, his and Ibn al-Qayim's works were actually their 'textbooks' and Ibn Abd al-Wahhab quotes both of them repeatedly. Some of Ibn Taimiya's works have survived, copied by Ibn Abd al-Wahhab.[54] Ibn Ghannam cites the *ulama* of the fourteenth century.[55] According to Ibn Abd al-Wahhab's son, Abdallah, 'We consider the books by Ibn al-Qayim and his shaikh [Ibn Taimiya] most valuable and often quote their sayings.'[56]

Wahhabism revived the line of the absolute rejection of all *bida* and returned to the Quran and the 'unsullied' Sunna. The Wahhabis seem orthodox from a dogmatic viewpoint. This is their own opinion, as well as that of the majority of objective experts, both in the Arab world and outside; it is also the view of contemporaries of the initial movement and of later scholars.

Burckhardt reports that the Cairo *ulama*, who were generally opposed to the Wahhabis, stated that they had found no heresy in their teaching. Since this statement was made contrary to the *ulama*'s 'own will', it hardly causes any suspicion. After reading Ibn Abd al-Wahhab's book, many Cairo *ulama* declared unanimously that if it expressed the Wahhabis' opinion, they too (the *ulama*) were wholeheartedly of their faith.[57] Abu Ras al-Nasiri, an Algerian *alim*, asserted that the Wahhabis' dogma was entirely orthodox.[58] Ibn Sanad, a chronicler from Basra, noted that the Wahhabis were the Hanbalis of the past.[59] According to Corancez, Wahhabism is Islam in its original purity.[60] The twentieth-century Arab writers Muhammad Hamid al-Faqih[61] and Hafiz Wahba[62] share that viewpoint. According to Taha Husain, 'this *mazhab* [is nothing but] a strong appeal for genuine Islam, for its purification from polytheism and idolatry'.[63]

In the present writer's opinion, however, the Wahhabis were sectarians precisely because they opposed Sunnism in its then dominant form, even though from the position of wanting to 'purify' it. They relied on Ibn Taimiya in their struggle against the orthodox Sunnis, whose pillar was al-Ghazali. Opposition to widely accepted dogma, even from ultra-orthodox positions, was as much sectarian as the attempts to destroy, 'purify' or change some of the fundamentals. It was not until the twentieth century, when the most extreme manifestations of Wahhabism had died away or been obliterated, that the movement itself lost its irreconcilable sectarian nature.

The description of the Wahhabis as the 'puritans' or 'Protestants' of Islam is widespread in the European and Arab literature. Corancez,[64] followed by Burckhardt,[65] was the first to coin it. Wahhabism is compared with medieval Europe's Reformation on the purely formal basis of the outer striving to 'purify' the original, 'genuine' religion from the later admixtures. It is only in this sense that one may speak of any outward resemblance between two phenomena whose socio-political and even theological content is entirely different.

Wahhabism appeared in an atmosphere of widespread popular dissatisfaction in the area of religion. It was a reaction to the spiritual crisis of Arabian and, in particular, Najdi society, where strivings for some kind of new ideals were widespread.

Ibn Abd al-Wahhab was not alone in feeling the need to 'purify' Islam in Arabia. It was not by chance that his teacher, Abdallah ibn Ibrahim ibn Saif, had prepared an 'ideological weapon' to transform religion. When Muhammad ibn Ismail – an *alim* from Sanaa (d. 1768/69) who advocated the 'genuine religion' in his works – learned of Ibn Abd al-Wahhab's preaching, he wrote a *qasida* (poem of praise) in his honour.[66] Muhammad al-Murtadha, a Yemeni *alim* (d. 1790), denounced dervishes.[67] Later, another Yemeni *alim*, al-Shawkani (d. 1834), rejected pilgrimages to graves and idolatry as manifestations of polytheism in his comments on Ibn Taimiya's works and in his own treatises. It is likely that he was connected with Ibn Abd al-Wahhab.[68]

The list of potential Wahhabis and participants in the elaboration of the teaching could undoubtedly be extended. As occurs during all important socio-political developments, their ideological basis was already 'in the air'. The seeds of Wahhabi propaganda fell on soil that was generally prepared to adopt the new teaching and germinated where conditions were most favourable to the realization of Wahhabi socio-political ideas.

Although scholastic theology and dogma form a considerable part of the Wahhabi teaching, it cannot be disputed that its socio-political content is original. The fact that 90–95% of Ibn Abd al-Wahhab's works consists of quotations from the orthodox *hadiths* and works by the *ulama* of the first centuries of Islam does not contradict this judgement.

The social content of the teaching

Statements that unequivocally reflect the interests of the feudal-tribal nobility to the detriment of those of the poor, together with slogans advocating social harmony and stability, are all found in Ibn Abd al-Wahhab's works. Ordinary people must obey the authorities,[69] he proclaimed, in accordance with the original spirit of Islam. Mutinies and revolts against the emirs must be punished with infernal tortures.[70]

Wahhabism made the payment of *zakat* (an alms-tax) obligatory rather than voluntary, thus elevating revenue-collection by the authorities from all groups of the population, including the nomads, to the status of an unchallengeable religious principle.[71] Those who joined the Wahhabis were not exempted from their obligations to their masters or creditors. According to Ibn Abd al-Wahhab's son Abdallah, the assertion made by those who opposed Wahhabism that 'one who joins us [the Wahhabis] is treated as free from all obligations and even debts' was a 'slander'.[72]

At the same time, Wahhabism required the emirs and the nobility to be just to their subjects, appealing to them to take care of slaves, servants and hired workers.[73] They flattered the sentiments of the poor by glorifying poverty, denouncing greed and claiming that access to paradise is easier for the poor.[74] In practice, the Wahhabis strongly condemned usury.[75]

Muhammad ibn Abd al-Wahhab and his Teaching

As mentioned above, Wahhabi teaching preached social harmony:

> Each of you is a herdsman and is responsible for his herd [subjects]. An imam takes care of his subjects, a man takes care of his family and herd, a woman takes care of her husband's house, son and livestock, a boy must take care of his father's property and livestock, a servant takes care of his master's property and livestock. Each of you is a herdsman and must take care of his herd [subjects].[76]

The preaching of the Brotherhood of all Muslims partly served the same purpose.[77] The idea of brotherhood would be used in a somewhat modified form some one and half centuries later in the Ikhwan movement. Abdallah ibn Muhammad ibn Abd al-Wahhab asserted, 'Arabs are equal to Arabs, and the practice to the contrary, which is widespread in some countries, is merely a manifestation of arrogance . . . and the true reason of great libertinism.' He appealed to people to 'forbid and abolish hand-kissing, which is widespread in some towns',[78] in other words, condemning some people's outer servility and others' haughtiness.

Naturally, the teaching included a series of moral standards to be followed. Wahhabism taught people to be kind and circumspect,[79] always to keep their promises,[80] to be patient,[81] not to lie, not to slander others, not to gossip, not to be indiscreet and to help the blind. It condemned meanness, envy, perjury and cowardice.[82] Wahhabism regulated even minor details of human behaviour. For example, it advised people how they should laugh, sneeze, yawn, joke, embrace and shake hands when meeting a friend and so on.[83]

Wahhabism may be seen as having some of the features common to all movements for greater social justice. It was by no means indifferent to the peasants, for example, and always sided with those who spoke out against exploitation. Thus the Wahhabis won the sympathy of a sizeable part of the Najdi peasants in the mid-eighteenth century. However, the centre of gravity of the Wahhabi doctrine lay in politics rather than in the social sphere.

Fanaticism and jihad

The Wahhabis considered all Muslims of their time who did not share their teaching to be far worse polytheists than the people of the *jahiliya*.[84] Muhammad ibn Abd al-Wahhab's brother Sulaiman, who led the anti-Wahhabi struggle in many Najdi oases for a long time, noted that intolerance of all opposing views was a characteristic feature of Wahhabism. According to the Hijazi historian Ibn Zaini Dahlan:

> Sulaiman once asked his brother Muhammad, 'How many are the pillars of Islam, O Muhammad ibn Abd al-Wahhab?' 'Five', he answered. Sulaiman replied, 'No, you have added a sixth one. It reads that one who does not follow you is not a Muslim. To you, it is the sixth pillar of Islam.'[85]

The Basra chronicler Ibn Sanad also mentions that kind of extremism:

> When Tuais, a black slave, killed Thuwaini [the shaikh of the Muntafiq tribe in the lower reaches of the Euphrates], Saud's supporters praised the murder not only because they were convinced of Thuwaini's infidelity; they were similarly convinced of the infidelity of all people on earth who did not share their convictions.[86]

In opposing the dominant form of Islam, the Wahhabis went much further than ordinary sectarians. In the words of E. Belyaev, 'According to the firmly established notion of the Muslims themselves, the followers of all directions, trends and sects in Islam are treated as Muslims.'[87] To the Wahhabis, however, all believers in heterodox sects were polytheists, not Muslims. They held that everybody who had heard their appeal and did not join them was a *kafir* (infidel). Subsequently, the Wahhabis treated even Jews and Christians less harshly than non-Wahhabi Muslims, allowing them to pray at home. The only restriction on their rights was the *jizya* (poll tax) of 4 piastres.[88] Ibn Abd al-Wahhab's followers seem to have been guided by the fact that the Prophet had recommended showing tolerance towards the 'People of the Book'.

When the Wahhabis seized an oasis or a town, they destroyed gravestones and monuments at the graves of saints and pious people and burnt books by *ulama* who disagreed with them.[89] Abdallah, Ibn Abd al-Wahhab's son, justified these actions.[90] The Wahhabis' religious practice might differ from their doctrine, however, and from Ibn Abd al-Wahhab's formal prescriptions. Many *ulama* charged the Wahhabis with disrespect for the Prophet. All later Wahhabi writers deny this charge outright, but the desire to deprive Muhammad of the attributes of 'Allah's companion' might, in practice, have led to belittling his role in Islam and a demonstration of 'lack of respect' for him.

There is a widespread belief that the Wahhabis forbade the consumption of coffee.[91] The facts belie this assertion, but it is not impossible that some particularly zealous adherents might have done so.

Wahhabism led easily to fanaticism. The conviction that the Wahhabis' opponents were 'infidels' and 'polytheists' was seen as justifying their cruelty towards them. Fanaticism simultaneously united and disciplined the Wahhabis, inspiring them to military exploits and campaigns of conquest against the 'polytheists'. That is how the ideological preconditions were created for declaring *jihad* (holy war) on all non-Wahhabis.

An emir derived clear advantages from adopting the Wahhabi teaching as his weapon. From a mere leader of a raid upon his neighbours, he became a fighter for the 'purity of the faith', while his enemies were 'the devil's servants', 'idolaters' and 'polytheists'. Making the *jihad* against the 'polytheists' its most important postulate, Wahhabism was an ideology of military expansion and raids from the outset.

Centripetal trends

Wahhabism was both the banner under which wars of conquest were fought and an ideological justification for centripetal trends in Arabia.[92] Opposing the cult of saints, destroying pious people's graves and felling holy trees amounted, under Arabian conditions, to the destruction of the ideological and spiritual basis of political fragmentation. Deprived of a saint of their own, the nobility of an oasis could no longer claim exclusiveness and lost the income from the pilgrimage to the saint's grave.

The Wahhabis asserted that people should obey their local ruler, except on occasions when they were ordered to 'commit a sin'.[93] The supreme arbiters in determining what constituted a sin and what did not were the champions of monotheism, led by Ibn Abd al-Wahhab. A vassal's opposition of whatever kind to the emir of al-Diriya released his subjects from the obligation of obedience and destroyed the basis of his power.

The most important centripetal trends within Wahhabism were those of the unity of Najd and its nobility in the struggle against their traditional adversaries, the Hijazi nobility. The new teaching banned pilgrimages to the holy places of Mecca and Medina (with the exception of the *hajj* to the Kaaba), and particularly to the Prophet's mausoleum, which would deprive the people of Hijaz of a sizeable part of their income. At that time, the inhabitants of Hijaz sympathized with the official form of Islam in the Ottoman empire, from where the bulk of pilgrims came. The Hijazi *ulama* were all too aware of the probable loss of their authority, and thereby of their privileges and incomes, in the event of the Wahhabis' success. Naturally, the *ulama* of the holy cities, who prided themselves on their knowledge of Islam, could not find themselves in agreement with a Najdi who had taken it into his head to teach them 'genuine' Islam.

The provisions and practice of Wahhabism gave rise to its marked anti-Sufi content or, to be more accurate, to its condemnation of the form of Sufism that was widespread throughout the Ottoman empire in the eighteenth century. It is true that the Wahhabi teaching did not openly attack the Sufis. Abdallah ibn Muhammad ibn Abd al-Wahhab even said once that he did not oppose Sufism.[94] But this statement seems a tactical reservation. To a true Wahhabi who relies on the Quran, the Sunna and the *ulama* of the first three centuries of Islam, Sufism is *bida*, and therefore a mortal sin. The denunciation of the cult of saints, sorcery and magic was essentially targeted at the Sufi dervishes. It should not be forgotten that Wahhabism's most important taboos in the spheres of ritual and everyday life included the prohibition on tobacco, hashish,[95] rosaries, music, loud singing, the *zikr* (ecstatic group worship) and dancing.[96] (These taboos were applied in practice, although the Wahhabis' treatises mention them far less frequently than European travellers do.)

Opposing *bida* in principle and taking the provisions of Hanbalism to extremes, the Wahhabis rejected Hanafism, the official Sunni school under the Ottoman empire. Thus one may say that they rebelled against the form of Islam that existed in the empire. The prohibition on tobacco, silk clothes and noisy festivals was not merely an expression of the Wahhabis' attitude to *bida*. It was the Najdis' reaction to the outer manifestations of the Ottoman nobility's way of life. 'The Wahabys beheld the gaudy robes of the Turkish pilgrims with disdain,'[97] notes Burckhardt. He writes that the Arabians were indignant at the corrupt courts and arbitrary rule in the Ottoman empire, at the sexual perversions that the Turks practised openly and at their presumption.[98] Raymond, a French artilleryman who served the Baghdad pasha, notes that anti-Turkish sentiment was widespread in Arabia. An Arab told him, 'The day will come when we see an Arab sitting on the throne of the caliphs; we have tolerated the usurpers' oppression too long.'[99]

Subsequent developments demonstrated that the Wahhabis' rebellion against Turkicized Islam far exceeded the sphere of religion and came to acquire a military-political character. It was a collision between Arabian statehood and the Ottoman empire. Wahhabism became the banner of the Arab national movement against Turkish influence in Arabia. The Wahhabis' militant anti-Shiism also contained a germ of the struggle against the Persians as carriers of the Shia 'heresy', but this was not a significant factor in the course of future developments in the military or political field.

In summary, Wahhabism as an ideology was the product of a profound spiritual crisis in Arabia, caused by economic and socio-political factors. As mentioned above, Wahhabism was an extreme form of Hanbalism: it rejected all *bida* and pressed for a return to the Quran and the original Sunna, to the exclusion of all else. Although Wahhabism served the interests of the nobility, it also demanded the fair treatment of the lowest social groups. Thus it contained the elements inherent in all egalitarian movements.

Contrasting the Wahhabis to all other Muslims, Ibn Abd al-Wahhab's teaching moulded them into a united sect and kindled a spirit of fanaticism. The necessity of undertaking *jihad* against the 'polytheists' made Wahhabism the banner under which raids were undertaken and conquests won. Wahhabism thus became the ideological weapon of the movement for centralization in the Arabian peninsula. It also endorsed the Najdi nobility's political and military struggle for predominance in Arabia, first against Hijaz. Opposing the dominant form of Islam in the Ottoman empire, Wahhabism served as the ideological justification behind the peninsular Arabs' national struggle against the Turks.

Many provisions of Wahhabism, especially the compulsory collection of *zakat*, were anathema to the bedouin, particularly to the 'noble tribes'. However, the notion of *jihad* – in other words, raids under the banner of Islam – was attractive to the bedouin. It made possible an alliance between the Wahhabis and the tribes, between the settled and the nomadic nobility, under certain conditions and for a certain period. Subsequent developments demonstrated that Ibn Abd al-Wahhab, who came from the *ulama* circles of Najd, strove constantly to win the support of the Najdi nobility for his teaching and that Wahhabism did not become a powerful movement before their support was enlisted.

Muhammad ibn Abd al-Wahhab and his Teaching

Ibn Abd al-Wahhab's first steps in politics

When Ibn Abd al-Wahhab came to Uyaina in 1740/41, he hastened to win the support of the emir, Uthman ibn Hamad ibn Muammar. The annals report that the shaikh told him, 'I want you to spread "There is no deity but Allah" [i.e. monotheism] and capture Najd and its bedouin.' The proposal was acceptable to the emir. Soon afterwards the families of Ibn Abd al-Wahhab and the ruler of Uyaina became related through marriage.[100]

Following Wahhabi doctrine, they started destroying local holy places. Ibn Abd al-Wahhab felled a sacred tree with his own hands.[101] Next came the turn of the grave of Zaid ibn al-Khattab, one of the Prophet's Companions, in al-Jubail. Numerous pilgrims gathered at the holy place. The oasis dwellers were about to resist the destruction of the object of their worship but Ibn Abd al-Wahhab was followed by Emir Uthman with 600 armed men. Ibn Abd al-Wahhab himself destroyed the gravestone.[102]

Thereafter an event occurred in the oasis that is described in rapturous terms by pro-Wahhabi Arab historians. A woman had committed 'fornication' in Uyaina, and Ibn Abd al-Wahhab, interpreting the *sharia* literally, ordered her to be stoned to death.[103]

> Emir Uthman and a group of Muslims appeared and stoned her until she died [Ibn Ghannam writes]. Uthman was the first to throw a stone. Ibn Abd al-Wahhab ordered her [body] to be washed and wrapped in a shroud and that a prayer should be said.[104]

It was a serious event. Word of it spread throughout the area, reportedly 'horrifying' those who had, in Ibn Ghannam's opinion, deviated from genuine Islam.[105] Wahhabism thus declared its intention of putting its principles into practice not only through propaganda and the destruction of tombstones but also through calculated acts of violence.

The news of the stoning reached Sulaiman ibn Hamad ibn Ghurayar al-Humaidi, 'the ruler of al-Hasa and the nomads of the environs'. Uyaina was in a dependent relationship with him and its trade was carried on partly through the ports of al-Hasa. Besides, the emir of Uyaina owned palm groves and other rich properties in al-Hasa. Sulaiman al-Humaidi ordered Uthman to kill Ibn Abd al-Wahhab, threatening that he would end the supplies of food and clothes and seize the sources of his income if he declined.[106] Sulaiman al-Humaidi's actions may be explained by the pressure brought by the local *ulama*, who resented the popularity of the new teaching, which undermined their position. The Shia in al-Hasa were utterly opposed to Wahhabism. Besides, the shaikh of the Bani Khalid might have felt threatened due to the Wahhabis' growing might.

However, the emir of Uyaina did not venture, or perhaps did not wish, to kill Ibn Abd al-Wahhab and he sent him into exile instead.[107] Uthman ibn Muammar might have been hoping to wait for some time and then invite the religious leader back. Ibn Abd al-Wahhab settled in al-Diriya in 1744/45.[108] He had a group of followers in the oasis, including the local emir Muhammad ibn Saud's two brothers and his wife. Ibn Abd al-Wahhab lodged at the house of one of his disciples and immediately contacted the ruler of al-Diriya. The emir's brothers and wife encouraged their *rapprochement*.[109] Muhammad ibn Saud, who nurtured ambitious plans, was already acquainted with the renowned religious leader's teaching and had evaluated the prospects of Wahhabism.

Ibn Abd al-Wahhab's need for military support and the ambitious emir's interest in religious backing led them to unite their efforts, and an alliance was concluded. Muhammad ibn Saud asked Ibn Abd al-Wahhab not to leave al-Diriya and tried to win his consent for a continuation of the earlier taxation system in the oasis. 'I collect a tax from the people of al-Diriya in the fruiting season and am afraid that you will tell me, "Don't collect it,"' the emir is reported to have said. Although Ibn Abd al-Wahhab did not object to the first condition, he rejected the second, promising Muhammad ibn Saud that his share in the returns from raids and the *jihad* would far exceed the proceeds from taxation.[110] This fact demonstrates that the emir tried to retain the right to tax his subjects, a right that was presumably against the *sharia*. But the more perspicacious Ibn Abd al-Wahhab suggested that Muhammad ibn Saud should lift the tax. In doing so, he was pursuing two purposes: to preserve the 'purity' of the doctrine and to win the support of the local population, whose life was immediately made easier.

So ended the initial period of the history of Wahhabism. From the time that Ibn Abd al-Wahhab moved to al-Diriya, his life was inseparable from the destinies of the emirate of al-Diriya and the future state of the Saudis.

CHAPTER 3

The Rise of the First Saudi State (1745-1811)

After Muhammad ibn Abd al-Wahhab had moved to al-Diriya, Uthman ibn Muammar realized the opportunity he had missed to strengthen his emirate and tried to encourage the religious leader to return.[1] But the founder of the Wahhabi sect remained loyal to his alliance with Muhammad ibn Saud and Ibn Abd al-Wahhab's numerous followers started to move to al-Diriya from Uyaina and other Najdi oases. The capital of the future vast Saudi state was then dragging out a miserable existence and Muhammad ibn Saud could not even provide Ibn Abd al-Wahhab's closest disciples with food. The religious leader had nothing at his disposal but his powers of persuasion.[2]

Ibn Abd al-Wahhab acquainted his followers and adherents with the basic tenets of his teaching and inculcated the idea of the need for a *jihad* against 'infidels'.[3] After the very first raids on their neighbours, the spoils were distributed 'justly' among the people of al-Diriya in accordance with Wahhabi doctrine: one fifth went to Muhammad ibn Saud and the rest to the fighters (one share to an unmounted and two shares to a mounted man). Thus the adherence to Wahhabism brought clear material rewards. Earlier a *ghazu* had been merely a valiant raid; now it became a seizure of the property of 'polytheists' and its transfer to the hands of 'genuine Muslims'.

The Wahhabis' method of undertaking hostilities did not differ from the usual internecine wars between oasis-states. A swift raid, the ambush of several dozen armed men, the seizure of several dozen head of camels or sheep, felled palms, looted fields or houses – these were the Wahhabis' 'achievements' in the first years under the leadership of Ibn Abd al-Wahhab. But the banner of the 'purified' religion conferred authority and prestige on the emir of al-Diriya; he came to be referred to as the imam (spiritual leader) in the Najdi annals. He was now considered the head of the Muslims (meaning all those who became Wahhabis) and stood in front of the community of believers during prayers.

The establishment of al-Diriya's hegemony in central Najd

Al-Diriya's allies were the people of Uyaina, led by Uthman ibn Muammar. The emir of Uyaina even commanded the united forces in the early years.[4] Uthman ibn Muammar became related to the Saudis through marrying his daughter to Abd al-Aziz ibn Muhammad ibn Saud. (Their son Saud ibn Abd al-Aziz, under whom the Wahhabis were to reach the zenith of their power, was born in 1748.)[5] Mortal hostility among relatives was so common in Arabia, however, that one should not be surprised at subsequent developments. Ibn Abd al-Wahhab's position was decisive in the rivalry between the rulers of al-Diriya and Uyaina and he had not forgotten his exile from Uyaina. The mutual suspicion between the two emirs soon led to an open clash.[6]

Uthman ibn Muammar was accused of maintaining a secret correspondence with Muhammad ibn Afaliq, the ruler of al-Hasa, and of preparing a plot against his allies. In June 1750 the Wahhabis of his oasis killed Uthman after Friday prayers. He was succeeded by his relative Mishari ibn Ibrahim ibn Muammar, who was dependent on al-Diriya.[7] Ten years later, Uyaina finally lost its independence. Ibn Abd al-Wahhab removed Mishari, settled him in al-Diriya together with his family and replaced him by a ruler who was subservient to the Saudis. Ibn Abd al-Wahhab himself arrived in Uyaina and gave the order for Ibn Muammar's family castle to be destroyed.[8]

Five years after Ibn Abd al-Wahhab and Muhammad ibn Saud had concluded their alliance, the latter's authority was still disputed, even in the nearest oases. Between 1750 and 1753 the emirates of Manfuha, Huraimala and Durma, which were among the Wahhabis' first allies, tried to end their dependence on al-Diriya.[9] Muhammad ibn Abd al-Wahhab's brother Sulaiman inspired the insurrection in Huraimala. He sent his theological messages throughout Najd, denouncing his brother's teaching. The unrest spread even in Uyaina under the impact of the anti-Wahhabi propaganda.[10] However, Abd al-Aziz (the son of Muhammad ibn Saud) managed to seize Huraimala with 800 unmounted and 20 mounted men, and Sulaiman fled to Sudair.[11]

Dahham ibn Dawwas, the emir of Riyadh, remained the Saudis' principal rival. Mutual raids between al-Diriya and detachments from Riyadh took place almost every year. The people of the regions and oases of Washm, Sudair, Sadiq and Huraimala joined Dahham by turns. The Wahhabis were the attacking party on most occasions. This is clear from the fact that Dahham had to conclude an armistice in 1753/54, which lasted nearly two years, and to declare his allegiance to the 'purified' Islam.[12] In 1757/58 the al-Diriya detachments built a fortress in front of Riyadh to curb its activities.[13]

In the late 1750s the energetic Arayar ibn Dujain from al-Hasa, who had assumed the leadership there some years previously, again appeared in the area of Najd. He won over the enemies of al-Diriya – Riyadh, Washm and detachments from Sudair, Munikh,

The Rise of the First Saudi State (1745-1811)

Sadiq and Mahmal. Yet Arayar's raid was unsuccessful and some of his temporary allies from Najd hastily declared their allegiance to al-Diriya.[14] In the early 1760s the Wahhabis successfully attacked al-Kharj, Tharmida, Ushaiqir, Sudair and several bedouin tribes and penetrated far into the territory of al-Hasa. Dahham ibn Dawwas had to submit to al-Diriya and make a substantial payment to its ruler.[15]

At the end of 1764 Hasan Hibbatullah,[16] the shaikh of the bedouin tribes of Najran, attacked al-Diriya at the request of the inhabitants of southern Najd and the Ajman bedouin. Abd al-Aziz's forces were routed, with 500 men killed and 200 captured. Ibn Abd al-Wahhab addressed words of consolation to the fighters and then negotiated with the Najranis. Demonstrating great diplomatic skill, he quickly concluded an armistice and specified the payment of a contribution and the exchange of captives. The Najranis departed without waiting for Arayar, who was coming from al-Hasa.[17]

Arayar's detachments, armed with guns, approached al-Diriya in early 1765. Many Najdis, including Dahham from Riyadh and Zaid ibn Zamil, the emir of al-Kharj, joined him. But the siege of al-Diriya ended in failure.[18] Muhammad ibn Saud died in the same year. He was succeeded by Abd al-Aziz ibn Muhammad ibn Saud. Ibn Ghannam and Ibn Bishr note that Abd al-Aziz was both the heir to the throne and the imam of the Wahhabi Muslims. According to Mengin, the people of al-Diriya 'elected' him emir.[19]

The Saudi emirate soon recovered from the shock caused by the defeat in the battle with the Najranis and the raid from al-Hasa. It continued to expand ever faster and, by the late 1760s, the Wahhabis had subdued Washm and Sudair, attacked the al-Zilfi oasis to the north-east of Qasim, a rich province of Najd, and successfully raided the nomads to the south and east of Najd. Some subdivisions of the Subai and Zafir nomadic tribes submitted to the Wahhabis. In 1769/70 the majority of the population of Qasim swore allegiance to the 'purified' religion and the Saudis.[20]

Surrounded on all sides by vassals or allies of the Wahhabis, Riyadh's position seemed hopeless. Dahham's two sons were killed in a clash with the people of al-Diriya and the old emir's fighting spirit was crushed. When the Wahhabis approached Riyadh in the summer of 1773, they found the town almost deserted. The emir fled with his family, and most of his subjects followed him, fearful of their old adversaries' inevitable revenge. Many of them died en route, either killed by the Wahhabis or overcome by heat and thirst.[21]

The struggle for predominance in central Najd was over. Although unrest continued for nearly a quarter of a century, it did not exceed the scale of an internecine war. The chroniclers give the figure (perhaps an underestimate) of 4,000 or 5,000 people killed, of whom more than half were Dahham's followers. One may agree with Philby: "Abd al-'Aziz had by this time been exactly eight years on the throne of Dar'iya, which was still little more than primus inter pares among the numerous city-States of Arabia."[22] But the Wahhabis now had a firm base from which to expand their state further.

The Saudis' authority did not rely on weapons alone. Whenever an oasis was annexed to al-Diriya, Wahhabi *ulama* were sent there to preach 'genuine monotheism'. A part of the Najdi population began to consider al-Diriya both as the capital of a strong emirate and as a spiritual centre. Its ruler acquired the status of a powerful emir and champion of the 'purity' of the faith. It should not be forgotten that the *ulama* and other supporters of Wahhabism undermined the resistance of hostile emirates from inside, often divided the nobility, won over a part of the people and sometimes acted as the Saudis' spies. It was not by chance that Dahham severed his alliance with the Wahhabis whenever he noted their growing influence over his subjects. He could oppose the Wahhabis' military might, which was combined with religious conviction, only by force of arms and terror. (An Arabian chronicler reports that, on learning that an oasis dweller had become a Wahhabi, Dahham ordered one of his hands and one of his feet to be amputated. The unfortunate man died soon afterwards.)[23]

In spite of all their efforts, the Saudis only crushed the independent emirs' resistance with difficulty. The forces of decentralization, fragmentation and tribal anarchy were making themselves felt. After the fall of Riyadh, it took al-Diriya some ten or twelve years to establish its power over the whole of Najd.

The unification of central Arabia

After the annexation of Riyadh in 1773, the Saudis' main enemy in Najd was Zaid ibn Zamil, the cunning, courageous emir of Dilam and the whole of al-Kharj. He tried to persuade the Najrani tribes to take up the struggle against the Wahhabis again. To that end, he asked the emir of Najran to send forces to his aid in return for payment. The Najranis came but, instead of helping the emir, engaged in extortion and plunder. The planned alliance did not materialize. Zaid ibn Zamil declared his allegiance to the Wahhabis, only to betray them shortly afterwards.[24]

Led by Arayar, the Bani Khalid invaded Najd from al-Hasa in the mid-1770s, seized Buraida in Qasim and plundered it with great cruelty. Uneasy at the Saudis' growing power, many Najdi rulers were ready to support al-Hasa, but Arayar died suddenly. A leadership struggle broke out among the Bani Khalid nobility. Saadun, one of Arayar's sons, won it temporarily, but the al-Diriya emirs encouraged his brothers to oppose him.[25] Subsequently, detachments from al-Hasa appeared in Najd almost every year. The nomads of the Subai and Zafir tribes joined the Bani Khalid raids. Certain Najdi oases – Harma, al-Majmaa, al-Zilfi and many others – sometimes joined the Wahhabis, sometimes broke away from them and acted independently and at still other times joined al-Diriya's enemies, Saadun ibn Arayar and Zaid ibn Zamil.[26]

The behaviour of the people of Yamama in al-Kharj may be considered characteristic of the period. They sent a delegation to al-Diriya, led by their emir, and asked Abd al-Aziz to count them as his subjects. The ruler of al-Diriya sent a *faqih* (legal expert) to their oasis to act as judge and to 'turn their minds onto the right path'. But as soon as the *faqih* had settled in Yamama, the local people engineered a plot to kill him together with all the adherents of Wahhabism. The *faqih* escaped, but Abd al-Aziz had to send his son Saud to Yamama with an armed detachment in order to curb the dissatisfied population and leave a garrison there.[27]

The Rise of the First Saudi State (1745-1811)

The manner in which hostilities were conducted is clear from a curious episode described by Mengin. The Wahhabis erected a fortress near Dilam to hamper Zaid ibn Zamil's activities. It was difficult to approach the fortress as it was protected by crack Wahhabi troops. To dislodge the enemy, the people of Dilam, guided by a Persian inhabitant of the oasis, built a movable tower with four wheels and coated it with lead to make it bullet-proof. Men entered it, and it was rolled towards the fortress. But the structure became stuck while approaching the fortress and only a desperate sally by the Dilam daredevils saved the men in the movable tower.[28]

In spite of resistance, the Saudi state gradually expanded its influence and territory. After the Wahhabis had seized the al-Majmaa oasis, the most active anti-Wahhabi preacher, Sulaiman ibn Abd al-Wahhab (the brother of the sect's founder), had to cease his activities. Together with his family he was taken to al-Diriya, where he stayed until his death.[29]

The fate of Qasim was finally sealed in the early 1780s. Unrest and internecine wars in the province had lasted for several years, combined with the struggle against al-Diriya. The old feud had not died down; indeed, the earlier allegiances, antipathies and alliances continued. Saadun ibn Arayar invaded Qasim in 1782, leading the Bani Khalid, the Shammar and the Zafir, and determined to drive out the Wahhabis. Zaid ibn Zamil and his troops joined him. For some weeks they besieged Buraida (which remained loyal to the Wahhabis), but this time without success. The anti-Wahhabi coalition disintegrated and the al-Hasa forces had to leave Najd.[30] Zaid ibn Zamil was killed in 1783 and was succeeded by his son Barrak. But the new emir's position was unstable because of the rivalry within the ruling family.[31]

Najd experienced a devastating drought between 1783 and 1786, leading to famine. The situation of al-Kharj, surrounded by the Wahhabis, was desperate. When Dilam was taken by storm in 1785, its emir and some of his followers were killed. The whole of al-Kharj swore allegiance to the Saudis and Sulaiman ibn Ufaisan, a Wahhabi military commander, was appointed ruler of Dilam.[32] In almost the same years, al-Diriya subdued al-Aflaj and al-Dawasir, though anti-Wahhabi insurrections continued for a long time in the latter province.[33]

The most powerful Arabian nomadic tribes were now feeling the heavy hand of the ruler of al-Diriya. When the Wahhabis defeated the Zafir bedouin in 1781, they seized all their property and camp equipment, 17,000 head of sheep and goats, 5,000 head of camels and 15 horses.[34] The Wahhabis also raided the Bani Murra, the Qahtan, the Subai and the Bani Khalid. They penetrated into the north and subdued Jabal Shammar in the late 1780s.[35]

The consolidation of the central Arabian lands around al-Diriya was now complete. Although anti-Saudi rebellions occurred in some regions, the local emirs could no longer be considered as rivals. They were semi-dependent vassals at best, but most of them were al-Diriya's direct placemen and played the role of governors. For example, Saud visited Anaiza, one of the main towns of Qasim, in the late 1780s and removed the emir (who had displeased him) without meeting any resistance. The ex-emir and many members of the Anaiza nobility were taken to al-Diriya as hostages.[36]

In 1788 the general strengthening of the Saudis' power and influence led Imam Abd al-Aziz and Ibn Abd al-Wahhab to take an important step: they ensured Saud ibn Abd al-Aziz's hereditary right to the throne during Abd al-Aziz's lifetime. Ibn Abd al-Wahhab undertook to swear in the towns and provinces of the state. Saud was already a popular leader, thanks to his courage, military successes and involvement in solving matters of state.[37] The proclamation of the heir to the throne strengthened the Saudi dynasty, ensuring a smooth transfer of power from the emir to his son. Inheritance from father to son is common in Arabia but by no means obligatory. Power was transferred on the basis both of seniority in the kinship group and of the closest relatives' personal merits. The decisive say in electing a new emir belonged to the elite. Ibn Ghannam's persistence in justifying the legitimacy of Saud suggests that the transfer of power from father to son might have provoked some resistance. But the system of direct inheritance continued until the collapse of the first Saudi state.

Relying on the resources of central Arabia, the Wahhabis began a successful offensive in all directions: to al-Hasa and Lower Iraq in the east and north-east, to Hijaz in the west, to Yemen in the south-west, to Oman in the south-east and towards the Syrian frontiers in the north. Sometimes they launched several large campaigns within a year and sometimes they alternated their attacks upon the various regions.

The Wahhabis in eastern Arabia

The Wahhabis' offensive against al-Hasa was helped by internal feuds in the rich province. A conspiracy against Saadun ibn Arayar matured among his closest relatives in 1785/86. They won over Thuwaini ibn Abdallah, the shaikh of the Muntafiq, who came as their ally, and hostilities began. Saadun was defeated in a decisive battle, and he then fled. He asked for asylum in al-Diriya and was received with honour. According to some reports, he died soon afterwards. Diwaihis became the ruler of al-Hasa for a time.[38]

The Wahhabis' pressure on al-Hasa eased off for a while because of an unexpected raid on Qasim in 1786/87 by Thuwaini, the shaikh of the Muntafiq. He gathered a large army with artillery and some Shammar subdivisions; the people of al-Zubair also took part in the raid. The raiders looted several villages in Qasim and besieged Buraida, but were repulsed.[39]

Returning to the region in which the Muntafiq roamed, Thuwaini tried to seize Basra and proclaim himself its ruler. At his insistence, a delegation of the Basra nobility was sent to Istanbul to ask the sultan to issue a *firman* (edict) confirming Thuwaini's appointment as governor. But this did not coincide with the plans of the ruler of Baghdad, Buyuk Sulaiman Pasha, who was virtually independent of the Porte. He attacked Thuwaini in the autumn of 1787, defeated him near the town of Suq al-Shuyukh and then ordered three towers to be built of his enemies' skulls. Thuwaini fled and Hamud ibn Samir became the new shaikh of the Muntafiq.[40]

The Arabian chroniclers who describe the initial period of the history of the Saudi state repeatedly mention clashes between the Saudi troops and the bedouin. But by the late 1780s certain bedouin tribes were participating ever more actively in the Wahhabis' campaigns. Ibn Bishr frequently reports examples such as, 'In that year, Saud ibn Abd al-Aziz led the victorious armies of the settled people and bedouin of Najd [to such-and-such a locality].' Some years later, the bedouin occupy first place in the phrase or are even mentioned as an independent force.

The Wahhabis raided deep into al-Hasa every year, reaching as far as the Gulf coast. In 1787/88 Sulaiman ibn Ufaisan broke through Qatar and then looted several oases and the port of al-Uqair in al-Hasa.[41] Besides the oases of eastern Arabia and the Bani Khalid, the Wahhabis raided the Muntafiq to the north of al-Hasa.[42] They suppressed all resistance with great harshness. Ibn Ghannam reports that once, when invading an oasis, they found 'most of the village men, who numbered 300, in a house and killed all of them'.[43]

Some subdivisions of the Bani Khalid were already fighting on the Wahhabis' side in the autumn of 1788. Zaid ibn Arayar, the henchman of al-Diriya, became the ruler of all the Bani Khalid. Al-Hasa as a whole was not yet pacified,[44] however, and its people's subsequent stubborn resistance and repeated insurrections showed the strength of anti-Wahhabi sentiment there. Among the explanations might be the strong Shia elements in al-Hasa and its nobility's habit of considering the Najdis as a legitimate object of their attacks, combined with their refusal to reconcile themselves to a subordinate role. It was no coincidence that the Wahhabis stressed religious motives in justification of their raids – Ibn Ghannam writes that the purpose of Saud's campaign was the destruction of idols and the places of devil worship.[45]

In 1791/92 Saud swept through the east Arabian oases with fire and the sword and occupied al-Qatif. Meanwhile, Sulaiman ibn Ufaisan again raided Qatar.[46] However, the whole of al-Hasa soon rose in revolt. The Bani Khalid removed the Wahhabi shaikh, and the new shaikh – Barrak ibn Abd al-Muhsin – immediately started raids on those bedouin and oases that were subject to the Saudis. Yet the Bani Khalid were defeated in a battle, losing more than 1,000 people, and Zaid ibn Arayar returned. The al-Hasa oases now pledged their allegiance to Saud. The Wahhabis stayed in the province for a month, destroying the domes above mausoleums and all Shia places of worship. Wahhabi *ulama* were sent to the towns and oases.[47]

It was when the subjugation of al-Hasa was in full swing, in 1791/92, that the founder of the Wahhabi movement, Muhammad ibn Abd al-Wahhab, died.[48] A prominent figure of his era and his society, he was a man of great courage and passion. A remarkable boldness was needed to challenge the entire religious system of Arabia at that time and face the advocates of the old. His life was constantly under threat and he was sent into exile three times, but this did not crush his will. Through his passionate speeches and his eloquence, Ibn Abd al-Wahhab made a major contribution to the success of the religious movement he had started and to the expansion of the Saudi state. According to Ibn Bishr, Ibn Abd al-Wahhab 'raised the banner of *jihad*, though there had been nothing but riots and murders before him'.[49] Mengin notes that 'he was extremely persuasive and won hearts by his speeches'.[50] The author of *The Brilliance of the Meteor* mentions another important detail, claiming that it was Ibn Abd al-Wahhab who taught the people of al-Diriya to make and handle firearms.[51] If this is true, his role in the rise and military successes of the emirate of al-Diriya was even greater than appears in the Najdi annals.

It is reported that Ibn Abd al-Wahhab 'was fond of women, had 20 wives and begot 18 children',[52] though this may be an exaggeration. Five of his sons and numerous grandsons became renowned *ulama*. In his last years, Ibn Abd al-Wahhab grew physically very weak and could appear at prayers only if supported by 2 disciples. Ibn Abd al-Wahhab bequeathed to his heirs land with palms, fruit trees and fields, which yielded an annual income of 50,000 *zahabs*, and a library of several hundred volumes. After his death, his son Husain became the mufti of al-Diriya. Husain was almost blind and was soon succeeded by his brother Ali, who was famous for his fondness for women. He had some 50 or 60 wives before finally choosing 4 of them.[53] The family of *ulama* that came to be named the Al al-Shaikh has preserved its influence and honoured status in Saudi Arabia up to the present day, but none of Ibn Abd al-Wahhab's later descendants has played the role of *eminence grise* that their forefather enjoyed in the emirate of al-Diriya.

Meanwhile, a new insurrection against the Najdis began in al-Hasa. The people of Hufuf killed thirty men from al-Diriya, including the governor, some officials and several Wahhabi *ulama*, dragged their bodies through the streets and mutilated them in public. Several other oases supported Hufuf. Zaid ibn Arayar, the Wahhabis' henchman and the shaikh of the Bani Khalid, betrayed his masters and took part in the insurrection.

In the autumn of 1793 Saud left for al-Hasa with large numbers of armed men. His bedouin detachment looted everything on their way, mercilessly killed all who resisted, destroyed palm groves, carried off dates and grazed livestock in the fields. Zaid ibn Arayar's rival and the Wahhabis' former adversary, Barrak ibn Abd al-Muhsin, took their side. The whole of al-Hasa expressed allegiance to them. Barrak ibn Abd al-Muhsin was appointed emir of the province,[54] but tried to throw off the Wahhabi yoke in the spring of 1796, taking advantage of their preoccupation with hostilities to the west and south-west of Najd.[55] Some months later, Saud arrived in al-Hasa with a strong army and suppressed the insurrection again.[56] Ibn Bishr describes the conquest of al-Hasa as follows:

> When morning came and Saud went on his way after the prayer, when they [the Wahhabis] rode camels and horses and shot their hand-guns at once, the sky darkened, the earth shuddered, puffs of smoke rose in the air and many pregnant women suffered miscarriages. Then all the people of al-Hasa came to Saud, throwing themselves on his mercy.
>
> He ordered all of them to appear before him and so they did. He stayed there for some months, killing, exiling and jailing everybody he wanted to, confiscating property, destroying houses and erecting fortresses. He demanded 100,000 dirhams from them and received that sum. It was a punishment for having often failed to

The Rise of the First Saudi State (1745–1811)

implement the treaty, having rejected the Muslims and having been involved by the [Muslims'] enemies [in the struggle] against them. Saud increased the number of murders. Some people, including Najim ibn Duhainim, toured the markets and caught those who had led a dissolute life or rejected the treaty. Some people were killed in the oasis, others were taken to the camp and their heads were chopped off in front of Saud's tent until they were all destroyed with few exceptions. Saud seized countless [amounts of] money in that raid. When he decided to leave al-Hasa, he caught some noble people . . ., brought them to al-Diriya and settled there. He appointed the above-mentioned Najim, a man from among the common people of al-Hasa, the emir of the oasis.[57]

To pay off the sum imposed by the Wahhabis, the people of al-Hasa had to sell their property. They were ordered to hand over all their arms to the conquerors.[58] So ended the conquest of eastern Arabia by the Wahhabis. The Gulf territories belonging to the Al Khalifa, the ruling family of Bahrain, also became dependent on the Saudis.[59]

In the early 1790s, hostilities to the west of Najd were also in full swing.

The Saudi emirate and Hijaz before 1802

After the start of the Wahhabi movement and the expansion of the Saudi emirate, there were no military clashes between the rulers of al-Diriya and the Hijaz nobility for a long period. The Saudis were preoccupied with subduing first Najd and then eastern Arabia, while tense internal struggles were being waged in Mecca.

The rule of Sharif Musaid (1752–70) was far from stable. Towards the end of his period, Mecca was threatened with the loss of the broad autonomy it enjoyed under the Ottoman empire. In 1769 Ali Bey, the ruler of Cairo, proclaimed Egypt's independence from the Porte and annexed Hijaz to his state. The following year, Ali Bey declared himself 'the sultan of Egypt and of both seas'; his name was mentioned in mosque *khutbas* (Friday sermons) in Egypt and Hijaz. His attempt to create an independent Arab state was unsuccessful, however, and Hijaz freed itself from Egyptian rule.[60]

According to the Arabian chroniclers, the Saudis tried to maintain friendly relations with the rulers of Mecca and even cherished the hope of persuading them to adopt the 'purified' religion. Soon after Ibn Abd al-Wahhab had moved to al-Diriya in 1744/45, thirty Wahhabi *ulama* arrived in Mecca to receive a permit for the pilgrimage and to conduct a theological dispute with the Meccan *ulama*. Dahlan reports that the Hijazis found the Wahhabis' teaching to be sheer heresy and godlessness. The sharif ordered messages to be placed everywhere with proofs to the effect that the Wahhabis had succumbed to heresy; the 'mean godless' were to be jailed and put in chains. Some of them managed to flee, however, and reported the events to al-Diriya.[61]

In the early 1770s Ibn Abd al-Wahhab and Abd al-Aziz maintained a correspondence and exchanged gifts with the sharif of Mecca. Another *alim* from Najd visited Mecca to explain the principles of the Wahhabi doctrine, but apparently had no success.[62] The sharifs permitted Wahhabis to undertake the pilgrimage now and then. When Surur became the sharif of Mecca in 1773, Abd al-Aziz sent him costly gifts as a token of his friendship.[63] Presumably, the rulers of Mecca and al-Diriya maintained moderately friendly relations as long as their interests did not come into direct conflict and while Hijaz was wary of Egyptian or Turkish interference in its affairs. As for the Wahhabis' teaching, the Hijazi *ulama* and nobility were probably hostile to it from the outset.

Mecca's new ruler managed to crush any opposition from the sharifian families and consolidate his position in Hijaz.[64] In 1788, however, Surur died and was succeeded by young Ghalib ibn Musaid, who had no real power and was for some time a mere tool in the hands of the late ruler's slaves and eunuchs. Through their oppressive measures, they set the local people against them, which helped Ghalib to make short work of the disobedient slaves and strengthen his authority. Ghalib was a valiant warrior and a perspicacious politician. By maintaining good relations with the neighbouring bedouin tribes, he could rely on them and on a new guard of slaves, some hundreds strong, in his raids of conquest.[65]

Ghalib's initial intentions regarding Najd are unknown. When he became the sharif of Mecca, he wrote to Abd al-Aziz asking him to send an *alim* who would explain the principles of Wahhabism. Abd al-Aziz did so, but the mission was again unsuccessful and Ghalib understood, perhaps, that the Wahhabis' teaching was incompatible with the interests of Hijaz.[66]

In 1790/91 the sharif of Mecca equipped an expedition against Najd: a 10,000-strong detachment with 20 guns was sent under his brother's command. Later, Ghalib himself led the campaign. But his attempts to seize the fortified oases of Najd were in vain and several allied bedouin tribes abandoned him. In summer 1791 Saud ibn Abd al-Aziz dealt the sharif's allies – the Shammar and the Mutair – a crushing blow in Jabal Shammar. The bedouin fled, leaving the Wahhabis a rich booty – nearly 100,000 head of sheep and goats and several thousand camels.[67] The Wahhabi detachments started raiding the regions between Najd and Hijaz and the oases and tribes that were dependent on the sharif. By May 1795 Saud was already besieging Turaba, an important strategic point on the approaches to Hijaz.[68]

In the summer of the same year, the Hijazis raided Najd in response to the Wahhabis' attack. Encouraged by their success, Ghalib equipped a large new detachment with guns in the winter of 1795/96 for an expedition into the depths of Arabia: it was routed by the united forces of the Mutair, Subai, Suhul, Dawasir, Ajman and, probably, some subdivisions of the Ataiba, the subjects of al-Diriya. Ibn Ghannam claims that the Wahhabis seized 30,000 camels and 200,000 sheep and goats.[69] When conducting their operations against the Wahhabis, the sharifs had to keep an eye on the Turks, realizing that their long absence from Mecca might encourage the Ottoman pashas to interfere with matters in Hijaz. The crushing defeat forced Ghalib to agree to a truce.[70] Nevertheless, his troops attacked the Wahhabi bedouin again as early as the following year. The Najdi forces were clearly superior. Continuing their advance southwards, they reached Najran and the northern frontiers of Yemen.[71] Their first contact with the people of Asir may date from that period.

The powerful tribe of Ataiba, earlier ruled by the sharifs of Mecca, joined the emirate of al-Diriya in 1797/98. The bedouin agreed to observe all the requirements of Wahhabism, and to pay *zakat* and a contribution for the earlier hostilities. Mengin reports that each nomad family paid 4 rials and each of their kin contributed a certain amount of arms and livestock.[72]

In 1798 Ghalib tried repeatedly to reach al-Khurma and Bisha with an army that included Turkish, Egyptian and Maghrebi mercenaries. The army was defeated, losing several hundred men; all their arms, equipment and large sums of cash fell into the Wahhabis' hands. The emir of al-Diriya established his control over Bisha. The sharif of Mecca again agreed to a truce and allowed the Wahhabis to perform the *hajj*.[73] Two years later, according to Ibn Bishr, Saud performed his first pilgrimage to Mecca with his family and troops and repeated it the next year. He distributed generous gifts and recruited followers there.[74] It was then that Uthman al-Mudhaifi, a relative of the sharif, contacted Saud and offered him his services.[75] In 1800 and 1801 the Wahhabi *ulama* arrived in Mecca to conduct yet another theological dispute.[76] The Wahhabis were obviously close to full control over Hijaz.

The pasha of Baghdad's unsuccessful expeditions to al-Hasa

Simultaneously with the conquest of al-Hasa, and with increasing frequency thereafter, the Wahhabi detachments raided the regions to the north of it. They attacked, in particular, the nomadic tribes and villages of Lower Iraq. Disturbing reports of the Wahhabis' activities reached Baghdad and even Istanbul. Instigated by the Porte, the pasha of Baghdad prepared to fight the invaders.

The Baghdad *pashalik* enjoyed a special status in the Ottoman empire at that period. After the devastating Turkish-Persian wars, and a long series of mutinies and internecine conflicts, the Mamelukes had seized power in Baghdad. Since 1780 it had been ruled by Buyuk Sulaiman, the Georgian Mameluke of the former pasha of Baghdad. In Longrigg's opinion:

> in the half-century now following [since 1780], the power of the Georgian Pasha, supported by the only civil and military organization in the country, was that of an independent monarch. A half-hereditary dynasty, neither Turkish nor helped to power by the government of Turkey, was now so firmly installed that for fifty years the Sultan could reckon Iraq but a respectful neighbour.[77]

The British East India Company supported the pasha of Baghdad against the Ottoman sultan.

The Baghdad *pashalik*'s virtual independence from Istanbul did not preclude permanent power struggles and rebellions by individual regions, towns and tribes. Disobedience to the weakening Porte did not mean that the *pashalik* was gaining in strength, however, as is clear from the blows dealt it by the Wahhabis. Their expansion in that region was aimed at the north-east, which had been the general direction of migration by the Arabian tribes for centuries. It is known, in particular, that the Shammar penetrated far into Iraq and even settled beyond the Tigris in the eighteenth century.[78] In the 1760s, during a devastating famine in central Arabia, the Najdis moved to al-Zubair and the area to the north of it.[79]

The bedouin tribes in Lower Iraq maintained close ties with the towns and villages of Iraq. The Baghdad rulers needed their help in ensuring the safety of the trade routes, villages and towns and for their supplies of horses and camels. Continuing the millennia-old traditions of Mesopotamia, the Baghdad pashas gave the bedouin shaikhs precious gifts and even arms to resist the raids from the depths of Arabia. The use of the Muntafiq and other tribes in the attempt to overthrow the Wahhabis in al-Hasa was in line with that policy.

The anti-Wahhabi campaign was led by Thuwaini ibn Abdallah. The former shaikh of the Muntafiq had been exiled after an unsuccessful attempt to establish his power in Basra, roamed for a long time and even spent some time in al-Diriya as a guest of honour. Then, according to some reports, he seized power again in his tribe and asked Buyuk Sulaiman Pasha to arm him against the Wahhabis.[80] According to another version, he persuaded the ruler of Baghdad to transfer the rule of the Muntafiq to him, promising to attack Najd and defeat the Wahhabis. Buyuk Sulaiman removed Hamud ibn Samir as shaikh and replaced him by Thuwaini.[81]

At the beginning of 1797, Thuwaini started to wage war against the Wahhabis. He led regular troops and detachments from Basra and al-Zubair and his troops had guns. Several subdivisions of the Bani Khalid, led by Barrak ibn Abd al-Muhsin, who had fled from al-Hasa, joined his campaign. Grasping the danger of the situation, Abd al-Aziz ibn Muhammad ibn Saud gathered all his forces and sent his best cavalry to al-Hasa 'under commanders who had become used to winning'.[82] He ordered the loyal bedouin to occupy the territory where the Bani Khalid roamed and to guard the main wells, since that tribe might join Thuwaini. Thereafter, the most reliable Wahhabi army, from among the settled people of al-Arid, was sent to al-Hasa.

Fierce battles broke out in al-Hasa between Thuwaini's troops and the Wahhabis, but fortune smiled unexpectedly on the ruler of al-Diriya. When the campaign was in full swing, Thuwaini was killed by his black slave Tuais, a fanatic Wahhabi. The assassin was hacked to pieces on the spot, but Thuwaini's death decided the outcome of the struggle. The Bani Khalid, led by Barrak, split from the Muntafiq, which was worrying for Thuwaini's troops. The panic-stricken Turkish and bedouin detachments retreated hastily northwards, leaving their arms and ammunition behind. The whole of Thuwaini's camp and artillery fell into the Wahhabis' hands in June 1797. Pursuing the enemy, the Wahhabi detachments appeared in the lower reaches of the Euphrates.[83] The following year, the Wahhabis penetrated into the Syrian deserts and moved towards the towns of Suq al-Shuyukh and Samawa in Iraq.[84] Populated by 'polytheists', Syria and Iraq were ideal targets to fire the imagination of the Wahhabi troops.

In the late 1790s the Porte repeatedly ordered the pasha of Baghdad to finish off the

The Rise of the First Saudi State (1745–1811)

Wahhabis. Buyuk Sulaiman Pasha's *kahya* (assistant), Ali Kahya, was appointed commander of the army. Historians differ in their dating of the Iraqi campaign against al-Hasa. Ibn Bishr and Mengin report that Baghdad's troops invaded al-Hasa in 1799.[85] Brydges claims to have witnessed the departure of Ali Kahya's troops from the environs of Baghdad in September 1798.[86] According to Corancez, the campaign was launched in 1798,[87] while Burckhardt gives 1797[88] and Ibn Sanad mentions 1798/99.[89] Raymond claims that the Ottoman army invaded al-Hasa as early as the beginning of January 1798.[90]

To determine the true date, one may begin with the testimony by Brydges, who was an eye-witness observer. At the time that Ali Kahya's army was leaving Baghdad in September 1798, Brydges had just arrived as Britain's political agent. The troops moved from Baghdad to the lower reaches of the Euphrates with big trains, absorbing bedouin detachments on the way. They could not have reached al-Hasa earlier than late 1798 or early 1799, which corresponds to the dates given by Ibn Bishr, Ibn Sanad and Mengin. Burckhardt may have confused Thuwaini's campaign with that of Ali Kahya. This would have been a natural error since he was in Hijaz, far from the theatre of war, particularly since he was writing one and a half decades after the events.

The army sent from Baghdad included infantry, cavalry and irregular detachments of the Shammar, Muntafiq and Zafir and was more than 10,000 strong. The people of Hufuf and other oases threw themselves on Ali Kahya's mercy. The Wahhabis ensconced themselves in fortresses and repulsed all attacks bravely. Kut put up a particularly stubborn resistance. Guns, siege machines and saps were of no help. The invaders were demoralized and began rolling back, pursued by the Wahhabis. Ali Kahya opened a correspondence with Saud and a truce was concluded.[91] His military failure had been caused by the soldiers' generally low morale and by the difficulty of marching through the arid regions controlled by the Wahhabis. In Brydges' opinion, Saud had spies in Ali's military council. Besides, the Wahhabis' fighting spirit was not yet exhausted: religious fanaticism coupled with stern discipline made them staunch fighters. Ibn Sanad reports that many of the inhabitants of al-Hasa fled to Iraq, fearing Saud's revenge.[92]

In 1799 a representative from al-Diriya arrived in Baghdad to have the agreement between Saud and Ali Kahya ratified by the pasha. Brydges, who was present at the meeting between the envoy from al-Diriya and the pasha of Baghdad, has left a description of it. To impress the desert dwellers, grand ceremonies were conducted in the pasha's palace. Buyuk Sulaiman's magnificently attired and haughty retinue met the envoy. They tried to take his arms and introduce him to the pasha. But the simply dressed Wahhabi pushed them aside, made his way to Buyuk Sulaiman (who was attired in silk, furs and jewels) and sat beside him, saying:

> Hoy Suleiman! peace be on all those who think right. Abdul Aziz has sent me to deliver to you this letter, and to receive from you the ratification of an agreement made between his son, Saoud, and your servant Ally; let it be done soon, and in good form; and the curse of God be on him who acts treacherously.

'If you seek instruction, Abdul Aziz will afford it,'[93] he added daringly, hinting that the Wahhabis considered Sulaiman's faith to be 'polytheism'. He held out a scrap of paper for the pasha with the treaty written on it.

It was obvious that the rulers of al-Diriya did not value the agreement with Baghdad and the pasha tried to secure more definite commitments from them. Sulaiman Pasha's special representative went to al-Diriya to negotiate with Saud. He wanted the Wahhabis to agree not to attack the Muslims' holy places in Lower Iraq. But Saud laughed and told the envoy, 'What is to the west of the Euphrates is mine, and I leave to the pasha what is to the east.'[94] The reports of the invasion of Egypt by Napoleon's army and the Porte's feebleness in the face of the conqueror must have bolstered the Wahhabis' courage.

In 1801 the British replaced the French in Egypt and Arabia became a remote periphery of the main theatre of war. This gave the Wahhabis a free hand in their plans for further expansion.

The fall of Karbala

The rulers of al-Diriya now planned to seize Karbala (in Iraq), with the Shia holy places, particularly the Husain mosque where the Prophet's grandson is believed to be buried. The bedouin traded regularly with Karbala and were aware of the situation in the town. The Wahhabis realized their plan in March–April 1802.[95] Most West European and Russian orientalists date the fall of Karbala to April 1801. This dating is based on Rousseau,[96] Corancez,[97] Burckhardt[98] and Mengin.[99] The Arabian historians and Philby[100] give the date as March–April 1802, a year later, relying on Ibn Bishr's chronicle. This date is confirmed by Ibn Sanad,[101] Raymond[102] and two anonymous Russian writers.[103] With the exception of the last source, the others were all written soon after the events occurred.

The present author believes 1802 to be correct, on the basis of a dispatch from Iraq that was written not later than the summer of 1803 and somehow reached the Russian embassy in Istanbul. Someone who lived in Iraq at the time and talked to witnesses of the attack could hardly have made an error of one year in dating such an important event.[104] A comparison of this dispatch from Iraq with the description of the Wahhabis' capture of Karbala in the book by Rousseau, which appeared six years later, reveals almost identical wording in the two texts (apart from the date). It is difficult to say how the Russian embassy in Istanbul could have taken possession of the French consul's dispatch. The erroneous date of the capture of Karbala in Rousseau's book might simply be the result of negligence on the part of the author or the compositor.

Alternatively, the primary source of the error might be the works by Rousseau and Corancez, who were not generally very scrupulous in dating events. Burckhardt and Mengin, who were acquainted with their works, reproduce the date without any additional checking. However, Driault, a French orientalist, writes in his preface to the publication of Raymond's dispatch that Corancez gave the date of the fall of Karbala as 1802 in his earlier works.[105] According to Rousseau, who was resident in Iraq:

> We have recently seen a horrible example of the Wahhabis' cruel fanaticism in the terrible fate of [the mosque of] Imam Husain. Incredible wealth was known to have accumulated in that town. The Persian shahs have, perhaps, never had something like that in their treasury. For centuries [the mosque of] Imam Husain was known to have received donations of silver, gold, jewels, a great amount of rarities ... Tamerlane spared that place. Everybody knew that the most part of the rich spoils that Nadir Shah had brought from his Indian campaign had been transferred to [the mosques of] Imam Husain and Imam Ali together with his own wealth. Now, the enormous wealth that has accumulated in the former has been exciting the Wahhabis' avidity for a long time. They have been dreaming permanently of looting that town and were so sure of success that their creditors fixed the debt payment to the happy day when their hopes would come true.
>
> That day came at last ... 12,000 Wahhabis suddenly attacked [the mosque of] Imam Husain; after seizing more spoils than they had ever seized after the greatest victories, they put everything to fire and the sword ... Old people, women and children – everybody died at the barbarians' sword. Besides, it is said that whenever they saw a pregnant woman, they disembowelled her and left the foetus on the mother's bleeding corpse. Their cruelty could not be satisfied, they did not cease their murders and blood flowed like water. As a result of the bloody catastrophe, more than 4,000 people perished. The Wahhabis carried off their plunder on the back of more than 4,000 camels.[106]
>
> After plunder and murders, they destroyed the imam's mausoleum and converted it into a cloaca of abomination and blood. They inflicted the greatest damage on the minarets and domes, believing that those structures were made of gold bricks.[107]

Mengin describes the sack of Karbala in almost the same terms. He reports that the Wahhabis committed carnage in the town, not sparing women, children, the infirm or the elderly. The dome of the mosque at Imam Husain's grave was destroyed. Countless wealth was stored there, due to the donations of rich Persians over the years. Hoping to save his life, a mosque attendant allegedly volunteered to show the Wahhabis the hidden treasure, but he was killed in the general turmoil and the accumulated riches were never found. The Wahhabis seized rich spoils, including jewel-encrusted sabres and a pearl as big as a dove's egg. Saud took both the sabres and the pearl. The spoils also included vases and lamps of precious metals, gold ornaments fixed into walls, Persian carpets and gilded copper from the roof. Besides, the Wahhabis seized a stock of cashmere and Indian fabrics, 2,000 plain sabres, 2,500 hand guns, black slaves and a huge sum in cash. The plunder continued for 8 hours before the Wahhabis finally left Karbala shortly after midday.[108]

Ibn Bishr, the Wahhabi chronicler, also describes the event:

In that year Saud made for Karbala with his victorious army, famous pedigree horses, all the settled people and bedouin of Najd, the people of Janub, Hijaz, Tihama and others . . . The Muslims surrounded [Karbala] and took it by storm. They killed most of the people in the markets and houses. They destroyed the dome above [Imam] Husain's grave. They took away everything they saw in the mausoleum and near it, including the coverlet decorated with emeralds, sapphires and pearls which covered the grave. They took away everything they found in the town – possessions, arms, clothes, fabric, gold, silver and precious books. One cannot count their spoils. They stayed there for just one morning and left after midday, taking away all the possessions. Nearly 2,000 people were killed in Karbala.[109]

The Wahhabis met almost no resistance. One reason was that part of the population had left for a pilgrimage to al-Najaf. It is also possible that the governor of Karbala, a fanatic Sunni, had not taken adequate measures to defend the Shia town.[110]

The fall of Karbala was a serious defeat for the feeble, aging Buyuk Sulaiman Pasha. The Ottoman sultan had long been waiting for a pretext to dismiss the independent pasha, who had numerous active young rivals even within Iraq. The Wahhabis' victory seemed to provide the ideal opportunity for them to launch a campaign against Buyuk Sulaiman. His situation was further weakened by the regular complaints made by the shah of Persia, Fath Ali, about Buyuk's inability to protect the Shia holy places and the threat of Persian troops being sent to Karbala.[111] In fact, Persia found itself at war with the Baghdad *pashalik* just some years after the sack of Karbala. Remembering the unsuccessful expeditions to al-Hasa, however, Baghdad deemed it impossible to defeat the Wahhabis in the depths of Arabia. The pasha therefore concentrated on fortifying Iraqi towns and restoring Karbala and the Husain mosque.

The temporary capture of Mecca by the Wahhabis and the Porte's reaction

After the fall of Karbala, Hijaz became the main theatre of war. By then, Saud had performed two pilgrimages with his family and troops, demonstrating his military might and gaining first-hand knowledge of the situation in Hijaz. The tribes of Asir, ready to support an attack on Mecca, joined the Wahhabis.[112]

The situation of Ghalib ibn Musaid, the sharif of Mecca, was by now precarious. His extortions and despotic rule had led to discontent in Mecca and other towns, and the ever-increasing duties levied in Jidda deprived him of the merchants' support. With the odds already in the Najdis' favour, the sharifs asked Istanbul for supplies of arms. But the Porte was facing more serious problems than the Wahhabi threat to Mecca. When the sultan's *firman* arrived in Mecca in late 1798, it ordered that the Hijazi towns were to be fortified in order to resist a possible French invasion. The city walls of Jidda were repaired and the population was given military training.[113]

In 1798 Admiral Blanquet's British squadron bombarded Suez, which was at that

The Rise of the First Saudi State (1745–1811)

time occupied by the French. On the way home, the fleet anchored in Jidda, where the British demanded that Hijaz should end its trade with Egypt. Although the sharif agreed to the demand, the trade continued. Ghalib even established contact with France, but did not prevent a detachment of Arabian volunteers from fighting against the French in Upper Egypt.[114] In spite of Ghalib's efforts to increase his guard and mercenary detachments, his military might diminished due to the secession of several nomadic Hijazi tribes.[115] But the loss was particularly severe when his relative and close aide Uthman al-Mudhaifi deserted to the Wahhabis and started immediately to rally the bedouin who had earlier supported the sharif.[116] Ghalib took the initiative and delivered the first blow, which was unsuccessful. The Qahtan, Ataiba and other Wahhabi tribes and reinforcements from the nearby regions of Ranya, Bisha and Turaba joined al-Mudhaifi, who started an energetic offensive against the sharif of Mecca. In 1802 the town and oasis of al-Taif were captured almost without a battle and looted mercilessly. The Wahhabis killed some 200 people and destroyed many houses. The bedouin appeared in the town every day, looted all valuable articles and destroyed thousands of books.[117] Seriously alarmed, Ghalib appealed to the Porte for aid. Rossetti, the Russian consul-general in Egypt, reported in 1803 that 'the sharif of Mecca's tyranny and extortions encouraged the victorious Wahhabis [to approach Mecca. They] captured al-Taif... The sharif is asking the pasha of Cairo and the Porte for aid.'[118]

The memory of the fall of Karbala was still fresh in the minds of the inhabitants of Istanbul. Fearful of the fate that might await Mecca, the Porte decided to take measures to counteract the Wahhabis. In the same year, Italinski, the Russian ambassador to Istanbul, reported:

> Receiving the sharif of Mecca's reports that a strong corps of the Wahhabi Arabs was approaching Mecca, the Porte has ordered its military department to build up to twenty warships immediately and send them to Egypt. Great care is taken as to the quality of the armaments produced, but there is such a shortage of sailors, in spite of the high salaries, that they are recruited compulsorily.[119]

In late March 1803 Italinski reported back to St Petersburg:

> In its present situation, the Porte fears only France's intentions and the rebel movement of some Arab tribes, called Wahhabis, who account for nearly 60,000 effectives. They plan to seize the wealth of the Mecca and Medina shrines and undertake to found a monotheist religion, defying Muhammadanism. To convert the [inhabitants] to the worship of the Quran, an *ulama* [*alim*] has been sent there who is an expert in the sacred books. Other measures have been taken too: an army has been formed to attack them from the line that runs from Basra to al-Arish, while the sharif of Medina will attack them from Hijaz.[120]

The fall of Mecca could not be prevented, however. Saud moved towards Hijaz with the main Wahhabi force in late March 1803. At the time, there were armed pilgrims from Syria, Egypt, the Maghreb, Muscat and other lands in Mecca. Notwithstanding Ghalib's requests, they declined to participate in the anti-Wahhabi hostilities. Left alone, the sharif fled to Jidda with a few loyal followers and hastily started to fortify the town. Saud sent the Meccans a message explaining the Wahhabi belief-system and promising to be merciful to the obedient. His agents spread a rumour that he had come there in person to prevent the bedouin's depredations and the sack of the holy city.

In April 1803 the Wahhabis entered Mecca in an orderly manner.[121] After performing the *hajj*, they destroyed all mausoleums and mosques with domes (which had been erected in honour of the early revered figures of Islam) and razed all buildings whose architectural features did not meet their precepts. They obliged the Meccans to pray regularly, to refrain from wearing silk and not to smoke in public. Piles of pipes were burnt in public squares and the sale of tobacco was forbidden. The prayer for the sultan in the mosques was abolished. The Wahhabis appointed Abd al-Muhsin, Ghalib's brother, governor of Mecca. Instead of the Turkish *qadhi* of Mecca, an *alim* from al-Diriya was appointed; he produced a favourable impression by his fair administering of justice, unlike his Turkish predecessor.[122]

European orientalists mention a letter that Saud allegedly sent to Selim III, the Ottoman sultan. The content is interesting:

> Sa'ud to Selim. – I entered Makkah on the fourth day of Muharram in the 1218th year of the Hegira [26 April 1803]. I kept peace towards the inhabitants, I destroyed all things that were idolatrously worshipped. I abolished all taxes except those required by the law. I confirmed the Qazi [*qadhi*] whom you had appointed agreeably to the commands of the Prophet of God. I desire that you will give orders to the rulers of Damascus and Cairo not to come up to the sacred city with the Mahmal and with trumpets and drums. Religion is not profited by these things. May the peace and blessing of God be with you.[123]

It is uncertain whether a letter of this kind was actually sent: the Arabian sources do not mention it. But the news of the capture of Mecca sowed panic in Istanbul. The loss of Mecca was a heavy blow to the sultan's prestige and to his authority as caliph, the custodian of the holy cities. He named himself officially as follows:

> We, the servant and custodian of Mecca and Medina, of the noblest cities, of the holy places whereto all nations turn with prayers, as well as of the holy city of Jerusalem, We, the supreme caliph and the happy monarch of innumerable kingdoms, provinces and towns, which evoke the envy of world sovereigns and are situated in Asia and Europe, on the White and Black Seas, in Hijaz and Iraq [and so on].[124]

Italinski reported back to St Petersburg in 1803:

[Ibn] Abd al-Wahhab has captured Mecca without facing any resistance from the citizens and has appointed the former sharif's nephew as the new sharif of the city; the ex-sharif fled to Jidda when the Wahhabis were approaching Mecca.[125]

The ambassador notes that the Porte would have disregarded the event 'had [Ibn Abd al-]Wahhab limited his activities in Mecca to the exile of the sharif and the appointment of a new one'. But, 'acting as the reformer of the Muhammadan faith', he started enacting his own rules in Mecca, which was 'extremely insulting to the Porte'.[126] The matter was not confined to an 'insult'. According to *The Memorandum on the Constantinople Reports and Revelations*, 'The discord that tears the Turkish empire from inside, the plunder of Mecca by the Wahhabis and the ever-growing taxes have caused universal discontent with the government among the populace of the capital.'[127]

It was high time to act, but the Porte was unable to send its own forces against the Wahhabis and asked Acca and Baghdad for aid. According to Italinski:

> The intention of a part of the government to use Jazzar Pasha [of Acca]'s help against the Wahhabis is substantially reinforced by an unforeseen circumstance. The Porte has received Jazzar Pasha's dispatch about [Ibn] Abd al-Wahhab's conquests, about the lack of obstacles to their further expansion, about the said conqueror's apparent intention of capturing Syria . . . Lastly, he expresses his readiness to combat the dangerous enemy of the faith and the throne and promises to defeat and disperse his troops within six months, returning the seized territories to the Porte. But his promise is given on condition that the Porte declares him commander-in-chief and grants him independence in all actions . . . [T]he decision to accept the pasha's offer is inevitable. In spite of his hatred for the vizier, he will not dare to oppose that decision, neither is he able to do so. Should [Ibn] Abd al-Wahhab capture Damascus, his importance and might will eventually reach a degree that may prompt him to declare the sultan a usurper of the caliph's throne and restore the caliphate of the Umayyads, whose descendants were ever considered the holders of the exclusive right as heirs to the spiritual guidance of the Muhammadan community; even in this capital, there are many of its supporters.[128]

These circumstances and the impossibility of performing the *hajj* 'evoke discontent in the city, which troubles the Porte with its potentially dangerous consequences'.[129]

The pasha of Baghdad reported to the Porte that he was:

> starting a campaign to seek them [the Wahhabis] in their own land with the purpose of destroying them, for which purpose he has a 5,000-strong cavalry, a 10,000-strong infantry and a 60,000-strong camel corps. He hopes to complete the expedition within six months.[130]

He asked the Porte to send artillery, gunpowder and tents. After receiving reports from the Syrian and Iraqi rulers, 'the Porte nourishe[d] the hopes of a full and imminent liberation from fear'. However, the Russian ambassador doubted Baghdad's ability to strike a blow and noted correctly that 'Jazzar thought about the capture of Damascus more than about a campaign against the Wahhabis.'[131]

Nevertheless, the Porte managed to send a small detachment of Turks to Hijaz under Sharif Pasha. This time the emir of al-Diriya, whose troops had been decimated by disease, could not consolidate his position in Hijaz.[132] According to Rossetti:

> The diseases that spread in [Ibn] Abd al-Wahhab's army made him raise the siege of Jidda. Sharif Pasha joined the sharif [of Mecca]; they made their way to Mecca and occupied it. The sharif of Mecca demonstrated great respect for Sharif Pasha, making him commander of the united troops.[133]

The Meccan citadel, where a Wahhabi detachment had ensconced themselves, resisted for some time before falling in July 1803. Italinski wrote on 15 September:

> On 25 August the Porte received Sharif Pasha's report from Jidda, which reached its destination in fifty days. It confirmed the earlier news both of the victory over the Wahhabis near Jidda and Medina and of their retreat to their capital al-Diriya.[134]

Sharif Pasha boasted of being able to take on the Wahhabis on his own.[135]

The death of Abd al-Aziz ibn Muhammad ibn Saud, the emir of al-Diriya, was a new blow to the Wahhabis. In the autumn of 1803 he was murdered by an unknown dervish in the Turaif mosque in his capital. The dervish identified himself as Uthman, a Kurd from a village near Mosul who had lived at the court as a guest. When Abd al-Aziz prostrated himself in the first row during prayers, the murderer threw himself upon the imam from the third row, stabbed him with a dagger and then wounded his brother Abdallah. Turmoil broke out in the mosque. The wounded Abdallah managed to stab the assassin with a sword and others finished him off immediately.[136]

According to some reports, the imam was killed by a Shia whose entire family had perished during the raid on Karbala.[137] According to Mengin, a letter in Persian had been found in the assassin's turban. It read, 'Your God and your faith charge you with the duty of killing Abd al-Aziz. If you manage to escape, you will be rewarded generously; if you die, paradise will open before you.'[138] The report's resemblance to the tactics of the medieval Ismailis, and to the legends connected with their activities, is striking. Ibn Bishr doubts that the imam's murder was in revenge for Karbala since the murderer was a Kurd and the Kurds are Sunnis.[139] The author of *The Brilliance of the Meteor* claims that the assassin was sent by the pasha of Baghdad, who thereafter rewarded his family generously.[140] The question of who killed Abd al-Aziz, and for what reasons, has never received a definitive answer. The Wahhabis had many embittered enemies.

Soon after the murder of his father, Saud hurried to al-Diriya whose people immediately swore allegiance to him. All the provinces also recognized the new ruler. Saud sent messages to the provincial rulers, promising to rule justly and to suppress rebellions and conspiracies with an iron hand. The news of the murder of Abd al-Aziz evoked 'great satisfaction' in Istanbul. The general mood was further improved by Ghalib's dispatch, in which he boasted of his successes in the war against the Wahhabis and 'undertook to penetrate up to their capital al-Diriya and capture it'.[141] However, it was to be the Turks' last success in the struggle against the Saudi emirate.

Hijaz under Wahhabi control

As early as the following year, the Wahhabis again started pressing their enemies in Hijaz. Their battles with the Turks and the sharif's troops continued all year long. Italinski reported back from Istanbul in 1804:

> Some days ago, His Majesty the Sultan strictly ordered the ministry to take all possible measures to ensure the security of Mecca and Medina. Mecca is besieged by an Arabian tribe named Bedda, who usually roam in the localities from where they can reach the said cities within a week; they belong to the Wahhabi sect.[142]

In 1805 Ghalib's detachments of nearly 10,000 men attacked a confederation of pro-Wahhabi tribes, led by Emir Abd al-Wahhab Abu Nuqta. The sharif was defeated, losing several hundred men, mainly Turks. The Wahhabis seized 2,500 firearms together with other weapons.[143] Perhaps the sharif's bedouin allies deserted him; the Turkish detachment in his troops was decimated. The Wahhabis then surrounded Mecca, hindering the pilgrimage.[144] By that time, enmity had flared up again between Ghalib and the Turks, and the latter refused to help him.

In the winter of 1805/06 Saud decided to deliver the final blow to Ghalib. Led by Abd al-Wahhab Abu Nuqta, Uthman al-Mudhaifi and Salim ibn Shakban (the emir of Bisha), the bedouin blockaded Mecca. They were ordered not to let the caravan of Syrian pilgrims pass. In that period (1804/05–1809) Arabia suffered a terrible drought. Thanks to the secure caravan routes, Najd received regular food supplies, which eased the lot of its inhabitants. But conditions in the besieged city of Mecca became intolerable and people were reduced to eating dogs and skin. The attempt to defeat the supporters of the agreement was unsuccessful, and Ghalib sued for peace. The Wahhabi troops entered Mecca in October/November 1805 and performed the *hajj*.[145]

For a time, Ghalib still hoped to preserve his independence. Some of the Turkish and Maghrebi soldiers, who had managed to reach Mecca with the pilgrim caravans, stayed on in the city. The fortification of Jidda continued. But Ghalib soon realized that all resistance to the Wahhabis was futile and he surrendered in 1806. In the same year, a group of Wahhabi *ulama*, led by Hamid ibn Nasir, arrived in Mecca to propagate the ideas of the 'purified' Islam.[146]

Another reason for Ghalib's decision to abandon all resistance was the successful establishment of Wahhabi power to the north of Mecca. As early as 1803, some shaikhs of the Harb tribe had embraced the new teaching and Wahhabi preachers were sent to them, but the attempt to capture Medina the same year was unsuccessful. With the bedouin's help, however, the Wahhabis took control of the caravan routes to Medina. Power in Medina was concentrated in the hands of the local *agha*, Hasan al-Kalay. Relying on a detachment of bedouin and Maghrebis, he established arbitrary rule, robbed the people mercilessly, extorted money from pilgrims and even laid hands on a part of the wealth that was preserved in the mosque at Muhammad's grave. When the *agha* saw that the Wahhabi forces were superior in might and Medina was threatened with famine, he surrendered the city in the summer of 1805,[147] stipulating that he should be retained as governor.[148] Simultaneously, the Wahhabis occupied Yanbu, which was ruled by the sharif of Mecca.

Some time after the occupation of Medina, Saud appropriated the jewels that remained in the mosque of Muhammad. He sold part of them worth nearly 10,000 thalers (rials) to Ghalib and kept almost the same amount for himself. Burckhardt estimates the amount plundered from the mosque by Ghalib at 40–50,000 thalers.[149] The Wahhabis took strong measures to enact all principles of their doctrine in Medina. Turkish officials were exiled from the city. When a respectable woman was caught smoking, she was forced to sit facing backwards on an ass, a pipe was hung around her neck and she was paraded through the streets in disgrace.[150]

Hijaz was annexed to the Saudi state though it was far less dependent on the Wahhabis than some of the provinces of Najd or al-Hasa. The sharif of Mecca retained a great deal of independence and he and his subjects were exempted from taxation. His returns from the customs duties in Jidda decreased substantially, however, since he could no longer impose duties on Wahhabi merchants. Income from his other sources also fell.

According to Burckhardt, the sharif retained considerable power in spite of the conquest of Hijaz. Owing to his honourable position, his personal influence over the many tribes who still resisted Saud, and the precious gifts that Saud received from him in Mecca, Ghalib found that many of his actions went unchallenged by the Wahhabis.[151] Saud's power in Mecca was balanced by Ghalib's influence and Jidda remained chiefly under the sharif's control. Al-Mudhaifi was appointed governor of al-Taif as a counterweight to Ghalib and ruled over several nomadic tribes in the vicinity. Nevertheless Saud's influence in Hijaz grew steadily while Ghalib's authority declined.

The end of Ottoman control of the hajj

From 1807 Saud performed the pilgrimage to Mecca with his troops every year. He usually ordered the Wahhabis to gather near Medina and then made his way southwards. Detachments from Asir and al-Taif, bedouin from the borderlands between Hijaz, Najd and Asir and armed men from various parts of Najd and Jabal Shammar, led by their emirs, joined him on the way. Every time that Saud came to Mecca, he distributed alms, exchanged gifts with Ghalib and brought a precious coverlet, known as the *kiswa*, for the Kaaba.[152] Ibn Bishr witnessed one of Saud's pilgrimages and left a detailed description of it.[153]

The Rise of the First Saudi State (1745-1811)

As mentioned previously, the Ottoman judges and other officials who had lived in Mecca and Medina were exiled from Hijaz. Saud continuously fortified the forts of Medina, kept a strong garrison in the city and replaced it every year. Since 1803 the Wahhabis had put all kinds of obstacles in the way of pilgrims from the Ottoman empire, particularly those from Syria and Egypt. The *hajj* caravans that came to Hijaz every year brought the *mahmal*, a richly decorated palanquin carried by a camel that was considered holy. The *mahmal* contained the *kiswa*, copies of the Quran and jewels. The pilgrims were accompanied by musicians, playing tambourines, drums and other instruments. Many pilgrims brought alcohol with them and it was not unusual to find groups of prostitutes in the caravans. All this could not fail to provoke the Wahhabis' hostility because of its incompatibility with their religious and moral standards.

The Wahhabis stipulated that the caravans come to Hijaz without the *mahmal* or musical instruments. Simultaneously they increased the *hajj* duty. In 1803 each Syrian pilgrim paid 8 piastres for the right to visit Mecca. Soon thereafter the duty rose to 10 piastres per pilgrim, 10 per riding animal and 7 per quintal of a load, and 100 purses for the passage of a whole caravan.[154] In 1805 the Syrian caravan paid 200 purses, but only individual pilgrims were allowed.[155] According to Corancez, in 1806 the Turks tried to buy the pilgrimage right for the huge sum of 2,000 purses (1m piastres), but the Syrian caravan was not allowed through to Mecca;[156] new restrictions were imposed every year.

To obtain a *hajj* permit, Yusuf, the pasha of Damascus, affected to observe almost all the prescriptions of Wahhabism. He prohibited wine and strong beverages, urged the closure of all the Damascus markets during prayers, imposed humiliating restrictions (for example, special clothes) on the Jews and Christians and even banned the shaving of beards. According to Bazili, 'the Wahhabis demanded – not without reason – that there should be neither boys nor other beardless persons in the caravans'.[157] In 1807/08 a Syrian caravan without a *mahmal*, arms or music tried to reach Mecca: it was unsuccessful.[158] The mass influx of pilgrims from the territories of the Porte virtually came to an end.

A belief spread in the Ottoman empire that the Wahhabis, being godless and non-Muslim, opposed the *hajj* in general. Yet not everybody believed this. The Egyptian historian al-Jabarti reports that the pilgrimages from Egypt and Syria ceased allegedly:

> because of the obstacles created by [Ibn] Abd al-Wahhab, but it is not true, because he prohibits coming for the *hajj* not on the grounds that are not provided for by the *sharia*, but prevents the penetration of those who come in a manner that runs counter to the law, with the innovations that are not permitted in the *sharia*, such as the *mahmal*, cymbals, drums, flutes and arms.[159]

In the same years the Maghrebis were never prevented from performing the *hajj*.[160]

The struggle with Britain over Oman

The Wahhabis' offensive was not confined to the hostilities in Hijaz and the north-east of the peninsula in the early nineteenth century. They gradually managed to establish their control over the whole Arabian Gulf coast, including Bahrain, and penetrated ever deeper into Oman.

The population of Oman proper was divided into two groups of tribes: the al-Hinawi (Ibadhis) and the al-Ghafiri (Sunnis). The struggle between the two groups had determined the history of Oman for centuries and helped the Wahhabis to penetrate the country. Without going into unnecessary detail, we begin in 1792, when Sultan, one of Ahmad ibn Said's sons, became the ruler of Muscat. His father, the shaikh of the al-Hinawi and imam of the Ibadhis, had driven the Persians from Oman in 1744. But Sultan was not recognized as the imam, or spiritual leader, which weakened his power. The tribes that inhabited the Omani coast of the Gulf, with its numerous channels, lagoons and sheltered harbours, engaged in sea trade, piracy, fishing and pearl-diving. They were Sunnis and kept somewhat aloof from both the al-Hinawi and the al-Ghafiri.[161]

In 1801 Sultan ibn Ahmad organized an expedition against Bahrain. Its people asked al-Diriya for help. The Wahhabis drove away the Muscatis, but made Bahrain dependent on the Saudi state, though they were hardly able to impose the principles of their teaching on the Bahrainis since they were mostly Shia.[162] A little earlier, Imam Abd al-Aziz had sent a copy of the works of Ibn Abd al-Wahhab to Oman, demanding that its people adopt the Wahhabi doctrine and submit to al-Diriya's authority. The Omanis, who were mostly Ibadhis, understood the content of the book in a very peculiar way. According to the Omani chronicler Ibn Razik:

> It is a small book, consisting mostly of sophisms and conjecture. It legalizes the murder of all Muslims who dissent from them [the Wahhabis], the appropriation of their property, the enslavement of their offspring, the marriage of their wives without first being divorced from their husbands, and without observing the *'iddah* [waiting period to see if a divorced woman is pregnant].[163]

The al-Hinawi rejected the demand,[164] but the al-Ghafiri allied themselves with the imam of al-Diriya. According to *The Brilliance of the Meteor*, as early as the 1790s the Wahhabis started raiding Oman together with Mutlaq al-Mutairi and Ibrahim ibn Ufaisan, making the al-Buraimi group of oases their strong point.[165] Al-Buraimi was the centre of the caravan paths that led to the Arabian Gulf coast, the Gulf of Oman and the Jabal Akhdar mountains.

In 1800/01 the Wahhabi army, led by Salim al-Kharq, one of Imam Abd al-Aziz's Mamelukes, successfully attacked Oman. Saqr, the ruler of the strategically important port and town of Ras al-Khaima, the centre of the Qawasim tribe, swore allegiance to the Wahhabis.[166] Other small shaikhdoms and emirates along the Gulf coast were also subdued. The ruler of Muscat, Sultan ibn Ahmad, found himself dependent on al-

The Rise of the First Saudi State (1745-1811)

Diriya. When he went to Mecca for the *hajj* in 1803, his relative Badr tried to seize power in his absence but failed and fled to the Saudi capital.[167] Trying to organize resistance to the Wahhabis, Sultan decided to strengthen his ties with the pasha of Baghdad whose emissaries had long been encouraging him to attack their common enemy. At the end of 1804 Sultan left with his fleet for Basra, whose people paid tribute to the rulers of Muscat, ostensibly as a token of gratitude for their help in the war with the Persians in the mid-eighteenth century. On the way back, Sultan was killed in a battle with the fleet from Ras al-Khaima.[168]

Sultan's relative Badr, who had been living in exile in al-Diriya, now returned to Muscat, hoping to establish himself with the help of his Saudi protectors. He retained power for some years and tried to inculcate the Wahhabi doctrine, but without any notable success.[169] Sultan ibn Ahmad's sons rebelled in 1807 and dethroned Badr. The new rulers of Muscat – Salim and then his brother Said – first observed obedience to the Saudis, but then refused to pay the tribute and began preparations for hostilities.[170] Saud sent a group of *ulama* to Oman to explain the Wahhabi teaching but again without success.[171] Said sought help from the shah of Persia, who responded by sending several thousand soldiers.[172] In 1808/09 Muscat started hostilities against Ras al-Khaima together with its allies from Sohar. After losing large numbers of their men, however, they finally pledged allegiance to the Saudis.[173]

United under the power of the Saudis, the inhabitants of the Omani coast, particularly the Qawasim tribe, ceased their mutual enmity and became a force to be reckoned with. Their fleet of several hundred vessels, both large and small, held sway in the Gulf. They imposed duties on and plundered the East India Company's merchant ships sailing between Bombay and Basra.[174] The inhabitants of the Omani coast seized and plundered the merchant ship *Minerva* with a cargo whose total value was 100,000 rupees.[175] (The Najdi chronicler makes no mention of this.)

Western historians have stressed the supposedly 'piratic character' of the inhabitants of the Arabian coast. But the truth is that they lived mainly by sea trade (though they were not averse to piracy if the opportunity presented itself) and saw the appearance of British vessels in their waters as extremely dangerous competition. Their acts of 'piracy' against the British should be considered, rather, as naval warfare against uninvited strangers.

The expansion of the al-Diriya emirate into Oman and along the Gulf coast clashed with Britain's colonial interests. In the late eighteenth century, Britain had finally established its dominance in India, defeating its European competitors after a struggle lasting almost two centuries. The British strove to keep the Gulf open to their trade and free from the influence of any power that might threaten India. In the second half of the eighteenth century and the early part of the nineteenth, France was Britain's most dangerous rival. The British in India saw Napoleon's invasion of Egypt in 1798 as a revival of the old menace. The French dreamed of using Egypt as a springboard in their offensive on India. Their subsequent defeat in Egypt did not put an end to their (somewhat problematic) plans to reach India via Syria, Iraq and the Gulf. Control over the remote approaches to the 'pearl of the British crown' became an issue of major strategic importance.

In the late eighteenth and early nineteenth centuries, British agents in the Gulf countries became political representatives one after another. In 1798 Britain concluded a treaty with the ruler of Muscat. Although directed against the French, it signalled Muscat's dependence on Britain. Two years later, a British representative arrived in the town.

Britain tried to maintain friendly relations with the Saudi state, which was steadily gaining strength. In the late eighteenth century, the Basra-based factory of the East India Company regularly sent gifts to Saud ibn Abd al-Aziz.[176] The British were interested in maintaining a lively trade between Bombay and Basra and a reliable postal service between India and Syria via Basra. They tried to persuade the Wahhabis not to harass the couriers who carried the post from Basra to Aleppo.[177] Britain did not hesitate to use military force when necessary, however. For example, the Wahhabi detachment that approached the British factory in the territory of present-day Kuwait had to retreat after being shelled from a British warship.[178] In an attempt to settle the conflict, Reinaud, a representative of the East India Company, was sent to al-Diriya.[179] He tried to obtain a promise from the Wahhabis that British interests in the Gulf would be safeguarded, but without success. The Wahhabis advanced on Kuwait in 1804. The following year, Britain tried to impose a protectorate on the Al Sabah, but Abdallah, the emir of Kuwait, preferred to remain independent.[180]

In the 1800s British warships engaged in direct hostilities with the Omani fleet and launched their first expedition against the Qawasim in 1805.[181] Muscat became their natural ally. When Said ibn Sultan's army and fleet, led by a British officer, attacked Ras al-Khaima in 1809, a British squadron was sent to the area. After defeating Oman's ill-armed fleet, the British landed troops. They razed the town to the ground, destroyed all the warehouses and shipyards and massacred the inhabitants, winning praise from the governor-general of India.[182] The defeat of the Saudis' allies and vassals was a blow for al-Diriya.

When the rulers of Bahrain and al-Zubair (who were from the Al Khalifa) began demonstrating their discontent with Wahhabi power, they were taken to al-Diriya as hostages. Their children fled to Muscat and asked the British for help. British warships routed the Wahhabi garrisons in al-Zubair and then in Manama. Al-Diriya's attempts to restore its rule in Bahrain were fruitless, though Bahrain paid tribute to the Saudis.[183]

After Britain's evacuation of Ras al-Khaima, the inhabitants rebuilt the town. In spite of its repeated rout in 1816, the Qawasim managed to gather a sizeable navy and appeared some 113 km from Bombay the following year.[184] But these are somewhat later events.

In the early nineteenth century, the British strove to establish naval dominance in the region. At the time, their policy did not envisage active interference in the developments in Arabia. They had insufficient forces and the prizes that awaited them in the Arabian deserts were too uncertain. France had been removed from the Arabian arena, though the Turkish historian Cevdet thought that Napoleon might try to contact the Saudis.[185] But France was engaged in the European theatre of war; in 1810 it lost Mauritius, its main naval base in the Indian Ocean.

The Rise of the First Saudi State (1745-1811)

The Wahhabis' influence in Oman reached a peak under their military commander Mutlaq al-Mutairi in the early 1810s. In spite of British support, Said ibn Sultan, the ruler of Muscat, had to pay the emir of al-Diriya 40,000 rials.[186] At around this time, it is likely that the Wahhabis moved south-west of Muscat and invaded Hadhramawt, where the first preachers from al-Diriya had appeared as early as 1803/04. Although their initial propaganda efforts had been unsuccessful, this time Hadhramawt paid tribute to al-Diriya.[187] In 1813 Mutlaq al-Mutairi was killed in a petty skirmish. At the same time, Egypt invaded Arabia and the Wahhabis withdrew their troops from Oman. They never established direct control over it. The remoteness of the country, the Ibadhis' hostility to Wahhabism, the death of Mutlaq, the Egyptian invasion of Hijaz and Britain's protection of the anti-Wahhabi forces – all these factors hampered the expansion of the al-Diriya emirate in south-eastern Arabia.

The advance to Asir and Yemen

Towards the beginning of the nineteenth century, Asir joined the Wahhabis. Thereafter the emirate of Abu Arish submitted to al-Diriya.[188] The Wahhabis' dominance in the areas south of Mecca was far from complete, however. The rulers of the region were the Saudis' unequal allies rather than their subjects. Asir's participation in the hostilities against Sharif Ghalib was in line with its interests.

When the Wahhabis advanced on Yemen, the situation was favourable to their expansion. The country was racked by internal differences and tribal anarchy, and the Zaidi imams had lost the coastal strip. But the Saudi troops' campaign against Najran in 1805/06 did not end in a decisive victory, though Wahhabi garrisons were left in the fortresses. Hodeida fell several times into the Wahhabis' hands. The mountain areas of Yemen remained virtually independent, though the Wahhabi troops besieged Sanaa in 1808.[189] The Wahhabis launched an active propaganda campaign in Yemen and sent *ulama* missions there almost every year, though without success. They could not even hold out in Hodeida.[190] The Shafii population of the coast – the Tihama region of Yemen – sympathized with the Wahhabi teaching because of their enmity towards the Zaidi imams of Sanaa. But they were not inclined to give up their virtual independence in favour of submission to the Saudis.

Hamud Abu Mismar, the sharif of Abu Arish, whose authority spread to a part of Tihama, joined the Wahhabis and probably even participated in the hostilities against the imam of Sanaa.[191] However, he was concerned at the rise of his neighbour and rival Abd al-Wahhab Abu Nuqta, the ruler of Asir, under the aegis of the Wahhabis. As Ibn Bishr reports, Saud invited the rivals to al-Diriya and tried to reconcile them, but failed. Feeling that Abu Mismar's rebellion was mature, he ordered him to attack Sanaa but the sharif declined.

Receiving proof of the unfaithfulness of his obstinate vassal, Saud ibn Abd al-Aziz began gathering detachments throughout Arabia to put an end to his activities. The Wahhabi army was said to be nearly 50,000 strong, though the figure may be exaggerated. Abu Mismar enjoyed the support of the nomads from Najran and Yemen. A fierce battle occurred at the end of 1809 and Abu Nuqta was killed. But Abu Mismar's troops were defeated. He fled and fortified his position in his capital, Abu Arish, which the Wahhabis failed to capture. Saud appointed his relative Tami ibn Shuaib in place of Abu Nuqta.[192]

Raids on Iraq and Syria

Turning again to the situation on the north-eastern frontiers of the Saudi state, developments there were, at first sight, favourable to the Wahhabis. As soon as Buyuk Sulaiman, the pasha of Baghdad, had drawn his last breath in August 1802, a bitter struggle started for his political legacy with the lively participation of the British and the French. Buyuk Sulaiman's relative Ali Kahya managed to make short work of his rivals and occupy the post of pasha for nearly five years. The *pashalik* was shaken by internal disturbances, popular insurrections and continuous revolts by the Kurds, however. In August 1807 Ali Kahya was knifed to death in a mosque. Soon afterwards, Kuchuk Sulaiman seized office and held power for some three years. He was preoccupied with the war against the Kurds and the Wahhabis until he was assassinated in October 1810. Clashes with the Persians continued in the second half of the 1810s.

After the fall of Karbala, the Wahhabis raided Iraq persistently for some years. At the end of 1803 and the beginning of 1804, Saud ibn Abd al-Aziz suddenly attacked the Muntafiq, took their shaikh prisoner and plundered the environs of Basra. Then his troops besieged al-Zubair. The Wahhabis invited the citizens to capitulate and adopt their teaching, but the local governor had their messenger's ears cut off and sent him back. All the holy places around the town were destroyed, including the Hasan and Talha mausoleums. But the people of al-Zubair defended their town courageously and repulsed the Wahhabis' attacks.[193]

In 1804/1805 Saud defeated the powerful Zafir tribe, which had tried to disobey him.[194] On orders from the Porte, Ali Pasha conducted a military operation against the Wahhabis, but did not dare penetrate into the depths of the desert.[195] In 1806 the Wahhabis tried to capture al-Najaf, but failed. Neither were they successful near Samawa or al-Zubair.[196]

In 1808 Saud appeared in the environs of Karbala, but the town was well protected and impregnable. He turned south, plundered the Muntafiq, raided the environs of Basra and al-Zubair and returned to al-Diriya without having made any substantial gains.[197] All further raids on Iraq, which continued up to 1810, were confined to plundering unprotected villages. In late 1809 the new pasha of Baghdad sent a regular army and Iraqi bedouin against the Wahhabis; the troops penetrated a short distance into the desert wastes, but were defeated by the Anaza and Zafir.[198] The Wahhabis achieved no success comparable to the sack of Karbala, however, despite Iraq's internal troubles. Their pressure on Iraq weakened towards the end of the first decade of the 1800s.

The Rise of the First Saudi State (1745–1811)

Neither did the raids on Syria yield any decisive victories, though the Syrian tribes started to pay tribute to the emir of al-Diriya in the early nineteenth century.[199] In 1808 Saud sent a letter to the shaikhs of Damascus, Aleppo and other cities demanding that they adopt the Wahhabi doctrine, submit to his authority and pay him tribute. There was widespread panic. The Wahhabi detachments ravaged villages in the environs of Aleppo and simultaneously penetrated into Palestine. Urgent measures were taken to defend the cities. However, the Wahhabis never dared to storm them.[200] In 1810 Saud made a daring raid on Syria with several thousand men, plundering dozens of villages and almost reaching Damascus.[201] It was his last large-scale campaign northwards.

The al-Diriya emirate had reached the limits of its expansion. The Saudis' authority now covered almost the entire Arabian peninsula. Even the sultan of Muscat, the imam of Yemen and the rulers of Hadhramawt paid them tribute. The tribes of the desert and semi-desert zone that bordered on the lands of the Fertile Crescent also submitted to the emir of al-Diriya. According to *The Brilliance of the Meteor*, the population of the territories ruled by the Saudis was as follows: Najd, 300,000; Hijaz and Tihama, 400,000; Yemen, 400,000 or more; eastern Yemen 200–300,000; eastern Arabia, 400,000; the tribes that migrated from Medina to Syria, such as the Anaza, some 400,000; and Oman and its coast (both the bedouin and the settled people), 200,000.[202] Thus the emirate of al-Diriya comprised nearly 2.4 million people. This figure seems plausible, although, in the case of Yemen, it is either an underestimate or the author consciously did not include the whole of Yemen in the Saudi state.

Chapter 4

The Social and Political System of the Emirate of al-Diriya

Wahhabism did not change the social structure of Arabia, although the tribal nobility became a more distinct social grouping within the population of the vast emirate of al-Diriya and their early state activities were somewhat regularized. The size of the ruling group's income from plunder, tribute, taxes, rent and the confiscation of property grew, but did not differ in essence from similar practices in the earlier feudal-tribal confederations.

Plunder and contributions

The aim of the Wahhabis' campaigns under the banner of the 'purified' religion was material: to increase the wealth of the rulers of al-Diriya, of the Arabian (and principally the Najdi) nobility who joined them and of the armed men who participated in the raids. There were several methods of seizing wealth and extracting an income from the conquered and annexed regions.

The easiest (but harshest) method was the *ghazu*, a raid involving plunder. It was used when the nomads and the inhabitants of an oasis refused to submit to the rulers of al-Diriya, and when the Wahhabis could not consolidate a position in a region beyond their control. Judging from accounts by the Arabian chroniclers and by European travellers, the *ghazu* was the principal method by which the nobility acquired wealth. When listing al-Diriya's proceeds from taxation, the Wahhabi historian Ibn Bishr comments, 'The *khums* [one fifth of the plunder] and spoils that were brought to al-Diriya were several times more.'[1] Burckhardt also mentions the *khums* as the main component of the ruler's income.[2]

The Wahhabis' first raids led to the seizure of dozens of camels and sheep, and to fields or date groves being pillaged. In the years when their power was at its zenith, one raid could yield several thousand animals. We have already noted that after the defeat of the sharif of Mecca's troops in 1796, the Wahhabis are said to have seized 30,000 camels and 200,000 sheep and goats,[3] though the figures may be exaggerated.

The methods of plunder did not vary greatly. According to Ibn Ghannam, in 1757/58 the Wahhabis ravaged fields in Manfuha.[4] As a result of a successful foray against the Zafir and Anaza tribal subdivisions, 'the Muslims [Wahhabis] seized all their [the nomads'] property, utensils, arms, sheep, goats and camels'.[5] After the fall of Buraida, the Wahhabis 'took away all available property.'[6] Ibn Bishr reports that in 1790/91, when the Mutair and Shammar tribes were routed, the Wahhabis seized 'rich spoils – camels, goats, sheep, utensils and goods'. Other bedouin soon met the same fate: the Wahhabis pursued them for two or three days, 'carrying off property and killing people'.[7] Such facts are widely reported in the Arabian chronicles.

The Wahhabis' plunder, just as the bedouin's *ghazu*, frequently led to starvation among the unfortunate victims. Together with the ordinary bedouin and oasis-dwellers, the nobility was looted too. But the latter often recovered its losses at the expense of the ordinary bedouin and peasants. The victorious Wahhabis usually spared the nobility, preferring to establish good relations with it. The defeated members of the nobility were deprived of their earlier independence, but became a part of the elite within the Saudi state.

The preponderance of spoils from raiding in the revenues of the Wahhabi state testifies to its military-expansionist character. The targets of the raids were those tribes, towns and oases that were not under Saudi rule or had tried to throw off al-Diriya's yoke. Wars, raids, plunder and unceasing expansion were the principal bases on which the Wahhabi state was established.

To maintain its sources of income, the emirate of al-Diriya had to expand continuously. Had this expansion paused, the returns that the settled and especially the bedouin nobility collected from its subjects would have diminished. Then there would have been no more incentives for the nobility to maintain a united state. This was the main internal contradiction of the first Saudi state, which carried the germs of its downfall from the outset.

The next source of wealth was the tribute – in money or in kind – imposed on those tribes and oases that had submitted to or joined the Wahhabis. Although this contribution was a single payment, its exaction might be extended for several years, making it a regular tribute or tax. By paying the Wahhabis a contribution or fine, the tribes and oases confirmed their allegiance to the 'purified' religion and to the ruler of al-Diriya. Basically, it was no different from the tribute paid by the oases or weaker tribes to the stronger bedouin in the pre-Wahhabi period. For example, a contribution of 2,000 rials was imposed on the people of the oases in Wadi al-Dawasir after their submission to the Wahhabis; half of the sum was to be paid immediately.[8] After Arayar ibn Dujain, the ruler of al-Hasa, was defeated by the Wahhabis, the emir of al-Diriya prepared to take reprisals against those of his allies who had deserted to al-Hasa. The

Mahmal and Sadiq oases pleaded with him for a pardon: it was granted, supplemented by a contribution 'in the form of fruit from their fields and palms'.[9]

In 1767/68 the people of Washm and Sudair joined the Wahhabis. They 'swore allegiance to the religion of Allah and His Messenger, and obedience and submission'. They committed themselves to paying the rulers of al-Diriya a contribution both in cash and in kind,[10] though it is not clear whether this was a single or a regular payment. When the people of al-Hawta, al-Hariq, Yamama, Silmiya and a part of al-Kharj submitted to the emir of al-Diriya in 1784/85, he imposed a tribute on them of 'as much money as he wanted'.[11] Impressed by the Wahhabis' military might, several nomadic tribes in the neighbourhood of Mecca joined them. A contribution was imposed on them in the form of money, arms, harness and their best horses.[12]

The seizure of landed property

Although the Wahhabi chroniclers' information on the capture of land from peasants and their conversion into tenant-farmers is scarce and fragmentary, some details nevertheless emerge. In 1754/55 the Wahhabis captured Huraimala and 'its [date] palms and dwellings were seized by the Muslims'.[13] It is clear that the dwellings were robbed. As for the palms, one may suppose that either they were seized from their owners or the spoils consisted of their fruit, in other words the current date harvest.

When 'Abd al-Aziz occupied Riyadh, he took possession of its houses and date palms, with some exceptions', reports Ibn Bishr.[14] This may mean that the citizens' houses became the property of the emir. One might ask what the use of owning these houses was when most of the inhabitants of Riyadh had fled. The emir probably just sold off the plundered household goods. Nor is it clear how the palms were disposed of. Who would look after them and what does the chronicler mean by 'some exceptions'? Some palms might have belonged to Wahhabi supporters among the Riyadh inhabitants; otherwise, Abd al-Aziz may have distributed them among his retinue.

We have more concrete information concerning the date-palm plantations in Harma. The Wahhabis subdued the oasis, whose people agreed to transfer the palms to the *bait al-mal* (state exchequer).[15] As for the other crops, grown between the rows of palms and in those fields without palms, they are not mentioned. (In practice, the agreed conditions were not implemented, since Abd al-Aziz did not think they were sufficiently harsh – the inhabitants of Harma were old and stubborn adversaries of al-Diriya. He ordered instead the walls around the oasis to be destroyed, some of the houses to be demolished and a group of the inhabitants to be exiled.)

When describing the revenues of the Saudi state, Burckhardt mentions that the exchequer was divided into two parts – the imam's privy purse and the state exchequer:

The most considerable portions of the Wahaby chief's revenues are derived from his own domains. He has established it as a rule, that whenever any of his districts or cities rise in rebellion, he plunders them for the first offence; for the second rebellion, he not only plunders but confiscates them, and all their land, to the public treasury. He then bestows some parts of them on strangers, but leaves most in the hands of the former proprietors, who now become merely his farmers, and are obliged to pay, according to circumstances, either one third or one half of the prudence. The property of those who took the most active part in the rebellion is farmed out to others, while they themselves either fly or are put to death . . . At present most of the landed property in Nedjd belongs to the Beit el Mal, or treasury; that of Kasym [Qasim], whose inhabitants have been constantly in rebellion, is entirely held in farm; and many villages of Hedjaz, and the mountains towards Yemen, are attached also to the treasury.[16]

The above excerpt reveals a fairly coherent system of extracting an income from the conquered population, though several points remain unclear, including the question of whether the rent was paid to the state exchequer or to the ruler himself. It is difficult to say whom Burckhardt means by 'strangers' – the peasants of the subdued regions who settled on the land that had been seized or the new landowners who rented out the land to its former owners.

Where reports by European travellers and the Arabian chronicles differ, there is reason to believe that the latter are more accurate. Ibn Bishr, for example, received information directly from the court's 'financial officials' whereas Burckhardt's European background meant that his judgement was inevitably somewhat biased. The Arabian chroniclers very seldom mention the confiscation of landed property to the *bait al-mal*. They refer to the existence of the *kharaj* (land-tax) on a few occasions, without specifying its nature. If it was the equivalent of rent for 'state-owned' lands, Burckhardt's reports are corroborated to some extent. Then one may speak about a drastic redistribution of landed property in the Saudi state and the coincidence of the rent with the land-tax on the *bait al-mal* lands.

When Mubarak ibn Adwan, the emir of Huraimala and the Wahhabis' ally, behaved obstinately, Ibn Abd al-Wahhab and the emir of al-Diriya told him, 'Take as much as you want from the Huraimala palms and live with us; we shall pay honour and respect to you and maintain you.' Ibn Adwan became the Wahhabis' honoured prisoner.[17] It was implied, presumably, that he would continue to receive the rent for his palm groves.

The burden of payments to the central exchequer was distributed unevenly in the al-Diriya emirate. The Najdi nobility was advantaged, but it may be supposed that the Saudi state's expansion and the influx of spoils weakened, if temporarily, the exploitation of central Arabia to the detriment of the areas on the outskirts of the emirate. In exchange, the privileged regions paid the 'blood tax', sending men for military campaigns.

Zakat

The most important innovation in the al-Diriya emirate was the regulated, centralized tax, imposed on the whole population in the form of *zakat*. This tax, which was for the benefit of the poor, was prescribed by the Quran and considered one of the pillars of Islam. The religious aim – the restoration of *zakat* – accorded perfectly with the needs of the Saudi state. When describing the collection of *zakat*, Ibn Bishr notes that, '"true Islam" spread in Najd. *Zakat*- and *kharaj*-collectors were sent from al-Diriya to tax fruit; they had earlier been called duty- and tithe-collectors.'[18]

The Najdi chronicler reports that seven-man teams were sent every year from al-Diriya to collect *zakat* from the bedouin. They comprised an emir, a clerk, a '*daftar*-keeper' (the equivalent of an accountant), an official who collected the proceeds from the sale of the camels, sheep and goats taken for the *zakat*, and three armed guards who gathered, drove and guarded the livestock. The rulers of al-Diriya sent more than seventy tax-collection teams to the bedouin every year. In addition, there were special agents to collect the *zakat* from peasants, towns and villages, as well as officials who taxed commodities.[19] Burckhardt reports, 'The collectors of revenues . . . are sent every year from Derayeh [al-Diriya] to the different districts or tribes, and receive a certain sum for their trouble and expenses on the journey.'[20] According to Ibn Bishr, the tax-collection teams lived at the taxpayers' expense,[21] which meant that the system was open to abuse.

The *zakat* rates were one tenth of the crops on unirrigated lands, one twentieth of those on irrigated lands and one fortieth of a merchant's capital.[22] The Anaza tribe paid 1 thaler for five camels, the price of one sheep for forty sheep and 7 shillings for one horse,[23] as Burckhardt reports, but the tax rates might differ between provinces. It is difficult to ascertain the total amount of the *zakat* returns in al-Diriya, though Ibn Bishr gives some estimates:

> Ahmad ibn Muhammad al-Mudliji told me, 'I was a clerk and worked with the tax-collectors who were sent to the Alawi [a subdivision] of the Mutair tribe during Abdul Aziz's rule.' Within a year, he collected 11,000 rials from them.[24]

The tax-collectors, led by Abd al-Rahman ibn Mishari ibn Saud, were sent to the Barikh (a subdivision of the Mutair tribe) and collected 12,000 rials from them; 7,000 rials were collected from the Khitaim. The Mutair's total *zakat* was 30,000 rials that year. Ibn Bishr continues:

> Besides, tax-collectors were sent to the Anaza of Syria, to the bedouin of Khaibar, to the Huwaitat bedouin and to the Anaza who lived in Najd. They returned with huge sums. A reliable person told me, 'Once . . . four teams [sent] to the Syrian bedouin stopped near Shaqra; each of them had 10,000 rials.'
> I said, 'The *zakat* collected from the Shammar and Zafir bedouin was nearly as high as that paid by the Anaza. Countless amounts were collected from the Qahtan,

the bedouin of the Harb, Ataiba, Juhaina tribes, of Yemen and Oman, from the Al Murra, Ajman, Subai, Suhul and other tribes.' Zakat was collected from them on legal grounds. Their most valuable properties were not taken away, with the exception of those who concealed a part of their camels or sheep [from taxation]. Such persons had to pay both the *zakat* and a fine. Abd al-Aziz advised the tax-collectors to be God-fearing, to collect *zakat* according to the legal prescriptions, to present the poor and sick with gifts and to spare them from anger and the seizure of their most valuable property.[25]

Under Saud ibn Abd al-Aziz, the amount of tax proceeds apparently grew still further. According to Ibn Bishr:

As for the *zakat* collection from the livestock-owning bedouin of the Arabian peninsula, who live beyond the two holy cities, in Oman, Yemen, Iraq and Syria, as well as the Najdi bedouin who live among them, a nobleman, who became Saud's clerk, told me, 'He sends more than seventy tax-collection teams to those bedouin every year, each team consisting of seven people . . .'

The same person told me that Saud sent agents to the Ghazz bedouin in Misr [possibly a place in the Sinai or the Negev desert near Gaza]. Besides, he sent agents to the Yam bedouin in Najran to collect the *zakat*. He told me, 'Those who collected the *zakat* from the Al Fidan [a tribe of the] Anaza bedouin, brought 40,000 rials, besides the agents' fees and 8 pedigree horses.' He said, 'It was the maximum return of a tax-collection team, the minimum being 2,500 or 3,000 rials.' Then he said, 'Saud collected 150,000 rials from al-Luhaya in Yemen, which was just a quarter of the tithe. The proceeds from Hodeida were close to it . . .'

I said, 'The returns [*amwal*] from al-Qatif, Bahrain, Oman, Yemen, Tihama, Hijaz and other lands, as well as the *zakat* imposed on fruit, commodities and their value in Najd, are uncountable.'[26]

Ibn Bishr does not mention the total revenues of the rulers of al-Diriya. The emirs themselves might have been ignorant of the amount. Burckhardt estimates the annual proceeds of the Wahhabi exchequer at 1m thalers (rials), while in the best year it reached 2m.[27] However, he does not indicate whether that sum included spoils and various fines or consisted of tax proceeds only.

According to *The Brilliance of the Meteor*, Saud's annual tax revenues at the zenith of his power were as follows: 400,000 rials from the nomads and settled people of Najd, 500,000 from the nomads of Syria, Yemen, Tihama and Oman, about 400,000 from al-Hasa, 200,000 from al-Qatif, 40,000 from Bahrain, 300,000 from Yemen (presumably, from its settled dwellers), 200,000 from the nomads of Hijaz and other regions, 120,000 from Ras al-Khaima (including the share in plunder), and 120,000 from the settled and nomadic dwellers of Oman, besides the expenses of the Wahhabi troops stationed there. The income from forays was 'uncountable'. Saud himself received a huge income in the form of gifts from notables and rich pilgrims; his landed property in Najd and al-Hasa yielded 300,000 rials.[28] To sum up, the emirate's annual tax revenues were close to 2m rials, which agrees with Burckhardt's report.

When the exchequer was short of money, the emir imposed a 'voluntary tax' on the settled people and the tribes.[29] This important detail shows that the rulers of the centralized Arabian state did not confine themselves to the framework of *zakat*, as prescribed by the *sharia*, but actually increased taxation. Although the Saudi rulers' income was enormous by Arabian standards, its real amount can only be understood in relative terms, since the considerable seasonal and regional fluctuations in prices need to be taken into account. It is sufficient to say that, according to Ibn Bishr, a bundle (*haml*) of firewood cost 5–6 rials and one palm tree up to 50 rials in al-Diriya.[30] The Saudi state also arranged for the centralized distribution of the collected wealth. The available data, however, permit only an approximate evaluation of both absolute and relative levels of expenses.

The Saudis' court

Maintaining the court and Ibn Abd al-Wahhab's family were among the emirate's main items of expenditure. The Saudis accumulated vast wealth in the form of land in oases, livestock, jewels and so on. According to Ibn Bishr, one third of the taxes collected in al-Hasa was spent on maintaining the Saudis' palace, Ibn Abd al-Wahhab's family and their entourage.[31]

The families of the Arabian nobility tended to be large. Their wealth enabled them to keep four wives, as permitted by the Quran, and also concubines. Among the well-off families, who enjoyed better nutrition and sanitary conditions than the rest of the population, there was a decrease in infant mortality. The Al Saud (the emir, with his brothers, children, uncles, cousins and nephews) were very numerous. Burckhardt reports that Saud had several wives and Abyssinian concubines.[32]

Although Saudi power was proclaimed under the banner of Wahhabism, which preached simplicity and moderation, the emirs of al-Diriya lived in great luxury by Arabian standards. Corancez notes, 'Saud became acquainted with luxury, which could not but influence him.' It was the way of all sects, which 'start with simplicity and restrictions to attract the masses and end in luxury for the leaders',[33] the French historian adds. According to *The Brilliance of the Meteor*:

> Saud had 6 Circassian concubines, bought by his agents in the Ottoman empire at a high price. He was said to have paid 3,000 rials or more for each of them, because they were beautiful. He had Abyssinian concubines as well. Some of them had been presented by Sharif Hamud Abu Mismar, the ruler of Abu Arish and Yemeni Tihama, while others were the gifts of the Qawasim as part of the spoils . . . Saud expanded his palace in al-Diriya and allotted each wife a room and maidservants . . . His wives wore precious Indian silks, decorated with gold, motley dresses and Syrian silks. They had precious gold adornments with jewels. He sent special agents

to Iran to buy jewels for his wives and concubines . . . Saud had become used to splendid food [and] special cooks made tasty dishes and delicate sherbets for him.[34]

Raymond gives the following description:

Saud likes to parade luxury in all its manifestations. Everything in his palace suggests the idea of greatness and splendour; nothing is rejected that may decorate the palace. Gold, pearls, expensive Indian materials – nothing is spared to make it even more beautiful. People say that Saud's cloak is an outstanding masterpiece that cost him at least 60,000 piastres. Seeing this conceit, one may suppose that the courtiers imitate him and strive to dress with the same magnificence, but he obliges them to retain simplicity.[35]

There are some exaggerations in Raymond's description. Nevertheless the rulers of al-Diriya did not stint themselves in their enjoyment of the pleasures of life. Besides livestock, lands, jewels, richly decorated arms and fortress-like palaces, they owned pedigree horses, the object of particular pride among the Arabian nobility. Saud was known to spend large sums on their maintenance. He owned some 2,500 pedigree horses,[36] of which 600 were reserved for the most courageous bedouin and Mamelukes.[37] Each of his sons owned between 100 and 150 horses, and Abdallah, the crown prince, had 300.[38] The rulers of al-Diriya seized horses during raids, received them as tribute, *zakat* and fines, and did not stop at extortion. Burckhardt writes, 'The Arabs complain that if a man has a fine mare, Saoud will find out some charge of misconduct to justify him in taking the mare as a fine.'[39]

The provision of traditional Arabian hospitality was expensive. Saud received several hundred guests every day.[40] They consumed 500 *saa* of rice and wheat a day (a *saa* is a dry measure, equivalent to 1–2.5 litres).[41] When Saud celebrated his son's marriage, the guests devoured 140 camels and 1,300 sheep during the 2-day-long feast.[42] Burckhardt estimates that the emir spent between £10,000 and £12,000 a year on maintaining his horses and his household.[43] Saud's numerous guests were usually from among the well-off. Few of the poor could leave their families, livestock and land and travel to al-Diriya, especially those who lived outside Najd. The guests were served different kinds of food according to their social standing: meat and rice for the notables and dates and *burghul* (boiled millet) for the poor.[44]

Saud owned large numbers of slaves. According to Ibn Bishr:

He had 500 male slaves – some people said they were 600 or even more than 1,000 – besides several hundred female slaves. At the end of Ramadhan, Saud appeared, surrounded by 1,300 servants, slaves and orphans, who lived in the palace.[45]

Compared to the rest of the population, which was frequently starving and poor, the emir's slaves enjoyed a privileged position. They formed the palace guard, the ruler's menial servants. Some of them, however, attained high office in the state. A slave called al-Harq, for example, led the Wahhabi troops into battle.[46] Many slaves were manumitted.

The Saudi court nevertheless retained a certain simplicity, or 'democratic atmosphere', especially in the early period. The separation of state power and the feudal ruler from the rest of the population was not yet obvious. Outwardly, the ruler of al-Diriya still resembled the shaikh of a bedouin tribe. Even simple bedouin addressed him unceremoniously: 'O, Saud', 'O, Abdallah's father', 'O, Moustached [One]' ('Abu Shawarib').[47] Corancez mentions the 'simplicity and crudeness of habits' at the court of al-Diriya.[48] Saud was available to all and any visitor could count on the emir's hospitality. The ruler investigated his subjects' complaints in person and he conducted trials in a patriarchal manner. Burckhardt writes that Saud sometimes beat liars with his own hands, but he regretted it for a long time afterwards and always asked his companions to keep his anger in check.[49]

The inhabitants of al-Diriya often gathered for theology classes: they were attended by all the members of the nobility, Ibn Abd al-Wahhab's sons, and Saud's sons and relatives. The ruler also came, surrounded by an entourage of black slaves with precious sabres encrusted with gold and silver: 'He was among them like the moon among clouds.' When he approached, people rose from the ground to clear the way for him, lest they be trampled by his slaves. He greeted everybody and then sat near Abdallah (Ibn Abd al-Wahhab's son), who started to deliver the lecture. Saud talked to the *ulama* and the notables. Then he went back to the palace to receive visitors and listen to their complaints until noon. After a rest, Saud talked to his retinue and studied theology again. Then he resumed his reception of visitors. A clerk sat near him and wrote down his orders. This continued for some two hours. Then the ruler dictated answers to letters, talked on religious subjects and prayed together with his relatives and the notables.

Saud was always accompanied by his guards. When he prayed at the palace mosque, two slaves guarded him. When he appeared at public prayers, six slaves with sabres surrounded him: two of them stood in front of him, two stood behind him and two stood behind the second row of believers.[50] These precautions were probably taken after the murder of his father Abd al-Aziz in the Turaif mosque in 1803. The permanent company of bodyguards near the ruler was a natural security measure, but it led to the emir becoming physically isolated from the people. Burckhardt's description of Saud's daily routine generally accords with the passage quoted above.[51]

Ibn Bishr notes the Saudis' simple lifestyle, approachability and closeness to the people. Nevertheless, one may conclude from the above-quoted excerpt that a special ceremonial developed at the court – the nobility became increasingly isolated from the people, and the people in turn were in awe of the splendour and magnificence of the court, with its special rituals and etiquette. Raymond, who knew of court life in al-Diriya only from eye-witnesses' accounts, reports that Saud:

> strove for gorgeousness and pomp . . . [While he is] outstanding for his luxury at

the court, he is even more notable when he leaves it; he impresses people with his numerous entourage who demand demonstrations of honour everywhere he passes.[52]

State expenditure outside the emir's court

Wealth was redistributed within the ruling elite of al-Diriya in the form of gifts from the ruler to the nobility, both in kind (pedigree horses, arms, livestock) and in cash. According to Burckhardt, the ruler of al-Diriya presented the nomadic shaikhs with between 50 and 300 thalers.[53] Ibn Bishr reports that the ruler 'gave generous presents to his subjects who visited him on business and [to] the emirs'.[54]

Data on the provincial budgets throw additional light on the character of expenditure in the Wahhabi state. Burckhardt deals with this question in detail, though his observations reveal an unconscious desire to find too much order in the Wahhabi state's nascent state apparatus:

> All these revenues, except the alms, or Zeka [*zakat*], from the Bedouins, are deposited in the public treasury, or Beit el Mál. Every city or village of any note has its own treasury, into which the inhabitants pay their quotas. Every treasury has a writer, or clerk, sent by the Wahaby chief with orders to prevent the sheikh of the place from partaking in illicit gain from the revenue. The sheikhs are not allowed to collect nor to account for the money paid.
>
> These funds are appropriated to public services, and are therefore divided into four parts. One fourth is sent to the great treasury at Derayeh [al-Diriya]; one fourth is dedicated to the relief of paupers ... for the pay of olemas [*ulama*] who are to instruct the Kadhys [*qadhis*] and the children; for keeping the mosques in repair, digging public wells ... One half is expended for the benefit of indigent soldiers, who are furnished with provisions when they set out on an expedition, or, in case of necessity, with camels; also for the entertainment of guests. The money thus allowed for guests is paid into the hands of the sheikhs, who keep a sort of public house, where all strangers may halt and be fed gratis; it is thought just that the whole community should contribute towards their expenses.[55]

The above quotation leaves many questions unanswered. It is unclear whether the local exchequer was replenished by part of the *zakat* or by additional taxation. Did the central exchequer participate in local expenditure? Burckhardt writes further that the central authority compensated the provinces for losses from natural disasters and enemy raids.[56] Was this an isolated instance of the central exchequer's participation in local expenditure or a permanent practice?

Ibn Bishr gives an example of a different distribution of the local budget in al-Hasa:

> His [the ruler's] proceeds from the *bait al-mal* of al-Hasa are divided into three

parts: one third goes on his frontier regions and fortresses and their population and garrisons; one third goes on his cavalry, his men, his aides and everything [that is needed] for the palace, his sons' houses, the shaikh's family's houses and others in al-Diriya; and one third is sold for money that rests with his confidants for gifts and monetary allotments . . . After all these allotments, al-Diriya receives 80,000 rials.[57]

Thus the local proceeds were distributed through several main channels. The greater part was spent for military purposes: salaries for the soldiers and garrisons, victuals, and maintaining the cavalry, i.e. the armed nobility. The next most important item of expenditure was the distribution of gifts to the local nobility, who occupied key posts in the nascent administration and disposed of a part of the expenditure. The expenses to the 'poor' covered the salaries of judges and the *ulama*.

Charity

Ibn Bishr notes that Abd al-Aziz, the emir of al-Diriya:

cared for the poor and sick. Some of them wrote to him on behalf of themselves, their mothers, wives, sons and daughters – one letter from each. And he [Abd al-Aziz] ordered a gift to be sent to each applicant. The sender of a letter might receive 20 rials or something of that order. When anybody died in a district of Najd, his children came to Abd al-Aziz or to his son and asked him to be a substitute for the [deceased] parent. He gave them generous gifts and, perhaps, granted them an allowance from the office [*diwan*]. He gave the inhabitants of the oases and villages huge amounts of alms every year in whatever season – about 1,000 rials, or more, or less. He inquired about the sick and orphans in al-Diriya and elsewhere and gave orders for them to be given gifts . . .

A clerk told me that Abd al-Aziz once suffered a headache. The ruler called him and said, 'Write a decree on alms to the people of [various] localities,' and dictated, '500 rials to the people of Manfuha, the same amount to Uyaina, 700 to Huraimala, 1,100 to Mahmal and similar amounts to all other districts of Najd.' The clerk said that the total amount of the grant was 90,000 rials.

Once 25 sacks of rials came to the palace. [Abd al-Aziz] was passing the sacks as they lay there. He pricked a sack with his sabre and said, 'The Lord has given me power over this, but He has not given this any power over me!' and started distributing the money.[58]

It is worth pointing out that the sum of 90,000 rials allotted to charity was insignificant in comparison with the accumulated wealth in the al-Diriya exchequer.

Ibn Ghannam describes a terrible famine in Najd in the mid-1780s when not only old people and children died, but adult men and women too: 'People were so emaciated that they fell down during prayers. Then Abd al-Aziz started giving food to the widows, the orphans and the weak.'[59]

The Social and Political System of the Emirate of al-Diriya

The Saudi state incorporated one of the tenets of Islam – charity – to serve its own ends. These charitable actions played an important political role: the welfare of the inhabitants of the central provinces was increased at the expense of the remote regions, thus encouraging the loyalty of the people (both the nobility and the ordinary people) in the central areas. A part of the sums allotted for charitable purposes was inevitably appropriated by the members of the local nobility, or served them indirectly by releasing them from the need to make large donations to the poor. The Wahhabi *ulama* and the rulers of al-Diriya could be seen as honest and sincere by the moral standards of Arabian society of the time, however, and as genuinely striving to ease the people's lot. Charity in the emirate of al-Diriya also helped to transform the earlier tribal solidarity in the face of many kinds of troubles. This is the aspect to which later pro-Wahhabi writers first paid attention.

The political structure of the state and the organization of power

Different provinces and nomadic tribes were united by force of arms under the emir of al-Diriya, whose power was sanctified by Wahhabism. Their dependence on al-Diriya was of a different character. Ibn Ghannam reports that the tribes and oases annexed by Ibn Abd al-Wahhab and Muhammad ibn Saud pledged themselves to wage a *jihad* against the 'polytheists' (i.e. non-Wahhabis) and to help the Wahhabis.[60] When the people of Harma and al-Majmaa joined the Wahhabis, they sent a delegation to Ibn Abd al-Wahhab and Abd al-Aziz, expressing their desire to 'embrace Islam' and fulfil all their obligations, including the payment of *zakat*, but asked for an exemption from *jihad* for two years.[61]

What did agreements of this kind mean? First, they were military alliances which obliged the party that joined the Wahhabis to wage hostilities against non-Wahhabis. It was not by chance that a deferment from the participation in *jihad* for two years was considered an exemption. An alliance with the Wahhabis committed the tribes and oases to pay a regular tax to the central exchequer and substantially limited their independence.

In 1865 Pelly, a British agent, visited Riyadh, the new capital of the second Saudi state, which had been restored to life after the defeat in the struggle with Egypt. He noted various forms of dependence on Riyadh among the tribes who had joined the Wahhabis, whether voluntarily or otherwise. One may cautiously assume that a similar situation obtained in the first Saudi state.

There were different 'categories' among the tribes. Some tribes paid the tax, participated in military campaigns and performed various duties. Others might graze their livestock in Najd and its outskirts, but the Wahhabis did not interfere when they were raided by a third party. The third group consisted of tribes who undertook not to attack those tribes ruled by the emir of Riyadh, in exchange for a similar obligation on their part. Lastly, the fourth group did not recognize the authority of the emir of Riyadh but paid him tribute.[62]

The central authorities took measures to abolish the traditional tribal methods of settling disputes and tried to resolve local disputes within the framework of the united state. Ibn Bishr writes that Faisal ibn Watban Al Dawish, the shaikh of the Mutair, and al-Humaid ibn Abdallah ibn Zahal, the shaikh of the Anaza, quarrelled in Saud's presence. The two powerful tribes had long been at loggerheads and a conflict between their shaikhs might have developed into a military clash. Saud hurried to reconcile the rivals, calmed their enmity and asked them to observe order and unity in the name of the common purpose – *jihad*.[63] Burckhardt reports that the ruler of the Wahhabi state settled intertribal conflicts in person and severely punished the instigators.[64]

The Saudis relied on their allies from among the local tribal nobility who joined them. In the early period, the emirs and shaikhs of tribes and oases sometimes retained their power, but as the Wahhabi state expanded and the central authorities grew stronger, al-Diriya increasingly replaced local rulers by people from rival kin and families who had previously had no prospects of power. Since they owed their position to the Wahhabis, the newly appointed shaikhs and emirs were more obedient to the Saudis than their predecessors had been.

There were many methods of appointment. Shortly before the Auda oasis in Sudair was captured, for example, a Wahhabi from among the local nobility asked Abd al-Aziz to make him the emir of the oasis if he was among the first to enter it: his request was granted.[65] Abdallah ibn Hasan, the conqueror of Buraida, was appointed emir of the whole region of Qasim.[66] When the emir of Durma executed three notables and seized their property, the local people rebelled and killed the ruler and his family. The Wahhabis, whom they called on for help, allowed them to elect a new ruler at their discretion.[67] The emirs of al-Diriya even appointed strangers to high positions.[68] According to Burckhardt:

> The Wahabys found it necessary to change the sheikhs of almost every tribe which they subjected to their domination, well convinced that in leaving the main influence in the hands of the ruling family, the tribe would never become sincerely attached to the new supremacy. They therefore usually transferred the sheikhship to an individual of some other considerable family . . . When Mohammed Aly Pasha subjugated Hedjaz, he replaced the ancient families and former sheikhs in their long-accustomed right, and thus created a formidable opposition to the Wahabys.[69]

To ensure the loyalty of the tribes and oases to the central authorities, the Saudis resorted to hostage-taking, a well-tried practice among conquerors in Arabia. Sometimes, after an oasis or a tribal subdivision swore allegiance to the Wahhabis, several notables were taken as hostages.[70] Some refractory shaikhs were forced to live permanently in al-Diriya; they were replaced by people loyal to the central authorities. To weaken the fighting capacity and organization of the bedouin, several *aqids* (tribal military commanders) were also held in al-Diriya.[71]

Thus the very character of local power changed: independent shaikhs and emirs were gradually replaced by the emir of al-Diriya's semi-dependent vassals or direct placemen. Burckhardt reports:

The Social and Political System of the Emirate of al-Diriya

> The great Bedouin Sheikhs ... receive from the Wahaby chief the honorary title of Emir el Omera ... The authority of those emirs over the Arabs is very limited, not much exceeding that which an independent Bedouin sheikh possesses, except that he can enforce obedience to the law by imprisoning the transgressor and fining him.[72]

This 'not much exceeding' is the important detail that distinguished a shaikh in the Saudi state from a tribal leader of the pre-Wahhabi period: there was an increasing consolidation of public power (jails, fines) and its separation from the nomadic population. That process was based on the centralized state's military power.

As the Saudis' vassals, the provincial emirs gathered armed detachments and assisted tax-collectors. Their authority was restricted by the judges who were sent from the centre.[73] *The Brilliance of the Meteor* reports:

> When Saud seized an oasis, he built a fortress there, dug a moat around it and stationed a garrison of between 500 and 1,000 men who lived at the population's expense. They might be either local people or soldiers from outside. They were supposed to be devoted to al-Diriya. They spent 2 or 3 years in the fortress. There were supplies and gunpowder there. Some fortresses had guns. Each soldier was paid 300–400 *zahabs*.[74]

The writer seems to be describing the garrisons in the largest towns. It is not known what the value of a *zahab* was. If it corresponded roughly to a rial, the sum mentioned might be a commander's salary rather than that of a rank-and-file soldier.

According to *The Brilliance of the Meteor*, the Wahhabis appointed both muftis and *qadhis* to oases, but only *qadhis* to smaller villages. They were paid directly from the exchequer. *Zakat*-collectors were sent to oases; sometimes there were four of them and sometimes seven. They were independent of the rulers who assisted them in tax-collection. An official known as a *muhtasib* was appointed to ensure the observance of religious rites, the rules of commerce and the established weights and measures; another of his functions was to supervise the work of judges and prevent bribery.[75] Thus the local representatives of the central administration were the emir (the commander of the garrison), the mufti, the tax-collectors and the *muhtasib*.

As noted earlier, in order to consolidate the power of the central authorities and of the Al Saud, Abd al-Aziz ibn Muhammad ibn Saud and Ibn Abd al-Wahhab decided on a step that somewhat contradicted Arabian traditions and customs: they made all Wahhabis swear allegiance to Saud ibn Abd al-Aziz as the crown prince.[76] The emirs of al-Diriya decided all important state matters after consultation with Ibn Abd al-Wahhab, his children and grandchildren, the *ulama*, the nobility of the tribes and oases and the members of the Al Saud.

Ibn Ghannam writes that when the victorious Saud returned from al-Hasa, 'he made his way to his father, people and children and began consultations with his father and most trusted subjects'.[77] Ibn Bishr reports:

If a matter was important to him [Saud] and he wanted to learn [his retinue's] opinion, he sent for the notables from among the nomadic shaikhs and heard their opinion. When they left him, he sent for the noble and wise people of al-Diriya and heard their opinion. When they left him, he sent for the shaikh's sons and the *ulama* from al-Diriya and consulted them. His opinion inclined to theirs, and he disclosed his opinion to them.[78]

Burckhardt writes:

In the time of war, the chiefs of the provinces, as well as the great Bedouin sheikhs, form a council; in the time of peace, Saoud consulted none but the olemas of Derayeh. These belong principally to the family of [Ibn] Abd el Wahab, founder of the sect.[79]

No details are available on the organization of the central administration in the first Saudi state. It is not known if there was a permanent council of the nobility under the rulers of al-Diriya. The Wahhabi chroniclers mention a *diwan* (consultative body) under the emir without specifying its functions. It is clear, however, that there were some central bodies. That is why we doubt Reynaud's report that the ruler himself managed all the affairs of state, helped by one clerk.[80]

Through the Al Saud, the Arabian feudal-tribal nobility pursued a policy that met the interests of their group as a whole, without regional differences. In Burckhardt's opinion, the ruling group in the Wahhabi state was:

an aristocracy, at the head of which stands the family of Saoud . . . He is, in fact, under the control of his own governors, all persons of great influence in their respective provinces, who would soon declare themselves independent were he to treat them with injustice.[81]

This opinion may be accepted only partly, to the extent that there was an interdependence between the rulers of al-Diriya and the nobility as a whole. But the Saudis' authority and influence were not based on 'just treatment' alone. They relied, above all, on military power, on the state apparatus, on the skilful exploitation of rivalries between the local shaikhs and emirs and on the ideological influence of the Wahhabi doctrine.

Ulama *and* qadhis

The Wahhabi *ulama* were an important source of support for the centralization policy of the rulers of al-Diriya. We have already given examples of their regular participation in the most important affairs of state. The sect's founder, Ibn Abd al-Wahhab, enjoyed indisputable authority. In the first years of his alliance with Muhammad ibn Saud, he was not only an *alim*, teacher and *qadhi*. He organized the troops, dealt with internal and external affairs, maintained a correspondence with the Arabian *ulama*, propagated his teaching and preached loyalty to the emir of al-Diriya.[82] He took an active part in the creation and guidance of the Wahhabi state. His preaching disciplined the Wahhabis, rallied them around the emir and encouraged an element of fanaticism. It was only after consulting Ibn Abd al-Wahhab that Abd al-Aziz distributed the spoils of war.

Ibn Abd al-Wahhab strove to maintain his reputation without taking a single rial from the spoils. After the capture of Riyadh, al-Diriya's main enemy in Najd, Ibn Abd al-Wahhab withdrew from affairs of state, transferred the supervision of the *bait al-mal* to Abd al-Aziz and devoted himself to religion, teaching and propaganda.[83] The shaikh's descendants wrote theological works in the spirit of his teaching and commented on his writings,[84] which is how the Wahhabi theological school emerged. It survived the Egyptian invasion of Arabia and supplied zealots for the short-lived Wahhabi renaissance in the mid-nineteenth century.

According to Ibn Bishr, the ruler of al-Diriya 'was generous towards . . . *qadhis*, *ulama*, students and experts in the Quran, muezzins and imams of mosques'. Young people were given expensive gifts after they had completed their education.[85] The pupils of Ibn Abd al-Wahhab's sons were maintained by the *bait al-mal*.[86] The expenditure on mosques and clergy was, naturally, an important item in the exchequer's expenditures. Mengin reports that 'the mosques are maintained on a part of the tithe and on the returns from the *waqfs* transferred to them. To manage them, the *ulama* appoint administrators.'[87] Unfortunately, there are no other data to confirm the existence and spread of *waqf* ownership in Arabia. According to *The Brilliance of the Meteor*, Ibn Abd al-Wahhab and his family owned large areas of landed property and received huge incomes from the state exchequer in addition to gifts from vassal rulers.[88]

Ulama were sent from al-Diriya to all the important oases, towns and tribes to conduct the ideological indoctrination of the population, eradicate all other teachings, impose religious dogma and evoke military enthusiasm and loyalty towards al-Diriya. Schools were opened where the *ulama* taught basic literacy and reciting of the Quran. Burckhardt reports that the *ulama* possessed large libraries in al-Diriya, where many historical works were preserved. Saud also had a valuable library.[89]

It may be assumed that there was no strict division of functions between the clergy and the judges. Ibn Abd al-Wahhab's descendants were sent as *qadhis* to the most important centres, acted independently from the local rulers and received a salary and gifts from the state. The Wahhabi *qadhis* followed the Quran, the Sunna and the Hanbali school of Muslim law in their judicial practice.[90] The *sharia* took root quite successfully in the oases. Among the bedouin, however, Muslim law found little application.[91] The Wahhabi judicial system was in direct conflict with *urf* (customary law). There are reasons to believe that *urf* maintained its predominance, though the expanding of some of the state functions of the nobility in the nomadic tribes increased the opportunities for the *sharia* to be applied. As late as the 1970s the present writer witnessed a lawsuit in Marib (North Yemen), where the governor settled intertribal disputes only on the basis of *urf*. The judicial prosecution and punishment of criminals also underwent some changes in the Wahhabi state. According to the *sharia*, a thief was liable under certain circumstances to a fine or to having his hand cut off.[92]

As in the time of the Prophet Muhammad, the Wahhabis strove to limit the institution of the blood feud, replacing it by a compensation payment of 100 camels or 800 thalers. (Giving these figures, Burckhardt does not indicate whether they were common to all regions of Arabia.) Presumably, the al-Diriya emirate managed to narrow the application of the blood feud, but not to eliminate it entirely.

The Wahhabis did not recognize the custom by which a criminal could be protected by individual members of a tribe. Judicial power belonged to the *qadhis*, who were appointed by the state. The *qadhis* paid special attention to violations of the prescriptions of the Muslim cult. Even slight deviations were punished severely.[93]

Trade and the economy (the positive aspects of centralization)

For the first time in centuries Arabia, especially its central regions, now acquired some measure of stability, even though it was temporary. The emirs took ruthless measures to ensure security on the roads, to guard the home trade from looting and to protect property. According to Ibn Sanad, a chronicler from Basra, the safety of travellers was among the Wahhabis' principal concerns.[94] According to Ibn Bishr:

> Abd al-Aziz was severe with bedouin who committed crimes, looted travellers or stole their property. When somebody did so, the ruler confiscated his property in full or in part, depending on the character of his crime, and punished him severely.[95]

The chronicler reports that when an Iranian pilgrim stopped close to the Subai bedouin's camp, somebody stole his bag with several small items amounting to 10 piastres. The victim sent a complaint to Abd al-Aziz. The ruler ordered the tribal shaikhs to send money to the pilgrim, who had already returned to Iran. Moreover, the emir called them and said, 'Unless you tell me the thief's name, I shall put you in chains and jail you and take a part of your goods as a fine.' The shaikhs promised to restitute double the value of what the pilgrim had lost. But Abd al-Aziz insisted on finding the culprit. The thief was found, his goods (70 female camels) were sold, the proceeds were confiscated to the *bait al-mal* and the bag was sent back to the pilgrim. Ibn Bishr notes that respect for the belongings of others, and fear of punishment for theft, reached an unusual degree. Once some hungry bedouin found an unknown person's goats, which had lost their way, but did not dare to slaughter them.[96]

It is obvious from Ibn Bishr's first story that the rulers of al-Diriya introduced a system of collective responsibility for security in a tribe's territory. Burckhardt also mentions this.[97] Moreover, the Wahhabis eliminated the duties for 'guards', 'convoys' and passage that the tribes had earlier imposed on the caravans crossing their territory. Merchants and travellers:

> are not afraid of an attack or theft by the bedouin who live in this country [Ibn Bishr writes]. No taxes or duties are imposed on them that are paid by pilgrims. Duties and taxes were abolished on the roads in the regions where nomads live, who [had] revived the usages of the *jahiliya*. When a rider starts alone from Yemen or Tihama, from Hijaz or Basra, from Bahrain, Oman or the Syrian desert, he carries no weapons. His weapon is a stick. He is not afraid of enemies who may do him evil ...[98]
>
> The subjects and villages enjoyed a safe and happy life in his [Abd al-Aziz's] time. He is really worthy of the title of Mahdi of his time, because one can travel with good money whenever he wants, in summer or in winter, to the left or to the right, to the east or to the west, in Najd, Hijaz, Yemen, Tihama and elsewhere. He fears nobody but God – neither a thief nor a robber.[99]

Ibn Bishr goes on to give an example: some tax-collectors were returning from remote regions with the *khums* (one fifth of the spoils for the emir) and the *zakat*. When camping, they attached travel-bags containing money to their tents or tied them to horse saddles in the night without any fear of theft.

The settled population of the oases and towns benefited from the new security and stability. Their palm groves and fields were no longer raided.[100] In a centralized state, the nomads could not collect the *khuwa* by relying on threats or military attacks. The preconditions appeared for the abolition of the tribute relations of 'brotherhood'. It is difficult to say how far-reaching these trends were. It would be wrong to claim that raids ceased altogether, but it is clear that the peasants could safely till their land and graze their livestock for the first time in many centuries. Ibn Bishr writes:

> In spring, the dwellers of all the oases of al-Arid, al-Kharj, Qasim, Washm, Janub and other places left their livestock – camels, pedigree horses, cows, sheep, goats and others – in steppes and pastures without herdsmen. When the animals felt thirsty, they came to the oases and then returned to their pastures, to stay there until spring ended and their masters needed them. Perhaps they procreated, but people did not know that until the animals came with their young. Pedigree horses were an exception. A special man was hired to water and hobble them.
>
> The people of Sudair leave their camels, pedigree and [ordinary] horses [in pastures] in spring and hire a man who waters them, visits their masters and returns to the livestock, while the owners do not leave their houses. The man puts the hobbles and chains straight and then returns. The pedigree and [ordinary] horses are treated in the same manner in the Washm pastures, as well as Abd al-Aziz's, his sons' and relatives' horses in various pastures. Only one man is hired to look after them. This practice is common in all regions ...
>
> There was a large camel pasture in al-Diriya for the camels that had lost their way and were found alone or in groups. A bedouin or a settled dweller of any part of the peninsula who found them brought them to al-Diriya, fearing that they would be found in his herd ... Abd al-Aziz appointed a man to supervise them and hire

herdsmen. The camels procreated in the pasture. The nomads and settled people whose camels were missing came there. When somebody recognized his camels, he either brought two witnesses or made an oath and brought one witness and then took the camels.[101]

In practice, however, the economic reality of the first Saudi state was far from the idyllic picture drawn by Ibn Bishr. It included raids on travellers on the roads (otherwise whom did the rulers of al-Diriya punish?), raids upon the orchards and fields of settled peasants, and frequent insurrections by nomadic tribes and oasis-dwellers. Ibn Zaini Dahlan, a historian from Hijaz, describes raids on the roads, which occurred when the Wahhabis were gradually establishing their control in Hijaz and when their henchman Sharif Abd al-Muin ruled Mecca.[102]

The measures taken by the Wahhabis to ensure security on the roads and the protection of property, together with the abolition of internal 'custom duties', created a favourable climate for intra-Arabian trade. Although already well-developed, this trade was now given an additional impetus. It should be stressed, however, that we mean domestic trade. The Wahhabis' policy in foreign trade, which was of primary importance in some regions of Arabia, was destructive, as will be shown below. Enormous fortunes (by Arabian standards) were made in trade, particularly in years of famine, when prices rose sharply.[103] According to Burckhardt:

> The principal trade of Nedjd is in provisions [Mengin confirms this]; and the tribes from the interior of the Desert purchased what they required; and as years of dearth often occur, the rich people hoard up great quantities of corn. With these Saoud never interfered; and in times of scarcity he allowed them to sell at their own prices, however they might distress the poor; for he said, that Mohammed never forbade merchants to derive from their capitals as much profit as they possibly could obtain.[104]

The Wahhabis prohibited usury, however, in accordance with the standards of early Islam.[105]

The development of trade within Arabia was conducive to the prosperity of al-Diriya, the state's capital. Ibn Bishr visited it during Saud's life and left a description of the town:

> I saw a great wealth, a lot of people, peerless arms, decorated with gold and silver, pedigree horses and Omani camels, rich clothes and other signs of prosperity beyond any description or calculation. Once I observed the seasonal fair, standing on a hill in the place known as Batin. It is between the western part of the town, called Turaif, where the Al Saud family dwells, and the eastern structures, known as Bujairi, which belong to the shaikh's sons. A market for men was on the one side, and opposite it I saw [the markets of] gold, silver, arms, camels, sheep and goats. Goods were bought and sold, money was taken and given. The market spread

The Social and Political System of the Emirate of al-Diriya

as far as my sight reached . . . The most frequently heard words were: 'Sold!' – 'Bought!' There are shops on the eastern and western sides with dresses, arms, fabrics . . .[106]

The might of this town, the grandeur of its buildings, the energy of its people, its populousness and wealth are beyond any description. One who knows cannot encompass everything with his knowledge. If I had tried to count the people who are hurrying and scurrying about the town, pedigree horses, camels of the Omani breed and the luxurious goods of various kinds the local residents and foreigners brought there, my book would not be sufficient to embrace it. I saw a lot of wonders there.

One who enters the seasonal fair will surely see people from various countries – Yemen, Tihama, Hijaz, Oman, Bahrain, the Syrian desert and Egypt, from capitals and from throughout the world. It would take too much time to enumerate all of them. Some people come, some people go, and some other people settle in the town for ever.

Houses were seldom sold, and their price was 7,000 or 5,000 rials. A low [mean] house cost 1,000 rials, and the price of other [houses] was close to it.

The monthly rent for some shops was 45 rials. Other shops were let at 1 or ½ a rial daily. I heard that when a caravan comes from Hadm, the daily rent for a shop was 4 rials.

A local inhabitant wanted to expand his house and make it more comfortable. He bought palm trees near his house to fell them and use in construction . . . Each tree cost 40 or 50 rials . . .

Firing and wood were very expensive there. The price of a bundle [*haml*] of firing was said to reach 5–6 rials and that of a thick palm stem was 1 rial per cubit.[107]

Al-Diriya became one of Arabia's major trading centres and trade routes from the entire peninsula met there. The abundant influx of goods caused an artificial boom, and a huge accumulation of people and wealth. There was as yet no economic base for the existence of such a large settlement. The fabulous prices of wood, palms and firing are an additional proof to that effect. Nonetheless, security on the roads ensured a certain, although temporary, strengthening of economic ties within Arabia.

The economic, political and ideological measures taken to centralize the state led to phenomena that were unprecedented in the history of central Arabia, with the gradual emergence of a supra-tribal community. This trend was so striking that Ibn Bishr exclaims in admiration, 'A man sits together with one who has killed his father and with the murderer's brother, as if they were his brothers.'[108] This statement may be a literary exaggeration, but it nevertheless describes a trend. Ibn Sanad notes that the Wahhabis put an end to mutual raids and all the bedouin, from Hadhramawt to Syria, became like brothers in spite of their differences. In some regions, the tents of the Anaza, Ataiba and Harb could be seen close to each other and their people lived in friendship.[109]

However, the main instrument of the policy of centralization and rallying of individual territories and tribes within the Saudi state remained the army. As long as it was strong and victorious, the existence of the al-Diriya emirate was assured.

The army

With the exception of a several-hundred-strong detachment of picked soldiers, who were kept in al-Diriya, Saud and his father had never had a regular army, according to Burckhardt.[110] All men aged 18 to 60 were liable for military service.[111] Virtually every bedouin or oasis inhabitant, if he was physically strong, was a potential conscript. Burckhardt reports that one out of every ten men was usually sent to join the troops.[112] Ibn Sanad and other authors do not specify the quota.

When preparing a raid, the emir of al-Diriya sent his messengers to the shaikhs of the bedouin tribes and ordered them to arrive at a particular well on a specified date, according to Ibn Bishr. Virtually nobody was late in arriving, 'neither high nor low, neither the bedouin of Hijaz nor those of Iraq, Janub, etc'. Those who were late had to pay a fine in the form of goods, horses and camels. It was collected by special officials sent by the ruler. Besides, the offenders were beaten and 'subjected to different tortures'. Nobody dared object to the officials' actions or plead for the offenders, but 'everybody was obedient and submissive'.[113]

Ibn Sanad writes, 'When a war was prepared, [Muhammad] ibn Saud called different tribes, specifying the number of men to be sent by each tribe and village.'[114] This is confirmed by Raymond,[115] Corancez[116] and Burckhardt.[117] According to Badia-y-Leblich (Ali bey), 'When the Sultan of the Wahhabis has occasion for troops, he writes to the different tribes, and indicates to them the number of men they are to send him.'[118] Here is Mengin's account:

> Before starting a military campaign, Saud demanded the necessary contingents from the provinces. The emirs transmitted his orders to those who were under their jurisdiction. The ruler of each town or province himself led the armed people to their destination. He commanded them as long as the war continued. Separate detachments were formed in each province under the emir's command with two clerks and an imam under him. The imam's functions were to lead prayers in the camp and to mediate in any disputes that might arise.[119]

The largest tribes of central Arabia – the Anaza, Qahtan and Mutair – obeyed orders from the rulers of al-Diriya, even if they lived far from the theatre of war.[120] Judging from the description of raids, however, it was usually only the nearby tribes that participated fully in them. But, when necessary, small detachments from all the other tribes joined the Wahhabi army.

The call-up was compulsory during a war. Thus there was a substantial difference between the Wahhabi troops and the earlier tribal confederations where bedouin took part in raids at their own discretion and joined whichever side they liked. In Mengin's words:

> Each man carried his own arms, victuals and munitions. Poor people were helped to equip themselves. The rich maintained the conscripts' families. A man whom the emir appointed to join the troops might provide a substitute, supplying him with all necessary items or giving him a camel or a horse. The infantry and camel corps were not paid, while the cavalry received fodder and a monthly salary.[121]

According to Badia-y-Leblich, the conscripts 'present themselves upon the day appointed, with their provisions, arms and ammunition; for the sultan never thinks of giving them anything; such is the force of their religious ideas'.[122]

Burckhardt reports that a soldier's provisions consisted of 100 lb [45 kg] of wheat, 50–60 lb [23–27 kg] of dates, 20 lb [9 kg] of oil, a sackful of wheat or barley for the camel and a full waterskin.[123] These provisions were undoubtedly the maximum a conscript could take with him, and their amount depended on the length of the campaign. According to Ibn Sanad's information, Saud himself decided how much livestock and munitions the conscripts could take with them. He did not like campaigns of more than one month, since the participants in shorter expeditions had to be self-sufficient, whereas the emir of al-Diriya was supposed to supply them in part if they fought for more than a month.[124] The conscripts who came with poor munitions were sent back, and the Wahhabi ruler punished the oases or tribes that had sent them.

Since the soldiers brought their own provisions, the state exchequer was released from this duty, which increased the troops' autonomy in a campaign. At the same time, conscription and the supply of victuals were a heavy burden for the poorer segment of the population. Unlike the rich, they could not hire a proxy, their households were deprived of their workforce, and if the bread-winner died, no financial compensation could make up for his loss. Rank-and-file fighters could count on nothing but a share in the spoils. Therefore, as Burckhardt reports, peasants and nomads not infrequently tried to evade participating in warfare.[125]

After reserving one fifth of the spoils for the ruler of al-Diriya, the rest was divided among the participants in the campaign. The rule was that a horseman (usually from among the nobility) should receive double the share of an infantryman. It may be supposed that the best part of the plunder was seized by the nobility. Raymond mentions that Abd al-Aziz's soldiers complained about the unjust distribution of spoils and about their commanders, who seized the lion's share of them. The emir had to intervene and restore 'justice'.[126]

Burckhardt writes that the rulers' guard of 300 top soldiers was the main reserve on the battlefield. They were well-armed and were maintained at the emir's expense.[127] The Najdi chroniclers do not mention the guard, but report only the presence of armed slaves. The emir's personal guard probably consisted both of armed Mamelukes and of free people.

When Saud was setting out on campaign, horsemen and the inhabitants of the capital would gather near his palace in al-Diriya. The emir usually went out from the palace, prayed at a nearby mosque, mounted his horse and left the town. He would stop at a point between al-Diriya and Uyaina and the sick, the weak and the poor would gather round him to receive gifts. Pleasing God by his charity and securing the support of the Most High, the ruler also strove to win his subjects' love and devotion.

The emir next arrived at the assembly place. After a prayer and consultations with his retinue, he went on his way. Following the bedouin's usual tactics, scouts (*uyun*) were sent out some days before meeting the enemy. The building of fires was prohibited on the night before engaging with the enemy. On the eve of battle, the ruler assembled his men again and reminded them of their duty to Allah. The conviction that the battle would be pleasing to God increased the Wahhabis' fighting spirit. Before the battle, they prayed once again.

From his childhood and into extreme old age, Saud enjoyed campaigns and *jihad*. *Ulama* from al-Diriya and nearby oases accompanied him on campaign. One of his sons, usually Abdallah, was left in the capital as caretaker ruler.[128] 'Saud filled his enemies with horror, and they often fled as soon as they heard that he was approaching.'[129] When he was preparing an expedition northwards, he pretended to be moving to the south, the east or the west. Mengin reports:

> A vanguard and rearguard were appointed during the day and night marches. The troops set out in one or more columns, depending on the situation. Emirs always led the people who were under their jurisdiction. Cavalry and camel troops led each column and brought up its rear. The centre was formed by artillery and infantry, two soldiers to a camel. [Corancez also mentions this.[130]]
>
> The Wahhabis fed on dates and camel's milk during the marches. They seldom ate bread and meat. [According to Raymond, Arabian fighters could do without water and food for three days. Mengin speaks of two days.[131]]
>
> The Wahhabis started battles in battalions [the writer might mean separate detachments]. The infantry left their camels behind under the servants' guard.[132] When the enemy approached or gained the upper hand, the camels screened the fighters. Each battalion consisted of inhabitants of the same region and was led by the emir and the nobility of the rural [oasis]. The soldiers launched battle in two files. When the first file tired or suffered heavy losses, the second one replaced it. The dead were carried away from the battlefield to be buried. Failure to pay the last honours to them was considered shameful. When defeated, the army retreated without panic. When the enemy suffered a defeat, the infantry did not pursue them, but the cavalry and camel corps did for a while.[133]
>
> [In the military camp] each knew his proper place. The commander was in the centre of the camp. The cavalry surrounded his tent. Infantry and cavalry posts were stationed at some distance from the camp. They were relieved every 24 hours. In the daytime everybody slept, getting up 5 times a day for prayers. In the night, people talked, recited the verses of the Quran and told stories.
>
> The Wahhabis' discipline was severe. A commander who failed to discharge his

duties or gave cause for complaint was degraded and sometimes fined. Rank-and-file offenders were beaten with a stick. For a serious offence, such as fleeing from the enemy, the offender would be beheaded.[134]

Badia-y-Leblich also notes that the Wahhabis' 'discipline is truly Spartan, and their obedience extreme'.[135]

With the exception of Mengin's latter observation, his data are undoubtedly accurate, though the Wahhabis' military campaigns might have been less organized and disciplined than his description. As to the beheading of those who fled from the enemy, this may be questioned. The bedouin's military tactics included flight as an element of battle: it was a device designed to save their forces from a superior enemy. The Arabians saw no dishonour in flight and it is unlikely that the Wahhabis could have drastically altered the earlier traditions.

When the Wahhabi troops failed to seize an oasis immediately, they built a fortress near it and left a small garrison there to constrain the enemy's activities.[136] The emirs of al-Diriya kept garrisons of loyal Najdis in the large oases and towns (al-Hasa, Qasim, Mecca, Medina).[137] They are mentioned in many Arabian sources, though Burckhardt denies this practice.[138] 'The soldiers from al-Diriya were superior to all others,' Mengin writes. 'Commanders of town garrisons were always appointed from among them.'[139]

Corancez reports that the Wahhabis' tactics were based on a surprise attack. If they heard that they had been detected and resistance would be offered, they retreated. The author claims that they did not keep to any particular order in battle and launched attacks only when the enemy was too weak to offer resistance. They were more interested in plunder than in hostilities. Even a slight resistance discouraged them. In such cases, they fled immediately and were then prepared to wait a long time for the opportunity to attack again.[140] In general, Corancez did not have a very high opinion of the Wahhabi troops and in some aspects he was correct. However, it may be assumed that the French historian confused the desert dwellers' specific order of battle with disorder and overlooked the Wahhabis' militant fanaticism.

The Arabian troops' armaments included pikes, swords, daggers, short spears for the infantry, shields, clubs, wick-guns and pistols.[141] The Wahhabis were able to make gunpowder.[142] Some of them wore helmets and protective clothing made of skins.[143] The nobility had chain mail.[144] Daggers and bags with cartridges were attached to the belts. Some fighters had pistols.[145] The wick-guns were seldom used and were not the main weapons. Ibn Bishr reports that Saud had thirty large guns and thirty small ones.[146] Most of them had been seized from the enemy and were almost never used.

The troops under the emir of al-Diriya's banner were 50,000 strong.[147] European sources are inclined to overestimate their strength and mention figures of 100,000, 120,000 and even 200,000.[148] Although the Wahhabis had no equals in the peninsula, this did not mean that they were invariably the victors.

Events leading to the disintegration and collapse of the first Saudi state

The task of subduing the entire Arabian peninsula ultimately proved to be beyond the strength of the rulers of al-Diriya. The vast territories, poor communications in the arid deserts and almost inaccessible mountains led to the isolation of individual regions and hampered military campaigns and supplies. The emirs' energy and troops were insufficient to conquer the mountain regions of Yemen and even of Hijaz, and the coastal regions of Muscat and Hadhramawt; and they were unable to consolidate their positions in Tihama and Najran. This created a permanent threat and a source of disturbance in the frontier regions and forced the Wahhabis to expend effort and resources on hostilities. These did not invariably end in the exemplary punishment of the 'polytheists' and the reward of rich spoils for the 'monotheists'.

Outside the Arabian peninsula and the desert areas, the Wahhabi troops were unable to wage successful large-scale military operations. It has already been noted that, after the capture of Karbala in 1802, the Wahhabis did not manage to seize a single fortified town in Syria or Iraq. Their cruelty not only sowed terror among the population, but also encouraged them to put up a fierce resistance. The defenders' courage and their commanders' military strategy made the fortified towns unassailable for the Wahhabi troops.

The Wahhabi offensives bore the imprint of medieval conquests. It is impossible to guess what the fate of their state would have been if it had been set up some centuries earlier. Beyond the boundaries of medieval Arabia, the Wahhabis faced more developed parts of the Ottoman empire. Some of its provinces were trying desperately and unsuccessfully to turn from the empire's 'full-dress turban' into modern states. First of all, they borrowed European military techniques and organization. In clashes with an army that had been trained and armed to European standards, the Wahhabis were inevitably the losers.

Halting the expansion even for a while might have threatened the very existence of the Saudi state, however. We have seen that participation in victorious raids and joint plunder was the main link that united the nobility of the isolated oases and tribes. When the military expansion of the al-Diriya emirate reached its natural boundaries, slowed down and then virtually ceased, political unity was no longer as attractive for the Arabian nobility as it had been before. The inflow of plundered wealth decreased. The feudal-tribal nobility might now count on greater returns by pursuing an independent policy and raiding neighbours in the traditional manner,

The oppression of the centralized state was particularly felt by the powerful nomadic tribes. Many bedouin, who had never known the meaning of a tax, paid the compulsory *zakat* only out of the fear of brutal reprisals and they often rebelled. Burckhardt notes that they were always ready to throw off the Wahhabi yoke and only recognized Wahhabism outwardly.[149] The spoils of war might compensate for the payment of taxes and the loss of income resulting from the various kinds of *khuwa*, but when successful raids ceased, the burden of the centralized state became unbearable. Taxes, tributes and fines sometimes weighed more heavily than the advantages of security and stability. Then whole tribes and provinces ceased to pay taxes.[150] Saud waged several campaigns every year against rebel tribes and provinces within his own state, besides raiding the disobedient outskirts of the peninsula and the provinces of the Ottoman empire.

Social inequalities continued to increase within the Saudi state. The central Arabian nobility, grown rich on the spoils of war, became accustomed to luxury: increasingly, its lifestyle diverged from that of the ordinary nomads and peasants. There was a growing gap between Wahhabi propaganda, addressed to the people, and the way of life of the nobility. The long campaigns distracted the Najdi peasants from agriculture, and this was not invariably compensated for by the spoils of war. The rent imposed by the rich landowners (sometimes the Saudis themselves) and the state on a part of the settled people, in addition to the *zakat*, increased their feeling of discontent.

The nobility became less interested in a centralized state once it had ceased to expand. Dissatisfaction at the Saudis' power increased among the bedouin and the tribal nobility, and the peasants also became disillusioned with Wahhabism and the emirs of al-Diriya. Taken together, these provided the preconditions for the collapse of the centralized Arabian state. The state's difficulties were aggravated by several political and economic measures – caused by the emirs' narrow fanaticism – and accelerated its decay.

The situation in the al-Diriya emirate was favourable to domestic trade. Conditions for foreign trade, however, were just the opposite. The Wahhabis' irreconcilable fanaticism had made them sever trade links with the 'polytheists', as they branded all non-Wahhabis. Trade with Syria and Iraq was prohibited until 1810.[151] When a merchant was found on a road leading to the lands of the 'polytheists', all his goods were confiscated.[152] Burckhardt writes:

> The offence which Saoud had most frequently to punish was the intercourse of his Arabs with heretics. At the time that the Wahaby creed was first instituted, the most positive orders had been given to interdict all communication between the Wahabys and other nations who had not yet adopted the new doctrine; for it was said, that the sword alone was to be used in argument with the latter.[153]

It is easy to imagine the terrible blow that the economies of some regions might suffer from a literal implementation of these orders. However, economic need proved stronger than arbitrary decisions and the dictates of religion. Badia-y-Leblich writes justly:

> But time will teach this people that Arabia cannot exist without the commercial relations of the caravans and the pilgrimage. Necessity will make them relax from this intolerance towards other nations.[154]

Arabia's trade with the 'polytheists' continued, though on a lesser scale. The grain trade with Egypt, Iraq and Syria did not cease even when the Saudis' relations with these areas were extremely bad.[155] The Wahhabis themselves sold in India some of the jewellery that had been seized.¹⁵⁶ Trying in vain to impose a 'blockade' on Arabia, the emirs could not survive without trade with the 'polytheists' and thus undermined their own authority.

The Wahhabis' policy was especially destructive for Hijaz. The heaviest blow was the sharp drop in the numbers of pilgrims coming from the Ottoman empire. The bedouin were deprived of payments for the passage of caravans through their territory and for the hire of pack animals. Numerous professional beggars, guides and attendants at places of worship lost their income. The Ottoman sultan's annual gifts were no longer sent to the holy cities.¹⁵⁷ As al-Jabarti writes:

> the people of Mecca did not receive what they had lived on – neither alms, nor food, nor money. Taking their wives and children, they left their homeland. Only those stayed to whom these incomes were not the means of subsistence. People left for Egypt and Syria and some of them for Istanbul.¹⁵⁸

The Wahhabis nevertheless maintained order and security on the Hijaz roads, and traders did not suffer attacks by robbers. When the numbers of pilgrims decreased, that fact prevented price rises. When a terrible drought led to a famine in Arabia that lasted for five or six years, food was brought to Hijaz from other countries. But the main forms of trade in Hijaz – 'middle-man' operations and selling goods to pilgrims – suffered. The transit of goods via Jidda decreased because of the sharp reduction in the number of pilgrims, for whom many items were brought. Traders in coffee and Indian fabrics were afraid to appear in the port, where they were treated as 'polytheists'. Trade with Egypt fell drastically. Both rich merchants and the ordinary townsfolk of Jidda, Mecca and other towns, who also depended on trade, felt the consequences. Many of them were ruined. Jidda became depopulated, with part of its buildings falling into decay.¹⁵⁹

The rulers of al-Diriya abolished many unjust tributes and put an end to the extortions of the sharif of Mecca and the *agha* of Medina. Yet they imposed *zakat* on those regions that were not governed directly by the sharif. One can imagine the feelings of the bedouin and the inhabitants of Medina, who had lost their income from pilgrims and still had to pay taxes. The sharif of Mecca retained his income, but it was drastically reduced due to the virtual cessation of the pilgrimage, the trade recession and the exemption of Wahhabi merchants from the duties, not to mention the loss of political independence. Participation in raids was a far from enticing prospect for the Hijazis, who had grown used to earning their living by less dangerous methods. It is enough to say that people in Medina who owned horses sold their animals as soon as possible to avoid conscription to the Wahhabi troops.¹⁶⁰

The strict morals introduced in Mecca ran counter to its people's customs and habits. The status of the holy city made its inhabitants feel superior to all other Muslims and led them to excuse a certain lewdness of behaviour. Whole blocks of Mecca belonged to prostitutes, who even paid a tax on their occupation. Homosexuality was widespread. Alcohol was sold almost at the gate of the Kaaba and drunkenness was not

The Social and Political System of the Emirate of al-Diriya

uncommon.[161] The new rules might meet with the approval of the pious *ulama* and sincere believers, but they were burdensome for the greater part of the population. No less burdensome was the humiliation caused by the submission to the Najdis for the first time in centuries.

All these facts, whether of an economic, a political or a psychological nature, created an anti-Wahhabi climate in Hijaz. The Wahhabis' authority and power relied only on the force of arms. A powerful impetus from outside was enough to start the process of disintegration of the Saudi state and widen the contradictions that were gradually undermining it from within.

CHAPTER 5

The Wahhabis Routed by the Egyptians (1811-1818)

Prelude to the Egyptian expedition to Arabia

The conquest of Mecca and Medina by the Wahhabis greatly damaged the prestige of the Turkish sultan, Selim III. The Commander of the Faithful and Custodian of the Two Holy Cities had proved unable to ensure that his subjects could undertake the *hajj*, one of the Muslims' five principal obligations.

Selim was assassinated in 1807, to be succeeded by Mustafa IV. The new sultan, who was a puppet in the janissaries' hands, strove to return Hijaz to Ottoman control at any cost. However, the attempts to prompt the Baghdad *pashalik* to active resistance against the Wahhabis proved hopeless. Preoccupied with internecine disputes and with a war against the Persians, the rulers of Baghdad were unable to confront the emirate of al-Diriya, nor did they wish to do so. Neither were the weak pashas of Damascus, who were subjected to regular attacks by the powerful pashas of Acca and who used their forces in internecine rivalry, able or willing to oppose the Saudi state. Finally, Genj Yusuf was appointed governor of Damascus. He managed to suppress the janissaries, make short work of the Syrian separatists and increase his power, yet he was reluctant to become involved in a military campaign against the Wahhabis.[1] The only real chance to rout the emirate was to use the troops of the Egyptian pasha, who was starting his rise to power.

When Muhammad Ali established himself in Egypt and was appointed ruler of Cairo in 1805, the Porte entrusted him with the task of reconquering the holy cities of Mecca and Medina from the Wahhabis. Preoccupied with several pressing issues – the strengthening of his power, the struggle against his rivals and against the Mamelukes, the protection of Egypt against British designs, and the necessity of internal reforms –

The Wahhabis Routed by the Egyptians (1811–1818)

the new pasha could not tackle the situation in Arabia for several years. He began serious preparations for an expedition in late 1809.[2]

The Porte's wishes were neither the sole nor the main reason that prompted the practically independent ruler of Egypt to undertake a protracted and expensive campaign in Arabia. By winning over the holy cities, Muhammad Ali hoped to strengthen his authority throughout the Ottoman empire and to win popularity. He planned, as Ali Bey had done earlier, to establish control over the trade in Indian commodities and Yemeni coffee via Jidda and then to conquer Yemen itself. In addition, Muhammad Ali intended to use the religious appeal of the call to liberate Mecca and Medina in order to remove his soldiers from Egypt – they had brought him to power but then become too dangerous a force and now constrained his actions. Lastly, it may be assumed that the Porte had promised unofficially to award the Damascus *pashalik* to one of Muhammad Ali's sons after Mecca and Medina had been liberated.[3]

Embarking on a ship-building programme, Muhammad Ali ordered timber, anchors and other materials. They were brought from Turkey to Cairo and then transferred to Suez by camel. The transfer was performed in great haste and many camels were driven to death: the road from Cairo to Suez was littered with their corpses. With hundreds of shipbuilders at work in Suez, two dozen vessels were ready by March 1810.[4] Thereafter, several more ships were built. The Egyptians made the Red Sea port of Qusai the main supply base of the expeditionary troops. They strengthened the fortresses along the northern part of the caravan routes between Egypt and Hijaz, sending garrisons of Maghrebi mercenaries. The bedouin tribes were given rich gifts.[5]

On 1 March 1811 Muhammad Ali launched a massacre of Mamelukes in the Cairo citadel and then continued it throughout the city. His dangerous rivals in Lower Egypt were destroyed. The war in Europe temporarily removed the threat of an invasion by a European power and favoured the Arabian campaign. Tusun, the Cairo ruler's young and courageous son, then aged 16 or 18, headed the expedition.[6]

To win the sharif of Mecca's support, Muhammad Ali started a secret correspondence with him: Ghalib promised his assistance. Just before Tusun set out for Hijaz, his father's scout was sent there to maintain contact with Ghalib, to make an on-the-spot appraisal of the situation and to ascertain the attitude of the nomadic tribes. The information received by Muhammad Ali seemed encouraging. The population of Hijaz was hostile to the Wahhabis and ostensibly saw the 'Turks' as liberators. (Initially, Muhammad Ali acted in Arabia as an arm of the sultan, and the people perceived his army as a Turkish one.) After receiving similar information from other sources, the Egyptian ruler decided that the right moment had come.[7]

Tusun routed in Wadi al-Safra

The offensives undertaken by the emirate of al-Diriya weakened notably around 1800. After the fall of Karbala and the conquest of Hijaz, the Wahhabis could not claim any real successes. In an alliance with Muscat, Britain inflicted several heavy defeats on the Wahhabis on land and sea and enabled Bahrain to put an end to al-Diriya's dominance. Permanent anti-Wahhabi insurrections were waged in Oman. In Iraq, the Wahhabis were powerless before the fortified towns.

The Saudi state was also weakened by long years of drought and a famine in Arabia, which lasted up to 1809, accompanied by a cholera epidemic. In al-Diriya alone, dozens of people were dying of cholera each day.[8]

The Saudis' power was also being undermined from within, owing to differences between members of the ruling family. Dissatisfied with their father's grants, Saud's sons Turki, Nasir and Saad left home and set off for Oman with a small detachment in 1810/11 in search of adventure and spoils. They gathered a sizeable army and penetrated the south and south-east of the peninsula far beyond Muscat. An enraged Saud ordered the Wahhabi troops to withdraw from Oman, leaving the young princes without any support. The emir's sons reached al-Hasa, but did not dare to appear in al-Diriya for fear of their father's wrath. The conflict finally ended in a reconciliation.[9]

For the first time in half a century, the imam's authority came to be disputed by his relatives. Saud sent away his full brothers, perhaps afraid of their rivalry, and drew closer to his half-brothers, born to Abd al-Aziz's other wives. This caused discontent among many members of the royal family. The opposition was led by one Abdallah, who is described as Saud's uncle by Raymond and Corancez. According to Corancez, he was the governor of the capital.[10] When, on Saud's death in 1814, his son Abdallah was to inherit the throne, a namesake of his (according to Burckhardt, he was Saud's brother) opposed him, supported by a part of the *ulama* of al-Diriya.[11]

The Saudi state retained some of its strength, however. The militant fanaticism of Wahhabism was not yet exhausted and the rulers of al-Diriya could still rely on the staunch detachments of the settled population of Najd and some bedouin tribes. They had not yet lost their reputation as victorious fighters. Lastly, Arabia's harsh natural conditions were themselves on the Wahhabis' side in the struggle against the outside enemy.

The Egyptian army consisted of Turkish, Albanian and Maghrebi mercenaries and had superior armaments, including artillery. Many of its commanders had experience of battles against the French and the British and were acquainted with European military tactics. However, discipline and morale in the army were low.

In August 1811 a detachment of troops was sent to Hijaz by sea to capture Yanbu. The cavalry, led by Tusun, set out in the same direction by land. Burckhardt reports that 1,500 soldiers were sent by sea and 800 cavalry and camel corps were led by Tusun. Relying on the Egyptian archives, Abd al-Rahim mentions 3,000 cavalry and camel corps, including the bedouin.[12] One of Muhammad Ali's most able commanders, Ahmad Agha, accompanied Tusun as a military adviser and was actually commander-in-chief. Muhammad al-Mahruqi, one of the richest Egyptian merchants, who was personally interested in the Red Sea trade and had visited Mecca several times, travelled with the expeditionary corps as Tusun's political adviser, appointed by Muhammad Ali. The Cairo *ulama* also accompanied the troops.[13]

The Wahhabis Routed by the Egyptians (1811–1818)

The Egyptian landing force occupied Yanbu in October of the same year. There were no Wahhabi troops in the town and the small detachment sent by the sharif of Mecca offered virtually no resistance.[14] 'The soldiers looted all goods, cash, cloth and coffee they found in Yanbu, dishonoured the women and girls, captured them and sold [them] to each other.'[15] Their behaviour could hardly be expected to win the goodwill of the local people. Yet the main goal of the first stage of the expedition had been achieved – an important bridgehead was seized for future actions against the Wahhabis.

In November, Tusun arrived in Yanbu with his detachment. Ibn Bishr writes that more than 14,000 people assembled in Yanbu.[16] Even if one takes into account that Burckhardt somewhat underestimates the strength of the Egyptian forces, the discrepancy between his and the Najdi chronicler's figures is striking. It is likely that some bedouin, together with the garrisons sent earlier by Muhammad Ali by the caravan route to the fortresses, joined Tusun on the way.[17] Tusun spent several weeks in Yanbu. After receiving reinforcements from Egypt, he led his army on to Medina.

Saud had been informed of Muhammad Ali's military preparations by his spies in Cairo. Apparently, this was why he had ensured that Medina was permanently fortified. When Tusun captured Yanbu, Saud mobilized his best forces and sent them to Hijaz under his son Abdallah's command. Eighteen thousand Wahhabis, including 600 horsemen, took up positions near Wadi al-Safra halfway between Yanbu and Medina.[18]

The decisive battle occurred in December 1811. While Tusun was pursuing the Harb bedouin, with whom he had not established friendly relations, his army entered a narrow mountain pass near Wadi al-Safra and was attacked by the Wahhabis' crack troops, of whose arrival Tusun was unaware. The 8,000-strong Egyptian army fled. Tusun's personal bravery did not save the situation and his army was routed, losing more than half its troops. It was only the Wahhabis' enthusiasm for plundering the vacated camp that saved the Egyptians from a massacre, and the remainder of Tusun's troops managed to reach Yanbu. But the Wahhabis did not attack the town and the Egyptians retained control of the important bridgehead.[19]

Here is al-Jabarti's description of the Egyptian soldiers' behaviour at the very first signs of defeat:

> The soldiers who were below suddenly saw the defeated soldiers descending from the mountains. They all took flight in search of salvation, leaving their tents, luggage and equipment and looting their commanders' lightest articles. Those who were stronger seized their weaker comrades' property and rode their horses and camels or, perhaps, even killed the weak to take their riding animals and flee. They rushed to Baraiq [a small port near Yanbu] to the few ships kept there for safety's sake. Their hearts were seized with horror. Since they retreated in disorder, none of them would have escaped if they had been pursued. On reaching the seashore, the soldiers shouted to call the ships. When a small vessel approached the coast, the soldiers crowded to get aboard and crushed each other. Those who managed to force their way to the vessel prevented their comrades from boarding it and did not hesitate even to use guns and bullets.[20]

As a representative of the al-Azhar opposition to Muhammad Ali, al-Jabarti provides his own explanation of the Egyptian troops' defeat:

> Some commanders, who were considered pious and devout, told me, 'How can we win when most of our soldiers belong to different confessions and some of them do not believe in anything and profess no religion? We are carrying boxes containing alcoholic drink, the *azan* [Muslim call to prayer] is never heard in our camp, the [Islamic] prescriptions are not fulfilled or even remembered, our people have no idea of religious rites. As for our enemies, as soon as a muezzin's call sounds, they perform their ablutions and line up behind their single imam humbly and obediently. When the time for prayer comes during a battle, they timidly perform the "fear prayer" [a shorter prayer] – one detachment goes forward and wages the battle while the others pray behind it. Our soldiers are astonished; they have never heard of it, not to mention seeing it. The Wahhabis shout from their camp, "Come and fight us, you pagans, you beard-shavers, who glorify libertinism and sodomy, you drunkards who have forgotten prayers, you usurers and murderers who permit yourselves forbidden deeds!"'[21]

Besides the purely military factors – the Wahhabis' unexpected assault, the Egyptian troops' poor position, the Wahhabis' still high militant spirit and the Egyptian soldiers' low morale – Tusun's inability to establish friendly contacts with the local nomadic tribes played a major role in his defeat. His army passed through territories whose inhabitants were the Wahhabis' allies and did not yet dare to oppose them, which explains why the Egyptian commanders were ignorant of the Wahhabi troops' movements and positions.

The occupation of Hijaz

To improve their situation, the Egyptians needed to bribe the local bedouin shaikhs. The necessary funds were soon sent from Egypt. C. Rossetti, the Russian consul in Egypt, reported back:

> The continuing export of food from here [Alexandria] to Malta and Spain allows him [Muhammad Ali] to improve the condition of his exchequer and comfortably bear the expenses for the further fortification of this town and for the important preparations in the campaign against Wahhab. Meanwhile, new troops arrive continuously in Alexandria from Turkey and are sent to Yanbu via Suez in small detachments. People insist that Wahhab, on his side, is taking active measures to meet the new expedition. There is a great discord between Wahhab and the sharif of Mecca.[22]

Rossetti also reported rumours about the forthcoming war between France and Russia.

The Wahhabis Routed by the Egyptians (1811–1818)

This allowed Muhammad Ali, for the time being, to pay less attention to the European powers.

Fresh reinforcements and military equipment arrived in Yanbu. By distributing rich gifts, Tusun won over the local nomads – the Juhaina and the Harb – and many of the settled people. Each tribal shaikh was allotted a monthly grant.[23] Discontent with the Wahhabis had turned to outright hostility in Hijaz and Tusun's policy proved fruitful. Ghalib maintained his correspondence with the Egyptians, though demonstrating all the outward signs of honouring Saud.[24]

In the autumn of 1812 Tusun set out with a huge army and approached Medina in October without meeting any resistance on the way.[25] The city was defended by a 7,000-strong Wahhabi garrison. However, as Ibn Bishr reports, most of the soldiers were ill and the citizens were not eager to fight for the Wahhabis. Tusun started by shelling the city, making breaches in the walls. Medina capitulated. The Wahhabi garrison took refuge in the fortress, but was forced to leave because of famine three weeks later, in November. Tusun promised not to obstruct an honourable evacuation of the remainder of the garrison.[26]

According to Mengin, the Egyptian soldiers behaved in a noble manner,[27] but Burckhardt, who was better acquainted with the course of the campaign, reports that Tusun's soldiers killed or robbed most of the Wahhabis they met on their way.[28] Tusun sent to Cairo: '4,000 ears [that his soldiers had] cut away from the Wahhabis' corpses, which ears will be presumably sent to Constantinople'.[29] Hasan, the *agha* of Medina, deserted to the Egyptians but was then arrested, brought to Istanbul and executed. Thomas Keith, a Scotsman who had been captured in Egypt and embraced Islam there, was appointed governor of Medina in his place.[30]

Sharif Ghalib was playing a double game. He was pleased at the Wahhabis' defeat and meant to throw off their yoke with the Egyptians' help, but an excessive strengthening of Muhammad Ali's positions in Hijaz was far from his interests. Ghalib would have preferred the Egyptians and the Wahhabis to have exhausted each other's strength, and for his true power to have been restored in Hijaz. Further developments were to frustrate all his hopes.

In the meantime, Ghalib again swore allegiance to Saud – who performed his last *hajj* in late 1812[31] – and began preparing to surrender Mecca and Jidda to the Egyptian troops. Then Abdallah's forces camped near Mecca. However, neither Ibn Bishr's chronicle nor other sources mention the Wahhabis' preparations for hostilities. Saud's and his son's passiveness did not mean that they were unaware of the danger threatening them. Their inactivity may be explained only by the domestic situation in the Wahhabi state, the instability of their rearguard and the unreliability of the bedouin.

In January 1813 a small Egyptian detachment captured Jidda without a battle. Aware of Ghalib's treachery, Abdallah withdrew the Wahhabi garrison from Mecca and retreated to al-Khurma with his army. Uthman al-Mudhaifi fled from al-Taif with his family. Mecca fell to Tusun without a fight, to be followed some days later by al-Taif.[32] First Ghalib and then the nomadic tribes of Hijaz swore allegiance to their new masters.

The Egyptians had taken Hijaz from the Wahhabis, in spite of their heavy defeat, virtually without any serious military effort. The decisive factors in their success were Hijaz's hatred for the emirs of al-Diriya and the Wahhabis, the Egyptian gold distributed freely among the nomadic nobility and all the bedouin, and, lastly, the sharif of Mecca's defection to Muhammad Ali.

A magnificent festival with fireworks and a gun salute was held in Cairo on the occasion of the capture of the holy cities. Muhammad Ali's messenger left for Istanbul with the keys of Mecca, Medina and Jidda. The Russian embassy in Turkey reported back:

> All the members of the Ottoman government gathered at the Eyub mosque to receive the keys and then bring them to the sultan's palace. This event was celebrated with three salutes of all batteries of the city, the fleet and the Black Sea straits. The festival continued for seven days.[33]

The sultan appointed Tusun as pasha of Jidda with three horsetails in his mace and sent precious gifts to Muhammad Ali and Sherif Ghalib.[34]

The events of the next months, however, were not encouraging for the Egyptians. The Wahhabis made successful forays into Hijaz in the spring and summer of 1813 and Saud himself appeared in the environs of Medina, though he failed to capture the town. The Asir tribes, who remained loyal to the Wahhabis, attacked the Egyptian detachments near the city walls of Mecca and Jidda. Together with the local population, the Wahhabi troops repulsed the detachments sent by Tusun to capture the strategically important oasis of Turaba; the Egyptians suffered heavy losses. Their sally from the outskirts of Medina towards al-Hanakiya was also a failure.

Fatigue, the heat, and constant illness caused by unclean water and poor nutrition, cost the Egyptian expeditionary force more lives than the battles did. According to Mengin's data, Muhammad Ali's army lost 8,000 men and 25,000 camels during the campaign. The loss of riding and pack animals hindered the Egyptians' manoeuvres, long marches and the regular supply of equipment, food and ammunition. Disappointed with the Egyptian pasha, the bedouin were reluctant to cooperate with his forces.[35]

In the autumn of 1813, however, military fortune smiled on Tusun once again. The Wahhabi commander Uthman al-Mudhaifi raided al-Taif but was defeated and fled. The Ataiba bedouin caught him and handed him over to Ghalib.[36] According to al-Jabarti:

> It was he [al-Mudhaifi] who besieged al-Taif, fought against it and captured it, killed men, raped women; it was he who destroyed the beautiful mausoleum of Ibn Abbas; it was he who fought the pasha's troops near al-Safra and al-Jadida, defeated and dispersed them. After his arrest, he was brought to Jidda and the sharif kept him in the dungeon to curry favour with the Turks.[37]

Al-Mudhaifi was brought to Cairo and then to Istanbul, where he was executed.

Despite a certain level of activity in Hijaz, the Wahhabis' overall military position

The Wahhabis Routed by the Egyptians (1811–1818)

deteriorated in the summer of 1813: their army was routed in Oman and its commander Mutlaq was killed.[38]

Muhammad Ali's policy in Hijaz

The Egyptian ruler understood that, notwithstanding the conquest of Hijaz, the Wahhabis were far from being defeated. He decided to come to Arabia in person, study the situation on the spot and at the same time perform the *hajj*. In the autumn of 1813, he arrived in Jidda with several thousand soldiers.[39] Ghalib greeted him and oaths of mutual friendship were sworn at the Kaaba, yet a serious conflict was about to break out between the pasha and the sharif.

First, Muhammad Ali tried to seize all the proceeds of the Jidda customs-house, depriving Ghalib of most of his income. Then the Egyptian ruler asked Ghalib to put pressure on the bedouin to make them supply pack animals for the Egyptian army. The shortage of means of transportation hampered regular supplies of equipment even between Jidda and Mecca. Ghalib resisted these demands. Several thousand armed slaves, mercenaries and loyal Hijazis, as well as his control of the Meccan fortress, made Ghalib's position strong enough to prevent open attempts to weaken his power.[40]

Muhammad Ali treacherously had Ghalib arrested in late 1813, however, ostensibly on orders from the Ottoman sultan. Under threat of being beheaded, Ghalib ordered his sons to cease their resistance and he was then sent to Cairo with all his family. He was replaced by Yahya ibn Surur, his relative and the Egyptian pasha's puppet. Muhammad Ali confiscated Ghalib's property – cash, furniture, various goods, coffee and spices to the total value of £250,000. However, the sultan ordered that a part of them be returned. Ghalib settled in Salonika and died there some years later.[41]

From the standpoint of his long-term political aim – full control over Hijaz – Muhammad Ali was undoubtedly the victor. He had deprived the sharif of Mecca of his power and ensured that he would not defect to the Wahhabis. All Ghalib's income now fell into Muhammad Ali's hands and helped to finance his expensive campaign. Lastly, he had deprived the Porte of the chance to take advantage of his differences with Ghalib.

But the immediate results of Muhammad Ali's treacherous behaviour were far from positive: the population of Hijaz, including the bedouin, was indignant; and many sharifian families, who went in fear of their lives, fled to the Wahhabis and took an active part in the war on their side. Sharif Rajih, a courageous commander, was among them. A part of Ghalib's guard also deserted to the Wahhabis.[42]

Initially, Muhammad Ali suffered a series of military failures. In late 1813 and early 1814 his troops were defeated near Turaba and Qunfudha. In the Turaba battle, the Wahhabis were commanded by a woman, named Ghaliya, to whom the Egyptians immediately ascribed the power of casting the evil eye. Tusun's troops were attacked from the rear and routed by the bedouin, led by Rajih.[43]

The end of the expedition to Qunfudha was no less disastrous. When the port was seized by the landing force, the soldiers killed many defenceless people and cut off their ears to send them to Istanbul as proof of their military valour. G. Finati, a participant in the landing, reported that several soldiers cut off the ears of people who were still alive in order to receive the promised remuneration.[44] Indignant at the Egyptians' behaviour, the population rallied around Tami, the emir of Asir. Tami cut off Qunfudha from the nearby wells, exhausted the besieged troops' forces and then started the attack. Shouting, 'Save yourselves!', the soldiers ran to the ships. Many were killed, or drowned or died of thirst on the way.[45]

Understanding that his position in Egypt would become precarious without a decisive victory in Arabia, Muhammad Ali took urgent measures to continue the campaign. Additional taxes were imposed on the Egyptian peasants. New reinforcements, ammunition, equipment and food were sent to Jidda, which became the main depot. Several hundred horsemen arrived from among the Libyan bedouin, who were loyal to the pasha. With their experience of desert warfare, they proved a great help to Muhammad Ali. His transport was replenished with thousands of camels, purchased in Syria or brought by the Libyan bedouin. He arranged with the imam of Muscat to hire ships to transport the troops.[46]

Steps were taken to improve relations with the local people. Muhammad Ali lifted some particularly burdensome taxes and reduced the custom duties in Jidda. He distributed money among the poor, repaired the holy monuments in Mecca, gave gifts to the *ulama* and demonstrated his piousness. He ordered his soldiers to refrain from plunder and to pay for any food they took. The people's attitude to the pasha's troops improved.[47]

The main event, however, was the resumption of the *hajj*. A Syrian caravan brought the bedouin the money that the Turkish authorities had withheld for ten years, and the influx of thousands of pilgrims restored the prosperity of the urban population in Hijaz.[48] Thereafter, even the introduction of a monopoly on the sale of foodgrain by Muhammad Ali and the forced coinage of depreciated Egyptian piastres could not seriously affect their welfare.[49]

The death of Imam Saud in al-Diriya in the spring of 1814 also played into the Egyptian ruler's hands.[50] Saud's talents as a military commander and a statesman were universally recognized. Ibn Bishr does not spare his words in extolling Saud's virtues: he portrays him as an ideal ruler, as canonized in many legends and in the Arab literature. The chronicler claims that Saud was loved by his subjects. Having studied for many years with Ibn Abd al-Wahhab, Saud had an excellent knowledge of the Quran and the *hadith*. He fought for Islam and waged *jihad* valiantly. He wrote advice for his subjects, demonstrating a surprising knowledge of theology and supporting his thoughts by quotations from the Quran, the *hadith* and the works of prominent *ulama*. He called on people not to commit forbidden deeds, such as fornication, the spreading of scandal, slander, lies and usury. He was modest, made substantial charitable donations and was without affectation in his treatment of both the people and his friends. He had a brilliant intellect and enjoyed great popularity.[51] The opinions of Raymond and Corancez are very different, however: 'Saud inherited his father's power,

The Wahhabis Routed by the Egyptians (1811–1818)

but not his virtues. It is true that he is not as fanatic as his father, but he is far more despotic.'[52]

Among Saud's possessions, Ibn Bishr mentions al-Hasa, al-Qatif, Bahrain, Oman, Wadi al-Dawasir, al-Kharj, Asir, Bisha, Ranya, al-Taif and Hijaz, Mecca, Medina, Yanbu, Jabal Shammar and Jawf, Sudair, Qasim, Washm and Mahmal.[53] This list – which contains whole provinces together with small towns – shows that the Najdi chronicler made no distinction between the regions and towns of the emirate as to their importance.

By the time of Saud's death, the whole of Hijaz, Oman, Bahrain and a part of Tihama had been lost. His son Abdallah inherited a state that was on the verge of collapse. Suppressing a certain amount of resistance, Abdallah established himself as ruler and started preparations for a further war with Muhammad Ali's army. Most historians note that, although Abdallah was a courageous warrior, he was not his father's equal in political flair, flexibility and other statesmanlike qualities. There may be some truth in this. Those who suffer a defeat are often branded by history as lacking in talent, whereas it is frequently circumstances that are unfavourable to them.

The victory at Basal and the Egyptians' advance on Asir

Muhammad Ali's policy in Hijaz now began to bear fruit and he managed to improve his relations with the bedouin. Ibn Bishr's report is important in noting that Abdallah made several attacks on the nomadic tribes of Hijaz, which were loyal to the Egyptian ruler. The imam of al-Diriya also sent a punitive expedition against a subdivision of the Mutair tribe, which had begun to show signs of disobedience.[54] In late 1814 Muhammad Ali contacted Sharif Rajih and persuaded him to return to his service, paying him a huge sum and awarding him a monthly salary.[55] By that time, Muhammad Ali had sufficient forces at his disposal. Burckhardt puts the strength of the pasha's troops at 5,000, whereas the pasha himself thought that they were 20,000 strong.[56] The true figure may lie somewhere in between.

In late 1814 and early 1815 the Wahhabis concentrated an army near Basal, close to Turaba, which was 30,000 (Ibn Bishr) or 20,000 (Burckhardt) strong. More than half of them came from Asir, led by Tami ibn Shuaib. Abdallah's brother Faisal commanded the united forces. In January 1815 the Egyptian troops won the battle in an alliance with the bedouin. Muhammad Ali paid 6 thalers for every head of an enemy fighter. He celebrated his victory by executing hundreds of prisoners in Mecca. The Wahhabis lost several thousand men.

Next Muhammad Ali's troops captured Turaba, Ranya and Bisha, reached the Red Sea coast and seized Qunfudha. Tami, the ruler of Asir, was delivered up to the pasha, brought to Egypt and then to Istanbul, where he was executed. Muhammad Ali appointed people who were obedient to him to rule the bedouin tribes.[57] As a result of his resolute action, the Wahhabis were routed in Asir and in the strategically important regions between Hijaz, Najd and Asir.

From Qunfudha, Muhammad Ali left for Medina. Some months later he returned to Egypt, from where he had received reports of disturbances. He was also aware of the possibility of a new landing by the British in Egypt or an attack by Turkey after the allies had captured Paris and Napoleon had been exiled.[58]

Tusun's invasion of Qasim and the armistice with Abdallah

Tusun's first attempt to penetrate into Qasim was unsuccessful. Learning that Abdallah had appeared there with a strong army, he turned back. But discontent with Wahhabi rule was already growing in the region, and the nobility of al-Rass contacted Tusun and promised him assistance in the event of an invasion. Without delay, Tusun came to al-Rass with a small detachment and occupied the town. He destroyed a part of the fortifications, imposed taxes on the population and camped nearby to ensure food supplies for his army at the expense of the local people. He could not arrange regular supplies from Medina.

Abdallah was in Anaiza with his troops. The Wahhabis made several sorties towards al-Rass and intercepted a part of the caravans from Medina. For example, the reinforcement detachment, led by Thomas Keith, was ambushed by the Wahhabis and annihilated.[59] Hostilities continued for some months until the summer of 1815.[60] Tusun's condition was desperate: the Wahhabis' powerful response might end in his rout. But it is probable that Abdallah was by now short of forces and fearful of a rebellion in Qasim. Both parties wanted peace. According to Ibn Bishr, the Egyptians were the first to test the ground; Mengin reports that it was Abdallah who took the first step. An armistice was concluded, but on terms that reflected the unstable balance of forces.

In line with the agreement, all hostilities ceased. Tusun's army left Qasim and the Egyptians promised not to interfere in Najdi affairs. Free trade and the *hajj* were guaranteed to all. Both Ibn Bishr and Burckhardt mention the above terms. Burckhardt adds further information on the agreement: all tribes to the east of al-Hanakiya were to submit to Abdallah, who, in turn, agreed to consider himself the sultan's subject. Abd al-Rahim corroborates this by references to documents from the Cairo archives.[61] Abdallah's envoys arrived in Cairo in the autumn of 1815 together with Tusun.[62]

After Tusun's departure, Abdallah started removing the emirs of Qasim who had vacillated during the time that the Egyptian troops had been in al-Rass or who had collaborated directly with Tusun. The emir and some other notables of Qasim were taken to al-Diriya as hostages. Large-scale works were undertaken to fortify the capital of the Saudi state. At the end of the year, Abdallah gathered a large number of troops from al-Hasa, Wadi al-Dawasir, Jabal Shammar, Jawf, Qasim and (as Ibn Bishr asserts) even Oman and began punitive expeditions against the Harb and Mutair bedouin, who had betrayed him. The bedouin scattered in the desert, avoiding direct clashes.

To the south, in the regions of Bisha, Turaba and Ranya, which were not, in Burckhardt's opinion, covered by the agreement between Abdallah and Tusun, clashes

The Wahhabis Routed by the Egyptians (1811–1818)

continued between the Wahhabis and the Egyptian troops.[63] Abdallah's actions led to discontent among the inhabitants of Qasim, not to mention the nomads, and complaints were sent to Muhammad Ali. The ruler of Cairo and his son regularly mentioned Wahhabi violations of the terms of the agreement in their letters to Abdallah.[64]

With the establishment of Egyptian control over Hijaz, Muhammad Ali's authority within the Ottoman empire grew and he began to demand Syria as a reward for his successes in Hijaz. He was now determined to consolidate his positions in Hijaz and in Arabia as a whole, and finally to destroy the Saudi state.[65]

Ibrahim conquers Najd

This time, the expedition was led by Ibrahim, Muhammad Ali's eldest son. There is an anecdote concerning Ibrahim's appointment as head of the new expedition. Before the start of the campaign, Muhammad Ali assembled his military commanders in Cairo to discuss the plan of operations. He pointed to an apple in the centre of a large carpet and said, 'The person who takes the apple and gives it to me without treading on the carpet will command the troops.' The pasha's retainers lay on the floor, but their hands did not reach the fruit. Then the pasha's son Ibrahim, who was not tall, approached the carpet, rolled it up and gave his father the apple. In that way, he hinted to Muhammad Ali that the Egyptian troops, under his command, would roll up the 'carpet' of the Arabian deserts, ensuring secure communication routes and good relations with the local population.[66]

These principles were indeed to become the basis of Egyptian policy in Arabia during Ibrahim's campaign. He understood that an advance into the depths of Arabia would be impossible without the assistance of the bedouin and strove to win them over. To that end, Ibrahim released the bedouin from *zakat*, which had been imposed by the Wahhabis, and paid in hard cash for all services. The expenses of the campaign were enormous; they required 'Croesus' and Human's treasures and Jabir ibn Hayyan's elixir',[67] according to al-Jabarti. (Human was a pharaoh's vicegerent in Ancient Egypt. Ibn Hayyan was an alchemist who allegedly discovered the elixir that transformed all metals into gold.) Ibrahim's victories were paid for by the Egyptian *fellahin*.

Ibrahim was aware of the hostile reaction caused in Hijaz by the pillage and licentiousness engaged in by his multinational army. He tried to make a favourable impression on the Arabs by his piousness and noble behaviour and by honouring all his promises. Up to the rout of al-Diriya, all hostile acts towards the local population were resolutely suppressed. Ibrahim also prohibited alcohol in the army.[68]

Meanwhile, the Saudi state was weakening rapidly and the main bedouin tribes were ready to betray it at any moment. Exhausted by the taxes and half a century of war, the settled population was grumbling. Abdallah's authority was not as absolute as that of his father. Only the Wahhabi *ulama* were an unfailing source of support for the emirs of al-Diriya.

Although the Egyptians could not send large numbers of troops to Najd, their soldiers differed from those who had gone to Hijaz six years earlier. They were now able to conduct regular sieges of fortresses, to build redoubts which protected them from surprise assaults and to use artillery with great skill. Instructors with experience of service in Napoleon's army, together with European physicians, travelled with Ibrahim's troops.[69]

Abdallah's troops remained the same tribal and oasis militia as they had been earlier. The Wahhabis were inferior to the Egyptians in military training. It is true that they were used to the climate and were defending their own homes, palm groves and fields, but their sense of 'Najdi patriotism' was not strong and their feelings for the Saudis were contradictory.

Perhaps Abdallah was aware of his difficult situation. He intended to rout Ibrahim's army in open battle or, in the event of failure, to retreat to central Najd and make the Egyptians lay siege to the fortified oases one by one. He hoped that the Egyptians would renounce their aim of conquering Najd since they were faced with the difficulties of a campaign in the very centre of Arabia, far from their supply bases.

In the autumn of 1816 Ibrahim arrived in Medina with numerous forces. New troops, food and equipment were being sent from Egypt. Ibrahim attracted the tribes around Medina to his service and started a slow advance into Najd. He captured al-Hanakiya and founded a fortified camp there. He approached the shaikhs of the neighbouring tribes, presented them with gifts and paraded his army. Meanwhile, a dispatch from Istanbul appointed him a pasha with three horsetails on his mace. Although he might have felt flattered, the appointment did not imply any support whatsoever. The Porte's influence on Arabian affairs was generally limited to demonstrative gestures.

In early 1817 Ibrahim tried to reach al-Rass, but was forced to turn back.[70] Meanwhile, the nomadic tribes deserted Abdallah one after another. In particular, Faisal Al Dawish, the shaikh of the Mutair, offered his services to Ibrahim in exchange for his future appointment as emir of al-Diriya. Abdallah arrived in Qasim and attacked the Egyptians, but was defeated. Many Wahhabis were killed; their ears were cut off and sent to Cairo. Travelling from al-Rass to Medina two years later, G. F. Sadlier saw many unburied skeletons. Further Wahhabi attacks on Ibrahim's army were repulsed with the help of artillery.[71]

In the summer of 1817 Ibrahim approached al-Rass and began a siege which was to continue for some months. The besieged troops defended themselves valiantly. From the fierce battle that ensued it seems likely that, understanding the town's strategic importance, Abdallah left his best forces there. During the long siege, he stayed close to al-Rass but was unable to give it effective support. Only two Wahhabi caravans were able to force entry into the town.

Ibrahim's losses reached 3,500, though some of these were caused by disease. The summer heat aggravated the difficulties facing the army, yet it had superior artillery, various types of siege hardware and skilful leadership. Even more important was the continuous influx of reinforcements. Abdallah could not cut off the enemy's supplies: Ibn Bishr does not even mention any attempt to that end. Ibrahim was also reaping the rewards of the gold he had distributed among the bedouin and his abolition of *zakat*.

In October al-Rass capitulated with honour and the remaining members of the Wahhabi garrison were permitted to go to Abdallah, carrying their arms.[72] According to Sadlier, the town's fate was different: it did not capitulate, but promised the Egyptians to do so after they had conquered Anaiza.[73]

The defence of Anaiza was led by close relatives of the imam of al-Diriya. Although the Wahhabi garrison was well equipped with food and munitions, the town was captured after a siege lasting several days. Some forts continued to resist, but after the powder magazine blew up in the fortress, the garrison capitulated with honour. The armed Wahhabis went to Abdallah with their arms.[74]

The Wahhabi imam gave up his attempts to defeat Ibrahim's army on the battlefield. Probably, he still hoped to exhaust the enemy in the successive sieges of the oases, but Ibrahim had the reserves of Egypt behind him and his offensive was slow but irresistible. After Anaiza, Buraida capitulated, and by the end of 1817 the whole of Qasim had sworn allegiance to Ibrahim.[75] The pasha wrote to his father that everybody in the province hated Hujailan, the aged emir of Buraida, and Abdallah.[76] Abdallah retreated first to Shaqra, where field defences were built rapidly, and then to al-Diriya.

Ibrahim stayed in Buraida for some two months to receive reinforcements. Then he moved towards Shaqra. Mengin claims that his troops were just 1,000 strong, which seems an underestimate. Later on, he mentions 4,500 soldiers without specifying whether they included the bedouin. What is beyond dispute is that Ibrahim conquered Najd with a relatively small force. However, the bedouin of the Mutair, Harb, Ataiba and Bani Khalid joined him on the march to Shaqra. These nomads were the last to submit to the Wahhabis and the first to split off from them. Ibn Bishr writes bitterly that many tribal shaikhs and the nobility of the Najdi oases followed Ibrahim, hoping for spoils and future independence, but were cruelly disappointed after the fall of al-Diriya.[77] On leaving the captured towns, Ibrahim destroyed all fortifications and took hostages with him.[78]

In January 1818 Ibrahim's army arrived in Shaqra. After some initial shelling, the town was stormed: it fell within a matter of days. The members of its disarmed garrison were released, having promised to take no further part in the war. The whole of Washm was in Ibrahim's hands.[79] Sudair with al-Majmaa was occupied virtually without a fight and Huraimala and Mahmal swore allegiance to the Egyptians.[80]

From Shaqra, Ibrahim moved towards Durma, which was defended by staunch warriors from al-Kharj. Even with his artillery and siege hardware, the pasha could not immediately force the garrison to capitulate. But the forces were uneven. When Ibrahim's soldiers burst into the town, they massacred its people as a punishment for their resistance and the town was plundered. As usual, ears were cut off from the corpses and sent to Cairo. These events occurred in February or March 1818.[81] The road to al-Diriya was now open.

The fall of al-Diriya

The last act in the tragedy of the first Saudi state came in April 1818, when the battle for al-Diriya started. Although the oases and towns of Najd fell into the conquerors' hands one after another, there were diehard Wahhabis in each of them who rejected the very idea of peaceful coexistence with 'polytheists' and were wholeheartedly devoted to the Al Saud. They gathered in al-Diriya to take part in the final battle.

The detachments from the capital and other central Arabian oases which confronted the Egyptians were led by Abdallah's three brothers – Faisal, Ibrahim and Fahd – and supported by contingents from Manfuha (under their courageous commander, Abdallah ibn Mazru), from al-Hariq and from Sudair. Old men from the capital defended smaller strongholds. The members of the house of Saud, the Al Muammar and other prominent commanders led separate detachments.[82] The Egyptian pasha disposed of some 2,000 cavalrymen, 4,300 Albanian and Turkish soldiers, 1,300 Maghrebi cavalrymen, 150 gunners with around 15 guns, 20 weapons technicians and 11 sappers.[83]

The oasis of al-Diriya lay along Wadi Hanifa like a ribbon stretching over several kilometres. The oasis and the town itself consisted of several continuous settlements. The citadel of Turaif, with its mosque and various extensions, rose above the locality. It was protected by a high rock on one side and by a canal on the other. Ibrahim began a slow offensive along the wadi. After the first skirmishes, those who vacillated left Abdallah, deserted to Ibrahim and informed him of the situation in the town. The Egyptians' superior artillery enabled them to destroy the Wahhabis' fortifications. To protect themselves from surprise assaults, they built European-style redoubts, as they had done earlier. It seemed for a moment that the Wahhabis would be victorious: Ibrahim's main powder-magazine blew up and the Wahhabis rushed into an attack, but their assault petered out.

Regular supplies of food, munitions and reinforcements ensured the success of Ibrahim's slow advance. His troops were supplied not only from Medina; the pasha of Baghdad also sent him a food caravan. Sick or wounded soldiers were sent to a hospital set up in Shaqra. Some of them recovered and returned to the ranks. Ibrahim made the emirs who had joined him send detachments to fight under his banners at al-Diriya. The casualties in his army were replaced by new soldiers, while the ranks of the defenders of al-Diriya were depleted. The food shortage was felt in the oasis.[84]

The Wahhabis' situation seemed hopeless and there were frequent desertions. The general storm of the town began in early September. Abdallah and some of his relatives took cover in the citadel of Turaif. On 9 September, feeling that all was lost, Abdallah decided to sue for peace. His uncle Abdallah ibn Abd al-Aziz, Ali (the son of Muhammad ibn Abd al-Wahhab) and Muhammad ibn Mishari ibn Muammar came to the Egyptian camp, where Ibrahim demanded that they capitulate. Abdallah's messengers agreed the honourable terms of capitulation of the oasis inhabitants, who continued their resistance for a further two days. Abdallah and his men, who had ensconced themselves in the citadel, fought courageously but Ibrahim brought up all his guns and Abdallah surrendered on 11 September.

The Wahhabis Routed by the Egyptians (1811–1818)

The 6 months of fierce battles were at an end.[85] The Saudi imam had lost some 20 close relatives, including 3 of his brothers. Ibn Bishr estimates the Wahhabis' total losses, strange as it may seem, at a mere 1,300 people and those of Ibrahim at 10,000 near al-Diriya alone.[86] Ibrahim reported to Cairo and Istanbul that the Wahhabis had lost 14,000 killed and 6,000 taken prisoner and that his troops had seized 60 guns.[87]

To celebrate the capture of al-Diriya, a festival with fireworks, public merry-making and cannonades was held in Cairo in October 1818.[88] Thereafter, 'learning about the defeat of the adversaries of the Muslim religion, the sultan expressed his profound satisfaction'.[89] The shah of Iran expressed his delight at the rout of the Wahhabis in a letter to Muhammad Ali.[90]

Abdallah was sent first to Cairo and then to Istanbul, where he arrived with two retainers in early December. The Russian embassy reported back:

Taken prisoner in al-Diriya and brought recently to the capital, the Wahhabi leader, his minister and his imam were beheaded last week. To make more glorious his triumph over the sworn enemies of the cities that are the cradle of Islam, the sultan ordered the *rakab* (the assembly of the topmost persons of the empire) to be convened in the old palace in the capital. Accompanied by a crowd of idlers, the three prisoners were brought there in heavy chains. After the *rakab* ceremony the sultan gave the order for them to be executed. The leader was beheaded in front of the main gate of St Sophia, the minister at the entrance to the palace and the imam in one of the main markets. Their bodies were displayed with their heads under their arms . . . and were thrown into the sea three days later.

His Majesty ordered that a prayer should be performed throughout the empire to thank heaven for the victory of the sultan's weapons and for the annihilation of the sect that had devastated Mecca and Medina and exposed Muslim pilgrims to fear and danger. All insolvent debtors were released from jail, and the government undertook to satisfy their creditors at His Majesty's expense. At his order, huge sums were distributed at mosques and *madrasas* (religious schools) to thank heaven for its mercy . . .[91]

Wahhabism outside Arabia

Muhammad ibn Abd al-Wahhab's teaching, which seemed a purely Arabian phenomenon, unexpectedly found followers thousands of kilometres away. It was disseminated by the pilgrims who visited Mecca in the early nineteenth century. The denunciation of idolatry and of the cult of saints, the opposition to *bida*, the holy war against the 'polytheists' and 'infidels', a combination of class and egalitarian slogans – all these elements of the Wahhabi belief-system and practice found acceptance in countries with different socio-political structures and were adapted to local requirements. Wahhabism penetrated as far as India, Indonesia and Africa.

In India, Muhammad ibn Abd al-Wahhab's teaching had a far-reaching influence.

Some of its elements were used by Said Ahmad Barelwi, a Muslim preacher and politician who was a disciple of Waliullah Shah, a renowned Muslim thinker. He started his preaching activities in the early nineteenth century and visited Mecca in the 1820s. After becoming acquainted with Ibn Abd al-Wahhab's teaching, he became a follower. On his return to India, he settled in Patna, where his numerous supporters began gathering. Adapted to local conditions, the Wahhabi slogans found a response among the Indian Muslims.

In 1824 Said Ahmad declared *jihad* against the infidels. In 1826 his forces invaded Punjab and started routing the Sikhs. By 1830 the Wahhabis had seized Peshawar, established a state of their own and even minted coins with Said Ahmad's name. But the following year, the imam of the Wahhabis was killed. His followers were active in the Muslim regions of India, especially in the north and in East Bengal, and declared *jihad* on the British authorities.

A nineteenth-century writer complained bitterly, 'The hatred which some Indian Moslems bore towards the English – fanned into flames by seditious preachers, who promised them deliverance or paradise – now became the text of every sermon.'[92] The Wahhabis' struggle against the British made a contribution to the Indian people's anticolonialist movement. Waxing and waning, it continued for some decades. The Wahhabis played an important role in the popular insurrection of 1857–59 against British rule.[93]

The Wahhabi centre in Sittan, on the northern frontier, witnessed two dozen expeditions by British colonial troops and was routed only in 1863. But the Wahhabis' activities continued thereafter. According to the British historian W. Hunter, all the governments of British India considered the Wahhabis a source of permanent danger to the Indian empire.[94] That factor may have encouraged the negative attitude to the Saudi state among British officials of the Indian Civil Service in the nineteenth century.

Wahhabism also inspired some Indonesian pilgrims who visited Mecca in the first decades of the nineteenth century. A religious-political movement began in Sumatra, using Wahhabi slogans. Initially it was directed against the local non-Muslims but it then acquired an anti-Dutch character. From 1821 the Dutch authorities waged a war against the Sumatra Wahhabis that was to last some fifteen years.

Some authors hold that Wahhabism exerted an influence not only on Uthman dan Fodio's movement in western Sudan – which led to the creation of the vast state of Sokoto in the early nineteenth century – but also on the Libyan Senussis.[95]

The sultan of Morocco, Moulay Sliman (1792–1822), who was known as a 'knowledgeable, devout and zealous Muslim', used Wahhabi ideas in his struggle against the feudal-tribal fragmentation of the country. He relied on the conception of united power, a united faith and a united state to oppose the separatist trends of the marabouts (local 'saints', heads of the religious brotherhoods). Imitating the Wahhabis, the sultan denounced annual festivals in honour of saints, abolished all taxes that were not stipulated by the Quran and sent Muslim *qadhis* to the Berbers to spread the *sharia* and eradicate the Berber tribes' customary law. Moulay Sliman's Wahhabi reforms threatened the material interests, the power and the very existence of the religious

The Wahhabis Routed by the Egyptians (1811-1818)

brotherhoods and the marabouts. With rare exceptions, they united against the government's Wahhabi policies: the sultan was defeated and forced to abdicate.[96]

In evaluating the place of the Wahhabi movement in the history of the development of Islam, it may be seen as a precursor of the Muslim reformation, i.e. 'the process of adaptation of the religious, philosophical and legal norms of Islam to the new historical conditions, which began in the middle of the nineteenth century and continue to this day'.[97] The fact that leading Muslim *ulama* considered Wahhabism as a religious trend rather than as an Islamic sect created a favourable precedent for the emergence, some decades later, of other reformist groups whose postulates have something in common with those of Wahhabism.

CHAPTER 6

From the Fall of al-Diriya to the Egyptian Evacuation of Arabia (1818–1840)

Egyptian policy in Arabia after the rout of the Wahhabis

After the fall of al-Diriya, the first Saudi state ceased to exist. There were no forces in Najd then to resist the conquerors, and the Egyptians became absolute masters of central Arabia and started to root out the influence of the Saudis and the Wahhabis by fire and the sword.

Emirs, military commanders and *ulama* were tortured, shot (singly and in groups), fastened to the muzzles of guns and torn to pieces. Sulaiman ibn Abdallah, the grandson of Muhammad ibn Abd al-Wahhab, was executed after being forced to listen to the *rabab* (a single-stringed violin), a punishment designed to offend his religious feelings.[1] Members of noble families and military commanders were killed in the towns and oases of Jabal Shammar, Qasim and Dilam and their lands and houses were confiscated.[2]

The members of the Saudi and Al al-Shaikh families and the Najdi nobility (some 400 people, including women and children) were exiled to Egypt. Some of them managed to flee, while others rose to high office in Egypt. One of Muhammad ibn Abd al-Wahhab's grandsons, Abd al-Rahman ibn Abdallah, taught Hanbali law at al-Azhar.[3] Captain G. F. Sadlier describes Ibrahim's campaign as a series of barbaric atrocities and violations of his most sacred obligations. Ibrahim grew rich by plundering the tribes who had contributed to his success and confiscated the properties of those defeated enemies who had once evaded his anger.[4]

Muhammad Ali ordered Ibrahim to raze the Wahhabi capital to the ground. Before destroying the town, the Egyptians extorted money from its inhabitants and looted them ruthlessly. Not only did Faisal ibn Watban Al Dawish not become the ruler of al-Diriya, but he was asked to pay the Egyptians – as the Saudis' legal successors – the arrears of *zakat* for the previous five years. The shaikh of the Mutair refused to pay and had to move to an area in the lower reaches of the Euphrates.[5] Taking advantage of the collapse of the Saudi state, some members of the Al Arayar family seized power in al-Hasa, but Ibrahim Pasha ousted them from eastern Arabia, confiscated the Saudis' lands and houses and plundered the oases.[6]

While feeling no sympathy for the emirate of al-Diriya, Britain nevertheless viewed the strengthening of the Egyptian position in Arabia with disquiet and the British squadron landed troops in al-Qatif.[7] According to H. St John Philby:

> [I]t is difficult to believe that the landing of a considerable force of British troops at Qatif just before or during Muhammad Kashif's occupation . . . was really intended to be a demonstration of cooperation with the Turks. Their establishment on the Hasa coast would clearly have been an indirect challenge to the British position on the 'Pirate Coast', where the Turks were technically entitled to the Wahhabi inheritance.[8]

Britain was anxious to discover Egyptian intentions in the Gulf and Sadlier was sent to meet Ibrahim Pasha. He was the first European to cross Arabia from east to west and visit the ruins of al-Diriya. Ibrahim left Najd in mid-1819, however, and made for Medina. Sadlier's proposal of joint actions against the Wahhabis was of no use to him. Besides, Egypt was generally anti-British. Ibrahim rejected the British offer of cooperation and expelled Sadlier from Jidda in the autumn of 1819. Soon afterwards, the British expeditionary corps evacuated al-Qatif, losing many soldiers as a result of disease.[9]

In late 1819 the British routed and destroyed Ras al-Khaima again. The British garrison was to stay there until July of the following year. The administration of British India prepared a so-called 'general peace treaty' and thereafter imposed it on all the littoral states and Bahrain.[10] In practice, it was a protectorate treaty, supplemented with new articles over the years.

During their conquest of Najd, the Egyptians were anxious to shift part of the expenses for the maintenance of their troops to the local population since the burden of the Arabian campaign was too onerous for Egypt alone. However, Ibrahim soon became aware that the returns from the conquered country did not cover the expenses of its occupation. The Egyptian troops were stationed thousands of kilometres from Cairo and hundreds of kilometres from their main operative base in Hijaz. The caravans with personnel and equipment had to cross vast deserts. Both settled and nomadic peoples were increasingly hostile to the conquerors. There was a shortage of camels and the bedouin often intercepted the food caravans. One can imagine the famine in Najd from the fact that sometimes even Ibrahim's soldiers ate grass. Mutinies occurred among the Egyptian troops.[11]

Finally, Ibrahim decided to evacuate most of his forces from Najd and eastern Arabia, knowing that his father's principal goal was to control the Red Sea basin rather than central Arabia. The Egyptian forces were concentrated in the al-Rass region.

Before leaving a locality, the soldiers destroyed all fortresses and defence structures, drove away livestock, felled palm trees and devastated fields. Sadlier writes that the people of Manfuha were in a more pitiable condition than at any time since the establishment of Wahhabi power. The protective walls around the oases had been razed to the ground. The Turks had taken the previous year's harvest, and neither wheat nor barley was available in the markets. All the horses had been taken away.[12]

Tribal and parochial rivalries revived, with the overt or covert connivance of the new masters, and raids and internecine clashes resumed. The caravan routes became dangerous and even the urban population preferred not to appear in the street unarmed. An impression arose that Egyptian policy was aimed at plunging central Arabia into chaos, decay and ruin and destroying the chances of a renaissance.[13] Small Egyptian garrisons acted as instruments of destruction and plunder rather than as a positive factor for centralization and order. Historians have not discovered even a single administrative act of that period concerned with improving the people's lot or promoting economic activity, not to mention ensuring security.[14]

The Saudi state lay in ruins; its military strength had been crushed and its administrative machinery was destroyed. Unleashed as a result of the rout of the Wahhabis, the forces leading to decentralization seemed to have destroyed the earlier hopes of unity. The process of social development within the framework of a centralized Arabian society was interrupted. The many long years of war had exhausted the scarce resources of central Arabia, and the Egyptian invasion and the ravage of Najd had severely damaged the economy. However, the same forces survived that had rallied central Arabian society more than half a century previously and led to the formation of the emirate of al-Diriya.

After the Saudi state was liquidated, the Najdi peasants, merchants and artisans grieved for the earlier times of stability, personal security and the protection of property and wealth. The Najdi nobility saw the Saudis as heroes: their successful wars had brought rich spoils. The surviving Wahhabi *ulama* bolstered reminiscences of the Saudi state's bygone glory and the earlier 'purity' of the religion.

Side by side with the feudal-tribal dissension, there was a trend towards consolidation, a striving to unite Najd in order to drive out the foreign occupier and restore favourable conditions for a normal life and economic activity. Subsequent developments showed that the small oasis-states had been an outdated form of social and political organization. Within a few years of the collapse of the al-Diriya emirate, the popular movement against foreign occupation had led to the restoration of the Saudi state with its capital in Riyadh.

Feudal-tribal dissension in Egyptian-occupied Najd

Ibrahim Pasha was replaced as governor of Arabia by Khalil Pasha, Muhammad Ali's nephew. Khalil died soon afterwards and was succeeded by his brother, Ahmad Shukri

From the Fall of al-Diriya to the Egyptian Evacuation of Arabia (1818–1840)

Yakan Bey, who remained in Arabia under the name of Ahmad Pasha until 1829, when Muhammad Ali recalled him to Cairo and appointed him head of the military department.[15]

Ahmad Pasha's main task was to stabilize the situation in Mecca and in Hijaz as a whole.[16] Feudal-tribal anarchy broke out in Najd and armed clashes between rival groups of the Hujailan clan occurred in the oasis of Buraida. In the autumn of 1819 Muhammad ibn Mishari ibn Muammar was appointed ruler of Najd. He came from the family who had ruled Ayayna in the days of the birth of the Wahhabi movement. Ibn Muammar tried to restore the ruined town of al-Diriya, thus gaining the sympathy of the people. The population of the neighbouring regions sent delegations to him to express support.[17] Plentiful summer rains ensured a good crop and helped Ibn Muammar to relieve the famine, although food was still short.

Ibn Muammar was not without rivals. For example, Majid ibn Arayar from a clan of Bani Khalid shaikhs regained power in eastern Arabia. The Al Arayar family ruled there up to 1830.[18] Then Turki ibn Abdallah ibn Muhammad ibn Saud appeared on the Najdi stage. He was from a collateral branch of the Saudis and had fled from the Egyptians after the fall of al-Diriya. He acted for some time on behalf of Ibn Muammar, while gathering forces for the future struggle.[19]

One of the last Saudi imam's brothers, Mishari ibn Saud ibn Abd al-Aziz, escaped while being brought from Medina to Yanbu by Egyptian guards. He appeared in Sudair, proclaimed himself imam and seized Washm in March 1820. He found some support in Qasim and other regions. However, Ibn Muammar relied on the Mutair tribe, routed Mishari and took him prisoner.[20]

Ibn Muammar's power remained shaky, with the malcontents grouped round Turki ibn Abdallah. There were soon to be decisive clashes between the rivals. Finally, Turki captured al-Diriya so swiftly that he was able to eat the lunch that the former emir had prepared for his own guests. Then he moved towards Riyadh, where he took Ibn Muammar's son captive. Father and son were both killed in captivity.[21] Ibn Muammar's rule continued for a year, but his reputation as an Egyptian puppet and the continued respect in which the Saudis were held worked against him.

Informed of the unrest in Najd, Muhammad Ali decided to strengthen his garrisons in central Arabia. In the autumn of 1820, Husain Bey arrived in Qasim with reinforcements and took steps to topple the emir from the house of Saud. Turki's supporters ensconced themselves in the Riyadh fortress but, after a short siege, agreed to be taken prisoner. The Egyptians treacherously killed almost all of them, however, although Turki managed to escape.[22]

In March 1821 Husain Bey ordered all al-Diriya citizens who had returned there to gather for a distribution of land. When 230 people had assembled, the Egyptian soldiers slaughtered them. Murder, imprisonment without trial, maiming and torture were common in Najd. The town garrisons robbed the population, and the soldiers felled palm trees and devastated fields. Many inhabitants moved to the desert or to areas outside Najd.[23] Ibn Bishr writes that 'the devil ruled the earth'.[24] The situation was aggravated by a cholera epidemic in 1821.

Before returning to Egypt, Husain Bey gathered hostages from many towns and kept them in a fort in Tharmida[25] until Hasan Bey, the new Egyptian commander, arrived in Najd in the spring of 1822. He was interested only in extortion and plunder. The situation was so intolerable that there were frequent rebellions and outbreaks of armed resistance. The punitive expeditions ended in failure one after another. The Egyptians were short of troops and confined themselves to keeping garrisons in a few key towns – al-Rass, Shaqra, Buraida, Anaiza, Tharmida and Riyadh.[26]

The first attempts to restore local rule – first by Ibn Muammar and then by two members of the Saudi family – failed. However, Wahhabism retained deep roots among the Najdis, who considered the Saudi family as the instrument of Allah's will on earth. As soon as the direct military pressure from Egypt weakened, forces arose that strove to restore centralization and order under the leadership of the house of Saud.

The restoration of Saudi rule under Turki

After escaping from the Egyptians in 1820, Turki hid for some years, presumably in the southern regions, and reappeared on the Najdi stage in May–June 1823, when Ibn Bishr mentions actions by his small detachment in al-Hilwa.[27] He then raided the areas to the north of Riyadh, preparing attacks against the occupation forces.

Turki gathered allies and supporters, including Suwaid, the ruler of Jalajil, a town in Sudair.[28] Detachments from several other areas came with Suwaid. Turki grew bolder and raided the nearby towns of Manfuha and Riyadh, which each had an Egyptian garrison of 600 soldiers. The emir did not yet enjoy the support of all the provinces; Ibn Bishr mentions that Tharmida, Huraimala and al-Kharj were hostile to him while most of the Washm and Sudair oases preferred to temporize.[29]

Meanwhile, a general rebellion against the Egyptians broke out in Qasim, caused by Hasan Bey's extortions. The Egyptians were forced to retreat to Hijaz, leaving garrisons only in Riyadh and Manfuha.[30] Taking advantage of the weakening Egyptian position in Najd in 1823–24, Turki expanded his influence in the environs of Riyadh and Manfuha, leaving the Egyptian garrisons isolated, and subdued Sudair, al-Majmaa and Washm. In late July 1824 Turki increased the pressure on Riyadh, Tharmida and al-Kharj. The Egyptian garrison was withdrawn from Manfuha. Riyadh, too, fell into Turki's hands after a siege lasting several months and the Egyptians retreated to Hijaz. Some areas of Qasim recognized Turki as their ruler. The whole of central Najd was now free of the occupier.[31]

The rule of Turki ibn Abdallah ibn Muhammad ibn Saud lasted from 1823, when he embarked on the conquest of Najd, to his death in 1834. Many historians consider Turki the founder of the second Saudi state because, while he formally recognized the Ottoman empire and in effect the suzerainty of Egypt, in practice he ruled independently. However, the revived emirate was not to achieve genuine independence until the Egyptians finally evacuated Arabia in 1840. It should be noted that the preceding imams had been the descendants of Abd al-Aziz ibn Muhammad ibn Saud,

From the Fall of al-Diriya to the Egyptian Evacuation of Arabia (1818-1840)

while Turki and all subsequent rulers, including King Fahd, Turki's great-great-grandson, were the descendants of Abdallah ibn Muhammad ibn Saud.

In late 1824 Turki settled in Riyadh, which remained the capital of Najd and later of the whole of Saudi Arabia. The construction started of a mosque, a palace and fortifications. In April-May 1825 the emir of Riyadh subdued the province of al-Kharj after several battles.[32]

Turki now controlled al-Arid, al-Kharj, al-Hawta, Mahmal, Sudair, al-Aflaj and Washm. In Qasim, however, only some oases had submitted to him, and Jabal Shammar was virtually out of the emir's reach. Perhaps Turki paid a nominal tax to the Ottoman authorities or to the Egyptians in Hijaz or Cairo,[33] although Ibn Bishr does not mention it. Within the territory under his control, however, he ruled without interference.

Some of the refugees returned to Najd, which was undergoing a temporary period of stability. The most prominent figure among them was Mishari ibn Abd al-Rahman ibn Mishari ibn Saud, who had fled from Egypt. In 1825 he was appointed governor of Manfuha. He was later treacherously to murder Turki. Abd al-Rahman ibn Hasan, one of Muhammad ibn Abd al-Wahhab's grandsons, also returned from exile. He was an outstanding *alim* and taught a whole generation of the younger members of the Al al-Shaikh family.[34] He immediately sent messages throughout Najd, calling on everybody, especially *ulama* and emirs, to return to the 'genuine Islam', to reject the polytheistic practice of the 'so-called Muslims' and to submit to the Imam of the Muslims. The shaikh used his famous grandfather's life as an example of genuine service to the faith.[35] The Finnish-Swedish traveller G. Wallin notes that Abd al-Rahman was a judge in Riyadh in 1845,[36] and W. G. Palgrave, who visited Riyadh in 1862, describes him as the 'chaplain of the palace'.[37] The Saudis' secular power was once more bolstered due to the impact of Wahhabism, though the previous fanaticism had disappeared.

Naturally, having conquered several provinces with relatively dense settled populations, Turki tried to take action against the bedouin. In 1826-28 he raided the subdivisions of the Bani Khalid, Hitaim, Dawasir and other tribes. Soon afterwards, many shaikhs of the Subai, Suhul, Ajman, Qahtan and (probably most pleasing for the ruler) Mutair tribes sent delegations to the emir to express their allegiance. This did not prevent him, however, from breaking his promise and resuming the raids.[38] An important event in 1827/28 was the flight from captivity in Egypt of Faisal (Turki's son).[39] He was twice to rule the emirate of Riyadh.

The lack of major rivals, and the temporary non-intervention in Najdi affairs by the Egyptians and the Turks, enabled Riyadh to subdue Qasim, though not completely.[40] Next came the turn of Jabal Shammar.[41]

As a whole, Hijaz remained beyond the reach of the emir of Riyadh, though his detachments appeared there. According to General Weygand, the historian of Muhammad Ali's military campaigns, the Wahhabis appeared in the suburbs of Mecca in 1826 and temporarily seized Medina, Mecca and al-Taif in October 1827; Ahmad Pasha retained only the sea ports.[42] However, Ahmad Pasha's problems seem to have been caused by local unrest, in which the emir of Riyadh had played a part. In 1827 Yahya, the sharif of Mecca, was killed. Muhammad Ali appointed Muhammad ibn Abd al-Muin ibn Aun in his place, a post that he held up to 1851.

Asir proved a hard nut to crack. Muhammad Ali conducted eleven expeditions against its population and always defeated them in battle, but he could never establish his control over the province with its mountains, valleys and indomitable people.

In 1832, at the height of the war between Egypt and the Turks, some troops rebelled in Jidda, led by a certain Muhammad Agha, nicknamed Turkche Bilmez. Sultan Mahmut II appointed him governor of Hijaz, but the Egyptians' victories in Syria prevented the new pasha from receiving aid from the Turks. Muhammad Ali sent new troops to Hijaz – an infantry regiment and over 1,500 cavalrymen. Turkche Bilmez retreated south to Yemen via Asir, sometimes clashing with the local shaikhs and sometimes concluding alliances with them. Finally, he seized the town of Mokha and was besieged by the Egyptians there. J. R. Wellsted, a British explorer of Arabia who was on board a British ship anchored in Mokha, and Ibn Bishr left descriptions of the battle. In spite of the Turks' desperate resistance, the town was captured and most of the defenders were massacred. Turkche Bilmez fled to a British vessel and managed to reach Istanbul. Muhammad Ali's army occupied Mokha, but did not hold out long.[43]

Eastern and south-eastern Arabia under Turki

There were no forces to the east of Najd to threaten the emirate of Riyadh as the Egyptians did in Hijaz. Naturally, when Turki consolidated his power in Najd he began raids eastwards into al-Hasa (the Eastern Province). By then, Muhammad and Majid, two brothers from the Al Arayar clan, had been ruling the province for some ten years. They may have been appointed formally by Muhammad Ali and even paid him tribute.[44]

In 1830 a strong bedouin alliance of the Bani Khalid, Subai, Anaza, Mutair and Bani Husain, led by the Arayar brothers, invaded Najd. Apart from the settled people of Najd, who were loyal to Turki, bedouin of other tribes supported him. A battle lasting several days was waged between the Najdis and their enemies: Majid was killed and his bedouin were defeated. The battle resolved the rivalry between the Saudis and the Arayars for dominance in eastern Arabia.[45] The town of Hufuf was seized without a battle. Muhammad, the surviving Arayar brother, barricaded himself in the famous Qut fortress, but finally surrendered.

Turki and Faisal stayed in eastern Arabia for forty days. They restored the Wahhabi doctrine and appointed *qadhis* to all important oases. Al-Qatif swore allegiance to the emir of Riyadh, though the Shia formed a sizeable part of its population.[46] The Bani Khalid's attempt to resist the Najdis was suppressed.

Unlike both their predecessors and their heirs, Turki and Faisal pursued a tolerant policy in al-Hasa,[47] which enabled them to strengthen their positions there. It is noteworthy that, while using the old Wahhabi banner, the Riyadh emirs nevertheless deviated from their predecessors' sectarian parochialism and fanaticism. Their

From the Fall of al-Diriya to the Egyptian Evacuation of Arabia (1818–1840)

followers could hardly be considered members of the sect. Therefore, we shall apply the term 'Wahhabis' only sparingly.

In late 1830 Turki imposed Saudi suzerainty on the ruler of Bahrain, Abdallah ibn Ahmad Al Khalifa (1816–43), who also controlled most of Qatar. He was asked to pay the annual *zakat*, to make an immediate payment of 40,000 thalers for the horses left in Bahrain as early as 1811 and to return the fortress of Dammam on the Arabian coast, occupied by Bahrain in 1826. It is not known with which of these demands he complied. Initially, the interests of the rulers of Riyadh and Muscat coincided in their joint opposition to Bahrain, but later they diverged. Within three years, the rulers of Bahrain had severed even the weak bonds of dependence on Riyadh. In 1834 Abdallah Al Khalifa went on the offensive and blockaded the Saudi ports of al-Qatif and al-Uqair.[48]

Even before Saudi control was established over the Eastern Province, the Najdis' old supporters had become active in south-eastern Arabia. In 1821 Saad ibn Mutlaq, son of the former Saudi governor of al-Buraimi, seized these strategically important oases once again and subdued part of Oman.[49] He had, perhaps, no direct ties with Najd at that moment. When Turki established himself as the ruler of Riyadh in 1824, Sultan ibn Saqr, the ruler of Sharja, and Rashid ibn Humaid from Ajman started negotiations with him. A considerable part of the population of Sharja and Ajman still sympathized with the Wahhabis.[50] Simultaneously, the rulers of the coastal states were negotiating with Britain, hoping for support against the Wahhabi threat. But Britain, at that time, adhered to a policy of non-interference in the internal affairs of Arabia.[51]

In 1828 the Wahhabis' supporters on the coast of the Arabian Gulf and the Gulf of Oman paved the way for a new invasion from Riyadh. Turki appointed Umar ibn Muhammad ibn Ufaisan as emir of al-Buraimi and the new ruler began raids on the inner areas of Oman and the coastal strip of al-Batina.[52] Said, the sultan of Muscat, sent a mission with gifts to Riyadh and expressed his readiness to pay tribute.[53] However, strong Najdi forces invaded Oman via al-Buraimi in 1832. Sultan Said agreed to pay the emir of Riyadh 5,000 rials and the two leaders arranged for mutual assistance in suppressing insurrections in their territories and divided up the Arabian coast between them.[54]

According to A. J. Wilson, a British diplomat and historian, 'by 1833 the whole coast of the Persian Gulf acknowledged Wahabi rule and paid tribute'.[55] The British authorities in India admitted that the emir of Najd had become the supreme force in central and south-eastern Arabia, but considered naval supremacy their main task, as it had been earlier.

The emirate of Riyadh under Turki

In the early 1830s Turki enjoyed a strong position in Riyadh. Exhausted by the previous occupation and ruined by the continuous wars, Najd submitted to his power. However, there was discord within the Saudi family. In 1831 Mishari ibn Abd al-

Rahman, the ruler of Manfuha, rebelled against the emir with some subdivisions of the Qahtan tribe. Failing to win wide support, he fled and tried to conclude an alliance with the shaikhs of the Mutair, with some subdivisions of the Anaza and with the emir of Qasim. When his enterprise failed, he took shelter in Hijaz, hoping for the support of Muhammad ibn Aun, the sharif of Mecca. Mishari received refuge in Hijaz, but not military aid. In 1832 he returned to Najd and was pardoned by the imam.[56]

The new state's limited resources and the scanty spoils from raids prompted the nobility to increase the exploitation of its subjects, and it was difficult for the emir to impose the principles of a 'just' treatment of the population. Ibn Bishr describes a characteristic episode. Returning from Hufuf to Riyadh in 1832, Turki convened a large assembly of emirs and reprimanded them severely for tyrannizing the people and taking from them what was not stipulated by the law:

> [Turki said]: 'When you receive my order to take part in a raid, you increase the taxes in your favour. Don't do this, because it is only my compassion for the people that prevents me from imposing an increased camel levy on them for participation in raids, and I collect fewer taxes from them than my predecessor usually did . . . Really, when my order reaches you, you are happy, finding something useful in it for you. You are like those who look at a palm tree and are happy when a strong wind blows because more dates fall down . . . I shall not allow you to take anything from the people. Those of you who are unjust to your subjects will be punished not only by dismissal, but by exile from the country.' Then he addressed the people over the heads of the nobility: 'If an emir oppresses you, report it to me.' Abd al-Aziz ibn Muhammad, the emir of Buraida, stood up and said, 'O, Imam of the Muslims, be concrete and don't speak in general terms in your speech. If you are angry with one of us, tell us about his deeds.' Then Turki said, 'My speech concerns you and people like you, who think that they rule these areas thanks to their swords, though actually it was the sword of Islam and the imam that seized these areas and subdued [them] to you.'[57]

In his letters, Emir Turki advised his subjects to fear Allah and demonstrate their devotion by the belief in monotheism, by prayer and by the payment of *zakat*. He stressed the importance of these three principles, as well as personal responsibility both for one's own behaviour and for that of the community or tribe. The emir denounced usury and warned against attempts to circumvent the prohibition of that practice, recommended all rulers to standardize weights and measures in their territories, and demanded that all agreements, once concluded, 'even with the *dhimmis*' (i.e. Jews, Christians and Zoroastrians), should be inviolable. Emirs were supposed to prohibit smoking, encourage religious education, build mosques and report those who shirked prayers.[58]

In spite of several crop failures, the economic condition of central Arabia stabilized somewhat during Turki's rule after a series of raids, internecine wars and murders. Yet in Sudair and Qasim in 1826–27 people died of famine, resulting from a drought. In the early 1830s prices fell and famine ceased thanks to good crops and relative stability.[59] But a cholera epidemic broke out in Najd first in 1828–29 and then in 1830–32. In April–May 1831 it spread among the pilgrims in Mecca, killing some 20,000 of them. One third of the people in the Syrian caravan died and half in that from Najd. The epidemic spread throughout Najd the following year. Ibn Bishr describes the catastrophe, with so many people dying that they could not be buried in the proper time. Nobody guarded the property left by the deceased. Domestic animals starved to death, finding no water or fodder. Many children died at the mosques to where they brought their sick parents, hoping that somebody would help them. There was nobody to take care of the children either. The oases became depopulated.[60]

The change of emir and Faisal's first rule

The nomadic tribes of central Arabia hardly ever reckoned with the authority of the emir of Riyadh. Two bedouin confederations clashed in the summer and autumn of 1833 close to Anaiza. One of them was led by Muhammad Al Dawish, the new shaikh of the Mutair, and the other was under Zaid ibn Mughailis ibn Haddal, the leader of the Anaiza. The latter were defeated. Turki either could not or did not want to intervene in the intertribal war.[61]

In the same year the ruler of Bahrain launched hostilities against the emir of Riyadh. In early 1834 he attacked the coastal towns of al-Hasa, relying on his fleet and on the fortress in Dammam, situated on the Arabian coast.[62] Faisal ibn Turki besieged the town of Saihat, where the supporters of Bahrain had fortified their position. But at that moment he received a report that his father had been killed in Riyadh by assassins sent by Mishari ibn Abd al-Rahman, who seized power in the capital. Faisal raised the siege immediately and hurried to Hufuf and then to Najd.

Some people hold that Mishari was instigated by the Egyptians. Others, including J. G. Lorimer, believe that the rulers of Bahrain were privy to the murder.[63] Yet Mishari's personal ambitions seem to have played the key role. On 9 May 1834, when Turki was leaving the mosque through the side door, he was surrounded by three men. One of them produced a pistol and shot the imam dead. Zuwaid, Turki's slave, tried to defend him, managed to wound one of the assailants and was then caught, but later fled to Faisal. Mishari appeared immediately with un unsheathed sword in his hand and asked people to swear allegiance to him.[64] Fuad Hamza describes it as 'the first political assassination of that kind in the history of the Saud family'.[65] One can hardly agree with him.

Turki had been a skilful ruler. He used violence and acted ruthlessly only when it was necessary. His attitude to Mishari (who was to be responsible for his murder) is an example of his lack of vindictiveness. However, to forgive one's enemies was not rare in Arabia. It stemmed from the need to find compromises with one's relatives and with strong personalities. Turki lived up to his reputation as a generous man, as the earlier rulers did, and tried to curb the predatory appetites of the nobility. Like his grandfathers and great-grandfathers, he demonstrated his religious zeal and devoted much time to theological studies.[66] It is interesting to note that he studied practical medicine and enjoyed a reputation as a good physician.[67] He hastened Egypt's withdrawal from Najd by his skilful actions. Central Arabia was united for eleven years under his rule.

Turki's assassination led to nine long years of internecine wars and unrest in Najd. During this period, four members of the Saudi family occupied the throne one after another. Mishari ibn Abd al-Rahman held out in power for little more than a month. Perhaps he did not believe that Faisal would dare to resist the *fait accompli* and try to win people's support, for which miscalculation he paid with his head.

Faisal convened his friends in Hufuf and told them of the murder of his father. His supporters – Abdallah ibn Ali ibn Rashid from Jabal Shammar; Abd al-Aziz ibn Muhammad, the ruler of Buraida; Turki al-Hazzani, the ruler of al-Hariq; Hamad ibn Yahya ibn Ghaihab; and Umar ibn Muhammad ibn Ufaisan, the emir of al-Hasa – recognized Faisal as the legitimate imam.[68] Deciding to leave for Riyadh immediately, they soon reached the city. Mishari was taken by surprise. On the night of 28 May 1834 Faisal sent some soldiers to Riyadh who had been born there, hoping that they would meet less resistance. Although they were recognized by Mishari's pickets, they were allowed to take up positions round the fortress. Hearing shots, Mishari barricaded himself inside. The next morning Faisal occupied the town and began the siege.

The defenders of the fortress, who numbered around 150, had sufficient reserves of food and the siege was long. However, Faisal's task was eased owing to the treason of some of the people under siege. His soldiers burst into the fortress, and Mishari was seized and executed.[69]

Faisal's rule began in 1834, when he was about 40 and at the height of his physical and spiritual powers. He hastened to make the capital's citizens swear allegiance and invited *qadhis* from different provinces to Riyadh, where they stayed as his guests for a month before returning home laden with gifts. Then the imam circulated his message in the oases and among the nomads, calling on everyone to be loyal to Islam. The emirs of the oases and the bedouin shaikhs came to Riyadh to express their loyalty to the new ruler. It was only then that Faisal sent tax-collectors to the desert.

Turki's murder had shaken the emir's power, however. Wadi al-Dawasir, al-Aflaj and the Qahtan tribe refused to pay tribute and Faisal had to send troops to suppress the unrest.[70] Soon afterwards, trouble began in eastern Arabia, where the Riyadh army, led by Mameluke Zuwaid, fought against Bahrain. The latter blockaded al-Qatif and al-Uqair again, but was faced with a new danger – the claims of Iran. The ruler of Bahrain agreed to pay Riyadh a symbolic tribute of 2,000 rials and Faisal pledged himself to protect Bahrain from external aggression. The blockade of al-Qatif and al-Uqair was lifted.[71]

Faisal enjoyed great influence in Oman in the mid-1830s. In the winter of 1835–36 J. R. Wellsted, a British naval officer stationed in India, and his companion Whitelock travelled in Oman under the protection of Said, the sultan of Muscat. They reported that in Oman the Wahhabis were sometimes stronger than the sultan.[72] However, the Ibadhis' hostility and Britain's counteraction made the Najdis' position there highly unstable. What Faisal found most disturbing were reports from Hijaz with unmistakable proof that Egypt was preparing for a new invasion of Najd. The emir of Riyadh had to concentrate his limited forces on the western border.

After new defeats in Asir in 1833–34, Muhammad Ali again tried to seize it in 1835, considering the province as the key to Arabia. He sent Ibrahim Pasha Kuchuk and Ahmad Pasha to Arabia with new troops, bringing the total number of Egyptian soldiers there to 18,000. Ibrahim Kuchuk and Sharif Ibn Aun undertook a new expedition, but it had no more success than earlier attempts: the Egyptians were defeated again and suffered heavy losses.[73]

Muhammad Ali sent new reinforcements, led by Khurshid Pasha, whose task was finally to conquer Asir and Yemen. According to F. Fresnel, the French consul in Jidda in 1837, Muhammad Ali may have divided Arabia unofficially into three *pashaliks*: the territories to the north and east of Medina, including Najd, were reserved for Khurshid; Mecca and Jidda were for Ahmad; and Asir and Yemen were for Ibrahim Kuchuk.[74]

The stabilization of Najd was a source of worry for Muhammad Ali, who saw the Riyadh rulers as threatening his plans in Arabia. According to M. Tamisier, a Frenchman in the Egyptian service, 'Muhammad Ali must fear the development of Wahhabism, because these sectarians plan . . . to restore the Arab nation on a new basis.' Fresnel notes that 'the Arabs [of the Arabian peninsula] are very attached to their nationality'.[75] Although Tamisier and Fresnel may have unconsciously projected notions from developed European societies onto Arabia, it is beyond dispute that the period witnessed a collision between the aspirations for Arabian statehood and the expansionist designs of the Egyptian pasha.

Before turning to the events concerning the final Egyptian invasion of Najd, we should mention a new and so far unobtrusive participant in the Arabian drama: the emirate of Jabal Shammar, which was to play an important role in central Arabia. After the emirate of al-Diriya was routed, an internecine struggle began in Jabal Shammar. The Al Rashid clan, who were related to the ruling family, put up an unsuccessful opposition to Emir Muhammad Al Ali. The head of the rebel clan, Ali Al Rashid, and his sons Abdallah and Ubaid were exiled from Hail, the capital of the emirate.[76] Some years later, Abdallah joined Turki's standards and formed a friendship with Faisal, the emir's son. He was among the commanders who swore allegiance to Faisal immediately after his father was assassinated.

Seeking an opportunity to repay his devoted friend's kindness, Faisal dismissed Salih ibn Abd al-Muhsin Al Ali, the ruler of Hail, on the pretext of the complaints made against him. However, it seems that he could not impose Abdallah Al Rashid as the successor and had to allow the people of Hail to decide who would be their next emir. This led to a power struggle that Abdallah and Ubaid were unable to win. Disappointed in Faisal, Abdallah left for Medina, where Khurshid Pasha was gathering troops for the invasion of Najd, and ensured the support of the Egyptians. Meanwhile Ubaid traced and killed Emir Salih. Having removed their rival, the brothers took power in Jabal Shammar and soon started to build a castle in the capital area, Barzan. The castle was later to become the symbol of the Rashidis' glory and might.

The Rashidi brothers swore allegiance to Emir Faisal, who appointed them to rule Jabal Shammar and sent a Wahhabi *alim* to Hail. But at the same time, they gathered camels and sent them to Medina for the Egyptians.[77] It should be noted, however, that different sources carry different accounts of the establishment of the Rashidis' power in Jabal Shammar, and some of them hold Faisal responsible for Salih's death. Philby repeats the same version.[78]

Faisal routed

The Egyptians demanded that the emir of Riyadh either participate in their expeditions against Asir, his secret ally, or supply camels for their troops. Faisal politely avoided doing either, while sending his brother to Mecca with presents for Ahmad Pasha.[79]

In 1835–36 the seasonal rains failed in central Arabia, resulting in widespread drought and famine, and a large number of Najdis moved to the regions of Basra and al-Zubair. Ibn Bishr mentions a comet which appeared in the constellation of Ursa Major as a herald of drought; he interprets this as a punishment for the sin of the assassination of Turki.[80] But, if one believes in omens, both the comet and the drought presaged far more troubles to come. Muhammad Ali decided to impose his power in Najd through his henchman Khalid ibn Saud, the son of the famous Imam Saud. The young emir, the eldest of the surviving brothers of Abdallah (who had been executed), had spent many years at Muhammad Ali's court in Cairo.

In July 1836 troops set out from Cairo, led by Ismail Bey, the former chief of the Cairo police. They consisted of Turks, Albanians, North Africans and Egyptian bedouin and were strengthened by artillery. Faisal tried to prevent the invasion, sending his representatives to the Egyptians with letters promising obedience. He offered to provide 5,000 camels for the Egyptian troops in Asir, but the Egyptians required 15,000, which he declined. The invasion of Najd became inevitable.[81]

After landing in Yanbu, Ismail proceeded to Medina and then to al-Hanakiya. Knowing that the invasion would be made via Qasim, Faisal occupied that region and camped in al-Rass, where the enemy was expected to appear. He remembered that al-Rass had fought valiantly against Ibrahim Pasha some twenty years before. Yet this time, Faisal's soldiers had no will to fight. They remembered their fathers' and elder brothers' fate too well, and everybody was seized by despair. When Faisal started withdrawing military hardware to Anaiza in April 1837, his troops were panic-stricken and scattered.[82]

Faisal returned to Riyadh with a group of loyal followers. He found that the citizens of the capital were in a defeatist mood and were by no means disposed to support him or to sacrifice their life or lands for his sake. Khalid's agents were active in the town and had managed to incite a part of the people against the imam.[83] Feeling that his position in the capital was untenable, Faisal made his way southwards to al-Kharj, and then proceeded to Hufuf, whose governor Umar ibn Ufaisan was loyal to him and placed the local troops at his disposal. Faisal stayed in Hufuf until July 1837. He probably even tried to fight the Egyptians near Riyadh,[84] as J. G. Lorimer mentions.[85]

Qasim recognized Khalid ibn Saud's authority and put up virtually no resistance. The Egyptians then sent a regular detachment and volunteers from Qasim to seize Jabal Shammar. Isa Al Ali, a member of the dynasty that had been dethroned in Hail, persuaded them to appoint him emir. Apparently, the Egyptians did not trust the Rashidi brothers. The town was captured almost without a battle and Abdallah and his brother Ubaid fled. Satisfying themselves with monetary contributions, most Egyptians returned to Qasim. However, Isa held out for some months in Hail. The extortions and atrocities committed by his Egyptian protectors reached such a degree that the people rebelled against the occupiers and their puppets, an additional factor being the influence of the Rashidi brothers, who had taken refuge in the desert. In Hail itself, no Egyptian dared to appear in the streets alone for fear of being killed. The Egyptians' situation became intolerable and they evacuated Jabal Shammar. Isa ibn Ali went with them. Abdallah ibn Rashid returned to Jabal Shammar as ruler.[86]

In May 1837 Ismail Bey and Khalid entered Riyadh. The first period of Faisal's rule (1834–37) had formally ended. None of the sources mentions any oaths of allegiance to the conquerors by the leading *ulama*; on the contrary, many of them went to the southern regions to promote resistance to the occupier.[87]

The Riyadh emir's rapid defeat and the easy occupation of Najd by the Egyptians may be explained by the cruel legacy of Ibrahim Pasha, his invasion and the calamities that befell the region. The Najdis were aware of the Egyptians' military superiority, especially in artillery. The whole of central Arabia had been weakened by the drought, famine and epidemics. Undoubtedly, the arrival of Khalid ibn Saud caused divided loyalties among those who were loyal to the Saudi family. In any case, the people of Najd only rebelled against the occupier when they realized that submission had not saved them from violence and plunder.

After capturing Riyadh, Khalid sent a letter to Turki al-Hazzani, the emir of al-Hariq, asking him to swear allegiance. The answer characterized the general attitude in the southern oases: 'We are your subjects, unless the Turkish soldiers come to our region. But if you ask us to submit to the Turks, we shall fight them.'[88]

Led by Ismail, the Egyptians and their allies, numbering some 7,000, set out southwards in July 1837 but suffered an outright defeat near al-Hilwa. The rout was so crushing that the Egyptians' bedouin allies seized their horses and fled from the battlefield. All the guns were left behind. Khalid, Ismail Bey and some Egyptian officers escaped with a small detachment. Thus a sizeable part of the Egyptian expeditionary corps in Najd was routed as early as July 1837.[89]

In an attempt to regain the capital, Faisal besieged it but he failed to capture it after a period of two months. The Qahtan and Subai bedouin attacked him from the rear and scattered his troops.[90]

The two parties' forces proved equal for the time being, though an Egyptian reinforcement, sent by Khurshid Pasha, came to Qasim in early 1838. The Egyptians reached an agreement with Faisal on dividing Najd virtually into two parts: Faisal retained his control over eastern Arabia, al-Buraimi and part of southern Najd, while central Najd submitted formally to Khalid.[91] However, Khurshid Pasha arrived in Najd in person in May 1838 and reached Anaiza in mid-June, meeting no resistance. As previously, one of the main tasks of his expedition was to collect camels to be sent to Hijaz, Asir and, probably, Egypt. Abdallah came from Hail to Anaiza and met Khurshid. He persuaded the pasha to recognize him as emir of Jabal Shammar on condition that he swore allegiance to the Egyptians.[92] Thus Abdallah abandoned his old friend Faisal, fearing to lose both his throne and his head.

Muhammad Al Dawish, the shaikh of the Mutair, and Fahd Al Suyaifi, the shaikh of the Subai, visited Khurshid to express their loyalty.[93] Khurshid fortified Anaiza as his main base for several months and built a strong fortress there. According to Philby, its ruins survived to 1925 and even then the local people still called it Khurshid's fort.[94]

In October 1838 the Egyptians set out for Riyadh, where a detachment led by Khalid ibn Saud joined them. Altogether Khurshid had 4,000 soldiers and 10 guns. They moved south to finish off Faisal, who had barricaded himself in Dilam. After a siege lasting over a month, Dilam was captured on 10 December 1838. Faisal was taken to Egypt as a prisoner for the second time. Central Arabia was routed again and lay under the heel of the Egyptians.[95]

The final period of the Egyptian occupation

Khurshid Pasha's rule as Muhammad Ali's vicegerent in Najd continued for eighteen months. He guaranteed the security of all those who had fought for Faisal, provided that the emir surrendered and kept his word.[96] One may agree with Alois Musil, a Czech orientalist, that Khurshid managed to establish law and order in inner Arabia.[97] This time, the Egyptians considered Najd as part of their permanent possessions rather than a hostile state that could be plundered. Khurshid planned to spread his power from central Arabia to al-Hasa, Oman[98] and, perhaps, Iraq.[99]

Ibn Ufaisan, the Wahhabi emir of al-Hasa, who was loyal to Faisal, fled. The rest of the population expressed its loyalty to the Egyptians, who sent garrisons to the towns of eastern Arabia and established effective control over it. Khurshid Pasha preferred not to antagonize the local people, but Muhammad Efendi, whom he appointed vicegerent of the province, unleashed a wave of extortions and plunder, and the acceptance of the new masters turned to hatred. Muhammad Efendi was killed and the Egyptians had to change their henchmen. The occupation of al-Hasa was anything but peaceful.[100]

Khurshid Pasha tried unsuccessfully to compel the ruler of Bahrain to resume the payment of tribute to the Najdi Emir Khalid, an Egyptian puppet, in order to allow the Egyptians to control the island of Tarut and the fortress of Dammam and to extradite Umar ibn Ufaisan, who had fled to Bahrain.[101] The British began to show signs of nervousness. As early as 1838 Colonel Campbell, the British consul-general in Cairo, warned Muhammad Ali against trying to strengthen his position in the Gulf region, especially in Bahrain. The British authorities in India ordered Admiral Maitland, the commander of the naval squadron in the Gulf, to protect Bahrain if necessary.[102]

From the Fall of al-Diriya to the Egyptian Evacuation of Arabia (1818-1840)

Hearing of Muhammad Ali's successes in Syria and Arabia, Abdallah Al Khalifa, the ruler of Bahrain, decided to pay Khurshid a symbolic tribute of 2,000 thalers a year, though he refused to admit his permanent representative to the island. Up to Egypt's evacuation of Arabia in 1840, Bahrain made advances to the Egyptians and the British,[103] but Weygand's assertion that the Egyptians occupied Bahrain[104] is erroneous.

In 1838 and 1839 the Egyptian presence was felt in Kuwait and Khurshid Pasha's agent appeared in the shaikhdom to purchase food. J. C. Lorimer supposes that the agent had also been charged with political and intelligence functions in connection with Khurshid Pasha's intention of seizing Iraq from the Turks. Jabir Al Sabah, the ruler of Kuwait, feared the Egyptians so greatly that he seated the Egyptian representative in the place of honour next to himself. On one occasion, the Egyptians sent a military cargo by a Kuwaiti ship around Arabia to al-Qatif.[105] Britain was becoming increasingly nervous.

At the same time, Khurshid Pasha started an advance on Oman. His henchman was Saad ibn Mutlaq, who served him no worse than he had served Faisal. Abu Dhabi and Sharja supported him, but Dubai and Umm al-Qaiwain avoided submitting to the Egyptians. Captain Hannel, the British resident, visited the coastal regions of Trucial Oman and signed agreements with four rulers, who promised to support the British. Hannel wrote to Saad ibn Mutlaq, advising him to return to Najd, and started instigating the Muscat tribes of Oman against him. Such was Britain's unease that a blockade of the Egyptian-controlled ports of the Gulf was considered in 1840.[106]

In Asir, Muhammad Ali's troops won several battles but they could not conquer the country and a new insurrection broke out there in September 1837. Although it was suppressed in May 1838, the hopeless campaign continued even as late as 1840, waged by Ahmad Pasha from Mecca and Ibrahim Pasha Kuchuk from Hodeida.[107] The attempts to hinder the Egyptian advance in Asir and Yemen, and to set up a naval base and a coaling station in the north-western part of the Indian Ocean, led to Britain's seizing Aden in 1839.

In 1840 Muhammad Ali's empire collapsed. In the opinion of many historians, the Egyptian ruler's decision to evacuate Arabia, Syria and Crete was the consequence, first, of France's failure to give him the expected aid and, second, his inability to resist British might. Egypt accepted the evacuation conditions in the autumn of 1840, but the country's growing weakness was felt in Arabia before this.

Muhammad Ali ordered the evacuation of Najd and Yemen in March 1840, and the withdrawal of Khurshid's troops from Najd and the Eastern Province and Ibrahim Kuchuk's forces from Yemen was in full swing by June. The Egyptian ruler needed to concentrate his troops closer to home in anticipation of a large-scale war between Egypt and France, on the one side, and the Turks, Britain and their allies, on the other. Although nobody knew it at the time, the Egyptians had left central Arabia for ever. Symbolic Egyptian garrisons were left in Najd to 'show the colours' and support Khalid.[108]

CHAPTER 7

The Second Saudi State (1843-1865)

In the 1840s Egypt was virtually removed from the Arabian political stage. The Sublime Porte was still unable to intervene actively in Najdi affairs, nor did it wish to do so. The British were preoccupied with the consolidation of their positions on the coast of the Arabian Gulf and the Gulf of Oman. With central Arabia again left to its own fate, the conditions emerged for a restoration of the Saudi state within a limited geographic area.

From the Egyptian evacuation to Faisal's return

Emir Khalid only remained in power for a year after Khurshid's troops had left central Arabia. In 1840, when Muhammad Ali capitulated, the Porte claimed Najd on the grounds that it had been conquered by the sultan's vassal and Khalid was therefore an Ottoman vassal. At least, this is the interpretation given by the renowned Turkish historian A. Cevdet.[1] But Khalid's position was growing steadily weaker and he was widely hated as an Egyptian puppet. During his exile in Egypt, he had been exposed to the concepts of a European education, which might actually have harmed rather than enhanced his reputation in Najd. He gave himself up to entertainment and pleasure, which was also injurious to his prestige. The Egyptian soldiers who remained in the country received no salary and engaged in extortions.[2]

Feudal discord resumed. In June-July 1841 Najd was subjected to a war which had been sparked off by raids by subdivisions of the Anaza tribe, Qasim's ally, and the reciprocal raids by a group of the Shammar tribe. There was a personal enmity between the rulers of Buraida and Jabal Shammar, based on the rivalry over the caravan routes that crossed central Arabia. The Rashidi brothers defeated two military expeditions from Qasim, which was a sufficient illustration of the rise of their emirate.[3] It was an important step towards the establishment of its future hegemony in Najd.

Khalid managed to retain some influence in the Eastern Province and even sent Saad ibn Mutlaq again to undertake operations in Oman, yet his plans did not bear fruit.[4] In August 1841, when Khalid had gone to say farewell to Khurshid Pasha, a distant relative of his, Abdallah ibn Thunayyan raised the banner of revolt. He was a great-great-grandson of the founder of the Saudi house and the only man from the Al Thunayyan branch to have ruled Najd for a time. Earlier, Ibn Thunayyan had taken refuge with the Muntafiq tribe in southern Iraq; he then appeared in Najd and enlisted the support of Turki al-Hazzani, the ruler of al-Hariq and Imam Faisal's former ally. The members of Muhammad ibn Abd al-Wahhab's family, as well as the Subai, Ajman and Al Murra tribes, supported the leader of the revolt. He called people to drive out the remaining Egyptian troops, who then numbered about 1,000. Feeling his position to be insecure, Khalid offered an *aman* (pardon) to Ibn Thunayyan, which the latter rejected. In the autumn Khalid withdrew his troops to the Eastern Province, either to save his life or to gather his strength. He was never to return to Riyadh.

After Khalid's withdrawal, Ibn Thunayyan established his control over Najd. Initially, he had a few hundred followers, but their number grew considerably. In late 1841 Ibn Thunayyan seized Riyadh. After the Egyptian garrison agreed to evacuate the fortress, Najd was liberated from all foreign troops. Other Egyptian garrisons apparently scattered; at least, there is no information on their destiny.[5]

Ibn Thunayyan tried to establish himself as the emir of Riyadh, but his power was virtually non-existent in Qasim, Jabal Shammar and the Eastern Province. His first raid was on al-Hasa, where Khalid was located with a detachment of Egyptian mercenaries. Khalid tried to resist with Bahrain's assistance, but was defeated. He fled to Bahrain, then to Kuwait and then to Hijaz via Qasim, settled there and received a pension from Muhammad Ali.[6]

Umar ibn Ufaisan was sent to Hufuf, gradually established control over the province on behalf of the emir of Najd and even seized al-Uqair from Bahrain. The main towns and oases submitted to Riyadh, but the new emir's attempts to advance towards Oman faced resistance from the British.[7]

Ibn Thunayyan sent gifts to Muhammad ibn Aun, the sharif of Mecca, and to Uthman Pasha, the new Ottoman governor of Jidda, appointed in January 1841.[8] Ibn Thunayyan's methods, probably inherited from the Egyptian occupiers, were cruel. He executed many of his adversaries, including members of the Al Sudairi clan, despite the Arabian tradition of pardoning one's enemies. He was hated by the people, perhaps because of the vast taxes he collected in the impoverished country. Dari ibn Rashid, a chronicler from Jabal Shammar, considers him 'a man of courage [but] a shedder of blood, who killed many of the pious . . . and whom, therefore, the people hated while they loved Faisal'.[9]

In 1843 Faisal ibn Turki fled Egypt, where he had been held prisoner since 1838. Some historians hold that he was helped by Abbas Pasha, Muhammad Ali's grandson, who either hoped for Faisal's future assistance or dreamed of an independent empire and wanted to enlist the cooperation of the people of Arabia. It is probable that both Muhammad Ali and his heirs understood that an independent emirate in the centre of Arabia would oppose the Ottoman empire.[10]

Faisal arrived in Jabal Shammar, where he received a cordial welcome from his old friend, Abdallah Al Rashid. G. A. Wallin writes that Abdallah and his brother Ubaid, who was notorious for his cruelty, enjoyed firm control over Jabal Shammar. Earlier, the people of Hail had been afraid to travel alone to a neighbouring oasis, but now 'one may go from one end of their land to another, bearing his gold on his head'.[11] Abdallah's power spread to many non-Shammar nomadic tribes:

> From Alkasim as far up as to Hawran, and from the lands of Ibnu Sa'ood in the eastern parts of Negd, as far as the mountains of Alhigaz, the nomads have all been subdued and obliged to acknowledge the sway of Ibnu Alrashid by paying him the Zaka tax.[12]

When Abdallah had a choice between Egyptian dominance (the emir probably did not know that the Egyptians were leaving Arabia for good) and a vassal dependence on Faisal, he preferred the latter, particularly as Faisal was his friend, and friendship is an important factor in Arabian politics. The ruler of Hail offered soldiers, animals and money to the emir. Faisal circulated messages throughout Najd, announcing his return and calling on people to support him. When Ibn Thunayyan learned of this, he mobilized his supporters, but desertions soon started among his troops.

Faisal's plans were hampered by Jabal Shammar's enmity for Qasim, especially for Buraida. Its governor might be expected to oppose Faisal, who was supported by Ibn Rashid. If the whole of Qasim had remained Ibn Thunayyan's ally, he might have retained power. However, the town of Anaiza entrusted its fate to his rival.

Najd sided gradually with Faisal – first Qasim, then Sudair and Washm – and Ibn Thunayyan fled to Riyadh. The Subai, Suhul, Ajman and Mutair tribes supported Faisal and his small army grew thanks to numerous defectors from Ibn Thunayyan. Faisal suggested that he leave the capital with all his property, settle anywhere in Najd and receive a generous pension. Ibn Thunayyan declined and ensconced himself in the fortress, though his situation had become hopeless. The capital's citizens joined Faisal.

Riyadh fell in the summer of 1843. Ibn Thunayyan was caught and died in jail in July, perhaps poisoned on Faisal's orders. According to an Arabian chronicler called Dari ibn Rashid, however, the dethroned emir was killed by warders in the jail whose relatives had been executed during his rule. By appointing them to guard Ibn Thunayyan, Faisal had in effect sentenced him to death.[13]

After nine years of chaos, internal struggle and foreign occupation, the emirate of Najd returned to life. Faisal once again became master of his own house: he was to rule for some two decades. The trend towards centralization was now so strong in Najd that the emirate could no longer return to the feudal-tribal internecine conflicts that had continued for some centuries before the Saudis' rise. Whenever a strong enough leader emerged and there was no direct intervention from outside, the centripetal forces quickly united the regions of central and eastern Arabia.

Faisal was indeed a strong ruler. He had experience of life in the more developed society of Egypt and of rule under Arabian conditions, and he knew how to combine cruelty with gentleness and inflexibility with a readiness to compromise. The growing contacts with the Egyptians, Turks and British made the emir of Riyadh take increasing account of the external world. He understood that central and eastern Arabia could not be isolated from developments in other countries.

The restoration of the Saudis' Riyadh emirate

The new Saudi state encompassed less territory than the emirate of al-Diriya did. Separatism was strong within Najd in spite of the growing stability. Philby observes that:

> Najd soon resumed the even tenor of its normal life. That was by no means synonymous with a life of peace, prosperity and harmony, whose blessings have always been rare or intermittent in the desert . . .[14]

After establishing control over the central regions of Najd, Faisal's next task was to regain the Eastern Province (al-Hasa). In the autumn of 1843 he besieged Dammam, which was controlled by the Bahrainis. A conflict had occurred within the ruling dynasty in Bahrain: the former ruler had fled to the mainland and settled in Dammam. Simultaneously, Faisal attacked the Manasir, Al Murra and Bani Hajir tribes, who supplied the fortress with all their needs.

The Bahraini garrison surrendered in March 1844 and the Najdi troops seized considerable spoils. The emir of Riyadh left his garrison of 100 men in the fortress in place of the Bahrainis. Muhammad ibn Khalifa, the new ruler of Bahrain, agreed to resume payment of the annual tribute to Riyadh and repay the arrears as a reward for the elimination of his rival. Thus Faisal started the new period of his rule from the liquidation of the small but troublesome Bahraini enclave and the restoration of his formal suzerainty over the island.[15]

Revolts broke out in the Eastern Province as a result of the struggle between the Bani Khalid and the Ajman. The nomadic Ajman followed the usual route of the Arabian tribes – from the south to the north or from the south-west to the north-east. They were weak and scattered during their migration from Najran. They had no pastures of their own, depended on other tribes and were their unequal clients. Emir Turki supported them, however, and allowed them to settle in the Eastern Province, in the area that traditionally belonged to the Bani Khalid. One of the reasons behind his support might have been to create a counterweight to the Bani Khalid and their nobility, who periodically rebelled against Riyadh and had once been its rivals.

The Ajman's strength gradually increased and they grew aggressive. In 1845 Falah ibn Hithlain, the supreme shaikh of the Ajman, angered the ruler of Riyadh and a punitive expedition was sent against him from Najd. This was in retaliation for an Ajman raid on a caravan carrying pilgrims, including Persians and Bahrainis, to Mecca. After being plundered, many pilgrims had died of thirst in the desert, left there by the bedouin, who carried off rich spoils. The emir of Riyadh could not ignore such a challenge to his power: it was a threat both to his authority and to his income from the pilgrim caravans.

In November 1845 Faisal led numerous forces against the Ajman and Ibn Hithlain fled to the Gulf. The junior shaikhs of the Ajman and Subai came to the imam and stated that they had had nothing to do with the raid on the caravan. Faisal forgave them, stipulating that they should leave the Bani Khalid's lands within ten days. Ibn Bishr, the famous chronicler, to whom frequent reference is made in the present book, accompanied Faisal in his campaign for a time.

In 1846 Ibn Hithlain returned with his tribe and contacted one of the Mutair shaikhs, but the latter helped Faisal to take him prisoner. The shaikh of the Ajman was chained, brought to Hufuf and executed. His son Rakan became the new head of the tribe. Together with the junior shaikhs, he asked for Faisal's pardon, promising to return the spoils and vowing loyalty to the emir. The Ajman clearly understood who had become the master of the desert and nothing more was heard of them for fifteen years.[16] Having established his control over the Eastern Province, Faisal turned to the south: al-Aflaj and Wadi al-Dawasir. In 1845 he sent troops to suppress the rebellion in al-Aflaj.[17]

While the emir of Riyadh was engaged in suppressing the Ajman and restoring peace and order in the southern provinces of Najd, the old enmity between Qasim and Jabal Shammar broke out again. In September 1845 the inhabitants of Anaiza raided the Shammar and seized their rich caravan. In response, the Shammar ambushed the Anaizis, killing hundreds of people and seizing numerous herds. Abdallah ibn Zamil, the emir of Anaiza, was taken prisoner. Abdallah Al Rashid's brother Ubaid had the emir and his relatives executed, in defiance of the traditional Arabian respect for prisoners' lives. Ubaid described his victory in verse. Later on, Charles Doughty, the great British traveller, heard these same verses recited in Arabia.[18] Ubaid's poem contained the usual boasts of the victor: he claimed to have killed ninety men, his hand tiring of holding his sword and his sleeves becoming caked with his enemies' blood.

Ubaid and Talal, the Shammar emir's son, returned to Hail and successfully raided the Anaza, Qasim's allies. It was difficult for Ibn Rashid to pacify Faisal, who was infuriated by the war between his vassals. The ruler of Jabal Shammar sent Faisal an explanatory letter, in the form of a poem, which allegedly made a favourable impression on the emir.[19]

As long as Abdallah ibn Rashid was alive, relations between Hail and Riyadh remained friendly. While retaining a broad autonomy, Abdallah acknowledged that he was Faisal's vassal. The emirs' friendship was supplemented by intermarriage between the families. Faisal's elder son Abdallah married Abdallah ibn Rashid's daughter, whose brother Talal, in his turn, was Faisal's son-in-law.[20] Ubaid spent two or three months every year in Riyadh as Faisal's guest. In 1847 Faisal even helped the

The Second Saudi State (1843–1865)

Shammaris to combat the Anazas, their traditional enemies. Jabal Shammar expanded northwards and in 1838 it annexed the large oasis of Jawf, some 350 km to the northwest.

Abdallah died in May or June 1847 and was succeeded by his son Talal, then aged 25, although it was Ubaid with his reputation as a strong leader who had been expected to occupy the throne of Hail. But Ubaid was allegedly reluctant to take power and ceded it to Talal. The latter's first action was to send camels and horses to Riyadh as a sign of his continuing dependence on the central government.[21]

The unsolved problem of Qasim and the struggle with the Ajman

Faisal never managed to establish full control over Qasim. According to C. Huber's calculations in the 1870s, the province included some 20 towns and villages. Buraida, with a population of some 10,000, lived mainly by the profits of the camel caravans.[22] Up to the early 1860s it was ruled by the Al Ulayyan, the biggest feudal lords in the region. The population of Anaiza was 18–20,000 with another 1,000 in the neighbouring villages.[23] It was ruled by the clan of Al Zamil, which belonged, like the other emir clans, to the settled bedouin nobility, but, unlike the others, enjoyed very limited power. Travellers described Anaiza as an 'urban republic' and its emir as *primus inter pares* or even an 'elected president'.[24]

The decisive say in town affairs belonged to the well-off inhabitants of Anaiza, each of whom sent one or two camels with two or four riders to the local troops and paid a regular tax for the maintenance of policemen from among the *abds*, for payments to herdsmen and for public hospitality. They participated in the government of Anaiza together with the feudal nobility through the emir's council.[25] Relations between the feudal and merchant nobility and the poor of the town were not free of tension, as is seen indirectly from Doughty's observation, 'But many a poor man (in his anger) will contradict, to the face, and rail at the long-suffering prudence of Zâmil!'[26]

In 1846–47, when the sharif of Mecca invaded Najd, the population of Qasim demonstrated their readiness to collaborate with him.[27] After the Hijazis left, the emir of Riyadh replaced the rulers of the principal towns. Yet a new revolt occurred in Qasim in the winter and spring of 1848–49. The local nobility did not recognize the emirs, who had been appointed from the centre and supported different branches of the old ruling families. Murders and treason alternated with peaceful periods, but the province remained unconquered.

First Anaiza and then Buraida opposed the central authorities. In the spring of 1849 Faisal gathered all available forces under the command of his sons Abdallah, Muhammad and Saud and his brother Jiluwi. The troops were accompanied by several *ulama*, including Muhammad ibn Abd al-Wahhab's great-grandson, Abd al-Latif. Ibn Bishr asserts that Faisal wanted to avoid bloodshed, in spite of his military superiority, and sent the following message to the people of Qasim:

Religion is useless unless it is expressed in a community, and a community cannot exist without subordination. You have refused to carry out our orders and ceased to obey us. You know that war is a fire that consumes men like brushwood, and I sicken at the idea of killing even one Muslim. Therefore do not make me shed your blood, but return to the obedience you and your fathers observed earlier.[28]

The rulers of Qasim were also inclined towards peace at that moment and started negotiations. Faisal stipulated that Qasim must pay *zakat* and take part in military operations. The negotiations ended in an agreement, which was soon violated by both parties, whose tribal allies took part in mutual raids. Faisal's son Abdallah defeated the forces of Qasim, led by Abd al-Aziz Al Ulayyan, the ruler of Buraida, in a battle near Yatima.[29]

Resistance was futile and the ruler of Buraida's attempts to gather strength were unsuccessful. He and other leaders of Qasim fled Anaiza, and the local nobility began negotiations with Emir Faisal with the mediation of Shaikh Abdallah Abu Butayyan, the local *qadhi*. A certain Muhammad ibn Abd al-Rahman ibn Bassam guaranteed the implementation of the peace terms by the inhabitants of Anaiza.[30] The family of Al Bassam, rich merchants of Anaiza, had trade partners even as far as Bombay. Doughty mentions one of the Al Bassam in his *Travels*.[31] Faisal promised to forgive the citizens and they recognized his suzerainty and allowed him to occupy the town. His troops entered Anaiza and the emir proclaimed a general amnesty.

Abd al-Aziz Al Ulayyan, the leader of the revolt, was still in Buraida. Faisal did not dare to dismiss the traditional ruler lest this strengthen the opposition to his power in Qasim. Abd al-Aziz's family begged for a pardon on his behalf and Faisal permitted him to continue as the ruler of Anaiza. At the same time, he appointed his brother Jiluwi as ruler of the whole of Qasim and left him in Anaiza with a detachment of loyal soldiers. It was a deviation from the old practice: earlier the province had no single ruler, and al-Diriya confined itself to appointing or approving the rulers of the two main towns.[32]

By the time that Faisal returned to Riyadh, the news of his victory had reached the Eastern Province and delegations of notables arrived from Hufuf and al-Qatif to confirm their submission and loyalty. Left to rule Buraida, Abd al-Aziz was apprehensive of Riyadh's revenge. He fled to Hijaz in 1850, sought the protection of Muhammad ibn Aun, the sharif of Mecca, and tried to persuade him to invade Najd. The sharif refused to take part in a campaign because of a shortage of forces. Faisal's son Abdallah raided the Ataiba tribe on the very border of Hijaz in the autumn of 1850. The presence of the fugitive emir of Buraida was an irritant to the sharif and, at Abd al-Aziz's request, he asked Faisal to forgive him. The imam agreed on condition that Abd al-Aziz take part in an expedition against Qatar with troops from Qasim. Abd al-Aziz returned to Buraida in early 1851. It appears that the emir of Riyadh could neither enlist the support of the Qasim nobility nor do without a compromise with its acknowledged leader.[33]

Over the next three years, the main problems faced by Riyadh were the raids by various tribes. Then in May 1854 Anaiza rebelled again. The local nobility, especially the Al Zamil clan, was dissatisfied with Jiluwi's rule in Qasim. Doughty reports that he 'daily vexed the people with his tyrannically invented exactions'.[34]

The Al Bassam family opposed the revolt, since hostilities would be harmful to their commerce. But Yahya al-Salih, a poorer member of the town council, agreed to lead the revolt and asked only for fifty swords to arm his followers. Having received the arms, his detachment approached the citadel and were able to drive Jiluwi away without bloodshed.[35]

The participation of the poor lent a new dimension to the revolt. On the one hand, the poorest part of the population opposed the oppression under the rule of the emir of Riyadh, while, on the other, a rich merchant family denied its support to the revolt. Shaikh Abdallah Abu Butayyan, who had served Riyadh loyally for a long time as the *qadhi* of Anaiza, left the town soon after Jiluwi. Abdallah ibn Yahya Al Zamil, nicknamed Sulaim, became the new emir of Anaiza.

Faisal began gathering forces and soon his son Abdallah appeared near Anaiza with troops. The attackers began felling palm trees. Several battles were waged without either party winning a decisive victory. Talal Al Rashid came to help Faisal with the settled and nomadic Shammar. The people of Anaiza sued for peace. Faisal gave them an *aman* and even allowed Abdallah Al Zamil to continue as the local emir. The revolt ended in late 1855, but Faisal had hardly increased his power in Qasim. He had to remove the ruler he had appointed earlier, while the leader of the revolt retained his post.[36]

In the mid-1850s abundant rains led to a bumper crop and food prices fell. But at the same time, a cholera epidemic broke out, carried by Indian pilgrims to Mecca in 1846. Ibn Isa, an Arabian chronicler, describes the grave consequences of cholera in Najd in the second half of the 1850s.[37]

In 1859 disturbances resumed in Buraida in the form of a blood feud between the rival clans of the nobility. Faisal was forced to intervene. Abd al-Aziz was taken prisoner and brought to Riyadh, but was again appointed emir of the town. Under the prevailing conditions, he was probably indispensable.[38]

In 1860 the Ajman started a new revolt and became increasingly bold. Strong troops, led by the emir's son Abdallah, were sent to the east. On 9 April 1860 they waged a battle near al-Mallaha, some 30 km south of Kuwait, following the best bedouin traditions of the pre-Islamic era. Seven Ajman girls, daughters or relatives of the shaikhs, sat in special palanquins on the backs of seven camels. Seven beautiful virgins from noble families appeared before the bedouin in their best dresses and with their hair down, shouting warlike slogans. The fighters were wildly excited, seeing that they would protect, in particular, the beautiful girls, who personified the tribe's honour. It was a bloody battle. The Ajman faced more disciplined and organized urban and settled people, who were supported by the Subai, Suhul, Qahtan and Mutair tribes. Some 700 Ajman were killed and the rest fled, leaving their virgins and camels and all their property. They took refuge in Kuwait. The event was celebrated in Riyadh, as well as in Basra and al-Zubair, which had suffered from the Ajman's raids and now sent

Abdallah precious gifts on the occasion of his victory.[39]

Yet a complete victory was far off. The Ajman were still strong and entered into an alliance with the powerful Muntafiq tribe of southern Iraq. Both tribes started raiding the environs of Basra, al-Zubair and Kuwait.

Faisal proclaimed a *jihad*. A battle was waged near Jahra on 27 March 1861 and the Ajman and Muntafiq were defeated again. The Najdis drove the enemy close to the Gulf shores; when the tide came in, the sea swallowed some 1,500 fighters, who were ignorant of the danger. The victory caused a new outburst of joy in Iraq and Najd.[40] Yet Abdallah's bloody victories over the Ajman led to their hostility over many decades and were later to cost him his throne.

After his victories in the east, Abdallah turned to Qasim. Fearing the worst, Abd al-Aziz, the ruler of Buraida, fled to Anaiza and then to Mecca. On the way, a detachment sent by Abdallah ibn Faisal intercepted him and both Abd al-Aziz and his son were killed. His other son, who had taken part in Abdallah's campaign against the Ajman, was caught and murdered in jail.[41]

In spite of two major victories in 1860–61, Faisal's emirate was threatened again. As before, the threat originated from Qasim, particularly from Anaiza. Its people described their rebellions against Riyadh in 1854–55 as 'the first war' and the hostilities that started in 1862 as 'the second war'. The formal pretext for the new revolt was the fact that Abd al-Aziz had been killed while leaving the town, accompanied by a detachment of its citizens, i.e. while he was a guest of Anaiza and enjoying its protection. The people of Anaiza began intercepting the small detachments of the emir of Riyadh.

The Anaiza troops appeared in the environs of Buraida and skirmishes occurred throughout the province. Faisal proclaimed a *jihad* again. A major battle was waged in the environs of Anaiza on 8 December 1862, described in detail by Doughty.[42] The Anaiza men were helped by the women, who brought them water and rescued the wounded. The Anaizis were armed with slow-match guns, while the Riyadh emir's soldiers relied mainly on spears and swords. At the height of the battle, it started to rain. The Anaizis found themselves without arms; they were defeated and almost completely annihilated. Some 200 of them were killed. The Riyadh emir's troops numbered about 1,000. These figures give an idea of the scale of hostilities.

The Anaizis had to take shelter in the town. In early 1863 reinforcements from Jabal Shammar and the Eastern Province reached the Riyadh imam's troops near the town. The besiegers had even obtained some guns. The Anaizis sued for peace.[43] Unable to rout the town, the emir of Riyadh forgave its people again and let the rulers continue their functions.[44]

Najd's relations with Hijaz and the Ottoman government during Faisal's rule

Relations between Najd and Hijaz were always complex. Both the Ottoman pashas in Jidda and Medina and the sharif of Mecca claimed the right to intervene in central

Arabian affairs. In 1846 Sharif Muhammad ibn Aun waged a campaign against Najd, ostensibly as a reprisal for Faisal's refusal to pay tribute to the Sublime Porte. It is believed that the emir of Riyadh paid 10,000 thalers, which was, perhaps, the condition of his 'flight' from Egypt.[45] Another pretext for the sharif's campaign was the rebellion that had broken out in Qasim: he hoped for the effective support of the population, which was displeased with Faisal.[46]

Muhammad ibn Aun's troops consisted of some 1,000 men, mainly bedouin, and included a small regular Turkish detachment. In the spring of 1847 the sharif reached Qasim, facing no resistance on the way. But Faisal was energetically preparing for war. The strength of both parties was approximately equal and they avoided a direct battle.

The emir of Riyadh sent his brother to Anaiza with gifts for the sharif – 8 Omani racing camels and 4 horses. But Ibn Aun returned the animals and presented Faisal's brother with clothes and a horse. According to Arabian custom, this was an insult. As soon as Faisal's representatives had left Anaiza's city gates, they sent back both the horse and the clothes. The emir of Riyadh evaded an open clash, however, fearful perhaps of an invasion from Turkey. He sent Ibn Aun a 'gift', which was actually a single instalment of the tribute – 10,000 rials, horses and camels.[47] The agreement may have provided for the resumption of the annual payment of 10,000 rials, but it is unclear whether it was implemented. In 1854–55, during unrest in Hijaz, Faisal delayed payment of the tribute.[48]

It was probably at this point that Khalid ibn Saud, who lived in Hijaz, addressed the Sublime Porte again, volunteering to lead a campaign against Najd. The Turkish historian Cevdet quotes his letter. Khalid wrote:

> When Sharif Pasha was governor of Jidda [in 1847], the annual tax on Faisal was fixed at 10,000 thalers. Although he has paid that sum regularly since then, his present intention to replace the annual tribute by livestock supply is not caused by financial difficulties . . . He received 80,000 thalers from Said ibn Sultan [of Muscat] last year. Besides, Faisal receives 5,000 thalers a year from the ruler of Bahrain . . . His refusal to pay the tribute is a testimony of rebellion . . . If you send me 1,000 infantry, 1,000 cavalry, 200 bedouin and 2 guns, I shall be able to seize the whole of Najd. I shall try to add 90,000 thalers to the tax and pay 100,000 thalers to the Jidda exchequer.[49]

Khalid ibn Saud's proposal remained unanswered.

In Asir and Yemen, the Ottoman authorities tried to achieve the goal that had eluded Muhammad Ali. In April 1849 Turkish warships landed troops in Hodeida. Another detachment arrived there, led by Muhammad ibn Aun, the sharif of Mecca. The Yemeni imam agreed to the presence of a Turkish garrison in Sanaa and the payment of tribute. But in 1851–52 the Turks were defeated in Asir and Yemen. The Najdis were delighted at the news since they feared a Turkish invasion.[50]

The sharif of Mecca strengthened his position by establishing good relations with the tribes of Asir and the Harb tribe in Hijaz and maintaining contacts with Abbas, the

Egyptian pasha. This aroused the suspicion of the Ottoman authorities and in 1852 the pasha of Jidda was instructed to send Sharif Muhammad ibn Aun and two of his elder sons to Istanbul. This was achieved by setting a treacherous trap for Ibn Aun. One Abd al-Mutalib became the sharif of Mecca.[51]

In the 1850s Hijaz was seized by serious unrest, caused, in particular, by a year-long delay in paying the Turkish soldiers' salaries. A revolt broke out in October 1855, when the slave trade was prohibited by the sultan's *firman*, a result of pressure from the European powers. In 1855–56 the Turks temporarily lost control of Mecca and only restored their power with difficulty. Ibn Aun was returned to Mecca, and two years later his son Abdallah succeeded him. The local insurgents attacked the Turkish garrisons in Mokha and Hodeida. However, their fall was prevented by a cholera epidemic in February 1856, which devastated the besiegers' camps. The Turkish garrisons were driven out of Asir. It was only the opening of the Suez Canal in 1869 that enabled the Turks to transfer their troops regularly to the Red Sea coast of Arabia and occupy Asir again in 1871.[52]

In 1858 the British and French vice-consuls and fourteen Christian subjects were killed in Jidda and their houses were looted. The survivors fled to the *Cyclops*, a British frigate. Britain and France demanded that the guilty be punished. Namiq Pasha, the Turkish governor of Mecca, did not comply with their demand immediately and the *Cyclops* bombarded the town; a small British detachment landed from the ship. Eleven people were beheaded in the presence of the British, and then the chief of police, the head of the Hadhramawtis and the *qaimmaqam* (head of the local administration) were executed.[53]

Although the emirate of Riyadh was practically independent of the Ottoman empire, Faisal behaved cautiously and avoided conflicts with the Turks. He did not raid Syria, Hijaz or Iraq. In 1855 and 1860 he claimed the status of a vassal of the Porte in his correspondence with Britain concerning the situation in the Gulf. This was advantageous to him in his relations with the British.[54] Ottoman officials also mentioned Turkish sovereignty over central Arabia when their interests required it. In early 1862, for example, the Turkish governor of Baghdad censured the British for their attack on a village that was under the jurisdiction of 'Feysal Beg, the Kaimmakām of Najd . . . part of the hereditary dominions of the Sultan'.[55] The British consul-general in Baghdad answered the governor:

> We had hitherto always maintained direct relations with Amir Feysal . . . and we had never acknowledged the authority and jurisdiction moreover which assuredly the Porte neither does exercise nor has ever exercised in that quarter.

When informing the Ottoman government of Britain's reply, the British ambassador in Istanbul stressed the point even more clearly, in spite of admitting the fact that Faisal paid tribute.[56] Recognition of the Najdi emirate's independence probably left Britain freer to expand its interests in the Gulf basin.

The Second Saudi State (1843–1865)

Conflict between Britain and the emirate of Riyadh in the Gulf

J. G. Lorimer formulated British policy towards the emirate of Riyadh as follows: non-intervention in Trucial Oman, moderate resistance in the sultanate of Oman and an uncompromising opposition in Bahrain. In his opinion, that policy was determined by the Wahhabis' systematic aggressive acts along the coast.[57]

However, the emir of Riyadh considered the coastal regions to be part of his territory. Emir Faisal described his state to Colonel L. Pelly, a representative of the British administration in India: 'This land of Arabia from Koweit, through Kateef, Rusulkhymah [Ras al-Khaima], Oman, Rasul Hud (Ra's al-Hadd) [the easternmost point of Oman and Arabia] and beyond, which God has given unto us'.[58] Later he said: 'Muscat is our tributary. We took it by force of arms.'[59] In the opinion of the emir of Riyadh, Britain had intervened in the affairs of others by granting its protection to the coastal rulers.[60] Mahbub ibn Jauhar, an official of the Saudi court who was attached to Pelly's group, described the British as 'successful pirates'.[61] But Faisal was aware of Britain's might.

Although the Najdi detachments raided the environs of Kuwait, they did not attempt to seize it and relations between Faisal and the ruler of Kuwait remained friendly.[62] Najd and Bahrain, however, waged a war lasting for many years. The conflict between the two states in 1845–46 did not end in victory for either side. The Bahrainis blocked the ports under the Najdis' control, but when the Bani Khalid deserted from Bahrain to Najd, the balance of forces changed in favour of Riyadh. Muhammad ibn Khalifa agreed to pay an annual tribute of 4,000 thalers.[63]

The peace was short-lived, however, and hostilities resumed in the autumn of 1850. Faisal's troops occupied Qatar. The emir of Riyadh received support from a splinter branch of the ruling family of Bahrain, which enabled him to create a fleet of his own and start preparing an invasion of the island. Only the arrival of a British squadron sent to protect Bahrain saved its ruler from defeat. Faisal restored peaceful relations with him on condition that he paid the tribute and cleared the earlier arrears. The ruler's rivals, however, were given the fortress of Dammam.[64]

In 1859 the ruler of al-Qatif, a vassal of Riyadh, and Muhammad ibn Abdallah Al Khalifa, appointed by Faisal in Dammam, resumed preparations for an invasion of Bahrain on the pretext that its ruler, Muhammad ibn Khalifa, supported the tribes of Qatar against the Najdi authorities. The British squadron was again sent to protect the island.[65] Captain Jones, the British resident in the Gulf region, informed Faisal that the British government considered Bahrain an 'independent emirate' and was ready to protect it against all attacks.[66]

In 1861, backed by the guns of the British squadron, Captain Jones imposed an agreement on the shaikh of Bahrain similar to those concluded earlier with the small states of Trucial Oman. Bahrain became a British protectorate and was never again claimed by the Saudi rulers. Nevertheless it continued to pay tribute to Riyadh for its possessions in Qatar.

In the same year Britain decided to prevent unexpected changes in the ruling dynasty of Bahrain and sent Faisal an ultimatum, demanding that the ruler's rivals be exiled from Dammam. When no answer was received, the British squadron bombarded Dammam and Muhammad ibn Abdallah Al Khalifa fled the fortress.[67] In 1867 another battle was waged between the troops of the emir of the Eastern Province and the Bahrainis. Al-Nabhani, a historian of Bahrain, notes that 'it was the last battle in Bahrain, because thereafter the British came'.[68]

Oman was also in the sphere of Najdi-British rivalry. In 1845, fairly soon after returning to power, Faisal sent Saad ibn Mutlaq with troops to al-Buraimi. The commander ruled al-Buraimi for almost three decades; he served Turki, then his son Faisal during his first reign, Khurshid Pasha, Khalid, then Faisal again and was fairly conversant with the affairs of Oman. The local shaikhs asked Britain for help, but Britain still avoided direct intervention in conflicts beyond the coastal regions. Faisal sent the British a letter, stressing his intention of maintaining the friendly relations that had existed between his father Turki and the British government.[69]

Soon after coming to al-Buraimi, Saad demanded tribute from some local rulers, including the sultan of Muscat and the ruler of al-Sohar. In order to ensure that his demands were met, he sent a detachment to Muscat. However, the British started patrolling the coast of al-Batina and Saad ibn Mutlaq left after Muscat had agreed to pay an annual tribute of 7,000 rials.

In 1848 the Najdi garrison in al-Buraimi dispersed because the routes along which supplies of food, arms and reinforcements arrived had been intercepted. Muscat refused to pay tribute and the ruler of Abu Dhabi seized the al-Buraimi group of oases. Abu Dhabi's occupation of al-Buraimi continued for eight months, but its ruler's rivals from Dubai and Sharja helped Ibn Mutlaq to recapture it. Ibn Mutlaq was dismissed by Faisal in 1850 and died soon afterwards.

In March 1850, when the Najdi garrison in the oases had shrunk to 50 men, Said ibn Tahnun, the ruler of Abu Dhabi, seized al-Buraimi again. In 1853 Abdallah, Faisal's son, arrived there with troops. The local tribal shaikhs and the rulers of the coastal states hastened to express their submission to Riyadh. Its influence was high, but Captain Campbell, the British resident, forced the local rulers to conclude a treaty on a permanent peace. The Najdi troops approached Muscat, which was saved by the British squadron again, but the rulers of both al-Sohar and Muscat pledged themselves to pay Riyadh 12,000 rials every year.

In December 1853 Abdallah left al-Buraimi, having appointed Ahmad Al Sudairi its ruler. The latter stayed there until 1857. Despite their dependence on Britain, Muscat, al-Sohar and the Gulf states continued to pay tribute to the emirate of Riyadh. Now and then the Najdis penetrated Jabal Akhdar, the mountain region of Oman. The territory under their control was not defined precisely – sometimes it increased and sometimes it decreased – and there was a period when their tax-collectors operated throughout a considerable part of Oman. Ahmad Al Sudairi was succeeded by his son Turki, who ruled al-Buraimi from 1857 to 1869.[70]

The Second Saudi State (1843–1865)

The socio-political and economic situation in the second Saudi state

As in the first Saudi state, the emir of Riyadh was the imam (leader of the Muslim community), the commander-in-chief, the supreme judge and the head of the executive. He personally took all major decisions on domestic and foreign policy, gave rulings on fiscal and military problems, took decisions on raids and the conclusion of peace treaties and supervised their implementation, controlled the reception and appointment of diplomatic agents, carried on official correspondence, and engaged in the problems of relations with allies, vassals, neighbours and nomadic tribes.

Faisal's court was small and informal and lacked a bureaucracy. On the most important questions the emir would consult his close relatives, whose loyalty was above any local interests. The Al al-Shaikh family also played an important role, although nobody enjoyed the status of Muhammad ibn Abd al-Wahhab.[71]

The distribution of lucrative, prestigious posts helped to satisfy the conflicting requirements of the family members. Abdallah was declared Faisal's heir and participated in military affairs and the government of Riyadh and the central regions. The second son Saud, Abdallah's rival, enjoyed considerable autonomy in the government of the southern regions. The third son Muhammad, who tended to support Abdallah in his conflict with Saud, was in charge of the northern part of the country. The youngest son Abd al-Rahman, who was to beget the founder of the new Saudi state, was born in 1850 and was too young for independent assignments.[72] However, the division of the emirate between Faisal's sons enabled them to acquire supporters in their provinces and thus to create the basis for future feuds, which were to tear the second Saudi state to pieces.

Faisal's health was poor in the last years of his life. He had caught an eye disease – probably trachoma – in Egypt and was completely blind when Colonel Pelly visited Riyadh in 1865. Faisal was then aged about 70 and was unable to play an active part in ruling the state. Abdallah was in charge of all affairs.

According to R. B. Winder, 'The Saudi family has thrown off, at crucial moments, men of strength, intelligence and character who could control the various divisive elements in the far-flung realm, who assured a stern justice.'[73] Faisal ibn Turki was a leader of that type. In spite of Britain's hostile attitude to the Saudi emirate, Pelly conceded:

> I could not but observe that all parties admitted the Ameer Fysul ben Saood to be a just and stern ruler who had been unprecedentedly successful in curbing the predatory habits of his tribes; and who was desirous of inculcating among them more settled habits, and of turning their minds toward agriculture and trade. No one seemed to like the Ameer, but all seemed to admire him, and he was spoken of with a sort of dread in which respect and hatred were curiously mixed.[74]

After the first meeting with Faisal, Pelly portrayed him as follows:

> I found the Imam seated at the upper end of the room, on a small handsome carpet, supported at his back by a heavy cushion . . . On my approaching him, the Imam rose, but with difficulty; took my hand and felt slowly over it; and then requested me to be seated close by him on the carpet. He was quite blind, but his face was remarkable, with regular features, placid, stern, self-possessed, resigned. He looked upwards of 70 years of age, and was dressed richly but with taste, wearing over the Arab cheffiah (head cloth) a turban rolled from a green cashmere shawl. His voice was well modulated, and his words calm and measured. He was dignified, almost gentle, yet you felt that he could be remorselessly cruel.[75]

The degree of central control varied in the provinces of the second Saudi state and was in inverse proportion to the distance from Riyadh, just as it was in the first state. It depended on the situation in each province, the province's relative importance and the people's religious convictions. In the central regions, the emirs, *ulama* and *qadhis* were appointed by the ruler of Riyadh. Many of them belonged to the local nobility, but some were sent from outside.

The Riyadh emir's attempts to strengthen his power in Qasim were a major cause of unrest, and he had to allow the local nobility to continue their rule. Relations with Jabal Shammar were surprisingly smooth, however, in particular because Riyadh did not try to consolidate its positions or establish direct control in the region and was satisfied with nominal vassalage. The friendly relations between the ruling families were strengthened by dynastic marriages, and they needed each other's military support.

Only Najdis were appointed emirs of Hufuf. The population of the Eastern Province felt little sympathy for Riyadh and Wahhabism but, because of the area's strategic importance, the emir of Riyadh stationed permanent garrisons there. Al-Buraimi had both a Najdi garrison and an emir appointed from Riyadh, yet that group of oases retained more features of a front-line post than Hufuf did.

As earlier, the loyalty of the various provinces and tribes was ensured by keeping hostages in the capital. Inviting Pelly to see the jail, Faisal said, 'You will see that there are at this moment more than 70 chiefs there.' He added, 'Yes, we are very severe; but we are just.'[76]

The states, both large and small, that paid tribute to Najd – Muscat, and the coastal emirates of Oman and Bahrain – remained semi-independent. Riyadh never appointed emirs there, though an agent with semi-diplomatic status might be sent to control the payment of tribute and to represent Najd's interests.

The nomadic tribes depended on the emir of Riyadh to varying degrees, but Faisal never achieved full control over them as had been the case during the first Saudi state. Endless bedouin rebellions continued throughout the period of his rule.

Wahhabism partly lost its fanatic and uncompromising character in the second Saudi state. The experience of life in Egypt had probably taught Faisal that the Egyptians and the Ottoman government were far stronger than the Najdis, and provoking them by manifestations of religious intolerance would amount to inviting his

The Second Saudi State (1843–1865)

own ruin. Yet religious sentiment grew acute at times.

When a cholera epidemic devastated Najd in the mid-1850s, the Wahhabi preachers explained it as a punishment for non-observance of the prescriptions of monotheism. A special tribunal of twenty-two 'zealots' was set up in Riyadh with the right to punish the violators of rigid religious requirements with fines and corporal punishment. The zealots acted ruthlessly, which caused deep resentment among the urban population of Qasim and Hufuf. The emir of Riyadh was forced to relax the religious rules governing everyday life and limit the zealots' authority.[77]

The military organization of the emirate of Riyadh under Faisal did not differ from that under the first Saudis. At call-up, each town or tribe had to send a stipulated number of armed men and animals. The quotas were fixed in registers, which were also the basis of taxation. When giving the order to mobilize, the emir reported the number of men he required to the local rulers, who were responsible for the conscripts' equipment. Usually half of the quota was required, but in an emergency all available forces were assembled. The men were supposed to come with arms and animals. The government was theoretically responsible for the supply of munitions. Cavalrymen were particularly valued and those who came on horses enjoyed certain privileges. Each tribe and town was represented by a separate detachment or unit in the troops, with its own flag.

When a military campaign ended, the troops were disbanded. They were not paid a regular salary, but four-fifths of the spoils were divided among the fighters – one share to an infantryman or member of the camel corps and two to a cavalryman. One-fifth was taken by the *bait al-mal*. The emir kept a detachment of almost 200 guards, slaves and freedmen, who also performed the functions of a police force, when necessary. The core of the Najdi troops was formed by settled people.[78]

The Najdis had some guns, but it is probable that they were seldom used. Faisal did not make serious attempts to create a navy. Instead, he counted on semi-vassals such as Bahrain. Naturally, the coastal rulers found reasons to evade complying with his demands. Besides, the treaties imposed on them by the British had limited their freedom to support Riyadh.[79]

Faisal's taxation system did not differ greatly from that of the first Saudi state. Peasants paid *zakat* only on cereals and the fruit that might be preserved and counted: 10% of the crops from non-irrigated lands and 5% of those from irrigated lands. The bedouin paid a livestock tax, whose rate was 2.5–5%. The value of gold and silver was taxed at 2.5%, as well as merchants' goods. Those whose annual income was below the stipulated level were exempted from the taxes. Additional taxes were collected during wars.[80]

As earlier, the exchequer was replenished by duties from pilgrims, tribute from Muscat, Bahrain and other vassals and proceeds from the Riyadh emir's own possessions. It is noteworthy that no distinction was made between the state exchequer and the imams' privy purse in nineteenth-century Arabia. The methods of tax collection remained unchanged up to the period after the Second World War and merely continued the practices of the emirate of al-Diriya.[81]

The total state revenues cannot be calculated with even a minimum degree of accuracy. Colonel Pelly gave an extremely approximate estimate of the Riyadh population, revenues and military potential. According to his calculations, the population of Najd and al-Hasa (probably the settled population only) was 115,000, the revenue was equivalent to 692,000 thalers and the number of potential servicemen was 7,900.[82] As for the nomads, they numbered 20,000 and the tax they paid was 114,000 thalers. Thus Pelly estimated the state revenue at 806,000 thalers, besides the tribute from Muscat, Jabal Shammar, Bahrain, and so on, and the 2m thalers in duties paid by pilgrims.[83] It would appear that the amount of revenue was overestimated and the settled and nomadic population underestimated, even if Pelly meant only adult males. Palgrave estimated the total state revenue at £160,000.[84]

The data on the expenses of the second Saudi state are even scarcer. After deducting the cost of maintaining the emir's family and the court, half of the expenditure was probably accounted for by military purposes and the rest was spent on public works – maintenance of wells and mosques, pensions to disabled and elderly persons, salaries of central government officials, subsidies to the local shaikhs and provincial emirs, and maintenance of the rather effective intelligence system.[85]

Most taxes were paid in kind, but monetary taxes were collected in some regions. Although the main currency was the rial (that is, the Austrian thaler), the British sovereign, and Turkish and Persian gold and silver coins also circulated. Indian currency was widely used in the Eastern Province. In the coastal regions of the Gulf, *tawilas* were used – these were long metallic coins, resembling a hair-slide, with an Arabic inscription chased on them. They were made either of copper with silver addition or of pure silver.[86]

During Faisal's rule, a stable source of income was provided by the export of Arabian pedigree horses, famous throughout the world. Horses were regularly supplied to India. The horses from Jabal Shammar were exported via Kuwait and from other places via al-Qatif and al-Uqair. In 1863, 600 animals were sold via Kuwait at an average price of 150 rials. Abbas Pasha sent several expeditions from Egypt to purchase horses. Two famous European travellers – G. A. Wallin and C. Guarmani – visited Arabia on the pretext of buying horses. However, there were very few left by 1864 and the animals Faisal sent to Istanbul were of such poor quality that the Sublime Porte protested and prohibited all exports of horses for four years,[87] though the ban could hardly be enforced in practice. A. Shcherbatov and S. Stroganov, Russian stud-owners, also tried to buy horses in northern Arabia at the end of the nineteenth century.

Before oil was discovered, the main occupation of the inhabitants of the Gulf coast was pearl-fishing. The Eastern Province lagged behind Bahrain, Qatar and Trucial Oman in that respect, however. The explanation might be the vast oases in al-Hasa and al-Qatif, which offered sufficient opportunities for agriculture. The pearls were sent to Bombay and then resold to Europe. Lorimer gave a detailed description of pearl-fishing in the Gulf, with its strict social and financial rules. Although his account dates from 1906, the picture had hardly changed since the 1860s and 1870s. The number of pearl-fishers was 22,000 in Trucial Oman, 13,000 in Qatar, 18,000 in Bahrain, 9,200 in Kuwait and some 3,400 in the oasis of al-Qatif.[88]

The Second Saudi State (1843–1865)

The second Saudi state was able to revive thanks to the end of foreign intervention in Najd's affairs. The interest in unity shown by a sizeable part of the Najdi nobility, merchants, craftsmen and peasants; the support of the Wahhabi *ulama*; and the prestige of the Al Saud – all these factors helped Faisal to bring many territories of central and eastern Arabia under Riyadh's control. However, the signs of the central authorities' weakness and sometimes impotence, and the bedouin tribes' separatism and wilfulness, were so obvious that no contemporary would have predicted a long life for the emirate of Riyadh. Jabal Shammar, which was gaining in strength, was an ally rather than an obedient vassal; Qasim maintained its autonomy in repeated revolts; the nomadic tribes challenged Faisal again and again; and the shadow of the British empire stretched from the Gulf to the Arabian Sea, virtually swallowing up the small coastal emirates. The situation was aggravated by the deepening split within the family of the emir of Riyadh.

CHAPTER 8

The Disintegration of the Emirate of Riyadh and the Rise of Jabal Shammar

The split in the emir's family

Faisal ibn Turki died in December 1865 and the power struggle between his sons started almost at his graveside. Crown Prince Abdallah became the new ruler, with the support of his younger brother Muhammad and the population of al-Arid. He had a rival, however, in his brother Saud. With an interest in weakening the emirate of Riyadh, Britain encouraged Saud's ambitions. Abdallah strove to increase centralization in the weak and unstable emirate, leading to discontent among the local nobility.[1]

According to Palgrave, Abdallah was courageous and energetic, yet strict and severe, which impressed the puritan-minded urban people. Saud was open, energetic, generous and liked spectacular gestures, which endeared him to the bedouin.[2] Philby generally agrees with these judgements.[3] The British resident, Colonel Lewis Pelly, on the contrary, writes that Saud was popular among the settled people and Abdallah among the nomads.[4] Saud's mother and one of his wives were from the Ajman tribe, who hated Abdallah and became Saud's most loyal allies. Abdallah was supported by the Qahtan.[5]

Abdallah's first preoccupation after becoming ruler was not the struggle against his brother (this was yet to come), but the affairs of Oman. Shortly before Faisal ibn Turki's death, Azzan ibn Qais, the ruler of al-Rustaq in Oman and a member of a collateral branch of the ruling family of Muscat, had rebelled against his relative, Thuwaini, the sultan of Muscat. Azzan had asked for support from Turki Al Sudairi, who was then in al-Buraimi. The latter sent a detachment and Thuwaini's troops were driven from al-Rustaq in late 1864. Taking advantage of the situation, Faisal ibn Turki tried to increase the tribute paid to him by the sultan of Muscat from 12,000 to 40,000

The Disintegration of the Emirate of Riyadh and the Rise of Jabal Shammar

thalers, sending troops to back up his demand.[6] On the advice of the British, Thuwaini refused to pay the increased amount. In the same year, the town of Sur was seized by the rebels acting together with a Najdi detachment, led by Abd al-Aziz ibn Mutlaq, brother of the famous Saad ibn Mutlaq. As always, the town was pillaged and several Indian merchants (who were British subjects) were among the victims. Unable to drive the Najdis away, Thuwaini gave them 10,000 thalers and then made a further payment of 6,000.

The British started helping Thuwaini and sent a protest to Riyadh. Abdallah, who had already seized the reins of government, agreed to release all those who had been taken prisoner in Sur and return all property to the owners, but made no mention of compensation.[7]

Pelly recommended that the British authorities in India should help the sultan of Muscat,[8] and soon afterwards the sultan was given British guns. Simultaneously an ultimatum was sent to Riyadh, demanding an apology, a promise that similar actions would never be undertaken, and the payment of compensation. If these conditions were not met, the emir's fortresses on the coast would be destroyed and his ships would be seized. From threats the British passed to deeds. The *Highflier*, a British warship, bombarded Ajman, which was used by the Najdis as a port on the Omani coast. In early February 1866 the fort of al-Qatif and some small ships in its harbour were destroyed. After an abortive attempt to land troops in Dammam, the *Highflier* bombarded the town. Next it shelled rebel Sur, destroying the local people's vessels. But Sultan Thuwaini was killed by his son Salim, which complicated Britain's political manoeuvres.[9]

A correspondence started between Emir Abdallah and Pelly. The emir of Riyadh strove to prevent the deterioration of relations, to have Britain recognize him as ruler and to prevent any pro-Saud intrigues by Britain. He made arrangements with Pelly through his representative to settle the claims.[10] The Saudis considered British messages as a kind of treaty which was binding on the sender.[11]

Aware of Britain's hostility, Abdallah played on his weak position, trying to use the British as a counterbalance to the Turks, a ploy which was finally to cost him dear. His ambassador, Abd al-Aziz al-Suwailim, arrived in Baghdad in March 1866 on the pretext of bringing four Najdi horses to present to the sultan. The British resident in Baghdad learned, however, that his true purpose was to enlist the Turks' aid. Governor Namik Pasha received al-Suwailim with honours and even took a diplomatic demarche, demanding that the British cease hostilities, yet no concrete action was taken to support the emir.[12]

Meanwhile, Saud was gathering forces to contest the Riyadh throne. He went to Asir to seek the support of Muhammad ibn Aid, the local ruler. Abdallah immediately sent a delegation to Abha, then the capital of Asir, to warn the ruler against an alliance with Saud and invite the latter to return to Riyadh, guaranteeing his safety. Saud declined to return. Feeling that Asir was unlikely to support him, he went to Makrami, the ruler of Najran. Then he gathered his supporters from among the Ajman and some other bedouin tribes and moved to Wadi al-Dawasir.[13]

Abdallah had already fortified his capital.[14] He mobilized the urban people and the nomads of Najd and sent them against his rebel brother. Saud was seriously wounded but escaped from the battlefield to the Al Murra bedouin. The emir of Riyadh made short work of Saud's supporters, punished the rebel tribes and oases in Wadi al-Dawasir and replaced emirs in some provinces.[15] After his wounds had healed, Saud went to al-Buraimi and became Turki Al Sudairi's guest in late 1866. Four years later he challenged Abdallah again. In 1870 Saud arrived in Bahrain and tried to enlist the Al Khalifa family's support in order to attack Qatar, where a Najdi garrison was stationed.[16]

The feud continues

The struggle within the Bahraini ruling dynasty resumed in the late 1860s, leading to the flight of one of its members to the Saudis, mutual raids and the intervention of the British, which again prevented the emirate of Riyadh from establishing control over Bahrain.[17]

After the murder of Thuwaini, unrest broke out in Oman. Salim's rule was short and ended in a new revolt led by Azzan ibn Aqis from al-Rustaq, who seized Muscat on 1 October 1868 under the conservative banner of Ibadhism. The new power did not survive past the year 1871 in the coastal areas of Oman, but persisted for decades in the inner regions.

In 1869 Turki Al Sudairi was killed in Sharja, where he had tried to intervene in the local feud. In June 1869 the local tribes made arrangements with Azzan and managed to seize al-Buraimi with his help. They marched under the banner of Ibadhism against the Wahhabis, considering them heretics. The members of the Najdi garrison asked for a pardon and were released.[18]

Britain recognized al-Buraimi as a part of the Saudi state. Colonel Disbrowe, the British agent in Muscat, wrote in August 1869, 'So far as I can see and judge, Beraymi was gratuitously and unjustly invaded by Syeed Azan and Azan must look for Wahhabi retaliation.'[19] After capturing al-Buraimi, Azzan refused to pay tribute to Riyadh. Abdallah's response was resolute. He wrote to Azzan:

> From 'Abdallah ibn-Faysal Imam of the Muslims to Sayyid 'Azzan ibn-Qays Imam of the Robbers: We have heard what you have done. We intend to pay you a visit with 20,000 men. We hope you will receive us suitably.[20]

The emir of Riyadh started gathering his forces in al-Hasa for a campaign against Oman. Muscat was seized by panic, yet Abdallah's troops did not appear there. The winter of 1869–70 was so dry that movements of large numbers of troops were difficult. Zaid ibn Khalifa, the ruler of Abu Dhabi, entered into an alliance with Muscat. Lastly, Saud ibn Faisal's intrigues and revolt forced Abdallah to consolidate his power in the capital: this was the main reason for cancelling the Muscat expedition.[21]

The Disintegration of the Emirate of Riyadh and the Rise of Jabal Shammar

Saud entered into an alliance with Azzan, forming an anti-Abdallah coalition, which also included the ruler of Abu Dhabi. Abdallah's brother tried to make a sortie to Qatar, but was repulsed and took refuge in Bahrain. An impression arose that Saud was backed by the British, who, although they did not support him directly, certainly did not object to his actions.[22]

In 1869 the death occurred of Abd al-Rahman ibn Hasan Al al-Shaikh, a grandson of Muhammad ibn Abd al-Wahhab and the most influential *alim* and *qadhi* in Arabia in the nineteenth century. He had been taken to Egypt by Ibrahim Pasha in 1818, but returned in 1825/26 to Riyadh, where he was appointed *qadhi* by Emir Turki. It is interesting to note that, according to the chronicler Ibn Isa, he mentioned among his teachers (besides his grandfather) Husain ibn Ghannam, a Wahhabi historian, Abd al-Rahman al-Jabarti, a famous Egyptian scholar and historian, and several other Egyptian historians.[23]

The further rise of Jabal Shammar

In March 1868 Talal Al Rashid, the ruler of Hail, committed suicide, which was an extremely rare event in Arabia. Ibn Isa confines himself to stating that 'Talal's mind was afflicted by a disorder and he killed himself.'[24] According to Islam, people who commit suicide burn in hellfire for having opposed Allah's will. Philby reports that the people had been told that Talal was examining his new pistol and had accidentally pulled the trigger. He was aged 45.[25]

Although Talal had ruled a large territory almost independently, he had never severed ties with Faisal or his son Abdallah, but gave them active military support. His death provided an opportunity to review relations between the rulers of Hail and Riyadh, especially a year later, after the death of Ubaid ibn Ali, Talal's old but influential uncle, who had advocated cooperation with the house of Saud. Whereas Palgrave describes Ubaid as a fanatic,[26] Lady Ann Blunt sees him as 'the principal hero of Shammar tradition'; 'he has left a great reputation among the Arabs for his hospitality, generosity and courage'.[27] Doughty also praises Ubaid as a military commander and as a poet whose *qasidas* were frequently recited.[28]

While Talal did not expand his territory to the south, to his suzerain's possessions, he never gave up attempts to advance in the north or the west and had established his control over Khaibar and Taima to the north of Medina. Although Talal behaved with a large degree of independence, his military might was hardly sufficient to challenge his suzerain. Palgrave is of the opinion that in 1862 Faisal could mobilize three times as many fighters as Talal could.[29]

The emir of Jabal Shammar was known for his religious tolerance. He allowed both Shia and Jews to live and trade in Hail and collected huge taxes from them.[30] Palgrave writes:

Merchants from Basrah, from Meshid 'Alee and Wasit, shopkeepers from Medinah and even from Yemen, were invited by liberal offers to come and establish themselves in the new market of Ha'yel. With some Telal made government contracts equally lucrative to himself and to them; to others he granted privileges and immunities; to all, protection and countenance.[31]

Using the proceeds from taxes, the pilgrimage and raids, Talal completed construction of the fortress-palace of Barzan, enclosed the capital within a 7-metre-high wall and built a market area, a large Friday mosque and many public wells.[32]

Tribal solidarity, not religion, was the main cementing force in Jabal Shammar. Even the settled people in Hail and other towns considered themselves Shammar first and 'monotheists' second. In some oases, the emir of Jabal Shammar did not appoint governors since the oases were ruled by the local shaikhs. The nomads played a more important role in Jabal Shammar than in the emirate of Riyadh. The dominance of a single tribe ensured stability within a limited territory, but was an obstacle to the expansion of Jabal Shammar, causing the envy of other powerful tribes.

Talal paid Faisal and Abdallah a tribute consisting of horses, a share of the taxes collected from the Persian pilgrims in Hail and a share of the spoils. However, Riyadh's influence in central Arabia was declining while the green and red flag of the emirate of Jabal Shammar rose ever higher. Wallin writes as early as the time of Abdallah Al Rashid:

> I regard the Shammar as unquestionably one of the most vigorous and youthful tribes at present in Arabia, and their power and influence extend yearly more and more over their neighbours.[33]

Talal was succeeded by his brother Mitab. Ten months later Mitab was killed at a *majlis* (council) meeting by Talal's eldest son Bandar, who became emir. But the new ruler had a dangerous rival – his uncle, Muhammad ibn Abdallah Al Rashid (also known as Muhammad ibn Rashid or simply Ibn Rashid), the third son of the dynasty's founder. Bandar appointed his uncle to the lucrative and honourable post of head of the pilgrims' caravan,[34] an arrangement which functioned up to 1872, when Muhammad killed Bandar. Fearful of a blood feud, the new emir started persecuting Bandar's five brothers and made short work of four of them – the fifth, a boy named Naif, survived. Jabal Shammar recognized the new emir. Although Muhammad's rule opened with the bloody extermination of his rivals, it ushered in a period of prosperity and strong power in the state.[35] In Philby's opinion, 'never was the government in more sufficient handling'.[36]

The most important source of information about the history of the Rashidis from Talal's death to the seizure of power by Muhammad is a work by Dari ibn Rashid, quoted abundantly by R. Winder. In that period, the emirate of the Rashidis was mostly confined to Jabal Shammar proper and the closest oases – Khaibar, Taima and Jawf. Travellers estimated the population of the territories ruled by Hail in the late nineteenth century (before the annexation of Najd) at 20–50,000 settled people and almost the same number of nomads. According to other data, the bedouin might have numbered twice as many.[37]

The ruler of Jabal Shammar had the title of emir or 'the shaikh of shaikhs', in other words he remained the leader of the confederation of Shammar tribes, on which he relied.[38] The Rashidis ruled through their relatives and guards. In a setting of almost unceasing struggle within the dynasty, the emir mistrusted his relatives and relied increasingly on the guards and on Egyptian and Turkish mercenaries. The emir's guard was some 200 strong;[39] travellers from the 1860s to the 1880s give the figure of 500–600. Of them, the 20 most reliable men were the emir's personal bodyguards, some 200 remained in Hail and the rest accompanied merchants, pilgrims and tax-collectors and served periods of duty at the garrisons in the annexed regions of the emirate.

There were rank-and-file soldiers and 'the men [*rajail*] of the shaikh of shaikhs' among the ruler's guards. The term *rajail* was applied to the top-ranking guards, as well as to court officials and generally to those who enjoyed the emir's confidence. Many of them were former *abds*. 'The emir's men' were senior officials and commanders of his guard, palace attendants and managers of his possessions.[40] Travellers who visited the emirate in the 1870s and 1880s mention the most influential individuals – the manager of the palace guest-rooms, the chief treasurer, the chief scribe, the standard-bearer and, lastly, the *jalis*, a kind of major-domo and simultaneously chief councillor of the Rashidis.[41]

The emirs of Jabal Shammar followed the tradition of large-scale hospitality, whose symbol was a massive copper pan which could only be lifted with difficulty by 4 strong men. In the 1880s there were frequently between 150 and 200 people staying and having their meals at the palace regularly at any one time. That number reached 800–1,000 when large caravans arrived in the town.[42]

As statehood developed, the *sharia* was increasingly applied to the detriment of customary law.[43] The punishments included: the cutting off of a hand and the confiscation of property for rebelling against the emir; imprisonment for theft and the evasion of *zakat*; beating with a stick for inflicting blows and wounds; and fines.[44] The Rashidis' old residence was used as a jail, but even in the 1860s honoured prisoners and hostages were kept in the guest-rooms of the new palace.[45]

The structure of local government depended on the degree of a province's submission to the emir, as was the case in the Saudi state. Some provinces were ruled by the direct vicegerents of Hail, but most of them by the local nobility. In the nomadic tribes, all power belonged to the shaikhs: the Rashidis almost never intervened in their affairs.[46]

Aware of the unreliability of the bedouin detachments, the Rashidis relied mainly on the towns, oases and the *abd* guard. Guarmani estimates the maximum strength of Jabal Shammar's troops in the 1860s at 6,500, which might be increased to 9,000 by people from the annexed regions.[47] According to Nolde, in the 1890s the emirs could mobilize 40,000 people.[48] The conscripts rode camels and the nobility served in the cavalry. The arms mainly consisted of lances, swords and firearms but there were some guns.[49]

During the rule of Muhammad Al Rashid (1872–97) Jabal Shammar reached the apex of its might. In the 1870s it conquered al-Al and villages in Wadi Sirhan up to the boundary of Wadi Hawran. The continuing decay of the emirate of Riyadh and the alliance with the Porte enabled Muhammad to begin spreading his power to the towns of Qasim. In 1884, when the struggle intensified within the Saudi family, Muhammad became the ruler of the whole of Najd.

The rise of Jabal Shammar was possible only in the conditions of decay of the emirate of Riyadh, with its larger population and undoubtedly greater military potential. The Saudis' wars at the beginning of the century, the Egyptians' disastrous invasions, the exhausting feuds – all these affected Jabal Shammar less than central Najd proper. Several gifted rulers took advantage of the favourable conditions and made Hail the master of the whole of central Arabia for a short period.

The disintegration of the emirate of Riyadh and the seizure of al-Hasa by the Turks

In the autumn of 1870 Saud ibn Faisal concluded a new alliance with the Ajman and Al Murra tribes, attacked al-Uqair and captured al-Hasa. Abdallah sent troops under the command of his brother Muhammad to restore control over the province and its capital, Hufuf. In December 1870 a battle was waged in the desert near Juda. At the decisive moment a group of Subai nomads, who had come with Muhammad, deserted to Saud and the latter's victory was complete. Muhammad ibn Faisal was captured and jailed in al-Qatif, where he remained until the Turks released him. The entire Eastern Province swore allegiance to Saud.[50]

Aware that the citizens of the capital were hostile to him, and that this might cost him his life, Abdallah ibn Faisal left the town with his family and a group of supporters and made for Jabal Shammar. In despair, he applied for aid to Midhat Pasha, the Ottoman governor of Baghdad, and to the sharif of Mecca.[51] By his desperate attempts to elicit outside support, the emir of Riyadh actually hastened the collapse of his emirate.

Muhammad Al Rashid helped the imam materially but, as Doughty reports, did not allow him to enter Hail.[52] The Qahtan tribe came to the aid of Abdallah and he was able to return to Riyadh. A terrible drought occurred that year, leading, naturally, to new unrest and rebellions.[53]

In April–May 1871 Saud finally moved towards Riyadh. Abdallah fled to the south, where the Qahtan roamed, but Saud's detachment intercepted his equipment and property.[54] Then Abdallah was defeated by Saud again.[55] When Saud's bedouin troops entered Riyadh, their rapacious plunder of the town and its citizens aroused universal hatred. Feuds resumed in Najd. According to Ibn Isa:

> The bond of authority was loosened; disorders increased; famine and high costs grew worse; people ate the putrid bodies of donkeys; many died of hunger; and the people were largely given over to famine, hunger, trials, plunder, killing, dissension and rapidly stalking death.[56]

In Winder's opinion, however, it should not be forgotten that Ibn Isa was a supporter of Abdallah.

At this point, the crumbling emirate was faced with a new danger: the governor of Baghdad, Midhat Pasha, a famous Ottoman reformer and the promoter of an active foreign policy, decided to take advantage of the situation and add new territory to the disintegrating Ottoman empire. His activities in eastern Arabia caused a diplomatic crisis between London and Istanbul.[57] Midhat Pasha claimed that Ottoman sovereignty spread as far as Najd and that Abdallah was a mere Turkish *qaimmaqam*. The pretext of the invasion was 'to restore order, and to maintain the said Caimakam against his rebellious brother'.[58]

To conquer al-Hasa, the Turks sent their navy, augmented by 300 vessels they had received from the ruler of Kuwait. The regular troops consisted of 4,000 men, chiefly infantry, as well as cavalry and artillery. The Muntafiq sent 1,000 men by land. In May 1871 the Turkish troops landed in Ras Tannura (now the site of a large oil-processing plant) and moved towards al-Qatif, encountering no resistance.

After a short period of hostilities, the Turks occupied all the province's main towns and fortresses. Nafiz Pasha, the commander of the Turkish forces, circulated an address 'To all the people of al-Hasa, al-Qatif and the provinces of Najd', declaring that Najd and its dependencies were a part of Turkey's possessions, similar to Iraq, Yemen and Egypt. He claimed that the Turks supported the legitimate local ruler, the *qaimmaqam* Abdallah – appointed by the sultan and subordinate to the governor of Baghdad – against his rebel brother Saud.[59] Thus the Saudi brothers lost the Eastern Province as a result of the family conflict. Around the same time, they lost control over the oases of al-Buraimi. In autumn of the same year Midhat Pasha arrived in al-Hasa, but his attempt to seize Riyadh was unsuccessful. Many of the Turkish troops died from disease and the heat.[60]

The struggle within the Al Saud family continued. Abdallah appeared in the territory occupied by the Turks, while Saud was temporarily driven out of Riyadh by his uncle, Abdallah ibn Turki, the brother of Emir Faisal. Saud mobilized his allies – the Ajman and the Al Murra – and started attacking Turkish garrisons, but without success.[61]

Abdallah ibn Faisal stayed in Hufuf as the Turks' honoured prisoner but fled when he was warned that he would be taken to Baghdad. In late 1871 or early 1872 he returned to Riyadh, but the emirate's situation was hopeless. The famine continued; as reported by Ibn Isa, people ate carrion, skin and leaves.[62] The brothers tried unsuccessfully to forge an alliance against the Turks.

In March 1873 Saud returned to Riyadh again. The hostilities between the brothers continued with variable success, accompanied, as always, by plunder and killings. Aware that Abdallah ibn Faisal relied on the Turks, Britain increased its support for Saud and even sent him food supplies.[63]

In the mid-1870s Abd al-Rahman ibn Faisal, the fourth son of Emir Faisal, appeared on the scene. Winder is of the opinion that he supported Saud, while Philby believes that he sided with Abdallah.[64] It is not impossible that Abd al-Rahman merely vacillated between his two elder brothers. It is known that the young emir negotiated on Saud's behalf with Rauf Pasha, the new Ottoman governor of Baghdad, who kept him as a hostage until August 1874.[65]

In March 1874 the Turks gave up direct rule over al-Hasa to reduce their expenses. The tool of their policy became a certain Bazi Al Arayar, the shaikh of the Bani Khalid. Nasir Pasha ibn Saadun, governor of the newly created province of Basra and shaikh of the Muntafiq, appointed him *mutasarrif*. The Turkish regular forces were withdrawn and replaced by an Ottoman police detachment. Yet in spite of the traditional influence of the Bani Khalid nobility in the province, Bazi was unpopular and some people favoured the restoration of the emir of Riyadh's power. After being released by the Turks, Abd al-Rahman ibn Faisal led a revolt against them in the Eastern Province in 1874. A part of the Ajman, Al Murra and other nomadic tribes joined him. Nasir Pasha ibn Saadun responded vigorously: he landed 2,400 regular soldiers with 4 guns in al-Uqair and the rebels were defeated. Abd al-Rahman fled to Riyadh. The victors were allowed to plunder Hufuf for 3 days. Nasir Pasha left the province in February 1875, appointing his son *mutasarrif*.[66]

Saud's power in Najd was fragile. Towards the end of his rule, Jabal Shammar and Qasim ceased to obey him and Riyadh became the centre of a small central Arabian emirate, which was torn to pieces. Saud's alliance with the Ajman caused discontent among the urban people and the inhabitants of the oases. Central Najd was plunged into ever-deeper chaos.[67]

Saud was unable to control the other nomadic tribes of Najd. The Ataiba, Abdallah ibn Faisal's allies, attacked the oases. Saud's attempt to punish them was unsuccessful; he was defeated owing to the treason of the Qahtan and wounded in a battle. He died in January 1875, presumably of smallpox, though some sources report that he was poisoned.[68]

Abd al-Rahman ibn Faisal became the new ruler of Riyadh. He waged battles against his elder brothers and their bedouin allies, while the sons of his brother Saud, whom he had succeeded, opposed him in the capital. Fearing his nephews, Abd al-Rahman went to Abdallah and the three brothers decided to create a united front, led by Abdallah, against Saud's sons. The latter held out in Riyadh for some weeks and then fled. They retained allies in al-Kharj and al-Hasa.

Next Abdallah entered Riyadh again. In the eleven years after Faisal's death, it was the eighth change of power.[69] Philby gives a chronology of the rulers of Riyadh after Faisal's death:

2 December 1865–9 April 1871: Abdallah ibn Faisal;
10 April 1871–15 August 1871: Saud ibn Faisal;
15 August 1871–15 October 1871: Abdallah ibn Turki;
15 October 1871–15 January 1873: Abdallah ibn Faisal;
15 January 1873–26 January 1875: Saud ibn Faisal;
26 January 1875–28 January 1876: Abd al-Rahman ibn Faisal;
28 January 1876–31 March 1876: Saud ibn Faisal's sons;
from 31 March 1876: Abdallah ibn Faisal.[70]

The Disintegration of the Emirate of Riyadh and the Rise of Jabal Shammar

In 1878 a revolt against the Turks began in the Eastern Province but, after some initial successes, it was defeated.[71] Meanwhile there was internal discord in Qasim. The rival clans fought in Buraida and Anaiza, and both the Saudis and the Rashidis intervened in the conflict. The balance of forces was favourable to the Shammar and Abdallah was forced to recognize Hail's preponderance in that key province.[72]

According to Doughty:

The town of er-Riâth [Riyadh] with her suburbs, and the next village country about, is all that now remains of the Waháby dominion; which is become a small and weak principality, – such as Boreyda. Their great clay town, lately the metropolis of high Arabia, is silent; and the vast guest-hall is forsaken (the Waháby Prince's clay castle is greater than the Kasr at Hâyil): Ibn Saûd's servants abandon his unfortunate stars and go . . . to hire themselves to Mohammed ibn Rashîd. No Beduins now obey the Waháby; the great villages of East Nejd have sent back Abdullah's tax-gatherers.[73]

The reports by Blunt[74] and Huber[75] are similar.

In 1880 a son – named Abd al-Aziz ibn Abd al-Rahman ibn Faisal Al Saud – was born to Abd al-Rahman ibn Faisal, the fourth son of Faisal ibn Turki; the boy's mother was Sarah, the daughter of Ahmad Al Sudairi.[76] Abd al-Aziz's education started when he was 7 (his teacher was the *qadhi* of Riyadh), but the boy was more interested in playing with swords and rifles than in religious exercises, though he mastered reading the Quran at around the age of 11. The future king of Saudi Arabia (generally known in the West as Ibn Saud) started the more serious study of theology and other subjects at 14, when his father had already emigrated to Kuwait (see below). His teacher was Abdallah ibn Abd al-Latif, who was to become the chief *qadhi* and mufti of Riyadh.

The months that Abd al-Rahman ibn Faisal's family spent wandering with the Al Murra allowed the young emir to become familiar with the bedouin's customs and habits and their military methods and stratagems. With or without his father, Abd al-Aziz attended the *majlises* of the shaikh of Kuwait and acquired first-hand knowledge of the intricacies of Arabian politics and the emir's legal decisions. Abd al-Rahman's material situation was so desperate that it was only through the help of his friends that he was able to marry off his elder son. It was against this background that Abd al-Aziz nurtured the ambitious dream of restoring the family's honour and returning to the house of Saud their possessions, glory and wealth.[77]

Jabal Shammar: the heir to the Saudi emirate

Oases, provinces and nomadic tribes broke away from Riyadh one by one, surrendered (voluntarily or otherwise) to the Rashidis' protection and paid them tribute. Abdallah's attempts to evade the Rashidis' heavy hand were fruitless. Muhammad Al Rashid was playing a cat-and-mouse game with the emir of Riyadh, waiting for an opportune moment to deliver the fatal blow.

Rivalry flared up in Qasim between the former ruling family of Buraida, the Al Ulayyan, and the new rulers from the family of Muhanna, supported by Hail. The balance of forces was as follows: Riyadh cooperated with Anaiza and relied on the support of the Ataiba and Mutair; Hail supported Buraida and cooperated with the Harb.[78]

In 1882 al-Majmaa and the whole province of Sudair refused to obey the emir of Riyadh. Abdallah gathered his small detachments and the men from the Ataiba and moved towards al-Majmaa. Its inhabitants asked the emir of Hail for help. Muhammad Al Rashid moved his forces to Buraida, where the people of Qasim, Jabal Shammar's dependency, joined them. The very fact of the troops' approach caused Abdallah to flee to Riyadh. The governor of al-Majmaa was appointed from Hail.

Meanwhile, Saud ibn Faisal's sons tried to launch a challenge against Muhammad Al Rashid. They gathered a part of the Ataiba tribe and some inhabitants of the al-Arid oases, but were defeated.[79]

The winter of 1883–84 was rainy and the valleys turned green. Yet although the herds put on flesh, the Najdis, exhausted by plunder and raids, saw no improvement in their lot. In January 1884 Abdallah again tried to annex al-Majmaa but, abandoned by the bedouin, he was defeated. The oases and small towns of Washm and Sudair submitted to Jabal Shammar. Tired of raids and feuds, the population preferred a strong power.[80] Abdallah's small emirate was literally falling to pieces.[81]

In October 1887 Saud ibn Faisal's sons established control over Riyadh and al-Arid and captured the emir of Riyadh. He had previously managed to apply for help to the ruler of Hail, who plucked the ripe fruit without hesitation. Abdallah's appeal gave Muhammad Al Rashid an opportunity to extend his power to the whole emirate on the pretext of 'saving' its ruler. He made for Riyadh with a strong contingent of troops, and Saud's sons fled to al-Kharj. The emir of Jabal Shammar released Abdallah from jail and brought him to Hail, his capital, 'for his safety', leaving Salim Al Subhan, one of his most loyal and ruthless commanders, as the emir of Riyadh.[82]

Abd al-Aziz Al Saud believed that his uncle, Emir Abdallah, had fallen from power for three reasons:

> First, his brother Saud's sons were in al-Kharj and instigated the tribes against him. Second, he supported the family of Al Ulayyan, former emirs of Qasim, in their struggle against the family of Al Muhanna, who possessed real power then. This was due to Abdallah's ignorance of the situation . . . Siding with a defeated family was not a wise policy. Thus he weakened his influence in Qasim. Third, Muhammad ibn Rashid appeared on the scene and strove to rule Najd. He tied himself to the family of Aba al-Khail . . . and all they united against the Al Saud.[83]

The second Saudi state formally existed until the end of 1887. In August of the following year, Salim Al Subhan, the governor of Riyadh, managed to defeat Saud ibn Faisal's sons. The true extent of their strength is clear from the fact that the detachment sent against them by the Shammar consisted of a mere 35 men. Three sons were killed,

The Disintegration of the Emirate of Riyadh and the Rise of Jabal Shammar

the fourth had perished earlier and the fifth fled to Hail to throw himself on Muhammad Al Rashid's mercy. According to another version, Saud's youngest son was already an honoured prisoner in Hail.[84] The people of Riyadh complained against the merciless governor and Muhammad Al Rashid replaced him by Ibn Ruhayis in 1888/89.[85]

In the autumn of 1889 the Shammar went on a raid, reaching as far as Hijaz. When Muhammad Al Rashid returned to the capital, he found that Abdallah ibn Faisal, his guest and prisoner, was seriously ill. The ruler allowed him to go to Riyadh with his brother, Abd al-Rahman ibn Faisal. Abdallah returned to his depopulated capital and died in November 1889.[86] A quarter of a century earlier, when he occupied the throne, the emirate of Riyadh had extended from Jabal Shammar to the inner regions of Oman, from the Gulf to Hijaz and the boundaries of Yemen. When he was dying as a vassal of Hail, Abdallah ruled only the area of al-Arid and was the nominal sovereign of Washm and Sudair. He spent at least one third of that period as a homeless refugee while others ruled the disintegrating state. Philby describes him as an 'incompetent' ruler. However, the decisive factor in the ruin of the Saudi state was a combination of unfavourable circumstances rather than the ruler's personal weaknesses.[87]

Abd al-Rahman ibn Faisal became the next emir of Riyadh, though Muhammad, the middle brother, was still alive. Muhammad Al Rashid reappointed the cruel Salim Al Subhan as governor of Riyadh, perhaps to keep a watch on the new ruler. In 1890 Abd al-Rahman clashed with Salim and stirred up a rebellion. Ibn Rashid's troops besieged Riyadh, but the town was well fortified. The siege was in vain and the parties concluded an armistice. Abd al-Rahman remained the ruler of Riyadh and some neighbouring areas, virtually as Muhammad Al Rashid's vassal.[88] At that time the population of Anaiza and Buraida in Qasim – who had seen that the Shammar's power was increasing, taxes were rising and their own privileges were diminishing – preferred to unite with Abd al-Rahman against Jabal Shammar.

At the end of 1890 a broad coalition of anti-Rashidi elements was formed between Abd al-Rahman ibn Faisal, the population of Qasim and the Mutair. Ibn Rashid gathered all his forces, including detachments of the Shammar and their allies – the Zafir, Harb and Muntafiq. He sent forty messengers to the Shammar clans, who were then camped between Karbala and Basra. The messengers' camels were covered with black cloths as a warning that Emir Muhammad's subjects would disgrace themselves if they failed to come immediately to the aid of their ruler.[89] A large-scale battle was waged in Qasim near Mulaida with many thousands on either side; it was perhaps the biggest battle since the Egyptian conquest.

The fighting lasted for a month with no sign of victory for either party. However, for some unknown reason, Abd al-Rahman did not come to the aid of his allies, leaving them face to face with the Shammar. Finally, in January 1891 Muhammad Al Rashid resorted to a ruse: he pretended to retreat and then delivered a sudden counter-attack. Gathering thousands of camels in the centre, he moved them forwards after firing at the enemy. The camel corps was followed by the infantry, who simultaneously attacked from the flanks. The Qasimis lost between 600 and 1,200 people and many of their men fled to Kuwait, Iraq and Syria.[90] Within a decade, Ibn Rashid had established himself as the undisputed ruler of central Arabia.

When Abd al-Rahman ibn Faisal learned the news of his allies' defeat, he fled to the desert. After an abortive attempt to recapture Riyadh and a long period of wandering, his family settled in Kuwait in 1893 under the protection of its shaikh, Muhammad Al Sabah. The Ottoman government granted Abd al-Rahman a modest monthly pension of 60 gold liras.[91] Power in Riyadh was then seized by Ajlan, Muhammad Al Rashid's slave, and Najd was divided into several provinces, all subordinated to Jabal Shammar. The chroniclers left few reports about the period, mentioning only the deaths of renowned individuals, minor appointments to administrative posts by Muhammad Al Rashid and the usual winter raids against the bedouin tribes.[92]

The ruler of Jabal Shammar became the master of an exhausted and devastated country, deprived, moreover, of access to the sea. All the travellers, without exception, who visited central Arabia in the second half of the nineteenth century describe withered gardens and palm groves, sanded-up wells and ruined villages. The weakened state authorities were unable to protect the plantations and fields from bedouin raids. Thousands of people emigrated to Iraq or to the Gulf coast and commerce suffered greatly. According to Amin Rihani:

> Take a merchant from Bahrain who would be going to Al-Hasa for trade. Before he set foot on the Ojair [al-Uqair] coast he had to pay tribute to the 'Ujman; from Ojair to the first palms – five miles [8 km] – and fifty reals tribute to the Munasir; from the palms to Umm'uz-Zarr five miles and fifty reals tribute to Benu Murrah; from Umm'uz Zarr to 'Alat – another fifty reals to Benu Hajir; and so on . . . Moreover, much of his merchandise was often stolen.[93]

The dangers faced by the caravans during the transportation of goods caused price fluctuations, undermined economic ties and ruined artisans and merchants, especially small traders, who could not organize a reliable guard for their caravans.

In the last decade of the nineteenth century, it was only Muhammad Al Rashid's military strength that prevented the outbreak of revolts. As soon as he died, unrest began and was brutally suppressed by Abd al-Aziz Al Rashid, the new emir of Jabal Shammar. He plundered towns and villages ruthlessly and imposed exorbitant levies on them. Engaged in a struggle with Kuwait, he was unable to stop the tribal feuds which flared across the whole country or to prevent the bedouin from devastating the oases. Musil notes, 'All settled people longed for a strong power that would be able to protect their property and lives.'[94]

In evaluating the situation in central Arabia at the turn of the twentieth century, one may share Pershits' conclusion:

> The restoration and development of the economy of northern and central Arabia required the suppression of feudal-tribal anarchy, the curbing of the bedouin shaikhs and the creation of a firm, centralized state.[95]

The Disintegration of the Emirate of Riyadh and the Rise of Jabal Shammar

The Rashidis at the turn of the century

In the opinion of the chronicler Khalid al-Faraj:

> The policy of the Al Rashid might be characterized as 'divide and rule'. The rulers of Hail relied on their tribe, the Shammar, which was one of the most famous for valour and courage on the battlefield . . . They courted the Turks and indulged their wishes, because both the beginning and the end of the Iraqi pilgrims' way to the holy cities were in their hands, and the emir of Shammar depended on the proceeds from the pilgrims. Ibn Rashid recognized the suzerainty of Sultan Abdul Hamid. The Sublime Porte considered him one of his most devout vassals, and the force that had removed the Al Saud and destroyed their emirate. The sultan showered gifts and decorations upon him and provided him with assistance. In 1897 the ruler of Jabal Shammar died childless.[96]

The ruler was succeeded by his nephew, Abd al-Aziz ibn Mitab Al Rashid, then aged about 30. A courageous fighter and adventurer, he was described as easily roused to anger and hasty in taking decisions. He handled a sword more easily than politics, and acted first and reflected later.[97] Within a decade, he had lost most of the inheritance left him by his powerful uncle. Lorimer has left the following description:

> The impression at first formed of the Amir by our officials was that he was of a harsh and impetuous disposition, without prudence or judgement, and that his administration, especially in his outlying dependencies, was excessively severe and provocative of disloyalty; but the result of later enquiries was to modify this opinion, and to show that he was in the end the victim rather of ill-fortune than of his own folly. His courage and skill as a military leader . . . have never apparently been called in question.[98]

Jabal Shammar could not play the role of a stable state formation. Based on the supposed superiority of the Shammar, it was seen by other groups in the population as a tool for the dominance of one particular tribal confederation rather than a supratribal, all-Arabian power. With its growing dependence on the Ottoman empire in the late nineteenth century, Jabal Shammar became an instrument of Turkish influence in the peninsula. The people's general discontent with Turkish rule and policy in Arabia thus spread to the emirs of Hail. By strengthening its positions on the Gulf coast and hampering Turkey's attempts to restore its control over the region, Britain supported Jabal Shammar's rivals. Lastly, after Muhammad Al Rashid's death, the endlessly feuding ruling family failed to produce even a single ruler who could match Abd al-Aziz ibn Abd al-Rahman Al Saud, the future founder of Saudi Arabia. All these factors – later compounded by the Al Rashid's participation in the First World War on the side of Turkey – led to the inevitable decline and fall of the once-powerful emirate.

Great-power rivalry in the Gulf basin at the turn of the century and the situation in Arabia

The history of the first and second Saudi states has demonstrated the interweaving of Arabia's destiny with general developments in the region. The future of state formations in Arabia was determined not only by the balance of forces in the desert: it was sometimes influenced to a greater extent by the decisions taken in London, Istanbul, Cairo, Berlin, St Petersburg and Paris.

Britain – the strongest colonial power in the late nineteenth century – strove to control the whole of the Arabian peninsula, whether directly or indirectly, after the Suez Canal was opened in 1869 and Egypt had been occupied in 1882. The British colonial empire in India was imposing its will on the sultanate of Muscat, the princely states of Trucial Oman, Qatar and Bahrain, thus increasing their dependence on Britain. Kuwait, which was formally under Ottoman suzerainty, was the next to be subdued.

Although the Gulf was theoretically an international waterway, it became in effect a British lake. The imperial telegraph communications with India and Australia were maintained via the Gulf. Some 40% of the Gulf countries' exports and 63% of their imports were accounted for by Britain and British India. Almost all goods were imported and exported aboard vessels under the British flag.[99] The British navy dominated the Gulf and the Indian Ocean.

The chief British representative in the Gulf area had the title, 'Her Britannic Majesty's Political Resident in the Persian Gulf and Consul-General for Fars and Khuzistan'. Lord Curzon, the viceroy of India, described him as the uncrowned king of the Gulf.[100] The resident was appointed by the government of India from among officials of the Indian Civil Service. His subordinates were based in Muscat, Kuwait and Bahrain as political agents. As political resident, he was responsible to the government of India; as consul-general, he was subordinate to the British ambassador in Tehran, appointed by the Foreign Office. British global interests, as stipulated by the Foreign Office, often conflicted with the regional interests of the British authorities in India and the so-called 'Middle Eastern grouping' of the British ruling class.[101] They were united on all the cardinal questions, however.

British policy in the Gulf had the dual aim of controlling naval and other communications on the route to India and maintaining the Pax Britannica in the Gulf. This implied that British trade interests must reign supreme and that other powers must be prevented from penetrating into the region.

In the late nineteenth century, the antagonism of the great powers and their colonial expansion spread to the Gulf basin. The Kaiser's Germany was particularly energetic in its search of 'a place in the sun'. Kaiser Wilhelm II declared himself 'the protector of Islam' and Germany established close ties with the Ottoman empire and strengthened its economic, political and military positions there. In the late 1880s the idea arose of building a railway from Istanbul to Baghdad and then to the Gulf, which would enable Germany to penetrate the region, bypassing the British-dominated sea routes. In 1899 Germany was granted a preliminary concession for the construction of the Istanbul–

Baghdad–Kuwait railway. The creation of a continuous strategic railway from Berlin to the Gulf was an immediate threat to British dominance in the Gulf, Arabia and the entire Middle East. The Germans helped the Turks to build a railway in Hijaz, connecting Damascus with Medina. German diplomacy helped Turkey to increase its dominance (which was largely nominal) in the Arabian peninsula.

In the late nineteenth century, Russia – France's ally – was also seen in London as a dangerous rival in the region. A project to build a railway to the Gulf via Caucasia was seriously discussed in St Petersburg and there were vague proposals to build a Russian railway from the Mediterranean coast to Kuwait. It was no coincidence that Russian and French warships, visiting Gulf ports to 'show the colours' and find a location for a coaling station, were seen by the British authorities in India as a direct challenge.[102] A dispute arose between Britain and France over Muscat, where the French tried to establish a coaling station in 1899. The year 1903 witnessed a joint visit by Russian and French warships to the Arabian and Gulf ports.[103]

In the late nineteenth century, Britain started to change its traditional policy towards Turkey. London had earlier striven to retain the Ottoman empire's territorial integrity, hoping to subdue the whole empire and use this against Russia. But gradually the focus of British interests in the eastern Mediterranean and the Middle East shifted from Istanbul to Egypt and Mesopotamia. The growth of German influence in the Ottoman empire played a considerable role in that change. Lord Salisbury, who became British prime minister in 1895, started talking of a division of the Ottoman empire. It was implied that Arabia and the basins of the Tigris and the Euphrates would enter the zone of British dominance, as Egypt and Sudan had done. In line with these plans, London saw the retention of its control over the Gulf as a top priority.

In May 1893 the British foreign secretary, Lord Lansdowne, stated before the House of Lords:

> I say it without hesitation – we should regard the establishment of a naval base, or a fortified port in the Persian Gulf by any other Power as a very grave menace to British interests, and we should certainly resist it with all means at our disposal.[104]

In 1903 a British flotilla visited the Gulf ports under Curzon's flag. It was the largest foreign fleet in Gulf waters since 1515, when a Portuguese squadron, led by Albuquerque, had conquered Hormuz. In his speeches, Curzon spelled out Britain's position in language characteristic of the 'white man's burden' of the colonial era.

Although the decay of the Ottoman empire continued at the turn of the century, Turkey's positions in Arabia strengthened somewhat owing to its improved army and the development of communications. The Turks remained the second most important factor in Arabian affairs after the British.

The opening of the Suez Canal in 1869 substantially altered Turkey's position in western Arabia. Earlier, columns of exhausted soldiers had arrived there after long marches through the desert, and the expenses had been very high. Now they could be brought by sea, via the Suez Canal. In the 1870s the Turks reconquered Yemen and Asir.[105]

The Turks living in Hijaz were under the jurisdiction of Ottoman governors and Turkish judges, whereas the Arabs were ruled by the sharif of Mecca. Naturally, the Ottoman governor and the sharif were in permanent conflict and relations between the governor of Jidda and Aun al-Rashid, the ruler of Mecca since 1882, became strained. The governor undertook public works in territory that was formally under the sharif's jurisdiction: he improved the water supply in Jidda, rebuilt the Zubaida aqueduct, and built a new governor's office, barracks and guardhouses. He allowed Aun to perform his judiciary functions only with respect to his own clan, to nomads and to non-Turks born in Mecca itself. The Turks began to gain control of the caravan routes and to send expeditions against the Harb without the sharif's consent. Aun's proceeds from custom duties fell. Such was the discontent that the sharif, some of his high-ranking relatives, several individuals from among the nobility and the merchants, the mufti of the Shafiis and other *ulama* went to Medina to protest: they persuaded the sultan to dismiss the governor.[106]

Jamal Pasha, the new governor, pursued a far more cautious policy. Aun al-Rashid's influence grew somewhat, but his conflict with the governor continued and the Arabs' attitude to the Turks deteriorated. After Aun's death in 1905, he was succeeded by Ali, a Turkish puppet. Then the Young Turks' revolution occurred in Istanbul, and the governor was dismissed as a supporter of the old regime. After a period of uncertainty, Husain ibn Ali was appointed sharif of Mecca. He had been living in Istanbul since 1893 as an honoured prisoner, with his sons Ali, Abdallah and Faisal.[107] Later on, he was to lead the Arab revolt (see chapter 10).

Another important event in Hijaz in 1908 was the opening of a railway from Maan to Medina. Its construction substantially improved the Turks' military-strategic positions in western Arabia. However, British countermoves, and the growth of anti-Turkish sentiment among the Arabs, prevented the Ottoman empire from strengthening its positions in the east of the Arabian peninsula.

Kuwait, which had become the main port for inner Arabia and a flourishing trade centre in the late nineteenth century, strove to decrease its dependence on the Turks, which was already a mere formality. Muhammad Al Sabah, the shaikh of Kuwait, started to play an active role in the internal struggle in Arabia, where Jabal Shammar, the Ottomans' vassal, represented the greatest danger to Kuwait. This explains Kuwait's offer of protection to Abd al-Rahman ibn Faisal, who claimed the Riyadh throne. The emir, who it will be remembered had fled from Riyadh, still maintained contact with the oases and tribes of central Arabia, encouraged their anti-Shammar attitudes and never lost sight of his ambition to return.

In 1896 Muhammad Al Sabah and his brother were killed by a third brother, Mubarak, who became the shaikh of the town and the neighbouring tribes.[108] The new ruler of Kuwait was to have a major influence on developments in Arabia for the next two decades.

The powerful Muntafiq tribe in southern Iraq, led by the aristocratic clan of Al Saadun, was also a factor in central Arabian politics. But the Muntafiq saw the desert as merely offering the opportunity for raids and did not claim a state formation of their own.

The Disintegration of the Emirate of Riyadh and the Rise of Jabal Shammar

Britain was alarmed at Germany's and Turkey's plans to restore direct Ottoman control over Kuwait and connect the Berlin–Baghdad railway with the Gulf coast.[109] In 1897 the Turks tried to seize Kuwait and exile Shaikh Mubarak to Istanbul. He frustrated their plans by bribing Ottoman officials in Basra and Baghdad, who reported to the Sublime Porte that it was 'inexpedient' to replace the shaikh of Kuwait at that moment.

The following year, the Turks sent a delegation of Basra officials and notables to Kuwait. They invited the shaikh to Istanbul as a member of the consultative council under the sultan. Realizing that he would never return from Istanbul, Mubarak sought protection from the British, although he had earlier avoided any close cooperation with them. In return, Britain imposed a secret treaty on Mubarak: signed on 23 January 1899, it provided for a virtual protectorate. In particular, the shaikh pledged himself not to grant concessions to any country but Britain.[110] The German mission that arrived in Kuwait the following year seeking a permit to extend the Baghdad railway left empty-handed.[111]

In the autumn of 1898 Abd al-Aziz Al Rashid, the new ruler of Hail, visited Najd. The local nobility and *ulama* expressed their loyalty to the sovereign, though discontent with Shammar rule was growing. Then Abd al-Aziz Al Rashid attacked the Dawasir tribe and returned with spoils. The next year, the emir of Hail appeared in Kuwait, defeated the local forces and their Muntafiq allies and pursued them as far as the Euphrates.[112]

As a loyal vassal of Turkey, the Hail emirate was a cause of concern for Britain; one of the aims of British policy in the peninsula was to weaken Hail, though on some occasions they used it for their own ends. Britain supported the Arabian adversaries of Turkey and Jabal Shammar: this had an important, if not decisive influence on the Saudi family's successful return to power in Najd.

CHAPTER 9

The Renaissance of the Emirate of Riyadh in the Early Twentieth Century (1902–1914)

A favourable climate for the renaissance of the Riyadh emirate emerged in Arabia again towards the beginning of the twentieth century. Hail relied on the military might of the Shammar and their allies, but enjoyed less support among the Najdi population in general. Britain began to intervene in Arabian affairs to weaken the local rulers' dependence on the Porte and finally establish its protectorate over them. In line with these aims, Britain supported the adversaries of Jabal Shammar on many occasions. The Al Saud family, who had settled in Kuwait, became a natural pole of attraction for all Najdis who were dissatisfied with Rashidi rule.

The young Emir Abd al-Aziz captures Riyadh and establishes control over the neighbouring provinces

In the autumn of 1900 Abd al-Rahman ibn Faisal led a successful raid on a subdivision of the Qahtan and reached Sudair. He then returned to Kuwait and started preparations for a more serious, large-scale military expedition to Najd.[1]

The threat of finding himself again depending directly on the Turkish authorities prompted Mubarak, the shaikh of Kuwait, to step up his actions against Jabal Shammar.[2] He formed an alliance with Saadun Pasha, the shaikh of the Muntafiq, on the basis of an anti-Rashidi policy.[3]

In late 1900 and early 1901, the ruler of Kuwait gathered the armed urban population and the bedouin and set out for Qasim. Abd al-Rahman and some other Saudi emirs joined him, leading a part of the Ajman and the Mutair.[4] Adamov, the Russian consul in Basra, reported, 'The army of Kuwait was successful and managed to capture Riyadh itself, from where the victorious Mubarak made for Hail, Ibn Rashid's capital.'[5] Mubarak seemed to have exaggerated his initial successes in his boastful reports, however. Abd al-Aziz ibn Mitab, the ruler of Hail, received further supplies of arms from the Turks, mobilized all his forces[6] and defeated the Kuwaitis and their allies near the al-Sarif oasis in February–March 1901.[7]

At that moment Abd al-Rahman's son Abd al-Aziz was attempting to seize the citadel in Riyadh, the capital of his ancestors. His detachment burst into the town together with the Kuwaitis but the governor, Ajlan ibn Muhammad, ensconced himself in the al-Mismak fortress and withstood the siege successfully. On learning the outcome of the battle of al-Sarif, Abd al-Aziz retreated hastily to Kuwait – not without having ascertained, however, that the capital's citizens resented the Shammar oppression and were sympathetic to the house of Saud.[8]

Britain supported the actions of Kuwait and its allies, whether directly or indirectly. In Adamov's opinion, Britain stood firmly behind Mubarak, since it was interested in weakening Jabal Shammar. The shaikh of Kuwait purchased substantial shipments of British Martini rifles in Bahrain.[9]

Ibn Mitab's victory was followed by a massacre of the inhabitants of Buraida and other towns in Qasim in revenge for their support for Kuwait and the Saudis. Then Ibn Mitab sent the cruel army commander Salim ibn Subhan to teach Riyadh a lesson.[10]

The Turkish authorities in Iraq began gathering their forces for an attack on Kuwait under the pretext of 'restoring peace and order', but the fear of a conflict with Britain made them hold back.[11] As a result of a complex diplomatic struggle, the Turks, supported by Berlin, reached an agreement with the other powers in September 1901 to retain the status quo in Kuwait and prevent its occupation by British forces.[12] It is clear from a secret instruction sent to Adamov that Russia was also striving to maintain the status quo in the Gulf basin at the turn of the century.[13]

The ruler of Hail reached an agreement with the Turks and attacked Kuwait, weakened after the defeat near al-Sarif. Ibn Mitab besieged al-Jahra, a village on the Gulf coast. However, Britain sent a warship to bomb the Shammar camp and British weapons were shipped to the shaikhdom. The British chargé d'affaires in Istanbul protested to the sultan about the Shammar's activities. After a hopeless siege lasting two or three weeks, Ibn Mitab retreated to Hail on the sultan's instructions. His successes proved short-lived and his adversaries seized the initiative.[14]

Kuwait and its allies, the Saudi emirs, decided to deliver the Shammar a new blow in central Arabia. Abd al-Aziz persuaded his father to allow him to try his luck once more in Riyadh. According to most sources, he started his campaign with only forty men, including his brother Muhammad ibn Abd al-Rahman and his cousin Abdallah ibn Jiluwi. In November–December 1901, when the Kuwait crisis was at its peak and involved London, Istanbul, Berlin and St Petersburg, Abd al-Aziz and his men moved southwards via al-Hasa to reach the Rub al-Khali. On the way, the detachment enlisted supporters from the Ajman, Al Murra, Subai and Suhul tribes and became several thousand strong. Abd al-Aziz raided the hostile tribes and the villages of Najd that remained loyal to the Rashidis.

When Ibn Mitab was informed of the situation, he wrote to the Ottoman authorities in Basra and Baghdad, asking them to remove Abd al-Aziz from al-Hasa. Fearful of the Turks, the bedouin abandoned the young emir, who was left with his initial group of forty supporters. Fearing that his son's actions were becoming a dangerous adventure, Abd al-Rahman demanded that he return to Kuwait and give up the plan to capture Riyadh. The Turkish authorities in al-Hasa forced Abd al-Aziz's detachment to leave the province and they spent the month of Ramadhan (December 1901–January 1902) in the Yabrin oasis.[15]

It is probable that Ibn Mitab did not attach great importance to the young emir's sallies, which played into Abd al-Aziz's hands. Disobeying his father's orders, he decided to risk appearing in the vicinity of the Saudis' former capital on 12 January 1902. He left a group of his armed men with their horses and camels resting in a small oasis, instructing them to flee if he had not returned by the following morning. The rest moved towards the town walls.

Leaving a dozen fighters in reserve, Abd al-Aziz and his companions climbed over the wall near the Shamsiya Gate in the dead of night and made for their friend Juwaisir's house near the governor's residence. (Governor Ajlan ibn Muhammad used to visit his wife, who lived in Riyadh, in the daytime and spend his nights in the al-Mismak citadel together with its garrison of some eighty men.) Juwaisir fed Abd al-Aziz and his men and then they broke into the governor's house. Failing to find him, they locked his wife and a female relative in a room. Abd al-Aziz sent one of his men to bring his brother Muhammad and ten people who had been left outside the town. The whole detachment gathered in the house. When Ajlan's wife told them that the governor might come after the morning prayer, they decided to wait. Tension was mounting, since the tiny group was aware how risky the undertaking was.

On the morning of 15 January 1902 Ajlan at last appeared from the fortress gate with a small group of guards. Abd al-Aziz and his fighters opened fire and threw themselves upon the governor. The Shammar tried to flee. At the very last moment Abdallah ibn Jiluwi killed the governor just near the fortress gate. The gate in which the tip of Abd al-Aziz's spear stuck, and the wall on which Ajlan's blood allegedly remained, still attract many visitors to Riyadh.

Taking advantage of their surprise attack, Abd al-Aziz's men made short work of the Shammar garrison in the fortress and then massacred all enemy soldiers in the town. Two dozen Shammar ensconced in the tower of the fortress, however, were released on parole. The young emir lost only two people killed and three wounded. His unexpected and brilliant success captured the Najdis' imagination and was later glorified in numerous legends and *qasidas*.[16]

The inhabitants of Riyadh swore allegiance to Abd al-Aziz, who immediately started to fortify the town walls. When Ibn Mitab learned of the fall of Riyadh, he flew into a rage and vowed to take revenge on his traditional enemies. He travelled from the lower reaches of the Euphrates to Hail to gather troops and lead them to Riyadh, but the preparations took some months.[17]

Meanwhile, reinforcements for Abd al-Aziz arrived from Kuwait: seventy soldiers led by his brother Saad. Before the Shammar came, the young emir made a raid southwards, conquered al-Kharj and raided the Qahtan in al-Majmaa. In May 1902 Abd al-Aziz's father, Abd al-Rahman, came to Riyadh. Both Arab and European historians agree that father and son understood each other well, and their mutual confidence increased the stability of the new state. The elderly emir seemed to be aware of his son's abilities. When Abd al-Aziz gathered the *ulama* and notables of the town and urged them to swear allegiance to his father, Abd al-Rahman declined the honour and declared his 22-year-old son to be the emir, remaining as his chief adviser and the imam during prayers.[18]

The daring seizure of Riyadh proved that Abd al-Aziz possessed the virtues needed by a shaikh and emir – courage, luck and the ability to lead. Subsequent developments showed that he was an outstanding figure on the Arabian stage: this is the unanimous opinion of all historians and travellers, both European and Arab. Abd al-Aziz had grown calmer and wiser in exile; he had studied the bedouin's habits and customs, their strong and weak points, and so was able to manipulate them. At the same time, understanding that his chief supporters would be the Najdis, he always showed them particular consideration. Conscious of the importance of religion, he established good relations with the *ulama* from the outset and used them to strengthen the central power.

In the European and sometimes in the Arab literature, the founder of contemporary Saudi Arabia is known under his kin name, Ibn Saud: we shall use it from this point onwards. Gertrude Bell, the British Arabist, gives a literary portray of Ibn Saud at a later period in *The Arab War*:

> His hands are fine, with slender fingers, a trait almost universal among the tribes of pure Arab blood, and in spite of his great height and breadth of shoulder, he conveys the impression, common enough in the desert, of an indefinable lassitude, not individual but racial, the secular weariness of an ancient and self-contained people, which has made heavy drafts on its vital forces, and borrowed little from beyond its own forbidding frontiers. His deliberate movements, his slow, sweet smile, and the contemplative glance of his heavy-lidded eyes, though they add to his dignity and charm, do not accord with the Western conception of a vigorous personality. Nevertheless, report credits him with powers of physical endurance rare even in hard bitten Arabia.[19]

Leaving aside the colonialist expression 'racial lassitude', it is interesting to note Bell's generally high evaluation of the emir's personality.

Using the respite granted by the Shammar, Ibn Saud mounted attacks in all directions, striving to subdue enough land to give him the minimum military and economic base and enable him to continue the war. Meanwhile, developments in Arabia were attracting the attention of Istanbul, London, Berlin and St Petersburg. Germany put pressure on the Ottoman sultan, trying to ensure access to the Gulf for the Baghdad railway. The ruler of Hail, confident of Turkey's support, tried to regain control over southern Najd. But his Kuwaiti rivals, as well as the Saudis, were backed by Britain.[20]

It was not until July or August 1902 that the emir of Jabal Shammar set out for Riyadh, raiding unfriendly tribes and oases on the way. His attacks upon Washm, Mahmal and Qasim proved that the population of these oases opposed him.[21]

Meanwhile, Ibn Saud began gathering troops from among the urban people of al-Arid and Dawasir, and the Al Murra and Shamir tribes. The Shammar were unable to capture Riyadh immediately as it was heavily fortified, so Ibn Mitab decided to cut off Ibn Saud's supply routes from Kuwait rather than storm the town. On learning this, the emir left his father Abd al-Rahman with a garrison in the town and escaped to al-Kharj with a small detachment. The Shammar followed him; but to ensure their advance, they had to take by force the fortified oasis-towns that had joined the Saudis. Lastly, Ibn Saud gathered some 2,000 people near Dilam and attacked Ibn Mitab, relying on the garrison besieged in the town. Most of the Shammar scattered throughout al-Kharj to plunder, fell palm trees and graze their horses and camels, and the ruler of Hail failed to take advantage of his numerical superiority. Clashes and skirmishes continued from September to November 1902, when an epidemic spread among the Shammar and ensured Ibn Saud's final success. Ibn Mitab had to withdraw northwards,[22] affording Ibn Saud a respite to consolidate the nucleus of the future state.

Returning from the unsuccessful campaign, Ibn Mitab resumed his raids. He decided to attack Mubarak, the ruler of Kuwait, whom he saw as the main enemy. This time, Ibn Saud came to Kuwait's help in January–February 1903 with several thousand troops. The Kuwaitis (led by Jabir), the Najdis (led by Ibn Saud) and some subdivisions of the Ajman, Al Murra, Subai, Suhul, Bani Hajir, Bani Khalid and Awazim tribes, who joined them, attacked the Mutair, who were loyal to the Rashidis. The Arab sources claim that the allies had 10–15,000 men, including 500 cavalry, but these figures seem exaggerated. Ammash Al Dawish, one of the Mutair shaikhs, and his son were killed in the battle,[23] whose outcome was unclear. The Russian consul in Basra reported back that the Mutair had defeated the alliance of Kuwait and Najd.[24]

At that moment, Abd al-Rahman ibn Faisal visited Kuwait and met the Russian consul in Bushire.[25] Rather than a genuine attempt to establish political ties with Russia, the meeting was mainly intended to blackmail the British and persuade them to help the emir of Riyadh. In the spring of 1903 the Shammar again tried to capture Riyadh, but were rebuffed by its garrison, led by Abd al-Rahman, Ibn Saud's father. Subsequent skirmishes were unfavourable to the Shammar. After learning that Ibn Saud had already advanced to Qasim, they raised the siege of Riyadh and moved northwards.[26] Ibn Mitab never again appeared near the walls of the Saudis' capital.

Ibn Saud's first successes meant the restoration of the nucleus of the emirate of Riyadh with the active support of Kuwait and the indirect assistance of the British.

The advance to Qasim

In January 1903 Ibn Saud's representative met the British political agent in Bahrain and asked Britain to prevent Turkish troops landing in the event of the emir of Riyadh's seizure of al-Hasa. No precise answer was given, but the British administration in India observed Ibn Saud's activities with growing benevolence.[27] With their blessing, the alliance was strengthened between Mubarak, the ruler of Kuwait, Ibn Saud, the ruler of Riyadh, and Saadun, the shaikh of the Muntafiq, against Jabal Shammar. In March these three leaders met in Kuwait to decide on joint action.[28]

In the spring of 1903 petty clashes occurred in Washm between Saudi and Rashidi detachments. In May Ibn Mitab retreated to Qasim and Ibn Saud arrived from Kuwait with his detachment. Ibn Jiluwi besieged the Shammar garrison in Tharmida and seized the oasis after two weeks, massacring everybody who resisted. In the summer and autumn of the same year, hostilities were waged in Sudair province. The Shammar were increasingly losing control over the regions to the south of Qasim.[29]

Meanwhile, there were major changes in the international situation and Britain reinforced its offensive in the Gulf basin against its German and Russian rivals. In November–December 1903 Lord Curzon, the viceroy of India, paid a state visit to the Gulf countries accompanied by a squadron. The Najd–Shammar war was part of the great-power struggle for influence in the Gulf basin. Istanbul understood that a sizeable part of the Ottoman possessions in Arabia was in jeopardy.[30]

The ruler of Hail insisted that Turkey should send aid. In early 1904 he went to Iraq to gather reinforcements from among the Shammar tribes and receive arms.[31] The emir of Riyadh immediately moved his troops to Qasim. In March 1904 his detachment burst into Anaiza and Fuhaid ibn Subhan, the Shammar commander, was killed in the main market.[32]

The town had not yet been captured, however. A battle was waged near Anaiza and Ibn Saud defeated the Shammar troops, led by Majid ibn Hamud.[33] Some of Ibn Saud's relatives took part in the battle on the Shammar's side – they were grandsons of his uncle, Saud ibn Faisal, who had claimed the Riyadh throne, and were known as the Araif. The bedouin used this word, which meant 'recognized', to denote the camels seized by their enemies and recaptured in a counter-raid. Demonstrating his traditional magnanimity – or, according to one's point of view, great flexibility and an ability to foresee the future and disarm enemies who were no longer dangerous – Ibn Saud granted these relatives an unconditional pardon and suggested that they should either stay with him or join the Rashidis. Although they accepted his offer of reconciliation, hospitality and cooperation, they were later to become dangerous enemies.[34]

Ibn Saud appointed Abd al-Aziz Al Sulaim as emir of Anaiza. He belonged to a noble family who had returned from exile in Kuwait with their armed supporters. The new emir began settling accounts with his adversaries, but did not forget to fortify the town walls.[35] Soon after the capture of Anaiza, Ibn Saud sent a letter to Shaikh Mubarak of Kuwait, describing the fall of the town. The letter fell into the hands of the British and has been preserved in the Foreign Office archives:

> May God preserve you . . . We sent word to your Highness before this by the hand of your servant Madi that it was our intention to set forth on an expedition. So we proceeded . . . and by the help of God and with your assistance, we halted our

camels over above Osheziye [Ushaiziya] at the break of day. And we abode there, we and the people of Kassim who were with us, for the rest of that day. And the people of Anaiza who were with us sent men to their friends furtively to announce our coming. And when it was the fourth hour of the night we bestirred ourselves and came to Anaiza . . . And after we had said the morning prayer, we sent against them Abdullah ibn Jiluwi, with him a hundred men of the people of Riyadh to assist. And we marched against Majid, and when he saw the horsemen, God lifted his hand from off his men and helped us against them. And we broke them and slaughtered of them three hundred and seventy men. And God restored to us our kinsmen of the family of Saud who were prisoners in their hands . . . And, by Almighty God, but two Bedouins on our side were slain. Then we returned to the villages of our friends. And they had taken the castle and laid hands on the family of Yahia and those with them and slain them, and emptied the houses of the family Bessam. And, by God, there went away with Majid but some fifteen camels and seven mares; and the rest of their army and their horses and their arms and their tents and their furniture we took as spoil, by the help of God . . . And our intention, by the Grace of God, is that we should speed to Buraida, if God wills.[36]

After the fall of Anaiza the population of Buraida sent a delegation to Ibn Saud, asking his permission to attack the fortress in their town, where a Shammar garrison was ensconced. The seizure of Anaiza had convinced the people of Buraida that the course of developments was favourable to the emir of Riyadh. Besides, the Al Muhanna family (one of the leading clans of Buraida, who were in exile in Kuwait) had arrived in Anaiza with a small detachment, waiting for an opportunity to return to power.[37]

With the way to Buraida now open, Ibn Saud sent a detachment led by Salih Al Muhanna Aba al-Khail. When Ibn Saud entered Buraida, its population swore allegiance to him. However, the 150-strong Shammar garrison remained in the fortress, hoping to hold out until reinforcements arrived. The siege, together with skirmishes and minor battles, lasted for two months. Finally, the Riyadh soldiers dug a tunnel under the wall and set off an explosion. Exhausted by the merciless heat and a shortage of munitions, the Shammar surrendered the citadel in June 1904. Ibn Saud allowed them to return to Hail with their arms.[38]

After capturing Anaiza and Buraida, Ibn Saud spread his control from Riyadh to Qasim, including Washm. However, Ibn Mitab persuaded the Turks to provide him with more effective support. Initially, the Ottoman authorities mistrusted his requests for aid, seeing them as the usual attempts by a vassal to extort money, arms and reinforcements. But when they learned that Ibn Saud had annexed Qasim to his emirate, they grew worried and a 2,000-strong Turkish detachment with 6 guns, led by Colonel Hasan Shukri, was sent to Najd.[39] In June 1904 Ibn Mitab camped almost halfway between Hail and Buraida near Qusaiba, where he met the Shammar garrison on its way back from the town.[40]

Before opening hostilities, Hasan Shukri sent a letter to Ibn Saud, who was still in Anaiza, to warn him of the grave consequences of attacking the ruler of Hail. The

The Renaissance of the Emirate of Riyadh in the Early Twentieth Century

Turkish colonel wrote, 'His Majesty the great caliph heard about the sedition in Najd, directed by foreigners' hands. Therefore he sent me here to prevent bloodshed and a foreign intervention in the Muslim country.' Next he lamented Ibn Saud's cooperation with Mubarak, who was supported by foreigners and 'infidels', i.e. the British. He suggested in a bombastic manner that Ibn Saud should make his complaints to the Ottoman authorities rather than to Mubarak, a rebel against the caliph. Shukri noted that he was an ally not only of the Rashidis, but of all who sought aid and support from the Ottoman empire; if Ibn Saud also desired it, he might enjoy the Ottoman government's benevolence on a par with the Rashidis.[41]

The ruler of Riyadh was perturbed, but stood firm. He wrote in his return message:

We do not accept your advice or recognize your suzerainty. If you do not want bloodshed, you had better leave this country. If you attack us, we shall undoubtedly treat you as an aggressor. If you were free and objective, you would note that the cause of my disobedience is mistrust for you.

To explain his actions, Ibn Saud then referred to the situation in Yemen, Basra and Hijaz and the behaviour of the Turks. He recalled the time that the Hijazi authorities had plundered pilgrims just near the Kaaba. In conclusion, he warned the colonel that should the Turks move to the region under his power, he would 'consider them aggressors and treat them accordingly'.[42]

In the summer of 1904, in an attempt to gain British support in his struggle against the Turks and their vassal, the young ruler of Riyadh contacted Major Percy Cox, who had recently been appointed British political resident in the Gulf. Cox had been aide to the political resident in Somalia from 1892 to 1901, and consul in Muscat from 1901 to 1904, and was to play an important role in British-Saudi relations up to his retirement in 1923. He was an important mentor for the renowned Arabists Wilson, Bell and Philby. Although believing, with a greater or lesser deal of sincerity, that they protected British colonial interests, many of them undertook serious research and were experts on Arabian affairs. Cox was the first to give an accurate assessment of the importance of Ibn Saud and to suggest to the British colonial authorities in India that they should increase their ties with him, a view that was initially rejected.[43]

Britain saw the arrival of Turkish troops in Najd as a violation of the 1901 agreement on maintaining the status quo and sent the Porte a vigorous protest.[44] Having failed to persuade Ibn Saud to submit to their demands, the Ottoman authorities and Ibn Mitab decided to open hostilities. The Turks had 8 (11 according to other sources) infantry battalions, some 2,000 strong; 6 light guns; and substantial amounts of money, munitions, arms and food. The Shammar troops were reinforced by subdivisions of the Hitaim and Harb tribes and by people from Hail. Hearing that the enemy was approaching, Ibn Saud decided to meet them in the open field. His troops, which consisted of inhabitants of Riyadh, Qasim and al-Kharj and a part of the Mutair, moved westwards from Buraida. The forthcoming battles of al-Bukairiya and Shunana were to play a no less important role in determining the future of central Arabia than Ibn Saud's capture of Riyadh.[45]

The struggle for Qasim (1904-1906)

The battle of al-Bukairiya, which took place in mid-July 1904, consisted of a series of major and minor clashes. According to Arab sources, the Ottoman regular forces lost 1,000-1,500 killed, Hail 300-500 and the Saudi troops some 1,000. These figures seem grossly exaggerated; in any case, they include losses caused by disease and the heat. According to the chronicler Dari ibn Fuhaid ibn Rashid, who witnessed the battle, Ibn Mitab lost 100 men and Ibn Saud lost 200.[46] By comparison, the capture of Riyadh had cost fewer than a dozen lives. Ibn Saud was seriously wounded in the battle of al-Bukairiya and was within a hair's breadth of death.[47]

The first minor skirmishes in mid-July ended unfavourably for Ibn Saud and his troops were apparently forced to retreat in confusion. In the desert setting, however, this did not mean the end of hostilities. While the Rashidi troops and the Turkish infantry engaged in plunder and pursued Ibn Saud's fleeing forces, a detachment of Qasimis and the Mutair, led by Ibn Jiluwi, delivered a blow from the rear and sowed panic in the enemy ranks. The tide of battle was clearly turning in favour of the emir of Riyadh. Lorimer reports that a Turkish commander and many soldiers were killed. All the Turkish guns and many prisoners of war fell into Ibn Jiluwi's hands.[48]

Ibn Mitab was engaged in plundering the villages of Qasim and had left all his foodstuff and hardware near al-Bukairiya with a small detachment. Learning that Ibn Saud's troops were approaching with reinforcements, he sent a part of his troops to save the victuals and hardware, but it was too late. Ibn Saud seized all his supplies and the town of al-Bukairiya.[49]

Ibn Mitab then made for the western part of Qasim, to the area of al-Rass and Shunana, and arrived there in August, probably hoping for Turkish aid from Hijaz. But al-Rass, earlier obedient to him, decided this time to join the emir of Riyadh and the Shammar camped in Shunana. Ibn Saud arrived there with the bulk of his troops, but neither party took further action, probably because of the summer heat. Cholera broke out in Ibn Mitab's camp, and the bedouin on both sides began scattering, finding no spoils. Only the Turkish detachments from Iraq and the urban people of Jabal Shammar remained with Ibn Mitab: the urban residents alone stayed in Ibn Saud's camp. At last, a battle occurred near Shunana in late September and the Turks and the Shammar fled. Although they lost only a few dozen men, their camp equipment, camels, sheep, food, arms and some boxes with gold coins were all captured by the victors.[50]

In the words of Khalid al-Farj, a Najdi chronicler, 'It was that battle [of Shunana] that strengthened Ibn Saud's position in Najd and put an end to Turkish influence. One of the Rashidis' supports was destroyed in the battle.'[51] The importance of Ibn Saud's victory was heightened by the fact that he had fought several battalions of regular forces, though it should be stressed that the Turkish troops suffered desertions and were fighting in unfamiliar and extremely unfavourable conditions, when the summer heat was at its peak.

Ibn Saud's victory had not removed the Turkish threat, however. The emir of Riyadh sent a letter to the governor of Basra, asking for a subsidy as an Ottoman vassal[52] in order to preempt a new Turkish expedition. While receiving Ibn Saud's assurances of loyalty to the sultan, the Ottoman authorities nevertheless sent 3,000 troops with guns from Samawa to Najd. They were commanded by Ahmad Faizi Pasha from the army corps whose headquarters was in Baghdad. Faizi Pasha was more interested in personal enrichment than in the success of the expedition. The pack animals he had bought cheaply were totally unsuited to transporting men and equipment into the depths of Arabia.[53]

The declared purpose of the expedition, which started out in January 1905, was to establish peace between the Rashidis and the Saudis rather than to punish Ibn Saud. A meeting was held in al-Zubair, to the north of Kuwait, between Ahmad Mukhlis Pasha (the governor of Basra), Shaikh Mubarak of Kuwait and Ibn Saud's father, Abd al-Rahman. The *wali* (governor) informed the Saudi delegation that the Porte had appointed Abd al-Rahman as *qaimmaqam* and had decided that Qasim must be a neutral buffer province between the Rashidis and the Saudis. The Turks demanded the right to keep garrisons in Buraida and Anaiza in order to guarantee the neutrality of Qasim. Abd al-Rahman resorted to evasive tactics, promising only that these proposals would be discussed by the people of Najd.[54]

Faizi Pasha's troops were already advancing towards central Najd, however, while a 750-strong detachment with a battery of field artillery was hurrying to their aid from Medina under the command of Sidqi Pasha. Ibn Mitab was unhappy at his growing dependence on the Turks and soon quarrelled with Ahmad Faizi Pasha, abandoning his strong protectors.[55]

After the defeat near Shunana, the ruler of Jabal Shammar lived with the nomads and swore not to return to Hail before having taken revenge on his enemy. According to al-Farj, the weaker he grew, the more cruel he became.[56] It is probable, however, that he was merely afraid to return to Hail for fear of intrigues within the ruling clan.

Ibn Saud's position was seriously undermined by Salih ibn Hasan Al Muhanna, the emir of Buraida, who was trying to eliminate both the Rashidis and the Saudis, preferring the status of Ottoman vassal. In April 1905 the Turks entered Buraida and some days later they occupied Anaiza. Turkish garrisons were stationed in both towns, Ottoman flags were hoisted, the Hamidiye march was played by military bands and the sultan's name was mentioned at Friday prayers.[57]

Najd was divided into administrative units in accordance with the usual Ottoman practice. Buraida became a *qaza* (district), ruled by Salih ibn Hasan Al Muhanna, and Anaiza was proclaimed a *müdürlük*, headed by Abd al-Aziz ibn Abdallah. They both depended administratively on Basra. Southern Najd also became a *qaza* and Abd al-Aziz ibn Abdallah was treated as *qaimmaqam* with his residence in Riyadh, formally subordinate to Basra.[58]

Aware that he was not strong enough to challenge the Turks, Ibn Saud ordered his detachments to refrain from all hostilities against them. He and his father met Faizi Pasha, who reiterated his demands: first, that the Turkish garrisons should stay in Buraida and Anaiza until a peace treaty was concluded between the Rashidis and the Saudis; and, second, that Qasim should be a neutral buffer zone. Ibn Saud and his father, however, avoided making any firm commitments.[59]

Turkey's attention was then distracted by developments in Yemen, where the Ottoman troops were unable to suppress the movement led by Imam Yahya ibn Hamid al-Din of Sanaa. It was decided to move Ahmad Faizi Pasha from Najd to Yemen; Sidqi Pasha succeeded him as commander of the troops in Qasim. Fruitless negotiations were conducted between Ibn Saud and the Turks in April 1905.[60]

The Turks' situation in Najd was difficult: food was short, the soldiers were decimated by disease and there were mass desertions. The Ottoman garrisons did not stabilize the situation in Qasim. The local tribal-feudal leaders strove for more independence, seeing an opportunity to rid themselves of both the Rashidis and the Saudis. Salih ibn Hasan Al Muhanna, the ruler of Buraida, was especially active. Ibn Saud continued to play for time. The Shammar resumed the raids on Qasim, whose people began to turn to the Saudis. Ibn Saud then received help from an unexpected source – he was joined by the Mutair. They were under an outstanding leader, Faisal Al Dawish, who was later to lead the Ikhwan (see below).[61]

On 13 April 1906 a battle was waged in Qasim between the Saudis and the Shammar, witnessed by Dari ibn Fuhaid ibn Rashid, a Shammar chronicler. At daybreak, the Saudis shelled Ibn Mitab's camp and then attacked it. The ruler of Hail tried desperately to restore order among his men. He forced his way through to the Rashidis' banner, which had already fallen into the hands of al-Arid fighters. Taking them for his men, Ibn Mitab shouted something in the Shammar dialect. He was immediately recognized and killed and the Shammar fled in panic. Ibn Saud's soldiers severed Ibn Mitab's head from his body, put it on display in Buraida and Anaiza and then threw it to the dogs.[62] That was the end of a courageous military commander and unlucky political leader whose death opened a period of instability in Jabal Shammar.

In June 1906 Ibn Saud reached Hail, but he failed to capture it. Returning to Qasim, the emir of Riyadh dismissed Salih ibn Hasan, the governor of Buraida, and put him and his brothers in jail in Riyadh. Shortly afterwards Salih was killed trying to escape. His cousin, Muhammad Al Abdallah Aba al-Khail, was appointed as emir.[63]

Soon afterwards Ibn Saud reached an agreement with Mitab ibn Abd al-Aziz, the new emir of Hail, on the division of central Arabia. The territory and tribes to the north of Qasim would be governed by the ruler of Hail, and Qasim and the territories to the south of it by Ibn Saud.[64] Yet Turkish troops were still in Qasim and clearly sympathized with the Rashidis. The Sublime Porte gave Mitab a monthly subsidy of 200 Turkish liras and food, whereas Ibn Saud received just 90 liras per month.[65] At that moment the Mutair, instigated by the Turks, rose against the emir of Riyadh. After defeating them, Ibn Saud made for Buraida, where a Turkish garrison was stationed.[66]

In the summer of 1905 Sidqi Pasha was replaced as commander of the Turkish forces in Najd by Sami Pasha al-Faruqi, but he only arrived in Qasim with a detachment of 500 infantrymen in July 1906. He tried to entice Ibn Saud to his camp, but the emir was wary of treachery.[67] Apparently, they met in August 1906 in an open field and tried to come to terms. According to Lorimer, Ibn Saud persuaded the Turkish commander to agree that each garrison should be only 100 soldiers strong.[68] A Saudi source described the situation as more complicated: when the Turks insisted on retaining control over Qasim, Ibn Saud feigned anger and left, shouting one of the most terrible Arabian insults at Sami Pasha: 'If you were not my guest, I should not spare your life.'[69]

The Ramadhan fast, which fell in October 1906, delayed the beginning of hostilities. Ibn Saud gave Sami Pasha a choice: move the Turkish troops closer to Riyadh, putting them under the emir's protection; withdraw the troops and their equipment from Najd; or prepare for battle.[70]

The Turkish troops had been in Arabia for more than two and a half years. They were starving and were short even of tobacco; their uniforms were worn to rags. Although Arabs formed a sizeable part of the troops, they hated central Arabia so much that they called it 'Satan's daughter'. In order to survive, many of the soldiers had sold their arms and equipment to the people of Qasim. Disease and desertions had depleted their ranks. In such a situation, Sami Pasha had no choice but to evacuate.[71]

Anxious to get rid of the Turks, the emir of Riyadh guaranteed their safety and offered his camels to transport men and equipment. Sami Pasha was supposed to go to Medina with the Syrian contingent, but not to transfer them to Hail. A detachment from Iraq was left in Buraida as hostages.[72] In late October 1906 Sami Pasha left his fortified camp near Buraida and made for Medina. Some 800 Turkish troops from Iraq with guns began the evacuation in November. They reached Kuwait and were then transferred to Basra.[73]

According to Lorimer's estimate, the Ottoman troops sent to central Arabia in 1904–05 numbered some 4,500. Only 1,000 returned to Medina and Iraq: desertions, disease and battles had led to the loss of 3,500 men.[74] It was an overwhelming defeat. According to the chronicler Saud ibn Hizlul, the Ottoman troops were 'grateful' for being allowed to leave Qasim.[75] The Turks failed to retain even an illusory control over the region.[76]

The consolidation of Riyadh's power in southern Najd and Qasim (1906–1912)

On 26 December 1906 Sultan, Saud and Faisal, the nephews of Mitab Al Rashid, the new ruler of Hail who had been in power for less than a year, killed the emir and three of his brothers. Only his youngest brother, a boy named Saud, survived. He was saved by his uncle – a member of the Al Subhan clan – and sent to Medina, which was then under Ottoman control. The subsidies that the Sublime Porte had paid the Rashidis were now sent directly to Medina, which showed the Turks' attitude to the usurpers in Hail.[77]

The organizer of the coup, Sultan ibn Hamud, was unpopular and held out in power only until January 1908. He proved a failure as a military commander, too, finding no opportunities to reward his followers with spoils. Aware of his precarious position, he loaded the contents of the emirate's exchequer on to a camel and tried to flee to Egypt, but was intercepted by Saud ibn Hamud, who jailed him and later had him strangled. Saud became the new ruler of Jabal Shammar and Faisal was appointed governor of Jawf.[78]

The Rashidis' emirate was steadily weakening. Jawf was claimed by Nuri Al Shaalan, the shaikh of the Rwala tribe. He had considerably expanded his *dira* (territory controlled by a tribe), located in the south of present-day Syria and eastern Jordan. The Saudis took advantage of the instability in Jabal Shammar to attract Iraqi and Persian pilgrim caravans to Qasim. The struggle intensified among the ruling clans of Hail and there was a rapid succession of rulers. Saud ibn Hamud was replaced by a minor, Saud ibn Abd al-Aziz, who was returned to power in 1909 by the powerful family of Al Subhan – it was they who were the true rulers of the emirate. Jabal Shammar had a dozen emirs and regents before it finally collapsed in 1921. Saud ibn Abd al-Aziz Al Rashid's regent was Hamud Al Subhan. He married the boy's sister, but was poisoned several months later and was succeeded by his cousin, Zamil Al Subhan. To strengthen his position, Zamil married Emir Saud's mother: he was her fourth husband, coming after Muhammad ibn Rashid, Abd al-Aziz ibn Rashid and Sultan ibn Hamud, who killed and succeeded Mitab, her adopted son.[79]

The greatly weakened emirate of Jabal Shammar was unable to take advantage of the temporary halt to Saudi expansion, though Qasim rebelled, encouraged by Hail. The people of Buraida again tried to restore their independence; their new emir, also from the Al Muhanna clan, intrigued behind Ibn Saud's back. His campaign against Jabal Shammar was unsuccessful. Faisal Al Dawish and other Mutair leaders split from the emir of Riyadh, forging a secret alliance with Abdallah Aba al-Khail, the ruler of Buraida. When Ibn Saud learned of this, he gathered troops, mainly from among the Ataiba, who were considered the natural enemies of both the Shammar and the Mutair. Fearing for his life, Aba al-Khail defected to Ibn Saud. The emir of Riyadh was unable to subdue Buraida, having to concentrate his efforts on the action against Faisal Al Dawish.[80]

In April–May 1907 a battle occurred between the Mutair and Ibn Saud's troops (the latter consisted chiefly of Ataiba) near the town of al-Majmaa in Sudair. The Mutair were defeated. Wounded in the battle, Faisal Al Dawish sued for peace and agreed to submit to Ibn Saud. He was still the leader of a powerful tribe, and Ibn Saud needed live allies more than dead enemies at that difficult time. This explains his acceptance of Faisal's expression of allegiance.[81]

In August–September 1907 Sultan ibn Hamud of Hail appeared in Qasim, where he was joined by the people of Buraida, led by Aba al-Khail, and a part of the Mutair. His activities were unsuccessful, however, and there were few spoils. Hearing about his foray, Ibn Saud gathered troops from among the Qahtan, Ataiba, Subai and Suhul, joined by contingents from al-Arid. In the subsequent battles of September 1907 Ibn Saud defeated the Mutair again.

The decisive battle was waged near Tarafiya, some 12 km to the north of Anaiza. Fearing a defeat, the bedouin deserted Ibn Saud, only to return when the scales tipped in his favour. The Shammar, the people of Buraida and the Mutair fought against Ibn Saud. Tarafiya is considered one of Ibn Saud's decisive battles and is counted as a great victory by Saudi historians. However, the emir of Riyadh failed to capture Buraida and contented himself with plundering the environs. It should be stressed that Ibn Saud restricted plunder in his state in order to stabilize his power. The Shammar, on the other hand, engaged in merciless plunder, acting as bedouin raiders rather than as a long-term political force. After the battle of Tarafiya, they retreated to Hail and Faisal Al Dawish fled to the desert.[82]

The pro-Saudi faction grew stronger in Buraida. When Ibn Saud approached the town with troops in May 1908, his supporters opened the gates for him. Aba al-Khail and his followers took cover in the fortress, but then asked for an *aman*, seeing that their cause was hopeless. Aba al-Khail was allowed to go to Kuwait and then to Iraq. Ahmad ibn Muhammad Al Sudairi was appointed the new emir of Buraida. He belonged to a clan that had long-established connections with the Saudis and his brother commanded the permanent garrison, stationed in Buraida.[83] Meanwhile, Sultan ibn Hamud was killed in Hail and was succeeded by Saud ibn Hamud.[84]

In October–November 1908 several important events occurred in Hijaz. First, the Ottoman authorities replaced Ali ibn Abdallah by Husain ibn Ali as ruler of Mecca. Husain ibn Ali had spent his childhood among the bedouin before being exiled to Istanbul. In the year that the Hijaz railway opened, he returned to Mecca, nourishing secret ambitions of becoming king of the Arabs and in any case of establishing himself as a serious player in Arabian politics.

A terrible drought occurred in central Najd in 1908 and lasted for several years, according to Philby,[85] although some Arab sources give different accounts. What is certain is that, while rains may have fallen in other regions, it was central Najd that was affected by the drought.[86] Significantly, many inhabitants of central Arabia considered the drought in Ibn Saud's state as a sign of Allah's disfavour. Musil writes that this natural calamity was conducive to internal warfare in the emirate of Riyadh. In Jabal Shammar, however, there were abundant rains and some tribes left Ibn Saud and roamed to the regions ruled by Hail.[87]

The decay of agriculture, the famine and the general ruin of the bedouin undermined Ibn Saud's still feeble power. A sign of the emirate's general instability was the revolt between February and April 1909 against Ibn Saud in al-Hariq province, where Emir al-Hazzani was killed by rivals from his own clan. The province was seized by disturbances and it was only with great difficulty that Ibn Saud was able to restore law and order.[88]

The authority of the emir of Riyadh was still far from undisputed in his own state. The absence of strong enemies was helpful to him, but tribal rivalries and the trend towards decentralization undermined the central authority. The bedouin detachments often betrayed Ibn Saud; nor could the loyal nomadic tribes be relied on unconditionally. There was permanent unrest in Buraida.

While Ibn Saud was preoccupied with internal affairs, Husain, the sharif of Mecca – who was under constant pressure from the Ottoman government to take action against Najd – began threatening him from the west. Ibn Saud did not overlook the fact that he was surrounded by Ottoman possessions and hostile Turkish vassals on the west, north and east. It was obvious that his attempts to create a strong state in central Arabia would collide sooner or later with Turkey's interests. His daring raids on remote localities showed that the Wahhabi state might be restored to its previous wide territorial area, which worried both the Turks and those Arabian rulers who depended on Britain or the Ottoman empire.

Low-key hostilities continued in 1910 against the Araif, Ibn Saud's three relatives. They raided the tribes who were loyal to Riyadh and then took refuge among the Ajman in al-Hasa. Although their actions had no serious consequences, they heightened the internal instability caused both by the slowing of the expansion of the emirate of Riyadh and by the terrible drought. All three brothers belonged to the senior branch of the Al Saud family and claimed the throne of Riyadh.[89]

In March–April 1910 Ibn Saud took up the shaikh of Kuwait's call to attack the Muntafiq, who were led by Saadun Pasha and had formed an alliance with Jabal Shammar against Kuwait. In June 1910 Saadun Pasha defeated the united Kuwaiti-Saudi forces and seized huge spoils.[90]

Jabal Shammar's relations with the Ottoman authorities in Hijaz developed unevenly. In June 1910 Zamil Al Subhan even expelled the Turkish detachment from the Taima oasis. But in 1909 Nuri ibn Shaalan of the Rwala tribe seized Jawf and held it for a time, putting pressure on Jabal Shammar from the north and north-east. It seems that there was close cooperation between Nuri ibn Shaalan and Ibn Saud against the common enemy.[91]

In the first two years of his rule, Sharif Husain of Mecca tried to demonstrate his loyalty to the Sublime Porte by his campaign against Asir, while the Turks were preoccupied with suppressing Imam Yahya's revolt in Yemen. Husain conquered Asir for his masters and returned to Mecca via the Bisha, Ranya and Turaba oases on the border of Najd, establishing his suzerainty over them.

In the late summer of 1910 the sharif gathered bedouin troops and invaded Najd. On the way he accidentally took Saad, Ibn Saud's brother, prisoner. Both parties started cautious manoeuvres. Husain hoped for Jabal Shammar's aid and began a correspondence with Zamil, the regent of Hail, who planned to regain Qasim. Husain did not expect a large-scale war – his forces were insufficient – but Saad was in his hands. A certain Khalid ibn Luwai mediated between the emirate of Riyadh and the sharif of Mecca. He was to play an important role in the seizure of Hijaz by the Najdis. After the negotiations, Ibn Saud pledged himself to pay the sultan 6,000 rials a year and to recognize the Turks' formal suzerainty over Najd. Thereafter Saad was released and Husain returned to Mecca.[92] The emir of Riyadh had no intention of implementing the terms of the agreement, however: he failed to pay the tribute and his verbal acknowledgement of the sultan's suzerainty had no practical effect.

After concluding the peace treaty with the sharif of Mecca, Ibn Saud made again for al-Hariq to suppress the revolt led by one of the Araif. He executed all members of the Al Hazzani clan who had been captured for their part in the mutiny. However, he pardoned the leader of the revolt, his cousin's son Saud ibn Abdallah ibn Saud, who served him loyally until the end of his life. The other Araif fled to Hijaz, where the sharif gave them shelter.[93]

In early 1911 Shaikh Mubarak of Kuwait asked Ibn Saud to attack their common enemy, the Zafir tribe. Simultaneously, however, he warned the tribe's shaikh, Ibn Suwait, that Ibn Saud's troops were approaching, thus eliminating the element of surprise from the raid. Ibn Suwait fled and informed Ibn Saud of Mubarak's double game.[94] From the Kuwaiti ruler's viewpoint, helping the weak house of Saud against the powerful Jabal Shammar, and helping the emirate of Riyadh which was rising again from the ruins and was soon to become the main force in central Arabia, were two entirely different matters. Mubarak himself dreamed of establishing control, in particular, over Qasim, Washm and Sudair, hindering the expansion of the emirate of Riyadh.[95] After Ibn Saud's successful raid on the Zafir and other tribes of Lower Iraq, however, Mubarak preferred to reach an understanding with the young emir and restore good relations with him.[96] In spite of their acute rivalry, Mubarak continued to address him as 'my son' while Ibn Saud answered with 'my father'.[97]

In 1910 Captain Shakespear, the British political agent in Kuwait, visited Ibn Saud. His diaries, maps and photographs have not survived, although his reports have. According to Skakespear, the emir of Hail, Imam Yahya of Yemen and the ruler of Asir were engaged in a correspondence in order to organize an anti-Turkish revolt. Ibn Saud wanted to drive the Turks from al-Hasa and sought Britain's support.[98] In 1911 the Ottoman government still referred to the ruler of Hail as 'the emir of Najd'; whereas British correspondence was addressed to 'Shaikh Abd al-Aziz, the son of Shaikh Abd al-Rahman Al Saud'.[99]

Al-Hasa, or the Eastern Province, always attracted the attention of the emirs of Riyadh, not only because they considered it their legitimate possession. The rich oases of al-Hasa and the customs duties might improve the Saudis' financial position. Moreover, the emirate of Riyadh needed access to the sea. The situation in al-Hasa was favourable to Ibn Saud's plans because its people hated the Turks. But Ibn Saud had learned from his time in Kuwait that the chief force in the Gulf was Britain: he had been trying to establish friendly ties with the British since 1903.[100] In May 1904 he even sent a letter to Sir Percy Cox, the British political resident in the Gulf, expressing his discontent with Turkey's aid to the Rashidis.[101] The appointment of a British political agent to Kuwait did not mean the establishment of formal relations with Ibn Saud. Although the emir reported his plan to capture al-Hasa to the British and tried to enlist their support, Britain continued its policy of non-intervention in Najdi affairs and avoided making any direct commitments.[102]

In 1911 Ibn Saud visited Kuwait, had friendly talks with the British agent and agreed on areas of cooperation. Waiving all claims in Muscat and Oman, the emir of Riyadh was entitled to establish his control over al-Hasa, al-Qatif, Darin and the port of al-Uqair, while Britain pledged itself to prevent intervention by any other power from the sea. In exchange, Ibn Saud recognized the British protectorate over his emirate and pledged himself not to start wars without Britain's consent. Britain was entitled to exploit the peninsula's mineral resources. The British government promised to send troops and arms to Ibn Saud at his request. To wage war in the peninsula, however, Britain did not need the emir's prior consent.[103] Although the agreement was not concluded, it corresponded to the character of earlier negotiations (i.e. Britain's policy of not hindering Ibn Saud in his seizure of al-Hasa) and the general provisions of the future treaty of 1915. In practice, Britain treated the emirate of Riyadh as a virtual or potential protectorate within its sphere of influence in the Gulf.

In 1911 an anti-Turkish revolt began in Asir, led by Muhammad ibn Ali Al Idrisi, and the Turks tried to persuade Ibn Saud to attack the rebels. The emir answered that as an Arab he would not join the Turks in their war against Muhammad Al Idrisi, whom he considered his ally and brother. On the contrary, he gave some military support to Asir. The Asiris' old religious sympathies for the Wahhabis strengthened the alliance that was forming between them.[104]

In early 1912 the Porte, preoccupied with the Balkan war, tried to obtain support from its remote Arabian provinces or at least ensure their neutrality. A delegation was sent to Ibn Saud, asking, in particular, for Najdi troops to be sent to al-Hasa to support the Turkish garrison. Ibn Saud felt that al-Hasa would soon fall into his hands like a ripe fruit.

With its string of defeats in the Balkans, the Ottoman government tried persistently to make Ibn Saud its ally in Arabia. A Turkish delegation came to Riyadh and asked the emir to specify his demands and complaints. Ibn Saud told Sulaiman Shafiq Pasha, the governor of Basra, that the Turks:

> should convene a meeting of all the chiefs, great and small without distinction, at some place not actually under Ottoman administration, so that there might be absolute freedom of speech. The general object of the meeting would be the establishment of harmony in the Arab lands, and friendship between them and the Ottoman Government; and their specific task would be a choice between two alternatives. Either the Arab countries should form a single group presided over by a ruler of their own choice; or the existing arrangement of separate political entities should continue on the basis of complete local administrative independence, each under its own rules functioning as a Wali in a Turkish province.[105]

The emir's proposals were in direct conflict with the policy of the Young Turks: it was only their military and political weakness that prevented them from reacting to Ibn Saud's daring claims with a military expedition.

Ibn Saud's correspondence with the governor of Basra continued, however. The Russian consulate in Basra reported back on 17 July 1912:

> Ibn Saud, the emir of Najd, has written a letter to the local *wali*, demanding that the Turkish government should recognize his independence. The *wali* answered him hastily, persuading him that he should remain loyal to the sultan–caliph as a Muslim. Essentially the Turks' power in Najd is merely nominal even now. There are no Turkish officials or soldiers in Riyadh, its capital. Nonetheless, Ibn Saud expresses his submission and loyalty to the sultan at least in words . . . It should also be remembered that he has long claimed the coastal strip of al-Hasa . . . Probably, Captain Shakespear, the British agent at Shaikh Mubarak's court, is also in on this matter.[106]

The Renaissance of the Emirate of Riyadh in the Early Twentieth Century

In the late spring and early summer of 1912 Sharif Husain of Mecca raided Najd again, leading a detachment of the Ataiba. Ibn Saud's brother Muhammad attacked a subdivision of the Ataiba who were subordinate to Husain.[107] Relations between the two rulers deteriorated sharply: their mutual accusations even reached Istanbul. Husain prohibited the Najdis from performing the *hajj* in November–December 1912.[108] The religious and economic consequences of that decision can hardly be overestimated. It infuriated the Najdis, particularly the merchants, who were deprived of their income from the pilgrims. Husain's agents incited the people of Qasim against Riyadh, and the governor Ibn Jiluwi even had some Qasimis executed. Ibn Saud had suffered a serious blow, but the Najdis' hatred turned first against the sharif of Mecca.[109] Thus were laid the foundations of the future conflict, which was finally resolved by Najd's conquest of Hijaz.

The beginnings of the Ikhwan movement

Despite his initial successes, Ibn Saud lacked stable, broadly based support in central Arabia: this was to be provided by a religious-political movement similar to that which had rallied people around the house of Saud in the time of his ancestors. The Al Saud were connected with a religious idea that sanctified raids and the struggle for centralization, in the interests of the emir and the ruling nobility, and under the banner of 'the true religion'. But the first decade of Ibn Saud's activities had shown no signs of a particular emphasis on religion, whether as a means of legitimizing his power, strengthening people's loyalty or lending dynamism to his campaigns of conquest.

At that moment, the movement of the Ikhwan (Brethren) emerged in Najd. Ibn Saud was hardly among the authors of the Ikhwan's ideas or one of the founders of the movement. The spiritual fathers of Ikhwanism were Abdallah ibn Muhammad ibn Abd al-Latif from the Al al-Shaikh family, the *qadhi* of Riyadh; Shaikh Isa, the *qadhi* of al-Hasa; and one Abd al-Karim al-Maghrebi, who had come to Arabia at the turn of the century and settled in the area of al-Artawiya, a future *hijra* (settlement).[110]

Besides strict observance of the five fundamental tenets of Islam, the Ikhwan were required to be loyal to the 'brethren' (their fellow participants in the movement), to obey the emir–imam, to help each other in every way possible and to reject contact with Europeans and the populations of the countries they governed.[111]

The exact date of the foundation of al-Artawiya, the first *hijra*, is unknown, but it seems to have emerged in the first half of 1913.[112] *Umm al-Qura*, the semi-official Saudi newspaper founded after the annexation of Hijaz, reported in 1929 that the first *hijra* was founded in January 1913.[113] The first Ikhwan settlers lived near a group of wells in a wadi with good pastureland and numerous trees. The valley was situated in the territory of the Mutair, one of the proudest and most powerful tribes of central Arabia, on the caravan route from Kuwait to Qasim. *Lughat al-Arab*, a Baghdad periodical, claimed that 'plunder and murder run in the Mutair's blood'.[114]

Some Mutair voluntarily sold a part of their camels and the equipment that was necessary to maintain the bedouin way of life. They settled in al-Artawiya and began building houses, having decided to devote themselves to agriculture and the study of monotheism. A subdivision of the Harb – the Uraimat, also known as Araimat – joined the Mutair and played a major role in building the settlement thanks to their skill in handicrafts, building and agriculture, unlike the ex-bedouin. Many wells were dug in the Uraimat area.[115] The traditional bonds of mutual assistance within kin and tribes became the basis of the Ikhwan's solidarity: when one of them lost his property as a result of disease or a raid, the 'brethren' collected donations for him.[116]

After al-Artawiya, other *hijras* emerged. The Ataiba founded a *hijra* in al-Ghatghat, which was later destroyed. By 1918 many settlements of that kind had appeared in Najd.[117] There were 52 Ikhwan *hijras* in Arabia in 1920;[118] their number had reached 72 by 1923 and some 120 by 1929.[119] *Umm al-Qura* gave a break-down of the Ikhwan settlements according to tribe in 1929: Anaza, 7; Shammar, 16; Harb, 22; Mutair, 12; Ataiba, 15; Subai, 3; Suhul, 3; Qahtan, 8; Dawasir, 4; Bani Khalid, 2; Ajman, 14; Awazim, 2; Bani Hajir, 4; Al Murra, 4; Hitaim, 3; and Zafir, 1.[120] But only a tenth or, at most, a fifth of the ex-nomads settled in *hijras* even during the maximum upsurge of the movement.

Naturally, the *hijras* were founded near wells or in oases, where agriculture was possible. Both droughts and the crisis of nomadism, i.e. economic necessity, prompted the bedouin to settle. Their migration to the northern areas, controlled by the Ottoman authorities, was limited by their reluctance to depend on the Turks and then the British.

In order to encourage the process of sedentarization, Ibn Saud gave the Ikhwan money, seed, agricultural equipment and materials to build mosques, schools and settlements, and sent *mutawwas* (religious instructors) to educate them. Their conscripts received arms and equipment for 'the defence of the faith'. The emirs of the *hijras* came to Ibn Saud at least once a year with their entourages, receiving subsidies and enjoying his hospitality. The emirs' names were registered in special books; the amount of their subsidy depended on their record of service and the number of their followers. The Ikhwan who were liable to conscription were entered in the registers at Ibn Saud's court office and received an annual payment. When they needed money to buy food or livestock, to repay a debt, to arrange a wedding or to build a house, they received grants.[121]

Formally, a person who wanted to be admitted to a *hijra* was supposed to give up the habits and duties of the tribal way of life. This requirement was not observed in practice, however, and *hijras* were populated mainly on the basis of tribal affiliation. The Ikhwan's settlements became virtually the headquarters of the shaikhs of the largest tribes. Thus Ibn Saud's attempt to deprive the tribes of their traditional leaders with the help of the Ikhwan movement failed. Faisal Al Dawish of the Mutair settled in al-Artawiya, Ibn Bijad of the Ataiba in al-Ghatghat, Ibn Nuhait of the Harb in Duhna, and Ibn Jibril and Ibn Thunayyan of the Shammar in al-Ajfar.[122]

The Ikhwan's religious enthusiasm was supposed to be directed towards the worship of Allah and, naturally, to the service of His representatives on earth. Their religious and secular zeal was rewarded by spoils, but not in intertribal raids and plunder on the caravan routes, as had been the case earlier, but in wars against the 'polytheists'. In the nomads' transition to agriculture, economic and social necessity combined with religious zeal and military requirements, but these tasks might be in contradiction and some *hijras* collapsed. Of course, former bedouin could hardly be expected immediately to give up the earlier habits of nomadism and become good farmers. Their religious enthusiasm was often insufficient for prolonged labour in the field, and the former bedouin preferred 'fighting for monotheism' to agricultural work. The Riyadh *ulama* even issued a *fatwa* (official ruling) in favour of agriculture, commerce and the settled life.[123] Sedentarization was usually voluntary, but cases of forced 'Ikhwanization' were not rare, especially after 1918. According to Rihani, 'The work of conquest and that of proselytising went practically hand in hand, although the one sometimes preceded and sometimes followed the other.'[124]

Elements of caste difference between the 'noble' tribes, who fought against enemies, and the 'unnoble' ones, who were responsible for handicrafts, construction and the functioning of the new settlements, persisted in the *hijras*.[125] For example, a section of the Harb, considered one of the 'most noble' tribes of Arabia, settled in al-Artawiya together with the Mutair and the 'unnoble' Uraimat.[126] In *hijras*, too, the latter were subordinate and humiliated.

Craftsmen and small traders were often considered non-combatants. Their military duty consisted in shoeing horses, and making and repairing arms and agricultural implements. When a war started, they remained in the *hijras*.[127] As for the *mutawwas* (the lowest echelon of the *ulama*), they were the disciples of *ulama* who had been trained in Riyadh and other centres. The *mutawwas* acted both as preachers and as agents of the central authorities – the Riyadh *ulama* and the emir himself.[128] Ibn Saud appointed *qadhis* to the largest *hijras*, usually from among the Al al-Shaikh family.

Those *hijra* inhabitants who were subject to the draft were divided into three categories. The first included those who were permanently ready for action as soon as an appeal for *jihad* was made. The second category included reservists. The final category comprised those who usually stayed in the settlements during a war, but might be conscripted in an emergency by decision of the *ulama*. When called on to join a campaign, the Ikhwan came with their own camels, arms and food. Only a few *hijras* in central Najd received periodic subsidies from the exchequer for military needs.[129] According to Pershits:

> The Ikhwan became 'the white terror' of Arabia. Relying on their assistance, Ibn Saud had mainly suppressed the resistance of the strongest bedouin tribes by the early 1920s and established an order described as 'unprecedented' by Philby. The bedouin called the new regime 'the muzzle period'. The old privileges of the shaikhs – exemption from *zakat* and the *khuwa* collection from the weaker neighbours – were abolished [though they survived in different forms to a limited extent]. Raids, their traditional means of subsistence, came to be punished so unhesitatingly and so strictly that the nomadic nobility had no choice but to submit or to emigrate from the emirate of Najd. Montagne quoted a characteristic poem, written down by emigrants from Najd:

229

> 'The battle camels have fattened, they are somnolent.
> They have forgotten how to tear along in battle.
> O, Abu Zaban! Battles are waged no longer:
> The authorities have banned them.
> So many angry people
> Have been buried in alien tribes' land,
> For they have lost the skill of raiding,
> Fearing imprisonment.'[130]

The bedouin who settled in *hijras* maintained that they had forsaken the *jahiliya* (the state of pre-Islamic ignorance) and embraced the genuine Islam. They demonstrated their zeal by defeating the supposed non-Muslims – the nomads and settled people who did not join them. The situation took such a serious turn that Ibn Saud had to ask the *ulama* in October 1914 to issue a special *fatwa* with an appeal for tolerance in order to restrain the Ikhwan's ardour. The *ulama* confirmed that compelling people to wear turbans instead of *uqals*, and to give up the earlier way of life and join the Ikhwan, contradicted the *sharia*, since neither Allah nor His messengers had required people to do so.

The impact of the *fatwa* was insufficient, however, and a year later the emir sent experienced *ulama* to *hijras* to smooth over the damage inflicted by the fanatical preachers.[131] Since the bedouin had previously had only a vague idea of Islam, the change, as well as the replacement of tribal customary law by the *sharia*, was dramatic. Musil notes, for example, the increase in religious sentiment among the Rwala who took part in the Ikhwan movement. Many bedouin were already able to recite some *suras* from the Quran.[132]

Neophytes are generally more resolute and fanatic than are the traditional followers of a religious doctrine, and the Ikhwan were no exception. The bedouin, who had earlier been ignorant or almost ignorant of Islam, now zealously followed the religious prescriptions, such as the five daily prayers; those who evaded the prayers were beaten with a stick. To distinguish themselves from other Muslims, whom they considered 'polytheists', the Ikhwan wore white turbans instead of the usual *kufiyas*, shaved the sides of their moustaches, shortened their beards and sometimes hennaed them. Their *dishdashas* (long shirts) reached only to the knee, while other men wore full-length *dishdashas*. As H. R. P. Dickson notes, they looked mere ragamuffins.[133]

The Ikhwan banned all kinds of music except military drums, did not drink coffee because it was unknown in the Prophet's time, and avoided tobacco as if it were poison.[134] All alcohol was prohibited, as well as men's clothing made of silk or with gold embroidery. People who engaged in gambling, fortune-telling or magic were condemned to eternal damnation.[135] It should be noted that many of the Ikhwan's prohibitions, as well as those in Wahhabism, were of an egalitarian character. They can be seen as a form of protest by the lower strata in society against the 'luxury' (by Arabian standards) enjoyed by the ruling classes.

Only greetings from other 'brethren' were answered by the Ikhwan. When they met a European, an Iraqi Arab or an inhabitant of the Gulf states, they buried their faces in their hands lest they be defiled. Once, when Dickson came to Ibn Saud's *majlis*, a group of Ikhwan shaikhs walked out, covering their faces so that the Englishman could not see them. Although he was the imam's guest, he heard their low, muttered curses.[136]

The Ikhwan held that all who did not join them – both the nomads and the people of the oases and towns – were 'polytheists'.[137] In the name of the 'purified' religion, the members of the Ikhwan committed many atrocities, though their fanaticism strengthened the fighting capacity of Ibn Saud's troops.[138] According to Dickson, *furusiya*, the bedouin code of honour, collapsed as a result of the Ikhwan movement.[139]

Many authors stress that Ibn Saud himself was never a fanatic. He used the Ikhwan movement pragmatically for his own ends, skilfully bypassing its more extreme requirements. During the First World War, when Ibn Saud agreed to the British protectorate and received a monthly subsidy from the British government, he explained that it was *jizya*, the tax that the first Muslim caliphs had collected from the Christians.[140] But he did not trust the Ikhwan fully, even in the initial stage of their movement, due both to their bedouin origin and to the spread of egalitarian trends among them. Among the emir's entourage, his cousin and fellow-fighter Abdallah ibn Jiluwi was particularly vigorous in his opposition to the Ikhwan.[141]

The annexation of al-Hasa

On hearing of the Turks' defeat in the Balkan war, Ibn Saud began preparations for an expedition to al-Hasa. In early 1913 he moved to Qasim and proclaimed a general mobilization.[142] There were Ikhwan among his troops, but they did not form the majority. Gathering the settled Najdis and the bedouin, Ibn Saud made for al-Hasa. Before starting out on his military campaign, he met the British officer Colonel Leachman and may have warned him about his plan to attack the Turks.[143]

Weary of the Turks' extortions and oppression, the people of al-Hasa saw the Najdis as their saviours. As early as 1903 the Russian consul in Basra reported back that the Ottoman *mutasarrif* had 'driven the Arab population of the *sanjak* [district] to exhaustion by his corruption and arbitrary rule'.[144]

The Turks were worried by the strong forces that Ibn Saud had gathered in the area of pastures and wells between Riyadh and Kuwait. Jamal Pasha, the governor of Baghdad, threatened to send two battalions to Najd, saying that they would march from one end to the other. The emir of Riyadh answered daringly that he would soon make Jamal Pasha's task easier by decreasing the distance the battalions had to cover before meeting him.[145] Nadim Bey, the Turkish *mutasarrif* of al-Hasa, sent his representative to Ibn Saud to discover his intentions. Ibn Saud claimed that he was going only to attack a tribe in Kuwait. Simultaneously he sent people to Hufuf to purchase a large amount of rice and dates. Through his agents in al-Hasa, the ruler of Najd learned of the location of the Turkish garrisons and established contacts with the local population.[146] The Russian consulate in Basra reported back:

The Turks' power over al-Hasa was illusory. It was almost non-existent outside the towns . . . In early May [1913] Ibn Saud suddenly invaded al-Hasa with 8,000 well-armed Arabs and attacked Hufuf. It was not very difficult for him to capture the town.[147]

The attack on Hufuf began at night. The Najdis used the trunks of palm trees, ropes and ladders, all prepared beforehand. The town soon fell, as did the Kut citadel, with the exception of the Ibrahim mosque in the fortress, where the *mutasarrif* and a part of his garrison ensconced themselves. There were 1,200 Turks in Hufuf at the time.[148]

The mosque was mined, and the people inside were warned that the mines would be detonated and the mosque stormed unless they surrendered. The *mutasarrif* decided to lay down his arms. The men of the garrison were led out of the town by an escort headed by Ahmad ibn Sunayyan, a distant relative of Ibn Saud. The Turks left for Bahrain by sea.

Some days later, however, they landed in al-Uqair in an attempt to regain control over al-Hasa. Some of them were taken prisoner, but the rest again fled to Bahrain. Then the Najdis seized al-Qatif. Ibn Saud wrote the British a letter, complaining that they had allowed the Turks to use Bahrain as a base against him. He seemed to be sure of British support and their passiveness disappointed him.[149] Now the Eastern Province was in his hands. The Russian consulate in Basra reported back, 'It is quite possible that all these events occurred with Britain's knowledge or even advice. Their intrigues among the Arab shaikhs are well known.'[150]

Wasting no time, the emir of Riyadh began to 'pacify' the Shia, who were traditionally hostile to the Saudis and the Wahhabi doctrine. Abdallah ibn Jiluwi, Ibn Saud's cousin, was appointed governor of al-Hasa and was ruthless in his repression of the Shia, especially in al-Qatif.[151]

Under the Ottoman administration, an annual revenue of 37,000 liras had been collected from the province and 52,000 liras went on maintaining the garrison and for administrative purposes. The Russian consul in Basra wrote that the revenue might now be increased:[152] this was what Ibn Saud decided to do. He expelled foreign merchants from al-Hasa and al-Qatif and imposed an 8% duty on maritime imports to the Eastern Province.[153] Abdallah ibn Jiluwi stamped out raids on the caravan routes with an iron hand, and merchants could travel in the province in relative safety.[154]

Riyadh had seized a relatively rich Arabian province from the Ottoman empire and had gained access to the Gulf from Kuwait to Qatar. The importance of al-Hasa for the emirate of Riyadh can hardly be overestimated. The territory previously controlled by the Saudis was devoid of natural resources: the date crop barely covered the needs of the nomads and the settled people, and the shortage of foodgrain meant that it had to be imported. The settled population depended almost entirely on imported cloth and the troops needed imported arms. The seizure of al-Hasa, together with access to the Gulf, ensured the vitality and further consolidation of the Saudi state.

Britain ultimately intended to make the emirate of Riyadh its protectorate and therefore did not oppose the Turkish garrison being driven from al-Hasa. The British representative in Bahrain paid a courtesy visit to Ibn Saud in al-Uqair after the fall of al-Hasa. In late 1913 Shakespear, who had already met Ibn Saud in 1910, visited him in Riyadh and then went on a long tour of Arabia and as far as Suez. Having no other instructions, he only discussed the general situation with the emir.[155]

Shakespear, however, either could not or did not want to tell Ibn Saud that Britain was playing a double game. In June 1913 Ibrahim Haqqi Pasha, the Ottoman ambassador to Britain, and Sir Edward Grey, the British foreign secretary, concluded a convention delimiting the Ottoman empire's possessions and the British protectorates on the Gulf coast – Kuwait, Bahrain and Trucial Oman. All these territories were connected in one way or another with al-Hasa, which was not mentioned in the convention. Formally, it amounted to treating it as a part of the Ottoman empire.[156]

In March 1914 Britain and the Ottoman empire agreed to divide the Arabian peninsula between them. According to the terms of the treaty, the border between the possessions of the two states was a straight line, drawn from the Qatar peninsula through the central Arabian deserts to the frontiers between the Aden protectorates and Yemen. The territories to the north of that line, including al-Hasa and even Najd, were considered parts of the Ottoman empire, while those to the south of it belonged to Britain.[157] The treaty was to lose its importance with the outbreak of the First World War, however.

After the fall of al-Hasa, Ibn Saud negotiated with representatives of the Ottoman authorities. The Porte had neither the strength nor the money to recapture the lost province and wanted only to save face:

Sending a Turkish expeditionary corps to al-Hasa looks absolutely impossible at present, for the Turks do not have a sufficient number of soldiers in Baghdad or Basra [the Russian consulate in Basra reported back on 27 May 1914]. Besides, the British government observes all developments in al-Hasa with great interest and will try . . . to hinder the Turks in reestablishing themselves on the Gulf coasts.[158]

According to Philby, the emir of Riyadh agreed to recognize verbally the sultan's suzerainty over his territory in exchange for Turkish arms and money. He needed to ensure the security of the coastal province of al-Hasa.[159] The Russian consulate in Basra reported back in June 1914, 'The governor-general has received a *firman* from Constantinople to be handed to Ibn Saud, who is appointed the *wali* of Najd and al-Hasa.'[160]

The American scholar Gary Troeller has asserted categorically that a formal Ottoman-Saudi treaty was concluded on 15 May 1914 which provided, in particular, that:

The Valet of Najd is to remain in charge of Abdul Aziz Pasha Al-Saoud so long as he is alive, according to the Imperial Firman.
   After him it will go to his sons and grandsons by Imperial Firman, provided that he shall be loyal to the Imperial Government and to his forefathers, the previous Valis.

According to the seventh article, 'The Turkish flag shall be hoisted on all Government buildings and places of importance on the sea and on the land, and also on boats belonging to the Valet of Najd.' The ninth article read, 'The said Wali and Commandant is not allowed to interfere with, or correspond about foreign affairs and international treaties, or to grant concessions to foreigners.' The twelfth article provided for the participation of the governor of Najd in any wars the Ottoman empire might wage.[161]

Philby was of the opinion that Ibn Saud retracted his 'verbal obligation' to the Turks when the First World War broke out. In any event, the emir's behaviour in that period shows that he took little notice of his obligations towards the sultan, who had few means to make Ibn Saud act in the Turkish interest.[162] According to the *Memorial of the Government of Saudi Arabia*, no document with the text of the Saudi-Turkish agreement has been found in the Saudi archives.[163] However, even if the document is missing from the archives, it proves nothing. Instead of a written agreement, there might have been a verbal understanding which could have been implemented by both parties if they wished. Troeller quotes the full text of the Turkish-Najdi treaty.

It was understood in Istanbul that, in spite of the treaty with Britain on the division of Arabia, and Ibn Saud's verbal assurances of his loyalty to the sultan, real control over Najd and al-Hasa had been lost. In response, the Ottoman authorities began fortifying Jabal Shammar and promised to supply its ruler with 10,000 rifles, food and money.[164] On hearing of the agreement, Ibn Saud realized that Istanbul was still backing Hail: the potential Turkish menace to Riyadh persisted.

CHAPTER 10

Najd and Hijaz during the First World War (1914–1918)

On the eve of the First World War, German influence was prevalent in the Ottoman empire. After a short period of hesitation, the Young Turk triumvirate decided to side with Berlin and entered the war against the Entente. As a result of the Turkish leaders' adventurism, the political situation in the Ottoman empire reached a crisis point and the population of most of the non-Turkish provinces – starting with the Arab lands – demanded self-determination. However, the Entente powers considered the whole collapsing empire to be their colonial spoils and treated the Arab nationalists as temporary and subordinate allies whose power should not be allowed to increase beyond a certain point.

Bloody battles were waged in the Middle East for four years. Almost all the countries of the Arabian peninsula were involved to varying degrees, although compared to other regions, Arabia was of third-rate importance as a theatre of war.

When Britain started military operations against the Ottoman empire, its immediate tasks included, first, the retention of its control over Egypt, the Suez Canal and the Red Sea and, second, the seizure of a stronghold in the lower reaches of the Tigris and the Euphrates in order to protect the Iranian oilfields from a possible German-Turkish invasion. The first aim was ensured by the presence of British troops in Egypt and their control over the approaches to the Suez Canal from Sinai. To attain the second goal, an expeditionary corps was sent to Mesopotamia. The British garrison in Aden was reinforced and troops were brought from India in order to hold the strategically important port without engaging in active hostilities against the Turkish troops who had invaded South Yemen.

Of all the rulers in the Arabian peninsula, Sharif Husain of Mecca attracted the Allies' keenest attention. As a member of the Hashemite clan of the Quraish tribe, he was among the most influential leaders of the Muslim world. He was considered to be a descendant of the Prophet and the Custodian of the Holy Places, appointed by the sultan's *firman*. Britain was aware that the sultan's call for *jihad*, the Muslim holy war against the Christians (in this case, the British and the French), might have a profound influence on Egypt, India, North Africa and other colonies with a Muslim population. In fact, however, the sultan's appeal met only a limited response and the fears of its impact proved exaggerated.

In the first two years of hostilities in Mesopotamia, the Allied forces brought from India suffered a series of defeats at the hands of the Turkish troops, who included many Arabs. The Turkish divisions in Gallipoli, where the Allies were also defeated, included Arab subjects of the Ottoman empire. It was therefore felt that British and French interests would be served by encouraging Arab nationalism, which also had a religious dimension.

The emirate of Najd and the First World War

When the war began, Ibn Saud wrote to Sharif Husain of Mecca, Saud ibn Salih of Hail and Sheikh Mubarak Al Sabah of Kuwait, suggesting that a meeting of Arab rulers be convened: the aim was to prevent the Arabs becoming involved in the European hostilities and to conclude a treaty with the great powers which would guarantee self-determination for the Arab peoples. The Arab rulers' interests did not coincide at that moment, however, and they failed to find a common platform. The ruler of Hail's response was that he would fight those whom the Turks fought and make peace with those with whom the Turks did. A meeting of Ibn Saud's representative and Abdallah, the son of Sharif Husain, was held at the border between Najd and Hijaz, but they failed to reach an understanding. As for Mubarak, he advised Ibn Saud to start negotiations with the British.[1]

Talib al-Naqib, a representative of the Ottoman authorities, was sent to Najd from Mesopotamia. He met Ibn Saud in Buraida, but his mission was not a success because it coincided with the British occupation of Basra. Simultaneously another Turkish delegation was sent from Medina, bringing 10,000 gold liras as weighty proof of the Ottoman authorities' desire to have Ibn Saud on their side. Mahmud Shukri al-Alusi, one of the delegation members and a historian of Hijaz and Arabia, tried to persuade Ibn Saud to support the Turks. Although the emir refrained from making any commitments, referring to his inability to oppose the British, he promised not to hinder Najdi merchants who supplied the Turkish army with food – Turkish caravans with arms and equipment passed from Syria to Asir and Yemen via his territory throughout the war.[2]

Even though they had decided to back Husain, the British could not ignore the strongest Arabian ruler – the emir of Najd – whose territory stretched from Kuwait and Jabal Shammar to the Rub al-Khali and from the Gulf to Hijaz. Above all, Britain wanted Ibn Saud to neutralize the emir of Hail, a Turkish vassal, who threatened the

British army's flank in Lower Mesopotamia. In the initial period of the war, the British hoped to win over Ibn Saud and persuade him to block the supplies to Hijaz and Syria from the Gulf coast via Kuwait. It was normal practice, however, for all Arabian rulers, in spite of their mutual enmity, to turn a blind eye to the caravans passing through their territories so that they could collect increased duties from them.[3]

When hostilities started in the Middle East, Major (later Sir) Percy Cox, the British political resident in the Gulf, recalled his agent Captain Shakespear from leave and sent him to Najd. On arriving in Riyadh, Shakespear insisted that Ibn Saud open hostilities against the Shammar.[4] In early January 1915 Ibn Saud marched north with 1,500 troops, mainly from al-Arid. He was later joined by the Mutair, Ajman, Subai and Suhul. Saud ibn Salih, the new ruler of Hail (Zamil Al Subhan had been killed), marched out to meet him, also with some 1,500 men.[5] Although these figures are not wholly reliable, they are a rough guide as to the scale of operations.

In some reports, Ibn Saud is said to have had several guns under Shakespear's command; according to another version, Shakespear was a mere observer.[6] Perhaps, in the atmosphere of Ikhwan fanaticism, Ibn Saud did not want a British officer, who was moreover reluctant to wear Arab dress, to remain in his troops. The emir tried to persuade the British agent to stay in al-Zilfi, but Shakespear insisted on participating in the campaign, either seeing it as a matter of honour or in order to control Ibn Saud and prevent him from evading the battle.[7]

In late January 1915 the enemies met near the Jarrab well to the north of al-Zilfi. The battle lasted for several days. Some sources claim that the only person killed was Captain Shakespear while others mention losses of almost 100 on both sides.[8] Under the influence of the Ikhwan, Ibn Saud's men shouted the Ikhwan's bellicose slogans. The Shammar, who formed the bulk of Hail's troops, were again spurred on by their tribe's slogans, shouted by beautiful girls, their hair down, and riding on camels. These facts are interesting not only as a picturesque detail. The very choice of warlike slogans demonstrated the difference between the social structure of the two emirates: Jabal Shammar's base was tribal whereas Najd's was pan-Arabian, based on the Ikhwan's Wahhabi monotheism. The Shammar encouraged each other by addressing the tribe's ancestor; the Saudi slogans promised paradise to those warriors who were killed in battle.[9]

Instead of fighting the Shammar, the Ajman warriors attacked Ibn Saud's troops and seized some of their camels. The Mutair forced their way to the Shammar camp and started plundering it.[10] According to Philby, the battle ended without victory for either side,[11] but it nevertheless discouraged the emir of Najd from engaging in a large-scale war for two or three years. He always tried to avoid active participation in hostilities, ignoring appeals by the British.

The British-Najdi treaty

Before his death, Captain Shakespear had conducted political negotiations with Ibn

Saud and a draft treaty was drawn up: it stipulated that Britain would guarantee the emir's positions in Najd and al-Hasa and protect him from Ottoman attacks by sea or by land, while he pledged himself to help the Allies. Thus Britain abandoned its policy of non-intervention in the internal affairs of the peninsula. In Philby's opinion,[12] Britain recognized and guaranteed Ibn Saud's full independence, while he agreed to refrain from entering into relations with other countries without preliminary consultations with Britain. The other articles of the treaty dealt with British financial and military aid for Ibn Saud's operations against his enemies, particularly Jabal Shammar.

To the contemporary reader, the notion of 'full independence' is hardly compatible with the renunciation of an independent foreign policy, but that combination was not found strange by British colonial officials. Troeller's analysis of documents from the British archives shows that Ibn Saud had a subtle understanding of these nuances. A comparison of the initial draft treaty, proposed by the British, with the emir's corrected version shows that all Ibn Saud's observations were aimed at increasing his independence and diminishing British control.[13]

While Ibn Saud negotiated with Shakespear, Turkish envoys continued to be sent to Najd. Istanbul had not lost hope of persuading the emir to join the holy war against the infidels.[14] After Shakespear was killed at Jarrab in January 1915, no new British agent was appointed for a period. The situation in central Arabia was unclear and Britain's attention was concentrated on the west of Arabia.

It was only on 26 December 1915 that Britain concluded a treaty with Ibn Saud. Since it was signed on Darin island, opposite al-Qatif, it is referred to as the Darin or al-Qatif treaty. Signed by Ibn Saud and Sir Percy Cox, it was ratified by the viceroy and governor-general of India at a council meeting held in Simla in July 1916. On the eve of signing the treaty, the British presented the emir with 1,000 rifles and a sum of £20,000 and permitted him to purchase military equipment in Bahrain.[15]

The British government acknowledged that 'Najd, El Hassa, Qatif and Jubail, and their dependencies and territories . . . are the countries of Bin Saud.' The third article stipulated, 'Bin Saud hereby agrees and promises to refrain from entering into any correspondence, agreement, or treaty with any foreign nation or Power . . .' The fourth article stated that Ibn Saud was not allowed to grant concessions to foreigners; and he agreed to have no dealings with any foreign power, other than on the advice of the British government. Neither might the emir of Najd 'cede, sell, mortgage, lease, or otherwise dispose' of the territory of his country or a part of it in whatever manner without Britain's consent. He pledged himself not to intervene in the affairs of 'Kuwait, Bahrein, and of the Sheikhs of Qatar and the Oman Coast'.[16] There was no mention of Najd's western frontiers in the treaty. Thus, in effect, it established a British protectorate over Najd and its dependencies. This was in line with the 'Pax Britannica' that London intended to establish throughout most of the Middle East, and in particular throughout Arabia, after the war. In exchange for concluding the treaty, Najd was to receive a monthly subsidy of £5,000 from 1916 onwards and a shipment of machine-guns and rifles.[17]

Najd and Hijaz during the First World War (1914-1918)

The Ajman revolt

Although a subdivision of the Ajman had fought with Ibn Saud at the battle of Jarrab in January 1915, the emir did not forget their treacherous behaviour and sought a pretext to punish them. The Ajman had been among the most unmanageable tribes for half a century and submitted to the central government only reluctantly. Soon after the battle of Jarrab, the Ajman raided several tribes who were ruled by Kuwait. Its ruler wrote to Ibn Saud, asking him to punish the robbers. It was the desired pretext: but Ibn Saud mistrusted the ruler of Kuwait, fearing that he might change his mind and give the Ajman asylum after their defeat in the campaign.

In the summer of 1915, before signing the treaty with Britain, Ibn Saud made for al-Hasa with a 300-strong detachment. The local fighters joined him. He caught up with the Ajman in June 1915 near Jabal Kanzana, but they were ready for battle and put up a stubborn resistance. The Najdis lost some 300 men, including the emir's brother Saad, and Ibn Saud himself was wounded. After this failure, he had to retreat to the oases of al-Hasa. His condition was so serious that he had to take refuge in the Kut citadel in Hufuf. The Ajman started plundering the neighbouring oases and besieged Ibn Saud for six months – until September or October 1915. They were helped by local emirs and the Araif, and also received support from Hail. Ibn Saud's father sent him reinforcements, led by his second son Muhammad.[18]

The appeal for aid from Kuwait yielded no immediate results, and it was only after the second request that Mubarak sent his son Salim with 200 men to support Ibn Saud. At the start of the following year, Ibn Saud was able to leave Hufuf and start attacking the Ajman.[19] He soon quarrelled with Salim ibn Mubarak, who returned to Kuwait. Pressed by Ibn Saud, the Ajman retreated to Kuwait and Mubarak gave them refuge, as Ibn Saud had feared. In early January 1916 Mubarak died and was succeeded by Jabir ibn Mubarak, who had been on good terms with Ibn Saud since their joint raids. The new sheikh even drove the Ajman from his state and relations between Najd and Kuwait grew warmer for a period. But when Jabir died in 1917, he was succeeded by his brother Salim, who opposed Ibn Saud.[20]

In 1916 Saud ibn Salih of Hail appeared in Qasim with troops and made an unsuccessful attempt to seize Buraida and restore his control over the province. The emirate of Jabal Shammar was crumbling despite Ottoman support. The widespread anti-Turkish sentiment in the peninsula was now directed against the rulers of Hail. According to Musil, the local population often joined the Saudis in attacking the Shammar garrisons.[21] The emir of Buraida managed to defeat the Shammar on his own.[22]

The anti-Turkish revolt in Hijaz[23]

The Arab revolt led by Sharif Husain against the Turks, the sudden changes of fortune connected with the division of the Ottoman empire, and Britain's violation of its obligations, have all been described in sufficient detail in the Russian, Western and Arab literature. We shall therefore confine ourselves to a schematic account of these developments, concentrating our attention on Najd, where the nucleus of Saudi Arabia was to form.

Western historians have taken a disproportionate interest in the Arab revolt owing to a single personality, Colonel T. E. Lawrence, and his literary talent. He arrived from Cairo as a liaison officer to the sharif of Mecca in October 1916, and in this capacity he participated in the military operations of the sharif's bedouin troops against the Turks. The Arabs' subsequent activities were confined to operations against the Turks to the east of the Jordan and railway diversions, in which Lawrence played an active role, though greatly exaggerated in his own writings. Although the Arab revolt contributed to the Allies' success and saved British soldiers' lives, the Arabs' sacrifice merely resulted in the division of their lands by the European powers. Lawrence knew this would be the result but he nevertheless prompted the Arabs to risk their lives:

> [N]ot being a perfect fool, I could see that if we won the war the promises to the Arabs were dead paper. Had I been an honourable adviser I would have sent my men home, and not let them risk their lives for such stuff. Yet the Arab inspiration was our main tool in winning the Eastern war. So I assured them that England kept her word in letter and spirit. In this comfort they performed their fine things: but, of course, instead of being proud öf what we did together, I was continually and bitterly ashamed.[24]

It may be reiterated that, during the First World War, the Allies paid much greater attention to the sharif of Mecca than to the emir of Najd. Hijaz lay along Britain's and its allies' major naval communication route through the Red Sea. The four Turkish divisions stationed between Maan and Yemen were pinned down by the Arab revolt.

Sharif Husain's policy corresponded to the upsurge of nationalist sentiment in the Arab parts of the Ottoman empire. In the early twentieth century, various societies and organizations for the protection of Arab rights appeared in the empire. In 1909, after the Young Turks' revolution, the so-called Qahtan League was set up in Istanbul, led by prominent Arab nationalists. The league worked among the Arab officers of the Turkish army. In 1912 the Ottoman Decentralization Party was created in Egypt: its goal was to establish autonomous governments in the Ottoman provinces. At the turn of the century, many Arab nationalists believed that Britain and France might help them to gain liberation from the Turkish yoke. They were to be bitterly disappointed and some of them paid for their naivety with their lives.

The Young Turks adopted a chauvinist, pan-Turkish ideology and accused the Arabs of acting in the interests of foreign powers. Although no Arab party had yet formally raised the question of secession from the Ottoman empire, the Young Turks felt that the trend towards autonomy might lead to demands for independence.

In June 1913 an Arab congress was convened in Paris to discuss the Arabs' rights within the Ottoman empire. Its participants, mostly Syrians, insisted on reforms, based on the principle of decentralization. Understanding the threat posed by the Arab nationalist movement, the Young Turks resorted to repression. Although the Ottoman government issued an edict in August 1913 that provided, *inter alia*, for the expansion of local authorities' rights and the introduction of Arabic-language education in those provinces with an Arab majority, all these reforms remained on paper.

Proclaiming *jihad* at the beginning of the war, the triumvirate that ruled the Ottoman empire tried to enlist the support of the sharif of Mecca: he was sent a series of letters urging him to declare his support for the holy war. Husain avoided giving a definite answer, referring to his vulnerability to British attacks and the threat of famine in the event of a blockade of the Hijaz coast. In his telegrams to Enver Pasha, the Turkish war minister and virtual head of the triumvirate, Husain demanded that he recognize the independence of Hijaz and pardon the Arab nationalists who had been arrested. The triumvirate could not afford to agree.

Even before the outbreak of war, Sharif Husain had contacted the British via Cairo. His son Abdallah, a deputy in the Ottoman parliament, met Lord Kitchener, the British high commissioner in Egypt, in 1913 and early 1914 to test British reaction to a possible Arab insurrection against the Turks. Abdallah was hoping for aid, including arms supplies. At the time, the British avoided giving a definite answer, but Abdallah's visit opened their eyes to the depth of nationalist sentiment among the Arabs.

When the First World War broke out, Kitchener was appointed minister of war and Henry McMahon succeeded him in Egypt. In January 1915 Ronald Storrs, secretary for oriental affairs under the British high commissioner in Egypt, and Sir Gilbert Clayton, head of British military intelligence in Cairo, began developing a plan for an Arab revolt in support of the Entente. In mid-October, Storrs' envoy came to Mecca to contact Abdallah. This resulted in a correspondence between the sharif and the British high commissioner in Egypt. Husain's son Faisal believed that France planned to seize Syria while Britain had its sights on the southern regions of Iraq. Kitchener's proposal, sent from London, included no obligations or guarantees against the division of Arab territories and only hinted at the recognition of Hijaz's independence. But Abdallah had contacts with underground societies in Syria and Iraq and supposed that Damascus and Baghdad would react positively to a call for *jihad* against the Turks.

The Arab nationalists, particularly those of the Al-Fatah and Al-Ahd societies, were also preparing a revolt in Syria and Iraq, which were shaken by anti-Turkish disturbances. In return for their cooperation, they demanded that Britain recognize the independence of the Arab countries, whose northern frontier was to pass through Mersin, Adana, Urfa and Mardin – only Aden was excluded from the notion of 'Arab countries'. Their programme provided for a defence agreement between Britain and the future Arab state and for Britain to be given economic preferences. They recognized the sharif of Mecca as the leader of the Arab nationalists.

In 1915 and 1916 the Ottoman authorities in Syria uncovered several underground Arab organizations, arrested their leaders and executed them in the presence of Faisal, who had been in Damascus since 1916 as the Turks' virtual prisoner. The Turks had probably also learned of the nationalists' ties with Faisal, but preferred not to touch him for the time being. In 1916 Arab nationalist organizations were uncovered in Iraq too. Ottoman detachments and units with large numbers of Arabs were transferred from Arab territories to the European front and replaced by purely Turkish ones.

Sharif Husain resumed negotiations with the British in 1915, reiterating the demands made by the Arab nationalists in Syria as the main conditions for his fighting the Turks. The tide of war in the Middle East was turning against Britain and its allies – the offensives in Gallipoli and Sinai had failed; the Turks were threatening Aden from Yemen; and the situation of the expeditionary corps in Iraq was grave. The Allies attached enormous importance to an Arab revolt, which would be helpful for their military efforts in the Middle East.

Letters were exchanged between Husain and McMahon, which later gave rise to bitter disputes. The sharif of Mecca set out his demands in a message dated 14 July 1915:

1. Great Britain recognises the independence of the Arab countries which are bounded: on the north, by the line Mersin-Adana to parallel 37° N. and thence along the line Birejik-Urfa-Mardin-Midiat-Jazirat (ibn 'Umar)-Amadia to the Persian frontier; on the east, by the Persian frontier down to the Persian Gulf; on the south, by the Indian Ocean (with the exclusion of Aden whose status will remain as at present): on the west, by the Red Sea and the Mediterranean Sea back to Mersin.
2. Great Britain will agree to the proclamation of an Arab Caliphate for Islam.
3. The Sharifian Arab Government undertakes, other things being equal, to grant Great Britain preference in all economic enterprises in the Arab countries . . .[25]

Then followed the conditions for a military alliance, the abolition of capitulations and other issues. The text of the message clearly revealed Husain's claim to become, with Britain's assistance, the head of an independent Arab state. This would include, besides all Arab (and partly Kurdish) and some purely Turkish territories of the Ottoman empire, all Britain's Arabian protectorates, with the exception of the British colony of Aden. McMahon's reply, dated 24 October 1915, read:

The districts of Mersin and Alexandretta, and portions of Syria lying to the west of the districts of Damascus, Homs, Hama and Aleppo, cannot be said to be purely Arab, and must on that account be excepted from the proposed delimitation.

Subject to that modification, and without prejudice to the treaties concluded between us and certain Arab Chiefs, we accept that delimitation.

As for the regions lying within the proposed frontiers, in which Great Britain is free to act without detriment to the interests of her ally France, I am authorised to give you the following pledges on behalf of the Government of Great Britain, and to reply as follows to your note:
1. That, subject to the modifications stated above, Great Britain is prepared to recognise and uphold the independence of the Arabs in all the regions lying

within the frontiers proposed by the Sharif of Mecca;
2. That Great Britain will guarantee the Holy Places against all external aggression, and will recognise the obligation of preserving them from aggression;
3. That, when circumstances permit, Great Britain will help the Arabs with her advice and assist them in the establishment of governments to suit those diverse regions;
4. That it is understood that the Arabs have already decided to seek the counsels and advice of Great Britain exclusively; and that such European advisers and officials as may be needed to establish a sound system of administration shall be British;
5. That, as regards the two vilayets of Baghdad and of Basra, the Arabs recognise that the fact of Great Britain's established position and interests there will call for the setting up of special administrative arrangements to protect those regions from foreign aggression . . .[26]

The obligations Britain assumed were so ambiguous and took so little account of Husain's demands that the sharif, who had spent long years in the highly politicized atmosphere of Istanbul, could not have had any illusions concerning the true nature of the proposals. But even the most restrictive interpretation of the British message seemed to him a sufficient guarantee of his future status as king of the Arabs, which was enough to start a revolt against the Turks. Husain interpreted Britain's obligations in a broad sense in his public declarations, propaganda and correspondence with the British. He claimed that Britain had recognized him as the independent king of the Arabs and calculated, perhaps, that he would be able to extort more than had been promised.

Even interpreting McMahon's message cautiously, neither the sharif nor his entourage could have guessed that almost all London's promises were false and that negotiations were already being conducted on the colonial division of the Arab countries. The Sykes-Picot agreement to that effect was signed some weeks before the revolt started. It made McMahon's obligations null and void.

Aware that the Turks planned to replace him by a more obedient ruler, Husain decided to bring matters to a head. On the eve of the revolt he warned his son Faisal, who managed to escape the Turks' surveillance with a small escort. Proclaiming independence on 5 June 1916, Husain began the revolt five days later, fearing a pre-emptive attack by the Turks. In July the Turkish garrison in Mecca surrendered and gradually all the other large towns of Hijaz were captured, with the exception of Medina, which was connected with Syria by rail. Foreign liaison missions appeared in Jidda: the British mission was led by Colonel C. Wilson, and the French by E. Bremont.

In late October 1916 the sharif proclaimed himself king of the Arab countries. His second son Abdallah communicated the news abroad, but nobody outside Hijaz recognized the sharif's claim to the all-Arab crown. In January 1917 the British and French governments informed Husain that they recognized him merely as 'king of Hijaz'.

In late 1916 Husain had 30–40,000 men under his banner in Hijaz, but they had only 10,000 rifles. Aziz al-Masri, an Egyptian officer, was initially responsible for the organization of hostilities but he was then replaced by Jafar al-Askari, an Iraqi officer who was subsequently to become Iraqi prime minister. The advice of officers with experience of service in regular armies was by and large irrelevant to Husain and his commanders, who preferred the traditional methods of waging war, but the nucleus of a regular army was created nonetheless.

In early 1917 the British navy and Faisal's detachment occupied al-Wajh, the last coastal village still under Turkish control. In July the insurgent Arabs seized Aqaba. British subsidies, distributed with largesse by Husain and his sons among the bedouin, attracted more and more supporters to the revolt. The Arab troops began advancing on Damascus through the territory of present-day Jordan, along the edge of the desert, which facilitated the operations of Allenby's troops in Palestine. The collapse of the Ottoman empire was imminent and Arab soldiers deserted the Turkish troops.

When the secret treaties between the Entente powers were published in Russia after the October revolution, the Turks sent King Husain the text of the Sykes-Picot agreement on the division of Arab lands. When he queried the authenticity of the text with the British, he was 'sincerely' assured that it was a forgery, but the assurances were again ambiguous. Husain either believed or pretended to believe the British and continued hostilities against the Turks. In reality, Arab blood was being shed for anti-Arab purposes. However, the government of Hijaz was completely dependent on British military, financial and food aid and was deprived of a free hand.

From the final stages of the war, it had become clear that Britain would not implement the vague promises made to Husain and the Arab nationalists and was even aggravating the problem by dividing up the Arab territories and by the Balfour Declaration of 2 November 1917 (which stated that the British government 'viewed with favour' the creation of a Jewish 'national home' in Palestine). This led to a serious deterioration in Husain's relations with the British. Britain nevertheless ensured its 'special interests' in Arabia at the Versailles peace conference.

On 30 September 1918 a group of Anaza were the first Arab troops to burst into Damascus: they galloped through the main square, waving the Arab flag. The following day, British troops, led by Allenby, entered the town. Faisal temporarily became the king of Syria, where an Arab government was formed. But the French were to oust Faisal from Damascus two years later, drowning the Syrian Arabs' liberation movement in blood.

The Hijaz revolt and Ibn Saud

After the anti-Turkish revolt started in Hijaz, Britain's main task in the Arabian peninsula was to persuade Ibn Saud to join Sharif Husain or, at the least, to prevent an exacerbation of the disagreement between them. Ibn Saud had mistrusted Husain from the very start, however. When the emir of Najd learned of the Hijaz revolt from Cox in June 1916, he was afraid 'lest the pretensions of Husain to the leadership of the Arabs might create a situation totally unacceptable to himself [Ibn Saud]'.[27]

Al-Zirikli, a pro-Saudi author, maintains that after the outbreak of the Arab revolt, the Najdis sometimes helped the Turks and sometimes Hijaz. He quotes three curious documents. The first is a letter from Faisal to Sharif Husain, dated 10 November 1916, with a complaint against the continuing trade between Qasim and Medina. The second letter was sent by Sharif Husain in late March 1917, asking the emir of Najd to attack Hail. The third letter is from General Fahri Pasha, the Turkish commander in Medina, who offered the Najdis arms and equipment in July 1918 to fight the 'rebel Husain'.[28]

According to Musil, Ibn Saud's detachments attacked the tribes who were subordinate to Sharif Husain, particularly in the frontier regions. Ibn Saud maintained contact with the Ottoman governor and the Turkish commander-in-chief in the region of Medina. He supplied the Turks with camels in return for hard cash. In late September 1917 a Najdi delegation went to Damascus to discuss various problems with the Ottoman authorities, though the emir himself visited the British in Basra in late November.[29]

By now, Ibn Saud had perhaps understood which way the wind was blowing. He confiscated 700 camels that a rich merchant had bought for the Turks and even handed them over to the British in Kuwait.[30] Noting that the British were unable to restrain his Najdi rival, Sharif Husain sent an envoy to Riyadh: he presented Ibn Saud with some gold and called on him to act against the common (Turkish) enemy.[31]

After the beginning of the Hijaz revolt, Jabal Shammar received regular consignments of Turkish arms. When Ibn Saud saw that Hail had regained its military might, he strove to improve his relations with Sharif Husain. The main cause of his changed attitude to Hijaz, however, was British pressure. In November 1916 Cox met Ibn Saud at al-Uqair and tried to persuade him that he should not be afraid of the sharif's claims, though the British were already aware that Husain had proclaimed himself king of the Arabs.[32]

On 20 November 1916 Cox organized the so-called Great Durbar in Kuwait, a meeting between Ibn Saud, Sheikh Jabir of Kuwait and Sheikh Hazal of the Muhammara settlement. While praising Sharif Husain for his actions and stressing that all true Arabs should cooperate to defend the Arab cause, Ibn Saud refrained, as usual, from any real promise of support. The British persuaded Husain to send a telegram expressing his good wishes to the rulers at their meeting.[33] At the Great Durbar, Ibn Saud ultimately decided to side with Britain. It was then that he and Sheikh Jabir were decorated with British orders. The three leaders took an oath to cooperate with Britain.[34]

After the Durbar, Ibn Saud visited Basra, where the British showed him their modern armaments, including planes which he saw for the first time. Although the emir was too discreet to express his admiration, he was presumably impressed by the modern hardware. It was then that Britain agreed to pay him a monthly subsidy of £5,000.[35] Cox managed to persuade Ibn Saud that Jabal Shammar was a threat to Najd, owing to the massive supplies of German and Turkish arms. Besides the subsidy, he offered the emir 4 machine-guns and 3,000 rifles with cartridges; in response Ibn Saud promised to send 4,000 troops against Hail.[36]

Although the British saw that it was impossible to persuade Ibn Saud to undertake direct hostilities against Jabal Shammar, they nevertheless hoped that the treaty would encourage him to blockade the Turks in Hijaz and Syria. Like the other rulers in Arabia, however, Ibn Saud was not averse to replenishing his exchequer by smuggling, which continued up to the end of the war. On one occasion a caravan of 3,000 camels brought goods to Hijaz, which caused complications in his relations with the British.[37]

When Sharif Husain declared himself 'the king of the Arabs', Ibn Saud protested and demanded negotiations concerning the Najd–Hijaz border and suzerainty over the frontier tribes. According to the Najdi annals, Husain answered, 'What kind of borders are you demanding? You are either mad or drunk.'[38] The emir of Najd never forgot that insult. He warned Britain that he would have to fight Husain.[39]

Since 1917 Cox had striven to detract Ibn Saud's attention from the Allies' activities in Hijaz and continued to instigate him against Jabal Shammar, which represented a potential threat to the British flank in Mesopotamia. (In the same year, Cox became British civil commissioner in Baghdad with the British expeditionary corps.) Britain again tried to put an end to smuggling across the Arabian deserts, but to no avail. Goods were smuggled both from Iraq, where British troops were stationed, and from the Gulf ports, including Kuwait. Then the caravans made for Qasim or Jabal Shammar en route for Medina or Damascus.

In the autumn of 1917 Husain's Arab detachments were listless and Reginald Wingate, the new British high commissioner in Egypt, decided to increase pressure on Ibn Saud and spur him to action against Jabal Shammar. His representative Ronald Storrs was sent to Baghdad to discuss the situation with Cox. On later arriving in Riyadh, however, Storrs suffered sunstroke and had to leave Arabia.[40] In November 1917 Cox's representatives, led by Colonel Hamilton, landed in al-Uqair and made for Riyadh to discuss the situation with the emir at the end of the month.[41]

The mission included Philby, who was to become the most prominent expert on Arabian affairs and to connect his life with Ibn Saud and Saudi Arabia. As Philby himself wrote, his tasks were to encourage Ibn Saud to undertake a campaign against Jabal Shammar, to prevent a worsening in relations between Najd and Hijaz and to find a solution to the Ajman problem. Ibn Saud promised to start energetic action provided that he received arms.[42] But by April 1918, Jerusalem had already been captured and the British no longer needed the liquidation of the Jabal Shammar emirate; they refused to supply even the arms requested by Philby the previous December. Ibn Saud was disappointed.[43]

Philby offered the emir of Najd £20,000 from the fund at his personal disposal for an immediate campaign against Hail.[44] The campaign started on 5 August 1918, with the participation of Philby, who left a detailed account of it. In September 1918 the Ikhwan moved towards Hail under their own banners. The Najdis had some 5,000 men. The situation on the Hijaz frontier had already been aggravated because of the situation in the al-Khurma oasis. Sharif Husain concluded a peace treaty with Hail, which was worrying for Ibn Saud. When the Shammar seemed about to capitulate, Britain concluded that Ibn Saud's success in Hail might cause an adverse reaction from Husain and ordered Najd to end the campaign. Ibn Saud was furious although the campaign yielded huge spoils – 1,500 camels, thousands of sheep and 10,000 cartridges. The emir understood that Britain was no longer interested in his actions against Hail, and even less so in his conquest of Jabal Shammar.[45]

During the siege of Medina by the Hashemites from March 1917 to October 1918, a quarrel broke out in Abdallah ibn Husain's camp between Fajir, one of the Ataiba sheikhs, and Sharif Khalid ibn Mansur ibn Luwai, the emir of the al-Khurma oasis. The Saudi chronicler claims that Sheikh Fajir slapped Sharif Khalid's face during the quarrel. Although Abdallah put Fajir under arrest for three days, Khalid did not forgive the insult.[46]

In the autumn of 1917 a large group of Najdis performed the *hajj* to Mecca, where Husain received them with honour.[47] The Najdis insisted on establishing a formal border between the two states, but Husain evaded the issue.[48] Perhaps Khalid was using the *hajj* to contact the Najdis and embrace their version of 'monotheism', a possibility that did not escape Sharif Husain's attention. He understood that siding with the Wahhabi teaching amounted to a political obligation and the swearing of allegiance to Riyadh.

Shortly afterwards Khalid expelled the *qadhi* (appointed by King Husain) from al-Khurma. When Husain urged Khalid to come to him with an explanation, the latter declined, fearing for his life. He may have tried to approach Ibn Saud for protection in November 1917, but the emir avoided making any definite commitments.[49]

In July 1918 Husain sent a detachment, led by Sharif Hamud ibn Zaid ibn Fawwaz, to seize al-Khurma. Ibn Saud had already sent some Ikhwan to support Khalid, however, and the troops dispatched from Mecca were decimated.[50] This was an open challenge to the sharif: he declared in August 1918 that al-Khurma belonged to him and his family, and its people should cease obeying Khalid, who had wallowed in heresy.[51] But Khalid had already gathered troops and raided the villages that obeyed the sharif. Medina was still in Turkish hands, and his policy amounted to cooperation with them. The Medina garrison finally surrendered in November 1918. The First World War had ended for Arabia.

Further developments centred on Turaba and al-Khurma, two oases between Hijaz and Najd. Turaba had a population of some 3,000 and many members of the sharif's clan owned lands there. The oasis was considered the gateway to al-Taif on the Najdi side. Al-Khurma had a population of some 5,000, some of whom were Subais while others were *abds*. Several dozen sharifian families also lived there.[52]

After the capitulation of the Ottoman empire, there were five independent states in Arabia – Hijaz, Najd, Jabal Shammar, Asir and Yemen. Their future was to be determined both by the struggle between them (eventually won by the strongest, the emirate of Najd) and by Britain's policy. Lord Milner, the British minister for the colonies, wrote on 16 May 1919 that Britain's policy was aimed at creating an independent Arabia within the British sphere of influence and free from European political intrigue, which meant that its 'independent' rulers should maintain relations only with Britain.[53]

Events in Yemen and Asir

Before returning to the main events of Arabian politics, which were increasingly dominated by the rivalry between Najd and Hijaz and by British arbitration in the dispute, let us turn briefly to developments in Yemen and Asir.

The imam of Yemen remained loyal to the Turks during the First World War, first, because he was reluctant to find himself dependent on Britain and, second, because he feared Emir Muhammad Al Idris, who had established control over Asir. Muhammad Al Idris opposed the Turks and concluded a treaty with the British resident in Aden in May 1915. After an unsuccessful attempt to capture al-Luhaya with 12,000 troops, Muhammad Al Idris managed to seize a sizeable part of northern Tihama. Al-Lihaya was finally captured by the British navy and a detachment from Asir in early 1917. Hasan Al Aid, the sheikh of the northern part of Asir (with its capital in Abha), remained neutral until June 1916 and then started small-scale military operations to support the Arab revolt.[54]

In evaluating the situation in the south of Arabia at the end of the First World War, it should be noted that both Yemen and Asir were engrossed in their internal affairs and did not influence the outcome of the struggle between Najd and Hijaz.

The battle of Turaba

The victorious Allies discussed their mandates and privileges in the Middle East at the peace conference, taking little interest in developments in the Arabian peninsula. A ferocious epidemic of Spanish influenza claimed more lives in Arabia in the winter of 1918–19 than hostilities had done. Among its victims were Turki, Ibn Saud's eldest son, two of his other sons and Jauhar, his senior wife.[55] However, the epidemic did not prevent a new border conflict breaking out between Najd and Hijaz.

King Husain sent Shakir ibn Zaid with a detachment of 1,200 bedouin and 500 regular infantrymen to capture al-Khurma, but his troops suffered a series of defeats. In early 1919 Husain sent a part of his son Abdallah's army of 8,000 men with other detachments to al-Khurma.[56] The British resident in Jidda understood that this was a direct clash with the Najdis and tried to prevent it. Perhaps he thought that Husain would try to capture al-Khurma and then invade Najd, and it was not clear at the time whether such a clash would be advantageous to Britain. But King Husain's behaviour, his discontent with British policy, his mentions of the obligations that Britain had violated, and his claims to the title of 'king of all the Arabs', prompted London to teach him a lesson. The British may well have been ignorant of the real fighting ability of the Najdi troops. According to Philby, almost all the participants at a meeting convened by Lord Curzon were sure that the Wahhabis would be routed and so decided to support Hijaz's claims to al-Khurma.[57]

Abdallah was opposed to his father's decision. He understood that the population of Hijaz had grown tired of hostilities and that actions against the elusive bedouin might continue for a long time without success. Obeying his father's orders, however, he moved east towards Turaba, some 120 or 130 km from al-Khurma. In late May 1919 Abdallah captured Turaba and allowed his soldiers to plunder the oasis.[58] A correspondence followed with Ibn Saud. The Najdi sources claim that Abdallah's letter was arrogant and threatening; Abdallah wrote later that, on the contrary, this was the tone of Ibn Saud's message.[59]

Meanwhile the Ikhwan detachments, led by Sultan ibn Bijad, came to Turaba from al-Ghatghat, together with a detachment of Qahtan, led by Hamud ibn Umar. Khalid ibn Luwai also arrived there from al-Khurma. According to the Najdi sources, they numbered some 4,000 men. Ibn Saud's envoys, who returned from Turaba, told terrible stories of the plunder, murder and violence engaged in by Abdallah's army; they claimed that Abdallah had boasted that he would start the Ramadhan fast in Riyadh and celebrate the *id* in al-Hasa.[60]

The Ikhwan attacked Abdallah's troops at night on 3 sides, defeating them utterly.[61] Abdallah admitted that only 3 of his 500 infantrymen and 150 of the 850 Hijazis survived.[62] Almost all his arms and munitions fell into the hands of the Ikhwan. Although they had participated earlier in Ibn Saud's raids, this was their first serious military operation. The battle showed that the emir of Najd had a fighting force at his disposal. The situation was dangerous for Hijaz. Abdallah himself – perhaps with hindsight – considered that King Husain's situation was hopeless after the defeat.[63]

Ibn Saud is reported to have arrived in Turaba in early July 1919 with 12,000 reinforcements, though the figure seems exaggerated. On 4 July a courier arrived from Jidda with a message from the British resident:

> The Government of His Majesty has ordered me to inform you that you must return to Najd as soon as you receive this letter, leaving Turaba and al-Khurma as neutral zones until you and King Husain define the frontiers. If you fail to retreat after receiving my letter, the Government of His Majesty will consider the treaty they have concluded with you null and void and take all necessary steps to hinder your hostile actions.[64]

The British urged Ibn Saud not to move towards al-Taif.

On receiving the ultimatum, the emir of Najd felt that he had gone too far and returned immediately to Riyadh. He ordered the Ikhwan to evacuate the oases in the region, replaced them by the detachment he had brought from the environs of Hail and restored the emir of Turaba to his post. However, he continued sending letters to the sheikhs of the nomadic tribes of the region, calling on them to join the struggle for 'monotheism'.[65] Many of them responded to his proposal. In practical terms, it was tantamount to the establishment of Najdi control over the frontier region.

In support of its ultimatum, Britain sent aircraft and soldiers to Jidda.[66] It was presumed that the subsidy to Riyadh would be discontinued in the event of Ibn Saud's new invasion of Hijaz. The British probably felt that King Husain had been taught a lesson and they were reluctant to untie the hands of the emir of Najd.

In November 1919 Faisal, Ibn Saud's adolescent son, visited Britain, accompanied by Ibn Thunayyan, an experienced diplomat who had been educated in Istanbul and knew Turkish and French.[67]

Although Ibn Saud submitted to Britain's demands, the relatively easy victory over Hijaz had convinced him of his strength and he came to the conclusion that Hijaz would ultimately be his. The battle of Turaba may be considered as marking the watershed between two epochs of Arabian history.

At the end of the First World War, Najd was simply one of several Arabian states. Jabal Shammar still existed, Kuwait was a British protectorate, Asir had not yet been annexed by Najd, and Hijaz claimed the whole of Arabia though it lacked the forces to 'swallow' it. Meanwhile the European colonial powers were carving out their mandated territories from the remnants of the Ottoman empire. In the words of Lloyd George, 'No one contemplated that foreign troops should occupy any part of Arabia. It was too arid a country to make it worth the while of any ravenous Power to occupy as a permanent pasture.'[68] The thought that fabulous oil deposits might be found there did not enter anyone's mind.

After the First World War, partly under the influence of the October revolution in Russia, many Arab countries were seized by national liberation struggles of various shades. In spite of the diverse backgrounds and aspirations of the participants in the movement, they were all directed against the colonial regimes established by Britain and France, against the imperialist division of the Arab countries and against the mandate system introduced by the League of Nations. The insurrections of 1919 and 1921 in Egypt, of 1918–20 in Iraq, of 1925–27 in Syria, of 1919 in Aden, and the mass anticolonial movement of 1918–24 in Syria and Lebanon, all influenced the situation in Arabia, whether directly or indirectly. It became clear that the colonial system had had its day.

Part Two

Part Two

CHAPTER 11

The Consolidation of the Arabian Territories around Najd (1918–1926)

The situation of the emirate of Najd was far more complicated after the First World War than it had been before. Earlier, the emir had been able to capitalize on the conflict of interests between the Ottoman empire and Britain, whereas now the British had become the only real force in the region – as Ibn Saud had realized when they prevented him from attacking Hijaz and Jabal Shammar. On the other hand, Britain still avoided direct intervention in the affairs of the Arabian peninsula and strove to reduce the expenses involved in paying subsidies to the various rulers.

Relations between Najd and Kuwait

The rulers of Kuwait viewed the rise of the emirate of Najd with concern. The affiliation of the Mutair (who traditionally raided Kuwait) to the Ikhwan movement was a direct military threat to the shaikhdom. On the pretext of protecting and propagating 'monotheism', the Mutair claimed the right to plunder Kuwait, the land of 'polytheists' and Britain's ally.

In 1915 the Kuwaitis helped the Ajman to avoid a rout by granting them asylum. The Ajman then submitted reluctantly to Ibn Saud and joined the Ikhwan movement, but Ibn Saud wanted to divide the tribe into two dozen small *hijras*, scattered throughout the inner areas of Najd. Although they had no objection to the Ikhwan movement, the Ajman categorically opposed settling outside their *dira* (traditional homeland) in al-Hasa.[1]

The deteriorating relations between Britain and the ruler of Kuwait proved an unexpected help to Najd. The British discovered that the Turks in Damascus were receiving supplies via Kuwait, whose Shaikh Salim made huge profits from smuggling.[2] Salim was aware of the Anglo-Turkish agreement of 1913, which established Kuwait's border in Jabal Munif,[3] but he did not know that the Anglo-Najdi treaty of 1915 had not determined the frontiers of Kuwaiti territory.[4] (He claimed a considerable part of al-Hasa.)

When Ibn Saud founded an Ikhwan *hijra* on the very border of Kuwait, but within the Mutair *dira*, Salim protested. A clash occurred between the Kuwaitis and the Ikhwan, led by Faisal Al Dawish, who defeated the enemy.[5] Mindful of the danger of an invasion from Najd, a defence wall was erected around the city of Kuwait within two months. Both parties then began negotiations. Salim asked the British for support, but they urged the two sides to accept their arbitration.[6]

In September 1920 the emirs agreed to the British suggestion, but hostilities continued. Kuwait asked the Shammar for help and an armed detachment arrived from Hail. Ibn Saud ordered Faisal Al Dawish to make for Kuwait. In September 1920 about 4,000 Ikhwan (from the Mutair) appeared several kilometres to the south of Kuwait.[7] At the same time, Sir Percy Cox was negotiating with Ibn Saud in al-Uqair,[8] trying to resolve the border conflicts in a manner acceptable to the British. But in October 1920 Faisal Al Dawish attacked and routed the Shammar and the Kuwaitis near al-Jahra, though his troops suffered heavy losses. Salim ensconced himself in the fortress and started negotiations to gain time, simultaneously asking the British for support. In October they decided to help their protégé, sent warships to the coast of Kuwait and threatened to intervene in the conflict on Kuwait's side.[9] Faisal Al Dawish was forced to retreat.

In late February 1921 Shaikh Salim died suddenly. The nobility of Kuwait, who had tired of the senseless war, chose Ahmad ibn Jabir Al Sabah – the eldest son of the late Shaikh Jabir ibn Mubarak Al Sabah – as his successor. The new ruler was popular in the country and advocated a compromise with Riyadh.[10] At that time, he was negotiating with Ibn Saud in Najd. Ibn Saud understood that the British would not give him Kuwait. For the time being, his attention was concentrated on the planned campaign against Hail and the opportunity to subdue the whole of Jabal Shammar.

The annexation of Jabal Shammar

Within two years, differences between the Subhan and Rashidi families reached boiling point. In 1919 Saud Al Subhan fled to al-Zubair. He was succeeded as vizier by one Aqqab ibn Ijil, who sought to establish contacts with Ibn Saud.[11] In late March 1920 Saud ibn Abd al-Aziz, the emir of Jabal Shammar, was killed by his cousin Abdallah ibn Talal, who was, in his turn, shot dead by Saud's servant. As a result, the throne passed into the hands of Abdallah ibn Mitab ibn Abd al-Aziz.[12]

The emir of Najd received information that there were many supporters of the sharifian family at the Rashidis' court, while the British were preparing the Iraqi throne for Faisal, the son of Sharif Husein; there was a real danger of an alliance between the

Saudis' old enemies.[13] In March–April 1921 Ibn Saud concluded a peace treaty with Kuwait and decided to launch a campaign against Hail. Central Arabia was again affected by a severe drought and the resulting rise in prices aggravated the difficulties of Jabal Shammar.[14]

In April–May 1921 Ibn Saud's detachments defeated the Shammar tribes and appeared near the walls of Hail. The ruler of Jabal Shammar (Abdallah ibn Mitab ibn Abd al-Aziz) decided to sit tight behind the solid walls of the town, but when the food supplies ran out, he sent a delegation to negotiate. He was ready to confine his emirate to Hail and the territory of the Shammar, but Ibn Saud now felt strong enough to demand an unconditional surrender.[15]

Skirmishes continued for some months without any real results. Reinforcements arrived for the Najdis with Ibn Saud's son Saud, who headed the Najdi troops. Although the population of Hail managed to procure the food needed to withstand the siege, the internal struggle continued unabated in the town. The urban nobility replaced Abdallah ibn Mitab by Muhammad ibn Talal (Abdallah ibn Talal's brother), who was then in prison. Abdallah ibn Mitab asked the emir of Riyadh for asylum. With the siege at a stalemate, Ibn Saud ordered his son to return to the capital.[16]

Meanwhile Winston Churchill, the British colonial secretary, outlined the post-war structure of the Middle East at a conference in Cairo. The British decided to make Faisal, son of Sharif Husain, the king of Iraq and he ascended the throne in 1921. Abdallah was to become emir of Transjordan. Ibn Saud felt that he had better act fast lest Jabal Shammar slip out of his hands.

Before beginning a new campaign against Hail, Ibn Saud convened an assembly of the Najdi nobility, tribal shaikhs and *ulama*, who decided to enhance the state's international status by henceforth naming the emir 'the Sultan of Najd and her Dependencies'. The British authorities in Iraq soon recognized this new title.[17]

In August 1921 Ibn Saud returned to the walls of Hail with troops, which were, according to some sources, 10,000 strong; they included the Ikhwan, led by Faisal Al Dawish.[18] The Shammar's situation became hopeless. After the 2-month-long siege, the nobility sent a member of the Subhan clan to engage in negotiations, which ended in surrender. The gates of Hail were opened to Ibn Saud's troops at the appointed time. Ibn Talal hid in the fortress and made a desperate appeal for help to King Husain and the British authorities in Iraq, but they did not react; he surrendered on condition that his life would be spared. Ibn Talal settled in Riyadh as an honoured prisoner and married his daughter to Ibn Saud. The last independent emir of Hail was murdered in Riyadh in 1954 by his own slave.[19]

On 1 November 1921 the independent emirate of Jabal Shammar ceased to exist. The following day, the people of Hail swore allegiance to Ibn Saud, who appointed Ibrahim Al Subhan as governor of the new province. The sultan of Najd banned plunder in the town and even provided the inhabitants with food. The Shia, in particular, were fearful of reprisals but Ibn Saud issued a special ordinance guaranteeing their safety.[20] Characteristically, the Ikhwan disagreed with the tolerance shown by their emir and criticized him openly for such connivance with the 'infidels'.[21]

With the fall of Jabal Shammar, the whole of central Arabia was now under the authority of Riyadh. Najd and the territories it had annexed became the main force in the Arabian peninsula. Jabal Shammar had been unable to withstand the force of its stronger southern neighbour, whose fighters were inspired by the slogans of the revived Wahhabi teaching. Relying mainly on a single, large tribe, Jabal Shammar had failed to become the nucleus of a united Arabian state; the struggle within the ruling dynasty and the lack of a strong leader had weakened the emirate in the face of its formidable and resolute rival. The rulers of Jabal Shammar had linked their destiny with the Ottoman empire, while the Arab nationalist movement had a pronounced anti-Turkish character. Britain did not then hold that the annexation of the northern part of central Arabia by Najd would materially threaten its interests in Iraq and Transjordan and preferred not to become involved, though the increase in Najd's power was to prove troublesome for the British.

Delimitation of the borders with Iraq and Transjordan

After the conquest of Jabal Shammar, the emirate of Najd faced three hostile states, ruled by the Hashemite family, on its western and northern borders. Since Iraq and Transjordan were controlled by the British, Ibn Saud took all further action with an eye to British policy.

The border of Jabal Shammar with Iraq and Transjordan had not been defined. Another problem was that the issue of clear-cut land borders was new to the Arabian rulers. Ibn Saud held that all the tribes of the Shammar and Anaza confederation submitted to him and therefore his suzerainty spread to territories that the British considered a part of Iraq. Besides, some Shammar and other tribes rejected the Saudis' claims over them and continued to migrate into Iraq.[22] According to Glubb Pasha, the future commander of the Arab Legion in Jordan:

> International boundaries had never been heard of in Arabia . . . In practice, the Baghdad administration had never made any attempt to extend its control into the desert to a distance of more than two or three miles [3–5 km] from the Euphrates . . . It was essential for the very survival of the Nejed tribes that they be able to move northwards towards Iraq or Syria . . . Conversely, the northern tribes might at times be obliged to migrate for a whole season to Nejed. To draw a hard frontier across the desert seemed to the Nejdis to threaten the very existence of those tribes.[23]

Intertribal differences and skirmishes increased the friction between Iraq and Najd. In the autumn of 1921, one Yusuf ibn Saadun was appointed commander of the newly formed Iraqi camel corps. He was an enemy of Hamud ibn Suwait, the shaikh of the Zafir tribe, who had fled to Riyadh and soon returned with *zakat*-collectors sent by Ibn Saud. An Ikhwan detachment of Mutair, led by Faisal Al Dawish, joined Hamud; they

The Consolidation of the Arabian Territories around Najd (1918–1926)

attacked Yusuf's camp in March 1922 and almost all his men were massacred. British aircraft were sent to help the Iraqis. Ibn Saud claimed that he had no knowledge of those events, though nobody took his statement seriously. The Iraqi government disbanded the camel corps and dismissed Yusuf ibn Saadun. The disgruntled commander fled to Riyadh and offered his services to Ibn Saud.[24]

In the spring of 1922 Ibn Saud's representatives met Cox in Muhammara. The British insisted on establishing a permanent border between Iraq and Najd: the Najdis demanded that the borders should be based on the nomadic tribes' traditional *diras*. On 5 May 1922 the Muhammara treaty was signed, which handed over the Muntafiq, the Zafir and the Amarat (a section of the Anaza) to Iraq and the Shammar to Najd. But Ibn Saud refused to ratify the treaty on the pretext that the Zafir, led by Hamud ibn Suwait, had accepted his protection and rejected submission to Iraq.[25]

In July 1922 the Ikhwan began an advance to the north-west, into Transjordan. After seizing the Jawf oasis in July 1922, they encountered Emir Abdallah's patrols. Then they captured the Taima and Tabuk oases and collected *zakat* from their inhabitants in favour of Riyadh.[26] Thereafter the Ikhwan moved to Wadi Sirhan, which had earlier been part of Jabal Shammar, before attacking the Bani Shakir oasis. They were approaching Amman, the capital of Transjordan.[27] Simultaneously, the Najdis reached the border of Syria, which was French-mandated territory and interrupted the territorial continuity of British possessions. At the time, Britain was considering building a railway from Palestine to Iraq via the very territories seized by the Ikhwan. Urgent action was required.

Cox decided to demand a clear-cut frontier and arranged a meeting with the sultan of Najd. On 21 November 1922 Cox and Ibn Saud began six days of talks in al-Uqair. These resulted in the al-Uqair protocols, signed on 2 December 1922, as a supplement to the Muhammara treaty. This represented a certain success for British diplomacy: the sultan of Najd had been persuaded to recognize the borders of Iraq, which was under British mandate.[28]

Protocol No. 1 defined the frontiers between Iraq and Najd and provided for a neutral zone, where the Iraqis and Najdis might both graze their livestock. The Najdi tribes that traditionally used certain wells in Iraq might continue to do so, provided that the water sources in the frontier region were not used for military purposes. Thus the agreement took the traditional *diras* of various tribes into consideration. Protocol No. 2 stipulated that any tribe was entitled to change its state affiliation.

Simultaneously with the delimitation with Iraq, Ibn Saud signed a convention with Kuwait on the border issue. It also provided for a neutral zone for the nomads from both countries where they might graze their livestock.[29]

The al-Uqair negotiations themselves are worth describing in some detail. According to Dickson, who took part in them:

> On the sixth day Sir Percy [Cox] . . . told both sides that, at the rate they were going, nothing would be settled for a year. At a private meeting at which only he, Ibn Sa'ud and I were present, he lost all patience over what he called the childish

attitude of Ibn Sa'ud in his tribal-boundary idea. Sir Percy's Arabic was not too good, so I did the translating. It was astonishing to see the Sultan of Najd being reprimanded like a naughty schoolboy by H.M. High Commissioner, and being told sharply that he, Sir Percy Cox, would himself decide on the type and general line of the frontier . . . Ibn Sa'ud almost broke down, and pathetically remarked that Sir Percy was his father and mother, who had made him and raised him from nothing to the position he held, and that he would surrender half his kingdom, nay the whole, if Sir Percy ordered.

. . . Sir Percy took a red pencil and very carefully drew in on the map of Arabia a boundary line from the Persian Gulf to Jabal 'Anaizan, close to the Transjordan frontier . . .

. . . that evening there was an amazing sequel, Ibn Sa'ud asked to see Sir Percy alone. Sir Percy took me with him. Ibn Sa'ud was by himself, standing in the centre of his great reception tent. He seemed terribly upset.

'My friend,' he moaned, 'you have deprived me of half my kingdom. Better take it all and let me go into retirement.'

Still standing, this great strong man, magnificent in his grief, suddenly burst out into sobs. Deeply disturbed, Sir Percy seized his hand and began to weep also. Tears were rolling down his cheeks. No one but the three of us was present, and I relate exactly what I saw.

The emotional storm did not last long. Still holding Ibn Sa'ud's hand, Sir Percy said:

'My friend, I know exactly how you feel, and for this reason I gave you two-thirds of Kuwait's territory. I don't know how Ibn Sabah will take the blow.'[30]

It should not be forgotten, however, that both Ibn Saud and Cox were good actors and though Cox held all the trump cards, since Britain could dictate its terms in Arabia, Ibn Saud managed to satisfy many of his own demands. He was planning to start a campaign in the west of Arabia, and Cox might have hinted that Britain would look the other way if Hijaz were captured.[31]

No agreement was reached over the borders with Transjordan and in early 1923 a small group of Ikhwan raided Transjordan again. They were captured, and eleven of them were executed in Amman.[32] Meanwhile the tribes who dwelled on the Iraq–Najd border, and whose fate had been sealed at al-Uqair, continued to square accounts. Yusuf ibn Saadun mobilized a group of Ikhwan to attack his Zafir enemies, but Ibn Saud learned of the raid and sent a detachment to punish him. Yusuf fled with his supporters (including the Ikhwan) and asked for asylum in Iraq.[33]

In evaluating British policy in the region in the early 1920s, it is clear that it was not in London's interests to bring the antagonism between Najd, Iraq and Transjordan to a head. Britain preferred to exploit its newly acquired possessions with as little trouble as possible. Besides, Britain was giving huge subsidies to all the rulers in the region, only discontinuing them on 31 March 1924.[34]

In December 1923 a conference between Transjordan, Iraq and Najd was held in

The Consolidation of the Arabian Territories around Najd (1918-1926)

Kuwait, on Britain's initiative, to settle the disputes but the parties failed to reach agreement. Mutual raids continued across the formal border and in March 1924 Ibn Saud ordered Faisal Al Dawish to punish the tribes who raided Najd from Iraq. The Kuwait conference resumed in March 1924 and continued until April, but again without results.[35]

In mid-August a strong Ikhwan formation made for Amman via Wadi Sirhan. They passed near the fort the British had recently built in Qaf, but its garrison lacked communications and the Ikhwan's appearance some kilometres from Amman proved a surprise. Using aircraft, armoured cars and detachments of the Arab Legion, the British repulsed the Ikhwan and inflicted sizeable losses on them.[36]

While the situation on the borders with Transjordan, Iraq and Kuwait remained tense in the summer of 1924, it was Hijaz that now attracted Ibn Saud's attention. The Najdis had looked longingly at the holy cities of Hijaz for many years and their leaders calculated the probable proceeds from pilgrims and the Jidda customs. Religious enthusiasm and fanaticism were combined with the Najdi ruling group's plans for expansion.

Following the battle of Turaba, relations between Najd and Hijaz had become extremely strained. After Ibn Saud sent an armed detachment in May 1920 to seize the town of Abha in northern Asir, Husain prohibited Najdis from performing the *hajj* in August–September 1920. The Najdis complained to Cox as their arbitrator. At Britain's insistence, Husain permitted the pilgrimage the following year, but limited the number of pilgrims from Najd, fearing a heavy Ikhwan presence in Hijaz. By 1923 the Najdis had consolidated their positions in Asir, to Husain's growing apprehension. He stated that he would not allow an increase in the quota of Najdi pilgrims if Ibn Saud did not withdraw his garrisons from the border regions and Asir.[37]

The capture of northern Asir

The Turks had governed Asir from 1871 to the First World War and a Turkish *mutasarrif* was appointed to the court of the Al Aid. When the war broke out, the Turks left Asir and Emir Hasan ibn Ali Al Aid became virtually independent. But many tribes, such as the Qahtan, Zahran and Ghamid, opposed him and moved to the inner regions of Arabia, simultaneously sending a delegation to Ibn Saud to express their loyalty to him. The emir sent six *ulama* to teach the Asiris 'monotheism'.[38]

Although most Asiris were Shafiis, they had sympathized with Wahhabism since the time of the first Saudi state and their ties with Najd had never been broken.[39] On receiving envoys from the tribes, Ibn Saud sent a letter to Emir Hasan, demanding that he respect their rights. Hasan urged Ibn Saud not to intervene in Asir's internal affairs.

In May 1920, 3,000 troops from the people of Arial and the Qahtan bedouin, led by Abd al-Aziz ibn Musaid ibn Jiluwi, appeared in the Asir mountains. Some of the local population joined them. Emir Hasan was defeated at the approaches to Abha, his capital, and Ibn Jiluwi occupied the territory up to the area controlled by Muhammad

Al Idrisi. Lacking sufficient forces to establish direct control over the emirate, Ibn Saud took Emir Hasan and his cousin Muhammad to Riyadh, only to return them to Abha some months later as Riyadh's vassal governors. The internal struggle continued in Asir, and finally one Fahd al-Aqili became emir, but Hasan engineered a revolt against him and captured Abha after a siege lasting several days. Sharif Husain of Mecca helped him against the Najdis' henchman.[40]

After the fall of Hail, Ibn Saud gathered some 6,000 troops under the formal command of his adolescent son, Faisal, but actually led by Ibn Luwai. They left Riyadh in June–July 1922 and were joined on the way by 4,000 Qahtan, Zahran and Shahran bedouin. Having seized the oasis of Bisha, Faisal approached Abha in September–October 1922 and took the town without a battle. Hasan Al Aid fled to the mountains. King Husain attempted unsuccessfully to intervene on his side; the detachment from Hijaz was routed by the Ikhwan.

Establishing his control over a part of Asir, Faisal appointed Saad ibn Ufaisan as emir of Abha, left a garrison with him and returned to Riyadh in January 1923.[41] Ibn Ufaisan died soon afterwards and was succeeded by one Abd al-Aziz ibn Ibrahim. Hasan Al Aid later surrendered and was sent to Riyadh as an honoured prisoner.[42] The Al Aid clan's attempt to create an independent state in the northern part of Asir had ended in failure.

The conquest of Hijaz

By 1923 it was clear that a military conflict between King Husain and Najd was inevitable. Discontent with the authorities was growing in Hijaz and corruption and bribery were corroding the state apparatus. When collecting the usual tax from the pilgrims, Husain increased *zakat* too, to strengthen his army. The attempts to use troops to collect the taxes caused resentment among the tribes and many malcontents fled to Najd. King Husain still considered Asir to be his possession, and a detachment from Hijaz besieged Abha unsuccessfully in April 1923.[43]

According to Hafiz Wahba, Ibn Saud decided to conquer Hijaz as early as 1923 but he was unsure what Britain's position would be. He well remembered that in 1919, after the victory near Turaba, they had made him withdraw his forces and warned him against advancing further.[44] Naturally, Ibn Saud was aware of the discontent with Husain's regime in Hijaz, which was among the factors that prompted him to action. At the same time, friction began between Husain and the Indian and Egyptian pilgrims over the poor sanitary and medical facilities provided for them.[45]

King Husain's relations with Britain also deteriorated. He refused to ratify the treaty of Versailles in protest at Syria being transferred to French control and Britain being awarded the mandate over Palestine. In 1921 Lawrence suggested that Husain conclude a treaty with Britain: the sharif of Mecca would receive British subsidies, conclude a military treaty with Britain and recognize Britain's special interests in Hijaz.[46] Husain stressed that there could be no peace in Palestine as long as the Arabs suspected that

Zionism's ultimate aim was the creation of a Jewish state on Arab territory at the expense of the Arabs' national aspirations. He refused to sign the proposed treaty and called on the British prime minister to fulfil the promises made during the war: his appeals fell on deaf ears.[47]

All these disputes were removed from centre stage after Husain proclaimed himself caliph in March 1924 (the caliphate had been abolished by the new Turkish republican government). By adopting the title of caliph, Husain hoped to consolidate his power and reinforce his claims to be the sovereign of all the Arabs, at least to the east of Suez. His move was extremely unpopular in Egypt (whose king was also eager to assume the caliph's mantle) and among the Muslims of southern Asia, while Najd saw it as a challenge to the Ikhwan's religious sentiments and Ibn Saud's policies. Besides, Husain's decision aggravated his relations with the British, who were worried that they might lose control over the king of Hijaz. They considered him an adversary who could challenge their colonial dominance in the Middle East.

In July 1924 a Soviet consulate-general was opened in Jidda, much to the irritation of the British. In the same month Husain again refused to sign the treaty with Britain[48] and recognized the USSR. It should not be forgotten that the formal treaty on the protectorate, concluded by Britain and Najd in 1915, was still in effect. The sultan of Najd understood that Britain would apparently remain neutral this time in the event of a conflict with Hijaz.[49]

In July 1924, during the festival of *id al-adha*, Ibn Saud convened the Ikhwan leaders in Riyadh to discuss the conquest of Hijaz. His appeal for *jihad* was welcomed enthusiastically.[50] The Ikhwan wanted to 'purify' the holy cities in the course of a holy war, also hoping that their religious ardour would be rewarded by material spoils.

Ibn Saud decided to make a preliminary attack on al-Taif, a mountain resort near Mecca, to test Britain's reaction. On 5 September 1924 the Ikhwan burst into al-Taif and then stopped, waiting for Ibn Saud's orders. The bulk of their forces was formed by contingents from the al-Ghatghat *hijra*, led by Sultan ibn Bijad, from other Ataiba and Qahtan *hijras*, and from smaller tribes. They were joined by a detachment from al-Khurma led by Ibn Luwai. The Ikhwan seized a munitions depot in al-Taif and the town was plundered for three days. There was widespread violence and many people were murdered. Large numbers of the inhabitants fled and those who stayed were massacred by the Ikhwan. The people of Hijaz shuddered.[51] As early as 22 September Ibn Saud issued a strict ordinance against any repetition of such atrocities and guaranteeing that the Hijazis' lives and property would be protected in the future.[52] According to some data, 400 men, women and children were murdered in al-Taif.[53]

King Husain's son Ali tried to gather troops in al-Hada to stem the advance of the Ikhwan on Mecca, but he was defeated again in late September.[54] Husain's situation had become hopeless: the nobility of Hijaz, including the sharifian clan, the *ulama* and the chief merchants, assembled in Jidda and decided to force Husain to abdicate, hoping to placate Ibn Saud. After much persuasion, Husain agreed to give up the throne and on 6 October 1924 Ali was proclaimed king of Hijaz. The nobility set up a national representative council, a kind of parliament, making Hijaz almost a constitutional monarchy. Three days later Husain was sent to Jidda with his belongings; in mid-October he sailed for Aqaba, from where the British took him to Cyprus.[55] (He was to die in Amman in 1931.)

All hopes of placating Ibn Saud were dashed, however: with the Ikhwan approaching Mecca, Ali was forced to retreat to Jidda with a 400-strong detachment. In mid-October 1924 the Ikhwan entered the holy city, turning the barrels of their rifles to the ground. It should be noted that Ibn Saud forgot his initial intention of waiting for Britain's reaction before capturing Mecca. However, he preferred to stay in Riyadh so that he could blame the Ikhwan for the attack on Hijaz in the event of British intervention. Although many houses of people from the sharifian clan were plundered after the capture of Mecca, there was no carnage. Sharif Khalid ibn Luwai became emir of Mecca and Ibn Bijad stayed in al-Taif.[56]

The nobility of Mecca and Jidda hoped to nullify the Najdi conquest by making Ali king, since many of the notables saw Ibn Saud's quarrel with King Husain as the main reason behind the war. But the sultan of Najd wanted to drive the entire Hashemite family from Hijaz and rejected all other conditions for peace.[57] The members of the Hijazi *majlis* (parliament) tried to negotiate, but Ibn Saud insisted that Ali leave Hijaz. The representatives of the Hijazi nobility returned to Jidda in October 1924 and asked Ali to abdicate. Negotiations started between his supporters and his adversaries, after which the *majlis* dissolved itself. In December many of Ali's antagonists were jailed.[58]

It is important to note that the foreign consuls in Jidda wrote Khalid ibn Luwai a letter, declaring their neutrality and demanding that he ensure the safety of their nationals' property if the war continued. Khalid answered that the Ikhwan guaranteed the security of foreign subjects.[59] In late October Ibn Saud left Riyadh at the head of a 50,000-strong army (the figure may be grossly exaggerated). It took him 3 weeks to reach Mecca because he feared British intervention in the conflict. But when the couriers of the foreign consulates in Jidda met him en route and assured him of their countries' full neutrality, he understood that Hijaz was his.[60]

On 5 December 1924 Ibn Saud entered Mecca. *Umm al-Qura*, the new official mouthpiece, published his statement on 13 December. His programme for Hijaz was as follows:

1. My greatest concern will be the purification of this holy area of the enemies of the faith, who hate the Islamic world, namely of Husain, his children and followers.
2. The question of the future of this holy land will be settled through consultations among the Muslims. We have already informed the Muslims and asked them to send their delegates to a pan-Islamic conference that will determine the form of government they will deem necessary to realize Allah's decisions in this sacred land.
3. The legal base of Hijaz will be the Quran, the commandments sent [from heaven] with Allah's Messenger and those established by the *ulama* through *qiyas* [analogy].

The Consolidation of the Arabian Territories around Najd (1918–1926)

4. We hereby inform all *ulama* of this country and those who served the holy places earlier that they will stay here as they did before.[61]

While Ali remained in Jidda, Ibn Saud held elections in Mecca in December 1924, ostensibly to create a form of self-government, thus attracting the local merchants and the nobility to his side. An eleven-member council was elected, headed by Shaikh Abd al-Qadir al-Shaibi. Hafiz Wahba was appointed governor of Mecca.[62]

Ibn Saud soon received further messages from the foreign consuls expressing their neutrality: it was the commitment he needed. When Ali sent a plane to fly over Mecca, distributing leaflets in which King Husain expressed his intention of recapturing the city, Ibn Saud decided that it was time to act.[63]

On 5 January 1925 the united troops of the Ikhwan appeared near the walls of Jidda and started a siege which continued without interruption for almost a year.[64] Ali fortified the city and surrounded it with minefields. Armed Syrians, Palestinians and Yemenis arrived in the city, probably recruited by the sharif's family.[65] According to al-Zirikli, the Saudi troops numbered 5–6,000 and consisted chiefly of the Ataiba, as well as the Mutair and the Hijazi tribes of Ghamid and Zahran. Ali had 500 Hijazi fighters and several hundred Palestinians, Egyptians, Yemenis and Syrians. The Medina garrison consisted of 200 bedouin, over 300 Palestinians, several Transjordanians and around 250 Yemenis. There were some 300 men from the Ataiba and Uqail tribes in Yanbu and several hundreds scattered throughout other areas. However, Ibn Saud's troops were depleted during the siege of Jidda, for the bedouin could not long withstand the coastal heat.[66]

Ali did not receive real support from Iraq or Transjordan. According to al-Khatib in *The Just Imam*, 'The British behaved as if they tried to ensure Ibn Saud's victory.'[67] Fearing that Ibn Saud would use Husain's presence in Aqaba as an excuse to invade, his son Abdallah, the emir of Transjordan, allowed the British to escort Husain from the Red Sea port. The ex-king was met in Suez in May 1925 by Abd al-Malik al-Khatib, the former Hijazi chargé d'affaires in Cairo, and his brother, the author of *The Just Imam*. Husain told them that it was the British who had banished him from Hijaz, betraying him in return for his reluctance to accept the Balfour Declaration and his refusal to renounce the Arabs' right to an independent state.[68]

In early 1925 representatives of the Khilafat movement in India and several foreign consuls tried to mediate between Ali and Ibn Saud. In April al-Khatib, the foreign minister of the Jidda government, held an inconclusive meeting with Ibn Saud.[69] The siege of Jidda was raised in June because of the heat. In August Ali again asked the British for help, but his request was turned down on the grounds that Britain could intervene only with Ibn Saud's consent.[70]

In mid-October Sir Gilbert Clayton, the British representative, who had earlier been chief secretary to the government in Palestine, visited Jidda. He noted in his diary that Ali had been crushed both physically and morally. The inhabitants of Jidda were starving. Clayton was surprised that Ibn Saud did not capture the city. The sultan of Najd may have feared bloodshed and preferred to wait for Jidda to capitulate.[71]

The raids on Iraq continued both during and after the conquest of Hijaz. The Ikhwan crossed Wadi Sirhan, reached the Syrian border and cut off Transjordan from Iraq. British possessions in the Middle East were again faced with the threat of territorial isolation.[72] When Ibn Saud occupied Mecca with Britain's tacit blessing, he felt that he had better restrict his appetite in the north of the peninsula.

These developments came on the eve of the Locarno accords, when relations between Britain and France deteriorated because of the Mosul oilfields in Iraq, and British positions were being undermined by the nationalist movement in Palestine. Britain was therefore reluctant to intervene openly in the Najd–Hijaz conflict.

In October 1925 Clayton arrived at Ibn Saud's headquarters in Hijaz. Demonstrating once again his political flexibility, the emir agreed to concessions in the north in exchange for a de facto recognition of his annexation of Hijaz. The meeting resulted in the agreements signed in Bahra and al-Hada on 1 and 2 November 1925 respectively. The Bahra agreement dealt with Iraq and Najd and stipulated that any raid across the border should be considered an act of aggression and punished by the government to which the guilty tribe submitted. A special tribunal was to be set up of representatives of both states to investigate the raids. A tribe might cross the border to graze livestock only after receiving permission.

The al-Hada agreement defined the de facto boundary between Najd and Transjordan for the first time. Ibn Saud ceded a corridor to Transjordan that connected it with Iraq. The agreement also declared raids to be acts of aggression and provided for a special tribunal to investigate such cases. The grazing of livestock required special permission. Lastly, both states agreed to abstain from religious propaganda in each other's territory, a paragraph that obviously referred to the Ikhwan's preaching.[73] Thus Najd's borders with Kuwait, Iraq and (de facto) Transjordan were defined, though border conflicts soon broke out again.

When King Ali of Hijaz learned of the Bahra and al-Hada agreements and Clayton refused to support him, he understood that the days of his rule were numbered. Seeing that his brothers in Iraq and Transjordan were more concerned to preserve their thrones than to help him, Ali decided to end the struggle. On 16 December 1925 he asked the British consul to discuss the terms of capitulation with Ibn Saud. Jidda surrendered on 22 December; Ali left the town and Ibn Saud entered it the following day.[74]

In early February 1925, when the siege of Jidda was just beginning, Ibn Saud had sent Faisal Al Dawish and his Ikhwan to Medina. The troops were under strict orders not to capture the city without the emir's permission. He was afraid that the Prophet's mausoleum and the holy places of Medina might be destroyed. When the siege became unbearable for the citizens of Medina, they sent a messenger to Ibn Saud, expressing their readiness to capitulate to a member of the Al Saud, but not to the Ikhwan. In October Ibn Saud sent his son Muhammad to Medina, but a telegram of encouragement from Ali seemed to promise a rescue for the garrison of Medina and they delayed capitulating. In mid-November the situation in Medina became critical: no help was expected and the local nobility decided to surrender the city.[75] On 6 December 1925 Muhammad entered Medina and prayed at the mosque of the Prophet. Imitating his father, he brought rice for the famished citizens and provided them with financial aid.[76]

As early as the eve of the fall of Jidda, the nobility and *ulama* of Mecca and Jidda had informed Ibn Saud of their readiness to swear allegiance to him as king of Hijaz. On 11 December 1925, after the Friday prayer, people assembled at Bab al-Saf in Mecca. The *khatib* (preacher) announced the text of the oath and a salute of 100 salvos was fired. Then the sharifs, *ulama*, members of the *sharia* court, imams, reciters of the Quran, members of the National Assembly, representatives of Medina and Jidda, pilgrimage guides, attendants of Zamzam and the Kaaba and other people from Mecca and Medina all swore allegiance. The text of the oath read:

> Glory to Allah! We pledge to you, Sultan Abd al-Aziz ibn Abd al-Rahman Al Faisal Al Saud, that you will be the king of Hijaz in accordance with the Quran, with the Sunna, brought by Allah's Messenger, and with the traditions of Prophet Muhammad's Companions [*sahaba*] ... that Hijaz will be only for the Hijazis, that its population will pay attention to its affairs, that Mecca will be the capital of Hijaz and that Hijaz will be a community under the authority of Allah and Your Majesty.[77]

Eldon Rutter, a British traveller who embraced Islam, witnessed the scene and left a description of it.[78] Ibn Saud came to be styled 'the King of Hijaz and the Sultan of Najd and her Dependencies'.

On 16 February 1926 the government of Hijaz was recognized officially by the USSR. The Soviet note to Ibn Saud read as follows:

> On the basis of the principle of the people's right to self-determination and out of respect for the Hijazi people's will as expressed in their choice of you as their king, the government of the USSR recognizes you King of Hijaz and Sultan of Najd and her Dependencies. On this ground, the Soviet government considers that it is in normal diplomatic relations with Your Majesty's government.

In his reciprocal note, the king wrote:

> To His Excellency, the Agent and Consul-General of the USSR. We have had the honour to receive your note No. 22, dated 3 Shaaban 1344 [16 February 1926] concerning the recognition of the new situation in Hijaz by the Government of the USSR, which situation consisted of swearing allegiance to us as King of Hijaz and Sultan of Najd and her Dependencies by the population of Hijaz. My Government expresses hereby its gratitude to the Government of the USSR and its readiness to maintain friendly relations with the Government of the USSR and its subjects ... Abd al-Aziz, King of Hijaz and Sultan of Najd and her Dependencies. Mecca, 6 Shaaban 1344 [19 February 1926].[79]

Other states followed the USSR in granting recognition to Ibn Saud.

Submitting to Ibn Saud, but at the same time fearful of the dominance of the 'Najdi bedouin' over the more developed region of Hijaz, the local Hijazi nobility tried to preserve rather broad rights. Fifty-six representatives of the local aristocracy, *ulama* and merchants formed a 'constituent assembly', which decided that Hijaz should be independent from Najd in its domestic and foreign affairs. The kingdoms were to be united only by their common monarch; a Muslim government was to be set up in Hijaz; and a constitution based on the Quran and the Sunna was to be introduced. The 'constituent assembly' was to develop the internal organization and administrative provisions in accordance with local conditions. Some Hijazis feared that Ibn Saud was still bound by the 1915 treaty with Britain, which provided for a British protectorate over him in defiance of the Hijazis' desire for independence.[80]

The Hijazi nobility tried to restrict the monarch's power but the balance of forces was unconditionally in Ibn Saud's favour. He took note of the nobility's wishes, but implemented them only if they did not contradict his absolute power. In 1926 he issued an ordinance setting up consultative councils in Mecca, Medina, Jidda, Yanbu and al-Taif, which later became municipalities. A thirteen-member consultative council was created in Hijaz.[81]

Although Ibn Saud's conquest of Hijaz was not yet recognized by those countries with a Muslim majority, this was merely a question of time. After the seizure of Hijaz by Najd, a Muslim mission from India arrived in Jidda and demanded that control over the holy cities be handed over to a committee of representatives of all Muslim countries. Ibn Saud did not tolerate the delegation for long and soon sent them back to India by sea.[82]

In 1926 Ibn Saud decided to convene a Muslim congress in Mecca in June, after the *hajj*, to 'legalize' his control over Hijaz once more. The new king of Hijaz sent messages to the kings of Egypt, Afghanistan and Iraq, the president of Turkey, the shah of Iran, the emir of the Rif Republic, Imam Yahya of Yemen, other Muslim rulers, the head of the Supreme Islamic Council in Jerusalem and the head of the Khilafat League in Bombay, pledging that he would care for the holy places and improve conditions for the pilgrims.

Sixty-nine people took part in the congress: they came from the Muslim organizations of India, Egypt, the USSR, Java, Palestine, Lebanon, Syria, Sudan, Najd, Hijaz, Asir, Afghanistan and Yemen, among other countries. Ibn Saud gave the participants to understand that he was the master of Hijaz and would not tolerate any intervention in his affairs. Those who were dissatisfied with him walked out, although they were powerless to change the situation. Those who remained accepted the status quo.[83]

The head of the delegation of Russian and Turkistani Muslims and chairman of the Central Spiritual Directorate of the Muslims, Mufti Rizauddin Sahreddinov, said in an interview with the Soviet news agency TASS that the congress had recognized Ibn Saud as the 'custodian of the holy places'. It had appealed for Aqaba and Maan to be returned to Hijaz and it supported the new king.[84]

The victories of the Najdi troops; Britain's benevolent neutrality during Ibn Saud's conquest of Hijaz, when it chose the lesser evil and sacrificed Husain; the new king of

The Consolidation of the Arabian Territories around Najd (1918–1926)

Hijaz's wise policies, showing a combination of firmness and flexibility – all these factors meant that any further discussion of sovereignty over the holy places was futile. The Soviet consulate-general in Jidda reported back in 1929:

> Possession of Hijaz with its returns from the pilgrimage, customs, etc enables Abd al-Aziz to use all these resources (the pilgrimage alone yields up to £2m annually) to strengthen his power in Najd to great political advantage by aiding new settlers and subsidizing the shaikhs of bedouin tribes . . . The main force in Hijaz are the merchants, who support the British empire and advocate agreement with the British. The bedouin are dissatisfied: they pay *zakat* of 2.5%, plunder is prohibited, imports of trucks have deprived them of their income [and] they no longer receive the sultan's subsidies. The *hajj* guides are also dissatisfied, being no longer able to fleece pilgrims, since the state regularizes the *hajj* and appropriates the proceeds from it.[85]

Ibn Saud was now threatened with a danger that was not external, but emanated from the very Ikhwan who had annexed Hijaz to his possessions.

CHAPTER 12

Increased Centralization and the Ikhwan Movement (1926–1934)

The situation in Hijaz

With the conquest of Hijaz, Ibn Saud was faced with governing a country that was far more developed than Najd or even al-Hasa. The administrative-bureaucratic machinery of Hijaz had been created in line with Ottoman standards and was the most advanced in Arabia. King Husain had even published the budget with a breakdown of expenditure (although it was never observed in practice). An embryonic regular army had emerged and secondary schools had been opened. *Al-Qibla*, the official gazette, showed a fair knowledge of developments outside Arabia and covered European events widely. It also carried reports on public works in Hijaz, such as the expansion of the telephone network and street cleaning. Ibn Saud decided to preserve the management structure that had been created by the Hashemites and put it at his service.[1]

The new ruler had yet to reconcile the *ulama* of Najd and Hijaz and persuade the Meccan *ulama* to recognize the superiority of their Riyadh counterparts. To smooth out the theological differences, the *ulama* of Riyadh held a series of consultations with their Meccan colleagues and then stated that there were no substantial differences between them. The overall situation was not so simple, however, and disagreements between Najdis and Hijazis persisted.[2]

Some of the public works that had been started by foreign companies under Husain were continued.[3] When Hijaz was captured, Ibn Saud had already understood the importance of telephone and radio as a means of strengthening his power and of motor transport for economic and military purposes. However, they were deemed the devil's inventions by the bedouin and the dogmatic *ulama*. Travellers and historians have left many anecdotes concerning the Ikhwan's attitude to the modern means of

Increased Centralization and the Ikhwan Movement (1926-1934)

communication. The question of their religious permissibility was solved when excerpts from the Quran were read by telephone and then broadcast on the radio.[4]

The Ikhwan also saw automobiles as the invention of the godless, if not of the devil. The first truck that appeared in al-Hawta was burnt and its driver barely escaped the same fate. In the *ulama*'s opinion, planes flew contrary to Allah's will. Society's practical needs proved stronger than conservatism and dogmatism, however, and radio, the telephone and cars were increasingly introduced into the kingdom. Within two or three decades, even the *ulama* travelled by plane.[5] Although the importing of gramophones and the building of cinemas were still prohibited, record-players and film-projectors started to appear in private houses.[6]

The king understood that he had to take account of the interests of the Hijazi nobility. When he appointed his son Faisal as viceroy of Hijaz in August 1926, he simultaneously promulgated 'the fundamental provisions', which were similar to a constitution. They defined the status of the viceroy, the *majlis al-shura* (advisory council) and the administrative bodies.[7]

The *majlis al-shura*, created soon after the promulgation of the 'constitution', consisted of Prince Faisal as viceroy, four of his councillors and six representatives of the Hijazi nobility. The Hijazi members of the council had clearly not been supporters of King Husain or of Ali or, if they had, had later renounced them. Consultative assemblies of nobility, *ulama* and merchants were established in Mecca in 1924 and 1925. Although they claimed a certain independence and could address complaints to the king, none of their members was included in the *majlis al-shura* in 1926, which leads one to suppose that Ibn Saud was irritated by their activities.[8]

There was a striking difference between the first consultative assemblies and the *majlis al-shura*, which consisted merely of ciphers. Ibn Saud's control over Hijaz now became complete. He was recognized as king of Hijaz both within the country and throughout the Muslim world. Besides, he probably felt that the 'constitution' of Hijaz might become an infectious example to the people of Najd and wanted to nip any possible sedition in the bud. In the years that followed, Faisal's government in Hijaz progressively acquired the character of a typical Middle Eastern bureaucracy rather than that of a constitutional monarchy. The Hijazis, more educated than the Najdis, ensured its functioning, though they were under the control of Prince Faisal and his closest advisers.

While Ibn Saud and a group of his more intellectual advisers tried to adapt the administrative machinery of Hijaz to their needs, the Ikhwan were resolved to 'purify' it of 'evil' and destroy the places of worship that they considered incompatible with Islam. According to Hafiz Wahba, 'Perhaps the greatest misfortune that ever befell the Wahhabi reform movement was the enthusiasm with which these ignorant people embraced it.'[9]

Relations with the Ikhwan became an acute problem for Ibn Saud during the pacification of Hijaz. The Ikhwan destroyed the memorial at the Prophet's birthplace and the houses of Khadija and Abu Bakr in Mecca.[10] Philby, who took part in the 1931 *hajj*, noted that all the tombs had been destroyed in Hijaz and grieved that future generations would forget the historical facts connected with those places.[11] Although the Ikhwan were motivated by moral and religious fervour, they also showed the typical bedouin hostility towards everything that the urban dwellers of Hijaz worshipped and enjoyed, in their supposed oblivion of 'genuine' Islam. When the Ikhwan occupied al-Taif and Mecca, they began smashing mirrors and using the door- and window-frames for camp-fires.[12] The behaviour one might expect from conquerors was at the same time a manifestation of the nomads' contempt for urban 'luxury'. Thus the Ikhwan's egalitarian trends were mixed with religious fanaticism and bedouin customs.

In 1924 Khalid ibn Luwai ordered the burning of a large quantity of tobacco which belonged to rich Meccan importers. The merchants complained to Ibn Saud, who cancelled Khalid's order, but prohibited tobacco imports in the future. (Later, imports were permitted again, but smokers were punished.)[13] This incident showed Ibn Saud's pragmatic approach – he held that trade in Hijaz must be taxed but not undermined. When Khalid ibn Luwai was removed as governor of Mecca in December 1925, soon after the fall of Jidda, this indicated Ibn Saud's determination not to leave important administrative posts in Hijaz in the hands of leaders of the Ikhwan. In September that year, carrying firearms was officially prohibited in Mecca in order to restrict the 'brethren's' ability to resist the authorities.[14]

Ibn Saud had reason to fear the Ikhwan's actions against the Muslim pilgrims. On one occasion, they attacked and wounded several pilgrims, leading to protests by foreign consuls. Soon afterwards, the Ikhwan tried to murder Muslim officials at various consulates.[15] The king took steps to channel the Ikhwan's energy towards the conquest of towns and ports between Jidda and the Gulf of Aqaba, but soon the whole of Hijaz was under his power and the Ikhwan became idle.

At the start of the *hajj* in the summer of 1926, a *mahmal*, accompanied by a band of musicians, was sent from Egypt to Mecca. When the caravan approached Mecca, unarmed Ikhwan, who wore *ihram* (special white clothes for the pilgrimage), heard music for the first time. Considering it an outrage, they rushed angrily to stop the camel carrying the *mahmal*. The Egyptian officer ordered his soldiers to fire and some twenty-five people were killed. Ibn Saud, who was in the vicinity, immediately sent his sons Faisal and Saud to restrain the infuriated Ikhwan. He ordered the Egyptian officer to be detained, prohibited him from accompanying the pilgrims and prevented him from bringing the *mahmal* to Mecca,[16] but did not dare to punish him seriously, since the Muslim Congress was being held in Mecca at that time.[17] However, the Ikhwan long reproached Ibn Saud for his failure to punish the Egyptian 'polytheist' who had killed twenty-five 'brethren'. Both Faisal Al Dawish and Sultan ibn Bijad later traced their conflict with the king to that incident,[18] stressing that Ibn Saud not only had not allowed them to destroy the *mahmal*, but had even protected the pagan article.

In order to pacify the Ikhwan and to consolidate his prestige and power, the king nevertheless started to introduce rigid Wahhabi regulations. For shirking a common prayer, a person could be fined and sent to prison for between one and ten days. Those who drank alcohol were jailed for one month and fined; if they repeated the crime, they were sent to prison for two years. Wine-producers and wine-traders were subject to severe reprisals. As mentioned previously, smoking was prohibited, but not the tobacco trade itself.

The introduction of Wahhabi principles was combined with repressive measures against the Al Saud's political opponents. Taking part in meetings with the aim of spreading 'harmful ideas', 'false information' and 'dangerous rumours', as well as participation in anti-government meetings, involved a two- to five-year prison sentence or exile from the kingdom of Hijaz. A meeting, even for charitable purposes, might be convened only with the authorities' consent.[19] Strict observance of these rules in religious and daily life did not continue for long, however. When the Ikhwan withdrew from Hijaz, the prohibition on smoking was relaxed, alcohol became available and few people paid attention to the length of men's moustaches.

To demonstrate his concern for the 'purity' of religion and, at the same time, to control the Ikhwan's religious zeal, Ibn Saud founded the League of Public Morality – or, to be more accurate, the League for the Encouragement of Virtue and the Denunciation of Sin – in the summer of 1926. It was led by two *ulama* from the Al al-Shaikh family.[20] Ibn Saud ordered the Ikhwan to inform the league about all deeds that were not permitted by the faith, although they were not allowed to take unauthorized reprisals.

The organization gradually acquired the functions of a religious police. (Indeed, the league's Committees of Public Morality were later placed under the control of the general directorate of police.) The league's responsibilities included: the prevention of cheating in markets, *zakat* evasion, non-observance of the fast, violation of the *hajj* rules, murder, mutilation and the consumption and sale of alcohol.[21] By the summer of 1928 the Committees of Public Morality were already taking an active part in government meetings and controlled the population of Hijaz with growing rigidity.[22] Feeling that the experiment was worth repeating throughout the country, Ibn Saud founded the directorate of public morality in Riyadh in the summer of 1929, when the Ikhwan revolt was in full swing.[23]

The leaders of the league anathematized Mustafa Kemal of Turkey and King Amanullah of Afghanistan for their reforms. Turakulov, the Soviet consul-general in Jidda, wrote:

> It is difficult to expect another attitude to Kemal Pasha and Amanullah in a country that exists on incomes from the holy places, a country where any free-thinking jeopardizes the material interests of the majority.[24]

With the assistance of the League of Public Morality, the Ikhwan were debarred from supervising the observance of religious prescriptions. Tribal democracy in its religious form was sacrificed to the state apparatus of the centralized feudal kingdom.

The Ikhwan's actions seemed 'unbridled fanaticism' and 'savagery' to some European travellers and the more educated people in the royal entourage, but they were a manifestation of the ordinary Arabian people's striving for the simple way of life preached by the Wahhabis. The people only adopted the egalitarian aspect of the teaching, however, and tried to practise their ideals in their own particular way. The Ikhwan could not create a new type of society: their ideals were a mirror of the old system, in which they claimed their earlier masters' position. It had been the destiny of egalitarian popular movements since ancient times – their aspirations and practices ran counter to the interests of the nobility and the merchants. The Ikhwan's aspirations and practices collided with the real interests of the feudal nobility. Therefore it may be too partial and even wrong to describe the Ikhwan's passion as 'frantic reaction' – they were as much 'reactionaries' as the participants of peasant revolts in the feudal epoch, the cruel and foredoomed popular movements of the Middle Ages.

When the disappointed Ikhwan withdrew from Hijaz to their *hijras* and tribes in central Arabia, it became clear that a conflict with Ibn Saud's centralized state was imminent.

The first period of the Ikhwan revolt

Ibn Saud's cooperation with the British in delimiting the frontiers with Kuwait, Iraq and Transjordan and his policy in Hijaz had brought relations between the central authorities and the Ikhwan to a crisis. The 'brethren' felt that they had not had their fair share of the spoils in Hijaz and Ibn Saud's prohibition on raids across the borders of Kuwait, Iraq and Transjordan deprived them of the opportunity to improve their material conditions by plundering 'infidels'. With the deepening crisis of camel-breeding and the underdeveloped state of agriculture in the oases, the Ikhwan saw raids under the slogans of the faith as a natural remedy for poverty and starvation.[25] Ibn Saud's tolerance of the Shia of al-Hasa and al-Qatif poured oil on the flames.[26]

One of the contradictions of the Ikhwan movement was the fact that it was led by feudal-tribal shaikhs who strove to become independent rulers. With its 'democratic' composition and series of demands, the movement served the interests of feudal-tribal separatism. One of the Ikhwan's principal leaders was Faisal Al Dawish, the chief shaikh of the Mutair and a brilliant warrior and commander. After joining Ibn Saud, Faisal Al Dawish had come to Riyadh, accompanied by 150 armed men. The king had called him his old friend and one of his best commanders. At *majlises* and feasts, he was seated near the king. He urged Abd al-Aziz to supply his *hijra* of al-Artawiya with all necessary provisions, from ropes for the wells, to arms, and even clothes for his wives and children.

In late 1925, however, after the fall of Jidda, Faisal Al Dawish withdrew to his headquarters in al-Artawiya, bearing a mortal grudge against Ibn Saud, who had not appointed him governor of Medina, contrary to his hopes.[27] The conflict was fuelled by the almost forgotten antagonism between the Mutair and the Saudis. The chronicler Khalid al-Farj notes:

> A study of the history of Najd reveals that the Mutair were always in the ranks of the Al Saud's enemies. They were the first to receive Tusun Pasha in Hijaz and help

Increased Centralization and the Ikhwan Movement (1926–1934)

his campaign in Qasim. They supported Ibrahim Pasha during the siege of al-Diriya and joined his troops . . . It was they who welcomed Khurshid Pasha and made for al-Kharj together with him. Lastly, they were in the ranks of the Rashidis until Ibn Saud defeated them.[28]

Other opposition leaders were Zaidan ibn Hithlain, the shaikh of the Ajman, the Saudis' old and stubborn adversaries, who had only recently been subdued and joined the Ikhwan; and Sultan ibn Humaid ibn Bijad, the shaikh of the Ataiba, though he owed his position to Ibn Saud's help. Ibn Bijad had hoped to become governor of al-Taif, but the king decided otherwise.[29] The Ataiba were the second strongest and most numerous tribe of central Arabia, after the Anaza. Later, one of the Rwala shaikhs joined the movement against Ibn Saud. Thus the tribes to the east, north, west and south-west of Riyadh were now hostile to the central authorities. It is important to note that the anti-Saudi opposition did not include the Anaza, the most powerful tribe (with the exception of their subdivision, the Rwala), the Harb and most of the Shammar. The nomad revolt did not become general, which saved the royal regime.

In early 1926 Faisal Al Dawish, Ibn Hithlain and Ibn Bijad met in al-Ghatghat and prepared a list of claims to be put to Ibn Saud. These became the basis of the charge-sheet adopted at a general meeting of the Mutair, Ataiba and Ajman leaders of the Ikhwan in November–December 1926 in al-Artawiya. The charge-sheet included the king's seven offences:

1. His son Saud's visit to Egypt as a result of the *mahmal* incident.
2. His son Faisal's visit to London in August 1926 for negotiations with the British, seen as an act of collaboration with an infidel power.
3. Importing the telegraph, the telephone and cars to the land of Islam. (This charge was a mixture of the bedouin's religious extremism and the popular protest against strengthening the centralized state.)
4. The imposition of custom duties on the Muslims of Najd – a protest against the growing system of centralized taxes.
5. Allowing the tribes of Transjordan and Iraq to graze their livestock in the Muslims' lands – a reflection of the intertribal struggle for pastures.
6. The prohibition on trade with Kuwait. If Kuwait's people were infidels, Ibn Saud should wage *jihad* against them; if they were Muslims, he should not obstruct trade with them.
7. Tolerating the schismatics (i.e. the Shia) in al-Hasa and al-Qatif. Ibn Saud should either convert them to Islam or massacre them.[30]

Feeling that the Ikhwan's discontent might turn into open revolt, Ibn Saud hurriedly left Hijaz and returned to Riyadh in January 1927. Late that month, he gathered some 3,000 Ikhwan in the capital. It was then that Faisal Al Dawish, Ibn Bijad and the other rebel Ikhwan presented their charge-sheet at a meeting. There was as yet no open revolt and Ibn Saud sought a compromise. He agreed to decrease taxes, but refused to prohibit the radio and cars. He even persuaded the meeting to proclaim him 'the king of Hijaz and Najd and its dependencies'.[31]

In February 1927 the Riyadh *ulama*, nervous of the Ikhwan's demands, issued a *fatwa* that was to become famous. The fact that it was signed by fifteen *ulama* proved that the situation was extremely complex. The *fatwa* covered several issues. The *ulama* pretended to take a neutral attitude to the telegraph. They recommended that the imam should destroy the Hamza mosque and either make the Shia embrace Islam or exile them from the country. (It should be remembered that the Wahhabis considered the Shia to be non-Muslims.) The *ulama* demanded that the king refuse to allow the Iraqi Shia to graze their livestock in Muslim territory. Insisting that taxes already collected should be returned, the *ulama* noted nevertheless that the imposition of unlawful taxes was not a good enough reason to destroy the unity among Muslims. Finally, they claimed that only the imam might proclaim *jihad*.[32]

In early April 1927 Ibn Saud assembled the tribal shaikhs and the Ikhwan again. Some 3,000 Ikhwan came to Riyadh, but Ibn Bijad was not among them. This time, Ibn Saud tried to isolate Faisal Al Dawish, whom he considered his main adversary. Perhaps it was then that Ibn Saud managed to split a section from the Mutair and make them oppose Faisal Al Dawish.[33] But the anti-Saudi movement was not confined to the Ikhwan tribes. In the summer of 1927 a conspiracy was discovered: its purpose was to kill Ibn Saud's son Saud in Riyadh and Abdallah ibn Jiluwi in al-Hasa. Ibn Saud's brother Muhammad and Abdallah ibn Jiluwi's son were allegedly among the conspirators.[34]

Not daring to challenge the king openly, Faisal Al Dawish started to make preparations for raids on Iraq. He hoped to reward his followers with spoils and make the king either join him or demonstrate his reluctance to fight for Allah's cause.[35] The king bided his time. According to Glubb Pasha:

> Caution had always distinguished the policy of Abdul Aziz Ibn Saud. He had been confident of his power to defeat other Arabian princes, like Ibn Rasheed or the Sherifs of Mecca, but he was not prepared to engage in hostilities with Britain.
>
> The Ikhwan were able to quote against him his own pronouncements of an earlier date. The Iraqis, they claimed, were renegade Muslims, enemies of God, whose lives and property were forfeit to the Ikhwan, the only true believers.
>
> The broad mind and clear intellect of Abd al-Aziz Ibn Saud were able to grasp the essentials of a situation, even in countries which might have been expected to be far beyond the range of his experience. He was a model of common sense and prudence. If he encouraged fanaticism, it was to use it as an instrument to achieve his object; he was never himself a fanatic. To a wild and unruly people, however, prudence and common sense offered few attractions.[36]

Although Ibn Saud's position in the kingdom was becoming precarious, the British still considered him the only real force in the peninsula and intended to cooperate with him. They abandoned the attempt to preserve or establish a protectorate over the kingdom

Increased Centralization and the Ikhwan Movement (1926-1934)

of Hijaz, Najd and its dependencies. The vast and sparsely populated Arabian kingdom was surrounded by British colonies, protectorates and dependencies. Even if it remained independent, Britain felt that the kingdom would be unable to hurt British interests.

In May 1927 Clayton entered into negotiations with Ibn Saud in Jidda. On 20 May a seven-year treaty of 'friendship and good intentions' was concluded. Known as the treaty of Jidda, it abrogated the treaty of 1915 and recognized the 'complete and absolute independence' of Ibn Saud's possessions. No special privileges were formally granted to Britain, but Ibn Saud recognized Britain's special relations with the Gulf states and the Aden protectorates. Without recognizing Transjordan's annexation of Aqaba and Maan, the king nevertheless agreed to observe the status quo up to the final delimitation between Hijaz and Transjordan.[37] The conclusion of the treaty was a substantial success for Saudi diplomacy and sealed the independence of the new state.

Soon afterwards Britain afforded the Ikhwan a pretext for action against Iraq. In September 1927 a small detachment of Iraqi police was sent to construct a fort near the wells at Busaya, a watering-place in Iraqi territory, fairly close to the border. Ibn Saud protested, on the basis of the Muhammara agreement and Protocol No. 1, signed in al-Uqair. The Iraqi government stated that the post in Busaya was 80 miles [130 km] from the border and that it was a police post, not a military one. To the Najdis, there was no difference between a policeman and a soldier.[38] Britain did not react to the Saudi protest, but Ibn Saud, under pressure from the Ikhwan, demanded that the fort be demolished.

Faisal Al Dawish considered the Iraqi action a suitable opportunity to isolate Ibn Saud from the Ikhwan and deliver the 'infidels' a blow. During the night of 6 November 1927 the Mutair murdered all the Iraqi policemen but one. British aircraft intervened on the Iraqi side and bombed the bedouin.[39]

In early December, 400 Mutair raided Kuwaiti territory to the north-east of al-Jahra. On 13 December Shaikh Ahmad Jabir Al Sabah asked British aircraft to intervene. Ibn Saud had already informed Iraq and Kuwait that the raids were contrary to his orders.[40] On 16 December the fort in Busaya was rebuilt and occupied by an Iraqi army platoon.[41] From 1927 British aircraft had been engaged in frequent attacks on the Ikhwan. It was difficult to distinguish between the Ikhwan and peaceful tribes in the ocean of desert, and many innocent people were killed during the bombing. The Ikhwan's raids continued up to February. According to Glubb, who took part in the events:

> The real change in the situation, however, was that in 1927 Ibn Saud was no longer in complete control. The Ikhwan, as a result of their victories in the Hejaz, were intoxicated with their own strength, and claimed that it was their fighting power which had made Ibn Saud great. They were perfectly aware that they were the backbone of his army and that he possessed no regular forces with which to discipline them ... Wahhabi religious feeling was too strong in Nejed to permit the Ikhwan to revolt. By challenging the king on the question of war with Iraq,

275

however, the Ikhwan were able to claim religious sentiments on their side. The Iraqis were not Wahhabis and were therefore renegade Muslims, against whom holy war was a duty. It was Ibn Saud who was guilty of religious laxity in being unwilling to engage in hostilities against the enemies of God. The Nejdis were not prepared to use force to prevent the Ikhwan raiding Iraq.

The King was also in a dilemma in his foreign relations. He was unwilling to confess to other governments that he was no longer in control of his own subjects. Yet to claim that he was still in perfect control would expose him to protests and reproaches, if the Ikhwan raided contrary to his wishes. Busaiya provided him with a useful pretext. He proclaimed loudly that all had been well until the Iraq Government had been guilty of the aggressive action of building a police post in the desert, contrary to the al-Uqair Protocol. In view of this outrageous breach of faith, he stated that he could not be responsible of any counter-action taken by his subjects.

The contest which followed was in reality a three-corner one. The Ikhwan were indirectly rebelling against Ibn Saud. Both claimed Iraq to be the villains of the plot, because both were anxious to win the support of public opinion in Nejed.[42]

Under the circumstances, the king of Hijaz and Najd again preferred to bide his time. In March 1928 the Mutair returned to their *hijras* after successful raids.[43]

In January 1928 the king's adviser Hafiz Wahba met Henry Dobbs, the British high commissioner of Iraq, after Britain had warned Ibn Saud that it would bomb the Ikhwan mercilessly unless they ceased their raids. At the same time, supplies of British munitions to the king continued. A British government spokesman told the House of Commons in March 1928 that Britain had permitted the export of munitions to the Saudi state three times within recent months.[44]

In April 1928 Ibn Saud wrote a long letter to the ruler of Kuwait, explaining that not all the Mutair were guilty of raids and that the Iraqis had also attacked Najdi territory. Ibn Saud was compelled to protect the Najdi tribes from the British, but he was reluctant to wage a war that he clearly could not win. The only solution was to start negotiations.[45]

In early April 1928 a new meeting with the Ikhwan was held in Buraida, but Faisal Al Dawish and Ibn Bijad did not come to the town and Ibn Saud refused to meet them in the desert. The king promised the Ikhwan that he would negotiate with the British and protest against the building of the fort.[46] In May Ibn Saud met Clayton, but the negotiations were in vain; the next meeting in August was also a failure. Britain felt that Ibn Saud was losing firm control over the country. Both parties understood that a mere six months remained before the new grazing season, when the border areas would again be plunged into chaos. An agreement was finally signed in Jidda, but it did not resolve the main problems.[47]

Ibn Saud stayed in Mecca throughout the summer of 1928, making propaganda attacks against Iraq, ostensibly to convince the Ikhwan of his orthodoxy. According to Philby:

Increased Centralization and the Ikhwan Movement (1926–1934)

He was at one with his subjects in condemning the attitude of the British Government; and his subjects, whose fanaticism had been fanned into flame by infidel insults and injuries, were ready to fight to the death for his cause. But he knew better than they that only disaster could come of the war with 'Iraq in the circumstances of the time; and he had already made up his mind that there should be no such war at any cost. He also knew that the desert was in ferment to the point of challenging his policy of accommodation with the infidel.[48]

The principal leaders of the Ikhwan movement were already drawing up plans to divide Ibn Saud's possessions between them. Faisal Al Dawish was to become the ruler of Najd, Ibn Bijad claimed Hijaz and Ibn Hithlain wanted al-Hasa. Nida ibn Nuhair, of a collateral branch of the Shammar, was promised the position of ruler of Hail, provided he joined the Ikhwan, but he preferred to bide his time, remaining loyal to Ibn Saud.[49]

In September 1928 the king returned to Riyadh to find that some subdivisions of the Ajman had joined Faisal Al Dawish and Ibn Bijad. Ibn Saud appointed a new assembly composed of members of the urban population and the Ikhwan in October, but it did not meet until 6 December,[50] with the participation of the Ikhwan leaders, tribal shaikhs, urban nobility and *ulama*. There were over 800 participants, including their escorts. Faisal Al Dawish, Sultan ibn Bijad and Ibn Hithlain were absent. However, Faisal Al Dawish had sent his son, Uzayiz. Ibn Saud delivered a long speech about his achievements, including the unification of the peninsula and the establishment of peace. He gave details of his negotiations with the British and referred to Faisal Al Dawish's raids as the reason for Britain's obstinacy. Then he resorted to a dramatic gesture: he offered to abdicate, provided that the assembly elected another king from among the Al Saud. He promised to support any new king chosen by the assembly.

The theatrical gesture of abdication influenced the audience, particularly the population of the Najdi towns and oases, who traditionally supported the Saudis and understood the implications if Ibn Saud withdrew and Faisal and Ibn Bijad triumphed. Shouting, 'We do not want any other sultan!', almost everybody supported Ibn Saud's policy and rejected the three rebel Ikhwan leaders.[51] Wahba notes that none of the assembly's participants imagined that Ibn Saud would surrender the throne without a struggle. They were fully aware that he was at the peak of his physical strength and intellectual powers and was ready to fight the Ikhwan.

The nobility from the oases felt that it was high time to put an end to the Ikhwan: the nobility was keen to protect its interests against the rebel nomadic population and was aware of the settled people's traditional hatred for the bedouin.[52] The issue was complicated by the fact that the movement was conducted under a religious banner; the three Ikhwan leaders claimed to be genuine defenders of the faith and accused Ibn Saud of ignoring the true religion and collaborating with the infidel British for the sake of his vested interests.[53]

When the grazing season began, it became clear that a civil war was unavoidable, though many tribes played for time. Instead of opposing Ibn Saud, however, the three Ikhwan leaders decided to attack Iraq, thus avoiding being accused of open revolt.

Their intention was to win the support of other tribes by their successes in Iraq.

Ibn Bijad raided the village of al-Jumaima on the Iraqi border and massacred many merchants there, including several from Najd, and then attacked the Shammar. The rebels antagonized the Anaza, the largest tribe, and the Harb of Hijaz. Ibn Saud, who had felt uncertain of his strength just a month ago, was now supported by the bedouin and the settled people of Najd. Faisal Al Dawish was a more subtle politician than Ibn Bijad. He attacked only Iraqis, posing as the king's loyal subject and not breaking off relations with him altogether. The differences grew between him and Ibn Bijad.

After the massacre in al-Jumaima, Ibn Saud arrived in Qasim and mobilized a double quota of Najdi fighters. They joined him readily because neither peasants nor traders felt safe from the Ikhwan bedouin's murder and plunder. Ibn Saud was followed by a part of the Ataiba, led by Abd al-Rahman ibn Rubayin, Ibn Bijad's rival; Mishari ibn Busayis of the Mutair; Dulaim ibn Barrak of the Hitaim; most of the Harb; almost all the Najdi Shammar; a sizeable part of the Zafir; a part of the Anaza from Hijaz; and the Wuld Sulaiman, Faqir and other tribes. The nucleus of the troops consisted of the settled people of Najd.[54]

In early March 1929 Ibn Saud opened the campaign. Faisal Al Dawish and Ibn Bijad gathered their troops at the wells in Sibila.[55] A period of negotiations followed. Faisal Al Dawish even visited Ibn Saud's camp and then returned to the Ikhwan.[56] The day after his visit, 31 March 1929, the battle of Sibila was waged. Putting the infantry of Najd in the centre and appointing his brothers and sons as column commanders, Ibn Saud began the offensive. The bedouin guard was on the flanks. The Ikhwan lost the battle and Faisal Al Dawish received a severe abdominal wound. The king's son Saud, with the Riyadh citizens and the royal guard, moved ahead to complete the victory. It was the settled Najdis who bore the brunt of the battle.[57]

Gravely wounded, Faisal Al Dawish fled to al-Artawiya and sent a group of his female relatives to Ibn Saud to plead for his life. When the king heard of his enemy's wound, his attitude softened: he forgave Faisal and even sent him his personal physician – perhaps not only to treat the patient, but also to see how grave his injury was. In any case, Ibn Saud no longer saw Faisal Al Dawish as a dangerous rival.[58]

As for Ibn Bijad, he returned to al-Ghatghat soon after the battle. The king sent him a letter, urging him to surrender together with the tribal shaikhs who had participated in the revolt. Ibn Bijad obeyed and was jailed in al-Hasa together with the other leaders of the uprising. They all died there. Ibn Saud ordered all arms in the *hijra* of al-Ghatghat to be confiscated and for the settlement itself to be demolished. It lies in ruins to this day.[59] Believing that the Ikhwan revolt was over, the king left for Medina and then for Mecca to participate in the *hajj* of May–June 1929.

The second period of the Ikhwan revolt

Faisal Al Dawish had survived, however. His fighting spirit was not crushed and he was planning new raids on Iraq. At that moment Abdallah ibn Jiluwi decided to take action

Increased Centralization and the Ikhwan Movement (1926–1934)

against the Ajman.[60] Although neither Zaidan ibn Hithlain nor his tribe had taken part in the battle of Sibila, Ibn Jiluwi considered their earlier behaviour deserved to be punished. He sent his son Fahd to capture Zaidan ibn Hithlain close to al-Sirar, his *hijra*. Fahd enticed Zaidan to a meeting in the open desert and took him prisoner. When their leader did not return, the Ikhwan surrounded Fahd's camp and learned that he had ordered the execution of Zaidan and five of his companions. Fahd was killed in the subsequent battle and Zaidan's relative Nayif ibn Hithlain, who had initially opposed the Ikhwan, deserted to the rebels. Understanding that after his son's death Abdallah ibn Jiluwi would soon attack them, the *hijra* shaikhs quickly gathered their livestock and camp equipment and fled to the north.[61] According to Dickson, the treacherous murder of Zaidan antagonized the bedouin of north-eastern Arabia against Ibn Saud, though he was not responsible for it.[62] A large group of Ajman, who had left Kuwait under British pressure, returned to al-Hasa and joined their tribesmen.

Although summer put an end to large-scale operations, the Ajman managed to receive some aid from Kuwait, buying arms in the local markets. Ibn Saud later accused Britain of having turned a blind eye to this activity.[63] The rebels had sympathizers in Iraq and Kuwait, however, and Britain's control over the area was not absolute. In order to achieve their ends in Kuwait, Iraq and Transjordan, the British decided to help Ibn Saud destroy the Ikhwan revolt and thus strengthen his regime.

Faisal Al Dawish decided to raise the banner of revolt once again and joined the Ajman, who intercepted the Riyadh–Hufuf road in mid-July 1929. The Ataiba cut all connections between Hijaz and Najd. The Ajman's initial purpose was an attack on al-Qatif and the coastal towns of al-Hasa. On their way, however, they came across the Awazim and could not refrain from attacking them, hoping for plunder: they were rebuffed. The defeat was seen as shameful by the Ajman and the Mutair because the Awazim were not considered a tribe of 'blue blood'. Two months later, the Ajman attacked the Awazim again near the wells of al-Naqira and gained a Pyrrhic victory.[64]

A civil war was now raging in the country. There were frequent murders of tax-collectors and the caravan routes through Hijaz, Najd and al-Hasa were no longer safe.[65] In July 1929 the king returned to Riyadh with 200 motor cars to use against the rebels. He had arranged to buy 4 planes and had developed plans to set up a radio network in the country. The planes arrived in al-Hasa towards the end of 1929, too late to be used in fighting the rebels.[66] It was only late the following year that the radio contract was signed with the Marconi company.

In September, Ibn Saud decided to put an end to the revolt. He asked the emirs of al-Qatif, al-Hasa, Qasim and Hail to send men, money and arms, mobilized the urban people and the bedouin of Najd and received aid from the *hijras* that had not joined Faisal Al Dawish.

Faisal Al Dawish suffered a heavy blow in September, when the troops led by Ibn Musaid defeated the Mutair, led by Faisal's son Uzayiz, and the young commander perished together with the elite of the Mutair in the battle.[67] Some days later, Faisal Al Dawish suffered another defeat. Those Ataiba who supported the Ikhwan were routed by members of their tribe who were loyal to Ibn Saud and by Ibn Luwai's detachment from al-Khurma. The Ikhwan detachments dispersed.[68]

It was the end of the revolt. Faisal Al Dawish fled to Kuwait in October 1929, seeking asylum for himself and his followers. He intended to leave his family there and persuade Britain not to bomb the Mutair, but the British delayed their answer and gave no guarantees. Numerous unorganized groups of Ikhwan crossed the Iraqi border to escape from Ibn Saud. The Iraqi troops were concentrated in the north of Kuwait; British armoured cars turned the Ikhwan back to Najd.[69]

In October 1929 Ibn Saud declared that all the insurgents' property, camels, horses and arms would be confiscated. Those who were caught in contact with the rebels, but had not participated actively in the revolt, would forfeit their riding camels, horses and arms; the confiscated articles and livestock would be distributed among those who had fought on the king's side. Inhabitants of the 'corrupt' *hijras* would be evicted and deprived of the right to gather again.[70]

In December 1929 Ibn Saud started pursuing Faisal Al Dawish with troops from the urban population of al-Arid, Washm and Qasim, and some loyal sections of the Mutair and Ataiba, the Harb, Subai, Qahtan and Dawasir. The Ikhwan were defeated in numerous skirmishes. Faisal Al Dawish sent a letter to Ibn Saud in late December 1929, asking his pardon and begging for generosity. The king answered that Faisal could not hope that his activities would be forgiven. The correspondence continued nevertheless.[71] Simultaneously Faisal sent messages to the king of Iraq and to Glubb Pasha, claiming that the Mutair were loyal subjects of Iraq. But the British, too, had decided to finish off the Ikhwan. In late December the remainders of Faisal Al Dawish's detachments were pressed between Ibn Saud's troops and the British at the junction of the borders of Najd, Iraq and Kuwait. Ibn Saud's troops outnumbered the rebels many times and they had armoured cars.[72]

The Harb defeated a part of the Mutair, who fled to Kuwait.[73] Faisal Al Dawish himself crossed the border in early January 1930. When Ibn Saud learned of this, he immediately sent a message to Dickson, the British resident in Kuwait, protesting at Britain's giving the Ikhwan refuge in Kuwait, Iraq and Transjordan. The next day he was assured that the insurgents would be driven out.[74]

It is not impossible that both Britain and the authorities in Iraq and Kuwait wanted to keep the Ikhwan leaders in their hands as a means of bringing pressure on Ibn Saud. *Umm al-Qura* commented in January 1930:

> Those who were yesterday the rebels' enemies have today become their best friends. His Majesty's government had to request the neighbouring governments once more to observe their obligations and not to protect the insurgents.[75]

On 10 January 1930 Faisal Al Dawish and the other Ikhwan leaders surrendered to the British. They were brought to Basra by plane and embarked on a British ship in the Shatt al-Arab.[76] On 12 January Ibn Saud demanded the extradition of the Ikhwan leaders. Although King Faisal of Iraq wished to grant the refugees asylum, Britain held a different opinion. A British delegation arrived at Ibn Saud's camp and reached an agreement on the extradition of the rebel leaders. The king promised to spare their

Increased Centralization and the Ikhwan Movement (1926-1934)

lives, prevent raids on Iraq and Kuwait, pay £10,000 compensation for the losses inflicted by the Ikhwan's actions and appoint his representatives at any time to the joint tribunal in accordance with the Bahra agreement.[77]

On 27 January the three rebel leaders were brought to Ibn Saud by plane. Although the king reproached his defeated mortal enemy, Faisal Al Dawish did not admit to any wrongdoing. The captives were put in prison in Riyadh.[78] Faisal Al Dawish died there on 3 October 1931. He retained his spirit to the last, and died pledging to defend his cause against Ibn Saud at the Last Judgement.[79] Thus ended the life of Faisal Al Dawish, one of the most prominent bedouin leaders and the last major representative of a bygone era. Dickson gives a somewhat romanticized portrait of the Ikhwan leader:

> Arabia has never produced a greater warrior than Faisal Al Duwísh, nor had Ibn Sa'ud a more devoted follower until politics or ingratitude drove Faisal to rebellion. The Mutair, his people, almost worshipped him, and no man mentions his name today but with tears in his eyes.[80]

The other leaders of the revolt died in prison soon afterwards, perhaps with the 'assistance' of their jailers.[81]

By January 1930 the Ikhwan revolt had practically come to an end. After playing such an important role in Ibn Saud's conquests and in bolstering his power, the movement was finally crushed. Even the moves to settle the bedouin and convert them to farming were halted.[82] The centralized feudal state had gained the upper hand over the nomads and over their leaders' feudal separatist aspirations.[83] Those 'noble tribes' who had not participated in the revolt supplied soldiers for the king's loyal armed forces. But it was impossible to predict with certainty whom the bedouin would side with in future upheavals.

On 20 February 1930 Ibn Saud arrived in Ras Tannura, where he met Sir Francis Humphrys, the new British high commissioner of Iraq, and King Faisal aboard a British warship. During the three days of talks, the kings reproached each other for their past actions, but finally the common interest prevailed and they arranged to conclude a treaty on friendship and good neighbourliness. It was signed some weeks later at Britain's insistence. Only a few years earlier, the two royal families had fought in Hijaz, which was still considered by the Hashemites as their patrimonial estate. Although the sharifian family never forgot the loss of Mecca and Medina and the humiliating defeat inflicted upon them by Ibn Saud, the requirements of *realpolitik* proved stronger. The two kings recognized each other as rulers of their respective states, agreed to exchange diplomatic missions and declared their respect for each other's sovereignty over their respective tribes and territories.[84]

The Saudi regime seemed to have successfully solved its domestic and external problems and might now expect a period of relative stability. But first, Ibn Saud was to pass through two new ordeals – armed insurrection in Hijaz and Asir, and a war with Yemen, though neither of them was a serious threat to his power.

Armed insurrection in Hijaz and Asir

Ibn Saud's rule, imposed on Hijaz by force of arms, led to discontent among a part of the local nobility. Many of its representatives, particularly the sharifs, still maintained close ties with the brothers of Ali, the last Hashemite monarch. Abdallah ibn Husain, the king of Transjordan, never forgot the defeat inflicted on him by the Ikhwan near Turaba. Although he did not dare help his brother Ali openly, he was dissatisfied with Iraq's recognition of the seizure of Hijaz by the Najdis. The subsequent treaty of friendship between King Faisal and Ibn Saud was even more irritating. In spite of the British presence in Transjordan and Britain's explicit recognition of the Saudi regime, Abdallah decided to provide the opposition elements in Hijaz with money and arms.

The general discontent in Hijaz in the late 1920s appeared to be favourable to the opposition. Drought struck Najd and Hijaz in two successive years, and the civil war between the Ikhwan and Ibn Saud's regime had ravaged the country and undermined its economy. Moreover the worldwide depression of 1929–33 had serious consequences for Arabia: exports of livestock, leather and dates decreased, the country could not pay for imported food and the number of pilgrims fell drastically (from 126,000 in 1926 to 29,000 in 1932).[85] The exchequer was empty, salaries were withheld for many months, officials fleeced the people and the subsidies to many tribal shaikhs were discontinued. There was famine in the country.[86] However, the grave economic situation and people's discontent were not enough to produce any successes for the movement against the Al Saud.

Soon after the fall of Jidda, the so-called League for the Protection of Hijaz was organized in Egypt. Among its leaders were Shaikh Abd al-Rawf al-Sabban and the al-Dabbagh brothers. The conflict between the Egyptian King Fuad and Ibn Saud had prompted the Egyptians to support the league.[87]

In the late 1920s the Hijazi oppositionists, encouraged by King Abdallah, founded the Hijazi Liberal Party whose purpose was to drive out the Najdis and create an independent state of Hijaz. Its leader was Tahir al-Dabbagh, secretary of the Hijazi National Party under King Ali. The party leadership also included Shaikh Shakir ibn Husain al-Dabbagh, Ali al-Dabbagh and Muhammad Amin al-Shunkaidi. The Hijazi liberals tried to set up party branches in various cities throughout the Arab world. Husain al-Dabbagh made for Cairo with a huge sum of money. He contacted Hamid ibn Salim ibn Rifada, nicknamed 'One-eyed', a shaikh of the Billi tribe, a part of which roamed from Hijaz to Egypt after the anti-Saudi rebellion in 1929.[88]

In an attempt to find sympathizers in southern Arabia, Husain al-Dabbagh visited Aden and met some émigrés from the Idrisi clan. He hoped that armed operations in the north might be supported by an uprising in Asir and then by a general revolt in Hijaz. On his return to Cairo, Husain al-Dabbagh assured Ibn Rifada that popular discontent had matured in the south and people were waiting for the signal to start a revolt. In mid-May 1932 Ibn Rifada and his tribe crossed the Egyptian border near Aqaba, where Saud al-Dabbagh provided him with food. Soon afterwards Ibn Rifada appeared in northern Hijaz with his armed detachment.[89]

Increased Centralization and the Ikhwan Movement (1926-1934)

The activities of the 'Hijazi liberals' were probably not unknown to Ibn Saud. On learning of Ibn Rifada's detachment in June 1932, he ordered the immediate arrest of all oppositionists in Mecca, including several members of the al-Dabbagh family, and banned all political parties in Hijaz.[90] Simultaneously Ibn Saud sent detachments by truck to Daba and al-Bid to surround Ibn Rifada. The king urged Britain to prevent supplies to the rebels from Transjordan. The British high commissioner in Amman stated officially that the rebels would not receive any aid from Transjordan. British units sealed the border and a British warship arrived in Aqaba to prevent the transportation of equipment and food to Hijaz. Ibn Saud also closed the frontier.[91]

Ibn Rifada and the Billi fighters received no support from the population and hid in the Shar hills, some 50 km from Daba town. Ibn Saud lured them down from the hills, telling the nobility of Daba to send a letter to Ibn Rifada promising to join his movement. The Billi shaikh descended from the hills only to fall into a trap. His detachment was surrounded and routed in a short battle. This time Ibn Saud made even greater use of motor cars and armoured cars than he had done when suppressing the Ikhwan revolt.[92] The adventurous actions of Ibn Rifada and the 'Hijazi liberals' were defeated even before their allies had started an armed struggle in Asir.

According to the treaty of 1920 with Ibn Saud, Muhammad Al Idrisi retained suzerainty over southern Asir and a part of Tihama, but the situation had begun to change drastically after the conquest of Hijaz. In the shadow of the powerful Saudi state, the Idrisis' 'independence' became a fiction. Taking advantage of the Najdis' preoccupation with operations in Hijaz, Imam Yahya of Yemen annexed Hodeida and a part of Tihama to his possessions. Relations between Ibn Saud and Yahya deteriorated.

After the capture of Hodeida, Yahya's son Ahmad made for the north with his troops and threatened the main centres of Asir – Jizan, al-Sabiya and Abu Arish. Imam Yahya obviously intended to annex the whole of southern Asir to Yemen.

Fearing the Yemenis, al-Hasan Al Idrisi, the new emir of Asir, signed a treaty on 21 October 1926 establishing a Saudi protectorate over his state. The Idrisis waived an independent foreign policy, but retained autonomy in internal affairs. This exacerbated the Saudi-Yemeni conflict. Imam Yahya withdrew his troops from Jizan and al-Sabiya. In June 1927 a Saudi delegation arrived in Sanaa. Yahya insisted that Asir was a part of Yemen, torn away by the Idrisis, who were 'strangers and usurpers'. The Saudis argued that the area in question had nothing to do with Yemen and demanded that the vast territories of Asir up to Bajil, occupied by the Yemeni army in 1925, be returned to Riyadh. Yemen was not prepared to extend the conflict. Frequent clashes were already occurring on its southern borders with British troops and troops from British protectorates. In 1928 British aircraft bombed several Yemeni towns.

On 27 October 1930 Ibn Saud imposed a new treaty on al-Hasan Al Idrisi, which made the emir's power a mere formality. The pretext for altering the emirate's system of government was the large-scale smuggling into Hijaz via Asir. The treaty stipulated that after al-Hasan's death Ibn Saud should enjoy absolute power in Asir. The Idrisis, however, began establishing secret contacts with Imam Yahya and the 'Hijazi liberals'.

In 1931–32 armed conflicts occurred on the Saudi-Yemeni border.[93]

In 1930 Husain al-Dabbagh, a representative of the Hijazi liberal party, appeared in al-Luhaya, a coastal town. He arranged for joint actions with al-Hasan Al Idrisi, who then began receiving supplies of food and equipment. In 1932 he tried to get rid of the Saudi protectorate.

The revolt started in November 1932. Al-Hasan's troops were defeated within a few days and he fled to al-Sabiya. The Soviet consulate-general in Jidda reported back:

> The movement in the south was prepared by the same organization that guided Ibn Rifada's actions in the summer of 1932 and was directed by Amman (Transjordan) . . . As during Ibn Rifada's attack against Hijaz, the organization's activities consisted of establishing contacts with the coastal regions of Asir, carrying on anti-Saudi propaganda, sending emissaries to 'some European countries' to purchase weapons and sending food and munitions to the coast of Asir by ship. After the revolt started . . . , a ship arrived in Jizan with Ali al-Dabbagh and Abd al-Aziz al-Yamani. They brought rice, flour and dates . . . However, three days later a government detachment came to Jizan and detained al-Yamani. Ali al-Dabbagh tried to flee aboard the ship . . . The authorities later reported that Ali al-Dabbagh had drowned at sea.[94]

Soon afterwards the Saudi troops, led by Khalid ibn Luwai and Abd al-Aziz ibn Musaid, occupied the whole of Asir. Taking advantage of the highlands, the Idrisis and the tribes loyal to them tried to resist, but then fled to Yemen. Ibn Saud demanded that the rebels should be extradited, but Imam Yahya agreed to send them back only if Ibn Saud forgave them. In May 1933 a number of Idrisis returned to Mecca and were kept under surveillance, also receiving a pension.[95] Riyadh appointed a governor to Asir.

As early as the summer of 1932, it had become clear that the Saudi regime had grown stronger and was now the unquestionable master of the vast territory of the kingdom of Hijaz and Najd and its dependencies. The easy suppression of the revolts in the north of Hijaz and then in Asir only corroborated that fact.

In September 1932 (even before the armed rebellion in Asir), eighteen officials of the Hijazi government, most of whom were members of the *majlis al-shura* between 1926 and 1936, met in al-Taif and sent a special petition to Ibn Saud. Noting that the kingdom of Hijaz and Najd and its dependencies was a single nation, united by faith, history and traditions, they proposed that a unitary state should be proclaimed, named the kingdom of Saudi Arabia. (Undoubtedly, the step had been prepared beforehand by Ibn Saud.)

On 18 September 1932 Ibn Saud issued a decree 'On the merger of the parts of the Arabian kingdom' and proclaiming the new name of the state to be the kingdom of Saudi Arabia. The decree noted that all international treaties, obligations and agreements concluded by the previous government remained in force, as did the earlier ordinances, instructions and laws. The decree charged the council of ministers, formed in December 1931, to draft the kingdom's constitution and determined the procedure

Increased Centralization and the Ikhwan Movement (1926-1934)

of succession to the throne.[96] In 1933 Ibn Saud appointed his eldest son Saud as crown prince.[97]

Following his usual tactic of outbidding the opposition and forgiving those adversaries who had ceased to oppose him, Ibn Saud proclaimed a general amnesty in 1935. Simultaneously, the 'Hijazi liberals' disbanded their party. Many of them returned to Saudi Arabia. Tahir al-Dabbagh became the head of the education department and Shaikh al-Sabban was coopted to the *majlis al-shura*. Other prominent opposition leaders also received a royal pardon.[98]

The Saudi-Yemeni war[99]

The rulers of Yemen and Saudi Arabia had much in common: they had led the movements for the unity of their countries at almost the same time; they had fought the Turks and won independence after the First World War; and they both felt the pressure of British imperialism. But the struggle for Asir led them into a military confrontation.

In April 1933 Prince Ahmad, who had suppressed an anti-imam rebellion among the tribes of North Yemen, seized Najran. His pretext was the help given to the rebels by its inhabitants, the Yam tribe, who were considered a section of the Hamdan, a Yemeni tribe. Negotiations initiated by a Saudi delegation sent to Sanaa to settle the conflict ended in failure. The imam was instigated both by the Italians, who promised assistance in order to increase their influence in Yemen, and by the British, who wished to detract Imam Yahya's attention from their protectorates in Aden.

In October 1933 the Yemenis resumed their offensive and occupied al-Badr. The Idrisis began instigating their supporters among the tribes of Asir against Ibn Saud. In November, Ibn Saud strengthened his troops on the Yemeni border and sent Imam Yahya an ultimatum, urging him to evacuate the occupied territory, restore the earlier borders and extradite the Idrisis.

Fearing a Saudi attack, Imam Yahya made partial concessions to Britain to make his position secure in the south. In February 1934 Sir Bernard Reilly, the British resident in Aden, concluded a treaty of 'friendship and mutual cooperation' with Yemen in Sanaa, later interpreted by Britain as the imam's consent to British dominance in southern Arabia.

In late February and early March 1934 a new meeting of representatives of both kingdoms was held in Abha. Ibn Saud softened his stance and proposed a neutral zone in the contested area of Najran. When Imam Yahya evaded giving a definite answer, however, the Saudis began an offensive.

Saudi Arabia was better prepared than Yemen for a war. It had received a loan from Standard Oil of California and was able to purchase weapons. The first units of a regular army emerged in the country. The Saudis advanced in two columns – along the Tihama plain and through the mountains. The former (led by Saud) soon captured Najran, but the advance through the mountains was slow since every village was a fortress.

Faisal's troops passed through Tihama and occupied Hodeida on 2 May without a battle. Some Saudi detachments appeared in the environs of Taizz. Faisal asked his father to allow him to attack Sanaa, but his request was refused. The mountains were difficult of access, and the Saudis' advance was hampered by lack of experience in such terrain. British, French and Italian warships approached Hodeida and the Italians, who supported the imam, landed troops there. Although the Saudis were to stay for a long time in Hodeida and had even ordered concrete to expand its port, they understood that the European powers would not allow them to annex the whole of Yemen or even Hodeida alone.[100] Ibn Saud decided to content himself with a limited success.

On 15 May 1934 Prince Faisal and the imam's aide, Abdallah al-Wazir, signed an armistice and agreed the terms of the peace treaty. It was initialled in al-Taif on 20 May 1934. 'The treaty of Muslim friendship and Arab brotherhood' was later ratified by Yemen and Saudi Arabia. It was published simultaneously in the official media of Mecca, Sanaa, Cairo and Damascus. The treaty included twenty-three articles and an arbitration clause. Its term was twenty years with the possibility of extending it in the future. The treaty proclaimed the Saudi and Yemeni peoples to be a single nation; it provided for the establishment of peaceful and friendly relations between them and for the mutual recognition of independence and sovereignty. Imam Yahya waived his claim to the territories of the Idrisi emirate, and the Saudi forces were to be withdrawn from the occupied territories. It was decided to demarcate the frontiers (this was completed in 1936). The imam pledged to pay a contribution of £100,000 in gold.

Relations between the two countries began to improve, though the following year three Yemeni pilgrims tried to stab Ibn Saud in Mecca during the *hajj*. Prince Saud, who protected his father, was wounded in the back and shoulder. The bodyguards killed the would-be assassins. After the war of 1934, relations between the dynasties of the Saudis and the Hamid al-Dins steadily became more friendly. An era of political cooperation began between the monarchs of Saudi Arabia and Yemen.

CHAPTER 13

The Socio-political Structure of Saudi Arabia after its Creation

The new kingdom of Saudi Arabia extended over most of the Arabian peninsula, absorbing several feudal-tribal groupings that had previously been dependent on the Ottoman empire. The creation of a centralized state corresponded to the overall interests of the feudal-tribal nobility, the merchants and the majority of the population, ensuring security and putting an end to tribal feuds. However, centralization brought growing taxes and strengthened the military-bureaucratic machinery, which substantially restricted the nomads' traditional 'democratic' freedoms. The preaching of a 'purified' Islam in its Wahhabi form reinforced the Al Saud's struggle to unite all the territories of Najd and gave it a religious cover. The movement for a renaissance of the emirate of Najd was led at the moment of greatest historical responsibility by Ibn Saud, who was not only a prominent leader and statesman but also a military commander.

The independent Najdi state needed appropriate external conditions and a favourable international situation to achieve centralization and to conquer some of the adjacent areas. In the early stages, Ibn Saud's successes were helped by Britain's support for his struggle against the Turks and their vassals and by the collapse of the Ottoman empire after the First World War. Later, Britain's increasingly weak economic position meant that it was unable to establish direct control over a sizeable part of Arabia, which now seemed a costly burden: this too was conducive to Ibn Saud's success.

Arabia's economic base in the first third of the twentieth century had not changed significantly since the eighteenth and nineteenth centuries. Even without reliable figures, it may be supposed that the permanent wars and revolts, combined with the ever deepening crisis in camel-breeding, meant an economic regress. Thus Saudi

Arabia in the early twentieth century had no new social groupings that were fundamentally different in character or organization from the social forces that had led to the creation of the first Saudi state in the eighteenth century under the banner of Wahhabism.

After the First World War, the issue of national independence arose in several Arab countries (Egypt, Syria, Palestine, Iraq, Algeria, Morocco). The character of their independent development would inevitably be determined by such factors as the balance of forces between the feudal and bourgeois elements, the level of economic development, the degree of 'Europeanization' (modernization), the emergence of elements of a modern middle class and the growth of a working class. In that period, even the germs of capitalist relations were non-existent in Saudi Arabia, and the politically independent state was created on the primitive feudal-tribal basis in what was essentially a medieval society.

Yet since Saudi Arabia was no longer isolated from the outside world, its society could not escape external influences: it had to adopt both the technical means of centralization and administration (radio, telephone, aviation, motor transport) and their organizational forms (a regular army, ministries and government departments, an education system). The collision between the traditional socio-political institutions, which had developed from within Saudi society itself, and the modernizing trends from outside did not upset the state's socio-political balance in the first decade. There were two main reasons for this: first, the impact of modernization, which came from far more developed states of the Middle East, was still weak; and, second, the traditional structures were still dominant. The situation underwent a radical change only in the late 1940s, when the sudden vast inflow of oil revenues undermined the earlier social balance in Saudi Arabia.

The very name of the country – Saudi Arabia – implied the Saudi dynasty's control over it. The green of the national flag was the symbolic colour of heaven and the Prophet's favourite colour. The white sword symbolized *jihad*. Below it, the Muslim credo was written in white letters: 'There is no god but Allah, and Muhammad is His messenger.'

The king's power. Relations between the feudal-tribal nobility and the ulama

The evolution of the ruler's political power was reflected, in particular, in his title. The Turks had addressed Ibn Saud as 'Abd al-Aziz Pasha, the ruler of Najd and military commander' while the British had addressed him as 'Shaikh Abd al-Aziz, the son of Shaikh Abd al-Rahman Al Saud'. In 1921 the emirs, tribal shaikhs and *ulama* proclaimed him 'the sultan of Najd and its dependencies', and he came to be referred to as His Majesty in all official correspondence.[1] In 1926 he became 'the king of Hijaz and sultan of Najd and its dependencies' and a year later 'the king of Hijaz and Najd and its dependencies'. On 22 September 1932 he became the king of Saudi Arabia. Initially, however, these titles were intended mainly for the outside world, to enhance the international prestige of the state and its ruler.

The Socio-political Structure of Saudi Arabia after its Creation

To the settled population, Ibn Saud was an emir – i.e. the feudal ruler of Najd and the countries it had conquered – and the transformation of his title into 'sultan' and 'king' appeared natural to them. The bedouin considered him *shaikh al-mashaikh*, or chief shaikh, the head of all the nomadic tribes. To strengthen their authority, the Saudis stressed that their genealogical tree went back to a branch of the Anaza, a tribe of 'blue blood', and the most numerous and powerful in Arabia. A skilful use of material support from the tribal nobility, combined with pressure and military reprisals, enabled Ibn Saud to ensure the obedience of the numerous (and previously ungovernable) nomads.

Saudi power was arrayed in patriarchal-democratic clothing. Even the poorest bedouin could in theory address the king without ceremony or titles. Ibn Saud liked to be addressed as Ibn Faisal, after his grandfather, or as Ibn Miqrin, after his remote ancestor, the founder of the house of Saud, or as Akhu Nura, i.e. the brother of Nura, his beloved elder sister. There is an ideal of the 'true' Arabian which is derived from the bedouin and romanticized not only in Arabian society but in some other Arab countries as well: it is of the courageous warrior, generous to the defeated, the protector of Islam, the sexually potent male. By identifying himself deliberately with these qualities, Ibn Saud acquired authority and prestige.[2]

The king's 'democratic' and 'patriarchal' behaviour did not mislead those who understood the true strength of the monarch's position in the centralized state, as can be seen from the statements of loyalty to the ruler quoted in the *Memorial of the Government of Saudi Arabia* concerning the al-Buraimi conflict. Although written in the early 1950s, they reflect the essence of the relations that were established between the ruler and his subjects in the 1920s and 1930s. For instance, Kirram ibn Mani, the shaikh of the Aal bu Mutair tribe, stated that he and his people had been and remained loyal subjects of King Saud ibn Abd al-Aziz. He mentioned the payment of *zakat* by his tribe in the form of camels, sheep, goats, dates and rice to the king's tax-collector under the provisions of Islamic law, as the tribe had done earlier for a long period. Swearing loyalty and submission to His Majesty on behalf of his tribesmen, he mentioned Allah as the most reliable witness to his statement, which was not authenticated by his fingerprint.[3]

Another statement, quoted in the same source and submitted by a number of persons, read that the inhabitants of al-Buraimi were subjects of the Saudi government, as their fathers and grandfathers had been for decades. They stressed that all the territory, lands and property in their possession, and even their lives, belonged to the king. The document declared that whatever oral or written statement to the contrary had been made in the past, or might be made in the future, it was invalid and unacceptable. On behalf of themselves and all their successors, the authors of the document swore loyalty to the king, again calling on Allah as their witness.[4]

Ibn Saud bore the title of imam, as his ancestors had done. Its significance was not confined to his guidance of the faithful during prayers. He led all 'monotheists' who opposed the 'polytheists' – the Muslims of other countries. Although the element of extremism in society lessened after the defeat of the Ikhwan, devotion to the imam as the religious leader was supposed to cement the society of Saudi Arabia and sanctify the supreme state power. The head of state of the 'monotheist Muslims' was ex officio commander-in-chief and led the *jihad*, the holy war against the 'polytheists'. This was an effective strategy during the wars of conquest; but when Saudi Arabia reached the limits of its expansion and political prudence required an end to territorial seizures, Ibn Saud's reluctance to head a further *jihad* was quite natural, since it might amount to political suicide. As we have seen, this led to a conflict with the Ikhwan. Yet, even after routing the Ikhwan, Ibn Saud was seen as the commander-in-chief who was in principle ready to wage a holy war.

Following his forebears' example, Ibn Saud derived arguments in favour of the consolidation of central power from Muslim tradition, especially from the teaching of Ibn Taimiya. The medieval religious thinker was of the opinion that there should be two groups of authoritative persons in an ideal society: the *ulama*, the guardians of the *sharia*; and the emirs who enjoy the political power necessary to enforce the laws.[5] The emir's subjects should obey him absolutely and unconditionally.[6] The emir is responsible for the correct implementation of religious duties by all Muslims, carries out court sentences, engages in charitable works, oversees economic activities, ensures the security of the community and the normal functioning of public services and, lastly, issues social and economic prescriptions that guarantee respect for each individual according to his position in society within the framework of the *sharia*.[7]

The emir should consult the *ulama* on his activities, but he may also act as his conscience dictates.[8] The emir is bound in his behaviour by the Quran and the Sunna as interpreted by the *ulama*. This means that the *ulama* are given considerable, though not unlimited, influence and means of control. Theoretically the emir is free to act as he pleases outside the framework of religious affairs, but in practice, Islam penetrates all spheres of life in Saudi Arabia and the *ulama* play an important role in Wahhabi society. Their authority is increased by the fact that the most influential of them belong to the Al al-Shaikh, who have long been related to the Saudis.

During the crisis of 1914–15, provoked by the Ikhwan's fanaticism, Ibn Saud issued an ordinance and the *ulama* adopted a *fatwa* denouncing the Ikhwan's intolerant, extreme behaviour.[9] But relations between Ibn Saud and the *ulama* deteriorated on several occasions. One example is the *ulama*'s resistance to the introduction of telegraph and radio.[10] Ibn Saud's will prevailed in all conflicts over major issues, however. On one occasion, the *ulama* interfered in a dynastic marriage, trying to prevent a girl from a noble family in Riyadh marrying a non-Wahhabi Arab. The king ignored their opinion and even expelled thirty of them from Najd[11] (although this might have been a pretext for him to get rid of *ulama* whom he disliked).

Every member of the community was expected to obey the emir and to give him advice when required.[12] Speaking at the opening of the *majlis al-shura* in 1950, Prince Faisal said, 'The subjects' duty is to help the agencies in charge of various matters and to facilitate the execution of their tasks in accordance with the orders and instructions sent to the said agencies.'[13]

Ibn Saud always showed respect for the *ulama*, inviting them to speak at his *majlises* and taking note of their advice. The *ulama* demonstrated their power when Ibn Saud decided to celebrate the fiftieth anniversary of his accession to the throne: when they claimed that there is no festival of that type in Islam, the king was forced to agree. However, Ibn Saud sometimes made fun of their objections. Once a member of the *ulama* saw the king in the palace wearing a long robe that touched the ground and said, 'Allah-Allah! Abd al-Aziz, you are obsessed by pride. Your clothes are dragging behind you.' The king immediately sent a servant to bring a pair of scissors and, when he returned, told the *alim*, 'Cut off as much as you deem exceeds the religious standards.'[14]

According to Philby, in 1918 there were six *ulama* in Riyadh, three in Qasim, three in al-Hasa and one in each of the other areas of Najd – a total of some twenty persons.[15] He probably meant only the most revered and outstanding *ulama*, since their total number must have been much greater. Those who lived in the capital were considered superior to their provincial counterparts. The number of *ulama* in Riyadh fluctuated constantly.

The authority of the Saudi *ulama* as experts in theology and law rested both on their personal piety and on their specialist training. Although anybody might become an *alim*, in practice most of them came from the 'noble' tribes or the clan of Sayids, who were considered the Prophet's direct descendants. The most authoritative *ulama* belonged to the Al al-Shaikh, though they were not Sayids. They had been related to the ruling family as early as the time of Imam Abd al-Aziz I and Muhammad Ibn Abd al-Wahhab. King Faisal, who was assassinated in 1975, was the son of Ibn Saud and his wife from the Al al-Shaikh family.

Travellers paid great attention to the area in Riyadh where the *ulama* lived – not all their descriptions were equally favourable. Rihani, for example, commented on the *ulama*'s hypocrisy and sanctimonious behaviour:

> But even in the most sacrosanct quarter of the Capital, where the *ulema* live, one is likely to find some tobacco, hidden in the bottom of a chest, for a surreptitious moment of keif [hashish]. Outwardly, of course, the law is strictly observed and enforced. Asceticism and piety are ever watchful and alert. If one is seen walking in that quarter through the street with a swing of the shoulders or a sweep of the garment, he is forthwith reprimanded for his arrogance. If one laughs freely in one's house, someone will soon knock at the door. 'Why are you laughing in this ribald manner?' No one in that quarter ever dares to miss, except for a reason of sickness, one of the five daily prayers in the masjid. And as for tobacco, the culprit, when he is discovered smoking, is summarily dealt with. No pity has the piety of the *ulema*; no mercy in their ascetic justice. 'But', said one from the Palace, 'they are secretly a lecherous people. The walls of their houses cry out against them.'[16]

Most travellers, however, praised the Riyadh *ulama*'s knowledge of dogma and noted their role in the development of schools and libraries.[17]

When the time came to modernize the feudal state in certain fields, the *ulama* opposed the changes resolutely. In June 1930 an assembly of *ulama* protested against including such subjects as technical drawing, foreign languages and geography in the curriculum drafted by the newly formed directorate of education. The *ulama* claimed that technical drawing did not differ from the drawing of pictures and that foreign languages enabled the Muslims to study the infidel's teachings. They were indignant at geography's teaching that the earth is round. Ibn Saud merely ignored their protests.[18] On other occasions, the *ulama* joined Ibn Saud in opposing the Ikhwan's extremism, but it was rather an example of solidarity between the political and religious elites who were interested in preserving and consolidating the centralized state.

By the early 1950s some elements of a hierarchy had emerged among the *ulama*. The grand mufti was considered the head of all the *ulama*. Among the most authoritative members were the head and several members of the Committee of Public Morality in Riyadh, the chief *qadhi* of Mecca, the *qadhi* of Dilam and two judges of the *sharia* court in Riyadh.[19]

An important role in creating the spiritual basis of the centralized state was played by Abdallah ibn Muhammad ibn Abd al-Latif. A member of the Al al-Shaikh family (he was their recognized head until his death in 1925),[20] he was a renowned legal expert and preacher who had studied in Medina, Tunis and Cairo and travelled in Morocco, Spain, India, Afghanistan, Iran and Iraq. He had joined the Al Saud during their exile in Kuwait and was Ibn Saud's teacher. According to Philby, it was Abdallah who delivered sermons at Shaikh Abdallah's mosque in the *ulama*'s quarter in the capital and at the main mosque. He was also the chief *qadhi* of Riyadh.[21] During prayers, Abdallah would stand in front of the community as the imam, with Ibn Saud's father on his right and the king just behind him.[22]

The creation of the kingdom of Saudi Arabia, the consolidation of its independence and the revival of several socio-political Islamic institutions led several non-Saudi Arabs to take a renewed interest in Wahhabism. Muhammad Rashid Ridha's group, which formed around the Egyptian periodical *al-Manar*, found common ground between their ideas and those of the Wahhabis. Advocating the 'modernization' of Islamic societies by borrowing the technical achievements of Western civilization, they nevertheless demanded an unconditional return to the values, ideology and institutions of the first centuries of Islam and their introduction into all spheres of life. Ridha's group had prepared the ground for a spreading of the views of Hasan al-Banna, the founder of the Muslim Brotherhood. Ridha himself wrote several works that were extremely favourable to Wahhabism. In Egypt, these might have been seen as an expression of opposition to King Fuad, because after the *mahmal* incident all relations with Saudi Arabia had been severed (they were resumed in 1936). The Saudi government's sympathies with and support for the Muslim Brotherhood were not accidental.

The Socio-political Structure of Saudi Arabia after its Creation

State power and the administration of Najd

When discussing the position of Najd and Hijaz in the united state, Fuad Hamza – one of Ibn Saud's advisers – wrote, 'As for laws and the legal system, Najd and Hijaz are two independent kingdoms, which share only the common throne and the person who occupies it.'[23] At the same time, the author noted that there was no demarcated border between the two states and no customs posts, they pursued a joint foreign policy and, most important of all, they had a joint army. Although there were substantial differences in the administration of Najd and Hijaz in the first two decades, they gradually decreased. Real power was concentrated in the hands of the king and his court.

The royal court in Riyadh acted as the government of the whole country and simultaneously as the government of Najd. Al-Zirikli, who was conversant with its structure, describes it as follows:

1. The *majlis*, or royal council. Its members were referred to as the *jamaa* (assembly or community). Chaired by the king, they met twice a day – before lunch and in the evening. The chief members were Prince Abdallah ibn Abd al-Rahman (the king's brother), Crown Prince Saud and Prince Faisal, the viceroy of Hijaz, when he was in Riyadh. Other members included *wazirs* (secretaries or ministers), councillors, leading members of the *ulama* and any Saudi ambassadors who were in Riyadh on the day of meeting. The emirs of the main provinces and tribal shaikhs might also attend the *majlis* meetings.
2. The political department, responsible for foreign affairs.
3. The royal *diwan*, equivalent to the ministry of interior.
4. The coding and telegrams department.
5. The department for the affairs of the bedouin and Najd.
6. The accounting and gifts department.
7. The delegations and hospitality department, responsible for the reception of delegations and for the special palaces for the king's guests. The guests were divided into three categories: VIPs, delegations from the settled people and nomadic delegations.
8. The department of royal properties, responsible for maintenance of the royal palace.
9. The *jihad* warriors department, which dealt with the problems of irregular conscripts.
10. The special exchequer department.
11. The special warehouses department.
12. The department of the royal entourage.
13. The horse-breeding department.
14. The department of royal camels.
15. The motor transport department.
16. The radio department (set up after radio was introduced in the country). Among

its functions were the collection of radio information and the preparation of summaries of broadcasts in Arabic and foreign languages for the king.
17. The royal guard.
18. The health department – responsible for health matters in the royal palace.[24]

Al-Zirikli's description roughly corresponds with Nallino's account,[25] though with some differences. According to Nallino, the affairs of Hijaz, Asir and al-Hasa were managed by the royal *diwan*. He also mentions the departments of *zakat* and the state exchequer, whose functions overlapped with those of the ministry of finance and the ministry of religious readings and muezzins. Subdivisions of the royal court might be created or abolished, merged or divided, upgraded or disregarded, depending on the calibre of their head and their relations with the king. There were no written rules concerning the structure of the royal court. The decisive say in all matters belonged to the king. He gave directions to the heads of all departments and was the supreme arbiter in their disputes.[26]

As for the administration of the main provinces, their governor–emirs were appointed and dismissed by the king. There were no codes or laws concerning the local administration in Najd and its dependencies in the 1930s. Minor emirs were appointed by the governors, but the king might interfere in their choice. According to Fuad Hamza, the territories outside Hijaz were initially divided into five large provinces – Najd proper (including al-Arid and the neighbouring areas); Qasim; Jabal Shammar; al-Hasa, ruled by the Al Jiluwi; and Asir.[27] The province of Wadi Sirhan was virtually separated from Jabal Shammar, and Asir was divided into Asir proper and centres in Abha, Tihama and Najran.[28]

The nomadic tribes were put under the control of the provincial authorities. According to MacKie Frood, the Ataiba, a part of the Mutair, the Dawasir, the Qahtan and the Subai were ruled by the governor of al-Arid; the Ajman, Bani Hajir, Bani Khalid, Hawazim, Manasir, Al Murra and another part of the Mutair by the governor of al-Hasa; and the Shammar, the Shararat and the rest of the Mutair by the emir of Jabal Shammar.[29] It is important to note that the Mutair, who resisted the Saudis' power, were divided into three parts.

The autonomy of al-Hasa (the Eastern Province) was not established by special decree, but by the late 1930s it had its own bureaucratic agencies under Ibn Jiluwi, whose close relatives ruled the most important oases. The departments of police, financial affairs, customs and the coastguard and a branch of the Jidda mining department were set up in Hufuf.[30]

State power and the administration of Hijaz

As mentioned previously, Ibn Saud preferred the creation of a more sophisticated system of state power in Hijaz. In August 1926 the king promulgated the 'fundamental provisions of the kingdom of Hijaz', sometimes referred to as the 'constitution'. They read:

> The kingdom of Hijaz within its defined boundaries shall be an integral whole, whose parts shall be interconnected and shall not be divided or separated in whatsoever manner. [Hijaz] shall be a monarchic state with consultative bodies, an Islamic state, independent in both its internal and external affairs . . . Holy Mecca shall be the capital of the state of Hijaz . . . The whole government of the kingdom of Hijaz shall be in the hands of His Majesty King Abd al-Aziz ibn Abd al-Rahman Al Faisal Al Saud. His Majesty shall be bound by the provisions of the glorious *sharia*.

All court decisions should:

> correspond to Allah's Book, the Sunna of His Prophet (Allah's blessing be upon Him) and the rules to which the Prophet's Companions and the first pious generations adhered.[31]

The 'fundamental provisions' stipulated that the king should appoint the viceroy of Hijaz and the heads of departments: the former was responsible to the king and the latter were responsible to the viceroy.[32] The affairs of Hijaz were to be divided into six main divisions: *sharia* affairs; home affairs; foreign affairs; financial affairs; educational affairs; and military affairs. A special article stressed that 'military affairs shall be managed and all related functions shall be performed under the guidance of His Majesty the King'.[33]

The *majlis al-shura* (advisory council) was to consist of the viceroy, his advisers and six representatives of the Hijazi nobility, appointed by the king 'from among experienced and able people'. The 'fundamental provisions' provided for administrative councils, with municipal functions, to be set up in the main towns. Their decisions would come into effect after approval by the king. The creation of councils was also planned for smaller administrative units.[34]

Ibn Saud considered that some provisions of the 'constitution' contradicted his absolute power. Articles 28–37, which dealt with the *majlis al-shura* and local councils, were ignored from 1927; and Articles 43–45, which provided for the setting up of bodies to control the exchequer's expenditure, were never applied and later became invalid. A notable feature of the 'constitution' was the almost complete lack of provisions concerning individual or collective rights and of those restricting the king's authority, exercised on the basis of the *sharia*.[35]

In al-Zirikli's opinion – based on a study of the practical activities of those bodies that exercised power in Hijaz – the *majlis al-shura* approved the budgets of the state services and municipalities, issued permits for economic projects and concessions, adopted ordinances and solved problems related to local officials and foreigners. From 1932 its functions included the care of pilgrims.[36] Al-Zirikli claims that the *majlis al-*

shura's functions were both consultative and legislative: it might point out errors made by the government (the author means the *majlis al-wukala*, or council of ministers, set up in Hijaz) in the implementation of laws and codes; and it could approve, reject or alter government bills.[37]

A royal decree, issued in July 1928, provided for the creation of a joint *majlis al-shura* for Hijaz and Najd: it was never set up.[38] Neither were any decisions taken to confine the *majlis al-shura*'s decisions to Hijaz or, on the contrary, apply them to other parts of Saudi Arabia. By 1950 the advisory council had adopted some hundreds of *nizams* (codes) and orders to deal with various situations, define the status of state and public services and organize courts, a health system and a post and telegraph service. In practice, many codes, orders and decisions of the *majlis al-shura* of Hijaz were applied throughout the country.[39]

Before the conquest of Hijaz, Najd's foreign relations had been largely confined to the Gulf countries. The king himself maintained the diplomatic correspondence, controlled all foreign relations and instructed his envoys in negotiations. After the annexation of Hijaz, the new kingdom's international affairs became more sophisticated. There were several permanent foreign consulates in Jidda. The arrival of pilgrims also faced the new ruler of Hijaz with many delicate problems. As early as 1925, what amounted to a department of foreign affairs emerged in Hijaz, headed by Yusuf Yasin, a Syrian who had joined Ibn Saud's service. Together with the Egyptian Hafiz Wahba, Yasin took part in the 1925 negotiations in Bahra and al-Hada and then in various other diplomatic missions. He edited *Umm al-Qura* in Mecca and was the head of the political department at the royal court. In 1930 Ibn Saud issued an ordinance on the creation of a ministry of foreign affairs. His second son Faisal, the viceroy of Hijaz, was appointed foreign minister.[40]

Saudi Arabia established diplomatic relations with the Soviet Union on 16 February 1926, with Britain on 1 March 1926, with the Netherlands, France and Turkey in March 1926, with Germany in 1928, with Iran and Poland in 1929, with the US in 1931, with Italy in 1932 and with Egypt in 1936, after the death of King Fuad. In 1950 there were two foreign embassies (of the US and Britain) and several foreign missions in Saudi Arabia.[41] The Soviet mission left Jidda in 1938, but diplomatic relations between the two countries were not formally severed; normal diplomatic relations were restored in 1990.

Initially, one Abdallah al-Sulaiman, who had no specially appointed staff, was in charge of the exchequer in the emirate of Riyadh. Each oasis and province had its own *idaras* (*zakat*-collection offices), which were independent of the other agencies and responsible only to the emir and the king. They were modelled on the taxation office in the first and second Saudi states.

In 1927 the *mudiriya* (general directorate of finance) was set up in Mecca, again under Abdallah al-Sulaiman.[42] In 1929 the directorate became a *wikala* (agency), in effect a ministry. The Saudi government invited Mr van Li, a Dutch financial expert, to put the state finances in some sort of order, but his stay was short and unsuccessful.[43] In 1932 the king decided to transform the financial agency into the ministry of finance with broad responsibilities and charged Abdallah al-Sulaiman to head it.[44] The new ministry acted virtually as the ministry of the economy. It oversaw the activities of the departments of supplies, pilgrimage, agriculture, public works and motor transport. The ministry's competence also included signing concessions for the extraction of gold and oil; a petroleum and mining department was set up under it. Experts from Syria, Lebanon, Egypt and Iraq worked at the ministry. It continued to expand and in 1949 some 4,500 people were on its pay-roll.[45]

The council of ministers of Hijaz, chaired by the viceroy Faisal, was set up in January 1932.[46] Its official name was the *majlis al-wukala*. Its functions were similar, but not identical to those of a cabinet of ministers. It included the head of the cabinet (the viceroy), the minister of foreign affairs, the minister of finance, the minister of interior and the members of the advisory council. The ministry of interior consisted of the departments of health, education, communications (post, telegraph, telephone and radio), judicial affairs, military affairs, *waqfs* and the Kaaba, municipalities, water resources, quarantine, the coastguard and the general police.[47]

As early as 1925 a general security board was formed in Mecca, and the general directorate of police emerged. The next innovation was the special morality police, with inspectors and agencies for control over foreigners. The general directorate of security spread its activities to the whole of Saudi Arabia and established branches in all large towns. A police school opened in Mecca in the early 1940s.[48]

Prince Faisal had his own *diwan* in Mecca. It included a special bureau for secret and private correspondence, a bureau for the reception and dispatch of official letters, a bureau of the permanent committee of the *majlis al-wukala*, a cavalry department, a department for the procurement of camels for the army and a department of motor transport.[49]

Wazir, the Arabic word for 'minister', was not unknown to the people of Najd but, unlike other Arabs, they used it to denote 'secretary'. Until the 1960s, the ruler of every province had his own *wazir*. The most important rulers had several *wazirs* in charge of financial and other affairs and correspondence. Thus the closest Saudi equivalent to the Western notion of minister was the head of a department of the royal *diwan*, who managed state affairs under the king's supervision.[50]

The general department of health was set up in 1925 and began expanding its authority and functions. Some years later, health departments were formed in all the main provinces.[51] In 1931 the directorate of coastguards was created in Jidda to be in charge of ports, coastal defence, the suppression of smuggling and regulations relating to navigation.[52] In 1926 a municipality was set up in Mecca with its own independent budget. Special regulations were adopted in 1929 and amended in 1938.[53] By 1934 Hijaz was divided into fourteen smaller provinces. The local emirs were subordinate to the ministry of interior and in effect to the viceroy, Prince Faisal.[54] The bedouin were under the control of the provincial administration.[55]

When Ibn Saud issued his decree 'On the merger of the parts of the Arabian kingdom' on 18 September 1932, Saudi Arabia formally became a unitary state under centralized control, but its administrative structure did not change. The fifth article of the decree read:

The present agencies of the government of Hijaz and of Najd and its dependencies shall preserve their current status temporarily until new agencies are established for the whole kingdom on the basis of the new amalgamation.

The council of ministers of Hijaz was charged to start drafting immediately the fundamental law (constitution) of the kingdom and the law on the organization of government,[56] but this was never done. The differences in administration between Najd and Hijaz persisted for many years and have not yet been eliminated.

The king's entourage

Although the administrative and bureaucratic machinery of Saudi Arabia had become more sophisticated, it was still the king and his close entourage who took the main decisions. Thus the people in attendance on the monarch were the most powerful in the state. According to Philby:

> practically all the men he [Ibn Saud] collected round him . . . to deal with the activities of the various departments on his behalf, remained not only in his service, but roughly speaking in charge of the same departments, to the end of his life . . . It certainly illustrates an important trait in his own character: a sort of mild xenophobia, whose symptoms were a lack of enthusiasm for strange society, easily disguised of course by his lavish hospitality and genuine friendliness, and a curious preference for having round him at all times, day in and day out, year in and year out, the same people, always the same people, whether members of the family, or officials, or boon-companions, or servants. It was only in their company that he could relax . . . These people he could trust because he knew them intimately, their virtues and their faults; and these people he bound to himself and his service with a boundless generosity, ever increasing with the augmentation of his resources.[57]

The head of the financial agency, Abdallah al-Sulaiman, only resigned after King Ibn Saud's death to be replaced by Muhammad Surur al-Sabban. Abdallah al-Sulaiman's personality and activities are worth describing in some detail. Born in Anaiza (Qasim) in 1887, he had visited India and lived in Bahrain and other Gulf countries before settling in Riyadh, where his brother served at Ibn Saud's *diwan*. When this brother fell ill, Abdallah replaced him. Ibn Saud liked him for his good handwriting, intelligence, active nature and resourcefulness. The emir of Riyadh made him responsible first for the silver coins fund and then for the gold coins spent on his court and guests.

Abdallah al-Sulaiman's functions gradually expanded and he was put in charge of managing the subsidy of £5,000 paid to Ibn Saud by the British government until 1924. Ibn Saud made al-Sulaiman the chief manager of the finances. Al-Sulaiman had friends among the merchants who loaned him money 'without interest', since interest was considered usurious profit by Islam. The loans were used to purchase goods for the court 'on instalments' at inflated prices.[58] Turakulov, the Soviet consul-general in

The Socio-political Structure of Saudi Arabia after its Creation

Jidda, reported back in 1929, 'Abdallah al-Sulaiman plays the decisive role in the economic problems of Hijaz and government supplies.' He noted that al-Sulaiman concluded contracts through figureheads.[59]

While Ibn Saud emptied the exchequer, it was Abdallah al-Sulaiman's duty to replenish it. When the Arabic equivalent of 'minister' – *wazir* – came to be used in Najd in the early 1930s, it implied Abdallah al-Sulaiman, since Faisal, the minister of foreign affairs, had a different title and was never referred to as His Excellency as al-Sulaiman was. The minister of finance had his own entourage and his own 'companions' – some 400 officials, slaves and guards, maintained at his expense. He owned palaces and land.[60]

The king seldom received people in private, but al-Sulaiman had access to the king's bedroom after the general council meeting, when he put his requests to the monarch. All coded messages from the royal *diwan* were in triplicate: one for Crown Prince Saud, one for Prince Faisal and one for al-Sulaiman. The minister of finance had an influence over the armed forces, since it was he who allocated funds for salaries and financed arms purchases. His critics claimed that he had become the uncrowned king of Saudi Arabia. After retiring in 1954, he became the owner of a chain of hotels and trading companies.[61]

Among Ibn Saud's advisers was an Iraqi from Mosul called Abdallah al-Damluji, who had come to Ibn Saud in 1915 as a physician and medical expert. Thanks to a slight knowledge of French, he was made responsible for receiving foreign guests at the court in Riyadh. After the conquest of Hijaz, he was appointed the king's personal representative in Jidda. He then became deputy minister of foreign affairs, a post he held until 1930. He was succeeded by Fuad Hamza, a Palestinian refugee, who worked in the ministry of foreign affairs until his death. During the Second World War, Fuad Hamza represented Saudi Arabia in Vichy and then in Ankara and tried to arrange a correspondence between Hitler and Ibn Saud.

As mentioned previously, Ibn Saud's team included Hafiz Wahba and Yusuf Yasin. Wahba had previously been sent into exile on Malta by the British for his involvement with the 1919 revolt in Egypt. He became director of the education department, then Saudi envoy to the Vatican and finally ambassador to London.[62] Yusuf Yasin, who was from Latakia (Syria), came to Arabia in 1924 and found favour with Ibn Saud. He was the king's political secretary before being made minister of state. He was responsible for the correspondence with Saudi representatives abroad.[63]

In the initial period of his rule, Ibn Saud refrained from appointing his sons and relatives to high administrative posts, with the exception of his eldest sons Saud and Faisal, who became viceroys of Najd and Hijaz respectively. (Ibn Saud might have remembered the fate of his grandfather Faisal ibn Turki's state, destroyed by his sons' rivalry.) Over time, however, that practice changed and members of the royal family came to occupy key positions in the state machinery.

Introduction of the sharia and the Wahhabi legal system

As we have seen, the dominant ideology of Saudi Arabia was the Wahhabi interpretation of Islam. One god, one ruler and one official school of theology (Hanbalism) implied one legal and judicial system. However, it was not an easy task in the fragmented society of Saudi Arabia, with its different social groups (for example, settled and nomadic people), who had been subject to different legal systems for centuries. The solution frequently required compromises.

By the early twentieth century, the nomadic tribes had forgotten the *sharia* that the Wahhabis had tried to introduce in the eighteenth and early nineteenth centuries, and returned to *urf* or *adat* (customary law).[64] The legal practice differed in the various tribes. Al-Zirikli notes that the bedouin had a judicial system of their own, with the rough equivalents of courts of first instance, appeal and cassation.[65] Tribal *urf* was based on precedent; in some tribes, for example among the Rwala, the precedent had to be at least five years old.[66] Sometimes court sentences were proclaimed in verse or rhyming phrases, reminiscent of the practice among the *arifs* (experts in customary law), the successors to the pre-Islamic soothsayers.[67]

Naturally, the two legal systems collided after the emergence of the centralized feudal state, which applied the *sharia* and had a machinery for enforcing court decisions. For example, *urf* allowed asylum to be granted to persecuted persons under certain conditions, whereas the centralized state did not recognize the right of asylum. The bedouin criminalized some deeds, such as plunder or murder, when they were committed against their own tribesmen, but considered them a manifestation of heroism and valour when the victims belonged to other tribes. This contradicted the needs and policy of the state. Another legal problem was what should happen to property and livestock captured during raids.[68] Lastly, many problems stemmed from blood feuds, which the government always tried to suppress.[69]

Practical steps to restrict the *arifs'* influence began around 1914, when *mutawwas* and *qadhis* were sent to the tribes. The *arifs'* prerogatives were reduced, but attempts were not made to replace them entirely by *qadhis* in the early years. The *urf* and *sharia* courts acted in parallel among the tribes on the temporary basis of a delimitation of their respective functions. The *arifs* followed *urf* in the cases within their jurisdiction in the narrow sense, such as intertribal relations, whereas such questions as inheritance were resolved by the *qadhis* according to the *sharia*.[70] It should be noted that the Ikhwan movement accelerated the replacement of *arifs* by *qadhis*.

Saudi governors preferred not to intervene in internal affairs. All thirty-six decisions of the administrative court quoted in *The Memorial of the Government of Saudi Arabia*, for example, dealt with intertribal relations and the restitution of seized property and livestock.[71] Gradually, the governors' and *qadhis'* judicial functions were delimited. The judges examined mutual personal claims, commercial disputes, and questions of religion, family law and inheritance. The emirs' jurisdiction comprised intertribal conflicts, taxation, conscription and administrative problems.[72] But according to the *sharia*, emirs were entitled to examine lawsuits outside the military, administrative and financial spheres.

The Socio-political Structure of Saudi Arabia after its Creation

The struggle to establish the *sharia* in its Hanbali form as a counterbalance to tribal *urf* was not the only obstacle to the development of a uniform legal and judicial system in the country. After the creation of Saudi Arabia, Hanbalism dominated in Najd, Shafiism in Hijaz and Hanafism in the towns which had been under the Ottoman authorities.[73] The Turks used to appoint four *qadhis* from the four orthodox schools of Islam, though the Hanafis were given priority. Vidal notes that the Hanafi legal school survived for decades in the former Ottoman administrative centres of al-Hasa, such as Hufuf.[74]

After the annexation of al-Hasa, the central government was faced with the problem of the Shia minority. There are no reliable data on their number in the early twentieth century, but Vidal notes that there were 130,000 Shia in al-Hasa in 1955.[75] Wahba estimates the settled population of al-Hasa in the 1930s at 90,000, of whom 60,000 were Shia.[76] This is not incompatible with Vidal's figures, which might have included semi-nomads. Besides, the population of the Eastern Province grew rapidly after the discovery of oil. According to Vidal, the percentage of Shia in the oases of al-Hasa was 40–45%.[77] Taking into consideration the fact that many Shia concealed their religious affiliation, their number in the Eastern Province might be greater than the experts supposed.

According to Harrison, the Sunnis (who were Wahhabis) formed a minority in al-Hasa and included the rulers, merchants and landlords. The majority, including pearl-divers, craftsmen and peasants, were Shia.[78] Vidal also notes that most craftsmen were Shia.[79] Thus there were serious social contradictions within the province, but under a religious guise.

Small groups of Shia also lived in Mecca and Medina. The Zaidis, a branch of Shiism, were concentrated in Asir. There were also members of various Sufi orders – Sanusis, Idrisis, Qadiris and Bektashis – in Hijaz. These orders underwent a decline under the pressure of Wahhabism, which rejected Sufism in principle.[80]

The position of the Shia in the state of 'purified', 'genuine' Islam was problematic. In 1927 the Wahhabi *ulama* issued a *fatwa*, under pressure from the Ikhwan, requesting Ibn Saud to prohibit the Shia from praying in public, from observing the anniversaries of the Prophet's and his relatives' deaths and from performing pilgrimages to Karbala and al-Najaf; and to make them attend the mosque five times a day. The *ulama*'s opinion was that the Shia should study 'Allah's true religion' from Muhammad ibn Abd al-Wahhab's *Three Principles*.[81] The *fatwa* called on the faithful to destroy all Shia places of worship.[82] These demands seemed too extreme to the king and were not accepted. But the Wahhabis considered the Shia of the Eastern Province as infidels and treated them as *dhimmis*.[83]

During 1926 and 1927 a uniform judicial system was introduced into the country by the king's ordinances; the courts were supposed to examine cases by following the canons of the Hanbali school of law. Accordingly, it was laid down that court decisions should be based on six treatises by Hanbali theologians, written in the first centuries of the Islamic era: *Persuasion* by Musa al-Jamawi, *The Interpretation of the Text of the Code of Persuasion* by Mansur al-Bahuti al-Hanbali, *The Limit of Desire* by al-Fatawhi,

A Commentary on the Limit of Desire by Mansur al-Bahuti, *The Detailed Commentary* by Abd al-Rahman ibn Quddam and the *al-Mufti* by Shams al-Din ibn Ahmad ibn Quddam. In 1928 *The Guidance for Those Who Seek Fulfilment of Desire* by Mari ibn Yusuf al-Karmi al-Maqdisi al-Hanbali was added to the list: it was an abridged version of *The Limit of the Limited* by the same author.[84] The introduction of the Hanbali school of law seems to have faced difficulties in Hijaz, Asir and al-Hasa. Thus the application of Hanbalism in judicial practice might have been less rigid than was prescribed by the royal ordinances. The judicial reform did not greatly affect the situation in Najd, and separate courts for the bedouin and the settled people were established only in Riyadh and other large towns.[85]

After the reorganization of the judicial system in 1927, three kinds of courts functioned in Hijaz.[86] *Al-mahakim al-mustajala*, courts presided over by one judge for the examination of urgent cases, dealt with lawsuits where sums of up to £30 were claimed and with those petty offences and crimes that did not involve the amputation of a hand or capital punishment. Subhi al-Muhammasani, an Arab jurist, sees this as a return to the classical form of the *sharia*, because civil and criminal cases had previously been examined by different courts.[87]

Al-mahakim al-kubra, the high courts, consisted of *qadhis* and their assistants. They examined cases beyond the competence of the *al-mahakim al-mustajala*, including serious crimes for which the amputation of a hand or capital punishment might be stipulated. Sentences for crimes of that sort were passed collectively.

The *hayat al-muraqaba al-qadhaiya*, the judicial supervisory collegium in Mecca, played the role of a court of appeal. It consisted of the *mudir* (director) and four members. The director supervised all the activities of the Hijazi courts and judges and acted as a mediator between the government and the judges. A sentence might be appealed against within twenty days (ten days, according to other data) from the date it was passed but it would come into effect if the collegium rejected the appeal.[88] If an appeal was approved, the collegium returned the case for re-examination to the same court. According to al-Zirikli, the structure of the *hayat al-muraqaba al-qadhaiya* became increasingly sophisticated and the number of appeals it examined rose.[89]

There were two 'urgent courts', one high court and the *hayat al-muraqaba al-qadhaiya* in Mecca, one 'urgent court' and one high court in Medina and one 'urgent court' in Jidda.[90] In 1932 an 'urgent court' for cases involving the bedouin was set up in Mecca.[91] Mecca's international character meant that the four orthodox legal schools continued to exist, though the Hanbali school naturally dominated in judicial practice.[92]

In the Eastern Province a judge's decision might be appealed against (with the emir's approval) at the council of judges; the grand mufti took the final decision. The judges received salaries from the *zakat* funds. Claimants paid *khidma* (legal costs) in favour of the exchequer.[93]

In 1927 the first notary offices were opened in Hijaz for the registration of legal instruments other than those concerning *waqfs*.[94] As early as 1926, before the judicial reform, a commercial court was set up in Jidda. It consisted of six members with business experience. Its competence embraced litigation between merchants, shroffs, brokers and warehouse owners; issues arising from currency exchange and the payment of commercial bills through banks; disputes between merchants and ship-owners concerning cargo loss, collisions between vessels and attacks on them; and arguments over contracts and price agreements. Later, the court followed the *nizam al-tijara*, the commercial code of 1931, which covered those questions not dealt with by the traditional *sharia* and was based on the commercial code of the Ottoman empire.[95]

Among the tasks of the Arabian *sharia* courts of the 1920s and 1930s was the attempt to abolish blood feuds by introducing *diya* (blood money) and compelling the victims and their heirs to accept it. Its amount varied, depending on the gravity of the injury sustained.[96] The purpose of the measure was the same as in the time of the first Saudi state – to calm intertribal conflicts and reduce the pretexts for intertribal wars. After the court sentence was proclaimed, the victim or his heirs were required to state that they forgave the guilty party.[97] However, the most noble clans, including the Al Saud themselves, still rejected *diya* and held that blood may be washed off only by blood.

As for the amputation of a hand in the case of theft, it should be noted that extreme punishments of that kind were applied far less frequently than some foreigners might believe, because of a series of restrictions. A hand could be amputated only if the occurrence of the theft was established beyond doubt and if the culprit was an adult and sane and had acted of his own free will. The object of the crime should be precious; water, wine, pictures, musical instruments and legal books were not included in that category. The stolen article should have been stolen from a place where it was usually kept under lock and key. If one thief broke the lock and the other took the article, neither of them was liable to have a hand amputated. Nor did the theft of a close relative's property involve that punishment. Two witnesses were required to establish the event of theft. Finally, the amputation of a hand was not applied in years of famine and price rises.[98]

Adultery was considered by the *sharia* as a crime against the family and public morality; both partners would be stoned to death if found guilty.[99] The consumption of alcohol was usually punished by whipping.[100] A whole system of severe punishments was applied to caravan robbers.[101]

Revenues and expenditure

Successful military campaigns replenished the exchequer with a fifth of the spoils. Unlike the first Saudi state, however, the emirate of Najd and then the united kingdom of Hijaz and Najd and its dependencies existed for many years without large-scale raids. Hostilities had become expensive and their success did not invariably bring in money. Thus the state exchequer depended increasingly on the regular collection of taxes, of which *zakat* was the most important. While prayer was considered an act involving a relationship between Allah and the individual believer, *zakat* was treated in the official ideology of Saudi Arabia as evidence of submission to the rulers who enforced the laws of the Most High.¹⁰² The payment of *zakat* was thus both the carrying out of a religious duty and an outer sign of loyalty to the ruler who watches over the observance of Allah's law.

In September 1925 Ibn Saud issued a decree on the taxation system. It prescribed that *zakat* paid in kind should be taken from among livestock of average quality, and that *zakat* paid in cash should be based on the average price of livestock.¹⁰³ It was further explained that animals bred for military purposes or carriage and those fed on specially gathered grass were not liable to taxation. For taxation purposes, the minimum number of camels was 5, sheep 40 and cattle 30.¹⁰⁴ *Zakat* was to be paid on all cereals and on all fruit that could be measured and preserved, such as dates and raisins, together with almonds, pistachios and other nuts. Other fruit and vegetables were exempt from taxation. The rate of *zakat* was 5% on crops grown on irrigated land and 10% on those grown on non-irrigated land. Silver was taxed at 2.5% of its price and gold at 2.5 or 5%, depending on the amount. Trade capital and its growth were taxed at 2.5%.¹⁰⁵

The provincial emirs were in charge of the collection of *zakat*.¹⁰⁶ Under Ibn Saud, *zakat*-collectors were divided into two main categories – those who were sent to oases and towns and those who visited the bedouin. The former were paid a commission out of the total sum collected and the latter received a fixed salary. Formally, *zakat* was to be collected at the end of every year; in practice, because of date shifts in the Islamic calendar, it was collected during a particular (changing) season. In the Eastern Province it was collected in spring or summer. The collectors knew the routes of the tribes' migrations and the places they set up their camps.¹⁰⁷ At the height of the Ikhwan movement, the *mutawwas* collected *zakat* in the *hijras*.¹⁰⁸ In that duty they represented the imam–emir. Sometimes the members of the Al al-Shaikh family oversaw the tax-collectors.¹⁰⁹

The tax-collectors were considered the government's supervisors among the bedouin and supported its authority, but they often abused their position and Ibn Saud once confessed to Philby that, in his opinion, only a third of the tax collected ever reached the exchequer.¹¹⁰ The people of Arabia had paid *zakat* before the restoration of the Al Saud. But, for example, the Rashidis, the rulers of Hail, exempted forty to eighty people from each tribe from the payment of *zakat*, in return for an obligation to come with arms at the first request.¹¹¹ According to Dickson, the Al Sabah family also collected *zakat* in Kuwait.¹¹² *Khuwa*, the tribute paid by the weaker tribes to the stronger, was abolished in the emirate of Riyadh, as it had been in the first Saudi state. Dickson notes, however, that this payment persisted in other forms.¹¹³

It was a controversial question as to whether the tribes' payment of *zakat* amounted to recognition of the Riyadh government's suzerainty and thus of the Saudi state's sovereignty over their territories. The issue acquired practical significance in the border conflicts with Iraq and then in the al-Buraimi conflict. Although the Riyadh *qadhis* answered the question in the affirmative, there were varying interpretations among the different schools of Islamic thought and among those Europeans with a knowledge of Arabia.

Dickson, the British resident in Kuwait and an expert on Arabian affairs, was of the

The Socio-political Structure of Saudi Arabia after its Creation

opinion that when the head of state was at war, he might mobilize everybody who paid him *zakat*. If the payer of *zakat* did not obey, the ruler might confiscate his livestock. According to the Wahhabi practice, if tribesmen were reluctant or unable to pay *zakat* to their legitimate ruler, he had the right: (a) to confiscate the tribe's property; (b) to deny responsibility for protecting them from other tribes he ruled; and (c) to deny them support in the event of an attack from outside. If, on the contrary, the tribesmen paid *zakat* in full, the ruler or head of state must protect them from all attacks. The head of state should not impose *zakat* on those foreign tribes who only came to his state for grazing and left it after a short period, since they paid *zakat* to their legitimate rulers. Dickson asserts that this old and well-established law was known to everyone in Arabia.[114] According to *The Memorial of the Government of Saudi Arabia*, Dickson's opinion characterized the political aspects of *zakat* collection in the period from the eighteenth century.[115]

After the conquest of the Eastern Province, the rate of customs duty was established at 8%, though Philby mentions that the tax on tobacco was levied at 20%.[116] A certain Muhammad Efendi, who had served for 30 years under the Turkish administration and preferred to stay in Ibn Saud's service, was responsible for all taxation affairs in al-Hasa. He had an excellent knowledge of the province's financial system. A special tax, the *jizya*, was imposed on the Shia, Christians and Jews in al-Hasa.[117] After the conquest of Hijaz, the tax on pilgrims brought huge revenues to the state exchequer. But the total amount of taxes in 1927 (£1.5 million) demonstrates the state's poor financial condition.[118]

In 1929 an attempt was made to draw up a budget for Saudi Arabia. The first budget appeared only in 1934: it was the first time that individual state agencies had drafted their expenditure and submitted their suggestions to the ministry of finance. The summary of requirements was submitted to the *majlis al-shura* and thereafter to the *majlis al-wukala*. In practice, the budget was not adhered to, but what should be noted is its very small size: expenditure was 14 million rials (£1.75 million) and revenues were close to the same figure.[119] Al-Zirikli had the opportunity to read a report by the Egyptian ministry of foreign affairs on the Saudi state's revenues in the late 1930s. The main source of revenue was the pilgrimage tax, followed by concession payments by the oil companies, proceeds from the gold mines and *zakat*. The total annual budget did not exceed 2 million Egyptian pounds (equivalent to little more than £2 million at that time).[120]

All tax proceeds went to the *bait al-mal*, the state exchequer. The main item of expenditure was defence, including the payment of grants to soldiers' widows and children, to the wounded and to the sick. Other expenses paid out from the *bait al-mal* included salaries for officials and the *ulama*, youth training and schools.[121] Hafiz Wahba notes that:

> the shaikhs sincerely thought that they were entitled to lay hands on the state exchequer. [The emir of Riyadh] spent the revenue for his own needs. He presented gifts to those who came to meet him. In those years it was not deemed necessary to spend on schools, health protection or municipalities out of the exchequer.[122]

A whole army of the poor lived in Riyadh at the king's expense. Between 1,000 and 2,000 people received 2 meals a day from the royal kitchen. Almost 100 families of honoured prisoners were kept in the capital. Ibn Saud maintained their houses, stables, camels and slaves and paid for their food and clothes.[123] According to Hafiz Wahba, the number of the king's permanent guests was 500 and it sometimes reached 10,000.[124]

Many bedouin travelled hundreds of kilometres to receive a royal gift. It is important to note that the distribution of gifts was seen as the ruler's duty. Every Arab, especially a nomad, who received a gift from Ibn Saud – whether it was lavish or not, whether it was in cash, clothes or food – held that he was entitled to receive a similar gift each year or every time he visited the court. If he was given a rial less or worse clothes or food than he had received previously, he would protest. If he was denied a gift altogether, he felt insulted and might even join Ibn Saud's enemies.[125]

As in the time of the first Saudi state, Ibn Saud used hospitality as a means of redistributing the revenue among the Arabian nobility, since ordinary nomads could not visit the royal court regularly. The ruler's 'guests' under surveillance were disgraced tribal shaikhs and emirs from oases and other areas. Food and small gifts for the poor bolstered the king's reputation as a generous, hospitable and 'democratic' shaikh, accessible to all his subjects, 'the father of the nation'.

The armed forces

By the early 1930s, the Saudi army had undergone certain changes. In the first years of the emirate, however, the ruler's troops were still recruited in the same manner as under his ancestors. According to Sulaiman al-Dakhil, writing in 1913:

> Not only disabled, old and sick people, but also those engaged in farming were exempted from military campaigns. If there were two brothers in a family, one went to fight and the other stayed at home to manage the household. During the wars the emir did not give his troops food or equipment, since everybody came with food, arms and equipment of his own. However, if a campaign became long, the ruler supplied them with horses or harnesses and arms, as well as food . . . As for the bedouin tribes, they also obey the emir's orders. He writes letters to their shaikhs, fixing the place at which they must gather. He finds them there at the appointed day and hour. That is how wars and raids are prepared in the emirate in AH 1331. It does not differ from the practice of earlier centuries. Nothing has changed within recent days and years, because they find it the best manner.[126]

According to *Umm al-Qura*:

> Every man in Najd is a warrior by nature. He has carried arms since childhood and is trained in handling them. When he is called to a campaign, he takes his rifle, rides his camel and goes to the war. Any Najdi aged 13 to 70 is considered fit for military

service. When the king wants to mobilize his army in full or in part, he sends orders to all or some areas. Then he sends instructions – sometimes secret ones – to the emirs, fixing the assembly place. They follow his instructions. There are no military barracks in Najd, because the whole of Najd is a barracks and all men are servicemen.[127]

According to *The Arabia of Ibn Saud*, the Najdi armed forces were divided into four categories: the people of al-Arid; the urban population; the Ikhwan; and the bedouin.[128] The people of al-Arid included the royal guard (bodyguards) and the guards of the princes of royal blood, who did not leave their arms even while sleeping; government officials (except foreigners), who were mobilized in emergencies; and armed '*jihad* warriors'. The royal guards were also considered '*jihad* warriors' and were distinguished from the others by their permanent service with the king or one of the princes. A special department of *jihad* at the royal palace was responsible for the warriors' armaments and allowances.

The category of urban dwellers included the males of the Najdi oases and towns. They formed the flanks in battle, while the people of al-Arid fought in the centre. There were four degrees of readiness for mobilization:

1. During the long peaceful periods, when there was no threat of war, every village sent a certain number of men with equipment and food for four months in a year. If there was no need to do so, the village paid the equivalent of the expenses for the men's maintenance to the state exchequer.
2. During minor military campaigns, every village sent a certain number of men with their own food. The exchequer provided them with arms and military equipment and, if they remained in service for more than four months, supplied them with food for the rest of the period.
3. To wage prolonged or hard campaigns, minor *jihad* was proclaimed and all villages doubled the quota of men they usually sent to take part in hostilities.
4. In an emergency, when the state faced a serious threat, the emir called up everybody who was able to carry arms.

Unlike the urban population, all the inhabitants of Ikhwan *hijras* who were able to carry arms took part in hostilities. Bedouin were used in the Riyadh troops chiefly as scouts and flying columns. Each detachment had its own flag (different from the commander's flag, which was usually hoisted in the centre) and its own war cry in order to recognize each other, besides the common Saudi war cry.

The royal guard and the '*jihad* warriors' enjoyed certain privileges: they were better supplied and armed and were given the best mounts from the royal horses. Those who were entered on the register of the department of the royal court were paid a salary, while the rest received casual grants and subsidies.[129] The king had a detachment of specially selected bodyguards. His loyal slave, armed with a rifle, a pistol and a dagger, always followed him like a shadow and stood behind the king at the *majlis* meetings.

At the mosque the slave never prayed with others, but kept watch, a practice that was introduced after the murder of Imam Abd al-Aziz I in the mosque in 1803.[130]

Naturally, the true organization of the troops was not as orderly as is described in *The Arabia of Ibn Saud*. It is sufficient to recall the military campaigns of the various rulers of Riyadh and the mixed composition of their troops, with an alternating preponderance of settled people, Ikhwan and bedouin. But undoubtedly, al-Arid and the neighbouring provinces were the basis of Ibn Saud's armed forces, a permanent source of reliable fighters. Later, most officers of the regular army came from that area. According to *Umm al-Qura*:

> At the beginning of his rule, King Abd al-Aziz relied on the '*jihad* army'. It consisted of the settled people of Najd. Besides, there was an Ikhwan army of bedouin nomadic tribes, settled in *hijras*, which became somewhat like military barracks. It continued until 1930, when the king deemed it necessary to develop the armed forces and ordered a department of military affairs to be set up. The nucleus of a regular army came into being.[131]

The idea of creating a regular army had occurred to Ibn Saud earlier than this. He had seen units from British India in Iraq during the First World War and had fought against Turkish regular units before that. The advantages of a disciplined and trained modern army were obvious to him. After the capitulation of Jidda, the king invited all officers of the Hashemite army to join the Meccan police, from whose ranks the first regular units were subsequently set up. Syrian and Iraqi officers were employed to serve in the directorate of military affairs.[132]

In 1930 three regiments – infantry, machine-gun and artillery – paraded in Jidda for the first time. They formed the nucleus of the regular army. It was divided into brigades and battalions and distributed among five military districts. A uniform and badges of rank were introduced and a military academy was opened in al-Taif. In 1935 the *wikala* (virtually, ministry) of defence, based in al-Taif, and the directorate of military affairs were founded. In 1938 the directorate was abolished and the following year the general staff was formed. In 1946 the ministry of defence was created, headed by Prince Mansur ibn Abd al-Aziz.[133]

The importance of military and civil aviation was obvious in a country with a sparse population and a wide geographic area. In 1931 ten young Saudis were sent to Italy to study aeronautics. When they returned, the king bought several planes. During the war the king purchased five Dakotas in the US and then nine more. The first air routes appeared within Saudi Arabia and flights began to Egypt, Syria and Lebanon. A school for pilots was opened in al-Taif.[134]

The king was quick to understand the importance of radio in hostilities, communications and the maintenance of law and order. Schools for radio operators were opened in Mecca, Jidda, Medina and Riyadh. After completing their course, the students were sent to Britain and other countries to continue their training. During Ibn Saud's rule sixty permanent radio stations and three main radio centres (in Jidda, Riyadh and

Dhahran) were set up in the kingdom.[135]

It is important to note that the Saudi regular army coexisted with the '*jihad* army' and then with the 'white army', formed of the 'noble' bedouin tribes who were loyal to the king. This particular structure of the armed forces was dictated by the character and level of development of Arabian society and at the same time lessened the danger of a military coup.

Secular and religious education

With the collapse of the Saudi state in central Arabia in the late nineteenth century, even traditional Islamic education fell into decay. Most private collections of books were moved from Riyadh to Qasim and Hail, few people went to study outside the country and there were no schools at all in central Arabia. In some towns, private education circles were run by mosques. Some people who were literate earned their living by teaching pupils at home.[136]

Soon after Abdallah Al al-Shaikh returned to the capital, a religious school opened there,[137] and many eminent *ulama* set up schools in their homes.[138] Naturally, most attention was paid to learning the Quran by heart and then to studying the Hanbali legal system as the qualification for becoming a *qadhi*.[139] The *majlises* with the participation of the emir of Riyadh included readings of the *hadiths* and a *History of the Arabs* by Tabari.[140]

Wahba notes that few emirs from central Arabia paid any attention to their sons' education. Some of them considered it beneath their dignity.[141] These views changed with the development of the Ikhwan movement, when reading the Quran was encouraged from above and spread by the Ikhwan themselves. Schools opened both in towns and in *hijras*.

With their conquest of Hijaz, the Najdis found a far more developed education system. Few people in central Arabia were literate, whereas in Hijaz a newspaper was published and some schools on the Turkish model functioned, not to mention the existence of several large private libraries. In the late nineteenth century, the *al-Hijaz* newspaper began publication in Arabic and Turkish. Two papers called *Shams al-Haqiqa* and *al-Islah* also existed for some months. Mecca had a private press,[142] one (Turkish-language) state school and two private theological schools.[143] After the Young Turk revolution of 1908, two private schools opened in Jidda and Mecca.[144]

When Sharif Husain established his independent power, Hijaz experienced a limited renaissance in the field of education. There were two types of schools under the Hashemite government – *amiri* (state-run) and *ahli* (private). There was even a military college and also a type of agricultural college. Most schools were located in Mecca.[145] *Al-Qibla* newspaper, which was published from 1915 to 1924, devoted particular attention to Husain's efforts in the educational sphere. The students of the agricultural college issued their own magazine for a period.[146] In the last months of King Ali's rule, a paper named *Barid al-Hijaz* appeared in Jidda.[147]

Ibn Saud was impressed by the education system of Hijaz and in 1926 he founded the directorate of education, which began inviting foreign teachers to the country. In the same year, 12 state and private schools opened in Riyadh and the adjacent regions. Their budget increased from some £6,000 in 1928/29 to £23,000 in 1929/30. In the 1930s new schools were founded in Riyadh and the large towns of Hijaz and then in Hail, Buraida, Anaiza, al-Qatif and al-Jubail.[148]

Even in 1950, religious studies accounted for 22 out of 28 lessons per week in the primary schools (i.e. 79%). In the last year of study in secular secondary schools, their share was 25%.[149] Such subjects as geography, technical drawing and foreign languages were included in the school curriculum with Ibn Saud's support and in spite of the *ulama*'s resistance.[150] But the *ulama* exerted a rigid control over the directorate of education and they controlled education in the schools since they appointed the teachers and *mutawwas*. As a rule, the presses in Mecca printed only religious literature. Semi-legal Shia schools were set up in the Eastern Province, paid for by the Shia communities. They existed in parallel to the state schools and have survived up to the present day.[151]

In December 1924 the semi-official *Umm al-Qura* weekly started publication in Mecca as the main source of the government's official statements. It also carried information about the king's journeys and the texts of his speeches and of the treaties and agreements concluded with foreign countries. Literary issues were also discussed. Over time, however, the size of the paper was reduced and its content was confined to official reports and information. The *Sawt al-Hijaz* weekly appeared in Mecca between 1932 and 1939 and was succeeded by *al-Bilad al-Saudiya*, which became the country's chief weekly publication in 1953. *Al-Madina al-Munawwara* was started in Medina in 1938. Several irregular periodicals were published in Mecca. As for Najd, the first weekly, named *al-Yamama*, was issued in Riyadh in 1953. The Saudi press had no real influence on the creation of public opinion or on developments in the country, however.[152]

We have no reliable data on the Saudi education system up to the early 1950s. According to al-Zirikli, there were about 50 rural schools with 2,000 pupils, 90 primary schools with 13,000 pupils and 10 secondary schools with 600 pupils in the kingdom in 1950. Thus the total number of pupils was 15,600.[153] Philby reported that, just two years later, there were more than 55,000 schoolchildren in the country.[154] He claimed that 705 Saudi students were sent abroad as early as 1935.[155] Al-Zirikli reported (without specifying the education level) that 192 Saudi students were sent to Egypt in 1950 and 19 to the US in 1951.[156] His figures seem more reliable, since Philby was often inclined to exaggerate in his descriptions of Saudi Arabia.

A certain modernization of the political/state structure of Saudi Arabia – as evidenced by the creation of a regular army, the introduction of elements of a modern education system, the setting up of ministries and the approval of the 'constitution' of Hijaz – was not dictated by the character of Arabian society or its level of development, but reflected the influence of the outside world. In analysing Ibn Saud's reforms, we come to the inevitable conclusion that his striving to organize the state and government system in accordance with the ideals of the first centuries of Islam was more in line with the kingdom's level of development than were the 'innovations' borrowed from 'polytheists' and 'infidels'. The Arabian peninsula had a different sense of time from that in more developed Middle Eastern countries. However, both Ibn Saud himself as an early feudal ruler, and the doctrines of the 'purified, genuine Islam' which appeared in Arabia, were many centuries too late for the region as a whole. Even without the subsequent oil boom and influx of petrodollars, which undermined the earlier social structure, Saudi society could not have withstood the new ideas that were destroying the traditional system. The best recent example of this kind is the fate of Yemen in the 1960s. The traditional social structures have been unable to survive in the modern, interconnected world under pressure from outside, experienced through market relations, the penetration of new ideas and attempts to change at least a part of the society (e.g. the armed forces) in order to ward off an outside threat.

Saudi Arabia was strongly influenced from outside. A combination of geographic, geological and historical factors was to turn it into a major oil producer. The oil-extraction industry itself, with its various related branches, and, in particular, the huge revenues from oil exports in the hands of the political elite, all put pressure on the traditional social structures. As we shall see, these structures inevitably underwent various transformations or, in some cases, disappeared altogether.

Chapter 14

The Oil Concessions

The *hajj* was the main source of the kingdom's revenue, and, as we have seen, the sharp reduction in the number of pilgrims due to the world economic crisis of 1929–33 had left the Saudi finances in a desperate situation. Having built the first radio stations, improved Jidda's water supply and purchased several motor cars, the government's indebtedness stood somewhere between £300,000 and £400,000. Payments to creditors ceased and requests for loans were refused.[1]

Taking advantage of his personal relationship with the king, Philby persuaded him to meet Charles Crane, an American millionaire who was travelling in the Arab world, supposedly on a philanthropic mission. In fact, he was probably connected with the American oil companies and was sounding out the opportunities for their penetration into this unknown region. Crane was accompanied by George Antonius, the future author of *The Arab Awakening*, who acted as interpreter. Crane had sent the geologist Karl S. Twitchell to Saudi Arabia, allegedly to prospect for water.[2] In the spring of 1932 Twitchell found a geological structure indicating the presence of oil in the area of Dhahran and returned to the US to inform the oil companies of his findings.[3]

A new era was approaching in the history of Saudi Arabia. It was to exert an influence on its society as profound as that of Islam. But the motive forces behind the changes lay outside Arabia and were caused by the global switch of the twentieth-century economy to a new source of power – oil.

American companies in the Middle East in the 1920s

Before 1920 American companies had either been indifferent to oil deposits abroad or

The Oil Concessions

had failed to receive concessions in the Eastern hemisphere because of the restrictive national and colonial policies of the European powers and the private oil companies. From 1920, however, they started to take an active interest, prompted by worries of two kinds – the prospect of an oil shortage in the US and the threat of a British-Dutch monopoly over the world's oil resources. The main reason was the fear of being debarred from the exploitation of cheap oil deposits, located close to the major international markets.[4]

In 1920 W. Fairish, later the president of the Standard Oil Company of New Jersey, stated that the oil deposits in Texas and Oklahoma were running out. In the same year White, the chief American geological expert, predicted that the country's oil resources would be depleted within eighteen years. The US navy was also worried because experts claimed that the US would either have to curtail oil consumption or import oil from overseas. Senator Henry Cabot Lodge warned Congress that Britain was gaining control over the world's oil supplies.[5]

It is not known whether the American companies really supposed that US oil resources were close to depletion or if it was a pretext for the US administration to become more actively involved in their expansion abroad. In the present author's opinion, the latter reason is more probable. The largest US companies joined the struggle for concessions in Central and South America and the Middle East in the early 1920s. They claimed that, with 12% of the world's oil deposits, the US produced more than half of the world's industrial output, but oil sources outside the US were controlled by British-Dutch monopolies.[6]

The US companies were afraid of missing out on their share of Middle East oil. The administration drafted a policy of support for the US corporations' bids for concessions abroad in order to encourage all government departments and agencies to help them. When the future of the Ottoman empire was discussed at the San Remo conference in April 1920, London and Paris reached an understanding on the division of Iraqi oil. The US government intervened, asking for American companies to be included in the pool. The US objected to anti-American 'discrimination' in commercial activities in the territory of Germany and its former allies and insisted on an open-door policy.

When Atatürk's government tried to challenge the annexation of Mosul to Iraq, the US found an opportunity to blackmail its allies, threatening that it would support Turkey's claims. As a result, an understanding was reached as early as 1921–22 that the US would receive 20–25% of the future oil company's shares. In 1921 the Council of the League of Nations transferred Mosul province to Iraq and the Iraqi government granted a concession to the Turkish Petroleum Company for 75 years. But by 1927, when oil extraction in Mosul had already started, the Americans had not yet received their share. It was not until July 1928 that an understanding was reached that later came to be known as the 'red line agreement'. The Turkish Petroleum Company (renamed the Iraq Petroleum Company, or IPC, in 1929) became the property of the Anglo-Persian Oil Company (later to become the Anglo-Iranian Oil Company and then British Petroleum), the Royal Dutch-Shell group, the Compagnie Française des Pétroles and the Near East Development Corporation, which included the Standard Oil Company of New Jersey (the future Exxon) and SOCONY-Vacuum (the future SOCONY Mobil Oil). Calouste Gulbenkian, the founder of the Turkish Petroleum Company, received 5% of the shares.[7]

US companies penetrated IPC, though as second-rate partners. The 'red line agreement' substantially limited their independent activities, since the participants in IPC pledged themselves to acquire shares in the territory of the former Ottoman empire in the same proportions as in Iraq. It should be recalled that Najd and al-Hasa were formally parts of the Ottoman empire on the eve of the First World War.

The first oil concession in Saudi Arabia

Standard Oil of California (SOCAL) was among the American oil companies which undertook serious oil exploration activities abroad after the First World War. Although it was among the biggest corporations in the US, its efforts were unsuccessful in the 1920s.[8] But personalities can determine the destinies of companies. The future of IPC was connected with Gulbenkian, while the search for oil and oil concessions in the Arabian peninsula was connected with Major Frank Holmes of New Zealand. The tireless major appeared in Bahrain in the early 1920s, allegedly to prospect for water. In 1922 he went to Najd to negotiate with Ibn Saud on behalf of the Eastern and General Syndicate, a British firm. Ibn Saud agreed to grant the syndicate a concession for 30,000 square miles [77,700 sq. km] in al-Hasa. The agreement provided for an annual royalty of £2,000. In 1925 Holmes was granted another concession in Bahrain.[9] Adventurism was not alien to the Eastern and General Syndicate managers. Lacking sufficient capital, they hoped to interest British oil companies in obtaining concessions. They felt sure that they could do without mediators. Failing to find the necessary support, however, Holmes withheld all royalties after paying just £4,000: the concession for a territory with the world's richest oil deposits was terminated in 1928.[10]

The concession in Bahrain, initially granted for two years, survived only because the syndicate won its prolongation. Having failed to interest British oil companies, it contacted the American company, Gulf Oil Corporation. In November 1927 Gulf Oil sent its geologist to explore Bahrain and prepare a geological map. The Americans decided that the game was worth the candle and bought the concession from the syndicate. Gulf Oil was faced with difficulties, however. The company was connected with the Iraq Petroleum Company, still known at the time as Turkish Petroleum. The 'red line agreement' covered Bahrain too. In December 1928 Gulf Oil transferred its rights in the assets of the Eastern and General Syndicate to SOCAL.[11]

The British oil companies' lack of interest in concessions in Bahrain and Arabia is explained by their belief that there was no oil there and their resulting reluctance to take risks. The oil-bearing geological structures in Iran and Iraq differed from those in Bahrain and Arabia. No oil had been found on the island of Keshm near Iran, where the geological structures were similar to those in Arabia. Britain nevertheless opposed the appearance of an American oil company in the Gulf. According to the 1914 agreement, the ruler of Bahrain had pledged himself not to grant concessions in his territory, or to accept any proposal to that effect, without Britain's consent.

One month before the concession was transferred to SOCAL, the British authorities informed the Eastern and General Syndicate that they would 'recommend' that the ruler of Bahrain prolonged the concession only if the syndicate pledged to transfer the concession to a company under British control and management. SOCAL found an easy way to circumvent these formal restrictions: in August 1930 they set up the Bahrain Petroleum Company Ltd and registered it in Canada, thus formally making it a British company. Meanwhile, two representatives of SOCAL – E. Davis, later chairman of the Aramco board, and W. Taylor – undertook preliminary explorations in Bahrain and recommended a trial drilling.[12]

Bahrain's geological structure, indicating the presence of oil, led SOCAL to take an interest in nearby Saudi Arabia. The company did not contact Ibn Saud directly in the spring of 1930, feeling that Holmes might be more successful. But by this time, Holmes was preoccupied with negotiations with the ruler of Kuwait on behalf of Gulf Oil. He promised to visit the king but delayed the meeting, knowing that he had forfeited Ibn Saud's trust after his failure to pay for the earlier concession. Two years passed before oil was discovered in Bahrain in June 1932. SOCAL then decided to contact the king without Holmes. Besides, they had learned that the government of British India had advised the Eastern and General Syndicate not to promote the interests of Gulf Oil or SOCAL in Saudi Arabia.

As early as 1930, representatives of SOCAL met the Saudi envoy in London to seek a permit for their geologists to visit the Eastern Province, a request that Ibn Saud initially refused. Since Twitchell had already visited Saudi Arabia and recommended seeking a concession, SOCAL then contacted Twitchell.[13] In October 1932 the directors of SOCAL sent a telegram to Philby, who was then living in Jidda, asking him to make arrangements with the Saudi government for the preliminary prospecting for oil in the Eastern Province. The Saudis preferred to negotiate a concession before the geological work started.

In early 1933 L. Hamilton, SOCAL's representative, arrived in Jidda. He was assisted in his negotiations by Twitchell, who had already explored the water and mineral resources in Arabia. Simultaneously, Stephen Longrigg of the Iraq Petroleum Company and Frank Holmes of the Eastern and General Syndicate also appeared in Jidda. The Saudis demanded that the future concessionaire pay £100,000 in gold on signature of the contract. The syndicate immediately dropped out of the game. IPC offered a maximum sum of £10,000, still doubting the existence of oil in Saudi Arabia. SOCAL finally won the concession for £50,000.[14]

One reason (though not the decisive reason) for the Americans' success in obtaining the concession was that they had no imperial past in the Middle East. Surrounded by British colonies and dependencies on all sides, and compelled to maintain friendly relations with Britain, Ibn Saud nonetheless mistrusted the British and was reluctant to allow British companies in his country.[15]

The period of negotiations followed the worldwide depression of 1929–33 and occurred in a period when the prospects for American business seemed gloomy. When agreement between SOCAL and Saudi Arabia had finally been reached on all points, the US suddenly embargoed gold exports on 20 April and then abandoned the gold standard. SOCAL found a simple solution by buying gold sovereigns on the British currency market. The agreement was finally signed on 29 May 1933 by Abdallah al-Sulaiman, the Saudi minister of finance, and Hamilton on behalf of SOCAL. It was ratified by Ibn Saud's decree of 7 July 1933 and came into effect one week later. In November 1933 the concession was transferred to the Californian-Arabian Standard Oil Company, a branch of SOCAL. In January 1944 it changed its name to the Arabian-American Oil Company (Aramco).

By 1936 SOCAL had a large production potential in the Eastern hemisphere, but its transport and marketing network was inadequate. At the same time, the system of oil distribution developed by the Texas Company (now Texaco) needed extracted oil. The two companies established joint interests in a vast area stretching from Egypt to Hawaii. Texaco received half of the shares in SOCAL's branch.[16]

Soon after the oil concession agreement was concluded, the Anglo-American Group received a concession for the exploitation of gold mines in Saudi Arabia. Gold extraction began in Mahd al-Dhahab, but the mines were depleted by 1954. There are many gold mines in the mountains of Hijaz, but it is possible that King Solomon and the Abbasid caliphs extracted large quantities of gold from them, and the mines became unprofitable after a short period of exploitation.[17]

The concession agreement granted SOCAL:

> 'the exclusive right, for a period of 60 years, to explore, prospect, drill for, extract, treat, manufacture, transport, deal with, carry away, and export' oil and oil products, and to create the facilities to carry out these activities. The company was granted an 'exclusive' exploration area of more than 400,000 square miles [1,036,000 sq. km], covering almost all of eastern Saudi Arabia. [The agreement] also provided for a 'preference right' to acquire additional concessions in the remaining area of eastern Saudi Arabia, as well as any rights that the government might acquire in the so-called Neutral Zone south of Kuwait.
>
> In return for these concessions the company agreed to meet the following conditions:
>
> 1. A loan of £30,000 gold or its equivalent, was to be payable within 15 days of the effective date of the agreement. An additional loan of £20,000 gold after 18 months, if the agreement was still in force. Repayment of those loans was to be made by deductions from one-half of the anticipated royalties owing to the government.
> 2. An 'annual rental' payment of £5,000 gold, was to be payable in advance until the discovery of commercial quantities of oil.
> 3. Upon discovery of oil in commercial quantities the company was to make an immediate advance royalty payment of £50,000 and another payment of the

The Oil Concessions

same amount one year later. Repayment was to be made out of anticipated royalties. Furthermore, the company agreed to begin relinquishment of areas it chose not to explore, within 90 days of the discovery of oil in commercial quantities.

4. Once oil had been discovered the government was to receive a royalty on all net crude produced, sold, and run from field storage:
   ... after first deducting:
   (a) Water and foreign substances; and
   (b) Oil required for the customary operations of the company's installations within Saudi Arabia; and
   (c) The oil required for manufacturing the amounts of gasoline and kerosene to be provided free each year to the government ...

   The rate of royalty was to be four shillings, gold, or its equivalent per ton. In addition, a royalty payment was stipulated 'equal to one-eighth of the proceeds of the sale' of natural gas produced, saved, and sold.

5. The company agreed to build a refinery as soon as practicable after oil discovery and to supply 200,000 gallons (US) of gasoline and 100,000 gallons (US) of kerosene to the government without charge.

6. The government agreed that 'the company and enterprise shall be exempt from all direct and indirect taxes, imports, charges, fees and duties (including, of course, import and export duties) ...'[18]

The terms of the agreement were undoubtedly extremely advantageous to the company and disadvantageous to Saudi Arabia, but they reflected the balance of forces between the partners. At the time that the Saudi government signed the agreement, it had no experience in oil affairs and badly needed money. The government's main efforts were directed towards obtaining financial advantages in the form of royalties and loans. The article that exempted the company from all direct and indirect taxes deprived the kingdom of a colossal source of income and granted the company huge potential profits on its investment.

The start of oil extraction

Having signed the concession agreement, SOCAL lost no time. The first two geologists came to al-Jubail in September 1933, less than four months after the agreement had been signed, and met Twitchell, who arrived from Jidda. Hamad al-Ghusaibi, a local merchant, became the company's agent and the geologists stayed at his house in Hufuf until 1936. As early as 28 September 1933, they discovered some signs of a dome structure. Initially, the geologists' equipment was transported by camels. Trucks came some months later. All the equipment and most of the food supplies were brought from the US via the port of al-Khobar. By the end of 1933 there were eight oil experts in Saudi Arabia.

317

In 1935 a promising structure was discovered and drilling started. The first well showed signs only of oil and some gas, and the first commercial deposit was not found until 1938. In September that year, oil was brought to the Bahrain Petroleum Company's oil-processing plant in Bahrain. The port of Ras Tannura was subsequently chosen for oil exports. The British Admiralty assisted by providing information on navigation conditions in the Gulf. In 1939 the king and his entourage visited the oil-extraction area in Dhahran, where a camp had been set up of 350 tents. The Saudi nobility celebrated the start of oil extraction for several days. On 1 May 1939 the first tanker with liquid fuel sailed from Saudi Arabia.

By the outbreak of the Second World War, the geologists had conducted preliminary explorations over an area of 175,000 square miles [453,250 sq. km] and detailed explorations over an area of 50,000 square miles [129,500 sq. km]. The area of seismic exploration and drilling was smaller. When work was suspended because of the war, the geologists already knew that they had discovered fabulous oil deposits, but had not yet determined their full amount. In 1934 the company drilled a well in Jawf: it proved dry and the area was recognized as fruitless.[19]

Aramco announced the discovery of oil in commercial quantities on 16 October 1938 and the first cargo of Saudi Arabian crude oil was shipped from Ras Tannura on 1 May 1939. According to Knauerhase:

Encouraged by these events, the government agreed to enlarge the original concession area in the northern and southern regions of eastern Arabia, and to grant the company the right of exploration in the Saudi portions of the Neutral Zones between Saudi Arabia and Iraq and between Saudi Arabia and Kuwait. This raised the size of the exclusive area to approximately 495,000 square miles [1,282,050 sq. km], of which 484,000 square miles were onshore and 11,000 [square] miles offshore. The new concession was granted for a period of 60 years, and the period of the Original Agreement was extended by six years. The company was granted a ten-year moratorium on the relinquishment of any portion of the exclusive area. In return for those additional privileges the company agreed to meet the following conditions:

1. Upon completion of the ten-year moratorium on relinquishment, the company would give up from time to time those areas of the exclusive area it no longer wished to explore.
2. An immediate payment of £140,000 gold and an additional £100,000 gold upon discovery of oil in commercial quantities.
3. An annual rental of £20,000 for the additional area payable until oil was found in commercial quantities.
4. An increase in the amount of free gasoline and kerosene to 1.3 million and 100,000 gallons, respectively.

The search for oil led eventually to the offshore areas. The right to explore offshore had been fixed in previous agreements, without distinction in the payments to be made for oil lifted in these areas. In October 1948 an agreement was signed covering royalty payments from offshore operations. The company agreed to pay the same amount of royalty as provided in the Original Concession Agreement plus five cents (US) on each barrel recovered offshore. Furthermore, Aramco guaranteed a minimum annual royalty from offshore oil of $2 million payable in advance. If Aramco elected to pay the royalty in gold pounds, the conversion was to take place at $35 per ounce of gold. The additional five cents per barrel, however, was always to be calculated in US currency. Aramco gave up its rights to the Saudi portion of the Kuwait Neutral Zone and set out a 22-year schedule of periodical relinquishment of those parts of the 'exclusive' area in which it did not want to carry out further exploration.[20]

The figures for oil extraction in Saudi Arabia from 1938 to 1986 are given in Table 1.

Table 1. Oil Extraction in Saudi Arabia, 1938–1986 (million barrels)[21]

Year	Aramco	Getty Oil	Arabian Oil Co.	Total
1938	0.5	–	–	0.5
1939	3.9	–	–	3.9
1940	5.1	–	–	5.1
1941	4.3	–	–	4.3
1942	4.5	–	–	4.5
1943	4.9	–	–	4.9
1944	7.8	–	–	7.8
1945	21.3	–	–	21.3
1946	59.9	–	–	59.9
1947	89.9	–	–	89.9
1948	142.9	--	–	142.9
1949	174.0	–	–	174.0
1950	199.5	–	–	199.5
1951	278.0	–	–	278.0
1952	301.9	–	–	301.9
1953	308.3	–	–	308.3
1954	347.8	3.0	–	350.8
1955	352.2	4.4	–	356.6
1956	360.9	5.8	–	366.7
1957	362.1	11.6	–	373.7
1958	370.5	14.7	–	385.2

Year	Aramco	Getty Oil	Arabian Oil Co.	Total
1959	399.8	21.2	–	421.0
1960	456.5	24.9	–	481.4
1961	508.3	28.7	3.8	540.8
1962	555.1	33.7	11.0	599.8
1963	594.6	33.1	24.1	651.8
1964	628.1	34.4	31.8	694.3
1965	739.1	32.6	33.1	804.8
1966	873.3	30.2	46.5	950.0
1967	948.1	25.1	50.6	1,023.8
1968	1,035.8	23.2	55.0	1,114.0
1969	1,092.4	22.7	58.8	1,173.9
1970	1,295.3	28.3	62.7	1,386.3
1971	1,641.6	33.7	65.5	1,740.8
1972	2,098.9	28.3	75.0	2,202.2
1973	2,677.4	23.4	71.9	2,772.7
1974	2,996.5	29.8	68.7	3,095.1
1975	2,491.8	31.2	59.5	2,582.5
1976	3,045.5	29.7	55.7	3,193.3
1977	3,291.2	32.0	43.8	3,367.0
1978	2,952.3	29.4	56.3	3,038.0
1979	3,376.4	30.2	72.6	3,479.2
1980	3,525.3	28.5	70.0	3,623.8
1981	3,512.7	27.1	40.1	3,579.9
1982	2,309.4	23.6	33.4	2,366.4
1983	1,596.6	60.3*		1,656.9
1984	1,435.5	57.4*		1,492.9
1985	1,110.0	48.8*		1,158.8
1986	1,711.8	34.4*		1,746.2

*Information from the Saudi ministry of petroleum and mineral resources.

From the late 1930s Saudi Arabia entered a new era – that of oil – though its impact on the country only really began to be felt in the late 1940s. Both the kingdom's international position and the development of its society were to be influenced henceforth by a powerful new factor.

CHAPTER 15

Saudi Arabia and the Second World War (1939–1945)

Unlike the previous war, the Second World War did not affect the Arabian peninsula directly but Saudi Arabia nevertheless felt its economic, political and military consequences. Hitler's Germany wanted to reach Iran, Afghanistan and India via the Arab countries, thus obtaining a springboard from which to attack the USSR and weaken the British empire. The Middle East also attracted Nazi strategists because of its oil resources. The war increased the demand for oil and oil products, which Germany and its allies badly needed.

In their political calculations, the Nazis took account of anti-British sentiment in the Middle East, caused by Britain's colonial policy. Germany portrayed itself as 'the friend of the Arabs' and declared its support for their nationalist aspirations. German propaganda proclaimed, 'Victory for the Axis powers will liberate the Middle Eastern countries from the British yoke.' Simultaneously, the Germans launched a campaign of espionage and subversive activities in the Arab countries. Germany's moves threatened Britain's dominance in the Arab East, weakened its global strategic position and hampered its mobilization of the region's human and material resources for military purposes. The threat of a German occupation of the Middle East was shown to be real and it was only the transfer of German troops for the invasion of the USSR that removed that menace from the Arab countries east of Libya.[1]

Saudi Arabia's neutrality

When the Second World War broke out, Saudi Arabia declared its neutrality, though Ibn Saud sent troops to the borders of Iraq, Kuwait and Transjordan. This supposed neutrality was actually pro-British, due to the kingdom's heavy dependence on Britain. The countries of the British empire and those within its orbit accounted for most of Saudi Arabia's foreign trade. British India was the main supplier of foodgrain. The bulk of the pilgrims came from Islamic countries that depended on Britain. Saudi Arabia's monetary system relied on the British pound. The country was surrounded by British protectorates and military bases and the British navy dominated the Red Sea and the Gulf. According to Hafiz Wahba:

> Ibn Saud knew very well that it was the British navy that supplied his country. If Britain were to blockade it, the population would be doomed to starvation. If Britain were to stop transportation of pilgrims to the holy places, how would Hijaz survive without their money?[2]

In general, Ibn Saud enjoyed firm control over the country's internal situation, though sporadic unrest did occur among the tribes. In 1939–40 many Shammar roamed from Saudi Arabia to Iraq. The Saudi government probably encouraged the Shammar shaikhs to do so, calculating that it could use them for its own ends.[3]

The Axis powers also put pressure on Ibn Saud and some of his advisers demanded that the country should expand its ties with Italy and Germany. After Italy occupied Ethiopia in 1935, the Italian navy appeared in the Red Sea. Italy enjoyed some influence in Yemen, whose people had traditionally been anti-British. Saudi Arabia had concluded treaties of friendship with Germany in 1929 and with Italy in 1932 and had established diplomatic and consular relations with them.[4]

In late 1939 and early 1940 Germany sought Italy's help in persuading Saudi Arabia to grant an *agrément* to Fritz Grobba, one of the heads of the German intelligence network in the Middle East, who disguised himself as a diplomat. He was German ambassador to Iraq until the autumn of 1939, when he was declared *persona non grata* for attempting to engineer a mutiny. He was then appointed an attaché at the German embassy in Ankara.[5] Probably informed about Grobba's intelligence activities, the British demanded that Ibn Saud deny him diplomatic status: the king yielded to British pressure.[6]

Nazi Germany's military successes, however, changed the attitude of the Saudi government. Grobba was allowed to come to Jidda with a large mission and began active work. Nazi propaganda, mainly of an anti-British character, was carried on among the pilgrims. The German envoy also set up subversive groups of people who were displeased with the king and supplied them with arms and money. Soon after his arrival, Grobba asked Ibn Saud to grant Germany a concession for the extraction of mineral resources on the Red Sea coast, but the request was turned down.[7]

After invading Yugoslavia and Greece, including Crete, Nazi Germany began advancing towards the Middle East, first of all to Iraq and Syria. On 1 April 1941 there was an anti-British coup in Iraq, led by Rashid Ali al-Gailani. Its leaders asked for Ibn Saud's support,[8] but the king refused, saying that it would be an act of treachery against the British, with whom he was linked by ties of friendship.[9] Hitler sent him a private message, suggesting that he should attack Britain and offering him 'the crown of the king of all the Arabs' in exchange. Ibn Saud again refused and recalled his ambassador Fuad Hamza from Switzerland – Hamza had tried to persuade the king to cooperate with the Axis powers and forwarded Hitler's message to him.[10] Grobba's agents committed a series of acts of sabotage in Saudi Arabia, in particular at the oilfields in al-Hasa. The British sent an air-force squadron to Saudi Arabia with fire-fighting equipment.[11]

By late May 1941 British troops had occupied the most important strategic points in Iraq. At the same time, British forces and Ethiopian guerrillas defeated the Italian occupation army in Ethiopia. In July 1941 British and Free French forces occupied Syria and ousted the pro-Vichy administration. Thus the situation in the Middle East had changed considerably. The German high command was preoccupied with preparations for the invasion of the USSR and could not allocate sufficient forces to attack the British in the Middle East. Britain preserved its dominance in the region and the question was raised as to whether British forces should be deployed in the strategically important centres of Saudi Arabia, as had been done in Syria and Iraq. However, the British government had to reckon with the US, whose corporations had commercial interests in Saudi Arabia. Besides, the occupation of a country with a long tradition of distrust for foreigners might pose many problems.

To avoid provocations on the borders with Iraq and Transjordan,[12] Ibn Saud moved his troops further inland.[13] Soon afterwards he abrogated the treaty of friendship with Germany and in September 1941 he expelled Grobba.[14] Diplomatic relations with Italy were severed as early as 1940. When an Italian TBD (torpedo-boat destroyer), escaping from the British, entered Saudi waters, its crew were interned in al-Taif but were not handed over to the British authorities. Rashid Ali al-Gailani, the leader of the abortive coup in Iraq, asked for asylum in Saudi Arabia. He was received as an honoured guest, in spite of British demands for his extradition as he had been sentenced to death by the Iraqi military tribunal.[15]

Although hostilities did not spread to Saudi Arabia, its economy suffered as a result of the war. The mobilization of troops ate up revenues and the men's long absence undermined agriculture. The country's financial situation worsened: in 1941 the budget deficit stood at £1,150,000. Proceeds from the *hajj* also decreased: on the eve of the war, the annual number of pilgrims stood at between 50,000 and 100,000, yielding $5-6m to the exchequer; during the war, only 20-30,000 people travelled to Mecca. The prices of imported goods rose and the annual deficit reached $10-15m in 1940/41.[16] Oil output did not increase in the first years of the war.

Ibn Saud insisted that SOCAL pay him an annual advance of $6m on the total royalty payment. Fearing that the concession might be withdrawn and awarded to Britain, SOCAL agreed to grant Saudi Arabia an initial loan of $3m and then increase the sum to $6m. It even agreed to pay a fixed royalty, though a decrease in oil extraction was anticipated.

Britain ensured that Saudi Arabia was financially dependent on it by supplying goods and gold and silver coins to support the circulation of money in the country.[17] To curb the US oil company's activities, Britain used the Middle East Supply Centre, which was in charge of oil supplies to Allied troops in the Middle East up to 1942 and the distribution of food to the various countries of the region. Britain ensured sales of Iranian and Iraqi oil to the Allied forces and restricted the markets for Saudi oil. Besides, all food supplies to Saudi Arabia were in Britain's hands.

Britain's growing economic influence in Saudi Arabia worried the American oil companies, and the US government decided to provide Ibn Saud with indirect aid. After granting Britain a loan of $425m, the US demanded that part of that sum should be transferred to Saudi Arabia, as Ibn Saud was informed by representatives of SOCAL.[18] However, the king depended first and foremost on those countries from whom he received direct aid. Fearing that Britain would further strengthen its position in Saudi Arabia, the US oil companies insisted that their government provide direct aid to Ibn Saud.

The oil factor in American Middle East policy from the start of the Second World War

Before the war, the US government had considered the Middle East as lying within the sphere of European, mostly British, dominance. The US administration had few real political levers to support American oil companies and other private companies operating in the region.[19] In 1939 American companies accounted for only 10% of Middle East oil.[20] During the war, however, US policy in the Middle East underwent profound and major changes. The US strove to replace Britain as the dominant power in the region, taking particular account of the area's oil potential. The role of oil in the international arena changed: what had previously been a commercial product now became a strategic commodity of prime importance.[21]

The US administration tried to establish state control over the American oil concession in the Middle East, but was faced with dogged resistance on the part of the companies, which were reluctant to share their profitable business with the authorities.[22] This did not prevent the companies from using the government for their own ends. Aramco strove to stabilize the Saudi regime and prevent the consolidation of British positions in the country. To cut down on expenses, it tried to shift them on to the US tax-payer.

On 8 February 1943 Harold Ickes, the US secretary of the interior, received a memorandum from Standard Oil of California with the following considerations:

> Concern is felt over the rapidly increasing British economic influence in Saudi Arabia because of the bearing it may have on the continuation of purely American enterprise after the war. Direct aid from the United States Government to the Saudi Arab Government instead of indirect aid through the British as at present would check this tendency and give some assurance that the reserve of oil in Saudi Arabia will remain under control of Americans . . . One manner in which direct aid might be extended to the Saudi Arabian Government by the United States Government is through the machinery of lend-lease.[23]

Saudi Arabia and the Second World War (1939-1945)

As early as 18 February 1943 Roosevelt instructed E. Stettinius, the assistant secretary of state, who directed the lend-lease programme, to organize lend-lease aid to Saudi Arabia. According to the president, the protection of Saudi Arabia was vital for US interests, though the kingdom was not participating in the war either formally or in practical terms.[24] In 1943 the US Senate special committee for national defence programmes estimated US aid to Saudi Arabia at $99m in the form of direct and indirect lend-lease and other supplies, of which only $27m had to be repaid. According to the committee's report, the aid had released Aramco from meeting the budgetary requirements of Saudi Arabia and removed the danger of British control over all concessions and incomes.[25] Thus the US oil companies managed to neutralize the influence of their British competitors with the help of the US government.

After an abrupt reduction in oil output, caused by the closure of West European markets and British discriminatory policies, growth resumed in 1943 owing to the increased demand for oil from the Allied armies in the Pacific and the Mediterranean and the cessation of oil exports from Burma and Indonesia after these countries were invaded by Japan. Aramco supplied oil products to the US government for military purposes. Oil output in Saudi Arabia stood at 4.9m barrels in 1943 and increased more than ten times in 1946.[26]

In March 1942 the US appointed a chargé d'affaires to Jidda. Previously, the US ambassador to Cairo had been accredited simultaneously to Saudi Arabia. From 1944 to 1946 the American diplomatic mission in Jidda was headed by W. A. Eddy, an experienced intelligence officer and an Arabist, the son and grandson of Presbyterian missionaries who had lived and died in Syria. (From 1947 to 1952 Eddy was an Aramco consultant.)[27] There was also an attaché for oil affairs in the US mission.

In the spring of 1943 Brigadier-General P. Hurley was sent to Saudi Arabia as President Roosevelt's envoy to study the position of the US oil companies there. In October Crown Prince Saud paid an official visit to Washington and remained in the US for one month. In the same year, Prince Faisal and his brother Khalid visited the US and met President Roosevelt, congressmen and members of the government.[28] Aramco in that period estimated the total oil resources of Saudi Arabia at 20bn barrels, which was equal to all the explored deposits in the US.[29] This was the oil companies' weightiest argument in mobilizing the US administration to support their interests.

In November 1943 a group of US geologists prepared a report on their trip to the Middle East. They stressed that the centre of oil extraction would shift from the Gulf of Mexico and the Caribbean to the Middle East.[30] According to their estimates, the world's largest oil reserves lay in the basin of the Tigris, the Euphrates and the Gulf. Oil production in that region was the cheapest in the world. We have no comparable data concerning the 1940s, but in the mid-1960s the average output of an oilwell in the Gulf was approximately 4,500 b/d, in Venezuela less than 300 b/d and in the US 15 b/d. Most oilwells spout, while American oil needs to be pumped. Besides, most oil is extracted close to the Gulf, which makes transportation easier.[31] All these facts were taken into account when the US oil strategy was drawn up in the 1940s and 1950s.

In 1943 Aramco secured funding for the construction of an oil-processing plant in

Ras Tannura with a capacity of 50,000 b/d. It went into operation as early as September 1945. In March 1945 an oil pipeline reached Bahrain, where another large oil refinery was in operation.[32]

The US government decided to leave the economic and financial aspects of oil extraction to the companies and concentrate their efforts on America's general military and political interests in the region. In 1944 there were plans for the Trans-Arabian pipeline (Tapline) to be built by the US government, but later it also became the property of the Aramco participants.[33]

In December 1943 General Roys, commander-in-chief of the US forces in the Middle East, visited Saudi Arabia and made arrangements for the construction of military airfields in Dhahran and Dawqa. The building of the air-force base in Dhahran began in 1944 and was completed two years later. A US military mission arrived in Saudi Arabia to train the Saudi army, together with a group of British military instructors also invited by Ibn Saud. During the war, the US supplied arms and military equipment to Saudi Arabia under the lend-lease programme.[34]

Ibn Saud's meeting with Roosevelt[35]

In February 1945 President Roosevelt met King Ibn Saud, a meeting that was to demonstrate the importance of Saudi Arabia to US Middle East policy. On his return from the Yalta conference, the head of the US administration established a personal contact with the head of a state that was traditionally seen as within the zone of Britain's imperial interests. The meeting was kept top secret, mainly from the British, who only learned of it at the last moment.

Ibn Saud and his entourage were brought by the *Murphy*, an American TBD, from Jidda to the Suez Canal, where President Roosevelt waited for him on board the *Quincy*, a US cruiser, in the Bitter Lakes (in the Suez Canal). A marquee was pitched on deck for the king and every day a sheep was slaughtered for him, since he only ate meat if it was fresh. In the daytime Ibn Saud was shown newsreels about the US army's operations. Roosevelt's meeting with Ibn Saud was on 14 February 1945. When the president tried to persuade the king to agree to a plan to settle the Jewish victims of Nazism in Palestine, Ibn Saud answered that it was Germany that had committed crimes against the Jews and should be punished for them. His main argument was that the Arabs had not harmed the European Jews and should not pay for the misdeeds of others. All the president's attempts to convince the king were to no avail.

On 5 April Roosevelt sent Ibn Saud a letter, promising not to do anything that might be hostile to the Arabs. He also guaranteed that there would be no fundamental change in US policy over Palestine without consulting both the Jews and the Arabs. In Eddy's opinion, the king saw these assurances as indicating a formal alliance.[36]

During his talks with Roosevelt, Ibn Saud had confirmed his agreement to the free use of Saudi ports in the Gulf by British and US ships and to the building of a large air-force base. But he laid down the condition that Saudi Arabia should, under no circumstances, be occupied as Egypt, Syria, Iraq and Iran had been, and that no part of its territory should be alienated. The areas needed by the US army were leased for a period of not more than five years; thereafter they were to be returned to the Saudi state with all the structures erected on them. The president failed to win a longer lease. In addition, Ibn Saud asked for part of the light weapons stored in Iran to be transferred to the Saudi government after the end of hostilities. In exchange, Ibn Saud assumed the obligation of declaring war on the Axis powers.[37] In March 1945 Saudi Arabia made such a declaration of war, thus enabling it to join the United Nations.[38]

When the king asked for the president's friendship and his support for Saudi Arabia's independence, he received assurances to that effect. Eddy opined that Ibn Saud considered the meeting a guarantee against Britain's eventual attempts on his independence. As for the oil question, Roosevelt won Ibn Saud's confirmation of the current concessions granted to American companies and his consent to the building of the Trans-Arabian oil pipeline between al-Hasa and the Mediterranean coast.

The British prime minister, Winston Churchill, met Ibn Saud immediately after Roosevelt's departure in an attempt to neutralize US influence, but their negotiations did not alter the situation or prevent the Saudi kingdom's freeing itself from British influence with US support. In consolidating its position in Saudi Arabia, Washington skilfully capitalized on the Saudis' deep-seated mistrust of Britain. It is noteworthy, however, that after the war, in the late 1940s and early 1950s, Washington's Middle Eastern strategic interests were concentrated in Turkey, Iran and Egypt. The Gulf, or at least the Arabian coast, was of secondary importance. The West's strategic interests in the Gulf and in Arabia as a whole were still ensured by Britain.

In 1945 the balance of US, British and French capital in the Middle East oil industry was as follows. The Anglo-Iranian Oil Company controlled oil deposits of 27.750bn barrels, the Royal Dutch-Shell group 2.750bn, Gulf Oil 5bn, Standard Oil of California and the Texas Oil Company 20bn, Standard Oil of New Jersey and SOCONY-Vacuum 2.750bn and the Compagnie Française des Pétroles 2.750bn. Total reserves were estimated at 61bn barrels.[39] The companies with British and British-Dutch capital accounted for most of the output. The situation was to change radically, however, with the rapid growth of oil production in Saudi Arabia, where new fields were regularly discovered, and as a result of the crisis in Iran in the early 1950s, which seriously weakened the position of British capital in the field of oil extraction.

CHAPTER 16

Domestic and Foreign Policy (1945–1958)

Any student of post-war Saudi Arabia faces a major obstacle – the scarcity of information on the true political situation in the country, in spite of numerous newspaper and magazine articles, statistical abstracts, vindicatory works and even some sociological studies. The political struggle within the ruling elite was waged between groups from the various branches of the Al Saud, whose members only rarely leak information on the genuine nature of the conflicts and changes in the top echelons of the Saudi hierarchy. It was only the intensification of the power struggle between King Saud and Crown Prince Faisal between 1958 and 1964, and the 'rebellion of free princes' within the framework of that struggle (see chapter 17), that gave any hint of the situation within the royal family. The opposition's actions, which took various forms, were weak and ill-coordinated (with the exception of the labour unrest of 1953 and 1956) and were easily suppressed. Information on the activities of the opposition is scarce, fragmentary and contradictory.

A considerable part of the known history of Saudi Arabia is confined to relations with the oil companies, international relations and foreign policy. The reasons are obvious. A dramatic intensification of the international struggle in the Middle East after the Second World War and Saudi Arabia's participation in this struggle, the rise and fall of the Arab nationalist movement, and the interconnected destinies of the Arab countries all increased the importance of international politics in Saudi Arabia's history. Both its domestic and its foreign policy were pursued under the influence of the new factor of oil. The desert kingdom was soon to become the world's major exporter of liquid fuel (the largest since the 1970s).

Domestic and Foreign Policy (1945–1958)

Relations with the oil companies

By the end of 1945 Aramco had discovered four large oilfields in al-Dammam, Abu Hadriya, Abqaiq and al-Qatif. In May 1951 the world's largest oil deposit, Safaniya, was found on the continental shelf of the Gulf. The world's largest deposit on land – Ghawar, some 240 km long and 35 km wide – was discovered in the early 1950s. Oil explorers expected to continue finding new deposits of liquid fuel in the unique geological structures of Saudi Arabia.[1] The oil terminal at Ras Tannura was enlarged and started operations in December 1945 with a capacity of 50,000 b/d. The annual capacity of the oil-processing plant in Ras Tannura had risen to 15m tons by the mid-1960s. Two more plants were built in Jidda and Riyadh.[2]

After the Second World War, industry's shift to liquid fuel in the industrialized countries and the spread of motor transport and the chemical industry created an unprecedented demand for oil, especially in the Eastern hemisphere. Many regions that had lagged behind the US in oil consumption were rapidly bridging the gap. Twenty-five years after the end of the war, the demand for oil had increased more than 2.5 times in the US and more than 8 times in the rest of the world, with oil consumption growing fastest in Japan and Western Europe. By 1965 the Middle East was the world's largest oil producer, with an output of close to 8.5 mb/d, more than the US.[3]

The oil-processing industry increasingly shifted towards the centres of consumption. The transportation of crude oil is cheaper than that of refined products; importers could buy more oil than oil products for the same sums, and the wastes of oil refineries were processed in the industrial centres. Economic considerations were bolstered by weighty political considerations: the oil companies avoided creating large oil-processing capacities in the developing countries, particularly after the attempt to nationalize oil in Iran in the early 1950s.

As early as the Second World War, Aramco had calculated that an oil pipeline between Saudi Arabia and the Mediterranean would decrease the transportation costs by one third or even a half compared to the cost of transporting oil to Europe by tanker. They decided to build a 1,712-km-long pipeline from Abqaiq to Saida (Lebanon) with an annual capacity of 15m tons to be raised later to 25m tons.[4] In July 1945 Aramco created the Trans-Arabian Pipeline Company (Tapline). At the height of the works, 16,000 people were employed and some 3,000 trucks and other vehicles were in use by Tapline.[5]

British companies and the British government were powerless to prevent the growth of oil extraction by Aramco, but they tried to hamper construction of the US pipeline to the Mediterranean coast, which would enable the Americans to export oil to Western Europe cheaply and rapidly. It would partly deprive the British of the proceeds from tanker transportation of oil and the dues imposed on tankers for passage through the Suez Canal. The political struggle in Syria, Lebanon and Iraq in the post-war period was connected, both directly and indirectly, with the competition between Britain and the US for Arabian oil, including the construction of the pipeline.

In March 1949 Husni al-Zaim came to power in Syria through a military coup. His government was supported by the US and by Saudi Arabia, which granted it a loan of $6m. Husni al-Zaim opposed the plans for a 'Greater Syria' and the 'Fertile Crescent', inspired by Emir (King since 1946) Abdallah of Transjordan – a supporter of the British – and he ratified the agreement signed earlier on building the pipeline across Syrian territory. After a second military coup, in August 1949, the new Syrian government, under Colonel Sami al-Hinnawi, pursued a pro-British policy. It declared the pipeline agreement null and void and favoured the idea of a Greater Syria. Adib al-Shishakli, who led yet another coup in Syria in December 1949, restored the position of the US oil companies and confirmed his country's consent for the pipeline. In 1950 the Trans-Arabian pipeline was completed and put into operation. Its construction had cost $230m.[6] When Shishakli was overthrown in February 1954, he fled to Saudi Arabia.

The rapid development of the oil industry in Saudi Arabia after the Second World War led SOCAL and Texaco to the conclusion that they had insufficient capital to exploit such gigantic oilfields, build pipelines and find markets for the huge volume of oil. They decided to cooperate with Standard Oil of New Jersey and Mobil Oil. The agreement on their participation in Aramco was reached in late 1946, but the British oil corporations opposed the decision for two years, referring to the 'red line agreement' signed by the said companies. The latter ignored the protests of the Anglo-Iranian Oil Company and the Royal Dutch-Shell Group and entered Aramco in November 1948. The 'red line agreement' was dead. By 1948 Aramco was owned jointly by SOCAL (30%), Texaco (30%), Standard Oil of New Jersey (30%) and Mobil Oil (10%).[7]

In 1948 Aramco waived the right of concession in the Neutral Zone between Saudi Arabia and Kuwait in exchange for the Saudi part of the continental shelf in al-Hasa. One reason was that the American Independent Oil Company (Amin Oil) had concluded an agreement on a concession in that zone with Kuwait on far more favourable conditions for Kuwait than those that Saudi Arabia had won under its agreement with Aramco. Aramco preferred to quit the Neutral Zone, fearing that acceptance of Kuwait's demands would lead to a sizeable increase in the payments to Saudi Arabia for the main concession. A more important reason was the discovery of huge oil deposits in the part of the continental shelf belonging to Saudi Arabia.[8]

In October 1948 a new agreement was signed on the royalty for oil extraction from the continental shelf. Aramco agreed to pay the same royalty as provided for in the initial concession agreement, plus 5 cents for each barrel extracted from the shelf. Aramco guaranteed an advance payment of $2m as the minimum annual royalty for operations there. It pledged itself to return within 22 years those parts of its 'special rights zone' where it would not continue to prospect for oil.[9]

Profits from the exploitation of the Gulf basin's oil resources were so high that some outsiders offered the local governments far more favourable terms for concessions to penetrate further into the region. Several such offers were made by independent US corporations, whose weight could not be disregarded since their assets and turnover exceeded those of the largest West European and Japanese firms. The appearance of outsiders showed the Saudi government how much more it could have demanded in the deal with Aramco and strengthened its position when bargaining for a revision of the concession agreements.[10]

In 1949 the concession in the Neutral Zone was transferred to the Pacific Western Oil Corporation (later renamed the Getty Oil Company) for 60 years at the expense of Saudi Arabia's share. In exchange for the right to explore and exploit the oil deposits within an area of 2,000 square miles [5,180 sq. km], including the continental shelf to within 6 miles [10 km] from the coast, the company agreed to pay $9.5m immediately and 55 cents for each barrel of crude oil plus 12.5% of the proceeds from the sale of gas and gas products. The sum of $1m was paid as the advance on account of the future royalty. Should the total royalty be less than that sum, the Saudi government was not liable to return the balance.

The agreement stipulated that if the company were to waive the concession, all structures erected by it should be transferred to Saudi Arabia free of charge. Other conditions included preference for Saudi citizens in employment, and the provision of schools, vocational training courses and free medical services for them.[11] The first gusher played in the Neutral Zone in 1953 and the first batch of crude oil was exported the following year. Both Amin Oil and Getty Oil had their own oil deposits, pipelines, ports and oil-tankers.[12]

In December 1957 an agreement was signed with the Japan Petroleum Trading Company of Tokyo. It set up the Arabian Oil Company with the exclusive right of prospecting in the continental shelf of the Neutral Zone at a distance of over 6 miles from the coast within 2 years. In the event of oil being discovered, the company would be granted a concession for 44 years. Drilling began in 1959 and oil extraction started in January 1960. The royalty was $1.5m per year until the discovery of commercial deposits, with a further $1m from the date of discovery, which condition was retroactive from the date of conclusion of the agreement to the discovery date. The minimum royalty was $2.5m. The company agreed to pay income tax on all its operations in Saudi Arabia and abroad, including crude oil sales, processing, transportation and supplies of petroleum. The minimum rate was established at 56% of its income. In 1963 this was increased to 57%.[13]

Italian companies were permitted to prospect for oil on the Red Sea coast. In 1965 the Oxirap Company of France was granted a concession: the agreement effectively entitled Saudi Arabia to participate in all the company's operations. Then the Petromin Corporation of Saudi Arabia concluded an agreement with Agip (a branch of the Italian state-owned company, ENI) and the Phillips Company on oil prospecting in the Rub al-Khali. In 1967 Petromin transferred the rights on the Red Sea coast to a group consisting of the Natomas International Corporation, the Sinclair Arabian Oil Company and a Pakistani state-owned company. The composition of the group later changed. But the prospecting in the Rub al-Khali and on the Red Sea coast was in vain.[14]

From the late 1940s the Saudi government, which had by now acquired a better knowledge of the international financial markets and was aware of the fabulous income that Aramco derived from the country's oil resources, demanded a fairer division of the profits. The Saudis knew of the success of Venezuela, which had won a considerable increase in the concession payment, and concluded an agreement with Getty Oil on much more favourable terms than that with Aramco.

In 1950 two royal decrees of 4 November and 27 December imposed income tax on the net profits of all foreign companies that operated in Saudi Arabia. Although Aramco protested, the unfairness of the initial agreement was obvious. Landowner and government were the same legal entity in Saudi Arabia, while in other countries, including the US, companies had to pay both rent to the landlord and tax to the government.

After tough negotiations, Aramco agreed to pay income tax as called for in the royal decrees of 4 November and 27 December 1950, provided that:

> in no case shall the total of such taxes and all other taxes, royalties, rentals and exactions of the Government for any year exceed fifty percent (50%) of the gross income of Aramco, after such gross income has been reduced by Aramco's cost of operation, including losses and depreciation, and by income taxes, if any, payable to any foreign country, but not reduced by taxes, royalties, rentals, or other exactions of the Government for such a year.[15]

The agreement also called for an increase in the annual free deliveries of gasoline and kerosene for government use to 2.6m and 200,000 gallons, respectively, and the delivery of 7,500 tons of road asphalt. Furthermore, Aramco agreed to pay $700,000 'per annum towards expenses, support and maintenance of representatives of the Government concerned with the administration of Aramco operations'. The agreement was supplemented by a letter from Aramco assuring the government that there would be no reduction in royalty and rental payments in the event that Aramco should suffer an operating loss.[16]

All this represented a considerable achievement – Saudi Arabia's oil revenues almost doubled between 1950 and 1957. However, the weakness of the agreement was that these proceeds were calculated on the basis of Aramco's net profit. The most obvious injustice was the deduction from the payments to Saudi Arabia in cases when the company was taxed in other states. The relevant article was cancelled on 13 February 1952.[17] The posted prices of oil were determined by the mother companies, which sold it cheap to their branches: trade and transport companies throughout the world. Thus the payments to the Saudi government were calculated on the basis of a sum that was less than the mother companies' real profit. A dispute started between Saudi Arabia and Aramco over the posted prices of oil. The Saudi government was reluctant to bear losses from Aramco's deductions from the price of crude oil.

Despite the increased payments to Saudi Arabia, the low cost of oil production and the low salaries ensured colossal profits for the oil corporations. Oil extraction in Saudi Arabia cost Aramco some ten times less than in the US and five times less than in Venezuela. Over the period 1952–63 the company's net income after paying taxes to the Saudi government was $2.8bn, or 57.6% of the capital invested; in 1961 that figure was 81.5%. In the US the net income was 10–12% of the investment.[18] In March 1963

Domestic and Foreign Policy (1945-1958)

Tapline agreed to increase the royalty on oil transported to Saida – which condition was made retroactive to 6 October 1953 – and to pay income tax on the additional profit.[19]

In February 1954 the government of Saudi Arabia granted the Greek ship-owner Aristotle Onassis the right to transport all the country's oil by sea, with the exception of oil exported in tankers owned by: (a) the concessionaire companies; (b) their mother companies and branches; and (c) the oil buyers. The agreement envisaged setting up a transport company co-owned by Onassis and the government of Saudi Arabia. Britain denounced the step in strong words, describing it as 'a most flagrant example of flag discrimination and a grave interference with normal commercial practice'. The US State Department spokesman also protested at the agreement. Oil companies boycotted Onassis' ships throughout the world and within a few months he was forced to waive the contract.[20]

From the early 1940s, and more so in the 1950s, Aramco felt that favourable conditions for the exploitation of the Saudi oilfields might be jeopardized unless the stability of the Saudi regime (which was friendly to the US) was ensured.[21] The US began encouraging the royal family to undertake limited reforms, to put the financial system into some sort of order and to develop the economy, the health system and education. Saudi Arabia became increasingly important in the list of US foreign-policy priorities.

The final years of King Ibn Saud's life

Towards the end of his life, Ibn Saud became increasingly unable to tackle the problems facing the kingdom. The founder of the Saudi state was the product of a bygone era and he failed to understand or accept the changes.

Thanks to the rapid growth of oil output and changes in the terms of the concessions, Saudi Arabia's revenue increased several times over, within the years immediately following the war. Nonetheless, the kingdom functioned as a large family estate whose incomes were destined, in the opinion of the ruling elite, first and foremost to satisfy the royal family's needs. The members of the Al Saud travelled abroad in the 1940s and 1950s, became acquainted with the way of life in Western Europe and the US and acquired a taste for luxury, combined with an inability to live within their means. Their reluctance to count money, combined with their habitual generosity, resulted in unprecedented waste in a country where the great majority of the population still lived in poverty.

A mad race for luxuries started in the country. Hundreds of the most expensive cars, including gold Cadillacs, were imported and palaces with expensive furniture, air conditioning, gardens, swimming pools and tennis courts appeared in the kingdom. King Saud (who succeeded Ibn Saud in 1953) built twenty-five palaces for himself, of which one, the Nasiriya, cost millions of dollars. Colossal sums were spent on women's garments and jewellery and on the maintenance of slaves, servants, drivers, bodyguards and mere spongers. Generous emoluments were paid to the poets who panegyrized the

Saudis, to the 'scholars' who made up a semi-legendary history of the kingdom and to the 'journalists' who created its contemporary political mythology.

From throughout the Middle East, businessmen with an eye to a quick profit crowded into Riyadh. Those who gave the highest bribes received contracts. There was widespread corruption at the royal court and among officials. It was then that money began leaking from the kingdom to be invested abroad. Grasping traders and contractors deceived the ruling elite, selling them goods and services at prices five to twenty times higher than the real ones. It was a risky enterprise, however, since the royal family merely refused to pay their debts when funds fell short.[22]

The abnormality of the situation and the dangers it posed to the regime were clear to some far-sighted people in the ruling family, but the king's measures to modernize the state were few and not far-reaching enough. Towards the end of Ibn Saud's reign, in October 1953, he issued a decree that was intended to reorganize the *majlis al-wukala* (council of ministers) and extend its functions – both formally and in practice – to the whole country, not only Hijaz. The decree mentioned the ruler's increased duties and the state's responsibilities and the need to regularize the government of the country, but the *majlis al-wukala* did not start functioning before Ibn Saud's death.[23]

One of the king's noteworthy decisions in the last years of his life concerned the repair and enlargement of the main mosque of Medina. It was the most fundamental repair since the time of the Umayyads and took several years. Ibn Saud also ordered that the square surrounding the Kaaba should be extended, but the work only started in 1955. Lastly, he allotted additional funds for water prospecting in central Arabia.[24]

In his youth and his more mature years, Ibn Saud was a strong and courageous man and many legends grew up about him. One of them is quoted by al-Zirikli with reference to Rashad Pharaon, Ibn Saud's personal physician before becoming minister of health, and one of the richest men in the kingdom. Once, when Ibn Saud was wounded in the stomach in a battle, Pharaon offered to perform an operation under chloroform. The emir took a scalpel, cut open his stomach, extracted the bullet and told the physician, 'Now suture it.'[25] Ibn Saud's leg wound troubled him, particularly in old age. He could not bend his knee, which gave him acute pain, and he was unable to sleep without having an hour's massage on his knee first. President Roosevelt presented him with a wheelchair, an exact copy of his own. Although Ibn Saud liked it so much that he never left it, it might have been a factor accelerating his death: the lack of exercise led to obesity and general decrepitude.[26]

Ibn Saud greatly feared the rivalry between his two eldest sons and made them vow shortly before his death that they would maintain good relations with each other. He remembered the fate of his father and uncles after his grandfather Faisal ibn Turki's death and was worried that a conflict within the family might destroy his kingdom.[27]

King Ibn Saud died on 9 November 1953 in al-Taif. Some 100 princes gathered round his body and swore allegiance to Saud as king and Faisal as crown prince. The body was flown to Riyadh and buried in a cemetery in the usual Wahhabi manner, without an inscription, sarcophagus or mausoleum. Ibn Saud's grave, barely distinguishable from the others, was near those of his relatives, including his beloved sister Nura. The Wahhabis, who destroyed domes and grave memorials everywhere, were true to their principles.[28] On 9 November the new King Saud confirmed the appointment of his brother Faisal as deputy prime minister and minister of foreign affairs, reserving the post of head of government for himself.[29]

According to al-Zirikli, Ibn Saud left 34 sons who were still alive at the time of his death. He had concluded dozens of marriages, either prompted by dynastic considerations or out of love. The total number of his sons, daughters and sons' children was close to 160 at the time of his death. If the number of his daughters' children is added, it exceeds 300.[30] Ibn Saud's first son was Turki, who died from influenza in his youth. Saud, born in 1902, was the second son. His mother came from the aristocratic family of Al Arayar, the shaikhs of the Bani Khalid. She died in 1969, having survived her son. Faisal was born in 1906. His mother was Ibn Saud's third wife, who came from the Al al-Shaikh. The rivalry between Saud and Faisal continued throughout their lives and did not cease after their father's death, in spite of the vow they had made to him.[31] By 1962 Saud had 40 sons, almost as many as his father had had. Faisal had only 8 sons, of whom 5 were sent to American schools and universities, 1 to Oxford University and 1 to the military academy at Sandhurst, just when Saud severed diplomatic relations with Britain.[32]

In March 1954 Saud made his first political statement as king at the first meeting of the *majlis al-wukala*. He proclaimed his loyalty to the established religious principles and expressed his readiness to continue his father's policies and methods of government. He said that the first purpose of his reign was to encourage religion and the *sharia*. Among his government's tasks he mentioned strengthening the army, combating famine, poverty and disease, improving the nation's health and setting up ministries of education, agriculture and communications. Saud promised to put the country's financial affairs in order and to set up municipalities or provincial administrative councils. The intention that was to become a commonplace in all the Saudi government's political declarations was expressed clearly in Saud's speech – that of stressing loyalty to the country's traditions, while simultaneously introducing certain innovations and improving the state machinery.[33]

As mentioned above, Faisal became deputy prime minister and minister of foreign affairs in the first cabinet. Eight ministries were formed in Saudi Arabia: of interior; defence and aviation; post, telephone and telegraph; education; finance and the national economy; health; commerce and agriculture; and foreign affairs. Among the ministers were several names that were long to remain on the Saudi political stage: Fahd ibn Abd al-Aziz, the minister of education; Sultan ibn Abd al-Aziz, the minister of post, telephone and telegraph; and Rashad Pharaon, the minister of health. King Saud regularly interfered in his brother's actions and restricted his power.[34] Their latent struggle intensified to such an extent in the late 1950s that the situation in the kingdom was sometimes described as 'dual power'.

After ascending the throne, King Saud reduced customs duties on a range of essential goods, including food and clothes, to win popular support. He declared that officials would be subject to strict controls. 'Let everybody know that the government's door is always open to all grievances,'[35] Saud said, trying to play the role of the 'father of the nation'. However, the programme to 'combat famine, poverty and disease' and 'put the country's financial affairs in order', not to mention 'control over officials', remained on paper.

The first signs of labour unrest

The late 1940s and early 1950s witnessed the first signs of the emergence of entirely new social forces on the political stage of Saudi Arabia. Social conflicts acquired an unprecedented character as oil workers put forward their demands for the first time. The first strike by Aramco workers, mainly foreigners, occurred in 1945. The company administration agreed to make temporary concessions, including an eight-and-a-half-hour working day, a six-day working week and two weeks' annual paid leave. But then the foreigners who had gone on strike were deported. New labour unrest occurred in the oilfields in the late 1940s.[36] Faced with this unprecedented situation, the Saudi government adopted a labour code in October 1947 which followed Egyptian legislation in many areas. An eight-hour working day and a six-day working week were introduced in all companies that employed more than ten workers.

In 1952 Aramco workers set up a committee that acted as a trade union, and a year later they started resolute action. They wanted union rights to be guaranteed, wages to be increased, racial discrimination to cease, workers to be given new quarters, workers' transport costs to be reimbursed and Arabic to be the medium of instruction in the company schools. The Aramco administration refused these demands. A special royal commission, set up by Crown Prince Saud, supported the company and 12 workers' committee members were arrested. On 17 October 1953 some 20,000 Arab workers at Aramco went on strike. The people of the Eastern Province sympathized with the strikers – the general attitude to the Americans, their wealth and their way of life was either negative or hostile.

Martial law was declared at the oilfields. Thousands of soldiers were brought to the Eastern Province, but they, as well as the local police, were reluctant to act against the strikers when ordered to do so. The strike in Saudi Arabia found a response in other Arab countries. The situation grew so dangerous that the Aramco administration had to negotiate with the workers' committee and accept many of its demands: wages were increased by 12–20%, workers were provided with overalls, food and transport, their qualifications were upgraded, and the arrested committee members were released and allowed to return to work. However, the workers' right to establish a union was not recognized. The strike finally ended on 1 November 1953.[37]

Negotiations between the workers' representatives and the company continued over the next three years and the conflict was investigated by a special royal commission with Prince Musaid ibn Abd al-Rahman, King Saud's uncle, as one of its members. Both the Saudi authorities and Aramco strove to prevent the beginning of an organized workers' movement. The Aramco management set up so-called liaison committees:

Domestic and Foreign Policy (1945-1958)

formally, their function was to examine workers' demands in order to avoid labour conflicts, but in practice, they were on the look-out for 'suspect' activists among the workers.[38]

In 1956, when the anti-Western movement was gaining momentum in the Arab world under the impact of the revolutionary events in Egypt, the Eastern Province became a natural focus for actions of that kind. When King Saud came to Dhahran on 9 July 1956, he was met by a mass demonstration; the participants carried anti-imperialist slogans and demanded the closure of the US base. The king was given a list of the workers' demands, which included official recognition of their elected committee, an increase in the dearness allowance and higher wages, a reduction in the working day, an end to arbitrary sackings, equal conditions for local and American workers, an end to racial discrimination and a law guaranteeing the rights of Aramco workers and the protection of their human dignity.[39]

Two days later, on 11 July, the king issued a decree banning all strikes and demonstrations under pain of imprisonment for three years. The activists in the workers' movement, whose names appeared on lists prepared by the Aramco security services, were arrested and beaten. On 17 July the central committee of the Arab workers declared a general strike. The workers' demands included the introduction of a constitution, the legitimization of political parties and national organizations, the right to set up trade unions, the withdrawal of the decree banning strikes, an end to Aramco's interference in the country's internal affairs, the closure of the US base in Dhahran and the release of all those who had been arrested. That level of political involvement was far from widespread among the workers of al-Hasa, however. Nor did the short strike paralyse the oil industry. Bedouin from Ikhwan *hijras* and the governor's personal guard of slaves and freedmen were sent against the workers. Hundreds of them were arrested, tortured, jailed for various terms or deported from the country. The central committee of the Arab workers acted illegally for a period, sending telegrams of protest to the executive committee of the International Federation of Arab Trade Unions and leaders of Arab and other countries. It launched a solidarity campaign with Egypt during the Suez war of 1956, when oil workers collected donations for the Egyptians. Finally, the committee's activities came to nothing.[40]

After the 1956 decree banning strikes, another strike occurred in 1958, when truck drivers protested against the introduction of overtime by the contractor who employed them.[41] It is important to note that the actions of 1956 were the last large-scale movement of Saudi workers in the second half of the twentieth century.

Deterioration of the internal situation in the late 1950s

King Saud neither enjoyed a comparable authority to that of Ibn Saud nor had as strong a personality as his father's. He still lived in the Arabian past and maintained a large harem and a court of some 5,000 people. He considered the national income as his personal property, was lavish in his hospitality and presented his guests with expensive gifts, gradually plunging the state into debt.[42] The expulsion of Philby in 1955 was an episode that characterized the atmosphere in the country after the old king's death. Philby survived his hero, Ibn Saud, and started criticizing corruption at the royal court and in the country as a whole, which angered King Saud. When abroad, however, Philby won a large audience and had numerous opportunities to publicize his observations on the regime: Saud chose the lesser evil and allowed Philby to return and spend the rest of his life in his second homeland.[43]

Bribery was common in the state apparatus. The leaders of the left-wing opposition to the regime gave an example in their *The Hell of Saudi Rule*: the governor of the Eastern Province received 30,000 rials for saving some major contractors from a one-year prison sentence and a whipping. They had been arrested for drinking alcohol.[44]

Many members of the royal family and provincial emirs engaged in illegal currency operations. The governor of the Eastern Province, for example, used his authority to buy foreign currency from banks at the official exchange rate (3.75 rials to the dollar) and then sold it on the black market, receiving 6 or more rials per dollar. This was at a time when the banks lacked foreign currency to pay for imports.[45]

In the first two decades of the oil era, the sharp rise in the ruling elite's incomes increased the demand for slaves as a workforce, but the custom persisted under which slaves were liberated when their master felt close to death. Islam treats manumission as a praiseworthy deed and as an atonement for sins. In the 1950s the slave trade and slave markets still existed in Saudi Arabia. Although most slaves came from Somalia, Ethiopia, Sudan and French West Africa, another important source was Baluchistan. Some poor Arabs from the 'low tribes' and freedmen sold their children as slaves to well-off families, hoping to save them from semi-starvation. The international campaign against slavery nevertheless had some effect in Arabia. In 1936 the Saudi government banned imports of slaves and the enslavement of free people on pain of being sentenced to one year in prison. The slave trade continued, however, with the 'live commodity' mainly being brought to Arabia as pilgrims.[46]

The corruption of members of the ruling group, their reluctance to make even an outward show of observing the puritan customs, and their expensive garments, palaces and cars, were denounced both by the ordinary people and by a part of the *ulama*, the guardians of the Wahhabi traditions, particularly by those who were not at the top of the religious hierarchy. They saw the introduction even of superficial elements of modernization as *bida*, or impermissible innovation. Their ideas clashed with the views of the group of *ulama* who were close to the court. Philby's description of the official *ulama* is as follows:

> The 'Ulama, who are responsible for the spiritual control of the country, seem to have abandoned the hopeless task of encouraging virtue and denouncing vice. Or, are their mouths too stopt with gold? One hears strange stories in connection with the disbursement by them of the vast sums entrusted to them for distribution to the poor and needy and on other charitable objects. No accounts are rendered by such high, and presumably impeccable, dignitaries; no receipts are taken from the

beneficiaries of such bounty for submission to the auditors; the opportunities for peculation are obvious; and even Wahhabi prelates are after all human.[47]

The need for reforms in the Arabian peninsula was clear as early as the 1940s to individual enlightened Saudis, Yemenis and Bahrainis, as testified by *The Arabian Peninsula Accuses Its Rulers*, a book that ran into several editions in Egypt. It is not known who its author was or whether he belonged to a group with elements of a political organization.[48]

In the early 1950s, under the impact of the Egyptian revolution, the germ of an illegal oppositional organization appeared in Saudi Arabia. It consisted of nationalists who professed anti-Western ideas with a mild touch of socialism. The first group of that kind, formed on the crest of the strike of 1953, was the Front of National Reforms, founded by young officers, officials and Aramco employees with some basic education. The front declared its purposes to be:

1. The full liberation of the country from imperialist domination and from the economic yoke of Aramco and the other oil companies.
2. The introduction of a constitution with guarantees of an elected parliament, the freedom of the press, the right to hold assemblies and set up parties and trade unions, and the right to engage in demonstrations and strikes.
3. The development of national industry, and the supply of cheap seed, fertilizer and agricultural implements to peasants.
4. The abolition of slavery.
5. The revision and amendment of agreements with the oil companies in order to use the country's resources for its social, economic and cultural progress.
6. The elimination of illiteracy, the establishment of schools for girls and the expansion of higher and technical education.

The Front of National Reforms considered its activities to be part of the liberation struggle of all the Arab people against imperialism and for cooperation and unity on a free and democratic basis. In the field of foreign policy, the front advocated the strengthening of diplomatic, economic and cultural ties with the Arab countries and the establishment of economic relations with the socialist states. The front supported the policy of positive neutrality and peaceful coexistence and opposed all imperialist doctrines and alliances.[49]

In 1956 the Saudi government declared that the front had been routed. Some of its leaders were arrested, as well as fifty-six young activists known for their democratic views. It became extremely difficult for the front to continue its activities within Saudi Arabia but its members engaged in propaganda in Egypt, Syria and Lebanon and spoke at international conferences.[50]

One of the active organizers of the Front of National Reforms was Lieutenant Abd al-Rahman al-Shamarani, who worked among the young officers in the regular army. He was jailed, together with four other young officers, and was later executed for a conspiracy against the regime. *The Hell of Saudi Rule* was dedicated to his memory.[51] Under the influence of radio propaganda from Cairo, anti-government sentiment found fertile ground among some of the officers, the nascent intelligentsia and high-school and secondary-school students.

Articles containing direct or indirect criticism of the government appeared in *al-Fajr al-Jadid* and *Akhbar al-Dhahran* newspapers. Yusuf Shaikh Yaqub, the owner and editor of *al-Fajr al-Jadid*, and the journalist Ahmad Shaikh Yaqub were jailed and their paper was banned. Abd al-Karim Juhaiman, the editor of *Akhbar al-Dhahran*, was whipped in public before being jailed.[52]

In 1956, for the first time in the history of Najd, a school students' organization was created in the towns of Anaiza, Buraida, Shaqra and al-Rass. Its main demands included the dissolution of the League of Public Morality (the League for the Encouragement of Virtue and the Denunciation of Sin), created as early as the 1920s, 'the source of putrefaction [and] dangerous for the children who strive for education'. The students demanded that the curriculum and education methods should be standardized with those in Syria and Egypt and that higher education institutions should be set up in the country. Clashes occurred in Buraida between students and adherents of the League of Public Morality, supported by the police. Dozens of people were arrested and whipped. The king stated that the students were 'infected with communism'.[53]

The need for specialists nevertheless forced the government to open secular schools and send students from well-off families to study abroad. These students were exposed to many elements of a Western lifestyle that were far from the Wahhabis' puritanism; they were also introduced to new ideas which could only be seen as subversive by the regime.[54] Influenced by the *ulama*, who were worried that some young people were deviating from Wahhabi values, King Saud issued a special decree in 1954, noting that the youth were taking a greater interest in secular issues than in religion and did not study the Quran. To promote religious sentiment, a prize of 2,000 rials was instituted for those who learned the Quran by heart. Fearing that the development of secular education and sending students to study abroad would bring 'subversive ideas' into the country, the king issued a decree in April 1955 recalling all Saudi students from abroad. Those who failed to return were threatened with being stripped of their Saudi citizenship. Students of engineering, law and medicine, however, were exempted from the decree.[55] The decision was in such contradiction with the country's needs that it became practically ineffective in subsequent years.[56] Resisting the new trends, the government and the *ulama* resorted to the tested weapon of religious extremism. The activities of the League of Public Morality were revived and its funding was increased.[57]

The Saudis learnt a lesson from the Egyptian revolution of 1952, which came in the form of a military coup. The lesson was that revolutionary attitudes in the regular army – namely, among the officers, who are susceptible to nationalist (anti-imperialist) and anti-royalist ideas – were dangerous to the regime. After the Second World War, there was a serious attempt to create a regular army. The battalion that was sent to fight against Israel in 1948 was left behind in Egypt for military training. American, British and then Egyptian missions trained the regular army.[58]

In the 1950s the king and his entourage came to the conclusion that the Ikhwan were no longer dangerous to the regime but were opposing the 'innovations' and 'temptations and seductions of modern civilization'. They began paying more attention to the bedouin militia, known as the National Guard. According to the authors of *The Revolutionaries' Voices*, 'The government mistrusts the regular army, and the tribes [Ikhwan] will kill the patriots if a revolution starts.'[59]

The bedouin National Guard had modern weapons and its members, known as *mujahidin* (warriors for the faith), received high salaries. Its units were deployed chiefly near large towns, particularly in the areas of the oilfields. In 1957 the National Guard numbered 10,000 in Hijaz, 5,000 in al-Hasa and 5,000 in the north. Its headquarters was in Riyadh and it had schools for officers and technical personnel in Hijaz and Najd.[60] F. Bouirbie, a French expert on the Middle East, has given an account of a special order issued in 1957 and entitled 'The Ikhwan, the rivals of the army'. According to the text, the Saudi state would continue to pay attention to the creation of a large regular army, but preferred to spend money on units that consisted entirely of bedouin.[61]

However, the measures designed to strengthen the armed forces were insufficient to consolidate the regime. The country was facing bankruptcy because of the general waste and embezzlement among the elite. Saudi Arabia owed $120m to foreign banks in 1958 and the exchequer's debt to local banks, traders, businessmen and contractors was counted in hundreds of millions of rials. Officials did not receive their salaries for many months and had to live on credit or invent other ways to survive. In late 1957 the value of the gold and foreign currency reserves was only 14% of the total amount of rials in circulation. The national currency depreciated by a half and the state budget deficit reached 300m rials.[62]

In 1956/57 concession payments fell sharply because of the closure of European markets to Saudi oil and a simultaneous fall in the posted prices. The reduction in imports, including food, caused price rises which, combined with the shortage of currency, led to inflation and currency speculation. The lack of currency for foreign goods and equipment threatened many Saudi merchants and contractors with bankruptcy and led to widespread discontent. Some of them tried to start trading with the socialist (Soviet-bloc) countries. In 1957, for example, a Saudi merchant called al-Ayasi purchased a large amount of Soviet cement. A group of Saudi businessmen visited Czechoslovakia and made arrangements for the purchase of industrial products, food and equipment for a sugar refinery. Aramco refused to deal with merchants and businessmen who traded with the socialist bloc and prohibited the use of Soviet cement at its projects, threatening local contractors that it would cancel their contracts. The US government put pressure on the king and he banned trade with the socialist countries.[63]

The government's domestic policy caused discontent among broad segments of the Saudi population. Both the ruling group and the opposition were forced to reckon with a serious factor that might determine the fate of the regime – the impact of the wider Middle East political context on the situation in Saudi Arabia.

The main directions of foreign policy

Al-Zirikli published an important secret document which outlined Saudi Arabia's foreign policy in the late 1940s and early 1950s: the document contained instructions for Crown Prince Saud, given him before his visit to the US in 1947. The text mentioned 'the numerous common interests and purposes which unite the two countries'. This theme was included in the official letter to President Truman. Saud was told to assure the president and members of the US administration of Saudi Arabia's resolution to 'take all measures required by the good relations and the tasks of encouraging friendship and economic and cultural ties'.

Saud was expected to demonstrate 'Saudi Arabia's satisfaction with the fact that the US has given up the isolationist policies it adhered to earlier and the kingdom's great hopes caused by active US involvement in Middle East politics'. In his talks with Truman and his ministers, the crown prince was instructed to underline the fact that Saudi Arabia was:

> Britain's loyal friend since the moment of its [Saudi Arabia's] emergence and is so now, though there are some problems, too, between the two countries . . . The Saudis and the British know each other, which facilitates their mutual understanding, though Britain has adopted an unfriendly attitude towards Saudi Arabia on several occasions . . .
>
> Britain strove to retain the Middle East in the sphere of its political and economic influence. However, the advent of the US in the region, and the implementation of its Middle East policy, was worrying for Britain. We noted this when Britain deviated from its traditional friendly policy towards Saudi Arabia, gave up its balanced course between Saudi Arabia and its enemies and encouraged the latter, whether directly or otherwise.

Saud was instructed to stress the need for mutual understanding with the US: 'We strive for it and should like to know to what extent the US is ready to move in this direction.'

The seventh clause of the instructions described Saudi Arabia's attitude to the Soviet Union. The USSR was considered an 'indirect threat' to the kingdom because of the 'firm relations' between communism and Zionism and because of the Orthodox Church's 'Russian propaganda': 'We oppose Zionism and communism and hold that the Orthodox Church should not be permitted to became a tool of Russian propaganda in the Arab countries.'

The eighth clause dealt with Zionism:

> We, the Arabs, are Muslims first of all. The Jews have been the enemies of our religion since the birth of Islam. At the same time, Islam does not share the principle of racism . . . We are not racists. We do not oppose the Jews just because they are Jews. However, we oppose the tyrannical policy preached by some Zionist Jews. The reasons for our opposition to that policy are numerous. Zionism is based

on a tyrannical principle. Zionism claims hypocritically that it is based on the liberation of oppressed Jews. How can one get rid of oppression by oppressing others, or eliminate injustice by committing a greater injustice? Zionism contradicts the Arab countries' current political interests. It threatens them from the military and strategic viewpoint.

The ninth clause read:

> The first problem we see is the need to liberate US policy from the influence of the local Jewish elements and Zionist propaganda. The second issue is the need to distinguish between the problem of oppressed refugees and political Zionism, since: (a) Palestine cannot absorb all the Jewish refugees and therefore their problems will remain unresolved; (b) no country may be compelled to receive refugees without its consent; (c) it is unjust that the US refuses to receive refugees and at the same time insists on imposing them on Palestine; (d) the problem of 100,000 refugees is not a humanitarian problem, but a disguise used to justify the creation of a Jewish majority in Palestine; and (e) it is unjust and illegal that the US government allows its Jewish citizens to pursue a dual policy, as if they were citizens of two distinct states. They should be loyal to the US alone and should not be US citizens and Zionists simultaneously.

The instructions quoted by al-Zirikli[64] are a unique document since nothing of that sort has ever been published officially. In it, the Saudi government stated plainly that its enemy in the international arena was Britain. For many years, Ibn Saud had been the ruler of a state within the zone of unchallenged British influence and had followed Britain's course in his foreign policy, while retaining a nominal independence. The appearance of the US, Britain's powerful rival, enabled Saudi Arabia first to weaken and then to break its dependence on London. The Saudis held that the US had no imperial past in the region and an alliance with it would not lead to the establishment of US colonial dominance.

The Saudis' most dangerous opponents in the Arab world were the Hashemite rulers of Transjordan and Iraq, backed by Britain. The plans for a Greater Syria and the Fertile Crescent, nourished in the Hashemite capitals, were a threat to Saudi Arabia.[65] In the Arabian peninsula, which Riyadh saw as the sphere of Saudi influence, the kingdom was still half-surrounded by British protectorates. Although Ibn Saud was too cautious to challenge Britain directly, he sought US support in opposing it.

The anti-British trend in Saudi Arabia's foreign policy led it to unexpected alliances in the late 1940s and 1950s. It should be remembered that the Arab nationalist movement at that time was also anti-British. Initially, its leaders did not see the US as their main enemy. The 1956 Suez crisis, with the failure of the tripartite (British, French and Israeli) action against Egypt, and the final stage in the decline of British colonialism in the Middle East, were yet to come. Thus the Saudi ruling elite's interests coincided temporarily with those of the national liberation struggle in other Arab countries in spite of differences in their social content.

Anti-communism corresponded to the Saudi elite's ideological stance. It was understood in a peculiar form (communism was supposed to be connected with Zionism and, moreover, to use the Orthodox Church as a tool of its penetration), a theory presumably dreamed up by Ibn Saud's advisers. It is possible that one of them was Fuad Hamza, who brought Hitler's offer of the 'crown of the king of all the Arabs' to Ibn Saud in exchange for his cooperation in the joint struggle against Britain. Although the interests of the Soviet Union and Saudi Arabia frequently coincided as regards major world issues, the Saudi leaders' deep-seated mistrust of Moscow prevented them from starting even a formal dialogue with the USSR or establishing normal diplomatic relations, thus weakening Saudi Arabia's international position.

Formally, Saudi Arabia adopted a consistent attitude to the Palestine problem. Ibn Saud told Dickson as early as 1937 that he was sure that the Zionists' final goal was to seize not only Palestine, but all the land up to Medina, and to spread their control in the east as far as the Gulf coast.[66] The Zionists tried to come to terms with the king on several occasions. For example, Chaim Weizmann (the future president of Israel) made a proposal that was communicated to Ibn Saud through Philby in 1940: realizing Ibn Saud's financial embarrassment, the Zionist leaders offered him £20m if he would alter his attitude to the Palestine question and settle all Palestinian Arabs in his country. Ibn Saud rejected the plan.[67]

The evaluation of Zionist influence in the US and of Zionist policy in Palestine in the above-mentioned instructions for Crown Prince Saud was realistic in some aspects and grossly exaggerated in others. After President Truman had gone back on Roosevelt's promise not to pursue an anti-Arab policy on the Palestine issue, relations between Washington and Riyadh became more difficult. However, both Ibn Saud's and his heir's approach to the fate of Palestine and the threat of Zionism was entirely pragmatic; priority was given to the concrete interests of the Saudis, who tied themselves increasingly to the US.

US policy in the Middle East and its relations with Saudi Arabia were complicated by Washington's support, first, for Zionist claims in Palestine and, then, for Israeli foreign policy in the years following the Second World War. As early as October 1945 President Truman told the heads of US diplomatic missions in the Arab world, who had expressed their fears over the pro-Zionist drift in Washington's foreign policy, 'I'm sorry, gentlemen, but I have to answer to hundreds of thousands of people who are anxious for the success of Zionism; I do not have hundreds of thousands of Arabs among my constituents.'[68]

In the early post-war years, Saudi Arabia continued to receive American economic and military aid. The kingdom was granted a first loan of $5m outside the lend-lease scheme in April 1945 for the purchase of US goods; a second loan of $10m for 10 years at an annual interest rate of 3% in August 1946 for the purchase of food and agricultural equipment in the US; and a third loan of $25m in 1946 for the purchase of American agricultural products. Saudi Arabia also received $10m in cash to re-equip Jidda's port and to bring electricity to the town itself. All loans were granted by the

Export-Import Bank of the US.[69] Saudi Arabia received a further loan of $2m in May 1946 from the Foreign Liquidation Commission (created for the liquidation of surplus US military property abroad) to purchase military equipment on normal commercial credit terms.[70]

In 1951 a railway was built between al-Dammam and Riyadh with US assistance. Under the fourth clause of the Truman programme, the US pledged to help Saudi Arabia develop its agriculture, transport system and natural resources, starting in 1952. The aid did not cover much more than the initial research, however, and the amount was insignificant ($1.7m, according to Saudi data). Besides, most of the sum was spent on maintaining the US mission. In 1954 Saudi Arabia decided to end cooperation with the US under the fourth clause of the Truman programme, with a formal reference to the fact that Israel received far more under the programme.[71]

The air-force base in Dhahran, whose construction was completed in 1946, was the main US military stronghold in Saudi Arabia. The agreement of 18 June 1951 prolonged the lease for a further five years. In exchange, the US agreed to supply the Saudi army with modern aircraft and tanks. A special supplement to the agreement provided for the training of Saudi pilots by US instructors. Dhahran became the headquarters of the US advisers who came to Saudi Arabia in 1952 and trained the air-force personnel in Jidda and al-Taif. The expansion of US military activities amounted to supplanting the British, who had trained Saudi military personnel since 1947.[72]

Relations with Britain and the al-Buraimi dispute

Saudi Arabia's borders with the British protectorates – Qatar, the Trucial States, Oman, the Aden protectorates (later the PDRY and then part of the united Yemen) and Yemen in the area of the Rub al-Khali – were not delimited and led to disputes. In the late 1930s and especially in the 1940s, when most of the Arabian peninsula was covered by oil-prospecting activities, the border question acquired particular importance. Rights to various parts of the desert, which had earlier been of no economic value, now became the focus of disputes because of possible oil deposits.

In the late 1940s a fierce conflict arose between Saudi Arabia and Britain over the al-Buraimi group of oases, which were claimed by Abu Dhabi, the sultanate of Muscat (both British protectorates) and Saudi Arabia. The nine villages of al-Buraimi were scattered over a territory whose total area measured almost 2,000 sq. km. The traditional crossing-point of the caravan routes in the south-east of the Arabian peninsula, the area had been annexed to the first Saudi state in 1795. The Saudis considered al-Buraimi as a part of the Eastern Province and claimed that their rule over the oases had lasted for 155 years. Britain questioned these claims, stating that the Saudi dominance was just a short episode in the history of al-Buraimi, which actually belonged to Abu Dhabi and Muscat.

Al-Zirikli comments, 'The oil explorers' noses smelt oil in al-Buraimi. King Ibn Saud did not object to oil prospecting there by Aramco geologists.' Oil prospecting started in 1949.⁷³ The British government demanded, on behalf of Abu Dhabi and Muscat, that prospecting should be halted 'in those lands whose ownership has not yet been agreed upon'. It warned that to continue the prospecting might lead to a clash between Abu Dhabi and Saudi Arabia. Preferring not to aggravate the conflict, Ibn Saud ordered the geologists to be recalled from the disputed territory until the borders were defined. The Aramco specialists left the region and an intense exchange of notes began between the British and Saudi governments.

In 1950, however, geologists from the Anglo-Iranian Oil Company (the future British Petroleum) started prospecting on some islands that Saudi Arabia considered its own territory. They next began explorations in the very territory whose ownership had not been agreed upon, according to the British. On 21 May 1950 the Saudi government lodged a protest. The British ambassador to Jidda answered on 3 October that Britain considered that Saudi claims to the territory in question were unfounded.⁷⁴

In August 1951 a meeting was held in London between the Saudi delegation (led by Prince Faisal, the minister of foreign affairs) and the British foreign secretary, Herbert Morrison. It was decided to convene a special conference, chaired by the British representative and with the participation of all the parties concerned, in order to reach an agreement on the borders. Both parties agreed to stop all geological prospecting and troop movements in the disputed area until the end of the conference.⁷⁵ The conference was held in al-Dammam in late January and February 1952 but produced no results.⁷⁶

Relations between Britain and Saudi Arabia deteriorated, going beyond the framework of the territorial dispute. British military advisers had been sent to Saudi Arabia during the Second World War: they proved ineffective and had been recalled even before the end of the war. The British military mission resumed its activities in 1947 to train 10,000 bedouin for service in the units modelled after the Arab Legion in Transjordan. Several Saudi officers, mainly the king's sons and retainers, had been sent to British military academies. The al-Buraimi dispute brought an end to that cooperation. In 1952 the Americans, with their strong economic position in Saudi Arabia, took on the training of Saudi military personnel.⁷⁷ Soon after the failure of the al-Dammam conference, a British political agent arrived in al-Buraimi 'to undertake administrative duties'.

Ibn Saud instructed the governor of al-Hasa to send a civilian mission to al-Buraimi. It was led by Turki ibn Utaishan, the head of the administration of the group of oases. In early September 1952 he arrived in al-Buraimi and settled in the village of Khamasa with a group of some forty people – scribes, technical experts, guards and servants. According to the Saudi version, there was no armed detachment in the mission. Besides several policemen of his own, however, Ibn Utaishan enlisted many inhabitants of the oases, including several who were armed.⁷⁸ A British political agent was immediately sent from Sharja to al-Buraimi with an armed detachment. It stopped 4 km from the Saudis and British aircraft began flying over Khamasa at low altitudes. Britain demanded that the Saudi government recall Ibn Utaishan's mission.⁷⁹

On 10 October 1952 the US ambassador in Jidda offered to mediate in the dispute, recommending that the parties involved in the conflict should refrain from provocative actions, stay at their positions in al-Buraimi and resume negotiations. The proposal was advantageous to Aramco, leaving at least half of the rights over al-Buraimi with the Saudis. Ibn Saud proposed a plebiscite in the oases, but Britain turned down the suggestion.[80] In 1953 British geologists returned to al-Buraimi. However, Ibn Saud feared that if the Americans were permitted to prospect for oil, it might aggravate the conflict with Britain. At the time of the king's death in November 1953, Ibn Utaishan was still besieged in the village and the British were undertaking intensive oil-prospecting activities.[81]

In July 1954 Saudi and British representatives signed an agreement in Nice, referring their dispute to a court of arbitration that was to meet in Geneva early the following year. In September 1955 the British representative to the court resigned, feeling that the decision would be unfavourable to Britain.[82] An American Arabist has claimed that the Saudis promised the brother of the shaikh of Abu Dhabi a huge amount of money 'if he would prevent the Iraq Petroleum Company from operating in the disputed territories and leave the field open for Aramco'.[83]

In October 1955 detachments from Abu Dhabi and Muscat, commanded by British officers, were deployed in al-Buraimi. The Saudi policemen surrendered after a token resistance and were repatriated via Abu Dhabi and Bahrain. Britain claimed that it was the armed forces of Abu Dhabi and Muscat which had occupied the oases. The Saudi government stressed that its disagreement was not with Abu Dhabi and Muscat, but with Britain. Saudi Arabia lodged a protest, demanding the withdrawal of British troops, and then preferred a complaint against Britain's actions at the UN Security Council.[84]

The US sided with Saudi Arabia on the issue but, fearing that the dispute might escalate, again offered to mediate in the conflict and persuaded the Saudi government to withdraw its protest from the UN and resume negotiations with Britain. In May 1956 the British deputy foreign secretary arrived in Jidda and held several meetings with Faisal. Then the British ambassador came to Jidda for negotiations. On 9 November 1956, however, Saudi Arabia severed diplomatic relations with Britain and banned oil exports to it because of its participation in the 1956 'tripartite aggression' against Egypt.[85] In 1960 a UN mission, led by Dag Hammarskjöld, tried unsuccessfully to mediate between the two countries.[86]

When Kuwait's independence was proclaimed in June 1961, the country was immediately threatened by an invasion from Iraq. In supporting Kuwait, Saudi Arabia found itself on the same side as Britain. Saudi and British troops were sent to Kuwait and remained there until January 1963. The following year, Saudi Arabia and Kuwait agreed on a division of the Neutral Zone, for administrative purposes, but retained the earlier agreement on the even distribution of oil resources.[87]

Saudi-British differences were gradually forced into the background by their common interest in combating the Arab nationalist movement, with its socialist overtones, in the Middle East and particularly in the Arabian peninsula. Prince Faisal met the British foreign secretary in September 1962 in New York at a session of the UN

General Assembly. They agreed to resume diplomatic relations and to conduct new negotiations over al-Buraimi. In July 1963 the Saudi ambassador returned to London. It should be noted, however, that Saudi Arabia was the last Middle East state to restore relations with Britain after the rupture caused by the Suez crisis of 1956.

In the 1950s Saudi-British relations were further complicated by events in Oman. Riyadh supported the Ibadhis, its former enemies, who tried to found an independent state in inner Oman and waged an armed struggle against the British and the sultan of Muscat's troops from 1954 to 1959. After the Omani imamate was routed, its leaders fled to Saudi Arabia in 1959.[88]

Saudi policy in the Middle East

The Saudi representative took part in negotiations held in Egypt in 1943 to set up a regional organization of the Arab countries. Crown Prince Saud signed the covenant of the Arab League in Cairo in 1945. Britain had encouraged the creation of the league, hoping to use it to keep the Middle East within its sphere of influence. Unable to secure the leading role in the Arab League, King Ibn Saud initially treated it with reserve. He feared the Hashemite dynasty's dominant influence in the organization and at the same time opposed Egypt's claims to leadership. Riyadh's conditions for joining the league included the preservation of Saudi Arabia's territorial integrity and the continued independence of Syria and Lebanon as a counterbalance to the Hashemites, in addition to a guarantee that the existing borders between the Arab countries would be preserved.

Initially the Arab League members consisted of Egypt, Iraq, Yemen, Lebanon, Saudi Arabia, Syria and Transjordan. They were followed by Libya and Sudan and subsequently by all the other Arab states. The league's tasks, proclaimed during its foundation, included: first, consolidating relations between the member countries; second, coordinating their policies in order to develop their cooperation and ensure their independence and sovereignty; and, third, joint responsibility for the interests of all the Arab countries. The Council of the Arab League set up a permanent headquarters in Cairo. Within the framework of that regional organization, a cultural agreement was signed in 1946 and a treaty on joint defence and economic cooperation in 1950, according to which the signatories would 'consider any act of armed aggression against one of them an armed aggression against all of them'. The agreement provided for a permanent military commission and a joint defence council.

In the years immediately after the Second World War, Ibn Saud saw the Hashemites as his adversaries. Naturally, the plans to create a 'Hashemite empire', consisting of Iraq, Lebanon, Palestine, Syria and Transjordan under the notion of the Fertile Crescent or (in a curtailed form) under the plan for a Greater Syria, led to resistance from Saudi Arabia. Cairo also viewed these plans with suspicion.

King Abdallah of Transjordan still hoped for a restoration of the sharifian family in Hijaz. In 1947 he convened the so-called congress of Hijaz, which supported anti-Saudi groupings in Hijaz. In response to his actions, the Saudi government threatened to raise once again the issue of the areas of Aqaba and Maan that it considered part of Hijaz. Abdallah temporarily gave up the plans for a Greater Syria, referring to the need for a joint Arab position on the Palestine question, and he ended the anti-Saudi propaganda in Hijaz.[89]

Within the period of the British mandate in Palestine, Britain announced its support for a 'Jewish national home' there. President Truman also declared his support for the Zionists in Palestine in October 1946 and called for 100,000 Jews to be allowed to emigrate to Palestine without any consultations with the Arab countries. Ibn Saud wrote to Truman as follows, 'I am surprised by the president's statement concerning his support for the Jews in the Palestine question, since it runs counter to earlier US promises.'[90]

By the time that the Palestine question was referred to the UN in 1947, relations between Jews and Arabs in Palestine had deteriorated sharply, but there was no unity on the issue among the Arab states. Transjordan claimed its part of the territory, whereas Saudi Arabia, Egypt and other Arab League members rejected these claims. King Abdallah's plans also met active resistance on the part of the US. On 29 May 1947 the UN General Assembly decided to annul the British mandate over Palestine and divide the territory into two independent states. The creation of the state of Israel on a part of Palestinian territory, and the first Arab-Israeli war, created a new situation in the region. Essentially, Saudi Arabia did not take part in the war. Ibn Saud sent only one battalion, headed by Lieutenant-Colonel Said Kurdi-bek, which acted as a unit of the Egyptian army. In June 1948 King Abdallah visited Riyadh and a formal reconciliation took place between the two monarchs. However, the differences were far from having been settled.[91]

The Arab states' defeat in the Palestine war highlighted the disagreements between the members of the Arab League. The governments of Saudi Arabia and Egypt wanted to expel Transjordan from the league for its plans to annex eastern Palestine, which seemed to them the first step towards the creation of a Greater Syria. However, the Arab League failed to take any resolute action. King Abdallah grew bolder and formally annexed the Arab part of Palestine in December 1949.[92] The 13 June 1950 session of the Arab League Council decided to consider Transjordan's annexation of eastern Palestine a temporary measure and to reconsider its future only in the context of a final solution of the Palestine problem. King Abdallah was assassinated on 20 July 1952, to be succeeded by his son Talal (who soon went mad) and then by his grandson Husain.[93]

Relations between Saudi Arabia and Egypt oscillated between a close alliance and a complete rupture involving military confrontations. As a result of the serious clash between the Egyptian pilgrims and the Ikhwan in 1926 (see chapter 12), the Egyptian government had refused to recognize the conquest of Hijaz by Ibn Saud. King Fuad had antagonized Ibn Saud by trying to have himself proclaimed caliph, and diplomatic relations between the two countries were only resumed after Fuad's death in 1936. After the Second World War, however, relations between Egypt and Saudi Arabia improved considerably. After his state visit to Egypt in 1946, Ibn Saud granted King

Faruq an annual subsidy of approximately £1m. Egyptian teachers, technicians and advisers arrived in Saudi Arabia and an Egyptian military mission was sent to the Saudi army.[94]

In his speech from the throne of March 1954, King Saud proclaimed the need to cooperate with the Arab countries within the framework of the Arab League in accordance with its covenant and the treaty on joint defence. The king proposed closer relations with the Islamic countries, promised a continuation of the anti-Israeli policy and declared his determination to improve relations with all states. He noted, however, that there were unsolved problems between Saudi Arabia and the 'friendly British government'.[95]

The call for Arab cooperation, the traditional hostility towards Israel and the anti-British trend of Saudi policy laid the grounds for a *rapprochement* with Egypt. King Saud adopted a realistic attitude towards the revolutionary changes in Egypt and recognized the new regime. He was the first Arab head of state to visit Cairo after the revolution of 23 July 1952. During his official visit to Egypt in March 1954 he met Naguib, the head of state, and Gamal Abdel Nasser.[96] In early August 1954 Nasser visited Saudi Arabia as a pilgrim and negotiated with King Saud, who joined Egypt's efforts directed against the planned Baghdad Pact. In February 1955 a conference of ministers of foreign affairs of the Arab countries was held in Cairo with the participation of Prince Faisal. Its communiqué read:

> The foreign policy of the Arab states is based on the covenant of the Arab League, the treaty on joint defence and economic cooperation of the Arab states and the charter of the United Nations.[97]

The participation of Iraq and Iran in the Baghdad Pact made Saudi Arabia wary and it temporarily drew nearer to Egypt, Syria and Yemen. It has been claimed that Saudi Arabia and Egypt were implicated in the unrest that rocked Jordan in the winter of 1955–56 and led to the downfall of Glubb Pasha, the commander of the Arab Legion, and to Jordan's refusal to join the Baghdad Pact.[98]

As a counterbalance to the pact, President Nasser strove to conclude bilateral military agreements with other Arab countries. A joint defence pact with Syria was signed in March 1955. The Syrian delegation came to Riyadh, and the Saudis supported the Egyptian-Syrian treaty. In October Saudi Arabia concluded a bilateral military treaty with Egypt. The supreme council of both countries was formed of the ministers of defence and foreign affairs. A joint military council and a joint military command were set up. The treaty was for an initial period of five years and was to be automatically extended unless either party declared that it had terminated it.

In early 1956 the Arab governments refused to participate in the joint defence pact for the Middle East, initiated by London and Washington.[99] In March that year, King Saud met Egyptian President Nasser and Syrian President Shukri al-Quwatli in Cairo. They decided to conclude a pact on cooperation and brotherhood: thus three states with different regimes and contradictory interests agreed to coordinate their policy on an anti-Western basis. In the mid-1950s a wave of nationalism and anti-Western (chiefly anti-British) sentiment swept the Arab East. On 20 April 1956 Imam Ahmad of Yemen met King Saud and Nasser in Jidda. The following day, they signed a joint defence agreement.[100]

The Saudi king's alliance with Nasser was also caused by the fact that the Egyptian president did not actively oppose the US before the nationalization of the Suez Canal. Egypt's policy was directed against the British and the Hashemites, Britain's supporters in the Arab world. Cairo agreed with the direction of Riyadh's foreign policy and with Sanaa's traditional anti-British stance.[101] During the 1956 Suez war, Riyadh supported Cairo, declared its readiness to provide Egypt with military aid, severed diplomatic relations with Britain and France and halted oil exports to these countries, and gave Egypt substantial financial aid.[102]

The further Saudi-Egyptian cooperation advanced, however, the more doubts arose within the Saudi royal family and among the influential *ulama*. Propaganda from Egyptian radio influenced some sectors of the Saudi population, whose anti-Western attitudes were combined with anti-monarchism. Nasser's growing popularity in Saudi Arabia worried the king and his retinue. According to some authors, a conspiracy among Saudi officers was discovered as early as May 1955. The officers (who had been trained in Egypt) apparently intended to overthrow the regime, with the alleged involvement of Egyptian military advisers.[103] With the strikes and unrest in Dhahran still fresh in the minds of the king and the princes, signs of revolutionary activity now appeared in Jordan and Iraq. The embargo on oil supplies to Britain and France harmed the state exchequer, and thus the princes' privy purses, making them doubt whether Egypt was worth such sacrifices. Last, but not least, Washington incited Riyadh against Cairo, the Americans' main Arab adversary.

After Egypt's political success in the Suez war, the US administration sought new ways of controlling the Arab nationalist movement and preventing certain Arab countries from increasing their cooperation with the USSR. The result was the Eisenhower Doctrine, proclaimed in January 1957. The doctrine claimed that a 'vacuum' had been left in the Middle East after Britain's and France's defeat in the Suez war. It promised that US armed forces would be used to protect the territorial integrity and independence of the countries of the region, if and when they were subject to aggression by a country 'dominated by international communism'. President Eisenhower demanded that he should be authorized to deploy US forces abroad without consulting Congress. Essentially, it was a bid to establish US dominance in the Middle East with the support of friendly regimes and backed up by force of arms when necessary. On 9 March 1957 the president signed a programme (approved by Congress), outlining US policy in the Middle East. The Eisenhower Doctrine was put into practice one year later, when US marines landed in Lebanon.[104]

In pursuing its policy in the Middle East, Washington counted on Saudi Arabia's support owing to its economic dependence on the US. That support was especially precious for the US in the light of Riyadh's influence in the Islamic world. In January 1957 President Eisenhower invited King Saud to visit the US. There was active opposition to the Eisenhower Doctrine in some Arab countries. On his way to Washington, Saud met the leaders of Egypt, Syria and Jordan in Cairo. Their communiqué described the Eisenhower Doctrine as 'a detailed programme of enslavement of the nations who have recently chosen the road of independent development.' They rejected the 'vacuum theory' and stated that their countries would never come within the sphere of influence of a foreign power. King Saud was charged with conveying their opinion to President Eisenhower.[105]

King Saud behaved in a different manner once he was in the US, however. At the official negotiations, he won a commitment from the US to supply Saudi Arabia with ground, aircraft and naval equipment, train Saudi pilots, send technicians and grant a loan of $25m. The US promised another loan for the reconstruction of the port in al-Dammam, and it was decided to double Saudi Arabia's 15,000-strong regular army. Saud promised to extend the lease of the Dhahran air-force base and try to persuade other Arab countries to adopt the Eisenhower Doctrine.[106]

On King Saud's return to the Middle East, he found that opposition to the Eisenhower Doctrine was growing in the Arab world, including Saudi Arabia itself. Nasser enjoyed such authority that his opinion could not be disregarded.[107] At a new summit between the leaders of Egypt, Syria, Saudi Arabia and Jordan held in Cairo from 24 to 27 February 1957, Saud tried to advocate the Eisenhower Doctrine. He was supported by King Husain of Jordan. But Nasser and al-Quwatli said that they would never give up the policy of neutrality, since they did not want to be guided by Washington and help to increase US influence to the detriment of the Arabs' interests. Nasser also noted that he would accept US military aid only if it came without any political conditions and Egypt was entitled to use it at its own discretion. Pressed by Nasser, al-Quwatli and public opinion in Saudi Arabia, Saud had to withdraw his support for the doctrine and join the states that rejected it. He agreed that 'the Arab world should be protected by the Arab countries themselves in the interests of their genuine security and out of the system of foreign alliances'.[108] Soon afterwards, on 23 March, Crown Prince Faisal said in an interview with the Middle East News Agency that:

> The policy of the Saudi Arabian Government has not changed since the visit of His Majesty the King to the United States. The views of the Saudi Arabian Government are in full agreement with the views of Egypt on all problems.[109]

Saud's and Faisal's declarations may be seen as tactical manoeuvres, aimed at calming public opinion in Saudi Arabia and other Middle East countries, and avoiding a dangerous confrontation with Egypt. It was clear to both Cairo and Riyadh that their temporary identity of interests had ended. During his visit to the US, King Saud had met Crown Prince Abd al-Ilah of Iraq, with American mediation.[110] The traditional enmity between the Saudis and the Hashemites receded into the background, yielding to the common interests of self-preservation in an atmosphere of growing revolutionary ferment in the Middle East.

Domestic and Foreign Policy (1945-1958)

In April 1957, when King Husain of Jordan dismissed Nabulsi's government for its leftist stance,[111] King Saud gave Husain military and political aid. Two brigades of the Saudi National Guard, deployed in Jordan since the Suez war, were put at the Jordanian king's disposal. The Saudi government paid its share of the annual subsidy of $30m to Jordan to replace British aid under the agreement between Egypt, Syria and Saudi Arabia of 1956, whereas Egypt and Syria withheld payment.[112] A polarization of forces continued in the Middle East, with Cairo and Riyadh increasingly finding themselves at opposite poles. Soon after the change of government in Jordan, King Husain visited Riyadh, which meant a further *rapprochement* between the two previously hostile dynasties. Under the influence of the US, King Saud favoured the idea of an alliance between the three kingdoms – Saudi Arabia, Jordan and Iraq – in order to encourage conservative forces. In 1957 he visited Iraq, but an official alliance was not established.[113]

King Saud did not dare to dissociate himself openly from Egypt and Syria, fearing serious consequences for his throne. In his official statements, he stressed his loyalty to the principles of positive neutrality and the decisions of the Cairo conference. In March 1957 some Palestinians were arrested in Saudi Arabia and explosives were found on them. They had allegedly been sent by the Egyptian government to blow up the Nasiriya, the royal palace in Riyadh. Egypt claimed that the terrorists had been sent to make an attempt on Iraqi Prime Minister Nuri al-Said's life with the consent of the Saudis. Egyptian-Saudi relations deteriorated sharply and the arrival of an Egyptian delegation did not lessen the tension.[114]

A propaganda campaign was launched in Saudi Arabia against 'world communism' as the motive force behind all manifestations of the national liberation struggle. James Richards, the US president's special aide for the Middle East aid programme, visited Saudi Arabia in the spring of 1957 and signed a communiqué that mentioned the need to oppose all 'communist activities'.[115]

In February 1958 the United Arab Republic (UAR) was formed as a union between Egypt and Syria. As a counterbalance, Washington and London promoted the creation of the Arab Federation of Iraq and Jordan and encouraged other Arab countries to join it. But Saudi Arabia saw the old Hashemite threat behind the federation and refused to join, declaring its neutrality towards both the federation and the UAR. Relations between Saudi Arabia and Jordan cooled. On 8 April 1958 Riyadh discontinued the subsidy paid to Amman under the agreement of 19 January 1957. In response, King Husain demanded that Saudi troops should be withdrawn from Jordan: this was done in May.[116] King Saud nonetheless saw the main threat to his throne as emanating from the UAR. Nasser's reforms were having a strong impact on the nascent public opinion in Saudi Arabia and his popularity was growing among the Saudis.

CHAPTER 17

The Struggle for Power and its Outcome (1958–1973)

The struggle for power between Saud and Faisal

The first stage: Faisal assumes power (March 1958–December 1960). Soon after the creation of the United Arab Republic in February 1958, King Saud was accused in public of a conspiracy aimed at assassinating President Nasser. Abd al-Hamid al-Sarraj, the former head of Syrian military intelligence, reported that he had been offered around £2m to send a Syrian jet fighter to bring down Nasser's plane. Photographs of three cheques made out in Riyadh and drawn on a Beirut bank for the total amount of almost £2m appeared in the press.[1]

Nasser enjoyed such popularity that the report of the Saudi conspiracy against him led to increased tension in Saudi Arabia, particularly in Riyadh. The situation was disturbing for the Saudi royal family and the higher echelons of the *ulama*.[2] The country's financial situation was extremely grave, due to the high level of spending by the king and his retinue and the drop in oil revenues. The labour unrest in the Eastern Province had occurred only recently and there was dissatisfaction among local officials, intellectuals and some of the military.

An idea of their mood can be gauged from *The Message to King Saud* by Nasir al-Said, published in 1958.[3] Its author, who was to become a leader of the Union of the People of the Arabian Peninsula, worked for Aramco and was one of the oil workers' leaders in the Eastern Province. He was jailed together with several other activists in 1953, was released after the strike and was then exiled to Hail. When King Saud visited Jabal Shammar in 1953, Nasir al-Said addressed him in public, calling on him to proclaim a constitution, fix the date of parliamentary elections, abolish the *majlis al-shura* and grant the freedom to organize trade unions. He regained his job at Aramco under pressure from the workers, but then had to flee Saudi Arabia, fearing for his life. In addition to his previous programme, the *Message* demanded better pay for the workers and called on the regime: to grant broad democratic rights, such as the freedom to hold strikes and demonstrations, freedom of the press and freedom of conscience; to release all political prisoners; to abolish such punishments as amputating the hands of thieves; to recognize the Shia's freedom and equal rights; to close the US base in Dhahran; to ban slavery; to restrict the influence of the Al al-Shaikh family; to disband the League of Public Morality; and to put an end to the activities of the US intelligence community and Aramco's 'propaganda centres'.

Most members of the Saudi royal family and the leading *ulama* inclined to the necessity of a palace revolution in order to transfer real power to Crown Prince Faisal. The king ensconced himself in the Nasiriya palace in Riyadh with his guard and bodyguards. Faisal was in the desert, contacting the bedouin shaikhs.[4] Faisal then demanded that absolute power be transferred to him as head of government and that the king should not interfere in the cabinet's affairs. Receiving no reply, he sent in his resignation.[5] Proshin comments:

> The numerous royal family was always heterogenous. Its individual members occupied different social positions and received different allowances from the exchequer. However, in Ibn Saud's lifetime the frictions within the family did not turn into open enmity. The princes were afraid of Ibn Saud, for he might deprive them of their allowances, as he did more than once when he was disobeyed. After Ibn Saud's death, the royal family split into different groups.[6]

Crown Prince Faisal, an experienced and astute politician, rallied his supporters (who were dissatisfied with the influence enjoyed by Saud's sons at court) and tried to portray Saud as an incompetent leader. Despite his long-established and close connection with the US, Faisal wanted to give the impression that he was in favour of reforms and a *rapprochement* with Nasser. Meanwhile he was preparing a palace revolution.

On 24 March 1958 a group of princes, led by Fahd ibn Abd al-Aziz, handed an ultimatum to King Saud, urging him to transfer power to Faisal. They also demanded that the exchequer be protected from embezzlement; that the king's most hated advisers, who had taken part in the anti-Nasser conspiracy, be dismissed; and that the king's brothers enjoy the same rights as his sons did. When Saud asked the Americans for help, it was not forthcoming. He was opposed by the majority of the Saudi royal family and was unpopular in the army. In such a setting, he had to accept the princes' ultimatum.[7] A royal decree was published on 31 March 1958, endowing the chairman of the *majlis al-wukala* (council of ministers) with 'full responsibility to supervise the exercise of all administrative power in domestic, external and financial affairs'. Faisal also became commander-in-chief of the Saudi armed forces.[8]

The crown prince's political astuteness, and his proclaimed nationalism and reformism, proved so successful that the first reaction of the Western media to developments in Saudi Arabia was adverse. These events were described as a serious blow to the West's positions in the Middle East. Shortly afterwards, however, US Secretary of State John Foster Dulles stated that Faisal's coming to power indicated a normal course of developments and would not cause changes in Saudi-US relations.[9]

Faisal's attitude misled not only the Western media. Some opposition leaders, too, pinned their hopes on him. The Front of National Reforms of Saudi Arabia published an address to Faisal in Damascus,[10] echoing the proposals that Nasir al-Said had made in his *Message to King Saud*. In April 1958 the leadership of the Front of National Reforms decided to form the National Liberation Front of Saudi Arabia on the basis of their organization. Soon afterwards the new front withdrew its support for Faisal and denounced his actions.[11]

On 18 April Faisal broadcast a foreign-policy statement. He expressed the desire to establish friendly relations with all states that were not hostile to the Saudi government and stated that he believed in positive neutrality and would not join any military bloc (clearly referring to the Baghdad Pact). He referred to the principles of the United Nations and to those of Islamic law. Then he stressed the difficulties in the relations with Britain, caused by the al-Buraimi conflict, and expressed his readiness to improve relations with France, provided that Algeria was granted independence. The statement claimed that there was no US base in Dhahran.[12]

The royal decree of 11 May 1958 partly changed the status of the *majlis al-wukala*, approved in 1954, and divided the prerogatives of the monarch from those of the council. The chairman of the *majlis al-wukala* enjoyed administrative power, but political power remained with the king. The decree set the task of putting the state's finances in order and fighting corruption. The members of the *majlis al-wukala* were prohibited from assuming any new functions in the government or otherwise without the prime minister's approval. Neither could they appropriate state property, whether directly or indirectly, or sit on boards of commercial companies.[13]

Saudi Arabia joined the International Monetary Fund as early as 1957. Following the advice of IMF experts, Faisal adopted a programme of financial stabilization which envisaged a reduction in state expenditures to the level of revenues, a reform of the currency system and an end to imports of all goods except food, textiles and medicine. It was decided to halt the construction of several royal palaces and to prohibit car imports for one year. The government drastically curtailed spending on social development, education and health. In 1959 all grants for industrial and agricultural development were discontinued.[14]

The rial was devalued: $1 was now equal to 4.5 rials instead of 3.75. The gold content of the rial was fixed at 0.2 g. In early 1960 a uniform exchange rate was introduced instead of the earlier official and 'black market' rates. Paper money was put into circulation, backed by gold and hard currency, to replace '*hajj* stocks' and gold coins, which were gradually withdrawn from circulation. The rial was divided into 20 piastres instead of 22.[15] By 1960 the gold and hard-currency reserves had increased several times over. The improvement in the balance of payments enabled the government to lift the most important restrictions imposed on the import and export of currency and the export of capital.[16] However, the new policy led to a slowing down of commercial activities, a cessation of public works and an abrupt growth in unemployment. Contractors and members of the middle class and commercial bourgeoisie suffered financial losses.

King Saud had been far from laying down his arms, however, when he transferred real power to the crown prince. When he visited Egypt in 1959, the king tried to belie suspicions of his hostility towards Nasser.[17]

Saud spent the entire year of 1960 travelling throughout his country, sometimes leaving the capital for several weeks at a time. He held receptions for bedouin shaikhs and presented them with gifts. Following the behaviour expected of a 'just and generous ruler', Saud rescued poor debtors from jail by repaying their debts and gave them money for medical treatment. He regularly met members of the *ulama* and invariably took part in the ritual washing of the Kaaba before the pilgrimage. He also made donations for the repair and building of mosques in Saudi Arabia and abroad, and gave funds for the provision of water in the villages, the building of roads and the maintenance of cemeteries.[18] Huge sums of money were still concentrated in his and his sons' hands. The king's sons and brothers, unless they held official posts, received an annual sum of 10m rials from the exchequer if they were married or 2m if they were not. Other princes received allowances whose amount depended on how closely they were related to the king.[19]

The decisive event in Saud's struggle against Faisal was the participation of a group of young princes from the Saudi royal family who were influenced by Nasserist propaganda and called for reforms. Saud contacted them and promised his support in a cautiously worded message. He avoided making concrete promises, for he was far from supporting reforms and was afraid of antagonizing the *ulama*. On a visit to Cairo in May 1960, Prince Nawwaf ibn Abd al-Aziz said:

> There is a trend towards convening a constituent assembly for the first time in Saudi Arabia, drafting the first constitution of the state and setting up a supreme court and a supreme planning commission. The problem is how to accomplish this experiment.[20]

Nawwaf articulated the opinions of a group of young princes, among whom Talal ibn Abd al-Aziz was the most authoritative. Prince Talal, one of Saud's younger brothers, was approximately twelfth in line to the throne. He promoted the idea of constitutional rule, hoping to come to power through the reforms. In June 1960 Talal proposed the establishment of a constitutional monarchy. Faisal rejected the proposal, thereby antagonizing Talal and his group.[21] In August and early September, the young princes submitted a draft constitution to the king. Saud rejected it for its excessive radicalism, but tried to maintain contact with the group.[22]

In May 1960 Faisal planned to go to Europe for medical treatment and appointed Prince Fahd ibn Abd al-Aziz as acting prime minister. Saud refused to approve the appointment. Some princes supported Faisal, while others, including Talal and Nawwaf, sided with the king. Faisal did not dare to leave the country. In November Saud demanded that Faisal should: inform him about government meetings; not appoint the emirs of regions, towns and villages, or appoint judges, without his consent; publish the budget only after his approval; increase the civil list; and pay the full allowances to those of his sons who were minors.

On 18 December Faisal submitted the draft budget to the king. Saud refused to sign it, complaining of a lack of detail. On the same evening Faisal sent the king a letter of protest which read, 'As I am unable to continue, I shall cease to use the powers vested in me as from tonight.' Faisal and his supporters later claimed that the crown prince's letter was not a statement of resignation, since that word was not used. Faisal probably calculated that the king would back down, but Saud interpreted the expression 'I shall cease to use the powers vested in me' as a resignation.[23]

The second stage: Saud returns to power (December 1960–March 1962). On 21 December King Saud accepted Faisal's and thus the government's 'resignation', assumed the functions of prime minister and appointed new ministers. Talal ibn Abd al-Aziz and Muhammad ibn Saud became the ministers of finance and defence respectively. Muhammad was considered Saud's most promising son and his probable successor. Talal's supporter Abd al-Muhsin received the portfolio of minister of interior and Badr became minister of post, telegraph and telephone. The renowned nationalist Abdallah Tariqi headed the ministry of petroleum and mineral resources. It was the first time in the country's history that most of the ministerial portfolios (six out of eleven), though not the key ones, belonged to people outside the royal family.[24]

King Saud's return to power in December 1960 meant a temporary revival of the anti-Western attitudes of 1954–56. Saud's suspicious attitude towards the Americans was combined with the nationalism of the 'free princes'. In March 1961 Saudi Arabia informed the US that it would not extend the lease on the air-force base at Dhahran, which was to expire a year later. King Saud gave the main reason behind the decision as US aid to Israel. On 2 April 1962 the US transferred the base, one of the largest airfields in the world, to the Saudi government. However, the US military returned six months later in connection with the events in Yemen.[25]

On 25 December 1960 Radio Mecca reported that the *majlis al-wukala* had approved the creation of a partly elected national council and decided to draft a constitution. Three days later, Radio Mecca denied the report. It was clear that King Saud would not yield to the young princes, his temporary allies. Hints of reforms nevertheless began appearing in the Saudi press.[26] The Lebanese paper *al-Jarida* published the draft constitution of 200 articles, prepared by Egyptian jurists at the request of Talal and the other young princes in his group. The draft seemed to have been leaked deliberately. However, the director of the Saudi broadcasting and press department denied the report that the king had proposed a draft constitution.[27]

In the course of the struggle for power, three rival centres formed within the Saudi royal family: King Saud relied on a group of princes and tribal shaikhs; Crown Prince

Faisal enjoyed the support of other princes, many *ulama* and the influential merchants of Hijaz; and Talal was supported by the nascent intelligentsia (the graduates of foreign universities) and some of the officials.[28]

The struggle within the royal family remained the main feature of political life in Saudi Arabia throughout 1961. There were frequent defections from one camp to another. Abdallah ibn Abd al-Rahman and several other uncles and brothers of the king soon sided with Faisal. Of the 'free princes', Talal, Badr and Abd al-Muhsin entered the government and Fawwaz became governor of Riyadh. Nawwaf rejected the portfolio of minister of internal affairs and remained neutral. Soon afterwards he was appointed head of the royal *diwan*.[29]

The king set up a supreme planning committee, with Talal as its first chairman. The government projected an increase in the number of schoolchildren and students to 100,000 and then to 200,000. Administrative tribunals were organized at state institutions to investigate malpractice by officials (including ministers). Talal tried to introduce strict planning, but lacked both experience and support. His attempts to increase his own power alienated Saud's sons and closest relatives.[30]

Unemployment rose in 1961. Talal tried to increase employment by public works, but the funds ran out and some of the money allocated was embezzled.[31] On 8 June the ministry of labour, workers' and social affairs was set up. It tried to prohibit overtime and restrict the hiring of immigrants.[32] On 25 July a royal decree was issued setting up the supreme defence council, chaired by the king, with several ex-officio members: the minister of defence and aviation (vice-chairman); the ministers of interior, finance and the economy, post, telegraph and telephone, and foreign affairs; the inspector-general of the army; and the chief of staff. The council's task was to draw up a long-term defence policy for the Saudi army.[33]

The growth of opposition prompted the king to issue a special ordinance on the protection of the royal regime; capital punishment or life imprisonment was introduced as the penalty for crimes against the royal family and the state. Those who tried to change the regime, endanger state security or cause a split in the armed forces were liable to capital punishment. Crimes against the general interests of the state, or attempts to undermine the national economy in collusion with a foreign state, involved a five- to ten-year prison sentence.[34]

Faisal's group concentrated its attacks on Talal, avoiding attacks on the king's reputation. Faisal's supporters, both overt and covert, suggested to the king that innovations would destroy him and warned him against the new ministers. At the same time, they sabotaged the actions of the 'free princes'. Conservative princes in the royal family and high-ranking officials formed a bloc with religious circles, which feared that reforms might diminish the *ulama*'s role in the country.

The *ulama* took the offensive, led by Muhammad ibn Ibrahim Al al-Shaikh, the grand mufti, and Amr ibn Hasan, the head of the League of Public Morality. The mufti sent King Saud a letter, reminding him of the mufti's right to examine all laws and government orders before they came into effect and to give rulings on whether they corresponded to the *sharia*. In particular, the mufti objected to the labour law, claiming that it ran counter to the spirit of Islam. In his opinion, a worker who suffered an occupational injury was entitled only to compensation for the day of injury. Contrary to the opinion of Minister of Finance Talal, the king agreed with the mufti in order to pacify the *ulama*. Soon afterwards the League of Public Morality demanded that all photographic studios in Riyadh be closed down. Although the king wanted the government to obey, implementation of the demand would have amounted to undermining the government's prestige, so the cabinet compromised by ruling that the studios should not have signboards or shop-windows.[35]

Talal's attempts to put the kingdom's financial affairs in order met with the resistance of Saud and his retinue. Talal alleged that King Saud had engaged in land speculation, causing losses to the treasury, seized a share in state contracts and received large sums of money against false receipts, acting through officials at the ministry of finance. The king rejected Talal's proposal to nationalize Riyadh's private power company, aimed at raising additional income. Faisal's group used the occasion to stir up opposition to Talal and the other 'free princes' in commercial circles, spreading rumours that Talal intended to nationalize all industrial and trading companies.[36] In an attempt to reach a compromise with Faisal, the king decided to sacrifice Talal.

In August 1961 Prince Talal told a press conference in Beirut that King Saud had formed a government to enact the changes needed by the country. He claimed that there were harmonious relations both among the members of the government and between the government and the king. Meanwhile, he pointed to his differences with Faisal. Talal was accused of exceeding his authority by speaking on behalf of the government. On 11 September the king published a decree removing Talal, Badr and Abd al-Muhsin from the cabinet. On 16 September Prince Nawwaf ibn Abd al-Aziz, who was considered neutral, was appointed minister of finance and the national economy. Saud's sons occupied the other posts.[37]

Another factor that intervened in the struggle between the brothers was the king's health. It deteriorated so much that on 16 November 1961 Saud was admitted unconscious to the American hospital in Dhahran and then had to go to the US for treatment.[38] The Americans might have been implicated in the departure of a monarch who was proving inconvenient for them. Before leaving for the US, Saud appointed Faisal as regent on 21 November at the insistence of leading members of the royal family. Faisal used his brother's absence to defeat his rivals.[39]

In March 1962 the poor state of the king's health prompted him to appoint Faisal as acting head of state. Faisal demanded that Abdallah Tariqi, the minister of petroleum and mineral resources, should be removed from the *majlis al-wukala* and Saud agreed. The Aramco management had triumphed. According to Talal, they saw the minister of petroleum as their principal enemy. In their reports to the Saudi government, they denounced Tariqi's activities and described him as a communist.[40] Thus Faisal had regained real power fifteen months after stepping down as prime minister. The wheel had turned full circle. Saud spent the rest of the year in the US and underwent several operations.

Talal continued speaking about the need for reforms. He called for transformations within the framework of the *sharia* on the basis of *ijtihad* (an individual's judgement on religious and legal questions, based on *qiyas*, or analogy). This amounted to the introduction into the *sharia* of additional legal norms to regulate new social phenomena. Opening the doors of *ijtihad*, the new groups in society might start to make demands and lend them legal force, interpreting the *sharia* in their interests.

Failing to find support in the country, Talal and his group emigrated. On 15 August 1962 Talal spoke at a press conference at the St Georges Hotel in Beirut. He criticized the Saudi regime without mentioning the king in his statement, which was published by the Beirut paper *al-Anwar*. He said, 'Our aim is to establish a constitutional democracy within the framework of a monarchy.' He was supported by four princes: Abd al-Muhsin ibn Abd al-Aziz, Badr ibn Abd al-Aziz, Fawwaz ibn Abd al-Aziz and Saad ibn Fahd.[41] Fearing the reaction from Riyadh, the Lebanese government made every effort to get rid of the rebel princes. The group left for Cairo, where Talal met Nasser. While in Egypt, Talal published a book expounding his ideas for constitutional reforms and proclaiming socialism as the main principle in Islam.[42] The Yemeni revolution (see below) led to an increase in the group's activities.

In the late 1950s and early 1960s the struggle for power was confined to the royal family, but it was influenced by various political trends. The programme of Talal's group reflected the ideas of the liberal and nationalist reformers and its fate demonstrated the lack of fertile ground for ideas of that kind in Saudi society. Although the royal family had many internal rivalries, they had no seriously organized adversaries. The young, educated generation was represented by a tiny group in al-Hasa and Jidda. To the best of the present author's knowledge, their activities were confined to the distribution of leaflets and to articles for publication in the foreign press.

The influence of the National Liberation Front of Saudi Arabia was limited. The front demanded the abolition of the monarchy and the introduction of a parliamentary regime, the adoption of a national economic policy, the revision of all oil agreements, positive neutrality and a termination of the US lease on the Dhahran air base.[43] The influence of the conservative groups (princes, *ulama* and tribal shaikhs) was decisive. This explains why King Saud was not present at the Belgrade conference of non-aligned countries in September 1961: in his view, Yugoslavia was a communist and atheistic country.[44]

On 28 September 1961 Syria seceded from the UAR as a result of a coup. The Saudi government immediately recognized the new Syrian regime. The propaganda war between Radio Cairo and Radio Mecca (which had been abandoned) resumed in late 1961. Egypt criticized the despotism and corruption of the regime in Saudi Arabia, and the latter charged Nasser with intervention in the affairs of other Arab states and with having betrayed the Arab cause in Palestine by failing to adopting a tough stance against Israel. Relations deteriorated so much that in 1962 the Saudi government refused to receive the *kiswa* (a coverlet for the Kaaba), the Egyptian Muslims' traditional gift.[45]

Simultaneously there was a *rapprochement* between the Saudi regime and Jordan. On 30 August 1962 King Saud and King Husain met in al-Taif and concluded an agreement to coordinate their foreign policy, develop economic, military and cultural relations and demarcate their borders. It was clear that the agreement – known as the al-Taif pact – was directed against Egypt.[46]

The Yemeni revolution and Saudi Arabia's reaction

On 19 September 1962 Imam Ahmad of Yemen died and his son, Crown Prince Muhammad al-Badr, was proclaimed ruler. One week later, a revolution occurred in Yemen. Taking advantage of the change of imam, a group of anti-royalist officers, led by Abdallah al-Sallal, overthrew al-Badr and took power. Egypt immediately expressed support for the republican regime. By early November 1962, twenty-six states had recognized the Yemen Arab Republic (YAR).

The republican government confiscated land, palaces and some other property belonging to the Hamid al-Din dynasty and their royalist supporters. The new regime proclaimed equal rights for all citizens of the YAR, irrespective of religious or tribal affiliation, and banned slavery. The *sharia* courts were replaced by civil courts and new secular schools were opened.

The Yemeni revolution was perceived as an ominous warning to the Saudi royal family. Saudi Arabia had all the elements that had led to the revolutionary outburst in the neighbouring country: a feudal-tribal regime, backed by religion; corruption among the elite; a largely poor and starving population, whose standard of living had fallen sharply after the 'reorganization' of the country's economy and finances in 1958–60; and, most important, the emergence of active groups among officers, officials, merchants, intellectuals, workers and students, who had imbibed the ideas of national and social liberation from Marxist, Nasserist, Baathist and other propaganda and were impatiently demanding change. The revolutionary turmoil in other Arab countries was experiencing an upsurge.

However, subsequent developments in Yemen (see below) showed that it was only a small minority among the population who wanted change, and an even smaller one that was prepared to take action to implement such change. The Saudi regime's relative stability showed that the situation in Saudi Arabia was no different. In both countries, the society was basically feudal-tribal; the majority of the population preferred the old social system, contented themselves with the old social institutions, followed the traditional (conservative) leaders and were reluctant to adopt any ideology but Islam in its medieval form. These factors facilitated both the survival of the Saudi regime, with powerful support from the US and other Western countries, and its cooperation with the royalist forces in Yemen.

The Yemeni republican regime lacked sufficient support outside the towns and some regions with a Shafii population. Saudi Arabia offered asylum to Imam al-Badr. Prominent Yemeni royalists and tribal shaikhs gathered in the regions that bordered Yemen. The Saudi government supplied the royalists with money and arms, paid subsidies to the anti-republican tribes and supported the opposition in Yemen.

The Struggle for Power and its Outcome (1958–1973)

In opposing the YAR, Saudi Arabia found itself in the same camp with Britain. Fearing Yemen's impact on Aden and the protectorates and worried at the growth of Nasserist Egypt's influence in Arabia, the British authorities supported the Yemeni royalists. Later, Jordan and Iran also came to their aid. In early October 1962 Egypt began sending troops to Yemen by both sea and air at Abdallah al-Sallal's request. On 5 October Saudi Arabia allowed the royalists to form a government in exile in Jidda. On 11 October Abd al-Rahman al-Baidani, vice-president of the YAR, was already speaking about the 'state of war' with Saudi Arabia.[47]

In the same month, some Saudi pilots who were transporting military cargoes to the Yemeni border landed their planes in Egypt and asked for political asylum. Earlier, a Jordanian pilot had defected to Egypt from al-Taif; he was among the pilots King Husain had sent to support the Saudi regime. The Egyptian air force bombed groups of royalists and their mercenaries. The Saudi government claimed that Egyptian aircraft had bombed royalist camps in Najran and Jizan in late October and early November. The bombing may indeed have occurred, but it is noteworthy that the foreign journalists brought to Jizan by the Saudis found no traces of bombs or rockets.[48]

A Saudi pilot who fled to Egypt told correspondents that there was an underground organization of officers and civilians in Saudi Arabia, waiting for an opportunity to start action, and that the group had been set up even before the Yemeni revolution.[49] The Saudi authorities stopped air-force flights for a period. All military airfields were controlled by units of the National Guard.

According to the American journalist D. A. Schmidt:

> The top echelons of Saudi society had been divided on whether to come to terms with the new regime in Sana or whether to support the Imam in the mountains. Six members of the Saudi cabinet, all commoners, had signed a memorandum recommending that Saudi Arabia recognize the republicans. Others, headed by Prince Khaled, were already busy helping the royalists. King Saud, as usual, 'waffled' between ardent support of the royalists and prudent recognition of the revolutionaries.[50]

In that uncertain situation, Crown Prince Faisal returned to Saudi Arabia on 24 October from New York, where he had headed the Saudi delegation to the UN after enlisting US support during his visit to the White House. Schmidt continues:

> The Crown Prince found the commoners in the cabinet, who in effect represented the new middle class of Saudi Arabia, a defeatist element. Having little faith in the future of the Saudi monarchy and its ability to reform and defend itself, they were inclined to anticipate that President Nasser would succeed in this evident strategy, which was to use the Yemen revolution combined with a threat of armed force to bring down the structure of the Saudi monarchy. This defeatism was shared by some of the younger members of the royal family.[51]

The royal family decided to close ranks in the face of the danger. Most princes were keen to deprive King Saud of an active role in politics. He had become widely unpopular as a result of his corrupt dealings and taste for luxury; at the same time, he had discredited himself in the eyes of conservative circles by his connection with the reformists and 'free princes'. Washington also preferred Faisal, remembering Saud's nationalist statements and actions in the first period of his rule and in 1961–62. Under pressure from the princes and the *ulama*, the king appointed Faisal as prime minister and minister of foreign affairs on 25 October 1962. Faisal formed a government on 31 October and declared his ten-point programme in November:

1. His Majesty's government holds that the time has come to proclaim the fundamental law of government of the country on the basis of the Quran, the Prophet's Sunna and the deeds of the righteous caliphs. That fundamental law must clearly outline the basic principles of government and relations between the ruler and the ruled, organize various branches of power in the state . . . and declare the citizens' fundamental rights, including the right to express one's opinion freely within the framework of the Islamic faith and general law and order . . . [Then followed various vague formulations with promises to 'develop' the *majlis al-shura*.] The elastic and well-developed fundamentals of our High *sharia* are helpful in achieving this supreme object. They are suitable for all conditions, are applicable everywhere and are always in accordance with the requirements of the place and time.
2. [In the second point, Faisal stated that the government had studied the question of the system of local administration and promised to issue regulations on that subject soon.]
3. The government strives to ensure the immunity and high status of the judicial bodies, which are the torches of law and the symbol of justice. [The third point also stated that the government intended to issue regulations concerning independent courts and set up a ministry of justice with the office of prosecutor-general attached to it.]
4. Whereas the texts of the Quran and the Sunna are certain and finite, and the realities of time and people's new situation in secular affairs develop and are not finite, and with regard for the fact that our young state is governed in accordance with the letter and spirit of the Quran and the Sunna, it has become necessary for us to pay great attention to jurisprudence. Our jurists and *ulama* must carry the torches that illuminate the right path and play a positive and effective role in discussing the new situations facing the nation in order to find *sharia*-based solutions in accordance with the Muslims' interests. Therefore His Majesty's government has decided to create a legal council of twenty members, selected from among the outstanding jurists and *ulama*.
5. The government is fully aware of the need to make serious efforts for the propagation and encouragement of Islam and its protection by words and deeds.
6. [In the sixth point, it was stated that the government had decided to reform the

Committees of Public Morality 'in accordance with the lofty purposes of the *sharia* and Islam'.]
7. [In the seventh point, the government declared that one of its most important tasks was 'raising the nation's social level', including the provision of free medical services and education, subsidies to the needy and national insurance.] When the state ... protects the workers from unemployment, we shall reach a social level that many civilized nations of the world still dream of. Then we shall achieve genuine social justice, without the state's attempts on people's personal freedoms or the seizure of their property and rights. The government strives seriously to introduce important changes into the forms of public life and make the means of entertainment available to its citizens.
8. The government holds that the economic, commercial and social development of our society in recent years still lacks regulation, therefore many important regulations will be issued. [Independent bodies were to be formed to supervise the application of those regulations.]
9. [A financial revival and economic development were declared 'the government's major concern'.] The government has taken and will take important and resolute measures to draft a programme of concrete reforms, which will promote a permanent economic upsurge.
10. [The tenth point of the programme provided for the complete abolition of slavery, its prohibition and the liberation of all slaves.][52]

Thus the new prime minister suggested a programme to consolidate and preserve the regime without introducing any fundamental changes. The purpose of the vague promises to elaborate a constitution based on the Quran and the Sunna, and to transform the judicial system and the League of Public Morality (the latter was denounced by many Saudis), was to eradicate all opposition among a part of the population and to satisfy the protagonists of moderate reforms. The head of government tried to attract the growing middle class by the promise of new legislation and 'independent bodies' to supervise its implementation, as well as the lure of an economic upsurge. To enlist the support of the ordinary people, Faisal promised to raise their standard of living, provide them with various social benefits and protect them from unemployment. In line with the spirit of the age, he abandoned an over-rigid puritanism and allowed some innocent entertainments. The same climate necessitated the abolition of slavery. Faisal's programme was never implemented, however. Official Saudi publications were silent on this important document lest they attract attention to the forgotten promise of reforms.

In practice, the measures taken by the government were very limited. The decree to abolish slavery was issued on 7 November 1962. The government pledged to pay $700 compensation for a male and $1,000 for a female slave. By 7 July 1963 slave-owners had claimed compensation for 1,682 slaves. Other slaves were automatically considered free after that date, the last date for the payment of compensation. The majority of redeemed slaves were owned by the royal family. Most slave-owners ignored the government's offer, since the compensation offered was half the market price of a slave.[53] As a rule, the liberated slaves either had to stay with their former masters because of the country's high unemployment or remained without any means of subsistence.[54]

Whether independently or following the recommendations of US experts, Faisal and his entourage came to the conclusion that more active state intervention was needed in the economy, i.e. the creation of a state sector. According to the decree of 22 November 1962, the General Petroleum and Mineral Organization (Petromin) was formed under the ministry of petroleum and mineral resources, with the minister as its ex-officio head. Its tasks included the extraction, transportation and sale of oil and other mineral resources. To that end, it was to set up companies or invest its capital in existing companies. The development of the petrochemical industry, based on natural gas, was also a function of Petromin.[55]

In early 1963 regulations concerning the industrial and agricultural banks of Saudi Arabia were published. The budget of 1962/63 provided for a sizeable increase in the allocations for education and health.[56] In his speech in al-Taif on 6 September 1963, Faisal listed the projects that were to be given priority: development of the telephone network, roads and airports; settling of the bedouin; a reduction in water charges; the construction of a metallurgical works, an oil-processing plant in Jidda and a paper and pulp mill; prospecting for and exploitation of other mineral resources; opening a college of petroleum and minerals; and a reduction in electricity prices.[57]

The head of the commission for drafting the decree on setting up a ministry of justice and other legal bodies was a representative of the Al al-Shaikh family, while other members were princes of the royal family.[58]

The end of dual power. Faisal becomes king

Having declared martial law on 1 January 1963, Faisal's government took steps to suppress the opposition. The reformist-minded Shaikh Abd al-Aziz Al Muammar, former Saudi ambassador to Switzerland, was arrested and several officers in charge of airborne divisions were charged with an anti-government conspiracy and jailed. The National Liberation Front then stepped up its activities abroad.[59]

In the autumn of 1962 King Saud went to Europe for medical treatment and Faisal prepared to seize power. He appointed his half-brother Abdallah as commander of the National Guard and another half-brother as governor of Riyadh and slashed the allowance to members of the royal family by 20%.[60] When Saud returned to Riyadh on 27 April 1963, he found himself isolated. His thirty-nine brothers delivered an ultimatum, demanding that he transfer all real power to Faisal, though remaining king. Saud left the country.

After the king's second departure, Faisal removed all Saud's sons from important administrative posts and replaced them with his own brothers – Princes Khalid, Fahd and Sultan – and his uncle, Prince Musaid ibn Abd al-Rahman, who was devoted to him. Then he removed most of the royal guard from the capital. It consisted of three battalions with tanks and anti-aircraft guns and most of its officers had been trained in the US. The soldiers of the royal guard received high salaries, houses with plots of land and loans to buy houses of their own. Faisal transferred two battalions of the royal guard (an infantry and an armoured battalion) to the south of the country, to the Yemeni border, and incorporated them into the regular army.[61]

King Saud was allowed to return to the country, provided he did not interfere in government affairs. He was forced to agree and returned to Saudi Arabia on 13 September 1963.[62] On 22 March 1964 Saud made a desperate attempt to regain control over the state, demanding that all executive power should be transferred to him. Faisal declined and mobilized the National Guard in his support. On 25 March the grand mufti recommended that Saud accept the crown prince's demands. The king declined, counting on the support of those units of the royal guard who remained loyal to him. Then Faisal ordered the National Guard to surround the palace. The forces were too uneven and the royal guard capitulated.[63]

On 29 March the *ulama* issued a *fatwa* on the transfer of absolute power to Faisal, leaving Saud with the title of king. The members of the royal family supported the *fatwa*. The *ulama* stressed that their decision was caused by Saud's poor health.[64] Soon afterwards the *majlis al-wukala* passed a series of decisions, depriving King Saud of control over the royal guard and his personal guard and placing them under the ministries of defence and interior, respectively. The *majlis al-wukala* liquidated Saud's court and halved the monarch's annual civil list, reducing it to 183m Saudi rials ($40.7m). Saud could no longer direct state affairs and all royal prerogatives were transferred to Crown Prince Faisal. Sixty-eight princes of the royal family signed a statement supporting the transfer of power to Faisal.[65] The events of March 1964 repeated the palace revolution of 1958 – the only difference being that Saud this time tried to resist and failed.

In the summer of 1964 Faisal began paving the way for the final dethronement of his half-brother. On 24 October he left Jidda and made for Riyadh, meeting bedouin shaikhs on the way. The princes, tribal shaikhs and *ulama* assembled in the capital and proposed that Saud should abdicate and give up all political activities. Saud and some of his sons tried to mobilize their supporters. On 28 October the leading *ulama* gathered at the house of the grand mufti, Muhammad ibn Ibrahim Al al-Shaikh, and then negotiated with the princes at the Sahara Hotel in Riyadh. According to Gerald de Gaury, some 100 princes and 65 *ulama* took part in both meetings – the entire top echelon of the Saudi political and religious hierarchy.[66]

On 2 November the *majlis al-wukala* approved two decisions – the *ulama*'s *fatwa* declaring Faisal to be king, and a letter signed by all members of the royal family, who swore allegiance to Faisal as their monarch. The members of the *majlis al-shura* and representatives of the major provinces also swore allegiance to Faisal. The members of the cabinet, led by Prince Khalid, met Saud on 4 November to inform him of their decision. On the same day, the National Guard swore allegiance to Faisal. Hoping for a miracle, Saud still vacillated. Threatened with house arrest and the confiscation of his property, he finally signed the abdication statement. He left the country in January 1965, swearing allegiance to his brother before his departure. In March 1965 Faisal appointed his half-brother Khalid as crown prince.[67]

So ended the six-year struggle for power that had rocked the Saudi royal family. In the very first year of his rule, Faisal decided that the king should be ex-officio prime minister, assumed real executive power, appointed and dismissed ministers and approved their resignations. All ministers were directly subordinate to Faisal, whose power was virtually as great as that of his father, Ibn Saud.

The opposition in the 1960s and early 1970s

The 1962 Yemeni revolution and the Egyptian-Saudi confrontation led to a temporary increase in the activities of Prince Talal's group (who represented the liberal elite and middle-class traders). On 23 October 1962 Talal proclaimed the creation of the Arab Liberation Front and publicized its programme. He said that the new organization would struggle for a democratic regime and the abolition of slavery in Saudi Arabia, demand a revision of the agreements on oil concessions in order to protect the country's interests and set up a national company for oil production. He advocated the unity of the Arab nations against the imperialist pacts and military bases. Many of his demands were reflected in Crown Prince Faisal's ten-point programme.

The so-called politbureau of the front included Badr, Saad and Fawwaz, all members of the royal family; Muhammad Ahmar Ibrahim, a leading businessman; Saud ibn Isa, a former radio announcer; Daihan Abd al-Aziz, former director of the labour administration of Riyadh; Hasan Nasif, the former minister of health; Ibrahim Abu Takiha, the shaikh of the Huwaitat tribe; and Salim Abu Damiq, the shaikh of the Atiya tribe. The other six politbureau members were allegedly still in Saudi Arabia and their names were not revealed.[68]

In the early 1960s another opposition organization was set up in Cairo: the Federation of the Sons of the Arabian Peninsula (later the Union of the People of the Arabian Peninsula). It was led by Nasir al-Said, the author of *The Message to King Saud*. Claiming to represent 'all detachments of the toilers', including peasants, workers, students, employees, soldiers, officers and doctors, the organization distributed anti-royalist leaflets in Jidda, Riyadh and Mecca. Speaking on Radio Cairo, its members called for the abolition of the Saudi monarchy and the convening of a national assembly that would represent all groups in society. They supported Nasser and denounced King Husain of Jordan.[69] After the Yemeni revolution, the leadership of the Union of the People of the Arabian Peninsula moved from Cairo to Sanaa, where they created a supreme command – with the participation of Nasir al-Said – for practical actions in Saudi Arabia.[70] The groups set up by Talal and Nasir al-Said differed in their social composition, political aspirations and methods of struggle; they criticized each other vigorously.

As for the National Liberation Front, it tried to unite the opposition forces and merged with the Arab Liberation Front in December 1962. The new organization was named the Arab National Liberation Front. Talal was elected its general secretary. The front published its views in the Lebanese paper *al-Kifah*, in a column entitled 'The Voice of the Front'. Its programme included, in particular: a constitutional, democratic form of government and elected organs of government; freedom of thought, speech and assembly; the right to set up political organizations and trade unions; the right to strike and hold demonstrations; a radical restructuring of the government machinery; the development of education, the elimination of illiteracy and the introduction of education for girls, based on equality with males; the industrialization of the country; the distribution of uncultivated land among the peasants; the development of health care and the provision of medical services for all citizens; the encouragement of agricultural cooperatives; the improvement of communications; the strengthening of the army and the modernization of its equipment; a revision of the oil agreements in favour of Saudi Arabia; the creation of a state company for oil extraction and processing; the encouragement of Arab unity; the struggle against imperialist alliances and military bases; the pursuance of a policy of positive neutrality and peaceful coexistence; and the establishment of diplomatic and economic relations with all countries.[71]

In August 1963, however, Talal's group left the Arab National Liberation Front, which adopted its old name of the National Liberation Front.[72] Relations between the 'free princes' and Nasser deteriorated, particularly after Radio Yemen's calls 'to kill all members of the Al Saud royal family without any exceptions'. In August 1963 Talal stated in Beirut that he and other princes would seek an accord with King Saud and Crown Prince Faisal. In February 1964 Talal said that his criticism of the Saudi government's internal and foreign policy was 'entirely wrong', hinting at his disappointment with Egypt. He promised to 'behave well' in the future and expressed his admiration for Faisal's reforms. Talal returned to Riyadh in February; his brothers had arrived there a month earlier.[73] The movement of the 'free princes' ended and nothing more was heard of their political activities.

The organized opposition within the country failed to secure any successes. In December 1962 forty young officers were arrested for having planned a coup. In February 1963 the security services discovered another leftist opposition group.[74]

From 1962 to 1966 there was labour unrest in the country. In 1962 Egyptian compositors stopped work in Jidda, in protest at attacks on Egypt by the Saudi press. In 1963 Saudi and Bahraini workers went on strike in the Eastern Province, but the contractor who had hired them brought in blacklegs from Iraq and Jordan. In the same year a strike was waged at the cement plant in the Eastern Province, but when the strikers were threatened with a lockout they resumed work. The oil workers of the Neutral Zone went on strike, demanding a reduction in the working week from 48 to 40 hours. In 1964 Aramco workers boycotted the company's cafeterias and stores and held demonstrations. In spite of the 1965 decree prohibiting all workers' unions and associations and even collective bargaining, 900 Aramco workers sent a petition with their demands to the board of grievances under the *majlis al-wukala*.[75]

The above-mentioned actions did not affect the majority of the population, however, and until early 1967 the Saudi regime faced no serious danger from the illegal opposition. From time to time, the authorities reported the arrest of individuals charged with 'subversive activities' or 'affiliation with underground organizations that oppose the regime'. In December 1965 the ministry of internal affairs announced that sixty-five people had been arrested on suspicion of 'subversive activities': thirty-five of them were accused of 'membership in a secret organization that deviated from the righteous path to undermine the country's security'. After the defendants had pleaded guilty in writing and asked for an amnesty, the king released them, prohibiting those who were Saudi citizens from working in government offices and expelling those who were foreigners. The second group (of thirty-one men) was accused of adherence to communism and 'destructive principles': nineteen of them were given prison sentences ranging from five to fifteen years.[76]

Among the opposition organizations, only the Union of the People of the Arabian Peninsula and the National Liberation Front remained viable in 1966–67. Another group then emerged: the People's Liberation Front of Saudi Arabia. The Saudi security services arrested hundreds of people, including Yemenis and Palestinians.[77] On 9 January 1967 it was announced that a group of 'trained saboteurs' had been arrested. They were accused of having plotted to put bombs in many government offices, including the ministry of defence, the office of the US military mission, princes' palaces and at a military base near the Yemeni border. The 'saboteurs' had allegedly been sent from republican Yemen and were not Saudi citizens. In March, 17 prisoners accused of acts of sabotage were beheaded in public in Riyadh and more than 600 Yemenis were expelled from the country.[78]

In December 1966 the former King Saud moved from Europe to Cairo. It soon became clear that he had not given up hope of regaining the throne – with Nasser's help.[79] The irony was that he had doggedly opposed the Egyptian president earlier and had been charged with involvement in an attempt on his life. Speaking on Radio Cairo, Saud described Faisal as an 'agent of imperialism' and accused him of having become 'an ally of colonialism against his Arab brethren'. Saud's claim that he intended to return to the country 'at any price' seemed to indicate that he planned a military invasion of Saudi Arabia, relying on the tribes who were loyal to him.[80]

In April 1967 Saud paid a three-day visit to Sanaa, where President al-Sallal welcomed him as 'the legitimate king of Saudi Arabia'. After the Arab-Israeli war of June 1967, however, when the Egyptian-Saudi *rapprochement* began and hostilities in Yemen ceased, Saud's campaign to regain his throne lost momentum and he left for Europe in September. In November he returned to Egypt, but nothing more was heard of his political activities up to his death in February 1969.[81]

During the June 1967 war, there were anti-Israeli and anti-American demonstrations in Ras Tannura and Dhahran, and the demonstrators in Dhahran attacked the US consulate. Several people were arrested and there were rumours that some of them had been killed while in custody. Hundreds of Palestinians were expelled from the country. In late June, the Arab employees at Aramco staged a selective strike lasting several days.[82]

The Struggle for Power and its Outcome (1958-1973)

In 1968 the anti-Faisal opposition temporarily weakened both at home and abroad. Egyptian troops were withdrawn from Yemen in exchange for Saudi Arabia's financial and other support, and Egypt virtually ceased its support for the Saudi opposition within the kingdom. King Faisal's policy of gradual and cautious change led to dissatisfaction among members of the royal family, both those who regarded the changes as too liberal and dynamic and those who found them too slow and hesitant. Both viewpoints had advocates among the princes, which led to friction and personal rivalries. King Faisal's poor health, and the latent struggle over who would be his successor, also caused a certain tension in the royal family. In October 1970 Faisal underwent surgery in Geneva. The question arose as to the outcome of the struggle between the princely groups in the event of his death or retirement. The third most important figure after Crown Prince Khalid was Fahd ibn Abd al-Aziz of the powerful group of Sudairi brothers. (Known as the 'Sudairi seven', these full brothers were all Ibn Saud's sons by his wife from the noble Al Sudairi clan.) King Faisal nevertheless remained master of the situation, both in the kingdom as a whole and in the royal family.[83]

Several underground leftist organizations operated in Saudi Arabia in the late 1960s and early 1970s: the National Liberation Front of Saudi Arabia, the Union of the People of the Arabian Peninsula and some new groups, including the Revolutionary Najdi Party (which declared its intention of opposing the 'reactionary ruling clique') and the National Democratic Front of Saudi Arabia, founded by former Baathists and Nasserists. Although their headquarters were outside the kingdom, they may have had active members in the country.[84]

On 5 June 1969 a large group of Saudi officers, many of whom served in the air force, plotted a *coup d'état*. The officers were allegedly planning to assassinate King Faisal and his brother Prince Sultan, the minister of defence and aviation, and seize the capital.[85] According to some sources, the CIA took a part in disclosing the revolutionary officers' conspiracy.[86] The security services arrested hundreds of officers, chiefly below the rank of major. The Union of the People of the Arabian Peninsula reported that Colonel Daud al-Rumi, the commander of the Dhahran base, and Said Umari, the commander of the Dhahran military district, were jailed and died after being tortured. Some oil workers, officials and bank employees who were connected with the revolutionary officers were also arrested. Yemeni workers and Palestinian technicians were among the conspirators. The National Liberation Front claimed that forty people charged with the coup attempt were executed in August.[87]

Reports of mass arrests, executions and torture in jails were published in the foreign press for some months after the conspiracy was discovered.[88] There were reports of other attempted coups in September and November 1969 and April–May and July 1970.[89] It is possible that the authorities claimed the existence of new conspiracies to justify their repressive measures.[90] According to estimates by some Saudi emigrés, there were some 2,000 political prisoners in the kingdom in 1973, though the figure seems exaggerated.[91]

The Libyan revolution of September 1969 greatly worried the Saudi royal family, for the socio-political conditions were similar in both countries. In response, the Saudi regime concentrated on strengthening its armed forces, particularly the airforce, the National Guard and the security services, which were divided into counter-intelligence and the general directorate of security. The second deputy prime minister and minister of interior, Prince Fahd, controlled all the security services. The army was scattered throughout the country and was never allowed to concentrate near the main centres. After 1962 pilots were recruited only from among the royal family and other powerful families. The coup attempt of June 1969 showed that these steps had not had the expected effect.[92]

King Faisal continued the measures to encourage economic development, including drafting a five-year plan, approved in late 1970. Communications improved and the radio and TV network was developed. The programme of settling the bedouin continued, social services expanded and health care and education improved.[93] As previously, all these reforms were undertaken gradually and cautiously in order to undermine opposition from traditionalists and the *ulama*.

The Saudi-Egyptian confrontation and the war in Yemen

Developments in Yemen extended outside the local context. Because of Soviet support for the UAR and American and British support for Saudi Arabia, the conflict acquired an international dimension.

When hostilities began in Yemen in 1962, Riyadh asked for Washington's help. In a letter to Prime Minister Faisal soon after his coming to power, President Kennedy assured him of US support in preserving the kingdom's security and integrity.[94] On 16 November 1962 US jet fighters performed demonstration flights over Riyadh, Jidda and Dhahran. Three days later, the YAR and the UAR concluded a defence pact. Egypt gave the republicans increasing amounts of military and economic aid. It is interesting to note that both the UAR and Saudi Arabia considered the joint defence pact they had signed with Yemen in Jidda in 1956 as the legal basis of the aid they gave to the Yemeni republicans and the royalists, respectively.[95]

On 1 January 1963 Prime Minister Faisal declared a general mobilization. Two days later, he announced on the radio that the mobilization was directed against the republican government of Yemen. Simultaneously, the Saudi government asked the US for help. In early January the US sent warships and aircraft to Saudi Arabia.[96] The US also agreed to help Saudi Arabia establish an air defence system along the Yemeni border near Najran. On 6 February joint exercises between American and Saudi paratroops started near Jidda; they were joined by 100 American paratroopers sent from West Germany (the Federal Republic of Germany).[97]

The civil war in Yemen and the conflict between Saudi Arabia and Egypt continued to grow. The Saudis supplied the royalists with money, munitions, food and medicine. Egypt increased the strength of its troops in Yemen to 13,000 in December 1962 and to 20,000 in February 1963. It also sent doctors, teachers, agronomists and technicians to the country.[98]

The Struggle for Power and its Outcome (1958–1973)

On 27 November 1962 President Kennedy sent messages to Prince Faisal, King Husain of Jordan, President Nasser and President Abdallah al-Sallal, putting forward suggestions for a solution to the Yemeni conflict. He ignored Imam al-Badr and his retinue. Kennedy suggested that the UAR should withdraw all its forces from Yemen, while Saudi Arabia, Jordan and the shaikhs and sultans of the South Arabian Federation (which had been created by the British in 1959 to unite the protectorates of South Yemen) should cease their aid to the royalists. Faisal turned down Kennedy's proposal the very same day. On 28 November, Nasser also rejected Kennedy's plan and stated that he would agree to withdraw his troops only after ensuring that republican Yemen was out of danger. The YAR president was alone in approving Kennedy's initiative.[99]

Washington probably concluded that the royalists' cause was hopeless. On 14 December 1962 the government of the YAR warned that it would close down the embassies and missions of all countries that had not recognized the republic. On 19 December the US State Department declared officially that the US recognized republican Yemen.[100] K. Trevaskis, the former British high commissioner to Aden, is of the opinion that a reluctance to aggravate relations with the UAR was among the reasons behind Washington's step.[101] Arthur Schlesinger, the biographer of J. F. Kennedy, confirms this opinion.[102]

In early 1963 the Yemeni republicans and the Egyptian forces waged fierce battles with the royalists and with mercenaries who had invaded the country from Saudi Arabia and the British protectorates of South Yemen. The royalist detachments, formed with Saudi and some British help, numbered almost 40,000. They had supply bases and military camps in Saudi Arabia and South Yemen. In February–March 1963 the Egyptians and republicans drove the royalists from the towns of Marib and Harib in the east of Yemen. However, the royalist detachments continued to infiltrate regularly into Yemen through the mountains and across the deserts. By now they were in full control of some areas in the Yemeni mountains. The civil war in Yemen grew virtually into a war between the UAR and Saudi Arabia, which exhausted both countries.[103] According to Schmidt:

> When we examine this four-year period closely, we discover that the convulsive efforts of both sides to break the stalemate have at four distinct stages indeed changed the shape of the conflict. The first of these great efforts was made by the Egyptians in February and March 1963, in what has become known as the 'Ramadhan offensive', which carried them into the Jawf in north-eastern Yemen and to the occupation of Marib and Harib on the eastern side of the country. The second effort, made by the royalists, followed a period of disengagement initiated by the United States. In January and February of 1964 the royalists succeeded for several weeks in closing the Egyptians' main artery, the road from Sanaa to Hodeida . . .
>
> The third effort, Egyptian again, began that summer with a concentration of men in the north-west, and came to fruition in August and September in the largest of all the Egyptian offensives, in the region of Harad, aimed at closing the border with

Saudi Arabia and capturing or killing the imam. In both of these objectives they failed. Meanwhile the royalists were building up in the north and north-east for their own biggest offensive, making the fourth notable effort in a period of more than four years. Following the complete breakdown of the Alexandria agreement between King Faisal and President Nasser, this stinging reverse for the republicans led to the Jeddah agreement of August 1965 and the withdrawal of the Egyptians from northern and eastern Yemen.[104]

In the spring of 1963 Riyadh and Cairo agreed terms on ending hostilities in Yemen and disengaging their forces. In April 1963 the UAR, Saudi Arabia and the YAR agreed to allow UN observers into Yemen. In July 1963 detachments of UN soldiers arrived in North Yemen and established checkpoints in several regions, while UN air and ground patrols surveyed the border regions.[105] They were to prove almost totally ineffective.

In early March 1964 the delegations of the UAR and Saudi Arabia made arrangements for a meeting between Faisal and Nasser to outline a concrete plan for the cessation of hostilities in Yemen. The meeting was fixed for April, but was postponed because of the intensification of the power struggle between Faisal and Saud. The UAR insisted that Saudi Arabia recognize the YAR and cease all aid to the Yemeni royalists, whereafter Egyptian troops would be withdrawn from Yemen. Saudi Arabia still recognized Imam al-Badr as the legitimate ruler of Yemen, delayed official negotiations (which would have amounted to an admission of its participation in the conflict) and insisted on the unconditional withdrawal of all foreign (i.e. Egyptian) troops from Yemen before negotiations started. The Saudi notion of foreign troops did not include the pro-royalist mercenary detachments, which formally were not units of any army. In such a setting, the activities of the UN mission, which had been in Yemen since July 1963, made no sense: the mission and the UN detachments left the country in early September 1964.[106]

The Yemeni conflict threatened to spark off a war between the UAR and Saudi Arabia. In an interview with the Beirut paper *al-Nahar* in early September 1964, Faisal said that the Saudi armed forces might enter Yemen at the imam's request.[107] It was a clear threat. However, Saudi Arabia lacked the military might for that kind of action. Although Egypt's position remained unchanged, an understanding was reached with Saudi Arabia during the Arab summit in Alexandria in September 1964 that both states would mediate in the conflict between the republicans and the royalists.[108] On 2–3 November 1964 a conference of representatives of the YAR and the royalists, held in Erkowit (Sudan), agreed on a cease-fire from 8 November. The armistice lasted for a mere two days.[109]

The protracted hostilities in Yemen created major problems for the YAR, as well as for Egypt and Saudi Arabia. The number of Egyptian forces in Yemen reached 50,000 (the initial figure was 3,000), and between October 1962 and the spring of 1965 almost 15,000 Egyptian soldiers were killed.[110] Many thousands of Yemenis also died in the war.[111] The war emptied Egypt's exchequer and undermined its economy.

The Struggle for Power and its Outcome (1958-1973)

Although the Saudi government did not reveal its expenses, they were undoubtedly very high.

Nasser had overestimated his strength when he sent the expeditionary corps to support the republicans. He probably assumed that the whole operation would take some weeks or at most several months. The potential consequences of his action had seemed worth the effort – ousting the British from South Yemen, including Aden; and a revolutionary outburst in Saudi Arabia, which might lead to the creation of a friendly, 'national-democratic' regime in a country with rich oil resources and weaken the West's positions in the Gulf region. But the war lasted too long and Yemeni society was not yet ready for the revolutionary changes that had started in the country. The royalists enjoyed strong positions within Yemen and had powerful support abroad. The Egyptian soldiers, the sons of peasants from the Nile Valley and the Delta, were unfit for operations in mountainous and desert terrain. In 1967 the expeditionary corps was increased to between 60,000 and 70,000.[112]

Having won some temporary military successes in Yemen, the UAR adopted a tougher attitude towards Saudi Arabia in late 1964. The Egyptian command's role in Yemen's domestic affairs increased.[113] In late June 1965 Nasser stated that unless negotiations between Saudi Arabia and the UAR yielded tangible results, Egypt would eliminate the bases of aggression by force.[114] Within the YAR, the future of the territories annexed to Saudi Arabia – Asir (the area of the town of Jizan) and Najran – was debated. The Egyptian press argued that they had belonged to Yemen from time immemorial.

However, Egypt's position in the YAR had weakened considerably by the summer of 1965. The anti-Egyptian conservative wing, which relied on tribal shaikhs, *ulama* and some groups among the merchants, had acquired growing influence in the republican camp. That grouping, referred to as 'the third force', was dissatisfied with the activities of left-wing elements, which were particularly strong in the republican army and received Egyptian aid.

In early May 1965 the conservative wing of the republicans held a conference in Hamir, with the participation of royalists and pro-royalist tribal shaikhs, in an attempt to reach an agreement. Anti-UAR attitudes were evident at the conference. Meanwhile, the situation had deteriorated on the cease-fire line with Israel, tying the Egyptians' hands. Egypt's hopes for a worsening of the political situation within Saudi Arabia were not realized. The royalist forces in Yemen, armed by Saudi Arabia and Iran, were on the offensive. The republicans and the Egyptians surrendered one strongpoint after another.[115] That was the situation when Nasser and King Faisal met in Jidda on 22 August 1965. Two days later, they signed the first agreement on a settlement of the Yemeni conflict. Neither the republicans nor the royalists took part in the negotiations.[116]

The Jidda agreement of 1965 stipulated that the Yemeni people should solve the question of their country's state system by a plebiscite not later than 23 November 1966; a conference of all national forces and influential political figures was to be convened in Harad on 23 November 1965, to take decisions as to the government system in the transitional period before the plebiscite; a provisional cabinet of ministers was to be formed to govern the country during the transitional period and to define the character of the plebiscite; and Saudi Arabia and the UAR were to be responsible for implementing the conference's decisions. Saudi Arabia should immediately cease all military support for the Yemeni royalists and not allow them to use its territory for military operations against republican Yemen. The UAR was to withdraw its armed forces from Yemen within ten months from 23 November 1965. Hostilities were now to cease in Yemen and a bilateral commission should be set up to reach a peaceful settlement.[117] An understanding may have been reached in Jidda on debarring both President al-Sallal and Imam al-Badr from political activities for a long period.[118] This assumption is supported by the fact that al-Sallal left for Cairo and al-Badr for al-Taif after the agreement was concluded.

The Harad conference opened on 23 November 1965. Both al-Sallal and Imam al-Badr were absent, but the UAR and Saudi Arabia sent representatives. The main purpose of the conference was the creation of a provisional government for the transitional period and the preparation of a plebiscite on the form of government. The YAR representatives strongly advocated the principle of inviolability of the republican regime, while the royalists were equally firm in rejecting it. The conference deliberations were suspended, never to resume.[119]

At the end of 1965 the US and Britain began selling large quantities of arms and jets to Saudi Arabia. Nasser perceived these actions as hostile to Egypt.[120] In early March 1966 the royalists resumed military operations, putting an end to the armistice established by the Jidda agreement. The actions undertaken by the Egyptians and the republicans were not a success, and they were hemmed in within the triangle of Sanaa–Taiz–Hodeida.[121] On 22 March Nasser expressed his intention of keeping Egyptian forces in Yemen until the republican army became strong enough to protect the country.[122] On 1 May he reiterated that the UAR would not only attack the bases in Najran and Jizan, used against Yemen, but even occupy them, if Saudi Arabia continued its aggressive actions against the YAR.[123]

On 21 June 1966 King Faisal paid a three-day official visit to the US. By the summer of 1966 the Saudi ruling circles had managed to improve relations with some Muslim monarchies and conclude agreements with the US and Britain on supplies of military equipment and armaments.

Differences grew within the YAR. In August 1966 the prime minister, General al-Amri, tried to prevent President al-Sallal returning from Cairo, where he had spent ten months. The general's attempt was suppressed[124] and al-Sallal returned to power. Saudi-Egyptian relations remained extremely tense. On 9 February 1967 the government of Saudi Arabia closed all branches of the Cairo Bank and Bank Misr in Jidda. The Egyptian government issued a decree confiscating all the property and financial assets held by King Faisal and the Saudi princes in Egypt. The capital of forty Saudi companies and thirty-one Saudi citizens was sequestrated.[125]

The Struggle for Power and its Outcome (1958-1973)

The end of the confrontation with Egypt

Egypt's defeat in the Arab-Israeli war of June 1967 radically changed the situation in the YAR. As early as 12 June, Egypt began the partial withdrawal of its forces from Yemen – 15,000 combatants, 150 tanks and all heavy artillery.[126] In the atmosphere of unprecedented growth of anti-Israeli sentiment in the Arab world, the members of the Saudi ruling elite had to demonstrate solidarity with Egypt, a 'victim of Israeli aggression', in order to preserve their prestige in the Arab world and retain power within the country.

On 31 August 1967 President Nasser and King Faisal signed an agreement on a peaceful settlement of the Yemen issue at the Arab summit in Khartoum. The agreement provided for the withdrawal of all Egyptian forces from Yemen within three months. Saudi Arabia pledged to end support for the Yemeni royalists. A committee of the ministers of foreign affairs of Sudan, Iraq and Morocco was set up with the aim of convening a national conference in Yemen in order to form a coalition government of representatives of all the groupings in the country.[127]

At the Khartoum conference, Kuwait, Saudi Arabia and Libya promised to provide the UAR and Jordan – which had suffered most in the war with Israel – annual aid of £135m, of which Egypt would receive £95m and Jordan £40m. Kuwait agreed to donate £55m, Saudi Arabia £50m and Libya £30m.[128] Saudi Arabia warned, however, that it would start payment only after the Egyptians had completed the withdrawal of their forces from Yemen. On 10 October 1967 Egypt declared that almost all its troops had been withdrawn from Sanaa and the last contingent would leave the port of Hodeida on 9 December.[129]

The Egyptian troop evacuation complicated the situation in the YAR, however, because Saudi Arabia continued to give the royalists considerable support – their tribal detachments were trained on Saudi territory. The Khartoum agreement, signed after the UAR's military defeat, meant that it was Saudi Arabia that would dictate the terms of any solution to the Yemeni conflict. The withdrawal of the Egyptian forces weakened the position of the republicans, particularly their left wing, and gave encouragement to the royalists.[130]

Saudi Arabia's relations with the YAR and South Yemen (1967-1973)

After the Khartoum agreement, the government of the YAR moved increasingly to the right. On 3 November 1967 al-Sallal left for Baghdad and during the night of 5 November the rightist forces established their control over Sanaa and other towns. Al-Sallal's fate was the inevitable consequence of the withdrawal of Egyptian troops from Yemen.[131]

Tribal leaders came to power in the country and they looked for cooperation with Saudi Arabia and the West. On 8 November 1967 the new prime minister, Muhsin al-Aini, said that his government was ready to negotiate with the royalists, including the imam's family, on condition that the republican system was preserved.[132] The difficult problem of the fate of the Hamid al-Din dynasty divided not only the royalists and the new leaders of the YAR, but also some of the powerful tribal shaikhs who had previously fought against the republic.

The Yemeni royalists took the offensive and besieged Sanaa. Understanding that it was a matter of life and death, the republicans formed resistance groups of students, employees, workers, craftsmen and traders in early December 1967. The 20,000-strong militia freed the army to undertake military operations at the front and reinforcements were sent there. The siege of Sanaa lasted for 70 days. The republicans prevented the royalists from capturing Sanaa, drove them back and took the offensive.[133]

General al-Amri dissolved the people's resistance detachments of the most loyal republicans, who had saved Sanaa in the winter of 1967–68. In May 1968 the tribal guards disarmed them. The leftist republicans' attempt at a coup under Major Abd al-Wahhab Abd al-Raqib was suppressed and the major, who had led the seventy-day defence of Sanaa, was expelled from the country. He returned in January 1969, tried once again to overthrow al-Amri and was killed.[134]

In February 1969 Saudi Arabia stopped insisting on the return of Imam al-Badr to the YAR,[135] since it was satisfied with the changes in the republicans' camp.

The conservative republican regime of the YAR acted as a counterbalance to the People's Democratic Republic of South Yemen (PDRSY), which was in line with King Faisal's overall aims. He decided to abandon the plan to restore the imamate and reduced his subsidies to the Hamid al-Din family. In mid-April 1970 hostilities ceased in the YAR. Under the terms of the agreement with Saudi Arabia of April 1970, the Yemeni government repealed many measures that were unpopular with Riyadh. The Yemeni army and security services were purged of leftists. Many royalists returned from Saudi Arabia; some of them were appointed to the supreme administrative bodies.[136] Saudi Arabia officially recognized the YAR on 23 July 1970[137] and Britain followed it six days later.[138] In early March 1971 the YAR signed a joint defence agreement with Saudi Arabia.[139]

In March 1973 al-Hajari, the prime minister of the YAR, visited Riyadh. Both states recognized their borders as permanent and final in the communiqué of 18 March, though under the al-Taif treaty of 20 March 1934 between King Ibn Saud and Imam Yahya, Yemen had transferred Asir, Najran and Jizan to the 'control' of Saudi Arabia. The al-Taif treaty had been signed for a period of twenty years and was extended by Imam Ahmad for a further twenty years. Thus, in 1973, when the treaty was about to expire, Saudi Arabia won an important concession from the YAR, compelling it to recognize Asir, Najran and Jizan as Saudi Arabia's possessions.[140] Saudi influence was predominant in the YAR in the 1970s. The *rapprochement* with Riyadh led to an improvement in North Yemen's relations with the US, Britain and West Germany and to a reduction in its cooperation with the USSR.

In the 1960s Saudi Arabia had mainly concentrated its attention in the south of the Arabian peninsula on North Yemen, but in 1967 South Yemen gained independence. Since the Saudis saw the whole peninsula as within their sphere of influence, they were not averse to taking part in the division of the British colonial heritage, particularly since Britain did not object to an increase in Saudi influence in its former possessions. London saw the Saudi royal family as its most desirable ally in the peninsula.

It is not impossible that Riyadh planned to create a federation under its patronage as a successor to the Eastern Aden Protectorate and, perhaps, even gain direct access to the Indian Ocean. Saudi Arabia planned to give financial aid to the South Arabian Federation (which consisted mainly of the princely states of the Western Aden Protectorate), to whose government the British authorities were to transfer power after leaving South Yemen.[141]

Many feudal-tribal rulers had to flee to Saudi Arabia even before South Yemen became independent. Instead of the federal government to which Britain intended to transfer power, the leftist National Front came to power in South Yemen. The South Arabian League, the feudal-tribal rulers' political organization, was outlawed and moved almost all its activities to Saudi Arabia. The Front for the Liberation of Occupied Southern Yemen (FLOSY) also gradually became a pro-Saudi organization. Banned in South Yemen, it set up its headquarters in Taiz (YAR).

Saudi Arabia used South Yemen's economic difficulties, differences within the National Front and the rightist forces' discontent to encourage anti-government rebellions in Hadhramawt, Beihan and elsewhere in the summer of 1968. After the left wing of the National Front came to power on 22 June 1969 and started to introduce Soviet-style socio-political changes, Saudi intervention grew. On 27 November 1969 detachments of the Saudi regular army attacked al-Wadiya, a place in Hadhramawt near the Saudi border. The South Yemeni forces rebuffed the Saudis, but border clashes continued.[142]

Saudi Arabia helped the creation of the so-called National Salvation Army of South Yemeni emigrés in its border areas. The struggle against the National Front government was waged under the slogan of 'saving the country from the influence of communism'. On 25 February 1971 FLOSY and the South Arabian League united in the Organization of the National Forces of South Yemen. It formed the Committee for the Salvation of South Yemen, which contacted the National Salvation Army. These organizations were financed by Saudi Arabia and supported by the YAR. Their armed detachments repeatedly invaded South Yemen between 1971 and 1972.[143]

In March 1972 the fifth congress of the National Front of the People's Democratic Republic of Yemen (PDRY), as the new state was named, declared the National Front to be a political organization. The congress proclaimed that the front's activities would follow the principles of 'scientific socialism' and that its purpose was the creation of a 'vanguard party of a new type'. Riyadh's enmity for the pro-Marxist leadership of South Yemen acquired an ever more pronounced ideological character.

In September 1972 a large-scale border war was waged between the YAR and the PDRY. *The Economist* commented, 'King Faisal of Saudi Arabia and Sultan Qabus of Oman would breathe easier if it [the South Yemen regime] disappeared, and there are several thousand expelled southerners in North Yemen dedicated to the same cause.'[144] However, the two Yemens agreed to cease hostilities on 29 October 1972, a month after they had started.[145] Realizing that it was impossible to topple the leftist regime in South Yemen by force, Saudi Arabia established diplomatic relations with it, but nevertheless remained hostile.

Saudi-British relations in the 1960s and early 1970s

In January 1963 Saudi Arabia agreed to refer the al-Buraimi question to the UN and restored diplomatic relations with Britain.[146] The Yemeni revolution of 1962, and the intensification of the nationalist movement throughout the Arabian peninsula, forced Riyadh and London to reach a compromise.

The character of US-British relations in the peninsula also changed and Washington's opposition to the restoration of British positions in Saudi Arabia was gradually replaced by a spirit of cooperation. In December 1965 the US and Britain concluded an agreement with Saudi Arabia on military supplies: Britain was to provide jets, radar systems and other hardware worth $280m and the US was to provide surface-to-air missiles worth $70m. It was planned to deploy the rocket-launchers on the border with the YAR. British arms companies appeared to have seized a very profitable deal from their American competitors, whereas, in fact, Britain had an amicable understanding with the US: the latter would supply modern US aircraft to Britain for the sums that Britain itself earned from military supplies to Saudi Arabia.[147]

In May 1967 King Faisal paid a visit to Britain. It indicated a substantial improvement in Saudi-British relations. Britain had started to supply *Lightning* aircraft to Saudi Arabia in 1966 and it began to train pilots for the Saudi air force. More than 1,000 British instructors were sent to Saudi Arabia and Saudis were admitted to British military academies. British pilots also took part in military operations. In 1963 British instructors reappeared in the National Guard. In the 1960s and 1970s the kingdom purchased 25 *Strikemaster* jet fighters from Britain. In 1970 a new contract was signed with Britain on supplies of air-defence equipment.

In early May 1973 Riyadh concluded a contract with London on supplies of new armament systems, aircraft and missiles for a total sum of £250m. Besides the aircraft, a group of some 2,000 maintenance personnel, advisers and instructors was to be sent to Saudi Arabia. At that time, the entire Saudi air force – from pilots studying at the academy in Riyadh to young technicians at the technical training institute in Dhahran – were trained by the British.[148] The British-US accord over arms supplies did not last long, however. In the 1970s the lucrative Saudi arms market led to fierce competition between the military-industrial companies of both countries.

Problems in the Gulf

The 1960s and early 1970s saw a considerable increase in Saudi diplomacy in the Gulf, particularly in the emirates. There were several reasons for this. The role, might and influence of the Shah's Iran was growing and Saudi policy towards Iran was an intricate combination of rivalry, fear and cooperation. During this period, Britain completed its military evacuation of the Gulf. Here, too, Saudi Arabia was among those countries that claimed the 'British heritage' in line with American strategic principles, which attached an ever-growing importance to the Gulf region. According to R. R. Sullivan, a former US ambassador to Saudi Arabia:

> Obliquely, this operational premise defines what Saudi Arabia considers to be her sphere of influence; it includes every state bordering on her, except Iraq. Saudi Arabia is not especially active in political conflicts that take place in states beyond those on her borders, mainly because their outcome cannot affect her vital interests.[149]

In the mid-1960s Saudi Arabia and Iran grew closer. Both countries were monarchies with an interest in suppressing revolutionary movements in the Middle East as a whole, and in the Gulf in particular. They also had a common interest in confronting Egypt, which was then the leader of the anti-royalist and anti-Western camp in the region.

The Shah of Iran, who ruled a country with a population of 30 million and claimed that his monarchy was 2,500 years old, was not ready to recognize King Faisal's leading role in the Islamic world, yet there were grounds for cooperation. Both monarchs supported the Yemeni royalists, though the extent of their support differed. The Shah was in favour of the idea of an Islamic pact, suggested by Faisal in 1965. Riyadh and Tehran jointly encouraged the radical change in Egypt's policy after Nasser's death. Their joint say became decisive in the Organization of Petroleum Exporting Countries (OPEC) in the early 1970s since they accounted for more than half of the world's oil exports. Although the Shah made tough public pronouncements on the question of oil prices, the two monarchs finally found compromise solutions and became joint leaders of the 'moderate' camp within OPEC. With a military capacity that was one fifth of Iran's, Saudi Arabia was extremely wary of Tehran's 'imperial' aspirations in the Gulf, but never allowed the tension to grow into a conflict or an open clash. The rulers of the small Gulf states manoeuvred between their two strong neighbours.

In January 1968 Britain's Labour government decided to terminate the protectorate treaties with Bahrain, Qatar and the seven states of Trucial Oman (Abu Dhabi, Ajman, Dubai, Fujaira, Ras al-Khaima, Sharja and Umm al-Qaiwain) and withdraw the majority of British troops from the area. The Conservative government, which followed Labour in June 1970, declared on 1 March 1971 that the evacuation would be completed by the end of the year.[150] In spite of the decision to withdraw, London actively sought opportunities to preserve its economic and political influence in the region. To that end, it suggested a plan for a federation of nine Gulf emirates – the former British protectorates – and tried to enlist the support of Saudi Arabia, Kuwait and to some extent Iran and Iraq for the plan. In February 1968 the rulers of nine Gulf emirates agreed in principle to create a united state.

Iran opposed the inclusion of Bahrain in the federation, however, claiming that it was Iranian territory. King Faisal, who enjoyed friendly relations with the shaikh of Bahrain, rejected Tehran's claims. There were other differences, too, between Saudi Arabia and Iran. In April 1969 *The Economist* reported that the Shah was trying to persuade King Faisal to adopt a more active, concerted policy in the Gulf, including military cooperation, a field in which Saudi Arabia would be in a subordinate position.[151] Realizing his lack of military strength, Faisal preferred to use financial aid as a means of increasing Saudi influence in the small Gulf emirates. In 1968 Faisal and the Shah started negotiations over the division of the continental shelf. The final agreements were signed on 24 October 1968. In the spring of 1971 the Shah stated that his country would assume responsibility for the defence of the Gulf after the British withdrawal.[152] Iran intended to establish its military dominance in the Gulf without taking Arab opinion into account.

The federation of nine Gulf states proved an impracticable venture. The emirs of Bahrain and Qatar wanted independence, and Iran opposed the projected federation. Britain decided to create a new state of seven emirates of Trucial Oman, in which Shaikh Zaid, the ruler of Abu Dhabi and an adversary of Saudi Arabia in the al-Buraimi conflict, enjoyed the greatest influence. Bahrain and Qatar proclaimed independence on 14 August and 1 September 1971, respectively, and declared that they would not join the federation. The new situation led Saudi Arabia to seek a compromise with Abu Dhabi over the al-Buraimi dispute.

After the independence of Bahrain was proclaimed, Iran formally waived its claims to the emirate and its differences with Saudi Arabia lessened. But Iran's plans in the Gulf were not confined to Bahrain. In November 1971 Iran concluded an agreement with Sharja on the virtual transfer of the island of Abu Musa to Iran, though formally it remained a part of the emirate. Iran was entitled to build a military base on the island, in return for an annual payment of £1.5m to Sharja, until the latter's annual oil revenues had reached £3m.[153]

Iran tried unsuccessfully to make the shaikh of Ras al-Khaima waive his rights to the strategically important islands of the Greater and Lesser Tunbs in the Strait of Hormuz, at the entrance to the Gulf. When Britain declared on 30 November 1971 that it was no longer responsible for the defence of the states of Trucial Oman, Iran sent troops to these islands and to Abu Musa. An understanding appeared to have been reached between London and Tehran on the question. In response to Britain's complicity in Iran's actions, Libya nationalized all property belonging to British Petroleum and withdrew all Libyan assets from British banks. Iraq accused Britain and Iran of collusion and severed diplomatic relations with both countries. Kuwait and Syria also denounced Iran's seizure of the islands. On 1 December 1971 Egypt raised the question of Iran's evacuation of the islands, but took no further action.[154] The seizure of the islands was a blow to Saudi interests, since it considerably bolstered Iran's military position in the Gulf, but Saudi Arabia never denounced the Shah's expansionist policy in an official statement.[155] It may be assumed that Saudi Arabia did not feel strong enough to risk an open confrontation with Iran and also calculated that the Shah's actions would prompt the federation members to cooperate with Riyadh.

The creation of the federation, named the United Arab Emirates (UAE), was proclaimed on 2 December 1971. It included Abu Dhabi, Dubai, Sharja, Fujaira, Ajman, Umm al-Qaiwain and Ras al-Khaima (the last-mentioned joined on 10 February 1972). Britain signed a new treaty of friendship with the UAE. Shaikh Zaid of Abu Dhabi became the president of the federation and its vice-president was Shaikh Rashid of Dubai.

Saudi Arabia did not establish diplomatic relations with the UAE for some years because its territorial dispute with Abu Dhabi – the federation's most influential member – had not yet been resolved, but this did not prevent Riyadh from adopting a generally favourable attitude towards the new grouping. King Faisal supported the UAE's admission to the UN and the Arab League, and Saudi Arabia conducted lively unofficial negotiations with the new federation and the other states of the peninsula. The Saudi government did not want Iran, which recognized the UAE as early as October 1972, to seize the political initiative.

After Sultan Qabus' visit to Riyadh on 14 December 1971, Faisal established diplomatic relations with Oman.[156] In October 1974 Saudi Arabia settled the dispute with Abu Dhabi over Liwa and the al-Buraimi oases, thus paving the way for Riyadh's recognition of the UAE.[157] Saudi Arabia managed to acquire substantial influence in the Gulf emirates and it gave large amounts of financial aid to the federation members, particularly those with no oil resources. Some UAE members relied on Saudi support in trying to prevent a dangerous increase in Iranian influence.

In spite of their differences, the Shah and Faisal both strove to suppress the revolutionary movement in the Gulf. Although Saudi Arabia was interested in increasing its influence in Oman, a neighbouring country of great strategic importance, Faisal was circumspect when Sultan Qabus asked for his help at the height of the rebel movement in Dhofar in 1972. Open intervention in Oman's affairs did not correspond to the general aims of Faisal's policy. At the same time, Saudi Arabia virtually connived at Iran's intervention in Oman. As early as April 1973 Iranian helicopters and ground detachments participated actively in battles in Dhofar. Then a several-thousand-strong Iranian expeditionary corps was sent to Oman. The Iranian troops fought in Oman for several years until the People's Liberation Front of Oman, a pro-Marxist organization, was defeated and ended the armed struggle. Denouncing Iran's actions in rather vague terms, the Saudi government opposed 'foreign intervention' in the sultanate, essentially meaning not Iran's intervention, but the actions of the forces that had helped the People's Liberation Front.[158]

Saudi Arabia and the Arab world (1967–1973)

The Khartoum conference of August 1967 had discussed and approved the principle of coordinating the policy of all the Arab states, first of all in order to achieve a Middle East peace settlement. The conference reiterated the well-known formula expressing the Arab countries' attitude to Israel: 'No peace, no direct negotiations, no recognition'. This was adhered to by all the Arab countries, including Egypt and Saudi Arabia, for many years.

Saudi Arabia restored outwardly friendly relations with Nasser's Egypt on condition that Cairo make substantial concessions. The balance of forces was no longer that of the mid-1950s. Freed from the burden of debt, Saudi Arabia was becoming an exporter of capital and a source of financial aid for the states that confronted Israel. With US and British assistance, it strengthened its not large, but well-equipped armed forces. Exhausted by the war in Yemen, defeated by Israel and deprived of the Sinai peninsula and the income from the Suez Canal, Egypt had to concentrate all its efforts on restoring its military potential, pursuing a more restrained foreign policy and reaching a compromise with Saudi Arabia.

For Riyadh, too, the establishment of an 'accord' with Cairo was forced upon it: Faisal never saw Nasser as his ally or shared his ideas. Despite the Arabs' defeat in the 1967 war, the revolutionary turmoil in the Middle East did not end – as evidenced by the coups in Libya and Sudan, the attempted coups in Saudi Arabia itself and the rise of the Palestinian resistance movement. The Saudis were unstinting in their support for rightist groups in Egypt and in their attempts to bolster the regime in Jordan. A Saudi brigade of 3,000 soldiers was sent to southern Jordan during the 1967 Arab-Israeli war. It was deployed far from the front, but close enough to the capital to support King Husain. Faisal may have seen Jordan as a buffer state between Saudi Arabia and Israel, and he repeatedly urged the US and Britain to support Husain.[159]

In May 1970 a Syrian bulldozer damaged the pipeline owned by Tapline. This sparked off a conflict between Syria and Saudi Arabia which nearly led to the breaking-off of bilateral relations and to a trade and transit war.[160] After Hafiz al-Asad became the Syrian president in late 1970, however, relations between Damascus and Riyadh were restored and the mutual claims were settled.

Even after the 1967 defeat, Nasser remained the central figure in the Middle East. As Egypt regained its military strength, its differences with Saudi Arabia increased. The participants at the Arab summit of December 1969 in Rabat failed even to issue a communiqué. Nasser was given clearly to understand that he could not expect an increase in the financial aid he received from Saudi Arabia, Libya and Kuwait under the terms of the decision of the 1967 Khartoum conference.[161]

The situation changed after Nasser's death on 28 September 1970. King Faisal immediately stepped up his struggle for leadership of the Arab world. Encouraging the new Egyptian regime, which was deviating from Nasser's course, corresponded to Faisal's aims. Striving to restore its position in the Arab world, and weakened, *inter alia*, by US support for Israel, Washington hoped that Saudi Arabia would become a bridge between the US and the leading Arab countries – first and foremost Egypt, which had severed diplomatic relations with the US in 1967. Anwar Sadat, the new president of Egypt, was interested in a *rapprochement* with Saudi Arabia, since he hoped for increased financial aid. When King Faisal visited Egypt in June 1971, he was given a triumphal reception. To please his Saudi guest, Sadat released several members of the Muslim Brotherhood from jail. During the negotiations, he apparently confirmed that Egypt recognized the Arabian peninsula as the zone of Saudi influence. Saudi Arabia presented Egypt with £30m and promised to increase its annual financial aid and lift the restrictions on Saudi citizens travelling to Egypt.[162]

Saudi Arabia's relations with Sadat's regime grew closer, particularly when Sadat started to dismantle much of the Nasserist legacy in internal and foreign affairs. The policy was prompted above all by domestic Egyptian considerations, but Saudi subsidies also played a role. Between 1970 and 1973 Nasser's most faithful supporters were removed from important state and party posts. The first signs of the policy of economic liberalization had appeared even before the war of October 1973, paving the way for the development of a market economy.

In spite of the 27 May 1971 treaty of friendship and cooperation with the USSR, Sadat expelled all Soviet military advisers and personnel from Egypt in July 1972. During King Faisal's visit to Egypt in May 1973, an understanding was reached that Saudi Arabia would allocate £250m for the rearming of the Egyptian army. A part of that sum was to be provided by Kuwait, Abu Dhabi and Qatar. Faisal persuaded Sadat to change his armaments sources in order to undermine the military cooperation between Egypt and the USSR.[163] Such an about-turn in Egyptian policy could not have occurred before the October 1973 war. Egypt could not have started to re-equip its army while preparing for a war with Israel, even if an alternative source of arms had been found, since it would have undermined the army's combat-readiness. The *rapprochement* with Saudi Arabia furthered Sadat's policy of ending cooperation with the USSR and led to a full shift towards a pro-US orientation.

The Islamic pact

In the mid-1960s the anti-Western ('anti-imperialist') foreign policy of some Arab states was supplemented by a range of internal reforms, coloured by a socialist-oriented search for new socio-political and economic structures. Egypt advanced further along that path than other Arab countries – it was the strongest Arab state and Nasser was the most influential Arab leader. Although Egypt did not create a stable bloc under its leadership, many members of the Arab League followed Cairo's course whether voluntarily or otherwise.

After appearing on the stage of Middle East politics in the early 1960s, Saudi Arabia became the main centre of opposition to Nasser's Egypt. Its ruling group tried to undermine the influence of Egypt, Syria and Iraq and sought for ways and means of strengthening its ties with those countries with moderate or conservative regimes. John Foster Dulles' idea of military pacts with the participation of the Western powers was by now too discredited to think of reviving it, and monarchies were unpopular in most Arab countries. Saudi Arabia turned to Islam to find an attractive alternative to the ideas of Arab nationalism and Arab solidarity and the calls for a transformation of society.

The influence of Islam had never died out, even in such secular and relatively Westernized states as Turkey. In the late 1960s and early 1970s there were signs of an Islamic 'revival'. The overwhelming majority of Arabs saw Islamic traditions, rites and institutions as their natural heritage. Religion might be used to both anti-Western ('anti-imperialist') and anti-Soviet ('anti-communist') ends. Naturally, the Saudi regime used Islam as a tool in combating both its internal and its external adversaries.

In proposing the idea of an Islamic pact, King Faisal hoped to make it an alternative to the Arab League. Washington and London, which traditionally treated religion as an obstacle to the spread of socialist and communist ideas, adopted a positive attitude to Faisal's initiative. In December 1965 Faisal visited Iran. During the negotiations, he formally suggested the convening of an Islamic summit and was supported by the Shah. On 31 January 1966 Faisal stated, during an official visit to Amman, that an Islamic committee would be set up to convene an Islamic summit. Anticipating objections to the creation of a political bloc, he stated that he did not advocate a formal Islamic alliance, since the bonds that united the Muslim world were stronger than pacts or treaties.[164]

Faisal faced difficulties from the outset. Iran's positive attitude to the idea of the pact worried many Arab monarchs, since the Shah was Nasser's foe and Israel's friend. In the end, only the Shah of Iran and the king of Jordan agreed to participate in an Islamic summit. All the other Muslim states opposed Faisal's initiative.[165] Speaking at a mass meeting at Cairo University on 22 February 1966, Nasser said that 'the Islamic pact is created by imperialism and reactionaries' and, like the Baghdad Pact and the earlier political blocs, 'is spearheaded against the national liberation movements'.[166] Algeria, the YAR, Iraq, Syria, Kuwait and many other Muslim countries of Asia and Africa denounced the idea of the Islamic pact in various forms. Some Arab and international organizations also opposed it. Even Iran's allies in the Central Treaty Organization (CENTO) dissociated themselves from the idea of the pact and it had to be abandoned. Saudi Arabia then resorted to the practice of convening Islamic conferences at various levels.[167]

The Arab-Israeli war of 1967 revived the plans for a *rapprochement* between all the Islamic states on an unexpected new base, on the crest of the Islamic 'revival'. The developing countries, irrespective of their regimes, all denounced the Israeli occupation of Arab territories. They saw Israel's actions as a repetition of the worst form of colonialism: the forcible removal of the local population and its replacement by colonists. Even states that were far from Palestine and the Middle East conflict considered Israel's actions to be a dangerous precedent. The rulers of predominantly Muslim countries had to reckon with the feelings of their people, who regarded the Israeli occupation of East Jerusalem (the site of the al-Aqsa mosque) as an outrage against Islam. The Saudi regime – based on the Wahhabi doctrine – governed the country according to the *sharia* laws, proclaimed the purity of 'genuine' Islam and was proud of its country's role as the cradle of Islam, where the Kaaba and the Prophet's mosque in Medina were situated. It could not therefore recognize the occupation of East Jerusalem without undermining its own position. The expulsion of the Palestinians from their homeland destabilized the Middle East, and Israel's advance into the Sinai and the West Bank of the Jordan brought its forces much closer to Saudi borders. To play the role of leader of the Arab countries, to increase his weight and influence in the Islamic world and to protect Saudi Arabia's interests, King Faisal had to adopt a clear-cut anti-Israeli stance. His appeals for Islamic solidarity needed a concrete enemy.

In August 1969 the al-Aqsa mosque in Jerusalem, the third most holy place of Islam, was set on fire. King Husain of Jordan called for an Arab summit to discuss the situation. King Faisal, on the other hand, suggested an Islamic summit.[168] By relying on Islamic solidarity as an alternative to the Arab summits, he probably aimed to weaken Nasser's position. Although Faisal was overshadowed at the Arab summits, he had influential friends and allies in the non-Arab Muslim world. The formal pretext for his rejection of King Husain's idea was that the decisions of the 1967 Khartoum conference were still in effect. Nasser had publicly to support King Faisal's appeal, though he had little interest in the Islamic conference and did not attend it in person. Turkey and Nigeria rejected Faisal's proposal, saying that they were secular states. Iran, too, initially adopted a cautious attitude, saying that it must study the situation and assess the aims of the proposed conference.[169]

The summit was nevertheless held in September 1969 in Rabat, the capital of Morocco. There were serious disagreements between the participants, mainly between the two most influential Arab countries, Egypt and Saudi Arabia. Some days before the start of the conference, on 1 September 1969, King Idris of Libya was overthrown in a military coup, which substantially weakened the positions of the Muslim monarchies. The Saudi regime was also facing serious problems at home. Some days before the Rabat conference, several people were arrested and charged with a conspiracy against the Saudi regime. The coup was allegedly scheduled for 7 September 1969.[170] A similar coup attempt had been foiled in June.

The Rabat summit led to a serious conflict between India and Pakistan: the latter protested at India's being invited to the conference. Of the thirty-five Islamic countries invited to the summit, only twenty-five sent delegations, of which only ten were led by heads of state.[171] However, the participants found a common language on some issues, demanding that Jerusalem should be returned to the status it had enjoyed before June 1967. The conference statement read:

> Since they are deeply affected by the tragedy of Palestine, the heads of states and governments and the representatives pledge their full support to the people of Palestine for the restoration of their usurped rights and for their struggle for national liberation, and emphasize their adherence to peace based on honour and justice.[172]

On 23–25 March 1970 the first conference of ministers of foreign affairs of the Islamic countries was convened in Jidda under the chairmanship of King Faisal: twenty-three countries were represented.[173] It was followed by a second conference in Jidda on 4 March 1972, with the participation of thirty-one countries. At King Faisal's initiative, this second conference decided unanimously to create a 'fund for the holy war' against

Israel. The participants denounced US support for Israel and called on the US to refrain from giving Israel military or economic aid. They welcomed Lebanon's and Syria's aid to the Palestinian fedayeen (guerrillas) and pledged to support the said countries in every possible way in the event of an Israeli attack upon them. The conference denounced Israel for its annexation of the Arab part of Jerusalem.[174]

After the 1973 Arab-Israeli war, issues of economic cooperation, joint anti-Israeli action and support for the rights of the Palestinian Arabs acquired increasing importance at the Islamic conferences of the 1970s. Saudi Arabia's growing financial power, and the loans and subsidies it granted, increased its influence in the Islamic world.

Saudi Arabia and OPEC

Having studied the international oil market, the Saudis realized that the oil companies earned colossal profits outside Saudi Arabia, in spite of the formal principle of 50:50. In April 1959 the first Arab oil congress was convened with the participation of Saudi Arabia. The petroleum-exporting countries felt the need for collective action. They were particularly concerned at the drop in the posted price of oil. Between 1957 and 1960, for example, it fell in Ras Tannura from $2.12 to $1.84 per ton and the incomes of the petroleum-exporting countries decreased accordingly.[175]

When OPEC was set up in Baghdad in September 1960, its founding members were Iran, Iraq, Kuwait, Saudi Arabia and Venezuela. Subsequently, Abu Dhabi, Qatar, Libya, Algeria, Indonesia, Nigeria, Ecuador and Gabon joined it. OPEC's main aims at that stage were to raise crude oil prices to their 1954 level, to maintain them at that level and to hold consultations between the states and the oil companies on price changes and controlling the volume of production. On 25 January 1965 the Saudi government signed an agreement with Aramco. The company agreed to consider the royalties as part of the cost of exploitation, deducted from the gross income, and to pay income tax on the rest. It increased Saudi Arabia's share in the income from crude oil exports to more than half.[176]

OPEC's initial claims were modest and did not exceed the purely commercial framework. At the time, few people believed that the new organization would be viable, since the political regimes in the member countries differed greatly and were divided on several major issues. The international oil companies tried to ignore the new reality. As long as there was a relative surplus of oil on the world market and the terms were dictated by buyers rather than by sellers, the OPEC countries' demands were moderate. However, they gradually became more experienced at bargaining and came to appreciate the advantages of collective action.

In 1969 Libya proposed that the concessionaires operating in the country should pay it 54–55% of the profit instead of 50%. When they refused, Libya lowered its production quotas in 1970. However, the international oil companies could not afford to boycott Libyan oil (which accounted for almost one fifth of consumption in Western

Europe) in case the Suez Canal were closed or the Trans-Arabian pipeline blown up by Palestinian guerrillas: the companies were forced to capitulate. Libya's success caused a chain reaction, and the Gulf countries also forced the concessionaires to pay the same share of their profits.[177]

When the OPEC countries of the Gulf started negotiations with the oil companies in Tehran on 12 January 1971, they acted as a united group. Although OPEC failed to achieve its aim of a regular increase in the reference price of oil over the next decade, the situation on the world market was becoming increasingly favourable to sellers. Although Washington and London hoped for Saudi Arabia's support, it sided with the other OPEC countries. The oil companies had to accept most of the demands made by the six petroleum-exporting Gulf states.[178]

According to the agreement signed in Tehran on 14 February 1971, control over the reference prices was virtually transferred to Abu Dhabi, Iran, Iraq, Kuwait and Saudi Arabia. The terms of the agreement were as follows:

1. An increase of the tax rate to 55%.
2. A uniform increase of posted prices by 33% per barrel plus a 2-cent-per-barrel increase 'in satisfaction of claims to freight disparities'.
3. Additional increases in posted prices of 5 cents effective 1 June, and thereafter on each 1 January from 1973 to 1975.
4. An adjustment of 2.5% of each price on 1 June 1971, and thereafter on each 1 January from 1973 to 1975, as a guard against loss of purchasing power through inflation.
5. Reduction of the 2-cent-per-barrel degree differential to 1.5 cents and gravity escalation of 0.5 cents per barrel of crude between 30.0° and 39.9°. API for each degree below 40°.
6. Elimination of the existing percentage allowance and marketing allowance.
7. The remaining in force of the agreement for five years ('leapfrogging' of financial terms based on events elsewhere and embargoes were prohibited).[179]

Having mastered the method of collective bargaining, OPEC achieved an outstanding result – seizure of control over the posted prices of oil. However, the US dollar was devalued by 12% in December 1971. In response, OPEC increased the reference prices in the Gulf by 8.49%. Appropriate principles and methods were drafted for oil pricing to take account of fluctuations in the exchange rate of the US dollar.[180]

The Tehran agreements demonstrated that the OPEC members had achieved their aims as outlined in 1960. Yet there was still no solution to the question of the petroleum-producing countries' participation in the ownership and activities of the oil companies, which would fundamentally change their relations. Negotiations on that issue started between OPEC and the oil companies on 21 January 1972. The government had three options for changing the concession agreement: a reduction in the length of the original concession agreement; full nationalization; or a renegotiation of the existing concession to include at least partial participation immediately, leading to eventual ownership of the oil industry.

Riyadh chose the third way. Shaikh Ahmad Zaki Yamani, the Saudi minister of petroleum and mineral resources, became OPEC's chief representative at the negotiations with the international oil companies.[181] The Saudi government and Aramco agreed as follows:

1. Saudi Arabia's share in the company's assets should rise by 5% every year (from the initial level of 25%) from 1979 to 1982, to reach 51% on 1 January 1983.
2. Aramco should be compensated for its investments. The initial compensation paid for 25% of the shares, which were to be transferred to Saudi Arabia, should be $500 million and should be liable to adjustments for inflation.
3. Saudi Arabia should be entitled to a share of the extracted crude oil, equivalent to its participation percentage.[182]

Saudi Arabia's relations with the oil companies went beyond the purely economic framework of a dispute over its share in the profits from crude oil sales. Its status as the leading member in OPEC, and the world's largest petroleum exporter, made the whole complex of oil-related problems – from control over its extraction and transportation to its distribution and prices – one of the key issues in international politics. The Marshall Plan, the Iranian oil crisis, the Suez crisis, the cessation of oil supplies in 1956–57, the oil boycott of 1973 and the new price hike of the late 1970s were all stages in the growth of the importance of the oil question in US foreign policy. To retain its influence over the Middle East oil producers, Washington spent billions of dollars, organized a worldwide administrative and military machinery, coordinated its actions with the multinational oil corporations, fixed the ocean routes of tanker fleets and violated its own anti-trust legislation.

In the 1950s US control over Gulf oil had ensured huge profits for the oil companies and enabled Washington to 'keep its hand on the tap' that fed the economies of the West and the Third World. In 1959 President Eisenhower had restricted imports of Middle East oil to 2.5% of total US consumption.[183] At the time, the US economy was virtually independent of Middle East oil, though the region acquired increasing strategic significance in the US administration's anti-Soviet plans. By the 1970s, however, the US had become the world's largest importer of oil. Saudi Arabia's role increased in line with its ability to maintain or increase the volume of oil production.

The 'oil weapon'

Riyadh was aware of the inconsistencies and changes of direction in American policy towards the Middle East. On the one hand, Washington had to ensure America's energy supplies, protect the interests of US companies and maintain control over Middle East oil supplies to its European allies and Japan. This necessitated closer ties with the Arab countries – at least with those conservative states, including Saudi Arabia, that accounted for the bulk of the world's oil resources. On the other hand, Washington gave Israel economic, military and political aid and supported its foreign policy, thus undermining the basis for closer relations with the Arab states.

Aware of its growing weight in the world of oil and international finance, Saudi Arabia claimed the role of leader of the Arab world, which made an anti-Israeli stance inevitable. The task of 'liberating East Jerusalem' corresponded to the propaganda aims and overall direction of Riyadh's foreign policy, as well as to the internal requirement to bolster the regime that was responsible for the maintenance of the two holy cities and that declared its constitution to be the Quran. In spite of its vital interest in US support and cooperation, the Saudi government nevertheless had to be seen to engage in a confrontation with Washington over the Arab-Israeli issue.

On 18 April 1973 Shaikh Yamani announced in Washington that his country would only increase its level of oil production to 20 mb/d by 1980, as the US demanded, if Washington put pressure on Israel to ensure a political atmosphere in the Middle East that would be favourable to the Arabs.[184] Talking with US newsmen in Jidda on 6 July 1973, King Faisal said that Saudi Arabia would find it difficult to cooperate closely with the US if it continued to support Israel. Some weeks earlier, the king had warned Aramco that Saudi Arabia would freeze its volume of oil production unless the US changed its policy towards Israel.[185]

On the eve of the 1973 Arab-Israeli war, King Faisal warned the US administration more than once that its support for Israel might undermine Saudi-US relations. The Saudi government's tone became increasingly resolute. Saudi Arabia called on Washington to put pressure on Israel to implement UN Security Council Resolution 242 of 22 November 1967 (on the evacuation of Arab territories seized in 1967) and threatened that the US would otherwise face the consequences of a drop in oil supplies.[186] The US and Western Europe did not take these warnings seriously[187] since the earlier oil boycotts of 1956 and 1967 had proved ineffective. But oil supplies had exceeded demand in the 1950s and 1960s and the oil companies had huge reserves of liquid fuel. Besides, the US could do without oil imports at that time. The situation in the early 1970s was radically different.

In the summer of 1973 Saudi Arabia hinted that it would support Egypt in the event of a new war with Israel. The war started on 6 October. In the early days, the Syrian and Egyptian armies carried out successful operations. The Israelis launched a counter-offensive, but they could not defeat the Arab armies. In the Middle East context, a lack of victory amounted to an Israeli defeat, at least from the political standpoint. The Arab states demonstrated solidarity, despite the differences between their regimes. Iraqi units participated in the battles on the Syrian front. Jordan, Morocco, Tunisia, Saudi Arabia, Kuwait and Algeria sent token detachments to the countries fighting against Israel. Saudi Arabia and Libya decided to increase their financial aid to Egypt and pay Syria a subsidy to compensate these countries for the financial and economic losses caused by the war.

On 7 October, the very day after the outbreak of the war, the US secretary of state, Henry Kissinger, sent Faisal a telegram calling on him to persuade Egypt and Syria to cease hostilities. Faisal answered that he fully supported Egypt and Syria and called on

Washington to exert all its influence to make Israel vacate the occupied territories.[188] On 9 October the Saudi command recalled all servicemen from leave and brought the army to a state of operational readiness.[189] Five days later, a Saudi detachment was sent to Syria.[190]

CHAPTER 18

Domestic and Foreign Policy (the 1970s and the early 1980s)

On 17 October 1973 a meeting in Kuwait of the oil ministers of the ten Arab oil-exporting states decided to reduce oil production by at least 5% every month until the Middle East conflict was settled. Saudi Arabia and Kuwait immediately slashed production by 10%.[1] When the US organized an 'air bridge' to supply Israel with arms, Saudi Arabia and other Arab countries resorted to more resolute action. Between 20 and 22 October they declared, one after the other, that they would cease oil supplies to the US and then to the Netherlands, which had adopted a pro-Israeli stance. They also embargoed oil supplies to those processing plants that usually exported their products to the US or sold them to the US navy.[2]

Simultaneously with the Arab oil ministers, representatives of the petroleum-exporting Gulf states, including Iran, met in Kuwait and decided to raise the reference prices of oil by almost 70%. In December 1973 the new price was doubled. Between January 1973 and January 1974 the reference prices and the real incomes of the petroleum-exporting countries, including Saudi Arabia, increased fivefold.[3] Iraq supplemented the embargo by nationalizing British and Dutch shares in Basra Petroleum.[4]

The oil boycott created a major problem for the US, where more than a quarter of all imported petroleum came from the Arab countries. Japan and Western Europe faced even greater problems: 90% of oil consumption in Japan and 85% of that in Western Europe were covered by imports from the Middle East.[5] On 5 November 1973 the ten Arab petroleum-exporting countries decided to reduce production in December by 25% as compared with the volume in September. Western Europe reacted immediately. As early as the morning of 6 November, the governments of the nine EEC countries declared that they were in favour of implementing the UN Security Council resolutions on ending the hostilities and Resolution 242 in full, including the withdrawal of Israeli troops from territories occupied in 1967. Japan made a similar statement.[6]

After hostilities ceased, many Arab petroleum-exporting countries opposed the export restrictions, claiming that they harmed the interests of countries that were friendly to the Arabs. In early December 1973 the members of the Organization of Arab Petroleum Exporting Countries (OAPEC, set up in 1968) decided in Kuwait to cancel the reduction of oil production by 5%, planned for December, in order to help the situation of those EEC countries which adopted a favourable attitude to the Arabs. OAPEC's communiqué also noted that the African and Islamic states would be supplied with oil under their current contracts. The embargo on oil exports to the US and the Netherlands was temporarily maintained.[7]

On 25 December 1973 the next OAPEC conference in Kuwait decided to increase oil production in January 1974 by 10% and resume the full volume of liquid fuel supplies to Japan, Belgium, Britain, France, Spain and the Philippines. It also concluded that the oil sanctions had not materially influenced the economic situation of the US and other anti-Arab states or changed their policy.[8] On 18 March 1974, at Saudi Arabia's insistence, the embargo on oil exports to the US was lifted.[9] Saudi Arabia's interest in its economic, political and military cooperation with Washington had prevailed.

The use of the 'oil weapon' both during and after the 1973 Arab-Israeli war, and the enormous increase in oil prices, enabled the kingdom to become the leader of the conservative Arab states of the Middle East. King Faisal encouraged the restoration of Egyptian-US relations, the 180° change of direction in Egypt's foreign policy and the growing influence of conservative forces within Egypt. Saudi Arabia was keen to support anti-Soviet forces throughout the Middle East and even outside the region. At the same time, the 'cheque-book' foreign policy demonstrated Saudi Arabia's weakness: it was not backed up by military strength, nor did it have sufficient personnel to carry through its policies. Cooperation with the US and the West was hampered by disagreements over the approach to Israel and by the anti-Western sentiment among ordinary Saudis.

In late 1974 and early 1975 there was a crisis in Riyadh's relations with Washington. President Ford, Secretary of State Kissinger, Secretary of Defence Schlesinger and the US media began mentioning a possible US occupation of the oilfields on the Arabian Gulf coast.[10] Washington had to make great efforts to convince Saudi Arabia that there were no definite plans of that sort. On 14 March 1975 Kissinger met King Faisal. The Saudi government affected to believe Washington's assurances for the simple reason that it had no choice.[11]

King Faisal's position in the country seemed secure and his authority had grown after the 1973 Arab-Israeli war. The blow, when it came, was from an unexpected quarter. On 25 March 1975, during a ceremony to receive congratulations on the occasion of a festival, the king's cousin's son, Faisal ibn Musaid (recently returned from the US, where he had spent some years at school and university), shot Faisal dead with a pistol. The crime may have been motivated by personal reasons. The young prince was engaged to a daughter of the late King Saud; his mother was a Rashidi; and his brother, a religious extremist, had been killed in a clash with the police during the demonstration against opening a TV station in the 1960s. Another possible explanation is that Ibn Musaid was mentally unbalanced. There was also a suggestion that the assassination was the Americans' revenge for Faisal's participation in the oil boycott and a warning to the other members of the royal family. Whatever might be the truth, the real motives behind the crime have never been disclosed and the assassin was beheaded.[12]

Prince Khalid took the royal oath and also became prime minister. Domestic and foreign policy was determined by Crown Prince Fahd, who became the first deputy prime minister and temporarily retained the post of minister of interior. Prince Abdallah became second deputy prime minister and commander of the National Guard. Fahd's brother Sultan led the ministry of defence and aviation. For four years after Faisal's assassination, there were no signs of a direct threat to the country's stability. However, the opposition was gaining strength within Saudi society.

The creation of the Communist Party of Saudi Arabia in 1975 meant that a new leftist opposition group appeared in the country, though it had little real influence. The party claimed to unite and guide the working class, the poor peasants, the settled and nomadic population and the democratic strata of the intelligentsia and students.[13] After the upsurge of the anti-Shah and anti-Western movement in Iran, which had religious overtones, similar blocs and organizations appeared in Saudi Arabia. They opposed the regime from a position of the 'genuine (i.e. pure) Islam' and led the popular anti-government movement in the autumn of 1979 and at the beginning of 1980.[14]

The Saudi authorities had been aware since August 1979 of the existence of secret cells in the army, illegal imports of arms and expressions of discontent even among the young princes. To stop illegal arms imports, the authorities prohibited the transit of Lebanese and Syrian goods by truck via Saudi Arabia. In September the government tightened up security measures and several officers from the air force, tank and motor rifle units were arrested. It was claimed that ten young Saudi princes from the royal family were questioned by the king and his retinue on suspicion of radical sympathies. The second series of arrests came in September, when the country was electrified by the distribution of numerous illegal leaflets. Some of them called for a restoration of the 'purity' of Islam, others urged the overthrow of 'the rule of despotic agents', still others demanded the expulsion from the kingdom of all foreigners. The authorities failed to disclose the names of the individuals and organizations behind the leaflets. In the last week of September, a state of enhanced operational readiness was declared in the National Guard and the regular army.

In mid-November 1979 an anti-government rebellion began in Hijaz. Small armed detachments engaged in surprise attacks on the regular troops and seized positions on the roads leading to Medina. There was also serious unrest in the Qahtan, Ataiba and Yamani tribes, whose lands had been partly seized by princes from the royal family. The rebels controlled a sizeable area of territory between Mecca and Medina. According to some reports, several soldiers of the regular army and National Guard joined the rebels on 19 November. It was estimated that some 3,500 people took part in the revolt. The leaders of the movement divided their forces into two columns: one made for Mecca and the other for Medina. However, government troops, deployed in Medina and the environs, repulsed the rebels on 20 November. Some sources claim that more than 250 people were killed in Medina.

The authorities in Mecca were taken by surprise. On 20 November 1979, the first day of the fifteenth century of the Hegira, the rebels seized the main mosque of Mecca. The Movement of the Muslim Revolutionaries of the Arabian Peninsula, a little-known organization, declared that it was leading the rebellion. The opposition's spiritual leader Muhammad al-Qahtani, who called himself the Mahdi (Messiah), stated that the movement's purpose was the 'purification of Islam' and the liberation of the country from the 'infidel clique' of the royal family and corrupt religious leaders.[15]

The movement's political leader was Juhaiman al-Ataiba. His speeches were recorded on cassettes and played from loudspeakers fixed to the roofs of mosques. Cassettes were distributed free of charge to all who wanted them. Al-Ataiba condemned Western civilization for having destroyed the fundamental values of Saudi society and denounced the government's 'hypocrisy', claiming that the authorities paid lip service to the true religion but engaged in 'oppression, corruption and bribery' in practice. Al-Ataiba criticized the princes who 'seized land' and 'squandered the state's money' and the 'drunkards' who 'led a dissolute life in luxurious palaces'. He called on people to return, under the Mahdi's guidance, to the society of the first centuries of Islam, describing it as 'the golden age' and the era of justice and equality.[16]

The royal family could not begin negotiations with the rebels on their terms: these included the dismissal of several high-ranking princes, a revision of the terms covering oil production and sales (initially, the rebels demanded that no oil at all should be sold to the West), a return to the canons of 'genuine' Islam and the removal of all foreign military advisers from the country. On his return from a visit to Tunisia, Crown Prince Fahd insisted that the rebellion be crushed by force. Some 1,000 rebels continued to put up resistance for a further two weeks. According to government figures, dozens of people were killed. Witnesses claimed, however, that there were hundreds of casualties. The Mahdi was killed and Juhaiman al-Ataiba was captured. He was executed on 9 January 1980, together with 63 of his followers, including Egyptians, Yemenis, Kuwaitis and other Arabs.[17]

During the clashes in Mecca, unrest also began among the Shia of the Eastern Province. In response, 12,000 soldiers of the National Guard were sent to surround the oilfields. Between 300,000 and 350,000 Shia live in the most strategically important region of Saudi Arabia. Over several decades, the oil workers there had set up illegal trade unions and led demonstrations and political strikes, including anti-US actions. Defying a government prohibition, the Shia decided to organize the religious ceremony of *ashura* on 27 November 1979. The National Guard tried to prevent religious processions by force. But numerous demonstrators rushed to al-Qatif and other towns of the Eastern Province, carrying portraits of Ayatollah Khomeini, and attacked army barracks. They set fire to industrial plants and banks and shouted anti-royalist slogans.

Domestic and Foreign Policy (the 1970s and the early 1980s)

They distributed leaflets calling on the people to overthrow the 'despotic regime' and proclaim a republic. The unrest lasted for three days. The National Guard reacted firmly and witnesses claimed that dozens of demonstrators were killed or wounded.

After an initial period of confusion, caused by the Shia's demonstrations and the revolt in Mecca, the government began taking measures to calm the situation and to suppress the opposition. Several high-ranking officers were dismissed for negligence or incompetence, including the commanders of the three branches of the armed forces and six security officers. The governor of Mecca was dismissed from his post. King Khalid, Crown Prince Fahd and other high-ranking princes hurried to visit influential tribal shaikhs and inspect the military bases. Thousands of 'suspect' foreign workers were expelled from the country. On 17 December Nasir al-Said, the leftist opposition leader, who had escaped to Beirut, was kidnapped there: nothing more has been heard of him.[18]

Saudi students were temporarily recalled from abroad in the middle of the academic year. To pacify the *ulama*, women's hairdressing salons and women's clubs were closed down and female announcers were dismissed from the TV, in spite of their very decent clothing. New regulations prohibited girls from continuing their education abroad. Simultaneously, in an attempt to satisfy the 'reformers', technocrats, officials and representatives of the middle class who wanted a share in power, Crown Prince Fahd promised to elaborate a 'Fundamental Law' that would envisage the setting up of the *majlis al-shura*.

Under the shadow of the Iranian revolution, the US was concerned that the reforms in Saudi Arabia – i.e. the adaptation of outdated political institutions to the new socio-economic realities – might come too late, as a CIA official stated in January 1980. Due to a slip of the tongue, the official quoted President Carter's statement saying that the existence of the Saudi regime could not be guaranteed for more than two years. That and other leakages led to the expulsion of a CIA official from Saudi Arabia.[19]

The Saudi security services were expanded and strengthened with the active assistance of advisers from the CIA and from the French and West German secret services. The salaries paid to the military and the National Guard were doubled over several months, and the government turned a blind eye to the 'commercial' activities engaged in by many officers.[20] As a security measure, regular troops were dispersed along the borders, armoured units were withdrawn from towns and issues of ammunition were reduced to a minimum.[21] In January 1980 joint US-Saudi exercises were held in Saudi Arabia as part of large-scale military manoeuvres in the region.

On 10 January 1980 the Shia organized peaceful anti-government demonstrations in the towns and villages of the Eastern Province. Another demonstration was held in al-Qatif on 17 January. On 2 February unrest resumed in al-Qatif, demonstrations were held under pro-Khomeini slogans and several people were killed or wounded.[22] But these mass outbursts of discontent were the last. After the stormy events of late 1979 and early 1980, a period of calm now began.

King Khalid died on 12 June 1982 of a heart attack. The reins of power passed smoothly to Crown Prince Fahd, who continued the policies of the previous king. His half-brother Abdallah became crown prince. On the international level, Saudi Arabia maintained close ties with the US. The dominance of US capital in the oil industry, US arms supplies to Saudi Arabia, the Saudi regime's vital interest in continued US support, and the impact of economic fluctuations in the US on Saudi investments – all these factors predetermined Riyadh's orientation towards Washington. Besides close economic, political and military ties, the leaders of the two countries maintained permanent personal contacts and exchanged visits. There were many Saudi students in the US, both from among the ruling elite and from other social groups.

To help Washington become the protector of Arab interests in its relations with the oil-exporting countries, Saudi Arabia played the role of a 'moderate' in OPEC. After the 1979 Iranian revolution, Saudi oil exports frequently amounted to half the total OPEC exports, which gave Riyadh a decisive voice in the organization. Verbally, Riyadh opposed the rise in oil prices, in line with Washington's position. In practice, however, the rise met the interests both of the US energy companies and of the US as a whole in its competition with Western Europe and Japan. After the 1973 oil price hike, Saudi Arabia considerably reduced its oil production to prevent a fall in oil prices on the world markets.

Saudi Arabia became the largest investor in US banks, treasury bonds and real estate. Some sources claimed that the true value of Saudi investments far exceeded the official figures. In Saudi Arabia's confidential 1978 report to the IMF, its foreign investments (mainly in the US) were estimated at $133bn.[23] In the opinion of experts, at least $100bn had been added to that figure by the end of 1981.[24] Saudi capital was invested in the US mainly through the Chase Manhattan Bank and the Morgan Guaranty Trust. Total proceeds (interest, dividends, rent, etc.) from Saudi investments abroad stood at some $10bn per year.[25] Riyadh granted the International Bank for Reconstruction and Development (IBRD) and the IMF credit worth billions of dollars and began to participate in the decision-making in both organizations. In 1978 Saudi Arabia became a permanent member of the IMF board.[26]

The secret treaty on financial, economic and military cooperation concluded between King Khalid and President Ford in 1977 was conducive to consolidating US-Saudi relations. Saudi Arabia pledged itself not to increase oil prices by more than 5% until 1984 (a promise it did not keep) and to invest most of its oil revenues in US treasury bonds. The US pledged itself to help Saudi Arabia in repelling military aggression, from whatever source.[27] When Washington was deprived of Iranian oil supplies, Saudi Arabia increased its own production and met the world markets' demand for liquid fuel.

On 15 May 1978 the US Congress approved the government's decision to supply aircraft to Egypt, Saudi Arabia and Israel. Saudi Arabia was to receive a total of 60 F-15 aircraft by 1983. Riyadh committed itself not to equip them for offensive operations or to deploy them at bases close to Israel.[28] On 28 November 1981, after protracted discussions, the US Congress approved the White House's proposal to sell military hardware to Saudi Arabia, including 5 AWACS, for a total sum of $8.5bn. The pro-Israeli lobby in Congress opposed the deal, as it did whenever modern weapons were sold to an Arab country. The majority of Congressmen, however, considered the deal to be in line with US interests.[29] Differences nevertheless arose between Saudi Arabia and the US on Middle East issues.

Although Saudi Arabia's relations with Western Europe and Japan never reached the level of those with the US, they were friendly and multifaceted. Saudi Arabia purchased military hardware and weapons from Britain, France and West Germany. The Common Market countries and Japan were among the main importers of Saudi oil, and a part of Saudi petrodollars was invested there. Saudi Arabia turned increasingly to Western Europe and Japan for its purchases of industrial equipment and arms. In the 1970s Riyadh signed economic and technical cooperation agreements with France, Italy, Denmark, Japan, Switzerland and Britain.[30] However, when a film entitled *Death of a Princess* was shown on British TV in March 1980, it was considered an insult to Saudi Arabia and led to a temporary cooling in Saudi-British relations.[31]

The kingdom's bursting exchequer, which gave grants and credits to Arab and Islamic states and other Afro-Asian countries, played a substantial role in supporting Saudi Arabia's foreign policy. Saudi Arabia was second only to the US in capital exports in the form of aid in the 1970s and 1980s.

After Zia ul-Haq seized power in Pakistan in 1975, Riyadh developed closer relations with Islamabad. The *rapprochement* was based on their joint opposition to the Iranian revolution and to the Marxist regime in Afghanistan. Riyadh paid for the US arms purchased by Pakistan and partly transferred to the armed opposition in Afghanistan. Military cooperation between Riyadh and Islamabad also increased and there were press reports concerning the presence of Pakistani pilots in the Saudi air force.[32]

Saudi Arabia was active in the Arab world too. After the Arab summit of October 1974 in Rabat, Riyadh recognized the Palestine Liberation Organization (PLO). The Saudis paid particular attention to Fatah, as the main component of the PLO, and gave it substantial financial aid, hoping to spread Saudi influence in the organization, though without any tangible success.

When civil war broke out in Lebanon in 1975, Riyadh's political sympathies were divided between the rightist Christians on the one hand and the Muslims and the PLO on the other hand. On 18 October 1976 King Khalid convened a conference in Saudi Arabia with the participation of Egyptian President Anwar Sadat, Syrian President Hafiz al-Asad and PLO leader Yasir Arafat. They signed an agreement to bring about a cease-fire in Lebanon. Syrian troops in Lebanon were put under the formal control of a committee consisting of members from Saudi Arabia, Egypt, Kuwait and Syria.

Riyadh's position on the Arab-Israeli conflict was contradictory. Its cooperation with the US – Israel's protector and ally – ran counter to its claims to leadership of the Arab world as 'the custodian of the two holy shrines' and 'the fighter against Zionism and Israeli aggression', and to its demands for the liberation of the Muslim holy places in East Jerusalem. According to the Rabat summit's decision of October 1974, Egypt and Syria received annual aid worth $570m each, while Jordan was given $300m and the PLO $28m from the special fund set up by Saudi Arabia, Kuwait and the UAE.[33]

In addition, Saudi Arabia gave direct financial aid to the 'confrontation states' in their struggle with Israel to cover their budget deficits and to purchase arms in the West.

Riyadh also gave substantial amounts of aid to Middle Eastern countries with conservative regimes. It supported the trend towards liberalization in those countries with a strong state sector and urged them to cease cooperation with the USSR and to pursue a pro-American policy instead. Saudi support enabled Sadat to carry out his *infitah* ('open-door') policy in Egypt, to radically revise his domestic and foreign policy and to denounce the treaty of friendship with the USSR in March 1976. However, when Sadat visited Jerusalem on 19 November 1977 and pursued the course towards a peace treaty with Israel that led finally to the Camp David accords, Riyadh felt unable to support the policy, at least in public. On 26 March 1979 the peace treaty between Egypt and Israel was signed at Camp David. The following day, the Arab ministers of foreign affairs met in Baghdad and decided to sever diplomatic relations with Egypt and apply sanctions against it. On 24 April Saudi Arabia ceased all financial aid to Egypt, but continued to use its Egyptian workforce.[34]

CHAPTER 19

The Socio-economic Structure of Saudi Arabia in the Oil Era (the 1950s to the early 1980s)

Saudi Arabia's oil revenues grew more than 8,500 times between 1938 and 1973 and experienced an immense increase afterwards (see Table 2).[1] Thereafter the revenues stabilized.

Table 2. Oil Revenues of Saudi Arabia, 1938–1992 (million US$)

Year	Total revenue	Year	Total revenue	Year	Total revenue	Year	Total revenue
1938	0.5	1954	236.3	1970	1,944.9	1983	42,809.0
1939	2.0	1955	348.0	1972	2,779.3	1984	34,243.0
1945	5.0	1956	290.2	1973	4,330.9	1985	24,180.0
1946	12.5	1960	333.7	1976	33,500.0	1986	16,975.0
1947	17.5	1961	377.6	1977	43,308.0	1987	19,271.0
1948	31.5[a]	1962	409.7	1978	40,332.0	1988	19,607.0
1949	39.0	1963	455.2[b]	1979	62,885.0	1989	24,096.0
1951	110.0	1965	586.2[c]	1980	105,813.0	1990	40,128.0
1952	212.2	1966	760.3[d]	1981	116,183.0	1991	43,658.0
1953	169.8	1967	879.8[e]	1982	75,534.0	1992	47,560.0

a. Plus special revenues of $19.32m.
b. Plus special revenues of $152.5m because of retroactive recalculations.
c. Additional revenues of $46.0.
d. Plus $29.4m.
e. Plus $29.3m.

In the 1940s and 1950s Saudi Arabia spent the great bulk of its oil revenues on domestic consumption, owing to the country's poverty and its traditional socio-political structure. Most of the money went to members of the ruling group; the ordinary people received virtually nothing.

The country's state apparatus might have corresponded to the needs of a medieval feudal-tribal society, but it was totally unsuited to handling huge revenues and performing the new socio-economic functions. There was no distinction made between the exchequer and the king's privy purse in the 1930s, the 1940s and even the 1950s. There was no fiscal or currency system, no industrial or commercial legislation, no state or public institutions and no skilled personnel in the country to tackle the issues raised by the new level of incomes. The religious system was not conducive to innovations or economic development.

With the exception of a very narrow group of educated people and oil workers, there was no organized public opinion in the country to urge the king to spend the funds in the interests of society as a whole. The monarch was supposed to make charitable donations, to be generous in his hospitality and to distribute part of his income as gifts and subsidies among the tribal and religious nobility who did not belong to his family. Few people expected and even fewer people urged the king to go beyond his traditional obligations towards his subjects.

In the late 1950s the royal family took half of the $300m in oil revenues and the merchants, government officials and advisers accounted for a sizeable part of the rest.[2] Philby, however, gives a lower figure, holding that only one fifth of the state revenue was spent by the Saudi royal family in the 1950s.[3] Officials who grew rich owing to the abuse of their power became a regular practice in Saudi Arabia, as in most countries of the Middle East. American Arabists have commented, 'Those who did not do so would be regarded as stupid or eccentric.'[4] The expansion of the bureaucracy and growth in oil revenues were accompanied by an increase in corruption. It reached such an extent that a sizeable part of the budget allocations landed up in the pockets of those who were responsible for spending them. Many state officials engaged in commercial activities and many merchants occupied administrative posts, frequently using their positions for personal ends.[5] Since the opportunities for capital investment, particularly in the long term, were limited in Saudi Arabia, huge sums leaked abroad in the 1940s and 1950s and were invested in banks or real estate.[6]

The financial system. Revenue and expenditure

Before 1952 there was no uniform monetary system in Saudi Arabia. Besides Saudi rials, British gold sovereigns and Egyptian pounds circulated in Hijaz, Indian rupees in the eastern regions and Austrian thalers (each equal to 3 Saudi rials) throughout the country.[7]

In 1952 the Saudi Arabian Monetary Agency (SAMA) was founded with the functions of a bank of circulation, to be succeeded some years later by the Central

Bank. It issued rials with a gold content of about 0.2 g, backed by gold and hard currency. One US dollar was equal to 3.75 rials (4.5 in 1960).[8] So-called '*hajj* stocks' (or 'pilgrim receipts') were issued, soon to be replaced by paper notes. The official exchange rate of the Saudi rial changed twice thereafter. Its actual rate against the US dollar rose in 1971, due to the devaluation of the dollar and the unchanged gold content of the rial, to reach 4.14 rials to the dollar. In August 1973 Saudi Arabia revalued the rial, increasing its gold content to 0.21 g. The official exchange rate became 3.55 rials to the dollar.[9] Thereafter the exchange rate fluctuated between 3.33 (1980) and 3.75 (1990) rials to the dollar, remaining within the same range in early 1994.[10] SAMA's headquarters was in Jidda and it then opened branches in Mecca, Medina and Dammam. Its main tasks were to stabilize and strengthen the Saudi currency, centralize the revenues and expenditure and provide assistance to the ministry of finance and national economy. The agency employed foreign experts.[11]

In 1957 Saudi Arabia became a member of the IMF and IBRD and in 1970 it joined the International Development Association (IDA).[12] Dominated by US capital, these international organizations guided the country's financial and economic policy, though their recommendations often proved impracticable. Before 1952 the leading bank in Saudi Arabia was the Netherlands Trading Society, through which SOCAL made its first payments for the oil concessions. It had been active in the country since 1926. In the 1940s and early 1950s the Banque de l'Indochine (France), the Jordan Arab Bank, the British Bank of the Middle East and the National Bank of Pakistan opened branches in Saudi Arabia.[13] By the mid-1960s Saudi Arabia had three banks of its own – the Jidda-based National Commercial Bank, the Riyadh Bank and the Agricultural Credit Bank (the last of these was founded in 1964).[14] The private National Commercial Bank was set up in the mid-1930s by the large trading companies of Jidda, which belonged to the al-Kaaki and Mahfuz families.[15] In 1974 there were twelve Saudi banks (with seventy-two permanent branches and offices) and ten foreign banks in the country.[16]

Direct payments from the oil companies accounted for more than four-fifths of the state revenue. Taking their indirect incomes into account, it is clear that the entire revenue – and virtually the whole economy of the country – relied on oil production and exports, and continues to do so. The secondary sources of state revenue were municipal, port, airport and other dues, railway and airway proceeds, road dues and *zakat*. The last-mentioned slightly exceeded $1m in 1954, being less than 1% of the total revenue. In the 1950s the government reduced its rate from 2.5% to 1.25% of a person's income. Believers were supposed to spend the rest on charitable purposes.[17] In the 1940s and 1950s the main items of state expenditure were maintenance of the royal family, the armed forces and the police, and subsidies to tribes and religious establishments.[18]

An IBRD mission visited Saudi Arabia in 1960. It recommended, *inter alia*, the setting up of a central planning organization to concentrate the government's efforts on the most important economic projects, particularly without the participation of private capital; and to continue prospecting for mineral and water resources.[19] The Supreme Planning Commission was set up in 1961 to draw up an economic development policy, together with various ministries and agencies on the basis of the IBRD recommendations, and to supervise the implementation of the economic projects. It was replaced in 1965 by the Central Planning Organization, under a chairman with ministerial rank. There was no clear-cut delimitation of functions between the Central Planning Body, SAMA and the ministry of finance and national economy, and serious differences often arose between them. None of the economic plans adopted in the early 1960s was implemented.[20]

Budget expenditure on transport, health, education, agriculture, settling the tribes and irrigation began rising in the 1960s. Expenditure on health care rose from 60m rials in 1959 to 499m rials in 1973/74; spending on economic projects rose from 55m rials to 14,263m rials; and the total budget expenditure rose from 1,112m rials to 22,810m rials over the same period.[21]

The state budgets of the 1960s and early 1970s provided for increased investment in economic development, health and education, but the development projects were to a great extent a cover for military expenses.[22] After 1967 direct and indirect allocations to the armed forces and the police rose to two-fifths of the budget instead of one third as in the earlier period.[23] Saudi Arabia spent 10–13% of its GNP on the army, higher than any NATO country, including the US, and coming second only to those Middle East states directly involved in the Arab-Israeli conflict.[24] The swollen state apparatus consumed a large part of the revenue.[25]

A new phenomenon could be observed in Saudi Arabia's financial practice in the late 1960s and early 1970s – the export of capital by the state through SAMA. The bulk of state deposits was in the Morgan Guarantee Trust Company and the Chase Manhattan Bank.[26] Sizeable sums were deposited in European banks too. Saudi deposits abroad totalled approximately $785m in 1969, $890m in 1970, $1,540m in 1971, $2,870m in 1972, $4,790m in 1973, $19,200m in 1974, $38,700m in 1975 and $49,590m in 1976.[27] (These figures are estimates and describe the trend rather than the exact amounts of capital.)

After the various hikes in the posted prices of oil in the 1970s, Saudi Arabia was unable to use or even consume its growing income and it increased the export of capital, investing dozens of billions of dollars abroad by the late 1970s. Most Saudi investments consisted of US treasury bonds, bank deposits, shares in various corporations and investments in the Eurodollar market and real estate. According to data provided by the First National Bank of Chicago, 70% of Saudi investments were denominated in US dollars.[28]

The origins and development of Saudi industry

Even in the early 1940s wheeled transport was not used in most regions of Saudi Arabia. Up to the early 1960s 'national production' was confined to the traditional necessities and was represented by handicrafts and home industry.[29] Saudi Arabia's traditional economy was in ruins even before the arrival of Aramco. The invasion of modern industry, combined with large-scale imports, was destructive to local handicrafts and the nomadic economy and accelerated their crisis. By the late 1950s:

> The small, craft industries, which until the beginning of oil exploitation formed a minimal industrial activity in Saudi Arabia . . . [had] declined in competition with foreign goods . . . Workers in crafts and trade undoubtedly surpass[ed] in number those employed in industry.[30]

Within what was still a traditional economy, Aramco had a profound influence on Arabian society. It hired a workforce, erected modern townships and towns, created auxiliary services and workshops with the participation of Saudi capital and built a road network. All these changes gave a boost to Saudi Arabia's economy and to the country's social development, but – needless to say – they were caused by the need to create the elementary economic, technological and socio-political conditions in which Aramco could function normally.

With the assistance of local capital, secondary branches of industry and construction appeared in the Eastern Province to serve Aramco. There were only 2 local contractors in 1944, 107 in 1947 and some 200 in 1955.[31] They employed several thousand workers. Many of these contractors were involved in the construction of the Trans-Arabian pipeline, the building of roads and railways, including the Dammam–Riyadh railway, the construction of the Dhahran airfield, schools, houses and hospitals for Arab employees, and the expansion and reconstruction of the port of Dammam.[32] Some Saudi contractors opened their own building and transport companies with dozens of trucks and repair shops. Although the contractors' initial share in Aramco's total construction expenses was not high, it grew steadily. Through its Arabian Industry Development Department, Aramco controlled local companies' activities by either granting or denying them profitable contracts.[33]

Small plants for the production of building materials, bottles, oxygen, ice and soft drinks, power stations and furniture workshops appeared in the Eastern Province and the number of trading companies and shops increased.[34] As V. V. Ozoling has justly noted, however, 'there was virtually no national industry in the country in 1960'.[35] With the exception of the oil refineries, which were owned by foreign companies, there were no enterprises in Saudi Arabia with more than 100 workers. The average number of employees in 'large' companies was 6, and the total number of workers was around 5,500.[36] Capital investment in Saudi 'industry' amounted to several million dollars, whereas Aramco's capital investment was close to $1bn. Almost all Saudi companies were private, with the exception of large, state-owned motor repair shops.

The ruling elite of Saudi Arabia showed little concern in the 1940s and early 1950s with the fate of national industry and Saudi handicrafts. It was only gradually that its most far-sighted and enlightened members became aware of the need for state regulation and encouragement. Such ideas were influenced by developments in the more advanced Arab countries, the criticism of the regime by the nascent opposition at home and the advice of American experts.

Ozoling has divided Saudi Arabia's post-war economic policy into four periods.[37] The first, from 1946 to 1956, was 'the period of intoxication with wealth'. Saudi Arabia was taking the first steps towards becoming a multisector 'bourgeois-feudal state'.[38] Oil extraction developed steadily and the income of the ruling elite grew rapidly. The second period, from 1957 to 1963, was 'transitional'. The government was compelled to take some measures to protect the national economy, imposed controls on currency operations, restricted imports and tried to balance the budget. In 1964, for the first time in the country's history, a stable and permanently expanding basis emerged for a rapid increase in national savings. This seldom happens in countries with a preponderance of feudal and semi-feudal sectors, which cannot serve as an accumulation basis by themselves. The mid-1960s – the third period – saw the emergence of state capitalism, a new sector in the Saudi economy. Lastly, the government, which had previously preferred short-term current planning within a fiscal year, adopted the first five-year plan (covering the period 1971–75) in the early 1970s. This could be considered as the fourth period.

In May 1962 the decree on the protection and promotion of Saudi industry was issued, which provided for the abolition of customs duties on imports of machinery, equipment, spare parts and some kinds of raw materials and semi-finished goods. The government promised to allocate sites for new plants. In 1963 the ministry of commerce was transformed into the ministry of commerce and industry. Its tasks were to draft measures to protect Saudi industry from foreign competition and to grant preferences to both Saudi and foreign capital in the areas of industrial equipment imports, taxation and credit.[39] Set up in 1965, the Central Planning Body prepared recommendations concerning the diversification of the Saudi economy and the first plan for economic development. It was then that the registration of all new companies with the ministry of commerce and industry became compulsory.[40]

As a consequence of the above-mentioned decree of May 1962, 188 Saudi firms had been set up by late 1971, each employing between 7 and 64 workers. The average capital of these firms was 1.1m rials. Most capital was invested in construction.[41] However, the majority of Saudi industrial enterprises could not work at full capacity because of the narrow market, foreign competition and a shortage of workers and raw materials. The only successful branch was the cement industry, whose output grew from 30,000 tons in 1957/58 to 911,000 tons in 1972.[42]

The directory of the Jidda chamber of commerce listed the companies in the town (the largest in Hijaz) in the late 1960s. Most of them produced soft drinks, ice, paper, bricks and other building materials, household chemicals, boilers, and so on. The following figures give an idea of their assets: a soft drinks company, 15m rials; a cement company, 25m rials; a brick company, 200,000 rials; and a company making household chemicals, 7.5m rials.[43] In the 1960s Saudi businessmen built a match-making factory in a village between Riyadh and al-Kharj, a soap works in Jidda and cement works in Riyadh and Hufuf, and increased the capacity of the Jidda cement works and the Dammam paper mill. Expansion was observed in the following areas: brick, glass, furniture, sweets and food production, small foundries, and mechanical and car repair workshops.[44]

The Socio-economic Structure of Saudi Arabia in the Oil Era

The state allocated considerable sums for urban construction, electrification and the setting up of modern utilities in towns. In the 1960s economic development was confined mainly to the expansion and improvement of the infrastructure. This increased the demand for electricity and building materials. Total investment in the national economy was estimated in late 1969 at 1bn rials, a 6.5 times increase within 9 years.[45]

R. Knauerhase has noted that there were 101,569 workers in Saudi towns in 1968 and 146,740 in 1971, without specifying whether these figures included immigrants. The total number of Saudi firms stood at 42,886 in 1968 and 60,929 in 1971. The majority were workshops (for the repair of cars and domestic appliances) and very small factories, most of which were concentrated in Hijaz.[46] In both 1968 and 1971 the average number of workers in a firm was 2.33, including 1.42 paid and 0.91 unpaid workers (family members).[47]

As in many underdeveloped countries, the Saudi government needed to attract foreign capital for the national industry. As early as 1957 the decree on 'Foreign Capital Investments Regulation' was issued; it applied, with some exceptions, to existing and future foreign investments in Saudi Arabia. The concessionaire companies and those 'of vital importance for the kingdom's economic development' were exempted from the provisions of the decree. It stipulated that Saudi capital should account for at least 51% of the assets of any foreign company. Saudis should form at least 75% of a foreign company's personnel and receive at least 45% of the total salaries. The companies should act in accordance with the *sharia*, keep accounts in Arabic and establish their headquarters in Saudi Arabia.[48]

In February 1964 a new law on foreign investment was approved, which extended some of the privileges enjoyed by national capital to foreign capital. Foreign companies were exempted from income tax for five years from the date that they started operating, provided that the share of national capital was not less than 25% throughout the said period. Foreigners were allowed to export profits and capital without restrictions. The presence of national capital was no longer mandatory in the companies they set up, though it entitled the companies to some additional privileges. Foreign investments in the oil and mining industries were to be made under special agreements.[49] In late 1971 there were 66 industrial firms in the country with a total capital of 103m rials. There are no exact figures on those firms' personnel.[50]

There were very few Saudi industrialists in the early 1970s and they had neither economic nor political influence. Industry yielded insufficient profits and involved too many risks to attract capital from Saudi merchants, the royal family or the topmost echelons of the bureaucracy. They preferred either to transfer their capital abroad or to invest it in the import trade, land speculation, housing, or contracting and construction companies. This explains why the government had to assume the task of planning the country's industrial development. A state sector had to be created, especially in the capital-intensive industries. To that end, Petromin (the General Petroleum and Mineral Organization) was set up in 1962.[51]

Petromin redeemed the Jidda oil refinery from Aramco and began expanding it, simultaneously taking control of the oil products distribution network. In cooperation with foreign companies, Petromin started building chemical plants, which produced fertilizers, sulphur, acids and plastics from casing-head gas (which had earlier been burnt off at the oilfields) and then invested in the development of metallurgy.[52] Besides the metallurgical works and fertilizer plant near Dammam, other large state-owned enterprises were put into operation in the early 1970s – for example, the oil refinery in Jidda with 500 workers, and 3 cement plants employing a total of 981 people.[53] A large (by local standards) complex of state-owned military plants was built in al-Kharj: in 1965 it employed 850 workers and 54 engineers and technicians, all Saudis.[54]

Besides oil, other minerals were found in Saudi Arabia – gypsum, copper, iron ore, uranium, rock-salt, silver, gold and rare-earth metals – but their extraction had hardly begun in the 1960s.[55] As mentioned previously, between 1934 and 1954 a US-British-Canadian company extracted gold in Mahd al-Dhahab from mines dating back to ancient times. Within these 20 years it extracted about 26 tons of gold before deciding that further exploitation of the mines was unprofitable.[56] In July 1972 Saudi Arabia adopted new laws to regulate the exploitation of non-petroleum mineral resources. The maximum area allotted for exploration was increased from 100 to 10,000 sq. km. The companies that started mineral extraction were exempted from taxation for five years. This led to a marked increase of activity in prospecting, mainly for copper.[57]

The Saudi government tried to control the newly founded companies' activities in the key, capital-intensive industries – with the inevitable participation of foreign capital – through Petromin. It invested state funds in these industries and had a controlling interest in most of them, and its representatives sat on the company boards. Owing to the Saudi representatives' lack of experience, however, the industrial projects often proved unprofitable and served merely to enrich local officials and foreign companies.

The problem of building a modern communications network, relying on imported technology and foreign personnel, was solved somewhat more successfully from the 1950s to the 1970s, though with huge over-expenditure. The vast, sparsely populated country, with its stony and sandy deserts, needed roads and railways. A 577-km single-track railway was built in October 1951 from Dammam on the Gulf coast via Hufuf and Dhahran to Riyadh.[58] Its economic expediency is still disputed. Significantly, no further railways have been built in the country, and plans to extend the rail link to Medina and Jidda and restore the Hijaz railway, destroyed during the First World War, were never realized.

Intensive road construction began in the 1950s. In the Eastern Province, Dhahran was connected with al-Khobar, Dammam, Ras Tannura and al-Jubail. Paved roads were built to reach Kuwait and along the Trans-Arabian pipeline to Jordan, Syria and Lebanon. An asphalt road was built from Jidda to Mecca and Medina, followed by a highway from al-Taif to Mecca via almost inaccessible mountains. The road-building programme was even more intensive in the 1970s. The highway from Hijaz to Najd and al-Hasa was put into operation and the country's main population centres were connected by road. The most important road construction project of 1971–75 was the completion of the al-Taif–Abha–Jizan highway, which was over 700 km long.[59]

Ports were built, expanded or reconstructed in Jidda, Yanbu (on the Red Sea),

The Socio-economic Structure of Saudi Arabia in the Oil Era

Dammam, al-Khobar and Mina Saud (on the Gulf coast). In the 1960s there were only two airports in the country: at Jidda and Dhahran. Large airports were then built in Riyadh, Medina and al-Taif. Saudi Airlines, in conjunction with the American company, Transworld Airways, began regular flights to dozens of countries. A telephone network connected the country's main towns and was automated in the 1970s. Large radio stations operated in Jidda, Riyadh and Mecca, and smaller ones opened in other centres. For many years, the only TV station belonged to Aramco. In the 1960s a national TV network was created in spite of the *ulama*'s resistance.[60]

Knauerhase has compiled data showing the growth in the Saudi economy from 1962/63 to 1972/73. In his table, GDP includes military expenses and services. (Knauerhase changed his calculation system in 1966/67.) Even allowing for the fact that many of his figures are estimates, they provide a fairly reliable overall picture. According to these data, GDP increased within the period under examination from 8.6bn rials to 21.3bn, i.e. by 147.6%. Oil production still dominated the economy. Agriculture developed very slowly and moved from second to eighth position (oil-processing was now second). Industrial output grew from 157m rials to 417m, and building from 311m to 1,415m. These figures do not allow for inflation and speculative price rises, nor do they reflect the share of imported raw materials and semi-finished goods in the total value of industrial output.[61]

Ozoling has noted that in the 1970s, as previously, the oil industry was:

> the foundation of the country's economy, its only developed sector which corresponded to modern technical requirements. However, since it belongs almost completely to foreign capital, chiefly that of the US, it should be treated as an isolated organism within the country, not as an organic part of the national economy. That sector's activities are isolated to a considerable extent from the reproduction process in the national economy proper.[62]

Outside the oil sector, Saudi Arabia remained among the least developed states in the world. In the mid-1970s, after fifteen years of official encouragement, Saudi industry's share in GNP was still negligible.

In the second half of the 1960s the national manufacturing industry produced slightly more than 2% of GNP.[63] The share actually decreased in the early 1970s because of the accelerated growth of the oil sector. In order to become profitable and competitive, companies needed a developed technological base, skilled personnel and markets with a sufficient consumption capacity, conditions that were lacking in Saudi Arabia. Huge capital and the government's readiness to invest in industry had produced no significant results. The economic problems were aggravated by the underdeveloped infrastructure, unreliable statistics, corruption in the state machinery and collusion between foreign companies that overstated their equipment and construction costs many times over and thus foredoomed the new enterprises to unprofitability.

Trade and the commercial bourgeoisie

In the early 1970s the life of the country, and the normal functioning of its economy and society, depended on imports. Saudi Arabia imported all kinds of industrial and power equipment, machines, spares, engines, instruments, chemicals, medicines, almost all consumer goods and nearly half its food. The Saudi economy was self-sufficient only in petroleum products, as well as being partly self-sufficient in building materials and some types of mineral fertilizers. After the financial crisis of 1958, imports of luxury goods had been controlled, but the restrictions were only observed for a couple of years. Imports of alcohol beverages were strictly prohibited, which gave rise to large-scale smuggling.[64]

Saudi Arabia's main trading partner in the 1960s and 1970s was the US, followed by Western Europe and Japan. Britain (which had enjoyed an almost complete monopoly over the kingdom's markets in the 1920s and 1930s) now had to give up first place, though still retaining a strong position. The main articles imported from other Arab countries were livestock, meat, fruit, vegetables, foodgrain and some consumer goods.[65]

The bulk of the wholesale and retail trade was in the hands of Saudi merchants. Increased imports and demand, and a diversification of the range of consumer goods, resulted in flourishing commercial activities, a development of the old trading houses and the emergence of hundreds of new companies. In Arabia and other Islamic countries, commerce had always been considered an honourable occupation – Muslims remember that the Prophet was a merchant at one period of his life. Trade, land speculation and house-building were the first areas to attract private Saudi capital, first of all in Hijaz. Trade relied on experienced personnel, well-established traditions and solid links with trading partners. Some trading companies from Hijaz and al-Hasa were run by naturalized Syrians, Palestinians and Arabs from Hadhramawt.[66]

The influx of traders from other Arab countries in the 1950s caused discontent among the local merchants. In the early 1960s a decree was issued to restrict foreigners' trade activities: every foreign merchant (provided he was a Muslim and the citizen of an Arab country) must have a Saudi partner who should own at least 51% of the capital. As a result, thousands of Arab traders had to leave Saudi Arabia.[67]

Large trading companies, such as Alireza, al-Ghosaibi, Juffali, Bughshan, Jumaih, al-Sulaiman, Khashoggi and Pharaon, expanded in Saudi Arabia as a result of their import operations.[68] They also acted as contractors, built apartments, hotels and supermarkets, set up shipping and transport companies and invested in industry. As a rule, they were family businesses rather than joint-stock companies. The annual turnover of the largest of them reached $1bn in the mid-1970s. They were surrounded by hundreds of small-scale importers with very little capital and two or three agents. It was a radical change in commercial activities if one remembers that just one or two generations earlier merchants had imported food, cloth and garments from Bombay or logs from Malabar.

The Alireza trading family, with its headquarters in Jidda, is probably of Iranian descent. The company was founded in the 1860s. Before the First World War a member of the Alireza family was a deputy from Jidda in the Ottoman parliament; another Alireza, who was governor of Jidda in 1925, surrendered the town to Ibn Saud. The Alireza Company had been the agent for Ford cars since 1940, and for Westinghouse, ITT, Omega and Tissot since the end of the Second World War. One member of the family was minister of commerce, another was deputy minister of foreign affairs and two others were Saudi ambassadors to the US and France. The Alireza family invested in real estate, industry, services, power generation, transport and the oil industry.[69] They participated in large state contracts; for example, they owned a share in the Arabian-Italian Engineering Contractors (ALCO), whose business was importing various kinds of equipment.

One method of making money was to stand as guarantor for a foreign company that had signed contracts for road, port or hotel building or the improvement of public utilities in towns. The Juffali family became very successful after receiving the contract for the electrification of al-Taif for a British company.[70] The family then became the agent for Mercedes cars, imported tires and spare parts and bought several farms.[71]

Inevitably, those people who supplied goods to the state or the royal family became rich within a short space of time. Listing the largest trading companies of Jidda and Mecca, the Saudi writer Fuad Shakir mentions the family of Salih Isa Bukari, who became very wealthy by supplying clothing to the royal court, the army and police officers and to state-run schools in Riyadh.[72]

A bourgeoisie was also created, deriving its wealth from real-estate operations. Controls over land prices and rents for apartments in large towns were abolished as early as 1955/56. Rents rose immediately by four or five times and went on rising. Large plots of land were bought in towns, and whole blocks of poor people's housing were torn down and houses were built in their place to be rented or sold.[73]

The four Suwaidan brothers set up a company in Riyadh that engaged in land development. In 1969 they bought large plots in promising areas of the capital to sell them some years later at a price many hundreds of times higher than what they had paid. They built and sold villas and apartment blocks, imported building materials and hoisting and lifting/transport machinery.[74]

Saudi Arabia's largest trading companies were concentrated in Hijaz. They gained most from the oil boom, the growth in imports and the provision of supplies to the state, and spread their activities throughout the country. In 1948 the chamber of commerce was founded in Jidda. It was open to traders from Medina, al-Taif, Jizan and Tabuk, where there were no chambers of commerce, as well as to some traders from Mecca and Riyadh. In the early 1970s it had some 2,000 members.[75]

Most of the major traders in the Eastern Province had begun their activities as contractors for Aramco. Some of them were former Aramco employees. Sulaiman Ulayyan, for example, was a truck driver at Aramco and then set up a transport company. A junior clerk at Aramco, a distant relative of the al-Ghosaibi family, bought a filling station and then became the agent for Pepsi Cola.[76]

Access to the international stage proved difficult for Saudi merchants, with the exception of four businessmen who became multimillionaires: Khashoggi, Ghaith Pharaon (both of whom were sons of Ibn Saud's physicians), Sulaiman Ulayyan, the head of the Saudi-British Bank, and Akram Uddajah, born in Syria and naturalized in Saudi Arabia. Khashoggi made a large personal fortune out of arms supplies to the Saudi army and created a conglomerate of companies, the Triad Holding Corporation, based in Luxemburg, with a capital of $400m.[77] Pharaon became the chairman of the Saudi Research & Development Corporation. His activities embraced machine trading, insurance and the production of food and other consumer goods. Uddajah's company, Technique d'Avant-garde, was also based in Luxemburg. Perhaps his most famous purchase was the *France*, an ocean-going liner, which was furnished with antique French furniture.

This group of businessmen invested both in foreign construction companies and in banks. But attempts by newly rich Saudis to establish control over the large Western banks faced resistance from the financial capital of developed countries and were hindered by lack of experience and administrative personnel. The four Saudi businessmen mentioned above invested in Asian, African and Latin American banks, tourist and hotel complexes, shipping companies and real estate throughout the world.

With their close connections to the Saudi royal family, the Saudi bourgeoisie formed an unusual kind of commercial-financial oligarchy. It had developed in hothouse conditions, protected from foreign competition, and had grown mainly on the basis of imports, paid ultimately out of the oil revenues. According to some press reports, the Saudi royal family tried to avoid publicizing their connection with this oligarchy, although several princes and government members engaged in commercial activities through proxies.[78]

The Saudi royal family and the related families distributed the oil revenues within the state machinery, where corruption became a semi-legal public institution. The oil revenues were spent on the army and the police, thereby enriching their highest echelons, middlemen and (mainly) foreign companies, and on various public works and economic projects, which favoured the same officials, foreign companies and middlemen. Saudi merchants also capitalized on the relative backwardness of Saudi society, swallowing up a sizeable part of the oil revenues in the course of secondary distribution.

Landownership and land tenure

How did the growth of oil revenues influence the traditional branches of the economy – agriculture and animal husbandry – in which the majority of the population was still employed? What was the impact on life in the oases and among the nomadic and semi-nomadic tribes? The bulk of the territory of Saudi Arabia was considered *miri*, i.e. lands owned by the state, as personified by the king. In practice, most *miri* land was used by the occupier – mostly tribes – or was in the form of *iqtas* (feudal estates), over which the usufructuaries did not enjoy full ownership rights. The non-*miri* lands belonged to individuals, clans, family groups, tribes or religious establishments. The *miri* lands (which comprised 80% of the country's territory) included pastures and deserts used by the tribes. In 1925 King Ibn Saud had restricted the tribes' traditional rights to the *dira* areas and thereafter changed their boundaries whenever he deemed it necessary.

The state – in the person of the king and government – owned all mineral resources and thus was entitled to move tribes from one territory to another when necessary: for example, for the exploitation of mineral resources. In other respects, the tribes continued to use their lands as they had always done. The nomadic tribes usually observed the *dira* boundaries, but when there were heavy rains, a tribe might migrate to the pastures of other tribes.

Property in large areas of land usually appeared when the government transferred the *miri* lands to *iqta* (feudal possession). Many military commanders and large merchants were given *iqtas*. The new owners rented out the land to sharecroppers. According to a royal decree of 1957, the acquisition and registration of *iqtas* required permission from the local emir and the king. It is unclear, however, whether the decree was retroactive. After registration, the landowner might dispose of the land by selling it, presenting it, renting it or transferring it to *waqfs*, or religious foundations (see below). Although the *iqta* lands formally remained the state's property, *iqta* was a form of transition to *mulk* (private ownership).[79] We have no data on the total area of *iqta* lands in Saudi Arabia. *Mulk* is the only form of private ownership of land recognized in the kingdom. A legal entity owns the land and has the full right to dispose of it. *Mulk* was particularly common in Asir, where agriculture was more developed, but it virtually did not spread to arid lands.

Mushaa (communal landownership) also existed. On some occasions, parts of a *mushaa* plot were redistributed among the extended family or clan members for cultivation. The son of the head of the clan was often appointed the manager of the collective property. Sometimes it was rented out to sharecroppers, and the proceeds were distributed by the head of the clan among its members. But the communal lands were redistributed within the community in accordance with the right of inheritance. *Mushaa* was considered to encompass about one sixth of the lands under cultivation and was found mainly in Najd and the Eastern Province. There were also non-kin and non-clan forms of *mushaa*. Oasis-dwellers might own land jointly. The practice of landownership, cultivation and harvesting by communities existed in Asir. The crop was distributed equally among the community members.

In Jabrin and Khaibar the oasis lands belonged to the bedouin tribes. Malaria was widespread in the oases, and the tribes appeared there only to spray the palms with insecticide and then to gather the dates. During the rest of the year the local farm-hands, mostly descendants of freedmen, looked after the palm groves. The crop was divided among the adult bedouin according to the size of their families.[80]

In Muslim countries, *waqf* is a specific form of landownership under which a Muslim may transfer his land for the maintenance of religious or charitable institutions. *Waqf* lands cannot be alienated or sold. Most *waqfs* are transferred directly to religious institutions, such as *madrasas* (religious schools) or mosques, which become their limited owners and may dispose of them, for example, by renting. *Waqf* property is not liable to confiscation by the government. According to an official US government estimate of 1956, *waqf* comprised 5% of the cultivated lands in Asir, 10% in Hijaz and 15% in Najd and the Eastern Province.[81]

The high mortality rate among the peasants, which for centuries had prevented any rise in their numbers, was a natural obstacle to the excessive fragmentation of plots of land. When that 'natural means of regulation' ended, families took measures to prevent the sale or fragmentation of cultivated plots. Heirs often agreed to own a plot jointly, with the elder of the clan being entitled to cultivate the land or dispose of it by renting, for example. The functions of cultivation and disposal might be transferred within the family by turns. The person who was vested with these functions received a payment, besides his share in the crop. Marriages between cousins were preferred in order to retain lands within the clan.[82]

In the 1960s, according to the *Area Handbook*, 60% of the land was rented and only 40% was cultivated by the owners. In Asir and Hijaz 70–80% of the land was rented.[83] Figures for the late 1950s were similar: 40% of the land was cultivated by its owners, 10% by cash-paying tenants and 50% by sharecroppers.[84] Ozoling has calculated that some 60% of the total cultivated land belonged to large and middle-sized owners (of 5 or more hectares), who rented it out either wholly or in part.[85] Other (obviously understated) figures give the amount of cultivated land that was rented out as only 20–22%.[86] The wide discrepancies in the estimates show that statistical data on Saudi Arabia require very cautious interpretation. According to American experts, rented plots formed just one tenth of all land in the late 1960s[87] (perhaps they included in their calculations only the plots rented for cash).

All categories of land – *miri*, *iqta*, *mulk*, *mushaa*, *waqf* and tribal lands – might be rented out. The renting agreement might be verbal or written. The 70% sharecropping agreements stipulated that the landowner should provide the tenant with land, water, seed and sometimes a dwelling. If the tenant worked all year round and had livestock, fertilizer, agricultural implements, food and a house of his own, he gave the landowner 50% of the foodgrain and 75% of the date crop. When the tenant gave nothing but his labour, however, the owner received 80% of the foodgrain and 95% of the dates. But agreements of that kind formed only some 5% of the total. About 10% of the agreements stipulated that the tenant should sow his own seed and receive most of the crop. The landowner's share depended on the quality of the land, the availability of water, the distance from markets and so on. The introduction of agricultural machinery enabled those tenants who owned such equipment to establish better conditions than those enjoyed by others.[88] In the event of a crop failure, tenants had to take out a loan to support their families. If they had to ask their masters for help, many of the tenants could not repay their debts and became completely dependent on the landowners.[89]

Renting agreements for palm groves and fruit gardens were concluded for between four and seven years. A special form of sharecropping, known as *mugharasa*, was applied in such cases. The tenant pledged himself to plant the trees and grow them until the first fruiting, for which he received everything that was grown between the rows of trees.[90]

The renting of *miri* lands was subject to stricter rules, depending on the location of the territory, the type of irrigation, the number of palms, the demand for the agricultural produce and so on. *Miri* lands were rented out for a long period, usually for five years, though it might be one year in Asir.[91] *Waqf* lands were controlled by the ministry of pilgrimage and *waqfs* in Mecca and were usually rented to sharecroppers.[92]

On most occasions, the rights to water might be bought, sold, rented or inherited separately from the rights to land. Thus when someone bought, inherited or rented a plot where water was scarce, he could buy or rent the rights to water. It was only in Asir and Tihama that rights to water were identical to the rights to land.[93] The regulations concerning the rights to water among settled people were sophisticated and well-developed. They included rotation in using the water, the timing of its use, the length of the irrigation season and the amount of water supplied to each plot. On many occasions, individuals appointed and paid by the water owners and users controlled the water distribution. Water from natural or drilled wells and sources might belong to a single person or to a group. The landowner usually had the right to all water sources on his plot and did not need a special permit to dig a well. But digging a well in a previously uncultivated plot that was transferred to *iqta* required a permit. The wells dug by nomads belonged to the tribe when it was in the area in question. When the tribe roamed further afield, the well became 'common'. There were complicated forms of ownership relating to underground canals. The rights to water from artesian wells – in the Eastern Province, for example – depended on the initial owner's contribution to building special water installations, reservoirs and distribution mechanisms. The distribution of the water from streams in valleys was subject to a special system of rights.[94]

According to Knauerhase, of 70,352 plots of land in the 1970s, 33,242 (47.3%) measured less than 0.5 hectares and 13,661 (19.4%) measured 0.5–1 hectare.[95] Thus some 67% of all peasant families owned small parcels of 1 hectare or less. Other sources give similar figures.[96] The small-scale commodity sector dominated Saudi agriculture.

Agricultural cooperatives were created in the early 1960s in al-Taif, Medina and Buraida. They engaged in various activities, from the lending of seed to the storage and sale of agricultural produce. Such cooperatives did not become widespread, however.[97]

In the relatively densely populated oases of Asir, Hijaz and the Eastern Province, landowners and their families cultivated their own plots, seldom hiring agricultural workers. The situation in some oases of Najd was the same. In Qasim and Jabal Shammar, however, agricultural workers were hired for both long and short periods. The workforce was insufficient in seasons of intense agricultural activity, especially in the Eastern Province, and workers were attracted from the less important industries.[98] Agricultural workers were hired on the basis of oral or written contracts, but the patriarchal-feudal exploitation of freedmen and some workers persisted.[99] In Najd more women than men cultivated the land. Men preferred to become traders, warehouse workers, mechanics, construction workers, cattle drovers or craftsmen.[100]

A poor peasant's average annual income was 1,500–1,600 rials in the early 1970s (without additional earnings).[101] There were wide fluctuations in incomes, depending on the area, the size of the plot, the crops grown and the availability of water. A permanent agricultural worker earned between 1,600 and 2,000 rials a year.[102] Skilled agricultural workers (tractor drivers and machine operators) could earn up to 3,500 rials,[103] but they were few and most of them were non-Saudis. As a whole, poor peasants and agricultural workers could not ensure a tolerable standard of living for their families.

'Middle' peasants with plots of 2–5 hectares formed 10.7% of all peasant families. Some owners of 0.5–2 hectares might also fall within this category, however, particularly if their fields yielded more than one crop a year. Most 'middle' peasants had a stable annual income of 3–5,000 rials, which ensured a minimum subsistence level for their families, but was not enough to modernize their way of working. The well-off families with plots of 5–10 hectares formed 4.8% of the total. Their average annual income was 6–10,000 rials, which enabled them to start an intensive system of agriculture, based on the use of irrigation facilities and fertilizer.[104] However, many plots of that size were owned by merchants, money-lenders and officials and were rented out on semi-feudal conditions. There were between 3,500 and 5,000 large estates (more than 10 hectares), representing 4.5–7% of the total.[105] Most of the big landlords were notables, tribal shaikhs, members of the royal family, merchants and religious institutions.

The overwhelming majority of the big landlords lived in towns and rented out their land. Only a few introduced intensive methods of agriculture, using modern techniques. Large estates yielded an annual income of up to 100,000 rials, which was often used, however, to buy real estate, consumer goods and cars, and in the 1960s and 1970s was very rarely invested in the expansion and intensification of agricultural production.[106] All the experts agree that the growth of big landownership was accompanied by the ruin of the small peasants. For lack of precise statistics, we shall confine ourselves to a description of the general trends. Ruined peasants, including those who had a share in a collective property, might sell their plots or shares. Other community members enjoyed the right of first refusal, and thus several plots might be concentrated in a rich peasant's hands. If none of the community members wanted to buy the land, it might be sold to strangers. If a peasant was unable to repay the loan on his mortgaged land, satisfy his creditors or pay the rent for additional plots, he was finally forced to sell his land or cede it to money-lenders as debt repayment. Most of the purchasers were urban merchants, officials and other newly rich individuals.[107]

According to Abdallah al-Dabbagh, director of a department in the Saudi ministry of agriculture and water, peasants increasingly became permanently indebted to merchants and big landlords as early as the beginning of the 1960s. The debt grew every year, so that the peasant was finally forced to sell his plot. Thus the number of landless peasants and agricultural workers rose.[108] In the mid-1960s the first attempts were made to protect the 'middle' group of peasants. In 1968 a royal decree was issued on the distribution of state-owned arable and pasturable wastelands. Any Saudi citizen was entitled to a plot on *iqta* conditions, provided he was able to cultivate it.[109] Peasants were allotted plots of 5–10 hectares and companies (including foreign ones) of up to 400 hectares. However, the decree did not yield the expected results. To attract settlers to the new lands, the state itself had to 'revive' them by improving irrigation and building roads and canals.[110]

The Saudi scholar Abd al-Rahman al-Sharif conducted a socio-economic survey of the Anaiza region in the mid-1960s.[111] He found that 45.3% peasant households in Qasim had small or very small land-holdings (0.1–2.5 hectares). One fifth of the farms were relatively large. According to al-Sharif, they were created as a result of 'reviving' the waste (state-owned) lands. But this did not necessarily imply that the land was ploughed or irrigated. A person only had to plant trees on the land to make it his property. Naturally, questions of inheritance and the boundaries of 'revived' plots gave rise to many disputes, which were settled according to the *sharia*. In 1961 the *majlis al-wukala* ruled that anyone who intended to 'revive' a plot had to receive the permission of the emir of the region. If any building was planned on the plot, the emir referred the application to the municipality and the latter to the ministry of interior and the *majlis al-wukala*. If the plot in question was agricultural land outside the municipal territory, the decision was taken by the ministry of agriculture and water and the *majlis al-wukala*. Anyone who was permitted to 'revive' the land but failed to fulfil his obligations would lose his rights to that land. The decision warned that the property in land would be transferred either by a royal decree or by an order of the chairman of the *majlis al-wukala* or his deputy.

Land might be rented for hundreds or even thousands of years, in other words virtually for ever. Thus a tenant became a kind of landowner, though he had to pay rent at the end of the year. A long-term tenant might rent his land to a subtenant or for building. Children inherited tenancy agreements of that type from their fathers. According to al-Sharif, that form of tenancy was most common in Anaiza.

When land was rented with trees on it (mainly palms), the rent was calculated with regard to the trees and the wells dug earlier by the landowner. When the land required additional investment, the tenant became its co-owner but he paid the initial owner – his partner – a certain share, which was usually a quarter of the crops. The owner might demand that the tenant should reserve some palm trees for him.

Another valuable description of the Saudi peasants' condition is provided by Motoko Katakura, a Japanese researcher who worked in Wadi Fatima (Hijaz) from 1968 to 1970.[112] According to her data, most of the settled bedouin of Wadi Fatima owned and cultivated areas of between 0.6 and 2 hectares. They preferred to rent out their tribal land. The division of land between heirs led to the fragmentation of plots. Some brothers cultivated their land jointly.

In 1946 the Ain Aziziya Company was founded in Wadi Fatima with private and state capital. It supplied water to Jidda and Mecca. Many owners of plots with water sources sold them to the company and moved to Jidda. Katakura considers this example as proving that control over water amounts to control over the economy of the desert.

417

Landownership and land tenure in Wadi Fatima were complicated by the separate ownership of water, subtenancies and rewholesaling of the produce.

Agricultural workers earned between 5 and 10 rials a day. A person who hired out his tribesmen paid them more. If there was no supervisor, the landowner and tenant shared out the income, though the division might be complicated by an intricate system of middlemen. Some tenant middlemen hired agricultural workers and set up farms.

Katakura gives an example of a rich merchant who rented peasants' waterless lands for next to nothing, dug deep wells, installed pumps and then rented out some plots for a sum ten times more than he had paid and started farming in some others. Sometimes the nominal landowner became a subtenant. *Waqf* lands might be rented to tenants and peasant farmers. When many water sources dried up in the late 1950s and early 1960s, some of those who had recently taken up farming returned to nomadism.

Some occupations were seen as *aib* (shameful, despicable) by the bedouin – for example, those of butcher, breeder of hens, barber, servant or navvy. When some bedouin began settling in Wadi Fatima, others jeered at them. All the bedouin refused to operate wells and pumps, though it was well-paid work; it was performed instead by Yemenis, who numbered 400 in Wadi Fatima in 1970. Besides the Yemenis, there were 64 Palestinians, 28 Jordanians, 12 Syrians, 8 Egyptians, 5 Iraqis and 4 Sudanese. Most of the Palestinians, Jordanians, Syrians and Egyptians were skilled workers, teachers and officials.

Most settlements in Wadi Fatima were formed on tribal lines. The total population was 20,000, with 3,744 households. The tribal distribution was as follows: Quraish 30%, Harb 30%, Lihyan 15%, Shiyuf 10%, freedmen 5% and others 10%. The authorities were represented by the emir with three officials. There was a *qadhi* with a policeman and two clerks. The *maktab al-din* (religious bureau) consisted of a director and seven inspectors. (What Katakura calls the *maktab al-din* may have been the local branch of the League of Public Morality.)

A cooperative society ran a filling station, distributed cement and participated in the construction of a coffee-house. There was a post office and a telephone exchange. Each village had a *majlis al-qarya* (village council) of between five and nine members. In 1961 a social development centre was set up to train people in new professions. It also gave lectures on basic medical knowledge and hygiene and held consultation sessions for women. There were thirteen primary schools for boys and five for girls, one intermediate school, four literacy schools for adult men and four for women. Primary education was compulsory and free. The state paid the teachers' salaries and supplied pupils with textbooks, pencils, notebooks and bags. Almost all teachers at the boys' schools were Saudis, but girls were taught by foreign female teachers.

Problems in agriculture

As a result of several surveys by Saudi offices and foreign missions, there is far more information on agriculture in the 1960s and 1970s than in the 1920s or 1930s, not to mention the beginning of the century. The statistical data are unreliable, however, and should be treated as very approximate estimates. According to various calculations, one eighth to one quarter of the indigenous independent population was occupied in farming. Agriculture as a whole, including semi-nomadic and nomadic animal husbandry, accounted for a half to two-thirds. The estimated indigenous population of the country (with a territory equal to two-thirds of Western Europe) was 3.5–4.5 million in the 1960s and 4–5 million in the 1970s.[113]

The area of cultivated land was 210–300,000 hectares in the mid-1960s.[114] (A different source gives a figure of 150–500,000 hectares.)[115] Only in Asir and southern Hijaz, which account for 20% of the total cultivated area, is precipitation sufficient for non-irrigated farming. The other cultivated land in oases depends on wells, water sources and dams in valleys. The most important crop is dates (Saudi Arabia is the world's fourth largest producer), followed by wheat, barley, sorghum, millet, maize, rice, alfalfa, vegetables and fruit. Coffee is grown in some parts of Asir.

Many attempts have been made to increase the country's agricultural potential. Even before oil was discovered, Ibn Saud invited foreign experts to prospect for water and insisted that foreign oil companies should also search for water and drill artesian wells. In 1937 a large farm was established in al-Kharj (where there are abundant water sources by Najdi standards), with the assistance of Iraqi and Egyptian specialists. Agricultural equipment and draught and pedigree animals were introduced. A modern irrigation system and some specialized farms were created on an area of some 2,000 hectares to produce wheat, vegetables, melons, barley, alfalfa and dates. Vegetables were supplied to the royal court.[116] The farms were run by Americans from 1945 to 1959 and were then transferred to Saudi administration.

In the 1960s the government set up five agricultural centres in Jizan, Medina, Qasim, Riyadh and Hufuf, where peasants might hold consultations with experts and receive equipment, seed, seedlings, fertilizer and instructions on pest control.[117] In 1964 the Bank for Agricultural Development was founded: by 1973 it had 8 branches and 37 offices in villages.[118] The government's measures benefited rich peasants, who were by now becoming more or less modern farmers. The wealthiest households began purchasing agricultural equipment. By the late 1960s there were 277 tractors and 21,000 mechanical pumps in the country.[119]

Agricultural production increased somewhat in the early 1970s, particularly in al-Hasa, in the regions close to the capital and in Qasim. Only large and middle-sized farms, which used machines and fertilizers, could satisfy the growing demand for vegetables and fruit. Poultry, meat and dairy farms were set up.[120] Large palm plantations in the oases of al-Hasa, Medina, Buraida and Anaiza and vegetable plantations and market gardens in al-Hasa, al-Kharj and Medina produced substantial quantities of foods for market.[121]

However, despite the government's efforts and the success of the new, privately owned farms, Saudi agriculture as a whole experienced difficulties in the 1960s and 1970s, caused by the market situation, backward farming practices and social conditions. Cheap foreign agricultural products flooded in, but the government did not dare to increase the customs duties, fearing public discontent if this resulted in price rises. Competition from imported foodstuffs undermined low-income and some middle-income households. Owners and tenants of small plots went bankrupt through lack of money to purchase equipment, fertilizer and seed and through ignorance of modern farming practices and the new market conditions. The most active young peasants sought jobs in urban construction, the service sector, state offices and trade, which led to a shortage of agricultural workers in the oases.[122]

The introduction of mechanical pumps on large farms, combined with the increased water consumption in towns and industry, led to a fall in the overall water level, the drying-up of wells and the destruction of fields, gardens, plantations and entire oases. The water supply was further impaired by the droughts of the 1950s and 1960s. Poor peasants could not afford to buy more powerful pumps or drill deep wells and were effectively pushed out of agricultural production by the large farms, which were owned by absentee landlords and managed by Egyptians or Palestinians, who hired Yemeni workers. Some ruined peasants became agricultural workers on the large, privately owned farms. Others abandoned or sold their land and went away in search of a living.[123]

Agriculture's share in GNP fell continuously. According to Ozoling's calculations, per capita GNP grew from $460 in 1964/65 to $1,300 in 1974/75 in the country as a whole, whereas the respective figures in agriculture were $80 and $105.[124] Allowing for inflation, one may assume that there was no real growth. A sizeable part of the peasants and nomads suffered from malnutrition, protein and vitamin deficiencies and disease. In evaluating the situation in the 1960s and 1970s, Ozoling writes, 'Both farming and animal husbandry remain the most backward and stagnant branches of the economy.' Yet his opinion that 'the rural population received virtually nothing from the development of oil production and the rapid increase in state revenues'[125] sounds too categoric, even for that period. Non-agricultural earnings, government subsidies, the eradication of illiteracy, the development of schools and the introduction of better communications all improved the lot of peasant and bedouin families in the 1960s and 1970s.

Saudi agriculture in the oil era fell victim to the various competing forces and trends. The effect of government projects, dam-building and well-drilling was limited because of corruption, the contractors' incompetence and the huge overstatement of the cost of the works by foreign companies. As a rule, the projects were loss-making.[126] The development of agriculture in the oases was hindered by the preponderance of small landownership and land tenure. The unprofitability of investment in agriculture, caused by competition from imported food, was combined with the migration of a part of the active population to the towns. The country imported almost half of the food it consumed.[127] The agricultural sector of the economy faced complex problems in the 1960s and 1970s.

The Socio-economic Structure of Saudi Arabia in the Oil Era

The further destruction of the traditional nomadic economy and the weakening of tribal organization

The millennia-old way of life of the Arabian nomads began changing rapidly in the 1940s. Even before the oil era, the development of motorized transport in Saudi Arabia and other Middle Eastern countries had deprived the camel-breeders of the main markets for their livestock. With the creation of the centralized state, they lost their income from raids on settled peoples and from the duties imposed on caravans. The catastrophic droughts of the late 1950s and early 1960s accelerated the destruction of the nomadic economy, causing a high loss of livestock and ruining the nomads. The country was forced to import sheep and camels. According to figures from the Arab League, the numbers of livestock in the Eastern Province decreased dramatically.[128] Several American authors are more cautious and calculate that the drought, the depletion of pastures and the migration of young bedouin to the towns reduced the livestock by some 20%.[129] Various sources estimate the number of camels in Saudi Arabia in the 1960s at 0.6–1 million, sheep and goats at 4–6 million and cattle at 0.25 million.[130]

It is generally recognized that the number of nomads decreased rapidly in the 1950s and 1960s in both absolute and relative terms, but the lack of reliable statistics makes it impossible to discuss the process in detail. On the basis of FAO estimates, Twitchell calculated that in 1956, 12% of the population were settled peasants, 66% were nomads and semi-nomads and 22% were urban-dwellers. He estimated the total population of Saudi Arabia at between 3 and 6 million, considering 4.5 million the most probable figure.[131] Nine years later, according to Arab League figures, bedouin accounted for 30% of the total population; they formed 50% of the population in Najd and 20% in the coastal regions of Hijaz.[132] According to American experts, animal husbandry was the main source of income for 50% of the population in the mid-1960s, though purely nomadic camel-breeders numbered 200–300,000 out of the total population of 4 or 4.5 million.[133]

Until the mid-1960s, the lack of attractive alternative economic activities meant that camel-breeding was the only reliable means of subsistence for the nomadic population. The state's policy of settling the nomads yielded only partial and very limited results. In the late 1960s, a 20-year programme was approved for the gradual sedentarization of some 60,000 bedouin families (400–450,000 people), but it was not implemented.[134] The available water sources could not ensure the irrigation of new territories without substantial investment, and the best plots were already under cultivation. Moreover, the bedouin were reluctant to settle, even if the state irrigated thousands of hectares at its own expense, as was done in Harad, halfway between Riyadh and Dammam. Sometimes the nomads, who had no farming skills, failed to achieve the expected improvement in their living standards within two or three agricultural seasons and resumed their earlier way of life. The bedouin's traditional contempt for peasant labour was also difficult to overcome.[135] However, the nomadization process was the exception rather than the rule in the 1960s. Although the bedouin found it difficult to adapt to farming, they found an ever-expanding field of occupations and/or government aid in the towns.

The development of the oil industry influenced the nomads no less than the other groups in society. In the 1930s Aramco employed bedouin first as guides and then as unskilled workers, but soon found that, whereas they proved successful in the former occupation, they were not suited to the latter. The profession of driver was very attractive to the bedouin: the replacement of a camel by a truck as a means of transport did not humiliate even a shaikh's son and corresponded to the nomads' traditional mentality.[136] Aramco opened special centres where young bedouin were trained in driving and truck maintenance.[137] In the 1950s and 1960s the government encouraged the sale of cars to the bedouin, and some of them sold their camels and bought trucks. Grants and gifts from the king enabled the tribal nobility to buy motorized transport of their own. Trucks replaced camels, where the terrain permitted their use. Trucks were also increasingly used to bring water to pastures and to move sheep and goats from one pasture to another.

Intensive prospecting for water by the oil companies and other firms led to the discovery of new water sources which were not considered the property of a specific tribe. Members of various clans and tribes pitched their tents around them. The boundaries of the traditional *diras*, which depended on the availability of pastures and water, were steadily obliterated. The government supplied the bedouin with clover seed to be sown in valleys after the rains. They were taught to store up hay in case of a drought, which prompted them to turn to semi-nomadic animal husbandry.[138] Former bedouin settled near oilfields to work there and engage in farming. The ex-nomads built mud houses; mosques, primary schools and shops appeared in their settlements.[139]

The development of towns, increased demand for meat, improved water supplies and use of trucks enabled many nomads to change the structure of their livestock. Whereas camel-breeding had been the main occupation of the largest tribes of Saudi Arabia until the end of the Second World War, they gradually turned to sheep-breeding in the 1950s and 1960s. Sheep-breeding requires smaller grazing areas (and therefore less wandering) and enables both men and women to engage in other activities, which are impossible for a camel-breeder. Sheep-breeding became a profitable occupation. Sheep- and goat-breeding had earlier been confined to semi-nomads and subordinate tribes and was a sign of lower socio-economic status. By the end of the 1960s, however, owners of large sheep and goat herds were among the richest and most influential nomads. A hired workforce was increasingly used to look after the herds.[140]

The Al Murra, for example, were considered among the last purely bedouin tribes of Saudi Arabia to live almost exclusively by camel-breeding. The isolated position and extremely harsh natural conditions of the Rub al-Khali, where they roamed, played an important role in their continuing their earlier economic activities. Only camels could survive in that region. A time came, however, when both the tribal nobility and the poor nomads turned to sheep-breeding as a source of traditional income. The 'middle' nomads preferred to continue their earlier way of life for the time being. The nobility began selling its camels or transferring them to its relatives and clients to start sheep-breeding, hiring labourers for that purpose. The sheep-breeding Al Murra were now treated as the social equals of camel-breeders. A sizeable part of the poor members of the tribe went to towns in search of a living and then returned home. Some of them bought trucks and turned to sheep-breeding.[141] If that was the case with the Al Murra, a purely bedouin tribe, one may assume that the same processes developed to an even greater extent in other tribes, which were closer to the centres where animal products were sold and had access to better water sources.[142]

Sheep-breeding and the use of trucks enabled some families to settle in villages. The kinship ties within the tribes began to weaken somewhat, for sheep-breeders and camel-breeders seldom roamed together. Some sheep-breeders returned to their old camps in summer, but most of them stayed near the new wells with the people from other tribes. The economic isolation from the camel-breeders, intercourse with other tribes and new occupations gave rise to new forms of social relationships and changed the nomads' outlook. Marriages between cousins, for example, became less widespread.[143]

The changes in economic activity and the atmosphere of relative security under the centralized state decreased the nomadic families' dependence on the tribal military-democratic organization. There was a decrease in the minimum size of an autonomous family or clan unit seen as necessary to maintain its existence.[144] Work in a town weakened the individual family's dependence on the tribe still further. Tribal attitudes were also influenced by the modern media – TV and radio sets started to appear in the tents. On some occasions, the exposure to new social values outstripped changes in economic activities.

Well-paid service in the armed forces and the police and easy jobs in the burgeoning state apparatus attracted the most active bedouin and made them leave their tribes. The tribal nobility supplied personnel for the administrative-bureaucratic machinery, the officer corps of the National Guard, the camel corps and the police. Some of them engaged in trade. The prestige of the new occupations and the high earnings came into competition with the pride in one's ancestors and noble genealogy.[145]

To maintain the loyalty of the nomadic nobility, the Saudi royal family granted them subsidies as compensation for the lost incomes from raids and caravan dues. The subsidies rose in line with the oil revenues.[146] The nomadic nobility's welfare and social status were now determined not only by their wealth in the form of livestock or oasis lands, their authority in the tribe and their reliance on the remnants of the military-democratic structure: an important new factor was their loyalty to the king and their closeness to his court. Some nomadic shaikhs settled in towns and engaged in business. The new position of the tribal nobility also weakened the traditional tribal bonds.[147]

Although there was a considerable weakening of the tribal organization, this did not amount to a disappearance of the tribal and kinship factor from Arabian society. Even if they migrated to the towns, tribesmen preserved their network of mutual assistance and solidarity; they preferred to work and live together and liked to distinguish themselves from the people of other tribes and from those 'without kith or kin'.[148] Clan and tribal bonds determined an individual's position, and his success or failure in the bureaucracy, the army, the police and even business.

In the 1950s only a small part of the royal subsidies reached the ordinary bedouin, a point that was mentioned, for example, by Prince Talal, the leader of the 'free princes', in his *Message to the Citizen*.[149] Philby also notes:

> The sudden spread of fantastic riches brought little real advantage to the desert, whose products, it is true, are sold at prices far above the level of former times, but whose requirements now cost far more than before. Medicine and education, for example, remained unavailable to the Badawin.[150]

The Saudi royal family was aware of the dangers created by the nomads' growing discontent, and as early as the 1950s measures were taken to alleviate the negative impact of the crisis in the nomadic economy. The oil revenues enabled the state to halve *zakat*. Thousands of bedouin pitched their tents around Riyadh and other towns and were fed for weeks or even months at the state's expense. Men, women and children attended the government kitchens and warehouses daily to receive rice and sometimes meat. In the early 1960s more than half a million nomads and semi-nomads received state subsidies. Their number rose steadily throughout the 1960s and 1970s.[151] This gave rise to an abnormal situation: a rather large sector of society either ceased its economic activities or reduced them to a secondary source of income, without replacing them by another occupation. Many thousands – perhaps even hundreds of thousands – of nomads and semi-nomads were forced to become parasites, living off a share of the oil revenues.

The appearance of a Saudi working class

The transformation from a basically nomadic society was completed extremely rapidly in Saudi Arabia – within the lifespan of one or two generations – and it was accompanied by a painful breakdown of the old social structures. Aramco needed a local workforce from the outset, but it was difficult to find workers in what was still a largely feudal-tribal society. However, the jobs offered by the company led to improved material conditions and higher status for those people who abandoned their earlier occupations and became the backbone of the workforce.

In 1965, 7.6% of all Aramco workers were of bedouin descent, 23.4% claimed some connection to a tribe, 44.8% were former peasants and the rest had been fishermen, seafarers, pearl-divers, craftsmen or traders.[152] Many of these workers came from the 'lower' tribes of Awazim and Shararat or were Shia peasants, agricultural workers or craftsmen from the Eastern Province.[153] They felt no aversion for occupations that were traditionally 'looked down upon' or seen as for 'infidel' employers. As for the 'noble' bedouin and the settled followers of Wahhabism, they were forced to work in order to escape poverty or even starvation.[154] Bedouin were considered to be effective guards, drivers and electricians, but were not fit for hard, tiring or monotonous physical labour.

Initially Aramco even employed slaves, whose masters took a part of their salary.[155]

Some tribal shaikhs, merchants and money-lenders acted as intermediaries in supplying the workers and received part of their salaries.[156] The practice did not spread and Aramco preferred to hire people who depended on the company rather than on middlemen from among shaikhs or slave-owners. The company set up special schools and courses to train specialists from among its Saudi employees.[157] The number of people employed by Aramco stabilized in the early 1970s at around 11–13,000.[158]

The concentration of a new workforce within one company, their harsh working conditions and the low wages encouraged the first steps towards labour organization and the struggle for workers' rights. Many of their leaders were workers from other Arab states and had a greater political awareness and better organizational skills. After the unrest of 1953 and 1956 the Aramco management and the Saudi authorities subjected the workers to reprisals. Politically 'suspect' activists were blacklisted and fired.[159]

Reprisals, surveillance, pressure and discrimination were just one aspect of the measures to prevent further unrest. The company's profits were so high and the number of workers so insignificant that Aramco could afford a considerable wage rise, first for its skilled workers. As early as the late 1950s they earned more than low-ranking state officials or policemen and four to six times more than unskilled workers. In subsequent years, too, the growth of Aramco employees' salaries and the improvement in their living standards far outstripped those of other hired labourers.[160]

In the late 1940s Aramco employed 10,000 Saudis, chiefly unskilled workers. Ten years later, two-thirds of its Saudi employees were skilled or semi-skilled workers. Within the same period, 44 Saudis held important posts at Aramco and 3,000 were employed in line management.[161] The percentage of Saudis among Aramco's permanent employees was 80% (out of a total workforce of 12,800) in 1964 and 83% (out of a total of 10,353) in 1970.[162] Many Saudis worked as geologists, engineers, technicians, doctors, drilling foremen and laboratory assistants. The changes in the general structure of the workforce were due to the greatly improved skills of the Saudi oil workers, who had been trained at special centres and workshops both at the oilfields and abroad. In 1971 technicians, foremen, engineers and supervisors accounted for 14.5% of all Saudis employed by Aramco (as contrasted with 0.1% in 1952), the percentage of skilled workers was 59.4% (3.0% in 1952) and that of unskilled workers was 26.1% (96.9% in 1952).[163]

Average annual salaries in Aramco rose from 3,800 rials in 1953 to 10,700 in 1964 to become the highest in the country. In 1971 the average annual salary of a Saudi employed by Aramco reached 17,800 rials.[164] The management began paying special bonuses and allowances, provided housing with modern conveniences and gave loans to buy apartments as a reward for many years of 'irreproachable' service.[165] The company partly repaid the loans on the apartments. In late 1970, 88% of all Saudis employed by Aramco owned apartments.[166] It made them the company's debtors and put an end to fluctuations in the workforce. Aramco ran hospitals, schools and polyclinics for its personnel and the management encouraged some of its workers to engage in business activities.

The creation of a true Saudi working class was hindered both by socio-political conditions and by the narrow market of hired labour, the result of under-population in the country. Out of an economically active population of 1 million, a quarter worked for hire in 1965.[167] The hired workforce might be divided into three categories: (a) hereditary hired workers in handicrafts, trade, services or agriculture; (b) state officials; and (c) those employed in modern industry and trade.

The government was the single largest employer (of 150,000 people) in 1965.[168] However, non-Saudis formed a high percentage of state employees. In the early 1970s the number of state employees (other than in the army and the police) exceeded 120,000.[169]

There were 18,000 industrial workers in 1965 in the towns of the Eastern Province (Dhahran, Ras Tannura, al-Khobar and Dammam, mainly in the oil and related industries) and in Jidda. In the same year there were 82,000 agricultural workers in the country.[170]

In 1970 the Central Planning Organization of Saudi Arabia estimated the economically independent population at 1,050,000 people (excluding state employees and the armed forces). Almost half of them were occupied in agriculture (476,000, including 145,000 nomads), 29,000 were employed in the oil and mining industry, 52,000 in the manufacturing industry, 142,000 in construction, 20,000 in the power industry and public utilities, 130,000 in trade, 62,000 in transportation, communications and storage and 138,000 in the service sector. It is noteworthy that, with the exception of the oil industry, few enterprises employed more than 50 people.[171] The percentage of people engaged in agriculture was lower, and that in the service sector higher, than in other developing countries.

The urban social structure was characterized by the low percentage of people employed in industry and by the burgeoning state sector. The least well-off among the urban population included various categories, but the majority were migrants from the countryside (peasants and bedouin) who were illiterate and unskilled. Some of them found permanent or temporary jobs in construction, industry, trade and services, but many lived on government subsidies.[172]

Although a daily minimum wage of 6 rials was introduced in the late 1960s, many employers ignored it, particularly in the case of immigrants. Even according to official government figures, the minimum monthly salary for Saudi workers in the trade sector was 200–210 rials (that of immigrant workers was 120–180); in the service sector, the figures were 130–170 and 140–150 rials respectively; in handicrafts, 100–120 and 90–110 rials respectively. The condition of semi-skilled workers was far better, since there was a permanent shortage of them in the country: their average monthly salary was 300–400 rials in the private sector (other than the oil industry) and 600–700 rials in state enterprises. Office employees' salaries were close to that level: 300–500 rials. Overall, that category of employees earned only the basic minimum for subsistence. Skilled workers earned a decent monthly salary by Saudi standards (700–1,000 rials), while highly skilled workers could earn up to 1,500 rials a month.[173]

Al-Sharif's survey of Anaiza in the mid-1960s gives a good picture of the social structure of a central Arabian town at that time. There were 216 craftsmen and 350 apprentices in the town. Al-Sharif concludes that handicrafts supported 560 families, i.e. 18–20% of the urban population. However, the true number of families may well have been less, since the apprentices probably included the owner's sons and/or brothers. The category of craftsmen included butchers, carpenters, bakers, tanners, builders, porters, dyers, fitters, weavers, barbers, garage and car-repair workshop owners, millers, launderers and electricians.[174] Other authors have mentioned an underdeveloped system of guilds among some Saudi craftsmen. Traders had their shaikhs, who represented them in the town council and supervised the application of standards and rules and the quality of produce.[175]

The population of Anaiza was 23,500 in the early 1960s, with women outnumbering men by 3,000. Many of the men had gone to other regions in search of a living.[176] Anaiza was one of the relatively large trade centres in Najd. Its merchant families had connections with Riyadh, Dammam, Jidda, Mecca and Medina, as well as Iraq, Kuwait and Syria.[177]

A separate bedouin block, with a population of 560, formed in the town. Many of these bedouin had come from the Ikhwan *hijras* and they became minor officials, soldiers or drivers.[178] Although some of them had to become construction workers, agricultural workers or herdsmen, the bedouin preserved their traditional disdain for physical labour. Besides, they continued to reject marriages with people from other tribes and were reluctant to marry their daughters even to rich settled people,[179] whose opportunities for economic advancement prompted many of them, in their turn, to look down on the bedouin.[180] According to Lipsky et al.:

> It has not been a mark of social distinction in the country among the Sunnite Moslems to be able to claim a job requiring great business or activity. A man achieves distinction rather by being able to enjoy leisure . . . Manual labour generally is associated with very low status, while supervisory or policy-making functions carry prestige. Government service, consequently, especially in its higher ranks, is considered the most desirable type of employment. Even on the lower levels, government employees enjoy considerable respect in the eyes of the public . . . As a rule, the higher the position, the more leisurely is the tempo of work. This is particularly true in government offices. Other correlates of high status include the privileges of arriving later than subordinates in the morning, or leaving earlier, and of devoting more time to entertaining visitors.[181]

Al-Sharif notes that craftsmen and apprentices were connected by patron–client relations.[182] As a whole, paternalism was a real factor in the relations between employers and employees in Saudi society of the 1950s and 1960s. Family connections and social status mattered more than considerations of efficiency and competence and played an important role in the selection of personnel.[183]

The traditional owner of a company personified power and authority and at the same time was required to pay attention to his workers' needs. He lost his authority unless he was exacting and strict. He lost respect and sympathy if he did not help a worker in the event of an illness or his son's marriage, or failed to give a worker advice in a difficult situation.[184] The traditional owner would hire workers from among his relatives, friends and acquaintances. That practice persisted in the smaller commercial and industrial companies, but the 'impersonal' selection of workers began in larger enterprises in the 1960s.[185] According to the *Area Handbook*:

> Moreover, qualities which the industrial employer sought in his employees – reliability, punctuality and a willingness to submit to impersonal authority and routine – were alien to the rural Saudi Arab, who was not accustomed to keeping regular hours and who expected his employer to assume a personal, paternalistic attitude.[186]

The oil boom, the crisis in traditional agriculture and animal husbandry, the emergence of new occupations in towns and the higher standards of urban life all led to a rapid urbanization of Saudi Arabia. The population had always been distributed unevenly over its territory. Most of the population was concentrated in the region between Medina and al-Taif, in the coastal plain of Hijaz, in Asir, between Buraida and al-Kharj in Najd and between Ras Tannura and Harad in the Eastern Province. Urbanization increased the uneven distribution of the population.

The population of Riyadh, the Saudi capital, was about 80,000 in 1955, 162,000 in 1962 and 300–350,000 in the early 1970s. The corresponding figures for Mecca were 100,000, 159,000 and 200,000; for Jidda, 80,000, 148,000 and 250–300,000; for Medina, 50,000, 72,000 and 100,000; and for al-Taif, 8,000, 54,000 and 100,000. The populations of Hufuf and al-Kharj had also reached 100,000 by the late 1960s, and those of Dammam and al-Khobar were 40,000 and 35,000 respectively.[187] It is not clear whether these figures include immigrants, however.

Immigrants

Although integration into Saudi society was difficult, there had always been numerous immigrants of both Arab and non-Arab origin in the country – slaves and freedmen, mostly Africans, as well as the descendants of the Muslim pilgrims from many countries who had settled in Mecca and Jidda.

The demand for a workforce increasingly attracted new immigrants to Saudi Arabia, particularly skilled workers.[188] There was also a need for unskilled workers: Yemenis, Sudanese and Somalis were hired. The Palestinians, Jordanians, Syrians and Lebanese were mainly traders, teachers, officials, doctors, engineers and craftsmen. Egyptians worked in the country in the early 1960s as teachers and officials, but the influx of Egyptians ceased temporarily after the deterioration and rupture of relations with Egypt.[189] After Riyadh had improved relations with Sadat's regime, this influx resumed. There were hundreds of thousands of Egyptians in Saudi Arabia in the late 1970s in all spheres – from engineers and doctors to unskilled workers.

In the early 1970s, according to Knauerhase, the percentage of non-Saudis was 15–20% in Mecca, Medina and al-Taif, 23% in Riyadh and 35% in Jidda.[190] He does not specify whether these figures included the descendants of freedmen and 'old' naturalized immigrants or only those who had come to the country recently.

Immigrants accounted for almost 33% of the urban workforce in 1964, 45% in 1968 and over 50% in subsequent years. They formed a high percentage of the country's engineers and technicians. In the 1960s, for example, 60% of the engineers at the ministry of post, telegraph and telephone were Egyptians, Jordanians, Lebanese and Syrians.[191] Almost all lecturers at universities and colleges, a large number of schoolteachers and many officials were foreigners. The percentage reached 60–70% in the manufacturing industry, particularly in Hijaz, 50% in transport and communications and 30–50% in construction.[192]

Aramco hired many foreigners. Although the share of Saudis increased, the company continued to recruit doctors from India, accountants from Pakistan, teachers from Jordan and Egypt and interpreters from Lebanon. Many engineers, technicians and middle-rank employees were Palestinians.[193] The Saudis' share was even lower in other companies and industries.

Foreigners were not permitted to work in the kingdom without an official work permit. These permits were only issued to immigrants who had entered Saudi Arabia legally, possessed the skills needed by the country and had made preliminary arrangements for employment; but there were many illegal immigrants, especially from Yemen.[194] The total number of registered foreign workers was 76,000 in 1963, 144,000 in 1965, 165,000 in 1967, 231,000 in 1969, 320,000 in 1970[195] and 700,000 in late 1972.[196] These figures include only the urban 'legal' workforce.

By the late 1970s, according to some estimates, the number of immigrants had reached 2 or 3 million, which was almost equal to the total adult population of the country. Yemenis alone numbered about 1 million.[197] People of some 50 nationalities worked in Saudi Arabia, including thousands of Americans and Europeans.[198] Other countries with a similar situation were Libya and the oil-producing Gulf states.

It is difficult to evaluate the consequences of the large-scale influx of foreign workers into Saudi Arabia but, inevitably, it accelerated social change and led to new tensions within the society.

Freedmen. 'Lower tribes'. Women

The emergence of the capitalist sector and a working class, the development of the oil industry, the dramatic increase in the incomes of the ruling elite and the expansion of the domestic market – all these factors led, paradoxically enough, to a temporary increase in the demand for slaves in the 1940s and 1950s.[199] Slavery was abolished in 1962 under pressure from outside rather than from inside, though demands for its abolition had also been voiced in the country. In practice, slavery persisted for some time in Saudi Arabia even after its abolition, though not as a sector of the economy but in the form of the illegal detention of slaves and concubines in the noble families. Even after liberation, the *abds* did not become equal citizens of Saudi Arabia, whose society retained some features of the caste system. Some ex-slaves did, however, rise within the official hierarchy, as they had done earlier.

The 'lower tribes' – the Sulubba in the north, the Hitaim and Shararat in Hijaz, the Awazim in al-Hasa, the Balahita in the south-west, the Fuyud and Bahhah in Asir and the Bani Hajir in Najd – continued to be seen as inferior. They were found in 'non-prestigious' occupations, such as barbers, butchers, musicians and tinsmiths. Even if a member of one of the 'lower tribes' became rich, he still could not intermarry with the 'noble tribes'. Abdallah al-Sulaiman, Ibn Saud's minister of finance, was a Bani Hajir and he founded one of the most powerful business groups in the kingdom; yet the people of 'blue blood' – the Anaza, Ataiba, Shammar and Quraish, not to mention the Al Saud and the tribal nobility – still refuse to enter into marriages with his descendants.[200]

There were many common features in the social status of immigrants, freedmen, 'lower tribes', *sunnaa* and Shia. They were tolerated only on the margins of society and had no political rights.

Among the reasons for the shortage of workers in Saudi Arabia was the preservation of rigid restrictions on female labour. Women's social status was determined by the *sharia* in its most uncompromising form, and the *ulama* (whose influence was diminishing in other spheres) obliged the authorities to heed their voice.

In the early 1970s schools of nursing were opened in Riyadh, Jidda and Hufuf. More and more girls attended urban and rural schools. In the 1960s, 5,700 women attended literacy, housekeeping and handicrafts courses at 17 development centres in rural communities. Women were expected to work in the purely female industries and professions, where they would meet almost no men.[201] The state administration institute trained some 10,000 officials between 1961, when it was founded, and the early 1970s: there were no women among them.[202]

Labour legislation

The new labour relations did not fall under the canons of the *sharia* and so required regulation. With regard to the nascent workers' movement, the government adopted a labour code in 1947 which copied that of Egypt in many aspects. It was amended repeatedly thereafter. Formally, the code applied to all industrial, trade and agricultural enterprises that employed more than ten workers. Even the formal introduction of this legislation, based on that of Egypt (whose workers had won certain rights as a result of a protracted struggle), was an important social advance.

The labour code introduced a 6-day working week and an 8-hour working day (i.e. a 48-hour working week), annual paid leave of 10 days and 5 days' paid sick-leave. It was declared illegal to employ children under the age of 10. Special articles specified the procedure and payment of overtime and compensation for occupational injuries. The code provided for a minimum daily wage of 5 rials. A labour contract might be oral or written. Employers should open special shops, schools, hospitals, libraries and kindergartens for their workers. The ministry of finance was entitled to inspect any company, receive information on general and working conditions from employers and employees and require employers to implement the provisions of the code. To hire workers, an employer had to have a special permit from the ministry of finance.[203] In 1950 the ministry of finance set up a department of labour in the Eastern Province. In 1953 the department became autonomous and in 1961 it came under the newly created ministry of labour and social affairs.[204]

The labour code did not give employees the right to organize trade unions. Strikes were prohibited by a special royal decree in 1956.[205] Employers were entitled to dismiss employees without giving any reasons. The labour code ignored the rights of female employees and made no mention of a pension. It was not until the early 1960s that national insurance and pensions were introduced.[206]

Labour disputes became more frequent with the increasing use of hired labour.[207] They were settled by an arbitration commission of two members, one appointed by the employer and the other by the state administration, with no representation for employees. If the two members disagreed, the government appointed a supreme arbiter. In practice, government officials tended to side with Aramco in its disputes with employees; otherwise they were charged with 'communist activities' and dismissed. The workers demanded in their petitions to the king that the department of labour should actually protect their interests.[208] Lipsky et al. note:

> Despite the ban, strikes have occurred; they have been most frequent in the industrialized, sophisticated oil sector in the Neutral Zone and in the Eastern Province. Although they have the best working conditions of all worker groups, oil workers have pressed their claims the hardest and longest.[209]

In the Neutral Zone strikes were organized by Kuwaitis, since there was no formal prohibition on strikes in Kuwait. The employees' discontent was particularly strong in the contracting companies, where exploitation was ruthless and the labour code was not observed.[210] According to Lipsky et al.:

> Workers have demonstrated, petitioned, appealed to top management, held sit-downs, walked off the job, and boycotted facilities. They have not employed violence. Arrests have been made and leaders jailed. In certain cases, workers have been dismissed and foreign workers deported for any form of protest. Work stoppages often have occurred.[211]

The employees' demands were of an economic nature and related to problems over bonuses, medical services, transport and catering.

In the 1960s rising salaries combined with repressive measures weakened the intensity of labour unrest. However, employees' discontent, together with criticism from abroad, forced the government to amend the labour legislation. The increased oil revenues and the economic boom enabled both the authorities and the employers to introduce some additional benefits for employees.

The new labour code of 1969, for companies employing 10 or more people, provided (as did the first labour code) for an 8-hour working day and a 48-hour working week (36 hours in the month of Ramadhan). At Aramco, other oil companies and Petromin, the working week was 40 hours with 2 days off a week. Annual paid leave was now 21 days. Sick-leave was 30 days on full pay and 60 days on 75% of the salary. Employees might be granted unpaid leave for domestic reasons. Within the oil industry, workers had 28 days' annual leave and office employees had 1 month. According to article 75 of the code, nobody might be dismissed without good reason. The minimum daily wage was set at 10 rials.

The 1969 code met some of the social requirements of the workers. First-aid stations were to be opened at companies with 50 or more employees and medical services were to be free. On some occasions, medical treatment was to be paid for out of special insurance funds. In remote areas, employees were to be provided with housing and three meals a day at fixed prices. Fair-price shops should be opened at companies with 500 or more employees.

The special article concerning female employees was of no particular importance, since the use of female labour was extremely limited. The code prohibited men and women from working together. The minimum age for employment was 13; an adolescent's working-day was limited to 6 hours. The code included requirements concerning safety arrangements and provisions for compensation for occupational injuries and disablement caused by industrial accidents.[212] Simultaneously, a national insurance system was outlined and made compulsory in spite of the *ulama*'s resistance. It was an attempt to combine the modern methods of national insurance with the Muslim charitable traditions. As early as the beginning of the 1960s, the national insurance fund came to be replenished by *zakat* and government subsidies. From 1969 both employees and employers had to make payments to the general organization of social insurance.[213]

A permit issued by the labour bureau or passport department was required for employment. All companies with 100 or more employees were to have at least 75% Saudis among their personnel and to pay them at least 51% of the total payroll. Petromin required all mixed companies to observe that provision.[214]

The limitations of the labour legislation were obvious: the great majority of Saudis were employed by companies with fewer than ten employees, and the labour code was really only applied by the largest companies. American experts came to the conclusion that 'many of the 1969 provisions still are on paper'.[215]

Articles 189–191 reaffirmed the prohibition on strikes and declared employees' collective actions to be a crime punishable by imprisonment for up to six years and high fines.[216] In 1969 commissions for the settlement of labour disputes were set up to act in parallel to the *sharia* courts. As previously, state officials acted as arbiters. If they failed to resolve the dispute, it was to be referred to the grievance bureau. The supreme commission for labour disputes was created in 1970.[217]

Education

In the late 1950s Lipsky et al. commented, 'Public education . . . is still in its infancy.' In 1956 the literacy rate was slightly above 5%.[218] In 1954 only 8% of school-age children attended school. King Saud founded a school in Riyadh on the British model for his sons, and their servants and slaves. The king's brothers Abdallah and Faisal also set up schools for their children. But even the royal family was aware of the need to educate at least a part of the population.[219]

In 1954 the ministry of education was set up and a uniform school system was introduced on the lines of those in the more developed Arab countries. Six years of primary education were to be followed by three years at an intermediate school and three years at a secondary school. Only a handful of children received secondary education in the second half of the 1950s.[220] As before, the Quran and theology occupied the first place in the curriculum, followed by technical subjects and mathematics.

King Ibn Saud started to send young Saudis to study abroad and subsidized their education. King Saud tried to discontinue the practice in the first years of his reign under pressure from the conservative *ulama*, but later had to admit that it was essential for the country's progress. By 1957 at least 600 Saudis were studying at universities and other higher education institutions in Egypt, the US, Syria, Lebanon and Western Europe.[221] The number of Saudi students abroad, particularly in the US, had reached 3–5,000 by the mid-1970s.[222]

The first Saudi higher education institution – the College of Islamic Law – opened in Mecca in 1949. Its curriculum consisted almost entirely of the Quran, *hadith*, Arabic and Arab history. Its task was to train teachers for the lycees, most of which followed an identical curriculum. Colleges of *sharia* and Arabic were opened in Riyadh in 1953 to train teachers, jurists and judges.[223] A secular university, modelled on the Egyptian pattern, opened in Riyadh in 1957. Almost all its professors and lecturers were foreigners. Education at the university was free: the students received state scholarships.[224] Many graduates of the university advocated the modernization of the country.

To raise the country's international prestige and to meet the society's need for specialists, the government began paying more attention to education. Two thousand foreign teachers were invited to work in Saudi Arabia in the early 1960s.[225] Their number grew tenfold within ten years[226] until the government set the task of the 'Saudization' of education, at least at the lowest stages. In 1973 the country had fourteen training colleges for primary-school teachers and two institutions where intermediate and secondary-school teachers were trained.[227]

Expenditure on education amounted to 118m rials in 1959 and 1,677m in 1973.[228]

There were a total of 143,000 pupils (in all types of schools) in 1960 and 739,300 in 1973, but there were more than twice as many boys as girls (in 1960 girls had represented less than 4% of the total).[229] Referring to information from the Saudi ministry of education, *The Times* reported that there were 600,000 boys and 200,000 girls at Saudi schools in 1973.[230]

Riyadh University grew rapidly: from some 500 undergraduates and 15 postgraduates in 1960 (at the religious institutions, the numbers were 2,200 and 260 respectively), the number of undergraduates had risen to 4,400 by 1973. The number of postgraduates is unknown, but it may be assumed that it exceeded 300. In 1968/69 a girls college was set up in Jidda and faculties of King Abd al-Aziz University were opened in Jidda and Mecca.[231] In 1971 there were some 11,000 undergraduates and 500 postgraduates at religious colleges and institutes. In 1973 there were 2,500 undergraduates at King Abd al-Aziz University, about 900 at the College of Petroleum and Minerals in the Eastern Province and 660 (mostly non-Saudis) at the Islamic University in Medina. Sixty per cent of the students at King Abd al-Aziz University were studying engineering, but many of them found jobs in the state sector after graduation.[232]

The first vocational school opened in 1949. In 1960 a model engineering school was set up in Riyadh with foreign teachers. Engineering schools opened in Mecca, Jidda, Dammam, Buraida, Medina and other towns.[233]

Boys and girls were educated separately at all stages. The library of Riyadh University had special 'girls' hours'. Female students at King Abd al-Aziz University listened to male teachers' lectures on short-circuit television.[234]

In developing the education system, the ruling elite strove to use it to bring up young people in a spirit of loyalty to the traditional state and public institutions and to the regime as a whole. Prince Faisal, the acting head of the state, said in 1963:

> The curricula in Moslem countries were infiltrated with malicious and dangerous trends which dissuaded the sons of Moslems from studying the history of their religion or making any research about it or about its rich heritage, or from carrying out any deep and thorough scientific investigation about the Moslem Shari'a Code as it really is. What does man aspire to? He wants 'good'. It is there, in the Islamic Shari'a. He wants justice. It is there, in the Islamic Shari'a. He wants security. It is there also. Man wants freedom. It is there. He wants the propagation of science. It is there. Everything is there, inscribed in the Islamic Shari'a.[235]

In 1970 a government programme, 'Educational Policy in the Saudi Arabian Kingdom', stipulated that the main task of education should be:

> the duty of acquainting the individual with his God and religion and adjusting his conduct in accordance with the teaching of religion, the fulfilment of the need of society and the achievement of the nation's objectives.[236]

But the requirements of the conservative *ulama* were no longer accepted

The Socio-economic Structure of Saudi Arabia in the Oil Era

unconditionally by all groups in society. The collision between conservative views, backed by Muslim traditions in their Wahhabi interpretation, and the striving for modernization and social transformation under the impact of education led to tensions within Saudi society. The growth in the Saudis' cultural level and their exposure to science and the humanities led to an increase in their socio-political demands. An additional factor was the expansion of their contacts with the outside world through travel abroad, foreign radio and TV programmes and the large numbers of foreigners in the country. More and more Saudis began to question the legitimacy of the old political system and the traditional social values.

CHAPTER 20

The Political Regime (the 1950s to the early 1980s)

The Al Saud and the system of power

The Saudi monarchy had been established by the early 1930s but underwent changes in subsequent decades. The royal family was already large in the period of the consolidation of the territory round Riyadh; with its various branches, it grew even larger owing to polygamy and was close to becoming the dominant tribe. In 1973 it numbered between 2,000 and 5,000 adult males.[1] It was they who allocated the country's principal resources and its oil revenues and filled the upper echelons of the state machinery. But the state mechanism itself grew, became more sophisticated, modernized to some extent and acquired new functions.

Naturally, the king remained the central figure in the system of power, being ex officio imam, military commander and supreme judge. Although he was not formally a legislator, because all laws had been stated in the *sharia* once and for all, he issued decrees to cover those situations not encompassed by the *sharia*. The monarch personified supreme executive, legislative and judicial power. In practice, the king delegated these functions to state agencies, institutions and individuals – the *majlis al-wukala* (council of ministers), the royal *diwan*, the deputy chairman of the *majlis al-wukala* (if it was headed by the king), the *diwan al-malazim* (grievance board) under the *majlis al-wukala*, the ministry of justice, the ministry of defence, the general staff of the armed forces, the commander of the National Guard and the *majlis al-shura* (advisory council), which prepared the recommendations on whose basis the royal decrees were issued.[2]

The king's power was limited by the need to take account of the interests and demands of the most influential groups within the royal family, the *ulama* and (in recent years) the new, often amorphous, social groups connected with the modern sectors of the economy, the armed forces and the bureaucracy. In principle, he might take important decisions only after sounding out the opinion of the main ruling groups,[3] using the traditional method of consultation. It was customary for the king to consult influential members of the Al Saud, the chief shaikhs of tribes or tribal confederations, the emirs of the main provinces and the *ulama*. It was they who formed the political elite in the narrow sense.

An official report of King Faisal's activities in 1974 read:

> His Royal Majesty is known for his ardent desire to respect the principles of the Muslim religion. One of these principles requires the ruler to consult. His Majesty never holds an arbitrary opinion, but learns the opinions of statesmen, *ulama* and the knowledgeable and noble people of the country, despite the fact that His Majesty's opinion is always the best opinion.[4]

One of the reasons for the stability of the Al Saud's power was the preservation of unity within the royal family. The members of the Al Saud remembered that the power struggle between Saud and Faisal in 1958–64, the rebellion of the 'free princes' and the royal family's split into mutually hostile groupings had weakened the regime and led to a serious internal crisis. Unity within the dynasty was achieved by consensus among its main leaders. Although the Al Saud had several thousand members, some 100 people at most took part in decision-making on the most important issues. The 68 signatures on the royal family's decision to transfer the throne to Faisal on 2 November 1964 give some indication of the number of individuals who took political decisions and selected the persons responsible for their implementation.[5] The latent power struggle between the leaders of the various influential branches of the Al Saud prevented any single grouping from monopolizing power.

The elder branch of the royal family was represented in the 1950s and 1960s by the three surviving brothers of Ibn Saud – Abdallah, Ahmad and Musaid. Abdallah mediated between Faisal and Saud during their power struggle, and Musaid (who was fifteen years younger than his nephew Faisal, the future king) became minister of finance and national economy in Faisal's cabinet in 1962.[6]

The major decisions on current issues were taken by a tiny group of the king's closest relatives. Faisal's team included his uncles and half-brothers – Crown Prince Khalid, Prince Fahd, Prince Abdallah, the commander of the National Guard, and Prince Sultan, the minister of defence and aviation. Including a sizeable number of the leading members of the Al Saud, the 'team' managed to ensure the smooth transfer of power after the assassination of King Faisal on 25 March 1975: Khalid became king and prime minister; Fahd became crown prince and first deputy prime minister; and Abdallah, the sixth surviving son of Ibn Saud, became second deputy prime minister.[7]

Khalid's enthronement violated both the principle of direct inheritance and that of seniority, since Faisal's next eldest brother was Muhammad, the fourth son of the kingdom's founder. The ruling group's choice was probably determined both by the personal qualities of the claimants and by the balance of forces between the rival groups.⁸ King Khalid's mother was descended from a powerful branch of the Al Jiluwi, who were semi-autonomous hereditary rulers of the Eastern Province. When Abdallah Al Jiluwi (Ibn Saud's cousin) died, he was succeeded by his son Saud and then by another son Abd al-Muhsin, who retained his post as ruler up to the mid-1970s.⁹ Other members of the Al Jiluwi also occupied important posts in al-Hasa. Jauhara bint Musaid, King Khalid's mother, belonged to the family, as did one of King Faisal's wives.¹⁰

Fahd, who became crown prince in 1975, led the so-called 'Sudairi seven', which included his six full brothers, Ibn Saud's sons by his wife from the powerful and noble Al Sudairi of Najd. With their close interconnections, they formed an influential group. Sultan, Ibn Saud's twelfth son, was minister of defence and aviation in the 1960s and 1970s; Turki, his twentieth son, was his deputy; Naif, his twenty-third son, was minister of interior; Salman, his twenty-sixth son, was governor of Riyadh; Ahmad, his twenty-eighth son, was vice-governor of Mecca; and Sattam, his twenty-ninth son, was vice-governor of Riyadh.¹¹ Ibn Saud married several women from the Al Sudairi and begot six other sons related to the clan.¹² Prince Abdallah, the third most important figure in the kingdom after the death of King Faisal, had no full brothers, but his mother was descended from the powerful Shammar tribe in the north of the country.¹³ The grouping of full brothers – Saad, Musaid and Abd al-Muhsin, the governor of Medina – had not yet showed their hand.¹⁴

Another influential branch of the royal family were the Al Thunayyan. They were the descendants of Thunayyan, the brother of Muhammad ibn Saud, who had founded the dynasty in the eighteenth century. Abdallah Al Thunayyan had ruled Najd from 1841 to 1843. The members of the dynasty lived in Turkey in the nineteenth and early twentieth centuries, but Ahmad Al Thunayyan returned to Najd, became Ibn Saud's confidant and accompanied Prince Faisal to Paris and London in 1919. He died in 1921. In 1930 Faisal visited Ahmad Al Thunayyan's wife on his way to Istanbul, invited her to Saudi Arabia and married her daughter Iffat, who became his most beloved and influential wife. Thereafter some of the Al Thunayyan moved from Turkey to Saudi Arabia and acquired wealth and influence. At the end of Faisal's rule, Iffat was referred to as 'queen': this was a token of special respect, since the wives of Saudi kings were never usually regarded as queens. She was actively engaged in business.¹⁵

Ibn Saud's grandsons formed a special group who began acquiring influence thanks to their level of education. They were known as the 'royal technocrats'. Some of them, chiefly King Faisal's sons, were co-opted into the system of power: Saud al-Faisal, a graduate of Princeton University, became minister of foreign affairs; Khalid was governor of Asir; Muhammad was head of the irrigation department; Abd al-Rahman commanded an armoured brigade; Saad was deputy director of Petromin; Bandar was an air-force officer; Turki was deputy director of the internal intelligence department; and Abdallah was a businessman (and poet).¹⁶

About forty sons of the dethroned King Saud were expelled from the ruling circle of decision-makers and formed a group of malcontents.¹⁷ After the movement of the 'free princes' ended in 1964, Talal took no further part in political life. Badr, however, became deputy commander of the National Guard.[18]

The Araif (the 'recognized') may come to acquire influence within the Saudi royal family. They are the descendants of Saud ibn Faisal, who ruled Riyadh in the 1870s during the mutiny among Emir Faisal's sons. Although the Araif opposed Ibn Saud on many occasions, they later had to join him. Their head, Muhammad Saud al-Kabir, regarded himself as the next senior prince after King Fahd.[19]

The Al Saud are related to the Al al-Shaikh (the descendants of the founder of Wahhabism), to the Al Sudairi and to the tribal aristocracy of most noble descent. Women have played an important role in establishing close ties between their sons and brothers.[20]

All publication of information on the royal family, other than official reports, is prohibited in Saudi Arabia. Differences within the royal family are kept secret and are not subject to public discussion. The religious, administrative and judicial authorities treat members of the royal family as above the law. When a prince killed the British consul at a reception in Jidda, he was sentenced to life imprisonment; in fact, the sentence was never carried out and the prince was allowed to live in comfort in the family villa.[21]

Under King Faisal, as mentioned previously, subsidies to members of the royal family were curtailed. According to official figures relating to the mid-1970s, the annual allowances granted to the Al Saud amounted to some $300m, but the true sum is unknown and may be several times higher. A prince could receive between $60,000 and $160,000 a year. It is not known how much was spent on the some 2,000 female members of the royal family.[22]

Many of the Al Saud engaged in business. The princes grew rich through land speculation, commissions on import deals and government contracts worth billions of dollars. Many of them owned plots of land near large towns. When these plots were selected for industrial or residential development, the princes earned huge sums by selling the land to the state or to private companies.[23] By the late 1970s the Al Saud had become the richest 'family' in the world. They virtually controlled the country's national income, which reached $90bn a year, and invested Saudi capital abroad. Hundreds of Saudi princes became multimillionaires.[24]

The *ulama*

The influence of the *ulama* decreased in the first two or three decades of the oil era as a result of the spread of education, the emergence of modern industries, new kinds of economic and administrative activities, the large number of Saudis who travelled abroad, the influx of foreigners and the use of transistor radios. However, the fundamental position of the clerical leaders – who, it must be remembered, were connected with the Al Saud – remained intact. The *ulama* were a conservative force that the government could never afford to ignore. When an attempt was made to introduce income tax in 1960, for example, the *ulama* forced the government to restrict it to foreigners. The 1964 decision to dethrone King Saud and replace him by Faisal was approved by a *fatwa* signed by twelve of the most prestigious *ulama*.[25]

The king always stressed his loyalty to Islam – he was the imam, the head of the Saudi Muslims, which implied consultations with the *ulama* and recognition of their high authority. When he was virtually head of state, Crown Prince Faisal said in Mecca in May 1963:

> We have to believe in God, in Islam as our religion and in Mohammed as our prophet, God's peace and blessing be upon Him. But what does faith mean? Faith means both belief and action. It is not sufficient for a man to say: I am a believer for him to be a true believer. Nor is it sufficient to say: I am sincere for him to be really sincere. All this has to be worked hard for. We possess the greatest and noblest heritage, that is the Koran. We have to follow its commands and refrain from what it prohibits. We must seek to understand the correct meaning of Islamic Law and its spirit. We must strive to understand this spirit correctly. We cannot accept our religion to be spoken of as a religion of backwardness, of inanimation and decadence, as some people describe it.[26]

The *ulama* retained a tool with which to influence Saudi society – the Committees of Public Morality. Established in the 1920s to impose the Wahhabi doctrine, the committees continued to dictate the acceptable standards of morality, everyday life and behaviour; they ensured strict female segregation and the prohibition on smoking, drinking and dancing.[27] In the 1960s the *ulama* became reconciled to record-players, tobacco sales, private viewings of films, illustrated papers and periodicals and female radio announcers,[28] but they refused to retreat any further from their position. In accordance with the *ulama*'s demands, the ministry of finance and national economy prohibited all imports of human images and all goods whose form or packing could remind people of the cross.[29]

The local Committees of Public Morality were subordinate to the provincial committees of Hijaz, Najd and the Eastern Province; these were subordinate, in their turn, to the grand mufti and the chief *qadhi*, usually the most influential member of the Al al-Shaikh. All this system was under the control of the king himself. Although no grand mufti was appointed after the death of the last holder of that post in 1970, the descendants of Muhammad ibn Abd al-Wahhab continued to enjoy great influence.[30] In 1971 Ibrahim Al al-Shaikh was appointed minister of justice, and the clan regained control over the judicial system.[31]

Saudi Arabia's status as the motherland of Islam and the site of two of its principal holy places objectively strengthened the position of the *ulama*. The maintenance of Islamic canons, institutions and morality corresponded both to the domestic task of preserving the most important bases of the regime – i.e. the Islamic faith, the king's authority as imam and the influence of the *ulama* as custodians of the *sharia* – and to the task of enhancing Saudi Arabia's international position. Mecca and Medina gave

The Political Regime (the 1950s to the early 1980s)

the country particular prestige within the Islamic world. Modern air, sea and land communications led to much greater ease of movement for Muslim pilgrims and caused a considerable increase in their numbers.

In 1972 the number of pilgrims exceeded 1 million for the first time in the history of Islam, though most of them were Saudis. A total of 479,000 foreigners participated in the *hajj*. The bulk of the pilgrims were elderly; almost one third were women.[32] They needed catering facilities, shelter, medical services and transport.[33] Highways, airports and hotels were built in Hijaz to receive the pilgrims. By the 1970s proceeds from the *hajj* no longer played a substantial role in the country's economy, whereas the expense of organizing the pilgrimage was rising dramatically. The repair and expansion of the holy places demanded huge sums of money.[34]

The security services and the armed forces

Although the Saudi regime faced no serious internal threats in the 1960s and 1970s, the ministry of interior was strengthened. The post of minister of interior was considered a key office: it was filled by the king's closest advisers or by people from the most influential groupings within the Al Saud. Crown Prince Fahd ibn Abd al-Aziz, for example, was minister of interior for a long period. The ministry included the general directorate of public security (which controlled the national police), the directorate of coastguards and border police, the directorate of fire brigades and the general directorate of criminal investigation. There was a separate department of internal intelligence. A police college was established in Mecca in 1960.[35]

The National Guard, which was highly mobile and well equipped, was directly subordinate to the king until the early 1960s. Thereafter it came under Abdallah ibn Abd al-Aziz, an influential member of the Al Saud. The National Guard helped the police to maintain law and order and acted as a counterbalance to the army. It was recruited from among the 'noble tribes', which were unhesitatingly loyal to the king, while the police and the army were recruited from all groups of the population. National Guard detachments were usually isolated from the ordinary people.[36] Besides the police at the disposal of the ministry of interior, each local emir–governor had a guard of his own: this was recognized formally until the early 1960s and continued in practice thereafter. For example, Al Jiluwi's personal guard was sent against the Aramco strikers in 1953 and 1956. Detachments of the army regularly patrolled the port areas and usually helped the police and the National Guard to maintain law and order during the Ramadhan fast and the pilgrimage season.

The development of the regular army started after the Second World War, and military expenses grew every year. Soldiers were sent to Egypt and Sudan to be trained as mechanics. British and American military missions started to appear in Saudi Arabia.[37] After the war, the officers' training academy reopened and schools to train communications experts, pilots and army doctors were established. Army motor repair shops were also set up. A military hospital with 500 beds was built in al-Taif.

Graduates of the pilots' school in al-Taif were sent for further training to Britain, while those who had been trained at the American base in Dhahran went to the US. The ministry of defence created the appropriate departments and directorates for the various branches of the armed forces.[38]

The army increased in size and sophistication in the 1950s. Although Saudi Arabia did not participate in any large-scale armed conflicts after the war with Yemen in the 1930s up to the 1990–91 Gulf war, its military expenses were among the highest in the Middle East both in absolute terms and as a percentage of GNP. In 1965 the Saudi armed forces numbered about 40,000: the regular army (including the army, a small air force and a very small navy) and the National Guard each had some 20,000 men. The former royal guard became an infantry regiment of the regular army in the spring of 1964: it was 4,000 strong.[39]

The supreme commanders of the army and the National Guard were members of the royal family whose loyalty to the king was beyond all doubt. Army officers were recruited chiefly in al-Arid. A special decree of 20 March 1960 prohibited the army from engaging in politics.[40] Saudi army garrisons were initially deployed near the main towns. After the outbreak of the civil war in Yemen, Saudi and Jordanian contingents were concentrated near Jizan and Najran.[41] The Saudi air force was concentrated at the two main airfields of Jidda and Dhahran.

After the Second World War, the US became Saudi Arabia's main supplier of arms and military instructors. Under the agreement of 1947, a training base opened in Dhahran. In the same year, Britain set up a motorized division, modelled on the Arab Legion in Jordan. In 1951 the US and Saudi Arabia signed a mutual assistance and defence agreement under which the US was to retain the Dhahran base and supply Saudi Arabia with modern arms and military equipment. After the British military mission was recalled from Saudi Arabia in 1951 as a result of the al-Buraimi conflict, the US sent a special mission there in 1952. In 1957 the Americans' lease on Dhahran was prolonged for five years and the US continued to participate in training the Saudi armed forces. In 1962 the Saudi government refused to grant the US an extension of the lease on the Dhahran base, yet the military mission of US instructors stayed in the country.[42]

In 1950 Saudi Arabia signed a joint defence pact within the framework of the Arab League. The following year, an Egyptian mission was sent to the Saudi air force. Yet Saudi Arabia undertook no military action under the pact. In October 1955 Saudi Arabia and Egypt signed a defence pact which provided for joint command of the armed forces both in peace-time and under combat conditions. Eighteen months later, King Saud expelled the Egyptian mission as a token of his opposition to the United Arab Republic.

As the *Area Handbook* for 1966 notes:

> the organization and tactical doctrine of the armed forces were patterned after those of the United States ... Training in the Saudi armed forces is patterned after that of the United States Armed Forces ... United States personnel advise and supervise the training programs of the army, navy and air force ...[43]

The Political Regime (the 1950s to the early 1980s)

With Washington's encouragement, military expenses reached fantastic sums in the early 1980s. Saudi Arabia replaced Iran as the world's largest single purchaser of US weapons. The 1981 military budget exceeded $20bn, or $4–5,000 for every man, woman and child in the kingdom. Per capita military expenses were ten times higher than in the NATO countries.[44] The money was spent mainly on infrastructure and the building of barracks, roads and military academies.

In 1979 the numerical strength of the Saudi troops reached almost 120,000: 58,000 served in the land forces, 15,000 in the air force, 3,000 in the navy, 3,000 in the frontier forces and 40,000 in the National Guard.[45] There were some 700 tanks of various types in the army. The air force had 200 aircraft (including F-5s from the US, *Lightnings* from Britain and *Mirages* from France), and 80 VTOL aircraft. The navy had 30 warships, including 2 assault landing ships and 4 minesweepers. The main air-force bases were in Jidda, Dhahran, Khamis-Mushit, Tobruk and al-Taif. There were naval bases in Jidda and al-Jubail.

The US military mission in Saudi Arabia numbered many thousands – some sources mention 20,000 in the early 1980s.[46] Half of their number worked in military construction. Britain helped Saudi Arabia to create an air-defence network. In 1975–77 Riyadh assigned $7bn to purchase British weapons and to pay for British aid in developing the Saudi air force. Two thousand British specialists were charged with training the air-force pilots and technicians and with the maintenance and repair of British-made aircraft.[47]

Between 1974 and 1978 Saudi Arabia bought 7.4bn francs' (approx. $1.5bn) worth of French weapons.[48] France established an air-force base and a college for armoured troops in the kingdom. French specialists trained Saudis to use *Mirage* aircraft and IMX-30 tanks. Under an agreement of 1979, 5 tank brigades were to be created in Saudi Arabia under French control. Saudi Arabia also invited military experts from Egypt, Sudan, Jordan and Pakistan.

Newsweek wrote in March 1978, however:

> For all the hardware they possess, the Saudis remain a second-rate military power. Their standing army is . . . fewer than Jordan's. The Saudis have no military tradition in the modern sense, and troops who were guiding camels across the sands not long ago are now being asked to cope with computerized missile systems and supersonic jet fighters. They have to rely on American advisers and technicians to grease their military machine, and that will remain the case for years to come.[49]

The Saudi troops, with their relatively low numerical strength, were unable to absorb all the weapons bought for them or to make effective use of the military infrastructure. According to the *Washington Post* on 2 November 1981, the US began creating fully equipped reserve bases on Saudi territory and at Saudi expense, designed to be used later by US forces. Five AWACS devices and other military equipment, purchased from the US, were under American control for a long period. It had already been decided that they were to become the main component in an air-defence system that encompassed

– besides Saudi Arabia – Kuwait, the UAE, Oman, Bahrain and Qatar. Electronic control stations were set up which were to become the 'nerve centre' of the US Rapid Deployment Force. The US stored military equipment, munitions, fuel and food at the reserve bases built in Saudi Arabia: they were to be used effectively by the US and its allies in the war against Iraq in 1990–91.[50]

The Saudi army was manned by volunteers who signed an initial contract for five years that could be extended. Most of them were rural migrants. As a rule, non-commissioned officers in the infantry were former soldiers, but in the engineering units there were many NCOs from among the more educated urban population. Most officers were the sons of officials, military personnel, merchants and businessmen and had a secondary education. Many of the officers were members of the tribal nobility and the ruling family.

The armed forces personnel were well paid. Besides the basic salaries, which roughly corresponded to the salary scale of officials in civilian life, the military received numerous 'obligatory' and 'engineering' allowances. The 'obligatory' allowances covered uniforms, accommodation and meals, plus a special servant's allowance for officers. The 'engineering' allowances were paid to members of the air force, the navy and the engineering branches of the armed forces. The total allowances amounted to 40–50% of the basic salary.[51] The military also enjoyed other privileges, including free medical services. Their incomes tended to be higher than those of civilian officials. Their salaries were frequently increased, as were the original allowances; new allowances were introduced in the 1960s and 1970s.[52]

The military's privileged position reflected the royal family's attempt to ensure the army's loyalty to the regime. The policy of granting privileges was combined with the victimization of all politically unreliable elements in the army. The number of conspiracies aimed at seizing power (particularly in the 1960s) showed that there was no absolute loyalty to the royal family within the army, however, and leftist sentiment found a response among the younger officers. This explains why the National Guard, manned by relatively uneducated bedouin, was strengthened in parallel to the army. In the 1970s the army was deployed in specially created cantonments and camps outside the populated areas; the National Guard replaced the army in all strategically important centres.

The mechanism of power. Administration. Propaganda

The administrative machinery of Saudi Arabia began to change and become more sophisticated from the early 1950s. The decree of October 1953 provided for the establishment of a *majlis al-wukala* for the whole kingdom. Earlier the competence of the council was formally confined to the affairs of Hijaz, though in practice some spheres of its activities embraced all regions of the country. After the death of Ibn Saud in 1953, no appointments were made to the posts of viceroy of Hijaz (Faisal was the last to occupy it) or emir of Najd (the last emir was Crown Prince Saud).[53]

The Political Regime (the 1950s to the early 1980s)

The departments of the royal *diwan* might, as before, interfere in the activities of the *majlis al-wukala*, but their interference was not regulated by law. It depended on the king's real power and on the influence of specific individuals in the palace departments. The royal *diwan* dealt with the king's private affairs and was responsible – together with the *majlis al-wukala* – for such central agencies as the ministry of foreign affairs and the ministry of finance and the national economy. The king also had several councillors for special affairs.[54]

The royal decree of 12 May 1958 laid down the new structure and functions of the *majlis al-wukala*. The government was to consist of the prime minister and deputy prime minister (appointed by the king) and the ministers (recommended by the prime minister). The prime minister's resignation would involve that of the whole cabinet. He was to be responsible for general state policy. The government was to prepare the budget and enjoy supreme authority in financial affairs under the king's guidance. The local administration was subordinate to the cabinet. International agreements were to be subject to the approval of the *majlis al-wukala* and then of the king. The procedure of cabinet meetings included a quorum of two-thirds of the members; decisions were to be taken by simple majority vote, with the prime minister having the casting vote. The king might veto the cabinet's decisions.[55]

When assuming his post, a minister swore the following oath: 'I swear by Great Allah that I shall be loyal to my faith, the king and the country, that I shall keep state secrets, protect the interests of the state and the regime and discharge my duties honestly, devotedly and loyally.'[56] The members of the cabinet were prohibited from buying or renting state property, whether directly or through middlemen, and from selling the state any goods or services during their term in office.[57] (In practice, many ministers made their fortunes by using figureheads.)

The *majlis al-shura* was preserved in Saudi Arabia and in the mid-1960s it had thirty-four members. It was the successor to the regional consultative council of Hijaz and spread its competence to the whole country. It prepared recommendations for the issuing of royal decrees and regulations.[58]

In the early 1960s the institute of administration was founded to train state officials, a measure that had been suggested by an IBRD mission. The institute trained more than 10,000 officials over a 10-year period.[59] Its official purpose was the improvement of the state machinery, but it resulted in an inordinate expansion in the number of staff.

All civil employees of state agencies were divided into two categories: 'classified', i.e. true officials; and 'unclassified', i.e. auxiliary and service personnel and workers in the state agencies and enterprises. Unlike the classified employees, those who were unclassified formed a heterogenous category. In 1966, of 45,500 unclassified employees, 4,000 were industrial workers and railwaymen, 14,000 worked in the service sector, 7,000 were guards and policemen and more than 3,000 served on the Committees of Public Morality.[60] Officials were given a rank depending on their education, post and seniority. Other employees were divided into categories, with a particular salary corresponding to each rank or category. Unclassified employees were paid 250–800 rials a month, lower officials 400–1,000, medium-ranking officials

1,200–3,500 and the highest officials 3,000–6,000. The monthly salary of a minister and his deputy ranged from 8,000 to 10,000 rials.[61]

In October 1963 a new regionalization was introduced, increasing the government's control over the local administration. The state was divided into four large provinces (*muqataa*), headed by governors (*hakim*) and vice-governors (*wakil hakim*). The governor was the administrative head of the province and represented the government there.[62] Candidates for a governorship were recommended by the ministry of interior, put forward by the prime minister and appointed by royal decree, though in reality it was the king who selected the principal governors. Governors swore to be loyal to the faith, the country and the king. Their functions included the carrying out of court sentences, the maintenance of law and order, and cooperation with provincial councils in municipal affairs.[63]

Provinces were divided into counties (*mintaqa*), each headed by a prefect (*muhafiz*), and districts (*markaz*), each headed by an attorney (*rais*). Besides the four main provinces of Najd, al-Hasa (the Eastern Province), Hijaz and Asir, there was the Northern Frontier Province, whose administration governed the bedouin in the regions on the border with Iraq and Jordan and along the Trans-Arabian pipeline.[64] In the 1950s Najran and Bisha were still considered to be emirates directly subordinate to Riyadh.[65] It is unclear whether their status changed after the 1963 statute on the provinces was introduced.

The *majlis al-wukala* appointed provincial councils of no more than thirty members on the recommendation of the minister of interior. The budgets of these councils were funded mainly by central government, though they also collected some taxes locally.[66] The boundaries of the provinces and districts could be changed and depended, in particular, on the governor's personality, his relations with the tribes, his prestige in a certain locality and his family connections.[67]

The post of provincial governor was considered lucrative and prestigious and was reserved for members of the Al Saud and the Al Sudair; the latter had traditionally been loyal to the ruling family.[68] The local administration retained great autonomy in certain areas.[69] The traditional influence of local clans, such as the Al Jiluwi in the Eastern Province, persisted. Many decrees and orders had a limited effect and were implemented only insofar as they corresponded to the interests of the local nobility.

In the mid-1970s Saudi Arabia was divided into eighteen provinces, of which five (Mecca with Jidda and al-Taif; Riyadh; the Eastern Province; the Northern Frontier Province; and Hail) were of primary importance and two (Qasim and Medina) were of secondary importance and came under the minister of interior. His deputy was responsible for the remaining eleven provinces.[70]

In each village there was an elder (shaikh) who occupied his post owing to clan connections, wealth, wisdom and maturity, combined with an ability to settle disputes within the village, maintain good relations with the neighbouring tribes and cooperate with the higher administration. Emirs and shaikhs of larger villages and oases tried to win recognition for their appointment from the noble citizens, *ulama*, *qadhis* and merchants. The appointment had to be approved by the head of the next largest administrative unit. The shaikhs of the villages where strong tribal ties persisted usually came from among the tribal nobility. This was necessary in villages with weaker tribal bonds.[71]

In the 1970s and 1980s more than half the Saudi population were still organized in tribes, and both rural and urban Saudis maintained their clan allegiances to a great extent. Even in the 1950s tribal shaikhs were hereditary or, to be more accurate, were selected from among the noble families. The central government controlled the nomadic tribes through the administration of the provinces. Agents of the emirs collected taxes from the tribes, as they had done in the 1930s and 1940s, but *zakat* had become a token payment. The king, as before, was regarded as the chief shaikh. Even in 1954, when King Saud visited the northern part of the country, he was hosted by the tribal nobility of the Syrian and Iraqi tribes, who crossed the border to greet him as 'the shaikh of shaikhs'. In the opinion of Lipsky et al., it was 'a clear case where tribal allegiance took precedence over purely geographical considerations'.[72] (The truth was probably that the tribal nobility expected generous royal gifts without troubling about the reaction of the Syrian and Iraqi authorities; or perhaps they hoped to receive good pastures in Saudi Arabia.)

The centralized distribution of the massive oil revenues had another implication: it seriously weakened, or perhaps even eliminated, the centrifugal forces in Arabian society. Before the oil era, several main regions could be distinguished in Saudi Arabia: Najd as the political centre of the state, the native land of Wahhabism, with a high concentration of the people most loyal to the Al Saud; Hijaz with its holy places and commercial activity during the pilgrimage season; Asir with its agricultural potential; and the Eastern Province with its commercial and economic importance (though less than that of Hijaz). But the development of the oil industry made the Eastern Province the economic heart of the country. Without it, all other areas of the state would have seen a dramatic drop in their incomes. This explains why the issue of separatism virtually died down in Saudi Arabia after the discovery of oil.[73] Its echoes persist, however, in the form of competition within the bureaucracy and other state services, for example between Najdis and Hijazis (the latter's cultural level is still considered to be higher).

In the 1960s several posts requiring a modern education came to be filled by Saudis who had received a secular education at home or abroad. W. Rugh sees this as evidence that a 'new middle class' was forming in Saudi Arabia consisting of people with a secular education.[74] This suggestion is not convincing, however, since the same 'middle class' included major wholesalers from Jidda, Saudi members of the Aramco board, skilled workers, engineers, technicians, doctors, teachers of modern science and perhaps even the lesser members of the Al Saud. What is undoubtedly true is that there were instances of friction and competition within specific social groups between the modernists, who had received a secular education, and the conservatives, most of whom had had a traditional education. It should be remembered, however, that these differences were not universal or determinative. It is enough to mention that there were people with a traditional education among Prince Talal's reformist group, and many 'traditionalists' had been educated at American and European universities.

In 1960 King Saud gave five ministerial portfolios (two of which had previously belonged to princes) to relatively young commoners. Of the five new ministers, four had graduated from Cairo University. The fifth, who headed the new ministry of petroleum and mineral resources, was aged only 35 and was a graduate of Texas University. When the ministry of information was set up in 1963, a Saudi graduate of Cairo University was appointed as minister. Members of the royal family retained only five of the fourteen ministerial portfolios. Needless to say, they were the most important ones (interior, defence, the National Guard, finance and foreign affairs), thus enabling the Al Saud to keep the reins of government in their hands. But increasing numbers of commoners with a secular education came to occupy lower posts in the key ministries; they were appointed at all levels in the ministries of petroleum, commerce, information, agriculture, communications and finance. These were the agencies that played an active role in the modernization of the country. As for the ministry of education and the ministry of labour and social affairs, which might have been expected to be the most open to modernization, they became the strongholds of the conservative *ulama*.

In the early 1970s King Faisal appointed a *qadhi* from Jidda as minister of justice. The new minister had a traditional theological education and was head of the mainly *sharia*-based judicial system. At the same time, he had acquired wide experience in solving secular problems among the business circles of Jidda. Next a Saudi from a merchant family of Jidda, a graduate of Cairo University, was appointed minister of pilgrimage and *waqfs*.

The portfolio of minister of education continued to be held by a member of the Al al-Shaikh, but from 1971 two of his deputies were graduates of American universities. Two more deputy ministers of labour and social affairs were appointed in 1971, also graduates of US universities. Of four secretaries of state with ministerial status, two held US degrees. They headed the Central Planning Organization and the personnel service. Other new appointees during that period were six princes, also graduates of American and British colleges, who became secretaries of state and governors.[75]

By expanding the education system and attracting people with a modern education to all levels of the administration, the regime strove to modernize the archaic system of power. Naturally, friction arose between the old bureaucrats and the new, Western-educated officials who easily obtained promotion. In the final analysis, however, family and clan connections were the most important factor.

In Saudi Arabia, as elsewhere in the Middle East, propaganda became a powerful tool by which the regime could influence its citizens. Its role was first discussed in the ruling circles in the 1950s and early 1960s, when it became clear that ordinary Saudis were being influenced by the propaganda from Radio Cairo. Whereas sermons in the mosques and the activities of the *mutawwas* might remain the principal channels of influence, radio and TV became the modern technical means of spreading the ideas of the ruling group. Powerful radio transmitters started to be built in 1963, to be followed two years later by the first Saudi television programmes. Transistor radios and TV sets

The Political Regime (the 1950s to the early 1980s)

became the main sources of information in a country whose population was still largely illiterate. Religious broadcasts and recitations of the Quran were the main items in radio and TV programmes.

The role of the press was insignificant. The first daily paper, *al-Bilad al-Saudiya*, was published in Jidda in 1953. By the late 1960s there were almost two dozen newspapers in Saudi Arabia but they had a very limited circulation. In the mid-1970s four Arabic papers were issued in Hijaz: *al-Madina*, *al-Uqaz*, *al-Nadwa* and *al-Bilad al-Saudiya*. *Umm al-Qura*, a semi-official weekly, and *al-Riyadh* were published in Najd; and *al-Yawm* in the Eastern Province. Several other papers and magazines were started in the 1980s and 1990s. The press was under the direct or indirect control of state officials. It should be noted that papers and magazines could not survive without state subsidies.[76]

Legislation and the judicial system

According to the Arab jurist Subhi al-Muhammasani, writing in 1962:

> Saudi legislation was confronted by old bedouin customs, as well as by a conservative group who perceive unacceptable *bida* in everything not found in the *sharia*. However, in spite of these difficulties, the caravan of new life is going ahead, meeting the needs of the modern society. Its advance is promoted by the oil-based industrial revolution, the spread of education and schools, the settling of the bedouin and new social and economic reforms . . . Saudi Arabia has covered a longer way within a quarter of century than in the preceding fourteen centuries.[77]

In the 1990s, however, it has become clear that the 'caravan of new life' has advanced far more slowly in the legal sphere than al-Muhammasani anticipated three decades previously. New commercial, criminal and even civil codes have been enacted in most Islamic countries in the twentieth century. Only personal relations (marriage, divorce, inheritance) continue to be regulated by the *sharia*, though in a modified form, in almost all countries with a largely Muslim population except Turkey and Tunisia. Saudi Arabia is among the few countries where the *sharia* has survived in its 'initial purity'.

The Saudi judicial and legal system, which was suited to a centralized feudal state, was not able to cope with the socio-economic problems created by the rapid transformation of Arabian society. The Wahhabi teaching confined itself to the canons elaborated in the first three centuries of Islam and rejected everything that emerged in Islam thereafter as *bida*.[78]

In the early centuries of Islam, legal experts used *ijtihad*, the right to interpret the fundamentals of law and find solutions to new problems within this framework. After the four orthodox schools of Muslim law were created, the doors of *ijtihad* were virtually closed. The Hanbali *ulama* reject *ijtihad* outright. Saudi legal experts have therefore been forced to find solutions to twentieth-century problems in the traditions of the seventh, eighth and ninth centuries, inevitably resulting in deadlock.[79]

Two examples may demonstrate the difficulty of applying a medieval system of law in the twentieth century. The Quran bans profit and interest on loans, but the modern capitalist economy cannot function without a money market governed by the profit mechanism. SAMA's rules prohibit the receiving of interest, and Saudi legislation on commercial banks simply ignores the question. To circumvent the religious dogma, the formulation of a 'service charge' was invented as a euphemism for interest.[80] Another problem was the absence of commercial legislation. There are numerous legal norms in the *sharia* to regulate trade, yet they do not cover many aspects of modern economic activities. The attempt to draw up a commercial code failed because of strong opposition from the *ulama*.[81]

Some Saudi statesmen have admitted that the *sharia* needs adapting to the requirements of modern society. Shaikh Ahmad Zaki Yamani, the minister of petroleum and mineral resources from 1962 to 1986, stated in a lecture to the American University of Beirut in February 1967 that 'it is too late for the *sharia* to regulate contemporary problems'. In Yamani's opinion, to apply the *sharia*, the state ought to:

> select principles from the various juristic schools with no exceptions, the criterion being what is more appropriate to the needs of that particular country. Such countries could legislate new solutions for novel problems, deriving such solutions from the general principles of the *sharia* and considerations of public interest and communal welfare.

This was an obvious rupture with Wahhabi dogma – it found no support among the *ulama* and remained the minister's personal opinion.[82]

Neither did Prince Talal's earlier call to expand the application of *ijtihad* meet with a positive response.[83] As for other social groups, including the leftist opposition, they sought a solution to the main problems outside the framework of the *sharia*.

The Saudi *ulama* nonetheless found a loophole in the *sharia* to approve the new legal standards which were necessary in order for the economy and society to function. According to the classification drawn up by the early experts in Islamic law, all human actions can be divided into five categories: (i) those clearly demanded by Allah; (ii) those recommended by Him; (iii) those to which He is (legally) indifferent; (iv) those denounced by Him; and (v) those prohibited by Him. The *ulama* decided that only those questions to which Allah is indifferent are open to state legislation. Using that loophole, the Saudi authorities have, since the 1920s, issued *nizams* (regulations) and *marsums* (royal decrees) which are actually, though not formally, laws.[84]

The *sharia*-based Saudi courts had to transfer part of their judicial functions to administrative bodies or such social institutions as chambers of commerce and industry.[85] Initially, all situations not covered by the *sharia* were examined on the basis of Ottoman civil law of the Tanzimat era; gradually, a virtually new system of law was elaborated on the basis of decrees, ordinances and decisions of the *majlis al-shura*. Examples are traffic regulations, the labour code and the decree banning strikes; and

The Political Regime (the 1950s to the early 1980s)

the decrees on taxation, on the activities of corporations and companies, and on foreign investment.[86] As early as 1926, a commercial council – a version of the chamber of commerce – was set up in Jidda. In 1931 'commercial rules' were applied, based on the Ottoman commercial code of 1850 with the exception of the articles on interest and profit. In 1954 the commercial council was replaced by the ministry of commerce, and chambers of commerce functioned in several Saudi towns. In the early 1970s insurance was applicable to all forms of ownership, with the exception of life insurance. In 1970 the universal rules for personnel of 1957 were replaced by the code of discipline, which was obligatory for all officials and state employees.[87]

The judicial system that was created in Saudi Arabia in the 1920s and 1930s continued to function thereafter, but the commission of juridical supervision was replaced in the 1970s by the ministry of justice and the supreme juridical council. For the examination of especially important and controversial cases, the *diwan al-malazim* was set up under the *majlis al-wukala* in the mid-1950s. It played the role of arbitrator to some degree. At the same time, it was an administrative tribunal which examined grievances against the administration, questions of bribery and the boycott of Israel, and serious disputes involving tribes and foreigners. In the opinion of several American and British scholars, the *diwan al-malazim* originated in the Persian, pre-Islamic judicial tradition and was adopted from it by the *sharia*. The renaissance of that board in Saudi Arabia and the expansion of its functions testifies to a certain flexibility even among the Hanbali *ulama*.[88]

Formally, all citizens of Saudi Arabia were equal before the law. However, as mentioned previously, members of the royal family, prominent *ulama* and members of the principal noble clans enjoyed virtual judicial immunity and stood above the law.

CHAPTER 21

Economy, Society, Politics (the 1980s and the 1990s)

In the early 1990s oil remained the long-term basis of the Saudi economy, determining the country's position in the world economy and in the system of regional and global international relations. But the rate of economic growth decreased and the priorities in economic development gradually began shifting. This was caused by a glut of oil on the world market, which became a 'buyer's market', a fall in oil and gas prices and Saudi Arabia's increasingly sophisticated economic structure.

A modern transport and communications system and a financial sector had been created in Saudi Arabia; several branches of the manufacturing industry were established or developed; commercial activities were becoming increasingly sophisticated; and state subsidies had led to rapid advances in agriculture. The patient and protracted encouragement of the private sector began to yield the expected fruits, though the state retained not only the functions of planning, coordination and financing, but also those of production. Meanwhile, the heterogeneity of the economy, the mobility and instability of some of its sectors, and the wide differences between the living standards of the various groups in society, all increased. Some changes, though hardly noticeable to the superficial observer, occurred in the population structure in the 1980s and early 1990s. The first generation of Saudis who had grown up in the 'oil boom' era and received a modern education, frequently in Europe or the US, entered the workforce and began ascending the social ladder.

The external threat to Saudi Arabia's security increased in the 1980s and early 1990s and the Saudi regime spent colossal amounts on arms and the armed forces. The apparently inexhaustible oil revenues were now proving insufficient for the implementation of the ambitious programmes of economic and social development.

Economy, Society, Politics (the 1980s and the 1990s)

Economic development

The oil policy of Saudi Arabia and other OPEC member states underwent significant changes after the 'oil boom'. The general strategy was to reduce the rate of extraction because of the falling demand for oil on the world market. Shaikh Yamani admitted as early as 1980 that Saudi Arabia's production of 3.5 mb/d (175m tons a year) was sufficient to ensure the normal functioning of the economy. However, Saudi Arabia's political and economic obligations to the West led it to increase oil production up to 1984: the annual total stood at 1,839.9m barrels in 1983. Then it decreased: to 1,714.5m in 1984 and 1,264.9m in 1985. Meanwhile, the proceeds from oil sales dropped dramatically from $116bn in 1981 to $18.4bn in 1985.[1]

State revenues diminished by 32% over the period 1982–86.[2] The most difficult year was 1986, when it proved impossible to approve the state budget. Speaking on Saudi TV on 11 March 1986, King Fahd said that the fall in oil prices from $28 to $15 per barrel 'had made it impossible to formulate meaningful revenue and spending guidelines'.[3] The balance between state revenues and expenditure was drawn up on a monthly basis and many projects were postponed. The government had drastically to curtail expenditure on all items in the budget.[4]

The industrial and social development of the country – planned on a grandiose scale by Saudi standards in the atmosphere of 'oil intoxication' – was halted or slowed down. However, while it was easy to stop work on a new building or to freeze projects that were already under way, it was difficult to abandon policies designed to maintain production, transport, health care and education or discontinue social guarantees, since many of these were prestige projects. The industrial and economic recession itself could be regarded, under certain circumstances, as a positive phenomenon. In essence, the 'Arabian version of industrialization' combined two processes, growth and development: in other words, the building of industrial and other projects, and the modernization of the national economy. The former process decelerated sharply in the early 1980s, but the latter could hardly be stopped. The uneven development of the Saudi economy was succeeded by a more balanced one.

The fate of the fourth five-year development plan (1985–90) is indicative. Some $276.7bn (about 1 trillion rials) were assigned for its implementation, including $90bn for defence, the largest single item, and $31bn for the development of 'economic resources'. At the same time, the fourth plan included many projects provided for by the third plan but which had not yet been completed or, in some cases, even started. The plan listed the principal tasks in order of priority: to improve the efficiency of production and the rational use of resources; to lessen the economy's dependence on oil sales by developing the manufacturing industry; to start economic integration with the countries of the Gulf Cooperation Council (GCC); to reduce the number of unskilled foreign workers by at least 600,000; and to promote a more active participation by the private sector in all spheres of the economy.[5]

In this context, the fate of the Qasim oil refinery is typical. Its construction was suspended in March 1985, when 90% of the design work and 15% of the construction work had been completed. Petromin paid compensation of between $500m and $800m to Bectel, the Saudi-US contractors. Earlier, Bectel had received $300m for the work actually carried out. In the opinion of experts, these sums were enough to complete the work. Petromin's reluctance to do so gave rise to the assumption that it simply did not need the refinery.[6] Saudi oil refineries (then producing 1.6 mb/d) were working at under 60% capacity. Following the example of Kuwait, Saudi Arabia began to acquire oil refineries abroad. Aramco's largest acquisition in 1988 was the purchase of three refineries in the US.[7]

Building contracts awarded to private companies in 1985 amounted to $3.9bn, less than half of the $8.3bn awarded in 1984.[8] The construction of an oil refinery in Rabigha and an international airport in the Eastern Province was halted, and the building of petrochemical works in Jubail and Yanbu slowed down.[9] The ending of over-ambitious prestige projects proved beneficial to the country, however, as did the abrupt decrease in the numbers of foreign workers, who formed the majority in the construction sector.

Banks also faced difficult times. The apparently successful expansion of the activities of private banks was shown to be artificial in many respects. These banks were far less active in financing production than in engaging in speculative operations or the provision of consumer goods for the well-off groups in society. In the late 1980s the average profits of private banks fell sharply.[10] In the same years many debtors of the Saudi commercial banks tried to evade or reduce payments for the credit extended to them earlier by appealing to the anti-interest provisions of the *sharia*. Many clients started to invest their deposits in securities or withdrew them altogether.[11]

The government had to seek domestic sources of finance. In 1985 the rates for gas and electricity were increased by 70% for the first time since 1972 and the price of petrol went up. The authorities increased the fees for issuing residence permits and exit visas and for the change of guarantors by foreigners. The car tax – earlier set at 75 rials for 5 years – was increased to an annual rate of between 100 and 700 rials. Import duties on cars, building materials, electrical appliances, shoes and jewellery rose by 4–7%. In the spring of 1985 additional payments and bonuses for 250,000 state employees were considerably curtailed.[12] The changes in the taxation system led to a substantial increase in budget revenues.[13]

The private sector's cautious attitude to participation in state projects essentially proved justified: the state simply suspended or ceased payments for works that had already been completed. Of 1,200 contracting companies, one third went bankrupt or found themselves in a grave financial situation in 1984/85. Hundreds of private JVs (joint ventures) were liquidated.[14] In 1982 the ministry of industry and electricity issued 2,424 licences, including 1,361 for industrial enterprises. The number of industrial licences issued in the first half of 1983 was only 180.[15]

The economic situation caused the government great anxiety. Speaking at the second conference of Saudi businessmen, with 900 participants, in March 1985, King Fahd said, 'I hope that your main purpose will be capital investment in Saudi Arabia or any friendly country, but this does not mean any restriction on free investment.' He called on Saudi businessmen to adapt to the reduced oil revenues and diminished state investment in the economy. He assured his audience that the dialogue between businessmen and the state would be continued in order to achieve further progress, for which there were 'sufficient resources and opportunities in various fields'.[16]

The difficulties continued to grow, however. In drafting the budget for the fiscal year of 1988, the government tried to balance revenues and expenditure. It provided for a further reduction in expenditure to 140bn rials ($38bn) and a deficit of 36bn rials ($9.78bn). Expenditure was slashed on virtually all items. For the first time in many years, the number of state employees did not rise. The government took the radical step of reimposing income tax on foreign workers and experts, who had been exempted from it in 1975. The tax rate was high: 30% on annual incomes in excess of 60,000 rials ($16,000). Import duties were increased from 7% to 20%, with the exception of food and agricultural produce. Duties on cement and other building materials were raised by 20%.[17] The authorities realized that an outbreak of inflation might be the first consequence of their measures. King Fahd warned, 'We want Saudi businessmen to make reasonable profits, but we shall not allow them to ignore the citizens' interests and to sacrifice them to the minority whose main purpose is the accumulation of wealth.'[18]

In practice, many of these measures were soon revoked. The authorities reduced gas and electricity rates a few months after they had been increased, 'to alleviate the people's financial burden'.[19] Similarly, the water rate for industrial enterprises was increased and then decreased soon afterwards. The initial plan to reduce state purchases from Saudi agricultural companies was cancelled. Most indicative was the fate of the income tax imposed on foreign experts: two days after its introduction, it was lifted by a special royal ordinance. The result of the inconsistent economic policy was that the cuts in state expenditure and the growth of non-oil revenues were insufficient to balance the budget deficit.

The government continued its support of private capital, however, even in the difficult decade of the 1980s, and protectionist measures were taken to support the competitiveness of some Saudi goods.[20] The consistent and generous support from state funds enabled national capital to grow and strengthen. In 1975, 1,181 companies (including 958 that were entirely Saudi-owned) had capital of 2,209.3m rials (including 1,088.9m rials of purely Saudi capital). In 1986 almost 7,000 companies (of which 5,406 were entirely Saudi-owned) possessed investments of 68,078.8m rials.[21]

In 1986 Shaikh Yamani was removed from his post as minister of petroleum and mineral resources, an indirect proof of the country's economic difficulties. In spite of a sizeable excess of real expenditure as compared with the target figures and the failure of individual projects, the fourth five-year development plan was nevertheless largely fulfilled: the oil industry, particularly oil processing, developed further in both the private and the state sector; and huge investments in agriculture and the application of modern farming methods and highly productive seed and livestock substantially reduced the country's dependence on food imports.

Agriculture became an object of Saudi national pride. Between 1970 and 1989 the annual production of fruit and vegetables increased from 706,000 to 2,600,000 tons;

of dairy products from 156,000 to 500,000 tons; of poultry meat from 7,000 to 226,000 tons; and of eggs from 5,000 to 103,000 tons. This was more than sufficient to meet domestic demand; the surplus was exported to the neighbouring states and to countries in Western Europe such as Switzerland, Britain and Italy.[22]

Within the short period 1986–90 the area under cultivation grew from 5.7m to 7.4m hectares. The wheat harvest rose from 3.5m tons in 1990 to some 4m tons in 1991. All foodgrain was purchased by the state at the guaranteed price of 2,000 rials ($553) per ton from small farmers and 1,500 rials ($400) from big farmers. The annual domestic consumption of foodgrain was around 1m tons; the rest was exported, resulting in huge financial losses for the state. Because of the climatic and other natural conditions in Saudi Arabia, only state aid could make agriculture profitable. Each ton of wheat grown in the country cost 5 or 6 times more than imported wheat. On Saudi farms, 70% of the fodder consisted of imported, high-quality concentrates. The cost of production was maintained at a level acceptable to farmers, since the state paid 60% of the cost of the imported concentrates.[23] Agriculture's share in GDP grew from 3.3% in 1985 to 6.6% in 1990. The respective figures for oil extraction were 34.2% and 23.6%, and for oil processing 3.9% and 5.0%.

The fifth five-year development plan (1990–95) provided for a reduction of the oil and gas sector's share in GDP of 20% by 1995 and an annual real growth rate of 3.2% (2.7% in the oil sector and 3.6% in other sectors). The share of the non-oil productive sectors was to grow from 38.5% to 43.3%. At the same time, opportunities existed for a sizeable increase in oil production. A new oilfield (with deposits of 30bn barrels) was put into operation near al-Dilam.[24] By the beginning of the 1990s, total oil deposits were estimated at 258bn barrels and natural gas deposits at 180 trillion cu. m.[25]

The petrochemical industry developed further. When large industrial zones with dozens of modern plants were created in Jubail (in the Eastern Province) and Yanbu (in the west), the national economy obtained a solid base for high-tech production. On 29 October 1977 King Khalid and Crown Prince Fahd laid the foundation stone of the industrial complex of Jubail, an area measuring 1,030 sq. km in the early 1990s. The population of the town exceeded 40,000. More than 900 large and medium-scale enterprises for the production of steel, aluminium, fertilizer, plastics, and so on, were planned. The scale of Yanbu is smaller: in the early 1990s it had 5 large petrochemical complexes and a population of 19,000. The government's strategy was that oil processing and the petrochemical industry should 'haul in their wake' medium and small-scale private enterprises.

The structure of foreign trade did not change greatly in the 1980s and 1990s, with oil and oil products accounting for some 90% of exports. Consumer goods formed the majority of imports, as they had done previously. The main export markets in the late 1980s were Japan, the US, the Netherlands, Bahrain, Singapore and Italy. The chief sources of imports were the US, Japan, Britain, Germany, Italy and France. The bulk of foreign currency assets were invested in the US and Western Europe. The end of the oil era told directly upon the country's foreign assets, especially those held by the state.[26]

Economy, Society, Politics (the 1980s and the 1990s)

The 1990–91 Gulf war was a serious blow to the country's economy. The government had to seek loans on the international capital market and from national commercial banks at high interest rates to cover the colossal spending on defence and payments to the country's allies. Despite the difficult situation, oil production reached 8.5 mb/d in 1990, which exceeded the OPEC quota by almost 3 mb/d. The average annual production was 6.2m tons.[27] However, petrodollars could no longer patch up the holes in the budget, as they had done a decade earlier. Higher requirements concerning quality and the growing costs of maintenance within the oil industry necessitated large-scale investment. In the early 1990s the conversion of oil refineries to the production of ethyl-free petrol for cars demanded many billions of dollars.

The planned deficit in the 1991/92 budget was 30bn rials, 5bn less than the previous year. Total expenditure reached 181bn rials, 30bn more than the year before. The growth in spending on defence and security was noticeably small – 54.3bn rials in 1991 (51.9bn in 1990). The sums spent on social welfare grew steadily: education, 31.1bn rials (26.2bn in 1990); and health care and social development, 12.2bn rials (11.8bn in 1990). The most impressive increase was in the development of economic resources: 8.0bn rials (4.8bn in 1990). Thus the structure of the budget showed the government's preference for domestic economic development.[28]

The fifth five-year development plan (1990–95) continued the main directions of the previous plans, but was more oriented to socio-political aims: the development of the workforce; the active participation of citizens in productive activities; a decreased dependence on the oil sector; the development of non-oil mining industries; the encouragement of private capital's participation in the country's development; and the balanced development of all regions and their integration into the economic system of the GCC states.[29] A total sum of 753bn rials was allocated for the fifth plan.[30]

The workforce

Due to the lack of reliable figures, there had been widely fluctuating estimates of Saudi Arabia's population for many years. The British experts G. Birks and S. Sinclair estimated the indigenous population in 1985 at 6,447,000.[31] The first official census was undertaken in 1992. According to its results, published in mid-1993, the total population of the kingdom was 16,929,294: 12,304,835 (i.e. 72.7%; 6,211,213 men and 6,093,622 women) were indigenous Saudis and 4,624,459 (27.3%) were foreigners.[32] In the early 1980s foreigners represented some 36% of the population and 52% of the workforce.[33] If the present growth rate persists, the population may reach 44,800,000 by the year 2025.[34] It should be remembered, however, that all figures relating to the country's population are questionable and reflect trends rather than facts.

In the years of the oil boom and rapid industrialization, a high natural growth rate was observed in Saudi Arabia, combined with a notable decrease in mortality. As a result, young people under the age of 16 formed up to 50% of the indigenous population in the 1980s and 1990s. The second notable feature, already mentioned above, was the influx of immigrants. Taking an active part in all spheres of economic life, they gradually became an inalienable part of the society, which could no longer do without them.

The national composition of the immigrant groups varied. In the 1950s and 1960s most were Arabs – Palestinians, Yemenis, Egyptians and others. In the mid-1970s Arabs formed about 75% of all foreigners, other Asians and Africans around 23% and Europeans 2.1%. These figures are based on official sources and do not reflect illegal immigration. The estimated number of workers from North Yemen alone was between 800,000 and 1,200,000.[35] The number of Palestinians and other Arabs decreased in the late 1970s and the number of immigrants (mostly workers) from South and South-East Asia rose. It was on them that local and Western industrialists relied, with the support of the state. South Koreans, Chinese and Filipinos were regarded as more disciplined and skilled workers and less dangerous politically than non-Saudi Arabs.

At the same time, the lessening of the country's dependence on a foreign workforce, and the stabilization and even reduction in their numbers, were mentioned as important tasks in all economic development programmes. It was extremely difficult for foreigners working under contract in the country to become naturalized. Only a few Arabs from the Gulf states were granted Saudi citizenship.[36] Yet a sizeable part of the immigrants who had lived and worked in the country for a long time inevitably became part of Saudi society, though at its lower levels. A new pidgin language, 'Araburdiya', emerged as a mixture of Arabic and Urdu.

The share of the economically active population engaged in agriculture fell from 71% in 1960, to 61% in 1981, and 48% in 1985. The respective figures in industry were 10%, 14% and 15%; and in the service sector 19%, 25% and 37%. In the 1980s and 1990s the number of people occupied in agriculture decreased rapidly, while the numbers employed in industry and the service sector rose. The percentage of oil-industry workers among all hired workers was a mere 1.3%, that in other industries 1.7% and in oil processing 0.1%.[37] Saudi nationals formed a majority (57%) only in the oil and gas sector. The government's energetic measures for the full 'Saudization' of the sector had not achieved much success by the mid-1980s and numerous Jordanians, Palestinians and Syrians were still employed. The percentage of Saudis working in the manufacturing industry was only 6–18%, according to various estimates.[38] The Aramco complex, which employs people from 80 countries, occupies a special place in the national industry. In 1990 there were 32,000 Saudis among its 43,000 employees. They accounted for 76% of the company management and 60% of its leading experts.[39]

Overall, the percentage of foreign workers in Saudi industry exceeded 80% in the early 1980s.[40] It was characterized by a high turnover, since foreign workers did not usually stay long in the country. During the same period, according to official data, 16–50% of Saudis in the largest industrial centres had been employed for 6 or more years, while only 2.4–3.6% of foreigners had been employed for the same length of time.[41] The share of Saudis was high in the transport and communications sectors (over 70%). Saudis represented a minority in construction, where a cheap workforce from Africa and Asia was mainly employed.

Economy, Society, Politics (the 1980s and the 1990s)

Restrictions on female employment persisted in the early 1990s, though the traditional approach of confining women to the home was increasingly questioned and many businessmen held that it was better to employ Saudi women than foreigners. Some companies set up segregated 'female sections' where women could work separately and be instructed by foremen over the telephone. Examples of that kind were the exception, however. Most working women were nurses, doctors, and teachers at kindergartens and girls' schools. In the early 1990s fewer than 10% of all employees were women.[42]

Labour legislation was considerably revised during the oil boom in favour of employees. Formally, this applied to foreign workers too, whose labour and stay in the country were also regulated by government ordinances. The main features of the 1969 labour code were a forty-eight-hour working week, an eight-hour working day, paid leave, sick-leave and compensation for occupational injuries and illnesses. The working week for women and for adolescents aged 15–18 was reduced and they were barred from some kinds of work. Measures to protect workers and to improve working conditions were observed in the state sector, but were sometimes ignored in the private sector. Special bodies were set up to settle labour disputes. The complete ban on strikes and lockouts persisted. Participants in any illegal assembly could be imprisoned for between six months and two years. Any call to cease work was punishable by imprisonment for between one and three years. The organizers of strikes were liable to imprisonment for up to six years.[43]

Urbanization

The growth of towns is characteristic of all countries in the East in the twentieth century, but in Arabia urbanization was connected with industrialization to some degree. The percentage of the urban population grew rapidly: it stood at 48.7% in 1970, 58.7% in 1977, 66.8% in 1982, and 77.3% in 1990.[44] Modern towns sprang up as industrial, administrative and cultural centres. The area of Riyadh had increased from some 110 sq. km in 1968 to 1,600 sq. km by 1992; its population rose from 160,000 to 2 million over the same period. The capital changed beyond all recognition.

Jidda, the industrial and commercial heart of the country, had an area of 1,200 sq. km and a population of more than 1 million in the early 1980s (risen from 350,000 in 1970). Other cities and towns had much lower populations: the total population of Dammam, al-Khobar and Dhahran was some 350,000, al-Taif 330,000, Buraida 184,000, Hail 92,000, Anaiza 68,000 and Najran some 60,000.[45] Mecca and Medina were adorned with magnificent new buildings in the 1970s and 1980s. In September 1988 King Fahd laid the foundation stone of the expanded building of the Great Mosque in Mecca. Its planned capacity was 695,000 people and that of the Medina mosque 650,000.[46] There was a substantial increase in the annual influx of pilgrims: 286,000 in 1960, 431,000 in 1970, 813,000 in 1980, 1,000,400 in 1983, 763,000 in 1988 and over 1 million in 1993.[47]

Petrodollars enabled the authorities to undertake prestigious building projects, attract the best architects and use the most expensive building materials, but shanty towns of foreign workers sprang up even at the height of the oil boom.[48] New urban forms of everyday life and social intercourse did not lead to the immediate or universal breakdown of traditions. On the contrary, the traditional culture and traditional social relations were introduced to the towns. Many apartment blocks were named after the family clans that lived there.[49] The authority of parents and of the tribal nobility persisted among the urban population.

Social transformations

The fall of the bedouin's share in the total population in the 1980s and 1990s did not mean that traditional social values or reference points were abandoned. The intense scale of economic modernization and the penetration of Western ideas led both to a partial erosion and, paradoxically, to a partial strengthening of tribal traditions. Individuals needed to preserve their traditional values and to be affiliated to a particular social group. This objective trend was supported by the government's well-thought-out social policies. This did not prevent the government from encouraging the sedentarization of the nomads as a continuation of Ibn Saud's policy. Bedouin tribes were allocated irrigated plots of land with houses and wells and given financial aid. Some bedouin families set up profitable agricultural and sheep-breeding farms, often hiring workers from countries in South and South-East Asia.

The situation of the bedouin in the early 1980s can be judged from a survey by American academics in Najd. The nomadic bedouin proper, registered at water-supply points, formed only 33% of the population. In the rural areas 72% of the workforce were occupied in agriculture and animal husbandry. The settled bedouin formed at most 48% of the population in the oases. In the oil-producing areas, the unskilled Saudi workers were mostly young bedouin who were working in order to buy a lorry or to save up enough money for the bride-price. More than 30% of the population of the main tribes (at least one man in each family) served in the police, the army, the National Guard or the frontier guard. At the same time, ex-bedouin were rare among traders and administrative employees. Tribal origins continued to play a role in society, but the bedouin's social status was lower than before. The highest illiteracy rate (96% among persons aged 10 or over) was observed among the bedouin.[50] The situation was changing, however. According to Katakura, about 70% of bedouin children attended school in Hijaz in the 1970s.[51]

Most branches of agriculture developed steadily on the base of the market economy. As early as the 1970s, all peasant farms were market-oriented. Many new farmers and dozens of big agro-industrial farms emerged in the countryside. By the mid-1980s the government had transferred 560,000 hectares of land to 38,000 farmers and set up more than 1,500 farms and 10 cooperatives.[52] Theoretically, any Saudi subject might receive land in the specially allocated areas, but his connections with the tribe that traditionally controlled the territory in question were important in the distribution of land.[53] However, state loans and technical assistance were often spent on consumer goods rather than on production or remained unspent. In the opinion of British experts, state aid, combined with high incomes that had no solid economic base, were strong incentives for the bedouin to continue their traditional way of life and loss-making economy in the rural areas.[54]

The indigenous Saudi bourgeoisie grew in numbers and in wealth. There were seven special state funds to extend financial aid and credits, on very favourable terms, for setting up companies in the fields of industry and the infrastructure and for the building of housing. The 1972 law that obliged foreigners to transfer their companies to Saudis was supplemented in 1978/79 by a law that stipulated the obligatory participation of a Saudi partner or agent in all new foreign companies set up on Saudi territory.[55]

Hisham Nazir, the minister of planning, stated in January 1981 that support for and financing of the private sector were the priorities of the government's development strategy.[56] Razman al-Zamil, the deputy minister of commerce, said in the spring of the same year that the state's strategic economic activities would be confined to national projects and the petrochemical industry and would never enter the sphere of interests of the private sector.[57]

Generous state financial aid, combined with the requirement that Western companies should cooperate with local business, might have been expected to encourage the development of a large Saudi bourgeoisie. However, there were several obstacles that initially prevented this. They included the high technological level and capital-intensive character of modern industry. Most Saudi capitalists lacked the relevant knowledge, experience and assets. Besides, local capital was reluctant to engage in sophisticated enterprises, since commerce, financial deals and land speculation already yielded large profits.

Among the main features of the major Saudi entrepreneurs was the family character of their enterprises. There were different degrees of personal participation in company management, with some families monopolizing all spheres of activity.[58] The knowledge and experience of a traditional Arabian trader were sufficient for commercial and middleman operations until the 1970s and 1980s. When a company was engaged in industrial production, finance and services, its managers tended to be Americans, West Europeans, Egyptians, Jordanians or Palestinians. JVs were set up, where the Saudi party supplied capital, materials and the workforce and the Western companies organized production and sales. Saudi businessmen born between the 1940s and the 1960s increasingly assumed all management functions; their children will perhaps further 'Saudize' the business sphere.

In organizational terms, the companies set up by these Saudi entrepreneurs were ramified financial-industrial or commercial-industrial corporations. They were usually based around several large companies, owned exclusively by one family or a holding company. Trade remained an important sphere of activity for almost all major Arabian businessmen because it guaranteed high profits. In the 1970s and 1980s the hotel business also came to acquire great importance. No Saudi millionaire would refuse to become the agent of a Western company, since dealership is still considered a prestigious occupation.

The financial activities of the major Saudi businessmen have attracted the attention of both scholars and the mass media. Markets in Saudi Arabia, and even in the Arabian peninsula, have become too narrow for many members of both the old and the new business class. For example, Khalid ibn Salih and Said ibn Salih al-Mahfuz of Hadhramawt, who headed the old family of Mahfuz, retained their positions in trade, middle-man operations and dealerships, established several new companies and printing houses and took part in the creation of several petrochemical and other industrial projects in both Saudi Arabia and Egypt. By the early 1980s they were concentrating their activities in the financial sphere. They expanded the activities of the National Commercial Bank, the oldest bank in the country, founded in 1938 by the al-Mahfuz (51.5%) and al-Qaqi families. Different branches of the family participated in the activities of many Western financial and industrial institutions in Brussels, Paris, Frankfurt, Luxemburg and Houston.[59]

The foundations of the modern state machinery were laid during King Faisal's rule. Following the recommendations of Western experts, new ministries and administrative bodies were set up on a national scale. The number of state employees grew rapidly: in 1970 there were 10 ministries in the country with 120,000 employees; a mere decade later, there were 20 ministries and 20 other government agencies with more than 300,000 employees.[60] The state machinery was extremely inefficient, however, because of widespread incompetence and corruption. In the early 1980s the share of people with a secondary or higher education among office employees was about 20% in the case of Saudis and more than 60% in the case of foreigners.[61] Western observers noted that the productivity of Saudi employees was five times less than that of their Jordanian and Syrian counterparts. The poorest performance was noted at the lowest levels of the hierarchy, manned for political reasons by bedouin who had recently moved to the towns.[62]

Social policy

The creation of modern education and health systems had been among the government's priorities since the 1960s. The school attendance rate was 31% in 1970 and 49% in 1979. The number of primary schools grew from 1,977 in 1970 to 4,467 in 1980. The total number of schoolchildren and university students rose from 1.2 million in 1980 to 2.8 million in 1989, with the numbers of teachers at all levels rising from 78,300 to 184,300 over the same period. The share of female education institutions grew considerably: by 1989, of 16,797 institutions, 9,061 (54%) were for boys and 7,736 (46%) were for girls.[63] Schoolchildren received free textbooks, uniforms, meals and school buses. Higher education was also free. Many students were awarded scholarships and were sent abroad either to start or continue their higher education.

However, the growing numbers of young Saudis in educational institutions did not lead to the expected increase in the number of competent specialists in the economy and the social services. After graduating, many young Saudis turned to business. According to R. Cordes and F. Scholz, the government's attempts to raise the standing of education were crushed by its own employment policy. Numerous workplaces were created that did not require a highly educated workforce.[64]

The higher-education sector expanded dramatically. By the early 1990s, the country had 82 colleges with 115,000 students. There were 7 universities: King Saud University in Riyadh, the Islamic University in Medina, the University of Petroleum and Minerals in Dhahran, King Abd al-Aziz University in Jidda, Imam Muhammad ibn Saud Islamic University in Riyadh, King Faisal University in the Eastern Province and Umm al-Qura University in Mecca. Female students accounted for some 40% of graduates.[65] Until recently, Saudi students have preferred to study economics and the humanities. In pursuing its policy of the 'Saudization' of the workforce, the government paid particular attention to the training of specialists in technology. In the 1980s the number of engineering colleges grew from 5 to 42 and the number of their graduates from 188 to 4,667.[66] The education of Saudi students in the West has continued on the basis of interstate agreements and direct connections between individual universities. Degrees from US universities are considered particularly prestigious. An American author has observed that anyone who contacts the Saudi government will find himself dealing with 1,000 graduates of US universities.[67]

The foundations of a modern health system were also laid in the 1960s and the situation had changed radically by the early 1990s. The number of hospitals increased from 74 in 1980 to 254 in 1990; over the same period, hospital beds rose from 9,000 to 41,000; dispensaries from 75 to 498; doctors from 1,172 to 20,136; and other medical personnel from 5,002 to 70,887.[68] Average life expectancy in Saudi Arabia has ceased to be among the lowest in the Middle East: by 1990 it had risen to 63.7 years (from 49 years in 1965).[69] Infant mortality remains high, however: 154 deaths per 1,000 births in 1970 and 121 in 1982.[70] Trachoma, tuberculosis and other social diseases are still widespread.

In spite of the economic recession, the state built 2,242,000 housing units in the 1980s, and 465,000 more were built with the aid of state funds. The country had 154 sports clubs, 19 youth centres, 14 sports centres and 6 stadiums.[71] In spite of the temporary recession, the general upsurge in the economy and the government's social policies have substantially improved the living standards of a sizeable part of the population. Certain groups in society have adopted Western patterns of excessive consumption.

Social life

The preconditions for socio-economic change were not present within Saudi society until the late 1970s. But the crisis in the traditional economy, the influence of both neighbouring and distant countries, and the development of the capitalist sector of the economy on the basis of the oil industry (first imported and limited and then progressively expanding), prompted the government to undertake reforms.

Numerous speculative forecasts about the impending collapse of all the monarchies in the Arabian peninsula appeared in the late 1970s after the Shah's regime was overthrown in Iran. These prophecies were based on supposed comparisons with Iran: the outward similarity of economic development in the two countries, based on the oil-extraction industry; the political structures; and, most important, the widespread dissatisfaction with rapid modernization, the appearance of Western values and the lessening hold of traditional mores.[72]

It has now become clear, however, that Saudi Arabia lacked any major social groups that opposed the regime itself rather than its individual measures. The Saudi leaders responded to popular sentiment and strove to enable a sizeable part of the population to enjoy the fruits of the authorities' social policies. The social conflicts in the 1980s and at the beginning of the 1990s touched on the fundamental issues of social development, but were usually of limited significance and did not involve large numbers of the population. Although there were profound changes in communications, the economy, transport, industry, technology, education and health, there was no widespread movement for political change.

Any left-wing forces, such as the Saudi Communist Party, were weak. In a press interview in 1985, a party leader spoke of the 'weakening of the toilers' militant spirit' after the 1960s: 'The main event was the emergence of the consumer society. The Saudi workers are the favourites of fortune.'[73] During the oil boom, Saudi workers – who had waged an active struggle for their rights in the early 1950s – received many benefits for which West European workers had fought for almost one and a half centuries.

The programme of the Saudi Communist Party, adopted in August 1984, proclaimed the following aims: the achievement of democratic freedoms; the release of all political prisoners; the establishment of a modern criminal and civil justice system; and the recognition of the equality of all citizens before the law, irrespective of their religious affiliation or political views.[74] The communists faced two major obstacles: on the one hand, the action of the security services and, on the other, a lack of interest in their ideas and values on the part of ordinary Saudis. The fall of the communist regimes and the collapse of the USSR have deprived the Saudi communists of the hope of even a minimum role in the country's public life.

Social conflicts occurred chiefly between foreign workers and employers. In the early 1980s, with the general recession and the bankruptcy of dozens of construction companies, their foreign workers demanded that they should be paid their salaries and sent back to their countries of origin. In 1984, when the government's decision to abandon the construction of a new university building in Riyadh led to the bankruptcy of the American Karlson Group, more than 2,000 Pakistani and South Korean workers remained without any means of subsistence.[75] The authorities took responsibility for settling the conflicts, but anyone who organized a protest action was expelled from Saudi Arabia immediately. The authorities saw foreign workers as a threat to the stability of the country. Minister of Interior Prince Naif ibn Abd al-Aziz said in 1984 that expatriates threatened the Islamic faith and culture and therefore their number should be kept to a minimum.[76]

After the 1979 Iranian revolution, and the events at Mecca in the autumn of the same year, the Saudi authorities paid increasing attention to the formal observance of Islamic canons and standards of behaviour. In 1984 the importing of dolls became a punishable offence. The religious police stepped up their harassment of women who did not wear the veil. Members of the League of Public Morality did not confine themselves to checking attendance at prayers, but smashed the shop windows of photographic studios, closed mixed-gender beaches and tried to prevent the celebration of Christian holidays by Westerners living and working in the country.

In early 1984 Shaikh Abd al-Aziz ibn Baz, an authoritative member of the *ulama*, issued a statement entitled 'A Warning about the Danger of Travel to the Heretical Countries for the Faith and Moral Fundamentals'. He strongly denounced the activities of tourist bureaux that encouraged Saudi young people to travel to Western Europe and the US, thus turning them towards the path of evil. King Fahd backed Ibn Baz's statement in public. Similar attitudes also developed among some young Saudi intellectuals.[77] In the late 1970s and early 1980s new non-government, religious-political organizations appeared in the kingdom – Jamaa al-Tabit (The Doomsday Warning), Ahl al-Dawa (The People of Appeal), The Movement of the Islamic Revolution in the Arabian Peninsula, and al-Fajr (The Dawn), among others. They were oriented towards the preservation of fundamental Islamic values rather than towards any religious reform.

Owing to their egalitarian tone, the appeals for the preservation of traditional values and the denunciation of the Western way of life met with understanding and approval among many of the middle class and a sizeable part of the lower groups in society. This phenomenon reflected, on the one hand, people's deep-rooted, firmly held religious traditions and, on the other, their fear of being severed from their roots and their social group in an atmosphere of unprecedented and rapid change. Thus the main tension within Saudi society became the latent conflict between modern, Western values and lifestyles and traditional Islamic ideas, values and norms. The overall picture was not altered by Saudi society's access to the technological achievements of the West. An outstanding example, though of course with political overtones, was the flight of Prince Sultan (the first Saudi astronaut and the son of Salman, the governor of Riyadh) in a US spacecraft in August–September 1988.

Their extreme conservatism and their rejection of all *bida* led many religious leaders to oppose the regime. This was far more worrying for the authorities than the politically impotent movement of the handful of Saudi liberals and leftist radicals, which came to naught in the late 1980s. The liberals had demanded the elimination of the most backward vestiges of the past and a relaxation of the *sharia* in everyday life. But the religious extremists were more numerous, relied on a broader social base and had more publication facilities and opportunities to propagate their ideas.

Fearing a new wave of Islamic extremism, King Fahd tried to curb it and put social obstacles in its way. While demonstrating his support for Islam, he nevertheless sided openly with the protagonists of moderate social reforms.

On 6 November 1990 a group of forty-six women in traditional clothes blocked the traffic in a Riyadh street, demanding that the king allow women to drive cars. (Whereas there was no formal prohibition on female drivers, policemen regularly detained women who drove cars and kept them at police stations until their fathers or husbands came to take them home.) The authorities reacted negatively to the demonstration: the women all lost their jobs and their passports were confiscated. But the king met four of the demonstrators in April 1991 and made it clear that he was ready to consider their demands. Six months later, they were restored to their jobs, were paid compensation and had their passports returned, yet it was still not made legal for women to drive cars.

The majority of the population shunned both the liberals and the religious extremists, since the status quo suited their interests well. The lack of access to political power and the severe *sharia* laws were compensated for by the wide opportunities for business, education and employment in the state sector. The majority understood that sustained economic and social progress was only possible under stable conditions and with the decisive role of the state, which used its position as 'social arbiter' to maintain social peace. An end to the status quo might cause a social upheaval with unpredictable consequences.

Changes in the political structure

On 13 June 1982 King Khalid died after a prolonged illness – Crown Prince Fahd had already taken all affairs into his own hands. He became king and prime minister on the basis of the consensus of the most important princes, and appointed Prince Abdallah ibn Abd al-Aziz, his half-brother and the commander of the National Guard, as crown prince and first deputy prime minister. The king's full brother, Prince Sultan ibn Abd al-Aziz, the minister of defence and aviation, became second deputy prime minister.

Problems relating to the modernization of the state structure were covered in the press. The seizure of the Great Mosque in Mecca in autumn 1979 demonstrated the extent of discontent of a part of the population with the royal family's excessive privileges. In response, a committee was set up in March 1980, chaired by Prince Naif ibn Abd al-Aziz, the minister of interior, to draw up a 'government system' based on Islamic values. After a protracted delay, King Fahd's decrees were published in March 1992.[78] The first of them, called the Basic Law of Government, proclaimed, 'The Kingdom of Saudi Arabia is a sovereign Arab Islamic state with Islam as its religion; God's Book [the Quran] and the Sunnah of His Prophet . . . are its constitution . . .' The state's flag and emblem and the monarchic form of rule remained unchanged.

The country was to be ruled by the sons and grandsons of King Ibn Saud, the founder of the kingdom:

> The most upright among them is to receive allegiance in accordance with the principles of the Holy Koran and the Tradition of the Venerable Prophet . . . The

King chooses the Heir Apparent and relieves him of his duties by Royal order . . . The Heir Apparent is to devote his time to his duties as an Heir Apparent and to whatever missions the King entrusts him with . . . The Heir Apparent takes over the powers of the King on the latter's death until the act of allegiance has been carried out.

'Justice, consultation [*shura*] and equality' should underline the rule of the Al Saud. The document continued:

All God's bestowed wealth, be it under the ground, on the surface or in national territorial waters, in the land or maritime domains under the state's control, are the property of the state as defined by law . . . The state protects freedom of private property and its sanctity . . . Alms tax [*zakat*] is to be levied and paid to legitimate recipients.

The state pledged to protect Islam and implement the *sharia,* ensuring human rights in accordance with the *sharia* and promoting 'the achievement of the hopes of the Arab and Islamic nation for solidarity and unity of word'.

The state establishes and equips the armed forces for the defence of the Islamic religion, the Two Holy Places, society and the citizen . . . The defence of the Islamic religion, society and the country is a duty for each citizen . . . The state provides security for all its citizens and all residents within its territory and no one shall be arrested, imprisoned or have their actions restricted except in cases specified by statutes . . . Information, publication and all other media shall employ . . . the state's regulations, and they shall contribute to the education of the nation and the bolstering of its unity. All acts that foster sedition or division or harm the state's security and its public relations or detract from man's dignity and rights shall be prohibited . . . Telegraphic, postal, telephone and other means of communications shall be safeguarded. They cannot be confiscated, delayed, read or listened to except in cases defined by statutes.

The country's judicial authorities should be independent and follow the *sharia* in their activities:

The King, or whoever deputises for him, is responsible for the implementation of judicial rulings . . . The authorities establish the formation of the Higher Council of Justice and its prerogatives; they also establish the seniority of the courts and their prerogatives . . . The appointment of judges and the termination of their duties is carried out by Royal decree by a proposal from the Higher Council of Justice . . . The King carries out the policy of the nation . . .; [he] is the head of the Council of Ministers; he is assisted in carrying out his duties by members of the Council of Ministers . . . [which] establishes the prerogatives of the Council regarding internal and external affairs, the organisation of and co-ordination between government bodies . . . The King appoints and relieves deputies of the prime minister and ministers and members of the Council of Ministers by Royal decree . . . The King has the right to dissolve and reorganise the Council of Ministers . . . The King appoints those who enjoy the rank of ministers, deputy ministers and those of higher rank, and relieves them of their posts by Royal decree . . . The King is the commander-in-chief of all the armed forces. He appoints officers and puts an end to their duties in accordance with the law . . . The King declares a state of emergency, general mobilisation and war, and the law defines the rules for this . . . The King may delegate prerogatives to the Crown Prince by Royal decree . . . In the event of his travelling abroad, the King issues a Royal decree delegating to the Crown Prince the management of the affairs of state.

The king issued a royal decree embodying the status of the *majlis al-shura*. He was to set up the council, determine its procedure and select its members. He might dissolve or reorganize it. The *majlis al-shura* should consist of the chairman and 60 members, chosen by the king, with their rights and duties stipulated by royal decree. The qualifications for a council member included Saudi nationality and a minimum age of 30. The council's term of office was to be 4 *hijri* years. The text of the decree continued:

The King or whoever deputises for him will deliver annually a Royal speech at the Shura Council [*majlis al-shura*] on the state's internal and external policy . . . The Shura Council will express opinions on the general policy of the state, which will be referred to it by the Council of Ministers. In particular, it can do the following: (a) Discuss the general plan of economic and social development. (b) Study international laws, charters, treaties and agreements, and concessions and make appropriate suggestions regarding them. (c) Interpret laws. (d) Discuss annual reports submitted by ministries and other government bodies . . .

The decisions of the Shura Council will be submitted to the chairman of the Council of Ministers for deliberation. If the views of both Councils are concordant, they will be issued following the King's consent; if the views are different, the King has the right to decide what he deems fit . . .

The *majlis al-shura* might suggest new bills or changes in the law on the initiative of at least ten members.

In September 1992 King Fahd appointed Muhammad ibn Ibrahim ibn Jubairi, former minister of justice, as chairman of the *majlis al-shura*. The council had some elements of a representative assembly, which enabled it to become an influential state institution under certain circumstances.

Economy, Society, Politics (the 1980s and the 1990s)

Foreign policy

The foreign policy of Saudi Arabia in the 1980s and 1990s continued its earlier course and reacted to the challenges that threatened both the kingdom's security and its very existence. It was pursued at several interconnected levels – the regional level (the Arabian peninsula, the Gulf and the Red Sea); the pan-Arab level, with a stress on the country's role in the Arab-Israeli conflict; the pan-Islamic level; and the global level.

The Saudi leadership in the 1980s had inherited an exaggerated fear of leftist and revolutionary movements and regimes from the 1960s and 1970s, the period of confrontation with Nasser's Egypt. Owing to the interplay of history and geography, several leftist regimes emerged on Saudi Arabia's borders or in the immediate vicinity. The marxist regime in the PDRY was actively accumulating large quantities of arms, and in 1974 there was a military coup, with communist overtones, in Ethiopia. The pro-Soviet marxists came to power in Afghanistan in April 1978, and in December 1979 Soviet troops entered the country. Riyadh viewed all these developments with alarm. Although the Soviet leaders had no real intention of controlling the Gulf or overthrowing the Saudi regime, the Saudi leaders saw the USSR as their enemy.[79] This hindered the restoration of diplomatic relations with Moscow and the opening of a normal political dialogue. Saudi Arabia gave financial, material and political support to the Afghan armed opposition; it mobilized public opinion and the leaders of the Islamic states against the pro-Soviet regime in Kabul and the Soviet intervention. Riyadh supported the opposition in the PDRY and the Eritreans' armed struggle against Addis Ababa. The awareness of an external danger was increased by the growing influence of Baathist Iraq, which made no attempt to conceal its plans to compete with Iran for hegemony in the Gulf.

However, the main threat to the Saudi regime did not come from leftist radicals or pro-Soviet marxists. The fall of the Shah of Iran in 1979 destabilized the regional situation to a far greater extent than the activities of marxist groups in Ethiopia and Afghanistan. The call to 'overthrow the corrupt, pro-US regimes' which emanated from Tehran and Qom found a response both among the Shia community of the Eastern Province and among wider sectors of the Saudi population, who were deeply religious, conservative and anti-Western. When the protracted and bloody war between Iraq and Iran broke out in 1980, the Saudi regime supported Iraq. For several years the main task of Riyadh's foreign policy was to prevent Iran's victory and to ensure that Saudi Arabia did not become involved in the conflict.

Meanwhile, Saudi Arabia continued to make its presence felt on the pan-Arab stage. In 1981 it became one of the mediators during the Lebanese crisis. Its efforts continued in subsequent years. Riyadh tried actively to find a solution to the Palestine problem and the Arab-Israeli conflict. On 7 August 1981 Crown Prince Fahd put forward an eight-point peace plan, known as the 'Fahd plan'; for the first time, it admitted Israel's right to exist.[80] Although the initiative did not win universal approval among the Arabs and was rejected by Israel, it became a working document for most of the Arab states.[81]

Above all, the regime wanted to ensure that the US remained Saudi Arabia's main ally and protector, believing that no other power could save the kingdom from the leftist or external fundamentalist threat. In the 1980s cooperation between Riyadh and Washington increased considerably, particularly in the military field, including the purchase of arms from the US. During the Israeli invasion of Lebanon and the blockade of Beirut in 1982, Saudi Arabia denounced Israel, but did not take practical steps to put pressure on the US to force it to curb Israel's activities. At the Arab summit of September 1982 in Fez, King Fahd helped to draft a joint Arab plan for a peaceful settlement of the Middle East conflict, virtually on the basis of his earlier plan.[82]

As before, Riyadh attached particular importance to the YAR, the most populous country of the Arabian peninsula, and to the PDRY with its marxist regime. After establishing diplomatic relations with the PDRY in 1975, Saudi Arabia offered to provide financial and oil aid, hoping to change Aden's political course. When it became clear that Riyadh's hopes were unfounded, relations between the two countries deteriorated.

After the president of the YAR, Ahmad al-Ghashimi, was assassinated in June 1978 and succeeded by Ali Abdallah Salih, Riyadh agreed to pay for the arms and military hardware that the YAR purchased from the US, but insisted that Sanaa cease military cooperation with the USSR. Saudi aid to Sanaa grew during the war between the two Yemens in March 1979. After the ceasefire and the normalization of relations, however, Riyadh's relations with Sanaa deteriorated to the point that Saudi aid was briefly suspended (it resumed in 1980). The merger of the two Yemens in 1990 did not meet with much enthusiasm in Riyadh. An extremely poor, but potentially strong rival to Saudi Arabia had emerged in the peninsula. This might complicate the solution of major outstanding territorial disputes between the two countries.

In the 1970s and 1980s Saudi Arabia concentrated on developing regional cooperation in the Red Sea area, hoping to increase its influence there. The Ethiopian revolution of 1974 and the establishment of a revolutionary regime in Addis Ababa led to an extremely negative reaction from Riyadh. Saudi Arabia gave Somalia financial aid, probably amounting to hundreds of millions of dollars, and supported it in the war against Ethiopia in 1977. However, the Somali invasion of Ethiopia ended in failure. Saudi support for the Eritreans, who fought for independence from Ethiopia, proved more effective. When Mengistu Haile Mariam's pro-marxist regime fell in May 1991, Eritrea finally became independent.

In the 1970s and 1980s Saudi Arabia pursued its policy of support for right-wing regimes that had close ties with the West.[83] Saudi aid was frequently made conditional on the recipients adopting an anti-communist, anti-Soviet stance. In 1976 Riyadh gave the Mobutu government of Zaire $50m for its war against Angola. In 1977 it supported the NATO intervention in Zaire (which saved Mobutu) and paid the cost of transferring Moroccan troops by US aircraft to that country.[84] Thereafter Saudi Arabia again provided Zaire with financial aid. When Zaire restored diplomatic relations with Israel in 1982, however, Riyadh recalled its ambassador from Kinshasa.

Meanwhile, Gulf security and attempts to contain the danger posed by Iran and Iraq remained the priority tasks of Riyadh's regional policy. Faced with the Iranian threat, the Arab countries of the Gulf set up the Gulf Cooperation Council (GCC) in 1981 (Iraq's refusal to join was significant). Officially, the GCC's main tasks were economic cooperation and the coordination of economic development plans and industrial projects.[85] Some results were achieved in that field in the form of bilateral and multilateral agreements on customs regulations, the use of the workforce and the construction of petrochemical plants.

The situation in the early 1980s forced the GCC member states to concentrate on multilateral military cooperation and to coordinate their efforts in the field of domestic security. In November 1982 the Gulf states declared that they would form a Rapid Deployment Force (RDF) on the US model. Saudi Arabia was the main contributor to its formation. In October 1983 the Arabian RDF carried out a joint exercise in Oman to coordinate defence action in case of external aggression. It was obvious, nevertheless, that the Saudi and other oil monarchies were not strong enough, either separately or jointly, to confront Iran or Iraq. Thus the increased US military presence in the Gulf was welcomed in Riyadh and the other Gulf capitals,[86] though Riyadh preferred not to identify itself in public with US policy and even criticized it sometimes.

In April 1984 the threat arose of Saudi Arabia becoming directly involved in the Iran-Iraq war, when a Saudi cargo ship was hit by an Iranian missile. In May, the Iranian air force attacked two tankers in Saudi territorial waters. The Saudi military command took measures to strengthen the AD system on the eastern coast with US assistance, built the defensive 'Fahd line' and arranged patrols of Saudi cutters in the littoral waters.[87] When Iran repeatedly threatened to close the Strait of Hormuz, its statements were taken seriously, though it was clear that the US would not tolerate such a development. The Saudi regime confined itself to protests and maintained contacts with its powerful neighbour. In early 1985 Saud ibn Faisal, the minister of foreign affairs, went to Tehran: his visit did nothing to reduce the tension between the two states. In May 1985 several bombs exploded in Riyadh, killing one man and wounding three others. The Iran-based group, Islamic Jihad, claimed responsibility for the explosions and threatened to start a 'bombing campaign' throughout Saudi Arabia. The security services eliminated that danger.

On 31 July 1985 a clash occurred in Mecca between Iranian pilgrims and the Saudi police during the *hajj*: 402 people were reported killed, including 275 Iranians. Iran accused Saudi Arabia and the US of a premeditated provocation[88] and mass demonstrations were held in Tehran under anti-Saudi slogans. Saudi Arabia stated that Iran had tried to use the pilgrimage for political ends.[89] In March 1988 the Saudi authorities introduced new rules covering the pilgrimage, including quotas for individual countries of 1,000 pilgrims per 1 million of the population. Iran's quota was 45,000, but Ayatollah Khomeini demanded 150,000. When the Saudis refused, Khomeini prohibited Iranians from performing the *hajj*. It was only gradually that some of the differences between the two countries were settled. In May 1993, however, unrest again broke out among Iranians in the kingdom, resulting in 13 deaths.

The end of hostilities between Iran and Iraq in September 1988 was viewed with mixed feelings in Riyadh. On the one hand, it was the end of a military conflict that might have led to the destruction of the kingdom itself. On the other hand, Saddam Husain's dictatorship had grown stronger during the war; Iraq had increased its military capability and almost immediately made a bid for regional hegemony and expansion. On 2 August 1990 Iraq occupied Kuwait; some days later, it declared that Kuwait had been annexed. Saudi Arabia faced a serious threat of being dismembered and eventually disappearing from the political map. The threat was eliminated as a result of Iraq's defeat in February 1991 in the struggle against the multinational coalition, led by the US and backed politically by the USSR. Since the vicissitudes of the 1990-91 Gulf war, together with the regional and global implications for Saudi Arabia's domestic and foreign policy, have been dealt with extensively in the voluminous literature, the present book will not dwell further on the topic: the analysis of its long-term consequences must be left to the next generation of historians. With the end of the Cold War, the collapse of communism and the disintegration of the USSR, the situation throughout the world – and in the Middle East in particular – changed radically. Again, the consequences are outside the scope of the present work.

One event connected with the 1990-91 Gulf war cannot be ignored, however: the restoration of diplomatic relations between Riyadh and Moscow. The Soviet diplomatic mission had left Jidda in 1938 (see chapter 13), when Kerim A. Hakimov, the first Soviet ambassador, was recalled (he was later executed). Although relations between the two countries had not formally been severed, in practice they were non-existent for a long period. In the years of the Cold War, the Saudi regime saw the USSR as a threat to the kingdom because of the supposed strong connection between communism and Zionism. As a result of the particular ideological orientation of Soviet foreign policy, Moscow, in its turn, supported those Arab countries whose leaders proclaimed socialist slogans and pursued an anti-American policy. In the 1960s Soviet support for the Arab countries in their confrontation with Israel led to a change in Riyadh's attitude towards Moscow. The respective heads of state resumed the exchange of congratulations on official holidays and bilateral consultations were conducted through diplomatic channels. The Saudi rulers repeatedly expressed their appreciation of the USSR's contribution to a Middle East settlement.

The Soviet military intervention in Afghanistan in 1979 increased the Saudis' fear of Moscow, however. It was only the change of Soviet leadership in 1985 and the revision of the USSR's foreign policy by Mikhail Gorbachev that led to a positive change in bilateral relations. The new Soviet policy on Afghanistan became a serious test of the genuine intentions of all parties involved in the conflict, whether directly or otherwise. On the one hand, Saudi Arabia was the first to recognize the Mujahidin government; on the other, it helped to arrange negotiations between Soviet representatives and opposition forces in Afghanistan. In January 1988 Yuri M. Vorontsov, the first deputy minister of foreign affairs of the USSR, met the Mujahidin leaders in al-Taif. The withdrawal of Soviet troops from Afghanistan on 15 February 1989 removed the last obstacles to the normalization of relations between Moscow and Riyadh, but the exchange of ambassadors was repeatedly postponed. The breakthrough was caused by the Iraqi aggression against Kuwait in 1990.

In September 1990 full diplomatic relations were restored between Saudi Arabia and the USSR. The Saudi embassy opened in Moscow and the Soviet embassy in Riyadh.[90] Thereafter Moscow received Prince Saud ibn Faisal, the minister of foreign affairs, Hisham Nazir, the minister of petroleum and mineral resources, and Prince Faisal ibn Fahd,[91] the chairman of the General Organization for Youth Welfare. After the disintegration of the USSR, Russia assumed all its rights and duties in relations with Saudi Arabia. Andrei V. Kozyrev, the Russian minister of foreign affairs, visited Riyadh in April 1992, followed by other prominent Russian political figures. Multi-faceted connections gradually developed between the two countries. In December 1991 Saudi Arabia recognized twelve post-Soviet republics as independent states. It paid special attention to the Central Asian republics, with their large Muslim majorities. King Fahd sent millions of free copies of the Quran to the Central Asian Muslims and facilitated the conditions under which they could undertake the *hajj*.

The traditional message of King Fahd and Crown Prince Abdallah to the pilgrims – and, at the same time, to the whole population of the kingdom – on the eve of the *hajj* season of 1992 was viewed as an important policy statement. The creation of the new Muslim republics on the territory of the former Soviet Union was described as a manifestation of the 'greatness of the Muslim religion'.[92] The Saudi rulers reaffirmed their striving 'to support these countries and to help these nations to revive' without intervening in their domestic affairs. Statements on the situation in Afghanistan and Bosnia-Herzegovina followed the same line. In November 1994 the Russian prime minister, Victor Chernomyrdin, paid a visit to Saudi Arabia and met with King Fahd.

Conclusion

The development of oil production, the increase in oil exports and, to some extent, the start of oil processing after the Second World War had a profound and multifaceted, though contradictory, influence on Saudi Arabia's economy, society and politics and led to significant socio-economic changes. A gigantic modern enterprise with advanced technology and modern labour methods was imported from the world's most developed country into a kingdom with a medieval economy and largely feudal-tribal social relations.

The growth of oil production, followed in the early 1970s by the dramatic rise in oil prices, increased direct payments to the Saudi government many times over. Even when a sizeable part of the oil revenues was spent on consumption, this stimulated the development of the market economy, hastened the destruction of the traditional sectors of the economy and encouraged the development of the capitalist sector. That process accelerated still further when the national accumulation fund began expanding rapidly and the regime was obliged to create a state sector.

Within a mere three or four decades, the country achieved many successes: the economy was transformed, a secular education system from primary to university level was created and the basis of a modern health system was established. Considering the amount of financial resources available, however, the results might have been more impressive. The upper echelons of society consumed huge sums of money and spent them unproductively on the armed forces, the security services and the bureaucracy. The government's socio-economic projects were inspired both by a striving for progress and by propaganda motives – attempts to convince the population that the oil revenues were being spent not only on the needs of the royal family and their entourage, but also on the people's welfare.

Conclusion

The objective development needs of Saudi society – from the creation of a diversified national economy, based on modern technology, to the sedentarization of the bedouin, from the expansion of female education to the training and rational use of local personnel – conflicted with the archaic socio-political context. The conflict was aggravated by the relative youth of the socio-political system itself – it had been set up a mere two generations ago. The centralized, feudal-tribal state, which had been created in the 1920s and 1930s, not only corresponded to the development level of Arabian society at the time, but was actually a step forward compared with the previous feudal-tribal fragmentation, internecine clashes and separatist trends. By the 1970s, however, both Saudi society and the new forms of its political organization lagged behind the modern era by many centuries. Modern capitalism burst upon Saudi Arabia, bringing high-tech enterprises, modern communications, mass media, the market economy, military technology and new forms of organization. This led to the emergence of new social groups and the introduction of new ideas.

In spite of the archaic nature of the Saudi regime, its members proved relatively stable; their hold on power was tenacious and they began to adapt to the changing conditions. One of the features of the ruling elite was the fact that it was indigenous. It was not imposed from outside, but had grown from the bosom of Arabian society. It was represented by the numerous members of the Al Saud, who played the role of 'dominant tribe'; by the feudal, tribal and clerical nobility, who were connected by socio-political and family ties to the Al Saud; and by the large traders and the new bourgeoisie. The relative stability of the Al Saud's power stemmed from the fact that, whereas they suppressed all opposition, particularly from the left, their 'tribe' satisfied the interests of the other groupings within the ruling elite, the bureaucracy and the military and ensured their loyalty. Another reason was the ordinary Saudi's interest in stability and improved living standards. The Al Saud maintained a cautious balance between conservative circles, who prevailed in the ruling group, and the growing ranks of the protagonists of reform and limited modernization.

The specific feature of the Saudi ruling group was that the overwhelming part of their income was not based on the private ownership of land, livestock and so on. Their wealth originated in their status as the Arabian feudal-tribal elite and in their reliance on the state machinery (where they formed the upper echelons), the security services, the army, the police, the legal system and the remnants of the military-tribal organization. The main source of their income came from land rent, which merged with the tax rent and was based on the huge amounts of oil on Saudi territory.

The ruling group in Saudi Arabia, as well as in other Arabian oil monarchies, has acquired another feature: it has become a part of the international financial oligarchy. The colossal sums invested by the Saudi elite in US and West European securities and banks have made them an influential grouping in the international financial system. (Their true influence is far less than the value of their accounts and securities, however, because of a shortage of specialists, the underdeveloped Saudi banking system and a lack of experience.) There has never been a clear distinction between the Al Saud's 'own money' and the state exchequer: thus it is not clear who exactly owns the funds

Conclusion

invested abroad. The ruling group participates – though often in a secondary role – in banking, company, trade and other activities in both developed and developing countries through the channels of international financial organizations and transnational corporations.

The dual character of the ruling elite of Saudi Arabia – a group with feudal-tribal origins that is now a major financial player on the international stage – helps to explain Saudi Arabia's foreign policy, which sometimes seems contradictory. As an ally of the US, the regime should support American foreign policy. But as the custodians of the holy places of Islam and the imams of the community of 'monotheist' Muslims, the Saudi rulers (in line with their interest in ensuring a stable regime) have had to oppose Israel's foreign policy, impose an oil embargo to the detriment of US interests, support the cause of the Arab people of Palestine, demand that East Jerusalem with the al-Aqsa mosque be liberated from the 'infidels' and denounce the 1978 Camp David accords between Egypt and Israel.

There was a centralized distribution of oil revenues in Saudi Arabia through the direct division of a part of the revenues among the ruling group or through corruption, which became a semi-legal practice. The bulk of the money moved downwards – from the monarch to his entourage, to the feudal, tribal and clerical nobility and to the merchants. (This was a continuation of the earlier practice in the feudal-tribal Arabian state.)

An indigenous bourgeoisie developed in the country, based on trade, land speculation, contracts, the construction of housing and some industrial activities. In the 1970s the status of the big trading houses in Saudi society was equal to that of the influential bedouin shaikhs, though the traders' wealth was immeasurably greater. The merchants had close links with the regime and with the Al Saud. The regime suited them insofar as it helped them to accumulate great wealth within a short space of time, ensuring the necessary social stability through the operations of the security services or through 'bribing' potentially dangerous elements in society. The state financed Saudi companies, whether directly or indirectly, granting them credits, subsidies and profitable contracts and exempting them from income tax, company tax and duties on imports of equipment, machinery and materials.[1]

The merger of merchant houses with the ruling group took two forms. Increasing numbers of the feudal-tribal nobility – from the Al Saud to minor tribal shaikhs – engaged in lucrative speculative and trade activities. But the Al Saud had to appoint representatives of the merchants to prestigious and lucrative posts. Members of the leading commercial families headed ministries, embassies and important agencies. Even though there was no intermarriage between the merchant families (who had no 'genealogical trees') and the feudal-tribal nobility (who were proud of their 'blue blood' and clearly traced ancestry), this was no obstacle to their cooperation in the fields of business, social relationships and politics.

The conservatism of the upper echelons of the great trading families resulted not only from domestic considerations. Their traditional cooperation with foreign capital made it easy for them to become agents as contractors and importers of ready-made

Conclusion

articles, raw materials and equipment. This applies both to the new middle class, which sprang up around Aramco in the Eastern Province, and to the old-established merchant families of Hijaz.

There is no information on any conflict of interest between the ruling elite and the growing bourgeoisie. It is likely, however, that those members of the bourgeoisie who were involved in trade and speculative activities were dissatisfied with the division of the 'oil cake', whose largest piece was consumed by members of the Al Saud. The bourgeoisie saw more clearly the danger of the growing gap between the 'top' and 'bottom' groups in society. They probably feared that the traditional character of the regime might lead to a social explosion that would destroy both the monarchical structure and the old and new merchant houses. That is why, in spite of their basic conservatism, they advocated reforms.

Nor is there any information on the attitudes of the middle class and middle strata in society, including medium-sized wholesalers and retailers, and the ex-bedouin, who now ran modern farms or owned small companies and workshops in light industry, or engaged in services and the repair of cars and domestic appliances. It may be assumed that these groups derived growing incomes from the economic boom, but were nevertheless dissatisfied with their lack of political rights. Unlike the big trading houses, they had no say even in decision-making at the 'technical level'. Less educated, usually loyal to tradition and influenced by the *mutawwas* and the *ulama*, they might form a conservative opposition to the regime due to their dissatisfaction with the extravagance of some members of the ruling elite and with the government's moderate reforms, interpreted as *bida* (unacceptable innovation).

The oil revenues benefited, directly or otherwise, the urban population and the intermediate groups in society, such as state employees, the army, the police, technical specialists and teachers. Some 'noble' bedouin tribes, who were loyal to the Al Saud, grew rich on government subsidies, thus expanding the regime's social base: part of these elements were incorporated into the lower echelons of the ruling group, their loyalty assured by generous allowances.

It was among the middle-class urban population that the few signs of political organization emerged. The leftist opposition – consisting of young army officers, journalists, teachers, employees and small traders, together with some Saudi oil workers – formed the backbone of several underground organizations. As mentioned previously, they borrowed the fundamentals of their ideology from outside and failed to win any broad support within Saudi society itself.

The enrichment of the top groups in society, and the newfound prosperity of the middle class, barely touched the bulk of the population. Peasants with little or no land, poor bedouin and small craftsmen bore the burden of the transformation of society. Their living standards did not rise significantly in spite of the state's vastly increased income. Imports ruined many producers. The transition to new occupations and hired labour was accompanied by a painful breakdown of the earlier way of life and did not automatically lead to improved social welfare. The majority of the population lived as if in two dimensions, both capitalist and pre-capitalist at the same time.

Conclusion

In the 1950s and 1960s thousands of foreign experts – managers, engineers, technicians, teachers, doctors, journalists and economists – were employed in the state sector, in business and in the liberal professions. They assumed the socio-political role that might have belonged to the middle groups within Saudi society. The situation was aggravated in the late 1960s and 1970s, when the growth in incomes and the increased rate of economic development brought in hundreds of thousands of skilled and unskilled immigrants.. The overwhelming majority did not become Saudi citizens and they inherited the role of the *sunnaa* (craftsmen) and freedmen of traditional Arabian society: thus they could become rich and influential in their respective fields, but never became equal to the ruling elite or enjoyed political rights. This created new social tensions, though the immigrants played no active political role, concentrating instead on increasing their earnings and aware of the tight control of the police and security services. Almost the same situation persisted in the 1980s and 1990s.

The creation of a centralized state, the ending of intertribal wars and raids, and the disappearance of tribes and their confederations as independent political entities, had already started to weaken the tribal structure in the 1930s. The process of replacing tribal solidarity by other social ties was greatly accelerated by the sedentarization of the bedouin, the growth of towns, the joint participation of members of different tribes in industrial and trade activities and the population migration within the country.[2]

Like other countries with strong kinship and tribal traditions, Saudi Arabia nevertheless retained many elements of these traditions even under the new socio-economic conditions. Kinship and the affiliation to a clan or tribe still determined an individual's place in society and his success or failure both in the traditional and in the new spheres of activity.[3] The interests and solidarity of a kinship group took priority over the interests of an individual or those outside the group. Favouritism towards the members of one's family, clan or tribe dominated the economic sphere, the state bureaucracy and the armed forces. The maintenance of the family's honour and reputation was considered the duty of all. Shaikhs and members of the tribal nobility continued to enjoy great authority and few people rose to the top echelons without suitable family connections.

It should be noted that we have deliberately avoided using the term 'tribalism' in the case of Saudi Arabia, since scholars apply it mainly to the societies of sub-Saharan Africa. Instead we have used the expression 'kinship and tribal ties'. Although Islam recognized the equality of all individuals, it coexisted peacefully for many centuries with the tribal structure of Arabian society. After the defeat of the Ikhwan movement in 1929, tribal and kinship ties found a place in the structure of the centralized state. Naturally, they did not disappear within the mere four or five decades of the oil era. Clan ties were still frequently considered more important than competence or other business qualities; personal trust and sympathies were more valuable than accurate accounting. Such an attitude was hardly compatible with the development of a market economy and the modernization of society. Mutual assistance within a tribe, and the patriarchal authority of a head of family or tribe, often proved stronger than the new social relationships.

Conclusion

Although family ties remained important in Saudi society, their character nevertheless began to change as large tribal confederations were gradually replaced by smaller family groups. These changes were particularly noticeable among those groups with a modern education, such as officials, traders, intellectuals and skilled workers. Educated Saudis started to prefer monogamy: polygamy disappeared both because of the increasing cost of maintaining a large family and because monogamy corresponded more to the modern lifestyle. 'Modern' families were increasingly inclined to educate their daughters and even their wives. The new kind of family reflected an evolution in the way of life and thought as a result of a modern education and the conflict between the generations. But a secular education combined with a high income was not sufficient to result in the universal creation of the nuclear family. On marrying and leaving his father, a son continued to demonstrate respect and gratitude for him and maintain close family connections. Members of the same family preferred to live near to each other, even in modern cities. Women continued to wear the veil in public and to avoid meeting men other than their closest relatives.

It should be remembered that in Arabia the word 'Arabs' denoted nomads, first of all bedouin tribes. It did not apply to *fellahin* (hereditary farmers), slaves, freedmen, 'lower tribes' or *sunnaa*. The extended sense of the word is a twentieth-century phenomenon.

A national consciousness – in other words, the sense of belonging to a Saudi nation – took time to develop.[4] However, the emergence of new means of communication and information, the growing economic interdependence of the provinces, increased contact with foreigners and travel abroad all revealed the differences between the Saudi culture and way of life and those of other countries: this, in turn, accelerated the formation of the nation and a feeling of national affiliation. Nevertheless the true formation of the 'Saudi nation', even as part of the vague concept, *al-umma al-arabiya* (the Arab nation), still has a long way to go before it reaches the level of Egypt or Syria. Despite a common language, culture, history and territory, and the growing economic unity, family, tribal and communal connections remain stronger than 'national' ones. One may agree with M. W. Wenner's assertion:

> It is important to emphasize that tribal organization, tribal values and norms, and the political 'weight' of the tribes within the context of Arabian society remained intact in the new order . . . It is this characteristic of twentieth century Saudi Arabia which makes it literally impossible to suggest that nationalism, as it is understood in the social science literature, may be found in that country.[5]

The idea of a national territorial state, of a 'motherland', was new to Arabian society. The very concept of a motherland, to which individuals owe their primary loyalty, contradicts the spirit of Islam, which stresses the universal solidarity of believers as against non-Muslims.

National consciousness and national feelings in Saudi Arabia were confined to a narrow group working in the modern sector of the economy and in the civil and military bureaucracy. Those who described themselves as nationalists were, rather, reformers and modernists who wanted to create a more modern society. But their sentiments were so vague that the left wing of the 'nationalists' even avoided using the name Saudi Arabia because of their attitude to the Al Saud. Thus the assertions of some scholars of a connection between the formation of the Saudi nation (and the manifestation of nationalist sentiment) and loyalty to the king cannot be supported.[6] One example is found in the *Area Handbook*: 'For most of the people awareness of national political life meant simply that they acknowledged the king as their sovereign and identified him as the imam (religious leader).'[7]

Besides kinship ties, Islam was another dominant force in Saudi society. It permeated the socio-economic structure (which had been created according to Islamic canons), the legal system and all aspects of everyday life. Islam's impact on Saudi society was perhaps felt more intensely than elsewhere in the Islamic world because Saudi Arabia is the birthplace of Islam and had remained isolated from the rival ideological and cultural trends. Saudi Arabia was never under the influence of a dominant foreign culture such as that of France in North Africa and Lebanon, France and Britain in Egypt, or even of Britain in the Gulf states and South Yemen. It was not until the late 1960s and 1970s that the wide-scale penetration of Western consumer values, together with the effect of several thousand Saudis studying in the US, prompted a growth of American influence. This influence was nevertheless limited and affected only a relatively small number of wealthy, educated Saudis.

In Saudi Arabia the Wahhabi (Hanbali) form of Islam was identified with traditional social institutions (such as the system of distribution of state revenues); with the system of power, personified by the Al Saud and the groups that supported them; with the outdated legal system; with the traditional education system, whose main subject was theology; and with the medieval way of thinking, combined with a sense of fatalism. Saudi 'modernists', from the 'free princes' to the new middle class and the small leftist opposition, demanded that Islam be modernized in accordance with the needs of the late twentieth century and the rapid socio-economic changes in Saudi society.

However, the Al Saud referred to the Islamic canons in order to legitimize and preserve their power. Prince Abdallah ibn Abd al-Aziz's reply to the 'free princes' in the Beirut papers *al-Safa* and *al-Hayat* in 1962 is significant:

> [Prince] Talal alleges that there is no constitution in Saudi Arabia which safeguards democratic freedoms. But Talal knows full well that Saudi Arabia has a constitution inspired by God and not drawn up by man. I do not believe there is any Arab who believes that the Koran contains a single loophole which would permit an injustice to be done. All laws and regulations in Saudi Arabia are inspired by the Koran and Saudi Arabia is proud to have such a constitution . . .
>
> As for his statement about socialism, there is no such thing as rightist or leftist socialism; true socialism is the Arab socialism laid down by the Koran.
>
> Talal talked at length about democracy. He knows that if there is any truly democratic system in the world it is the one now existing in Saudi Arabia.[8]

Conclusion

Islam in its Wahhabi form, together with tribal and clan ties, are still significant, long-term factors in Saudi society. Even with the rapid development of market relations, they will continue to influence the evolution of socio-political structures and the character of potential conflicts within society.

Saudi Arabia has experienced more rapid change than any other Middle Eastern country and the old social balance has been lost for ever. The country has faced acute domestic crises of a nature that it had not experienced earlier. These were caused by changes in its social composition, with the growth of a bourgeoisie, the weakening of kinship and tribal ties, the collision between the interests of different classes and social groups, and the clash between traditional notions and new socio-political ideas. Yet it is difficult to ascertain the degree of social tension in the country. The Saudi press has been silent on social problems. Political parties, trade unions, clubs and meetings are banned. The leftist opposition has had to go underground or emigrate.

Up to the 1990s the regime was fairly successful in dealing with social unrest. The ruling elite – including the Al Saud, at the apex of the social pyramid – demonstrated its reluctance to give up power. Nevertheless it was this elite that carried out limited reforms: it was not the middle class, the army or the bureaucracy (these groups had taken power in several Arab countries, but often failed to retain it). The Al Saud cautiously modernized Saudi society under pressure from the educated members of the bureaucracy, the armed forces and business circles. As early as the 1960s and 1970s, a new labour code was introduced, economic plans were set in motion, TV appeared, a secular education system was created, including girls' schools, and some changes occurred in everyday life. The evolution towards elements of a constitutional system could be observed in the 1990s. All these innovations (*bida*) would have been unthinkable earlier, but the regime used limited 'modernization' to protect itself from dangerous social upheavals. Realizing that they could not do without a modern education, the Al Saud ensured a first-class education for their members. At the same time, the regime coopted educated and loyal people from other social groups – especially from among the major merchants – into the topmost echelons of the bureaucracy.

To preserve their socio-political and economic positions and maintain social stability, the regime strengthened the security services and the armed forces. The army, the National Guard and the police took a sizeable part of the budget and the latest arms and equipment were purchased for them. Their numerical strength increased several times over. The Al Saud never hesitated to suppress leftist or other opposition.

The colossal oil revenues enabled the regime to 'pay off' those who demanded radical change. The inflated and ineffective, but prestigious and well-paid state machinery absorbed potential malcontents and political activists. The economic boom encouraged the aspirations of large groups within society. The regime managed to ensure a social base that was both broad and firm – it consisted of the urban middle class, the bureaucracy, the 'noble' bedouin tribes (who received royal subsidies), the conservative merchants and the growing number of businessmen. Another feature of Saudi society was that a sizeable part of those groups who might potentially be hostile to the regime were influenced by the traditional leaders – the shaikhs, the *mutawwas* and the *ulama*. In addition, they received some material support from the authorities. It is the combination of reforms from above, the increase in the security apparatus, the socio-economic support for a sizeable part of the population and the basic conservatism of Saudi society that has ensured the stability of one of the world's most traditional regimes.

Saudi Arabia has preserved, though in a new form, many values of Arab and Islamic civilization and the traditional system of power and government while, at the same time, adopting Western technology, a market economy and a modern state education, health-care and other public-sector services. Modern scientific and technological knowledge is accessible not only to a few individuals, but to a sizeable part of the population, who nevertheless continue to maintain their religious convictions and their traditional cultural and ethical background. It is difficult to say whether this combination of modern and traditional elements, of Western and Arab (Islamic) civilizations, will prove to be an organic synthesis or a mechanical sum of the different parts. There are no historical precedents. To draw parallels with similar countries and regimes would distort the picture out of all recognition. The socio-political and economic model of Saudi Arabia (and of the other Gulf oil states) is unique. With regard to Saudi Arabia's role in the areas of oil, finance and Islam, any serious changes or social unrest in the country may have far-reaching international consequences.

Notes

A 'short-title' system has been used throughout the notes. For full publishing details of the works mentioned, the reader is referred to the bibliography.

Preface

1. When a date is shown as, for example, 1796/97, this indicates that the original *hijri* date gives no month and so may be either of two years in the Western calendar. (In the later chapters a date such as 1994/95 indicates a financial year.)

Chapter 1
1. C. Doughty, *Travels*, vol. 2, p. 355.
2. G. A. Wallin, *Notes*, p. 25.
3. A. I. Pershits, *Khozyaystvo*, p. 28.
4. C.-F. Volney, *Voyage*, p. 203.
5. R. Montagne, *La Civilisation*, p. 45.
6. G. A. Wallin, *Narrative*, p. 198.
7. J. L. Burckhardt, *Notes*, vol. 2, p. 32.
8. H. Philby, *Heart of Arabia*, vol. 2, p. 97.
9. C. Doughty, *Travels*, vol. 2, pp. 6, 401.
10. F. Mengin, *Histoire*, vol. 2, p. 175.
11. For details on towns, see: A. I. Pershits, *Khozyaystvo*, pp. 47–66.
12. J. L. Burckhardt, *Notes*, vol. 1, p. 70.
13. R. Montagne, *La Civilisation*, p. 45.
14. G. A. Wallin, *Narrative*, p. 125; C. Doughty, *Travels*, vol. 1, p. 153; C. Niebuhr, *Voyage*, vol. 1, p. 247; J. L. Burckhardt, *Notes*, vol. 1, pp. 42–46, 191, 245–246; F. Mengin, *Histoire*, vol. 2, p. 174.
15. *Lam al-Shihab*, pp. 499–501.

Notes

16. Ibid., pp. 510–517.
17. A. I. Pershits, *Khozyaystvo*, p. 57.
18. C. Doughty, *Travels*, vol. 1, p. 480.
19. A. I. Pershits, *Khozyaystvo*, p. 89.
20. G. A. Wallin, *Narrative*, p. 140; A. Jaussen, *Coutumes*, pp. 236–238.
21. A. I. Pershits, *Khozyaystvo*, pp. 95–96.
22. Ibn Bishr, *Unwan*, part 1, p. 11; F. Mengin, *Histoire*, vol. 2, p. 450.
23. *Lam al-Shihab*, p. 287.
24. W. C. Palgrave, *Narrative*, vol. 1, pp. 315, 461.
25. C. Doughty, *Travels*, vol. 2, pp. 355, 388.
26. Ibn Bishr, *Unwan*, part 1, p. 12.
27. J. L. Burckhardt, *Travels*, vol. 1, pp. 40–41, 91, 436–438.
28. C. Niebuhr, *Voyage*, vol. 2, pp. 19–20, 176.
29. *Lam al-Shihab*, pp. 447–465.
30. F. Mengin, *Histoire*, vol. 2, p. 164.
31. R. Montagne, *La Civilisation*, p. 52.
32. A. I. Pershits, *Khozyaystvo*, pp. 69–72, on the basis of materials collected by J. L. Burckhardt, C. Doughty, C. Huber, A. Jaussen, A. Musil, R. Montagne, A. Boucheman, H. Philby and other explorers.
33. C.-F. Volney, *Voyage*, p. 205.
34. J. L. Burckhardt, *Notes*, vol. 1, pp. 228–229.
35. C. Huber, *Journal*, pp. 671, 674; A. Jaussen, *Coutumes*, p. 238.
36. H. Philby, *Heart of Arabia*, vol. 2, p. 13.
37. A. G. Shcherbatov, S. A. Stroganov, *Kniga*, p. 8.
38. C.-F. Volney, *Voyage*, pp. 211–212.
39. C. Doughty, *Travels*, vol. 1, p. 344.
40. C. Niebuhr, *Voyage*, vol. 2, pp. 210–217.
41. C.-F. Volney, *Voyage*, pp. 205–206.
42. A. I. Pershits, *Khozyaystvo*, pp. 77–79.
43. J. L. Burckhardt, *Notes*, vol. 1, pp. 167–176.
44. A. Musil, *Manners and Customs*, pp. 452–453, 471.
45. R. Montagne, *La Civilisation*, p. 66.
46. C.-F. Volney, *Voyage*, pp. 208–209.
47. Ibid., pp. 204–205.
48. J. L. Burckhardt, *Notes*, vol. 1, p. 69.
49. A. Jaussen, *Coutumes*, p. 273.
50. Ibid., p. 278; C. Guarmani, *Northern Najd*, p. 107.
51. J. L. Burckhardt, *Notes*, vol. 1, p. 246.
52. See: A. I. Pershits, *Khozyaystvo*, p. 126.
53. J. L. Burckhardt, *Notes*, vol. 1, p. 317.
54. C.-F. Volney, *Voyage*, p. 207.
55. A. Jaussen, *Coutumes*, pp. 199, 208–220.
56. On this question, see: G. E. Markov, *Kochevniki*, ch. 5–6; B. V. Andrianov, *Neosedloe*, part 1. The latter author gives some data on the numerical strength and roaming places of the Arabian nomads.
57. J. L. Burckhardt, *Notes*, vol. 1, p. 133.
58. C.-F. Volney, *Voyage*, p. 211.
59. C. Niebuhr, *Voyage*, vol. 2, p. 139.
60. J. L. Burckhardt, *Notes*, vol. 1, pp. 140–141; C. Guarmani, *Northern Najd*, p. 116; C. Doughty, *Travels*, vol. 1, pp. 251, 334.
61. C.-F. Volney, *Voyage*, p. 207.
62. A. Jaussen, *Coutumes*, p. 124.

Notes

63. J. L. Burckhardt, *Notes*, vol. 1, pp. 193–194.
64. G. A. Wallin, *Narrative*, p. 122.
65. Ibid.; C. Guarmani, *Northern Najd*, pp. 109–110; C. Huber, *Journal*, p. 592.
66. C. Guarmani, *Northern Najd*, pp. 109–110.
67. H. Dickson, *Kuwait*, pp. 102, 622; H. Dickson, *Arab of the Desert*, pp. 572, 573.
68. Ibn Bishr, *Unwan*, part 1, p. 126.
69. J. L. Burckhardt, *Notes*, vol. 1, p. 194; vol. 2, pp. 9, 34.
70. C. Niebuhr, *Voyage*, vol. 3, pp. 178–179.
71. A. Musil, *Manners and Customs*, pp. 280–282.
72. J. L. Burckhardt, *Notes*, vol. 2, pp. 19–20.
73. R. Montagne, *La Civilisation*, pp. 68, 107; C. Guarmani, *Northern Najd*, p. 120; A. Musil, *Manners and Customs*, p. 406.
74. R. Montagne, *La Civilisation*, p. 23.
75. C. Doughty, *Travels*, vol. 2, p. 136.
76. For details on slavery, see: A. I. Pershits, *Khozyaystvo*, pp. 97–107.
77. W. G. Palgrave, *Narrative*, vol. 1, p. 452.
78. Ibid., p. 453.
79. J. L. Burckhardt, *Notes*, vol. 1, p. 181.
80. Ibid.
81. Ibid., pp. 181–182.
82. G. A. Wallin, *Notes*, p. 26.
83. A. Musil, *Manners and Customs*, p. 277.
84. Pershits, too, holds that 'the edge of the shaikhs' exploitation was directed outside the nomadic tribes or their nomadic parts, perhaps even more than inside' (A. I. Pershits, *Khozyaystvo*, p. 140).
85. A. Jaussen, *Coutumes*, pp. 140–145.
86. J. L. Burckhardt, *Notes*, vol. 1, p. 117.
87. C. Doughty, *Travels*, vol. 1, p. 248.
88. J. L. Burckhardt, *Notes*, vol. 1, p. 117.
89. C. Doughty, *Travels*, vol. 1, pp. 248–249.
90. J. L. Burckhardt, *Notes*, vol. 1, p. 296.
91. A. Jaussen, *Coutumes*, pp. 128–129.
92. C.-F. Volney, *Voyage*, p. 208.
93. C. Doughty, *Travels*, vol. 1, p. 251.
94. J. L. Burckhardt, *Notes*, vol. 1, pp. 119–123.
95. The evolution of Pershits' views on this question may be traced in: A. I. Pershits, *Khozyaystvo*, pp. 153, 159; A. I. Pershits, *Nekotorye*, pp. 308–309.
96. C.-F. Volney, *Voyage*, pp. 207–208.
97. J. L. Burckhardt, *Notes*, vol. 1, pp. 116–117.
98. Some specific functions of nomadic kinship-tribal organization are described in: I. M. Reysner, *Razvitie*, pp. 115–116, and other sources.
99. A. Blunt, *A Pilgrimage*, vol. 1, pp. 260–261, 270.
100. C. Niebuhr, *Voyage*, vol. 2, pp. 29–31; J. L. Burckhardt, *Travels*, vol. 1, pp. 331, 405–408, 440.
101. C. Doughty, *Travels*, vol. 2, p. 50; C. Guarmani, *Northern Najd*, pp. 46–48, 91–92; R. Montagne, *La Civilisation*, pp. 151–158; W. C. Palgrave, *Narrative*, vol. 1, pp. 109–113.
102. C. Doughty, *Travels*, vol. 2, p. 368.
103. J. L. Burckhardt, *Travels*, vol. 1, pp. 415–417; Ibn Ghannam, *Tarikh*, part 2, p. 5.
104. R. Montagne, *La Civilisation*, p. 66.
105. Ibid., p. 141.
106. A. I. Pershits, *Khozyaystvo*, pp. 147–148.
107. C. Doughty, *Travels*, vol. 1, p. 251.

Notes

108. C.-F. Volney, *Voyage*, p. 207.
109. L. Pelly, *A Visit*, pp. 189–190.
110. R. Montagne, *La Civilisation*, pp. 110, 134.
111. Ibid., p. 18.
112. J. R. Wellsted, *Travels*, vol. 2, pp. 258–260; C. Doughty, *Travels*, vol. 1, pp. 280–282; H. Philby, *Heart of Arabia*, vol. 1, p. 268.
113. A. Musil, *Manners and Customs*, pp. 136, 281.
114. See: G. de Gaury, *Rulers*, pp. 147–153.
115. See: G. Goodwin, *Janissaries*.
116. See: C. Niebuhr, *Voyage*, vol. 2, pp. 16, 26–29, 178–179.
117. Ibn Bishr, *Unwan*, part 1, pp. 64–65.
118. Ibid., pp. 61, 85, 110–122.
119. H. Philby, *Saudi Arabia*, p. 18.
120. Ibn Bishr, *Unwan*, part 1, p. 223.
121. Ibid., p. 138.
122. Ibid., p. 218.
123. H. Philby, *Saudi Arabia*, p. 30.
124. *Lam al-Shihab*, pp. 58–59.
125. M. al-Ajlani, *Tarikh*, part 1, pp. 68, 77.
126. Ibn Bishr, *Unwan*, part 1, pp. 157, 160, 212, 223–224.
127. Ibid., pp. 234–235.
128. Ibid., pp. 99, 224, 229.
129. Ibid., pp. 234–235.
130. Ibn Ghannam, *Tarikh*, part 2, pp. 5–6.
131. M. Abir, *Relations*, p. 34.

Chapter 2

1. *Zhurnal Razlichnykh Predmetov Slovesnosti*, 1805, vol. 2, no. 1, p. 20.
2. Ibn Ghannam, *Tarikh*, part 1, p. 25; Ibn Bishr, *Unwan*, part 1, p. 6. The date given by F. Mengin (1696) is a result of an inaccurate conversion of AH 1116 to the Gregorian calendar, since AH 1116 is AD 1704/05 (*Histoire*, vol. 2, p. 449).
3. Ibn Ghannam, *Tarikh*, part 1, pp. 25–26; Ibn Bishr, *Unwan*, part 1, pp. 6–7.
4. Ibn Bishr, *Unwan*, part 1, p. 7.
5. Ibid.; Ibn Ghannam, *Tarikh*, part 1, p. 28.
6. Ibn Bishr, *Unwan*, part 1, p. 8.
7. Ibid.
8. Ibn Ghannam, *Tarikh*, part 1, pp. 29–30.
9. Ibn Bishr, *Unwan*, part 1, p. 8; Ibn Ghannam, *Tarikh*, part 1, pp. 29–30; F. Mengin, *Histoire*, vol. 2, p. 449.
10. According to F. Mengin, he stayed in Uyaina for eight years, i.e. he arrived there in 1736/37 (*Histoire*, vol. 2, p. 449).
11. *Encyclopédie de l'Islam*, 1924, vol. 4, p. 1144.
12. See: Abd al-Aziz ibn Abd al-Rahman's preface to: Ibn Abd al-Wahhab, *Mufid*, p. 13.
13. *Lam al-Shihab*, pp. 7–32.
14. A. Dahlan, *Khulasat*, p. 228.
15. *The Encyclopaedia of Islam*, 1971, vol. 3, pp. 677–679.
16. Munir al-Ajlani, *Tarikh*, part 1, p. 196.
17. *Lam al-Shihab*, pp. 47–48.
18. I. Goldziher, *Le Dogme*, p. 49.
19. Ibid., p. 224.
20. See: G. Goodwin, *Janissaries*.
21. C. Niebuhr, *Voyage*, vol. 1, pp. 393–394; vol. 2, pp. 21, 204. Twentieth-century travellers

Notes

also observed them. See: H. Philby, *Heart of Arabia*, vol. 2, p. 299.
22. C. Niebuhr, *Voyage*, vol. 2, p. 21; C. Niebuhr, *Description*, p. 298.
23. Ibn Ghannam, *Tarikh*, part 1, pp. 5–13.
24. Ibn Abd al-Wahhab, *Kitab al-Tawhid*, p. 118.
25. Ibn Bishr, *Unwan*, part 1, pp. 6–7.
26. See: Abd al-Rahman ibn Hasan's commentary to Ibn Abd al-Wahhab's *Kitab al-Tawhid* in: *Majmuat al-Tawhid*, p. 64.
27. W. G. Palgrave, *Narrative*, vol. 1, pp. 99–102.
28. C.-F. Volney, *Voyage*, p. 212.
29. J. L. Burckhardt, *Notes*, vol. 1, pp. 99–102.
30. W. G. Palgrave, *Narrative*, vol. 1, p. 9.
31. R. Montagne, *La Civilisation*, pp. 73–75.
32. W. C. Palgrave, *Narrative*, vol. 1, p. 33.
33. G. A. Wallin, *Notes*, p. 21.
34. [Davletshin], *Otchet*, p. 8.
35. A. Jaussen, *Coutumes*, p. 316.
36. Ibid., p. 174; A. Musil, *Manners and Customs*, pp. 571–573.
37. A. Musil, *Manners and Customs*, p. 509.
38. Ibn Abd al-Wahhab, *Kitab al-Tawhid*, p. 134.
39. Ibn Abd al-Wahhab, *Usul al-Iman*, pp. 167–170; Ibn Abd al-Wahhab, *al-Usul al-Thalatha*, p. 8; Abd al-Aziz I, *al-Risala*, p. 19.
40. Ibn Abd al-Wahhab, *Fadhl*, p. 198.
41. Ibn Abd al-Wahhab, *Kitab Kashf*, pp. 220–223, 232; Ibn Abd al-Wahhab, *Masail*, pp. 123–125.
42. Ibn Abd al-Wahhab, *Kitab al-Tawhid*, p. 56.
43. Ibn Abd al-Wahhab, *Kitab al-Kabair*, p. 206; Abd al-Aziz I, *al-Risala*, p. 5.
44. Ibn Abd al-Wahhab, *Kitab al-Tawhid*, pp. 60, 70, 86; Ibn Abd al-Wahhab, *al-Usul al-Thalatha*, p. 42; Ibn Abd al-Wahhab, *Masail*, p. 76.
45. Ibn Abd al-Wahhab, *Mufid*, p. 28; Ibn Abd al-Wahhab, *Masail*, p. 70; Abd al-Aziz I, *al-Risala*, p. 6.
46. Ibn Abd al-Wahhab, *Kitab al-Tawhid*, p. 67.
47. Ibid., p. 90; Ibn Abd al-Wahhab, *Kitab Kashf*, p. 226.
48. Ibn Abd al-Wahhab, *Masail*, pp. 91, 120; Ibn Abdul Wahhab, *Kitab Kashf*, p. 230. Ibn Abd al-Wahhab's grandson, Abd al-Rahman ibn Hasan's, commentary to *Kitab al-Tawhid*, p. 102; Abd al-Aziz I, *al-Risala*, pp. 10, 13; Ibn Abd al-Wahhab, *Kitab al-Tawhid*, pp. 74, 87, 207–209; Abdallah ibn Muhammad ibn Abd al-Wahhab, *al-Risala*, pp. 47–48.
49. Ibn Abd al-Wahhab, *Kitab al-Tawhid*, pp. 111, 118; Ibn Abd al-Wahhab, *Masail*, pp. 33, 144.
50. Ibn Abd al-Wahhab, *Kitab al-Tawhid*, p. 52.
51. Abd al-Aziz I, *al-Risala*, p. 5; Ibn Ghannam, *Tarikh*, part 1, p. 38.
52. C. Didier, *Séjour*, p. 179; [J. Rousseau], *Description*, pp. 129, 146.
53. Abdallah ibn Muhammad ibn Abd al-Wahhab, *al-Risala*, p. 53.
54. A. Krymski, *Istoriya*, p. 201; Ahmad Amin, *Zuama*, p. 13.
55. Ibn Ghannam, *Tarikh*, part 1, pp. 17, 19, 53.
56. Abdallah ibn Muhammad ibn Abd al-Wahhab, *al-Risala*, p. 53.
57. J. I. Burckhardt, *Notes*, vol. 2, p. 113.
58. See: A. Krymski, *Istoriya*, p. 195.
59. Ibn Sanad, *Tarikh*, p. 32.
60. [L. A. Corancez], *Histoire*, pp. 7, 18.
61. Al-Faqih, *Athr*, p. 4.
62. H. Wahba, *Jazirat*, pp. 308–309.
63. Quoted from: A. Attar, *Muhammad ibn Abd al-Wahhab*, p. 151.

Notes

64. [L. A. Corancez], *Histoire*, p. 18.
65. J. L. Burckhardt, *Notes*, vol. 1, p. 102.
66. Ibn Bishr, *Unwan*, part 1, pp. 53–54; Ibn Hasan, *Fath*, p. 4.
67. H. A. R. Gibb, *Mohammedanism*, p. 168.
68. Ahmad Amin, *Zuama*, pp. 21–23.
69. Ibn Abd al-Wahhab, *Sittat*, p. 275.
70. Ibn Abd al-Wahhab, *Kitab al-Kabair*, p. 225.
71. Ibn Abd al-Wahhab, *Mufid*, p. 37; Abd al-Aziz I, *al-Risala*, p. 33; al-Muammari, *al-Risala*, p. 68.
72. Abdallah ibn Muhammad ibn Abd al-Wahhab, *al-Risala*, p. 46.
73. Ibn Abd al-Wahhab, *Kitab al-Kabair*, pp. 238–239, 241.
74. Ibn Abd al-Wahhab, *Nasihat*, pp. 323–324, 328.
75. Ibn Bishr, *Unwan*, part 1, pp. 165–166; al-Jabarti, *Egipet*, p. 326.
76. Ibn Abd al-Wahhab, *Kitab al-Kabair*, p. 240.
77. Ibid., p. 243.
78. Abdallah ibn Muhammad ibn Abd al-Wahhab, *al-Risala*, pp. 48–49.
79. Ibn Abd al-Wahhab, *Nasihat*, pp. 281, 286, 299.
80. Ibn Abd al-Wahhab, *Kitab al-Kabair*, p. 213.
81. Ibn Abd al-Wahhab, *Nasihat*, p. 332.
82. Ibn Abd al-Wahhab, *Kitab al-Kabair*, pp. 212–214, 219, 222, 230.
83. Ibn Abd al-Wahhab, *Nasihat*, pp. 254, 260, 262, 278.
84. Ibn Abd al-Wahhab, *Kitab Kashf*, pp. 227–228.
85. A. Dahlan, *Khulasat*, p. 232.
86. Ibn Sanad, *Tarikh*, p. 23.
87. E. A. Belyaev, *Musulmanskoe*, p. 99.
88. [L. A. Corancez], *Histoire*, p. 16.
89. A. Dahlan, *Khulasat*, p. 230.
90. Abdallah ibn Muhammad ibn Abd al-Wahhab, *al-Risala*, p. 45.
91. See: I. Goldziher, *Le Dogme*, p. 225.
92. See: M. V. Churakov, *Novaya*, p. 89, where it is mentioned that Wahhabism reflected the trend of feudal unity.
93. Ibn Abd al-Wahhab, *Kitab al-Kabair*, p. 231.
94. Abdallah ibn Muhammad ibn Abd al-Wahhab, *al-Risala*, p. 54.
95. Ibid., p. 43; Ibn Bishr, *Unwan*, part 1, p. 151; [L. A. Corancez], *Histoire*, p. 17.
96. J. L. Burckhardt, *Notes*, vol. 1, p. 102; vol. 2, p. 115.
97. Ibid., vol. 2, p. 114.
98. Ibid., vol. 2, pp. 110–111.
99. J. Raymond, *Les Wahabys*, p. 34.
100. Ibn Bishr, *Unwan*, part 1, p. 9; see also Ibn Ghannam, *Tarikh*, part 1, p. 30.
101. Ibn Ghannam, *Tarikh*, part 1, pp. 30–31; Ibn Bishr, *Unwan*, part 1, p. 9.
102. Ibn Bishr, *Unwan*, part 1, pp. 9–10.
103. Ibid., p. 10; F. Mengin, *Histoire*, vol. 2, pp. 449–450.
104. Ibn Ghannam, *Tarikh*, part 2, p. 2.
105. Ibid.
106. Ibid., p. 3; Ibn Bishr, *Unwan*, part 1, pp. 10–11; F. Mengin, *Histoire*, vol. 2, p. 450; *Lam al-Shihab*, pp. 62–65.
107. F. Mengin, *Histoire*, vol. 2, p. 450.
108. Ibn Ghannam gives AH 1157 (part, 2, p. 4), and Ibn Bishr gives AH 1158 (part, 1, p. 15). See also F. Mengin, *Histoire*, vol. 2, p. 452.
109. Ibn Ghannam, *Tarikh*, part 2, p. 3; Ibn Bishr, *Unwan*, part 1, p. 11.
110. Ibn Bishr, *Unwan*, part 1, p. 12. Ibn Ghannam mentions only the first condition (part 2, p. 3).

Notes

Chapter 3
1. Ibn Ghannam, *Tarikh*, part 2, p. 4; Ibn Bishr, *Unwan*, part 1, p. 13.
2. Ibn Bishr, *Unwan*, part 1, p. 13.
3. Ibid., p. 14.
4. Ibn Ghannam, *Tarikh*, part 2, pp. 9–12; Ibn Bishr, *Unwan*, part 1, p. 21.
5. Ibn Bishr, *Unwan*, part 1, p. 23.
6. Ibn Ghannam, *Tarikh*, part 2, p. 12; Ibn Bishr, *Unwan*, part 1, p. 22.
7. Ibn Ghannam, *Tarikh*, part 2, pp. 13–14; Ibn Bishr, *Unwan*, part 1, pp. 23-24; *Lam al-Shihab*, p. 75.
8. Ibn Ghannam, *Tarikh*, part 2, p. 57; Ibn Bishr, *Unwan*, part 1, p. 43; F. Mengin, *Histoire*, vol. 2, p. 457.
9. Ibn Ghannam, *Tarikh*, part 2, pp. 6, 9, 12, 15, 17; Ibn Bishr, *Unwan*, part 1, pp. 18–26; F. Mengin, *Histoire*, vol. 2, pp. 451–454. Mengin dates these events to the second half of the 1740s.
10. Ibn Ghannam, *Tarikh*, part 2, p. 20.
11. Ibid., p. 45; Ibn Bishr, *Unwan*, part 1, pp. 29–30.
12. Ibn Ghannam, *Tarikh*, part 2, p. 19; Ibn Bishr, *Unwan*, part 1, p. 28; F. Mengin, *Histoire*, vol. 2, p. 454, where this event is dated to 1748.
13. Ibn Ghannam, *Tarikh*, part 2, p. 53; Ibn Bishr, *Unwan*, part 1, p. 40.
14. Ibn Ghannam, *Tarikh*, part 2, pp. 54–57; Ibn Bishr, *Unwan*, part 1, pp. 42–43. F. Mengin gives 1757, gradually moving closer to the Arabian annalists' dating, and the dates of the events since 1769/70 coincide (*Histoire*, vol. 2, p. 456).
15. Ibn Ghannam, *Tarikh*, part 2, pp. 57–63; Ibn Bishr, *Unwan*, part 1, pp. 43–47; F. Mengin, *Histoire*, vol. 2, pp. 457–461.
16. According to F. Mengin, he was considered an astrologer (*Histoire*, vol. 2, p. 462).
17. Ibn Ghannam, *Tarikh*, part 2, pp. 65–66; Ibn Bishr, *Unwan*, part 1, pp. 47–48; F. Mengin, *Histoire*, vol. 2, p. 462.
18. Ibn Ghannam, *Tarikh*, part 2, pp. 66–68; Ibn Bishr, *Unwan*, part 1, pp. 48–49; *Lam al-Shihab*, p. 77; F. Mengin, *Histoire*, vol. 2, pp. 463–464. Niebuhr, who visited al-Hasa in the mid-1760s, also reports the defeat inflicted on the Wahhabis by the Najranis and Arayar's invasion of Najd. However, he mentions a certain Makrami as the Najranis' shaikh. In his opinion, the clashes between the Wahhabis and the people of al-Hasa occurred before the hostilities against Najran (C. Niebuhr, *Description*, pp. 299-300).
19. Ibn Ghannam, *Tarikh*, part 2, p. 74; Ibn Bishr, *Unwan*, part 1, p. 49; F. Mengin, *Histoire*, vol. 2, p. 465.
20. Ibn Ghannam, *Tarikh*, part 2, pp. 75–82; Ibn Bishr, *Unwan*, part 1, pp. 49–58; F. Mengin, *Histoire*, vol. 2, pp. 465–470.
21. Ibn Ghannam, *Tarikh*, part 2, pp. 82–86; Ibn Bishr, *Unwan*, part 1, pp. 60–61; F. Mengin, *Histoire*, vol. 2, pp. 473–474.
22. H. Philby, *Saudi Arabia*, p. 62.
23. Ibn Ghannam, *Tarikh*, part 2, p. 9.
24. Ibid., pp. 88–94; Ibn Bishr, *Unwan*, part 1, pp. 63–64; F. Mengin, *Histoire*, vol. 2, pp. 474–478.
25. Ibn Ghannam, *Tarikh*, part 2, pp. 88–90, 94; Ibn Bishr, *Unwan*, part 1, pp. 61–63; F. Mengin, *Histoire*, vol. 2, pp. 475–478; *Lam al-Shihab*, pp. 156–159.
26. Ibn Ghannam, *Tarikh*, part 2, pp. 91–107; Ibn Bishr, *Unwan*, part 1, pp. 70–72; F. Mengin, *Histoire*, vol. 2, pp. 480–486. The general picture of Najd is similar in the three sources, but the details differ.
27. F. Mengin, *Histoire*, vol. 2, pp. 479–480.
28. Ibid., pp. 483–484.
29. Ibn Ghannam, *Tarikh*, part 2, p. 95; Ibn Bishr, *Unwan*, part 1, p. 65; F. Mengin, *Histoire*, vol. 23, p. 479.

Notes

30. Ibn Ghannam, *Tarikh*, part 2, pp. 91–114; Ibn Bishr, *Unwan*, part 1, pp. 75–76; F. Mengin, *Histoire*, vol. 2, pp. 485–486.
31. Ibn Ghannam, *Tarikh*, part 2, p. 119; Ibn Bishr, *Unwan*, part 1, p. 78.
32. Ibn Ghannam, *Tarikh*, part 2, pp. 120–124; 132; Ibn Bishr, *Unwan*, part 1, p. 78–80. F. Mengin dates the annexation of al-Kharj and Dilam to 1783 (*Histoire*, vol. 2, p. 492).
33. Ibn Ghannam, *Tarikh*, part 2, pp. 124–131; Ibn Bishr, *Unwan*, part 1, pp. 79–80; F. Mengin, *Histoire*, vol. 2, pp. 491, 496–499.
34. Ibn Bishr, *Unwan*, part 1, p. 75. Ibn Ghannam (*Tarikh*, part 2, pp. 110–111) also reports the fact, but gives no figures.
35. Ibn Ghannam, *Tarikh*, part 2, pp. 126–130; Ibn Bishr, *Unwan*, part 1, pp. 77–82. F. Mengin dates the annexation of Jabal Shammar to 1785 (*Histoire*, vol. 2, p. 496).
36. Ibn Ghannam, *Tarikh*, part 2, p. 136; Ibn Bishr, *Unwan*, part 1, p. 83; F. Mengin, *Histoire*, vol. 2, p. 499. From 1783 the difference in dates between the Arabian sources and Mengin's work reappears.
37. Ibn Ghannam, *Tarikh*, part 2, p. 137; Ibn Bishr, *Unwan*, part 1, p. 83. According to F. Mengin, it happened in 1787 (*Histoire*, vol. 2, pp. 499–500).
38. Ibn Ghannam, *Tarikh*, part 2, pp. 124–125; Ibn Bishr, *Unwan*, part 1, p. 80. F. Mengin dates it to 1784 (*Histoire*, vol. 2, pp. 492–493).
39. Ibn Ghannam, *Tarikh*, part 2, pp. 127–129; Ibn Bishr, *Unwan*, part 1, p. 81. F. Mengin gives 1785 (*Histoire*, vol. 2, pp. 494–495).
40. Ibn Ghannam, *Tarikh*, part 2, pp. 129–130; Ibn Bishr, *Unwan*, part 1, pp. 81–83; F. Mengin, *Histoire*, vol. 2, p. 496. F. Mengin dates the event to the autumn of 1785, and some details of his description differ from those found in the Arabian annals.
41. Ibn Ghannam, *Tarikh*, part 2, pp. 135–138; Ibn Bishr, *Unwan*, part 1, p. 83. F. Mengin's date is 1786 (*Histoire*, vol. 2, p. 499). Some sources (*Lam al-Shihab*, pp. 172, 175) give the Wahhabi commander's name as Ibrahim ibn Ufaisan.
42. Ibn Ghannam, *Tarikh*, part 2, pp. 138–139; Ibn Bishr, *Unwan*, part 1, pp. 84–85; F. Mengin, *Histoire*, vol. 2, pp. 500–501.
43. Ibn Ghannam, *Tarikh*, part 2, p. 141.
44. Ibid., pp. 142–153; Ibn Bishr, *Unwan*, part 1, pp. 85–86; F. Mengin, *Histoire*, vol. 2, pp. 502–503. The details of the events differ in the above sources and *The Brilliance of the Meteor* because of the rapid succession of events and frequent changes of side by many people, which created a kaleidoscopic picture.
45. Ibn Ghannam, *Tarikh*, part 2, p. 153.
46. Ibid., pp. 152–153; Ibn Bishr, *Unwan*, part 1, p. 88.
47. Ibn Ghannam, *Tarikh*, part 2, pp. 157–162; Ibn Bishr, *Unwan*, part 1, pp. 97–99; F. Mengin, *Histoire*, vol. 2, pp. 507–509.
48. Ibn Ghannam, *Tarikh*, part 2, p. 154; Ibn Bishr, *Unwan*, part 1, p. 89; F. Mengin, *Histoire*, vol. 2, p. 506.
49. Ibn Bishr, *Unwan*, part 1, p. 90.
50. F. Mengin, *Histoire*, vol. 2, p. 506.
51. *Lam al-Shihab*, p. 67.
52. F. Mengin, *Histoire*, vol. 2, p. 506. According to *Lam al-Shihab* [The Brilliance of the Meteor], Ibn Abd al-Wahhab left four sons and six daughters. This does not contradict Mengin's data, since some of the children might have died when their father was still alive.
53. *Lam al-Shihab*, pp. 265–266, 477–478.
54. Ibn Ghannam, *Tarikh*, part 2, pp. 158–166; Ibn Bishr, *Unwan*, part 1, pp. 97–101; F. Mengin, *Histoire*, vol. 2, pp. 508–509. Mengin does not give all the details, but Ibn Ghannam's data are more reliable, as he was a contemporary witness to the events he describes.
55. Ibn Ghannam, *Tarikh*, part 2, pp. 174–175.
56. Ibid., pp. 174–185; Ibn Bishr, *Unwan*, part 1, pp. 105–106.
57. Ibn Bishr, *Unwan*, part 1, p. 106.

Notes

58. Ibn Ghannam, *Tarikh*, part 2, p. 184.
59. *Lam al-Shihab*, pp. 184–186.
60. C.-F. Volney, *Voyage*, pp. 81–82; J. L. Burckhardt, *Travels*, vol. 1, p. 412.
61. A. Dahlan, *Khulasat*, p. 228; Ibn Bishr, *Unwan*, part 1, p. 23.
62. Ibn Ghannam, *Tarikh*, part 2, pp. 80–81; Ibn Bishr, *Unwan*, part 1, pp. 58–59; F. Mengin, *Histoire*, vol. 2, pp. 470–471.
63. F. Mengin, *Histoire*, vol. 2, p. 490.
64. Al-Shawkani, *al-Badr*, part 2, p. 4; J. L. Burckhardt, *Travels*, vol. 1, pp. 410–413; C. Didier, *Séjour*, pp. 171–172.
65. J. L. Burckhardt, *Travels*, vol. 1, pp. 415–417.
66. Ibn Ghannam, *Tarikh*, part 2, p. 144.
67. A. Dahlan, *Khulasat*, pp. 261–262; Ibn Ghannam, *Tarikh*, part 2, pp. 145–152; Ibn Bishr, *Unwan*, part 1, pp. 86–87; F. Mengin, *Histoire*, vol. 2, pp. 502–505.
68. Ibn Ghannam, *Tarikh*, part 2, p. 171; Ibn Bishr, *Unwan*, part 1, pp. 102–103; F. Mengin, *Histoire*, vol. 2, p. 510.
69. Ibn Ghannam, *Tarikh*, part 2, p. 173; Ibn Bishr, *Unwan*, part 1, pp. 103–105; F. Mengin, *Histoire*, vol. 2, pp. 510–511.
70. Al-Muammari, *al-Risala*, p. 55; Ibn Ghannam, *Tarikh*, part 2, pp. 200–203.
71. Ibn Ghannam, *Tarikh*, part 2, p. 174; Ibn Bishr, *Unwan*, part 1, p. 105.
72. F. Mengin, *Histoire*, vol. 2, p. 514; Ibn Ghannam, *Tarikh*, part 2, p. 245; Ibn Bishr, *Unwan*, part 1, p. 111.
73. Ibn Ghannam, *Tarikh*, part 2, pp. 242–247; Ibn Bishr, *Unwan*, part 1, pp. 112–117; F. Mengin, *Histoire*, vol. 2, pp. 516–517.
74. Ibn Bishr, *Unwan*, part 1, pp. 120–121.
75. F. Mengin, *Histoire*, vol. 2, p. 521.
76. Al-Shawkani, *al-Badr*, part 2, p. 7.
77. S. H. Longrigg, *Four Centuries*, pp. 199–200.
78. Ibid., p. 202.
79. Ibn Bishr, *Unwan*, part 1, p. 52.
80. F. Mengin, *Histoire*, vol. 2, p. 511; Ibn Ghannam, *Tarikh*, part 2, pp. 186–187.
81. Ibn Bishr, *Unwan*, part 1, pp. 107–108.
82. F. Mengin, *Histoire*, vol. 2, p. 511.
83. Ibn Ghannam, *Tarikh*, part 2, pp. 193–199, 233–235; Ibn Bishr, *Unwan*, part 1, pp. 107–110; F. Mengin, *Histoire*, vol. 2, pp. 511–514; Ibn Sanad, *Tarikh*, pp. 21–23.
84. Ibn Bishr, *Unwan*, part 1, pp. 111–112; F. Mengin, *Histoire*, vol. 2, p. 517.
85. Ibn Bishr, *Unwan*, part 1, pp. 118–119; F. Mengin, *Histoire*, vol. 2, pp. 518–519.
86. H. J. Brydges, *An Account*, vol. 2, p. 17.
87. [L. A. Corancez], *Histoire*, p. 23.
88. J. L. Burckhardt, *Notes*, vol. 2, p. 184.
89. Ibn Sanad, *Tarikh*, p. 24.
90. J. Raymond, *Les Wahabys*, p. 12.
91. Ibn Bishr, *Unwan*, part 1, pp. 118–119; F. Mengin, *Histoire*, vol. 2, pp. 518–521; J. Raymond, *Les Wahabys*, pp. 12–15; *Lam al-Shihab*, pp. 342–366.
92. Ibn Sanad, *Tarikh*, pp. 24–25.
93. H. J. Brydges, *An Account*, vol. 2, pp. 24–27.
94. Ibn Sanad, *Tarikh*, p. 27.
95. Ibn Bishr, *Unwan*, part 1, pp. 121–122.
96. [J. Rousseau], *Description*, p. 73.
97. [L. A. Corancez], *Histoire*, p. 27.
98. J. L. Burckhardt, *Notes*, vol. 2, p. 186.
99. F. Mengin, *Histoire*, vol. 2, pp. 522–524.
100. H. Philby, *Saudi Arabia*, p. 93.

Notes

101. Ibn Sanad, *Tarikh*, p. 28.
102. J. Raymond, *Les Wahabys*, p. 16.
103. *Zhurnal Razlichnykh Predmetov Slovesnosti*, 1805, vol. 2, no. 2, p. 25; *Vestnik Evropy*, 1819, no. 7, pp. 72–75.
104. [J. Rousseau], *Description*, pp. 72–75.
105. See: J. Raymond, *Les Wahabys*, p. 1.
106. J. Rousseau (*Description*, p. 74) gives a more realistic figure of 200 camels.
107. *The Archives of Russian Foreign Policy* (henceforth: *ARFP. The Office Section*), 1803, file 2235, pp. 38–40.
108. F. Mengin, *Histoire*, vol. 2, pp. 522–524.
109. Ibn Bishr, *Unwan*, part 1, pp. 121–122.
110. S. H. Longrigg, *Four Centuries*, p. 217.
111. J. Raymond, *Les Wahabys*, p. 21; H. J. Brydges, *An Account*, vol. 2, p. 28; [L. A. Corancez], *Histoire*, pp. 28, 186.
112. F. Mengin, *Histoire*, vol. 2, p. 525.
113. G. de Gaury, *Rulers*, pp. 181–182.
114. M. Abir, *Relations*, pp. 34–40.
115. J. L. Burckhardt, *Travels*, vol. 1, pp. 440–441.
116. Ibn Bishr, *Unwan*, part 1, p. 122/1; F. Mengin, *Histoire*, vol. 2, p. 526.
117. Ibn Bishr, *Unwan*, part 1, pp. 122/1-3; J. L. Burckhardt, *Travels*, vol. 1, p. 154; Ahmad Dahlan dates the capture of al-Taif to early 1803 (*Khulasat*, pp. 274–275).
118. *ARFP. The Office Section*, 1803, file 2234, vol. 1, p. 154.
119. Ibid., p. 251.
120. Ibid., p. 300.
121. Ibn Bishr, *Unwan*, part 1, pp. 122/2-3; F. Mengin, *Histoire*, vol. 2, p. 527; A. Dahlan, *Khulasat*, p. 277; J. L. Burckhardt, *Notes*, vol. 2, p. 184.
122. Ibn Bishr, *Unwan*, part 1, pp. 122/2-3; F. Mengin, *Histoire*, vol. 2, pp. 527–528; A. Dahlan, *Khulasat*, pp. 277–279; J. L. Burckhardt, *Notes*, vol. 2, pp. 195–196.
123. *A Dictionary of Islam*, p. 660. For more on the *mahmal*, see ch. 12 of the present work.
124. *ARFP. The Office Section*, 1804, file 2242, p. 202.
125. Ibid., 1803, file 2234, vol. 2, p. 580.
126. Ibid.
127. Ibid., file 2235, p. 249.
128. Ibid., pp. 184–186.
129. Ibid.
130. Ibid., pp. 211–214.
131. Ibid.
132. Ibn Bishr, *Unwan*, part 1, p. 130; A. Dahlan, *Khulasat*, pp. 280–285.
133. *ARFP. The Office Section*, 1803, file 2235, p. 407; J. L. Burckhardt, *Notes*, vol. 2, p. 196.
134. *ARFP. The Office Section*, 1803, file 2235, p. 260.
135. Ibid., p. 293.
136. Ibn Bishr, *Unwan*, part 1, p. 123.
137. J. L. Burckhardt, *Notes*, vol. 2, pp. 201–202; H. J. Brydges, *An Account*, vol. 2, p. 32; [L. A. Corancez], *Histoire*, p. 42; *ARFP. The Office Section*, 1804, file 2241, vol. 1, p. 95.
138. F. Mengin, *Histoire*, vol. 2, p. 529.
139. Ibn Bishr, *Unwan*, part 1, p. 124.
140. *Lam al-Shihab*, pp. 273–276.
141. *ARFP. The Office Section*, 1804, file 2241, vol. 1, pp. 95–96.
142. Ibid., file 2242, p. 94.
143. Ibn Bishr, *Unwan*, part 1, pp. 132–133; F. Mengin, *Histoire*, vol. 2, p. 531; A. Dahlan, *Khulasat*, p. 285.
144. A. Dahlan, *Khulasat*, p. 285.

Notes

145. Ibid., pp. 285–292; Ibn Bishr, *Unwan*, part 1, pp. 133–134, 144; F. Mengin, *Histoire*, vol. 2, p. 533.
146. Ibn Bishr, *Unwan*, part 1, pp. 133–134; A. Dahlan, *Khulasat*, p. 292.
147. Ibn Bishr, *Unwan*, part 1, p. 135. F. Mengin dates the event to 1809 (*Histoire*, vol. 2, p. 534).
148. J. L. Burckhardt, *Notes*, vol. 2, p. 203; J. L. Burckhardt, *Travels*, vol. 2, pp. 277–287.
149. J. L. Burckhardt, *Travels*, vol. 2, pp. 169–170; A. Dahlan, *Khulasat*, pp. 294–295, 303. F. Mengin dates the destruction of Muhammad's grave to 1810 (*Histoire*, vol. 2, pp. 535–536).
150. J. L. Burckhardt, *Notes*, vol. 2, p. 199.
151. Ibid., p. 203.
152. Ibn Bishr, *Unwan*, part 1, pp. 137–145, 151. His report differs from the data given by F. Mengin (*Histoire*, vol. 2, pp. 534–535).
153. Ibn Bishr, *Unwan*, part 1, p. 151.
154. [L. A. Corancez], *Histoire*, pp. 34–35, 74–81.
155. A. Dahlan, *Khulasat*, p. 285.
156. [L. A. Corancez], *Histoire*, p. 102.
157. K. M. Bazili, *Siriya*, p. 79.
158. [L. A. Corancez], *Histoire*, pp. 126–132.
159. Al-Jabarti, *Egipet*, pp. 210–211.
160. J. L. Burckhardt, *Notes*, vol. 2, pp. 204–205, 210; J. L. Burckhardt, *Travels*, vol. 2, p. 13.
161. For details, see: R. B. Winder, *Saudi Arabia*, pp. 92–93.
162. Ibn Bishr, *Unwan*, part 1, p. 122.
163. Salil ibn Razik, *History*, pp. 248–250.
164. Ibid., pp. 229–230.
165. *Lam al-Shihab*, pp. 201–206.
166. Salil ibn Razik, *History*, pp. 229–230; F. Mengin, *Histoire*, vol. 2, p. 522; J. G. Lorimer, *Gazetteer*, vol. 1, p. 424.
167. F. Mengin, *Histoire*, vol. 2, p. 522; Salil ibn Razik, *History*, pp. 232–233.
168. Ibn Bishr, *Unwan*, part 1, p. 131; Salil ibn Razik, *History*, pp. 169–170, 238–239; J. Raymond, *Les Wahabys*, p. 29; [L. A. Corancez], *Histoire*, pp. 56–59.
169. S. B. Miles, *Countries and Tribes*, vol. 2, pp. 305–309.
170. Ibn Bishr, *Unwan*, part 1, p. 136.
171. Ibid., pp. 141–142.
172. Salil ibn Razik, *History*, pp. 307–308, 314.
173. Ibn Bishr, *Unwan*, part 1, pp. 141–142.
174. J. G. Lorimer, *Gazetteer*, vol. 1, p. 181.
175. [L. A. Corancez], *Histoire*, pp. 48–49, 120–121, 143; H. J. Brydges, *An Account*, vol. 2, pp. 36–37.
176. H. J. Brydges, *An Account*, vol. 2, p. 15.
177. Ibid.; [L. A. Corancez], *Histoire*, pp. 49–50.
178. H. J. Brydges, *An Account*, vol. 2, p. 16.
179. [Reinaud], *Auszug*, p. 235.
180. See: Abd al-Rahim, *al-Dawla*, p. 91.
181. J. G. Lorimer, *Gazetteer*, vol. 1, p. 181.
182. Ibn Bishr, *Unwan*, part 1, p. 146; F. Mengin, *Histoire*, vol. 2, p. 541; [L. A. Corancez], *Histoire*, pp. 142–145; H. J. Brydges, *An Account*, vol. 2, pp. 38–44; J. L. Burckhardt, *Notes*, vol. 2, p. 208; J. G. Lorimer, *Gazetteer*, vol. 1, pp. 183–185.
183. Ibn Bishr, *Unwan*, part 1, pp. 147–148, 153–154.
184. R. B. Winder, *Saudi Arabia*, p. 38.
185. A. Cevdet, *Tarih*, vol. 6, p. 353.
186. Ibn Bishr, *Unwan*, part 1, pp. 146–147; Salil ibn Razik, *History*, pp. 324–326; *Memorial*, vol. 1, pp. 111–112.
187. Ibn Hashim, *Hadhramawt*, pp. 120–122.

Notes

188. F. Mengin, *Histoire*, vol. 2, p. 525; Ibn Bishr, *Unwan*, part 1, p. 121; al-Shakani, *al-Badr*, part 2, pp. 6–8.
189. Abd al-Rahim, *al-Dawla*, pp. 145–146.
190. Ibn Bishr, *Unwan*, part 1, pp. 136–149; F. Mengin, *Histoire*, vol. 2, pp. 533–534; J. L. Burckhardt, *Notes*, vol. 2, p. 202.
191. F. Mengin, *Histoire*, vol. 2, p. 533.
192. Ibn Bishr, *Unwan*, part 1, pp. 144–145. F. Mengin gives different details of that event and dates it to 1810 (*Histoire*, vol. 1, p. 541). See also J. L. Burckhardt, *Notes*, vol. 2, pp. 208–209.
193. Ibn Bishr, *Unwan*, part 1, p. 130; Ibn Sanad, *Tarikh*, p. 33; J. Raymond, *Les Wahabys*, pp. 27–29; [L. A. Corancez], *Histoire*, p. 54.
194. Ibn Bishr, *Unwan*, part 1, pp. 131–132.
195. [L. A. Corancez], *Histoire*, pp. 55, 61–63.
196. Ibn Bishr, *Unwan*, part 1, pp. 135–136; J. Raymond, *Les Wahabys*, p. 31; [L. A. Corancez], *Histoire*, pp. 87–90.
197. Ibn Bishr, *Unwan*, part 1, p. 140; [L. A. Corancez], *Histoire*, pp. 138–142.
198. Ibn Bishr, *Unwan*, part 1, p. 143.
199. Ibid., part 2, p. 126.
200. [L. A. Corancez], *Histoire*, pp. 133–135.
201. Ibn Bishr, *Unwan*, part 1, pp. 148–149; J. L. Burckhardt, *Notes*, vol. 2, pp. 209–210; F. Mengin, *Histoire*, vol. 2, pp. 542–544 (Mengin erroneously dates the expedition to 1811).
202. *Lam al-Shihab*, pp. 469–470.

Chapter 4

1. Ibn Bishr, *Unwan*, part 1, p. 173.
2. J. L. Burckhardt, *Notes*, vol. 2, p. 151.
3. Ibn Ghannam, *Tarikh*, part 2, p. 173.
4. Ibid., p. 52.
5. Ibid., p. 111.
6. Ibid., p. 94.
7. Ibn Bishr, *Unwan*, part 1, p. 87.
8. Ibn Ghannam, *Tarikh*, part 2, p. 136.
9. Ibn Bishr, *Unwan*, part 1, p. 42.
10. Ibid., pp. 51–52.
11. Ibn Ghannam, *Tarikh*, part 2, p. 124.
12. Ibid., p. 245.
13. Ibn Bishr, *Unwan*, part 1, p. 30.
14. Ibid., p. 61.
15. Ibid., pp. 71–72.
16. J. L. Burckhardt, *Notes*, vol. 2, pp. 154–155.
17. Ibn Bishr, *Unwan*, part 1, pp. 40–41.
18. Ibid., p. 90.
19. Ibid., p. 173.
20. J. L. Burckhardt, *Notes*, vol. 2, p. 158.
21. Ibn Bishr, *Unwan*, part 1, p. 173.
22. J. L. Burckhardt, *Notes*, vol. 2, p. 152.
23. Ibid., vol. 1, p. 104.
24. Ibn Bishr, *Unwan*, part 1, pp. 126–127.
25. Ibid.
26. Ibid., p. 173.
27. J. L. Burckhardt, *Notes*, vol. 2, p. 161.
28. *Lam al-Shihab*, pp. 466–469.

Notes

29. Ibid., p. 110.
30. Ibn Bishr, *Unwan*, part 1, p. 214.
31. Ibid., p. 173.
32. J. L. Burckhardt, *Notes*, vol. 2, pp. 121–123.
33. [L. A. Corancez], *Histoire*, pp. 66–67.
34. *Lam al-Shihab*, pp. 480–486.
35. J. Raymond, *Les Wahabys*, p. 26.
36. Ibn Bishr, *Unwan*, part 1, p. 171; J. L. Burckhardt, *Notes*, vol. 2, p. 129.
37. Ibn Bishr, *Unwan*, part 1, p. 171.
38. J. L. Burckhardt, *Notes*, vol. 2, p. 129.
39. Ibid., pp. 159–160.
40. Ibid., p. 130.
41. Ibn Bishr, *Unwan*, part 1, pp. 170–171.
42. J. L. Burckhardt, *Notes*, vol. 2, p. 131.
43. Ibid., p. 130.
44. Ibid.
45. Ibn Bishr, *Unwan*, part 1, p. 171.
46. J. L. Burckhardt, *Notes*, vol. 2, p. 169.
47. Ibid., p. 128.
48. [L. A. Corancez], *Histoire*, pp. 21–23.
49. J. L. Burckhardt, *Notes*, vol. 2, p. 126.
50. Ibn Bishr, *Unwan*, part 1, pp. 168–170.
51. J. L. Burckhardt, *Notes*, vol. 2, p. 126.
52. J. Raymond, *Les Wahabys*, p. 26.
53. J. L. Burckhardt, *Notes*, vol. 2, p. 158.
54. Ibn Bishr, *Unwan*, part 1, p. 127.
55. J. L. Burckhardt, *Notes*, vol. 2, pp. 155–157.
56. Ibid., p. 157.
57. Ibn Bishr, *Unwan*, part 1, p. 173.
58. Ibid., pp. 127–128.
59. Ibn Ghannam, *Tarikh*, part 2, p. 119.
60. Ibid., p. 9.
61. Ibid., p. 90.
62. L. Pelly, *A Visit*, p. 187.
63. Ibn Bishr, *Unwan*, part 1, p. 172.
64. J. L. Burckhardt, *Notes*, vol. 2, pp. 138–139.
65. Ibn Bishr, *Unwan*, part 1, p. 51.
66. Ibn Ghannam, *Tarikh*, part 2, p. 94.
67. F. Mengin, *Histoire*, vol. 2, p. 153.
68. Ibn Bishr, *Unwan*, part 1, p. 131; Ibn Ghannam, *Tarikh*, part 2, p. 102.
69. J. L. Burckhardt, *Notes*, vol. 1, pp. 287–288.
70. Ibn Bishr, *Unwan*, part 1, pp. 67, 130.
71. J. L. Burckhardt, *Notes*, vol. 2, p. 172.
72. Ibid., pp. 132–133.
73. Ibid.
74. *Lam al-Shihab*, pp. 102–104.
75. Ibid., pp. 105–107.
76. Ibn Ghannam, *Tarikh*, part 2, p. 137; Ibn Bishr, *Unwan*, part 1, p. 83.
77. Ibn Ghannam, *Tarikh*, part 2, p. 185.
78. Ibn Bishr, *Unwan*, part 1, p. 166.
79. J. L. Burckhardt, *Notes*, vol. 2, p. 133.
80. [Reinaud], *Auszug*, p. 241.

81. J. L. Burckhardt, *Notes*, vol. 2, pp. 131, 134.
82. Ibn Bishr, *Unwan*, part 1, p. 91.
83. Ibid., p. 15.
84. Ibid., pp. 93–94.
85. Ibid., p. 127.
86. Ibid., p. 92.
87. F. Mengin, *Histoire*, vol. 2, p. 176.
88. *Lam al-Shihab*, pp. 111, 267.
89. J. L. Burckhardt, *Notes*, vol. 1, pp. 249–250.
90. Ibid., vol. 2, p. 136.
91. Ibid., vol. 1, pp. 379–380.
92. Ibid., vol. 2, p. 145.
93. Ibid., pp. 137, 139–140, 145–148.
94. Ibn Sanad, *Tarikh*, p. 31.
95. Ibn Bishr, *Unwan*, part 1, p. 125.
96. Ibid.
97. J. L. Burckhardt, *Notes*, vol. 2, p. 137.
98. Ibn Bishr, *Unwan*, part 1, p. 126.
99. Ibid., p. 124.
100. J. L. Burckhardt, *Notes*, vol. 2, p. 143.
101. Ibn Bishr, *Unwan*, part 1, pp. 124–126.
102. A. Dahlan, *Khulasat*, pp. 279–280.
103. F. Mengin, *Histoire*, vol. 2, p. 174.
104. J. L. Burckhardt, *Notes*, vol. 2, pp. 149–150.
105. Ibid., p. 150; F. Mengin, *Histoire*, vol. 2, p. 452; al-Jabarti, *Egipet*, pp. 325–326.
106. Ibn Bishr, *Unwan*, part 1, p. 13.
107. Ibid., p. 214.
108. Ibid., p. 4.
109. Ibn Sanad, *Tarikh*, p. 31.
110. J. L. Burckhardt, *Notes*, vol. 2, p. 171.
111. Ibid., p. 163.
112. Ibid., p. 105.
113. Ibn Bishr, *Unwan*, part 1, p. 128; see also J. L. Burckhardt, *Notes*, vol. 2, p. 163.
114. Ibn Sanad, *Tarikh*, p. 32.
115. J. Raymond, *Les Wahabys*, p. 9.
116. [L. A. Corancez], *Histoire*, p. 44.
117. J. L. Burckhardt, *Notes*, vol. 1, p. 105; vol. 2, p. 163.
118. Ali bey, *Travels*, vol. 2, p. 136.
119. F. Mengin, *Histoire*, vol. 2, p. 177.
120. Ibn Bishr, *Unwan*, part 1, p. 172.
121. F. Mengin, *Histoire*, vol. 2, p. 177.
122. Ali bey, *Travels*, vol. 2, p. 136.
123. J. L. Burckhardt, *Notes*, vol. 2, p. 165.
124. Ibn Sanad, *Tarikh*, p. 32.
125. J. L. Burckhardt, *Notes*, vol. 2, p. 164.
126. J. Raymond, *Les Wahabys*, pp. 24–25.
127. J. L. Burckhardt, *Notes*, vol. 2, p. 171.
128. Ibn Bishr, *Unwan*, part 1, pp. 167–168.
129. Ibid., p. 166; see also J. L. Burckhardt, *Notes*, vol. 2, p. 170.
130. [L. A. Corancez], *Histoire*, pp. 11–12.
131. J. Raymond, *Les Wahabys*, p. 8; F. Mengin, *Histoire*, vol. 2, p. 180.
132. They might be special camel-drovers. It was usual among the bedouin for 'back-riders' to

guard the animals during battle and drive away any livestock that had been seized. The Wahhabis might have altered that tradition, making both riders active fighters. It may be noted that those authors who describe the Wahhabi movement of the period do not mention any auxiliary functions of the 'back-riders'.

133. F. Mengin, *Histoire*, vol. 2, pp. 178–179.
134. Ibid., pp. 179–180.
135. Ali bey, *Travels*, vol. 2, p. 137.
136. Ibn Ghannam, *Tarikh*, part 2, p. 35.
137. Ibn Bishr, *Unwan*, part 1, p. 140.
138. J. L. Burckhardt, *Notes*, vol. 2, p. 179.
139. F. Mengin, *Histoire*, vol. 2, p. 178.
140. [L. A. Corancez], *Histoire*, p. 64.
141. J. L. Burckhardt, *Notes*, vol. 1, pp. 53–56.
142. F. Mengin, *Histoire*, vol. 2, p. 179; J. L. Burckhardt, *Notes*, vol. 1, p. 179.
143. J. L. Burckhardt, *Notes*, vol. 1, p. 53.
144. Ibid., p. 237.
145. F. Mengin, *Histoire*, vol. 2, p. 179.
146. Ibn Bishr, *Unwan*, part 1, p. 171.
147. Ibn Sanad, *Tarikh*, p. 33. Ibn Bishr gives the same figure.
148. *Zhurnal Razlichnykh Predmetov Slovesnosti*, 1805, vol. 2, no. 1, p. 30; [Reinaud], *Auszug*, p. 241; [L. A. Corancez], *Histoire*, p. 118.
149. J. L. Burckhardt, *Notes*, vol. 1, p. 106.
150. Ibid., vol. 2, p. 168.
151. Ibid., pp. 140–141.
152. Ibn Bishr, *Unwan*, part 1, p. 79; J. L. Burckhardt, *Notes*, vol. 2, pp. 140–141.
153. J. L. Burckhardt, *Notes*, vol. 2, pp. 140–141.
154. Ali bey, *Travels*, vol. 2, p. 139.
155. J. L. Burckhardt, *Notes*, vol. 2, pp. 141–214.
156. Ibn Sanad, *Tarikh*, p. 35.
157. J. L. Burckhardt, *Travels*, vol. 1, pp. 355–360.
158. Al-Jabarti, *Egipet*, p. 211; see also J. L. Burckhardt, *Travels*, vol. 1, p. 349.
159. J. L. Burckhardt, *Travels*, vol. 1, p. 25.
160. Ibid., vol. 2, pp. 208–209.
161. Ibid., vol. 1, pp. 233–234, 361–363, 377.

Chapter 5
1. K. M. Bazili, *Siriya*, p. 79.
2. J. L. Burckhardt, *Notes*, vol. 2, p. 219; Abd al-Rahim, *al-Dawla*, pp. 284–285.
3. J. L. Burckhardt, *Notes*, vol. 2, pp. 218–219; F. Mengin, *Histoire*, vol. 1, pp. 342–343; M. Sabry, *L'Empire*, p. 46; Abd al-Rahim, *al-Dawla*, pp. 286–287.
4. F. Mengin, *Histoire*, vol. 1, pp. 342–343; J. L. Burckhardt, *Notes*, vol. 2, p. 220.
5. J. L. Burckhardt, *Notes*, vol. 2, pp. 220–221; F. Mengin, *Histoire*, vol. 1, pp. 343–344.
6. F. Mengin, *Histoire*, vol. 1, pp. 343–344; J. L. Burckhardt, *Notes*, vol. 2, p. 223; al-Jabarti, *Egipet*, p. 300; A. Dahlan, *Khulasat*, p. 301.
7. F. Mengin, *Histoire*, vol. 1, pp. 359, 373; J. L. Burckhardt, *Notes*, vol. 2, p. 221.
8. Ibn Bishr, *Unwan*, part 1, pp. 131–134; [L. A. Corancez], *Histoire*, p. 140; A. Dahlan, *Khulasat*, pp. 285–292.
9. Ibn Bishr, *Unwan*, part 1, pp. 152–154. Salil ibn Razik gives slightly different details of that event (see his *History*, p. 318).
10. J. Raymond, *Les Wahabys*, p. 31; [L. A. Corancez], *Histoire*, p. 46.
11. J. L. Burckhardt, *Notes*, vol. 2, p. 288.
12. Abd al-Rahim, *al-Dawla*, p. 362.

Notes

13. J. L. Burckhardt, *Notes*, vol. 2, pp. 223–225; F. Mengin, *Histoire*, vol. 1, p. 375 (the latter source dates Tusun's campaign to October 1811).
14. J. L. Burckhardt, *Notes*, vol. 2, p. 225; al-Jabarti, *Egipet*, p. 317 (in the latter source, the capture of Yanbu is dated to September).
15. Al-Jabarti, *Egipet*, p. 317; F. Mengin, *Histoire*, vol. 1, pp. 373–376.
16. Ibn Bishr, *Unwan*, part 1, p. 155.
17. G. Finati, *Narrative*, vol. 1, p. 136.
18. Ibn Bishr, *Unwan*, part 1, pp. 155–156; F. Mengin, *Histoire*, vol. 1, p. 382.
19. F. Mengin, *Histoire*, vol. 1, pp. 384–385; Ibn Bishr, *Unwan*, part 1, pp. 155–156; J. L. Burckhardt, *Notes*, vol. 2, pp. 230–232.
20. Al-Jabarti, *Egipet*, p. 320.
21. Ibid., pp. 325–326.
22. ARFP. *The Office Section*, 1812, file 2282, p. 128.
23. F. Mengin, *Histoire*, vol. 1, pp. 384–388; J. L. Burckhardt, *Notes*, vol. 2, p. 237; Ibn Bishr, *Unwan*, part 1, pp. 157–158; al-Jabarti, *Egipet*, pp. 321, 390.
24. J. L. Burckhardt, *Notes*, vol. 2, pp. 242–245; Ibn Bishr, *Unwan*, part 1, p. 157; Abd al-Rahim, *al-Dawla*, pp. 295–296.
25. A. Dahlan, *Khulasat*, p. 295.
26. J. L. Burckhardt, *Notes*, vol. 2, pp. 237–240; F. Mengin, *Histoire*, vol. 1, pp. 390–396; Ibn Bishr, *Unwan*, part 1, pp. 158–159; al-Jabarti, *Egipet*, p. 346.
27. F. Mengin, *Histoire*, vol. 1, p. 390.
28. J. L. Burckhardt, *Notes*, vol. 2, pp. 240–243.
29. ARFP. *The Office Section*, 1813, file 2285, pp. 67–68; according to Abd al-Rahim (*al-Dawla*, p. 296), the number of ears was 3,000.
30. J. L. Burckhardt, *Travels*, vol. 2, p. 386.
31. Ibn Bishr, *Unwan*, part 1, p. 159; A. Dahlan, *Khulasat*, p. 295.
32. F. Mengin, *Histoire*, vol. 1, pp. 391–399; J. L. Burckhardt, *Notes*, vol. 2, pp. 244–247; Ibn Bishr, *Unwan*, part 1, pp. 159–160; al-Jabarti, *Egipet*, pp. 391–393.
33. ARFP. *The Office Section*, 1813, file 2285, p. 325.
34. F. Mengin, *Histoire*, vol. 1, pp. 399–403; al-Jabarti, *Egipet*, pp. 393–398; A. Dahlan, *Khulasat*, p. 296.
35. Ibn Bishr, *Unwan*, part 1, p. 161; F. Mengin, *Histoire*, vol. 1, pp. 403–407; J. L. Burckhardt, *Notes*, vol. 2, pp. 248–250.
36. J. L. Burckhardt, *Notes*, vol. 2, p. 248; Ibn Bishr, *Unwan*, part 1, p. 162; A. Dahlan, *Khulasat*, p. 296.
37. Al-Jabarti, *Egipet*, pp. 406–408; see also A. Dahlan, *Khulasat*, p. 296.
38. Ibn Bishr, *Unwan*, part 1, pp. 162–163.
39. Ibid., p. 163; A. Dahlan, *Khulasat*, p. 296; F. Mengin, *Histoire*, vol. 1, pp. 407–408; vol. 2, pp. 1–2; J. L. Burckhardt, *Notes*, vol. 2, p. 251.
40. J. L. Burckhardt, *Notes*, vol. 2, pp. 251–260; F. Mengin, *Histoire*, vol. 2, pp. 2–3; Ibn Bishr, *Unwan*, part 1, p. 163; al-Jabarti, *Egipet*, pp. 450–451.
41. Ibn Bishr, *Unwan*, part 1, p. 163; al-Jabarti, *Egipet*, pp. 451–456, 477; J. L. Burckhardt, *Notes*, vol. 2, pp. 260–262; F. Mengin, *Histoire*, vol. 2, pp. 3–16.
42. F. Mengin, *Histoire*, vol. 2, pp. 3–16; J. L. Burckhardt, *Notes*, vol. 2, pp. 264–267; Ibn Bishr, *Unwan*, part 1, pp. 164–165; Abd al-Rahim, *al-Dawla*, pp. 302–304.
43. F. Mengin, *Histoire*, vol. 2, pp. 12–17; J. L. Burckhardt, *Notes*, vol. 2, pp. 268–272; Ibn Bishr, *Unwan*, part 1, p. 164; al-Jabarti, *Egipet*, p. 463.
44. G. Finati, *Narrative*, vol. 1, pp. 222–223; A. Dahlan, *Khulasat*, p. 300.
45. G. Finati, *Narrative*, vol. 1, pp. 226–232; F. Mengin, *Histoire*, vol. 2, pp. 17–19; J. L. Burckhardt, *Notes*, vol. 2, pp. 274–277; Ibn Bishr, *Unwan*, part 1, p. 177.
46. J. L. Burckhardt, *Notes*, vol. 2, pp. 252, 278, 280–284, 303–305; F. Mengin, *Histoire*, vol. 2, pp. 26–29.

Notes

47. A. Dahlan, *Khulasat*, p. 300.
48. Ibid.; J. L. Burckhardt, *Travels*, vol. 1, p. 82; vol. 2, p. 33; J. L. Burckhardt, *Notes*, vol. 2, pp. 286–287, 306.
49. J. L. Burckhardt, *Notes*, vol. 2, p. 287; F. Mengin, *Histoire*, vol. 2, pp. 20, 27–29.
50. Ibn Bishr, *Unwan*, part 1, p. 176; al-Jabarti, *Egipet*, p. 464; F. Mengin, *Histoire*, vol. 2, p. 20.
51. Ibn Bishr, *Unwan*, part 1, pp. 165–166.
52. J. Raymond, *Les Wahabys*, p. 26; [L. A. Corancez], *Histoire*, p. 66.
53. Ibn Bishr, *Unwan*, part 1, p. 175.
54. Ibid., p. 178.
55. Al-Jabarti, *Egipet*, p. 483; A. Dahlan, *Khulasat*, p. 300; J. L. Burckhardt, *Notes*, vol. 2, p. 286.
56. J. L. Burckhardt, *Notes*, vol. 2, pp. 290–292.
57. Ibn Bishr, *Unwan*, part 1, pp. 179–181; al-Jabarti, *Egipet*, pp. 487–491; A. Dahlan, *Khulasat*, pp. 298–301; F. Mengin, *Histoire*, vol. 2, pp. 30–32; J. L. Burckhardt, *Notes*, vol. 2, pp. 310–332.
58. J. L. Burckhardt, *Notes*, vol. 2, pp. 338–339; J. L. Burckhardt, *Travels*, vol. 1, pp. 133–136; M. Sabry, *L'Empire*, p. 48.
59. Ibn Bishr, *Unwan*, part 1, pp. 181–182; F. Mengin, *Histoire*, vol. 2, pp. 32–34; J. L. Burckhardt, *Notes*, vol. 2, pp. 339–343.
60. A. Dahlan, *Khulasat*, p. 301.
61. Ibn Bishr, *Unwan*, part 1, pp. 182–183; J. L. Burckhardt, *Notes*, vol. 2, pp. 343–345; F. Mengin, *Histoire*, vol. 2, pp. 34–48; Abd al-Rahim, *al-Dawla*, p. 312.
62. F. Mengin, *Histoire*, vol. 2, p. 57; al-Jabarti, *Egipet*, pp. 510–511.
63. Ibn Bishr, *Unwan*, part 1, pp. 184–185; J. L. Burckhardt, *Notes*, vol. 2, pp. 346–356; F. Mengin, *Histoire*, vol. 2, pp. 55–57.
64. F. Mengin, *Histoire*, vol. 2, pp. 56–57, 67–71.
65. M. Sabry, *L'Empire*, pp. 44–46.
66. Ibid., pp. 49–50.
67. Al-Jabarti, *Egipet*, p. 638.
68. G. F. Sadlier, *Account*, p. 484; F. Mengin, *Histoire*, vol. 2, pp. 77–82; M. Sabry, *L'Empire*, p. 49.
69. J. L. Burckhardt, *Notes*, vol. 2, pp. 356–357; Abd al-Rahim, *al-Dawla*, p. 318.
70. Ibn Bishr, *Unwan*, part 1, pp. 185–186; al-Jabarti, *Egipet*, p. 608; F. Mengin, *Histoire*, vol. 2, pp. 77–95; J. L. Burckhardt, *Notes*, vol. 2, p. 456; G. F. Sadlier, *Account*, pp. 484–486.
71. G. F. Sadlier, *Account*, pp. 484–486; Ibn Bishr, *Unwan*, part 1, pp. 186–187.
72. Ibn Bishr, *Unwan*, part 1, pp. 187–188; F. Mengin, *Histoire*, vol. 2, pp. 98–104.
73. G. F. Sadlier, *Account*, p. 486.
74. F. Mengin, *Histoire*, vol. 2, p. 105; G. F. Sadlier, *Account*, p. 486; Ibn Bishr, *Unwan*, part 1, p. 188.
75. Ibn Bishr, *Unwan*, part 1, pp. 188–189; F. Mengin, *Histoire*, vol. 2, pp. 106–107.
76. M. Sabry, *L'Empire*, p. 52.
77. Ibn Bishr, *Unwan*, part 1, p. 197.
78. F. Mengin, *Histoire*, vol. 2, pp. 107–111.
79. Ibid., pp. 111–112; G. F. Sadlier, *Account*, pp. 487–488; Ibn Bishr, *Unwan*, part 1, pp. 189–191.
80. Ibn Bishr, *Unwan*, part 1, pp. 190–192.
81. Ibid., pp. 192–194; G. F. Sadlier, *Account*, p. 488; F. Mengin, *Histoire*, vol. 2, pp. 115–117.
82. Ibn Bishr, *Unwan*, part 1, pp. 194–195.
83. G. F. Sadlier, *Account*, p. 488.
84. F. Mengin, *Histoire*, vol. 2, p. 118–131; G. F. Sadlier, *Account*, p. 488; Ibn Bishr, *Unwan*, part 1, pp. 196–203; al-Jabarti, *Egipet*, p. 634; A. Dahlan, *Khulasat*, p. 302.

Notes

85. Ibn Bishr, *Unwan*, part 1, pp. 206–207. It may be concluded from the detailed description of the battle, which lasted many long months, that the Najdi chronicler was either in the capital then or interviewed numerous informers who had witnessed the battle. F. Mengin (*Histoire*, vol. 2, pp. 139–140) dates Abdallah's capitulation to 9 September. This confirms Ibn Bishr's information because the Egyptians might consider that date the day of their victory. G. F. Sadlier (*Account*, p. 488) gives 4 September and M. Sabry (*L'Empire*, p. 55) dates the event to 15 September on the basis of sources that are unknown to us.
86. Ibn Bishr, *Unwan*, part 1, p. 207.
87. ARFP. *The Office Section*, 1818, file 2321, p. 439.
88. Al-Jabarti, *Egipet*, pp. 636–637.
89. ARFP. *The Office Section*, 1818, file 2321, p. 435.
90. Abd al-Rahim, *al-Dawla*, pp. 400–401.
91. ARFP. *The Office Section*, 1818, file 2321, pp. 479–480.
92. E. Rehatsek, *The History*, p. 361.
93. See: K. M. Ashraf, *Predstaviteli*.
94. Ibid., p. 145.
95. Madhi, *al-Nahdhat*, part 1, pp. 62–68.
96. N. A. Ivanov, *Marokko*, pp. 30–34.
97. *Islam v Novoe*, p. 108.

Chapter 6

1. F. Mengin, *Histoire*, vol. 2, p. 136; Ibn Bishr, *Unwan*, part 1, pp. 202, 210, 212–213.
2. Ibn Bishr, *Unwan*, part 1, p. 115; G. F. Sadlier, *Account*, p. 471.
3. G. F. Sadlier, *Diary*, p. 158.
4. Ibn Bishr, *Unwan*, part 1, p. 213; F. Mengin, *Histoire*, vol. 2, p. 231; A. Dahlan, *Khulasat*, p. 303; G. A. Wallin, *Narrative*, p. 186.
5. Ibn Bishr, *Unwan*, part 1, p. 213; F. Mengin, *Histoire*, vol. 2, pp. 151, 158–162; G. F. Sadlier, *Account*, pp. 474, 486.
6. Ibn Sanad, *Tarikh*, p. 50; Ibn Bishr, *Unwan*, part 1, pp. 212–213.
7. F. Mengin, *Histoire*, vol. 2, pp. 160–162; M. Weygand, *Histoire*, vol. 1, pp. 113–114.
8. H. Philby, *Saudi Arabia*, p. 148.
9. F. Mengin, *Histoire*, vol. 2, pp. 160–162; M. Weygand, *Histoire*, vol. 1, pp. 113–114.
10. J. G. Lorimer, *Gazetteer*, vol. 1, pp. 197–200, 658–677. For details, see: R. B. Winder, *Saudi Arabia*, pp. 46–49.
11. Ibn Bishr, *Unwan*, part 1, p. 212.
12. G. F. Sadlier, *Account*, p. 469.
13. Ibn Bishr, *Unwan*, part 1, pp. 210, 212–217; F. Mengin, *Histoire*, vol. 2, pp. 158–159.
14. H. Philby, *Saudi Arabia*, pp. 147–148.
15. A. Dahlan, *Khulasat*, p. 303; C. S. Hurgronje, *Mekka*, p. 161; M. Tamisier, *Voyage*, vol. 1, pp. 144–149.
16. M. Weygand, *Histoire*, vol. 1, p. 168.
17. Ibn Bishr, *Unwan*, part 1, pp. 217–219.
18. Ibid., pp. 218–219; A. Musil, *Northern Negd*, p. 270.
19. Ibn Bishr, *Unwan*, part 2, p. 56.
20. Ibid., part 1, pp. 220–222; A. Dahlan, *Khulasat*, p. 303.
21. Ibn Bishr, *Unwan*, part 1, p. 222; A. Dahlan, *Khulasat*, p. 303.
22. Ibn Bishr, *Unwan*, part 1, pp. 224–225; A. Dahlan, *Khulasat*, p. 303; A. Cevdet, *Tarih*, vol. 11, pp. 190–191.
23. Ibn Bishr, *Unwan*, part 1, pp. 226–227; A. Musil, *Northern Negd*, p. 270.
24. Ibn Bishr, *Unwan*, part 1, p. 227.
25. Ibid.; A. Musil, *Northern Negd*, p. 270.
26. Ibn Bishr, *Unwan*, part 1, pp. 230–232; A. Musil, *Northern Negd*, p. 271.

Notes

27. Ibn Bishr, *Unwan*, part 2, pp. 11, 56.
28. Ibid., part 1, pp. 231–232.
29. Ibid., part 2, pp. 11–12.
30. Ibid., p. 12; W. G. Palgrave, *Narrative*, vol. 2, p. 62.
31. Ibn Bishr, *Unwan*, part 2, pp. 13–17, 27.
32. Ibid., pp. 17–19; W. G. Palgrave, *Narrative*, vol. 2, pp. 62–63.
33. J. G. Lorimer, *Gazetteer*, vol. 1, p. 1094; R. B. Winder, *Saudi Arabia*, p. 65.
34. Ibn Bishr, *Unwan*, part 2, pp. 19–22, 62.
35. Ibid., pp. 23–26.
36. G. Wallin, *Narrative*, p. 186.
37. W. G. Palgrave, *Narrative*, vol. 2, p. 18.
38. Ibn Bishr, *Unwan*, part 2, pp. 26–30, 32–33.
39. Ibid.
40. Ibid., pp. 32, 62; A. Musil, *Northern Negd*, p. 271.
41. Ibn Bishr, *Unwan*, part 2, p. 32; F. Hamza, *Qalb*, pp. 141, 336.
42. M. Weygand, *Histoire*, vol. 1, pp. 169, 273.
43. J. R. Wellsted, *Travels to the City*, vol. 1, pp. 384–387, 391–393, 395; F. Mengin, *Histoire Sommaire*, pp. 35–36, 38, 40, 63; M. Weygand, *Histoire*, vol. 2, pp. 86–87; Ibn Bishr, *Unwan*, part 2, p. 46.
44. J. G. Lorimer, *Gazetteer*, vol. 1, pp. 950–951, 954.
45. Ibn Bishr, *Unwan*, part 2, pp. 35–37; J. G. Lorimer, *Gazetteer*, vol. 1, p. 954.
46. Ibn Bishr, *Unwan*, part 2, pp. 37–38, 62–63.
47. J. G. Lorimer, *Gazetteer*, vol. 1, pp. 954–955.
48. Ibid., pp. 856–857, 955–956, 1095; R. B. Winder, *Saudi Arabia*, pp. 78–79.
49. Salil ibn Razik, *History*, pp. lxxxi–lxxxii.
50. J. G. Lorimer, *Gazetteer*, vol. 1, p. 687.
51. J. Saldana, *Precis of Nejd*, pp. 9–10. Quoted from: R. B. Winder, *Saudi Arabia*, p. 79.
52. Ibn Bishr, *Unwan*, part 2, pp. 33–38.
53. J. G. Lorimer, *Gazetteer*, vol. 1, p. 461; Salil ibn Razik, *History*, p. lxxxiii; *Memorial*, vol. 1, p. 161.
54. 'Precis regarding Muscat and its relations with the Wahabee power'. Quoted by G. Badger in his preface to Salil ibn Razik, *History*, pp. lxxxi–lxxxii.
55. A. J. Wilson, *Persian Gulf*, p. 198.
56. Ibn Bishr, *Unwan*, part 2, pp. 38–39, 45, 48–49, 54; J. G. Lorimer, *Gazetteer*, vol. 1, p. 1094.
57. Ibn Bishr, *Unwan*, part 2, p. 44.
58. M. al-Alusi, *Tarikh*, pp. 97–100.
59. Ibn Bishr, *Unwan*, part 1, p. 219; part 2, pp. 28–30, 34, 38, 45.
60. Ibid., part 2, pp. 33, 39, 41; J. G. Lorimer, *Gazetteer*, vol. 1, pp. 2518–2519; J. R. Wellsted, *Travels in Arabia*, vol. 2, p. 253.
61. Ibn Bishr, *Unwan*, part 2, pp. 44–47.
62. M. al-Nabhani, *al-Tuhfa*, pp. 154–155; Ibn Bishr, *Unwan*, part 2, p. 48.
63. J. G. Lorimer, *Gazetteer*, vol. 1, pp. 857, 1095.
64. Ibn Bishr, *Unwan*, part 2, p. 49.
65. F. Hamza, *Qalb*, p. 236.
66. Ibn Bishr, *Unwan*, part 2, pp. 54–57.
67. R. B. Winder, *Saudi Arabia*, p. 95.
68. Ibn Bishr, *Unwan*, part 2, pp. 48–51.
69. Ibid., pp. 51–53.
70. Ibid., p. 65–66; *Memorial*, vol. 1, pp. 170–171.
71. Ibn Bishr, *Unwan*, part 2, pp. 68–69; J. G. Lorimer, *Gazetteer*, vol. 1, pp. 858, 956–957, 1097–1098.
72. J. R. Wellsted, *Travels in Arabia*, vol. 1, pp. 54–65, 96–97, 219, 223–224, 231; see also J.

Notes

G. Lorimer, *Gazetteer*, vol. 1, pp. 454, 1098–1099; *Memorial*, vol. 1, p. 173.
73. M. Tamisier, *Voyage*, vol. 1, pp. 360, 362, 370; vol. 2, pp. 82–83; F. Mengin, *Histoire Sommaire*, pp. 93–95; M. Weygand, *Histoire*, vol. 2, p. 88; Ibn Bishr, *Unwan*, part 2, p. 68.
74. F. Fresnel, *L'Arabie*, p. 251.
75. M. Tamisier, *Voyage*, vol. 2, p. 362; F. Fresnel, *L'Arabie*, p. 360.
76. G. A. Wallin, *Narrative*, pp. 180–184; G. Guarmani, *Northern Najd*, pp. 88, 92; C. Huber, *Journal*, p. 151.
77. R. B. Winder, *Saudi Arabia*, pp. 101–104.
78. Ibn Bishr, *Unwan*, part 2, pp. 67–68; H. Philby, *Saudi Arabia*, p. 172; C. Huber, *Journal*, p. 158.
79. Ibn Bishr, *Unwan*, part 2, pp. 68–70; J. G. Lorimer, *Gazetteer*, vol. 1, p. 1097; A. Cevdet, *Tezakir* 1–12, p. 139.
80. Ibn Bishr, *Unwan*, part 2, p. 69.
81. Ibid., p. 70; J. G. Lorimer, *Gazetteer*, vol. 1, p. 1097; F. Mengin, *Histoire Sommaire*, p. 95; R. B. Winder, *Saudi Arabia*, p. 108.
82. Ibn Bishr, *Unwan*, part 2, p. 70.
83. H. Philby, *Saudi Arabia*, p. 176.
84. Ibn Bishr, *Unwan*, part 2, pp. 69–72; F. Mengin, *Histoire Sommaire*, p. 95.
85. J. G. Lorimer, *Gazetteer*, vol. 1, p. 1097.
86. For details, see: R. B. Winder, *Saudi Arabia*, pp. 110–111; Ibn Bishr, *Unwan*, part 2, p. 72; F. Hamza, *Qalb*, p. 342; A. Musil, *Northern Negd*, p. 272.
87. Ibn Bishr, *Unwan*, part 2, pp. 72–73.
88. Ibid., p. 72.
89. Ibid., pp. 73–74, 79–80.
90. Ibid., pp. 74–76; A. Musil, *Northern Negd*, p. 272.
91. Ibn Bishr, *Unwan*, part 2, p. 77.
92. Ibid., pp. 80–81; A. Musil, *Northern Negd*, p. 272; F. Hamza, *Qalb*, pp. 336, 342.
93. Ibn Bishr, *Unwan*, part 2, p. 81.
94. H. Philby, *Arabia of the Wahhabis*, p. 170.
95. Ibn Bishr, *Unwan*, part 2, pp. 81–84; E. F. Jomard, *Etudes*, pp. 239–241; R. B. Winder, *Saudi Arabia*, pp. 118–120.
96. R. B. Winder, *Saudi Arabia*, p. 121.
97. A. Musil, *Northern Negd*, p. 273.
98. J. G. Lorimer, *Gazetteer*, vol. 1, p. 1099.
99. R. B. Winder, *Saudi Arabia*, pp. 122–123.
100. Ibn Bishr, *Unwan*, part 1, pp. 85–86; J. G. Lorimer, *Gazetteer*, vol. 1, pp. 957–958.
101. J. G. Lorimer, *Gazetteer*, vol. 1, p. 862.
102. Ibid., pp. 862–865; R. B. Winder, *Saudi Arabia*, pp. 125–128.
103. R. B. Winder, *Saudi Arabia*, pp. 127–128.
104. M. Weygand, *Histoire*, vol. 2, p. 89.
105. J. G. Lorimer, *Gazetteer*, vol. 1, p. 1009.
106. Ibid., p. 457; R. B. Winder, *Saudi Arabia*, pp. 129–131.
107. F. Fresnel, *L'Arabie*, p. 250; R. B. Winder, *Saudi Arabia*, p. 131.
108. Ibn Bishr, *Unwan*, part 2, p. 89; E. Driault, *L'Egypte*, vol. 2, pp. 176, 190, 323; J. G. Lorimer, *Gazetteer*, vol. 1, pp. 1104–1105; A. Cevdet, *Tezakir*, 1–12, pp. 139–140.

Chapter 7
1. A. Cevdet, *Tezakir* 1–12, pp. 139–140.
2. J. G. Lorimer, *Gazetteer*, vol. 1, pp. 1104–1105; R. B. Winder, *Saudi Arabia*, p. 112.
3. Ibn Bishr, *Unwan*, part 2, pp. 91–92.
4. Ibid., pp. 90–91; J. G. Lorimer, *Gazetteer*, vol. 1, pp. 705–706, 867, 959–960, 1107–1107; R. B. Winder (*Saudi Arabia*, p. 136) quotes other sources.

Notes

5. Ibn Bishr, *Unwan*, part 2, pp. 92–93, 95; A. Blunt, *A Pilgrimage*, p. 263; A. Musil, *Northern Negd*, p. 273; F. Hamza. *Qalb*, pp. 272–273.
6. Ibn Bishr, *Unwan*, part 2, p. 96; J. G. Lorimer, *Gazetteer*, vol. 1, pp. 1105–1106; A. Dahlan, *Khulasat*, p. 312; A. Musil, *Northern Negd*, p. 273; R. B. Winder, *Saudi Arabia*, pp. 139–140.
7. Ibn Bishr, *Unwan*, part 2, p. 97; J. G. Lorimer, *Gazetteer*, vol. 1, pp. 706, 867–870, 1108; al-Nabhani, *al-Tuhfa*, p. 159.
8. Ibn Bishr, *Unwan*, part 2, p. 97.
9. Quoted from: R. B. Winder, *Saudi Arabia*, p. 142.
10. Ibn Bishr, *Unwan*, part 2, p. 99; A. Dahlan, *Khulasat*, pp. 312–313; R. B. Winder, *Saudi Arabia*, p. 142.
11. G. A. Wallin, *Narrative*, p. 182.
12. Ibid., p. 179.
13. R. B. Winder, *Saudi Arabia*, pp. 143–147; Ibn Bishr, *Unwan*, part 2, pp. 99–103; A. Dahlan, *Khulasat*, p. 113; A. Rihani, *Tarikh*, p. 81.
14. H. Philby, *Saudi Arabia*, pp. 193–194.
15. Ibn Bishr, *Unwan*, part 2, pp. 108–110; J. G. Lorimer, *Gazetteer*, vol. 1, pp. 866–875.
16. Ibn Bishr, *Unwan*, part 2, pp. 111–112; R. B. Winder, *Saudi Arabia*, pp. 152–153.
17. Ibn Bishr, *Unwan*, part 2, pp. 111, 113.
18. C. Doughty, *Travels*, vol. 2, p. 42.
19. Ibn Bishr, *Unwan*, part 2, p. 112; R. B. Winder, *Saudi Arabia*, pp. 154–155.
20. J. G. Lorimer, *Gazetteer*, vol. 1, p. 1111.
21. Ibn Bishr, *Unwan*, part 2, pp. 114, 117; G. A. Wallin, *Narrative*, pp. 146–149; R. B. Winder, *Saudi Arabia*, pp. 153–156.
22. C. Huber, 'Voyage', *BSG*, vol. 6, p. 147.
23. Ibid., vol. 5, p. 494; vol. 6, pp. 147–148.
24. Ibid., vol. 5, p. 494; C. Doughty, *Travels*, vol. 2, pp. 340–341, 357.
25. C. Doughty, *Travels*, vol. 2, pp. 337, 395, 416, 433–434; C. Huber, 'Voyage', *BSG*, vol. 5, p. 494.
26. C. Doughty, *Travels*, vol. 2, p. 357.
27. Ibn Bishr, *Unwan*, part 2, pp. 114–115.
28. Ibid., p. 124.
29. Ibid., p. 123.
30. Ibid., p. 125.
31. C. Doughty, *Travels*, vol. 2, pp. 377–378; see also H. Philby, *Arabia of the Wahhabis*, pp. 161, 383–392.
32. Ibn Bishr, *Unwan*, part 2, p. 127.
33. For details of the affairs of Qasim, see: Ibn Bishr, *Unwan*, part 2, pp. 119–130; W. G. Palgrave, *Narrative*, vol. 1, pp. 168–169; R. B. Winder, *Saudi Arabia*, pp. 157–165.
34. C. Doughty, *Travels*, vol. 2, p. 458.
35. Ibid., p. 459.
36. C. Huber, *Journal*, p. 493; R. B. Winder, *Saudi Arabia*, pp. 165–168.
37. See: R. B. Winder, *Saudi Arabia*, p. 168; J. G. Lorimer, *Gazetteer*, vol. 1, p. 2519; W. G. Palgrave, *Narrative*, vol. 1, p. 407.
38. R. B. Winder, *Saudi Arabia*, pp. 169–170.
39. Ibid., pp. 170–171; H. Philby (*Saudi Arabia*, p. 208) dates the battle to 1859.
40. R. B. Winder, *Saudi Arabia*, pp. 171–172.
41. C. Doughty, *Travels*, vol. 2, p. 459; H. Philby, *Saudi Arabia*, p. 313; R. B. Winder, *Saudi Arabia*, pp. 173–174.
42. C. Doughty, *Travels*, vol. 2, pp. 459–463.
43. W. G. Palgrave, *Narrative*, vol. 2, p. 109.
44. For details of the 'second war', see: W. G. Palgrave, *Narrative*, vol. 2, pp. 108–111,

Notes

        171–174, 249–250; C. Guarmani, *Northern Najd*, p. 93; R. B. Winder, *Saudi Arabia*, pp. 174–178.
45. C. S. Hurgronje, *Mekka*, p. 164.
46. Ibn Bishr, *Unwan*, part 2, pp. 114–115.
47. Ibid.
48. J. G. Lorimer, *Gazetteer*, vol. 1, pp. 1110–1111; R. B. Winder, *Saudi Arabia*, p. 182.
49. A. Cevdet, *Tezakir* 1–12, p. 140.
50. T. E. Marston, *Britain's Imperial Role*, pp. 149–152, 157–159; R. B. Winder, *Saudi Arabia*, pp. 182–183.
51. G. de Gaury, *Rulers*, pp. 248–249.
52. T. E. Marston, *Britain's Imperial Role*, pp. 162–163, 216–217; A. Cevdet, *Tezakir* 1–12, pp. 101–129.
53. G. de Gaury, *Rulers*, p. 252.
54. R. B. Winder, *Saudi Arabia*, p. 207.
55. Quoted from: ibid.
56. Ibid.
57. J. G. Lorimer, *Gazetteer*, vol. 1, p. 1116.
58. R. B. Winder, *Saudi Arabia*, p. 217.
59. Ibid.
60. Ibid.
61. Ibid.
62. J. G. Lorimer, *Gazetteer*, vol. 1, p. 1111.
63. Ibid., pp. 877–880, 961, 1111–1112; R. B. Winder, *Saudi Arabia*, pp. 185–186.
64. Ibn Bishr, *Unwan*, part 2, pp. 130–132; *Memorial*, vol. 1, p. 207; J. G. Lorimer, *Gazetteer*, vol. 1, pp. 800, 961–962, 1112; al-Nabhani, *al-Tuhfa*, pp. 163–164; Salil ibn Razik, *History*, p. xc.
65. J. G. Lorimer, *Gazetteer*, vol. 1, p. 885.
66. R. B. Winder, *Saudi Arabia*, p. 189.
67. J. G. Lorimer, *Gazetteer*, vol. 1, pp. 887–890; C. U. Aitchison, *A Collection*, pp. 185, 192; R. B. Winder, *Saudi Arabia*, pp. 190–191.
68. Al-Nabhani, *al-Tuhfa*, pp. 183–184; see also J. G. Lorimer, *Gazetteer*, vol. 1, pp. 892–893, 899, 1113.
69. Quoted from: R. B. Winder, *Saudi Arabia*, p. 192.
70. Describing the developments in Oman, we follow R. B. Winder (*Saudi Arabia*, pp. 192–203), who used sources to which the present writer did not have access.
71. L. Pelly, *Report on a Journey*, pp. 35, 49; W. G. Palgrave, *Narrative*, vol. 2, p. 98.
72. H. Philby, *Heart of Arabia*, vol. 1, p. 99; H. Philby, *Arabia of the Wahhabis*, p. 141.
73. R. B. Winder, *Saudi Arabia*, p. 225.
74. L. Pelly, *Report on a Journey*, p. 7.
75. Quoted from: R. B. Winder, *Saudi Arabia*, pp. 225–226.
76. R. B. Winder, *Saudi Arabia*, p. 218.
77. W. G. Palgrave, *Narrative*, vol. 1, pp. 407–409.
78. H. Philby, *Saudi Arabia*, pp. 194–195; R. B. Winder, *Saudi Arabia*, p. 209.
79. W. G. Palgrave, *Narrative*, vol. 1, p, 399; vol. 2, p. 189.
80. L. Pelly, *Report on a Journey*, pp. 92–93; *Memorial*, vol. 2, pp. 323–330.
81. *Memorial*, vol. 1, pp. 139–140; L. Pelly, *Report on a Journey*, pp. 28–29.
82. L. Pelly, *Report on a Journey*, pp. 92–93.
83. Ibid., p. 34.
84. W. G. Palgrave, *Narrative*, vol. 2, p. 86.
85. L. Pelly, *A Visit*, p. 188.
86. L. Pelly, *Report on a Journey*, pp. 11, 91; W. G. Palgrave, *Narrative*, vol. 2, pp. 178–179; S. M. Zwemer, *Arabia*, pp. 115–116.

Notes

87. D. G. Hogarth, *Penetration of Arabia*, pp. 150, 160, 267, 277; L. Pelly, *A Visit*, p. 188; C. Guarmani, *Northern Najd*, p. 42; J. G. Lorimer, *Gazetteer*, vol. 1, pp. 2335–2340; A. Blunt, *A Pilgrimage*, vol. 1, p. 255; vol. 2, pp. 2–3.
88. J. G. Lorimer, *Gazetteer*, vol. 1, pp. 2220–2293.

Chapter 8
1. H. Wahba, *Jazirat*, p. 244.
2. W. G. Palgrave, *Narrative*, vol. 2, pp. 73–74.
3. H. Philby, *Saudi Arabia*, p. 218.
4. L. Pelly, *Report on a Journey*, p. 76.
5. H. Philby, *Heart of Arabia*, vol. 1, p. 99; H. Philby, *Arabia of the Wahhabis*, p. 141.
6. L. Pelly, *Report on a Journey*, pp. 33–34.
7. R. B. Winder, *Saudi Arabia*, p. 231.
8. L. Pelly, *Report on a Journey*, p. 52.
9. J. G. Lorimer, *Gazetteer*, vol. 1, pp. 473–476, 1121–1125; Salil ibn Razik, *History*, pp. c–civ; C. U. Aitchison, *A Collection*, p. 185; R. B. Winder, *Saudi Arabia*, pp. 232–234.
10. R. B. Winder, *Saudi Arabia*, pp. 234–237.
11. *Memorial*, vol. 2, p. 144.
12. J. G. Lorimer, *Gazetteer*, vol. 1, p. 1125; S. H. Longrigg, *Four Centuries*, p. 302; R. B. Winder, *Saudi Arabia*, pp. 237–238.
13. H. Philby, *Saudi Arabia*, p. 218.
14. Ibid.
15. Ibid., pp. 219–220; R. B. Winder, *Saudi Arabia*, pp. 238–239.
16. H. Philby, *Saudi Arabia*, p. 220.
17. J. G. Lorimer, *Gazetteer*, vol. 1, pp. 892–902; al-Nabhani, *al-Tuhfa*, p. 191; R. B. Winder, *Saudi Arabia*, p. 245.
18. J. G. Lorimer, *Gazetteer*, vol. 1, pp. 726–727; *Memorial*, vol. l, p. 44; R. B. Winder, *Saudi Arabia*, pp. 245–247.
19. R. B. Winder, *Saudi Arabia*, p. 247.
20. Ibid.
21. Ibid., p. 248.
22. A. Rihani, *Tarikh*, p. 84; al-Nabhani, *al-Tuhfa*, pp. 239–240; Salil ibn Razik, *History*, pp. cxv–cxvi; L. Pelly, *Report on a Journey*, p. 76; J. G. Lorimer, *Gazetteer*, vol. 1, p. 1128.
23. See: H. Philby, *Saudi Arabia*, p. 159; R. B. Winder, *Saudi Arabia*, p. 244.
24. Quoted from: R. B. Winder, *Saudi Arabia*, p. 242.
25. H. Philby, *Arabia of the Wahhabis*, pp. 135–136; A. Musil, *Northern Negd*, p. 240.
26. W. C. Palgrave, *Narrative*, vol. 1, p. 203.
27. A. Blunt, *A Pilgrimage*, p. 194.
28. C. Doughty, *Travels*, vol. 2, pp. 41–42.
29. W. G. Palgrave, *Narrative*, vol. 1, p. 174.
30. A. Musil, *Northern Negd*, p. 239.
31. W. G. Palgrave, *Narrative*, vol. 1, p. 130.
32. Ibid., p. 128; C. Guarmani, *Northern Najd*, pp. 53–54; C. Huber, 'Voyage', *BSG*, vol. 3, p. 357.
33. G. A. Wallin, *Narrative*, p. 179.
34. C. Doughty, *Travels*, vol. 2, p. 485; A. Musil, *Northern Negd*, p. 274.
35. J. G. Lorimer, *Gazetteer*, vol. 1, pp. 1163–1165; C. Huber, *Journal*, p. 190; R. B. Winder, *Saudi Arabia*, pp. 242–244.
36. H. Philby, *Saudi Arabia*, p. 224.
37. C. Guarmani, *Northern Najd*, pp. 90–91; C. Doughty, *Travels*, vol. 2, p. 20; H. Philby, *Arabia*, p. 196; C. Huber, 'Voyage', *BSG*, vol. 6, pp. 140, 141, 146.
38. W. F. Blunt, *A Visit*, p. 88.

Notes

39. G. A. Wallin, *Narrative*, p. 180; C. Guarmani, *Northern Najd*, p. 91; C. Doughty, *Travels*, vol. 1, pp. 23, 33, 35, 52; C. Huber, 'Voyage', *BSG*, vol. 5, p. 354.
40. R. Montagne, *Notes*, p. 78; R. Montagne, *La Civilisation*, p. 156.
41. C. Doughty, *Travels*, vol. 1, p. 588; E. Nolde, *Reise*, pp. 80, 86, 89; R. Montagne, *Notes*, p. 78; R. Montagne, *La Civilisation*, pp. 155–156.
42. G. A. Wallin, *Narrative*, p. 180; J. Euting, *Reise*, vol. 1, pp. 200–201; C. Doughty, *Travels*, vol. 1, p. 610.
43. G. A. Wallin, *Notes*, p. 43; G. A. Wallin, *Narrative*, pp. 179–180.
44. G. A. Wallin, *Narrative*, p. 80; C. Guarmani, *Northern Najd*, pp. 46–48; J. Euting, *Reise*, vol. 1, p. 203.
45. E. Nolde, *Reise*, p. 34; W. G. Palgrave, *Narrative*, vol. 1, p. 109.
46. For details, see: A. I. Pershits, *Khozyaystvo*, pp. 178–179.
47. C. Guarmani, *Northern Najd*, p. 91.
48. E. Nolde, *Reise*, p. 84.
49. C. Huber, 'Voyage', *BSG*, vol. 5, p. 357; J. Euting, *Reise*, vol. 1, p. 177; E. Nolde, *Reise*, p. 36.
50. H. Philby, *Saudi Arabia*, p. 219; R. B. Winder, *Saudi Arabia*, pp. 248–249.
51. R. B. Winder, *Saudi Arabia*, pp. 249–250.
52. C. Doughty, *Travels*, vol. 2, p. 50.
53. R. B. Winder, *Saudi Arabia*, pp. 250–251.
54. Ibid.
55. Ibid.
56. Quoted from: ibid., p. 251.
57. S. H. Longrigg, *Four Centuries*, p. 302; A. Midhat, *Life of Midhat Pasha*, pp. 56–57; A. Blunt, *A Pilgrimage*, vol. 2, p. 266; R. B. Winder, *Saudi Arabia*, p. 252.
58. A. Blunt, *A Pilgrimage*, vol. 2, pp. 266–267.
59. A. Rihani, *Tarikh*, p. 84; R. B. Winder, *Saudi Arabia*, pp. 253–254; A. Midhat, *Life of Midhat Pasha*, pp. 55, 61–62.
60. R. B. Winder, *Saudi Arabia*, p. 255.
61. A. Blunt, *A Pilgrimage*, vol. 2, p. 266; *Memorial*, vol. 1, p. 257; R. B. Winder, *Saudi Arabia*, p. 255.
62. See: R. B. Winder, *Saudi Arabia*, p. 256.
63. C. Doughty, *Travels*, vol. 2, p. 368; A. Musil, *Northern Negd*, p. 274; A. Rihani, *Tarikh*, p. 85; J. G. Lorimer, *Gazetteer*, vol. 1, pp. 1132, 1133.
64. H. Philby, *Saudi Arabia*, pp. 224–225.
65. J. G. Lorimer, *Gazetteer*, vol. 1, pp. 808, 971, 1131–1132; W. G. Palgrave, *Narrative*, vol. 1, p. 116.
66. J. G. Lorimer, *Gazetteer*, vol. 1, pp. 914, 917; A. Rihani, *Tarikh*, p. 85; A. Blunt, *A Pilgrimage*, vol. 2, p. 267; R. B. Winder, *Saudi Arabia*, pp. 259–260.
67. R. B. Winder, *Saudi Arabia*, pp. 260–261.
68. J. G. Lorimer, *Gazetteer*, vol. 1, p. 1132; C. Doughty, *Travels*, vol. 2, pp. 51, 453–455; R. B. Winder, *Saudi Arabia*, pp. 260–261.
69. H. Philby, *Saudi Arabia*, p. 226; A. Rihani, *Tarikh*, p. 86; J. G. Lorimer, *Gazetteer*, vol. 1, pp. 1134, 1137.
70. H. Philby, *Saudi Arabia*, p. 226.
71. J. G. Lorimer, *Gazetteer*, vol. 1, p. 983; *Memorial*, vol. 1, p. 267.
72. R. B. Winder, *Saudi Arabia*, pp. 263–264.
73. C. Doughty, *Travels*, vol. 2, p. 455.
74. A. Blunt, *A Pilgrimage*, vol. 1, p. 119; vol. 2, p. 268.
75. C. Huber, *Journal*, p. 114.
76. R. B. Winder, *Saudi Arabia*, p. 266. However, there are different data concerning the exact date of birth of the founder of modern Saudi Arabia.

Notes

77. F. Hamza, *al-Bilad*, pp. 3, 5–10; al-Mukhtar, *Tarikh*, part 2, p. 18; G. Kheirallah, *Arabia*, p. 74.
78. C. Huber, *Journal*, p. 162; A. Rihani, *Tarikh*, p. 87; C. Doughty, *Travels*, vol. 2, pp. 38, 51, 307, 315, 338, 394, 456; R. B. Winder, *Saudi Arabia*, p. 267.
79. H. Philby, *Saudi Arabia*, p. 229; A. Rihani, *Tarikh*, p. 87.
80. H. Philby, *Saudi Arabia*, pp. 229–230; C. Huber, *Journal*, pp. 650, 670, 720.
81. H. Philby, *Saudi Arabia*, p. 230.
82. A. Rihani, *Tarikh*, p. 88; J. G. Lorimer, *Gazetteer*, vol. 1, p. 1137; A. Musil, *Northern Negd*, p. 278; F. Hamza, *al-Bilad*, p. 6; H. Wahba, *Jazirat*, pp. 235–236. Strangely enough, Philby erroneously dates these events to 1885 (*Saudi Arabia*, p. 231). A. Adamov, the Russian consul in Basra, reported that they happened in 1886 (*ARFP. The Embassy in Constantinople Section*, 1902, file 1265, p. 84).
83. A. Rihani, *Tarikh*, p. 88.
84. R. B. Winder, *Saudi Arabia*, pp. 272–273.
85. A. Rihani, *Tarikh*, p. 88–89; R. B. Winder, *Saudi Arabia*, p. 273. Philby has erred again, dating these events to two years before they actually happened (see his *Saudi Arabia*, p. 232).
86. H. Philby, *Saudi Arabia*, p. 232; R. B. Winder, *Saudi Arabia*, p. 273.
87. H. Philby, *Saudi Arabia*, p. 232.
88. A. Rihani, *Tarikh*, pp. 88–89; A. Musil, *Northern Negd*, pp. 278–279; R. B. Winder, *Saudi Arabia*, pp. 274–275.
89. A. Musil, *Northern Negd*, p. 279.
90. Ibid., pp. 279–280; H. Philby, *Arabia of the Wahhabis*, pp. 272–273; J. G. Lorimer, *Gazetteer*, vol. 1, p. 1177; H. Wahba, *Jazirat*, p. 237.
91. A. Rihani, *Tarikh*, p. 91; H. Philby, *Saudi Arabia*, pp. 235–239; J. G. Lorimer, *Gazetteer*, vol. 1, p. 1140; R. B. Winder, *Saudi Arabia*, pp. 277–278.
92. H. Philby, *Saudi Arabia*, pp. 235–236.
93. A. Rihani, *Ibn Saoud*, p. 218.
94. A. Musil, *Zur Zeitgeschichte*, p. 68.
95. A. I. Pershits, *Khozyaystvo*, p. 202.
96. Quoted from: al-Zirikli, *Shibh*, p. 85.
97. Ibid., p. 119.
98. J. G. Lorimer, *Gazetteer*, vol. 1, p. 1170.
99. G. L. Bondarevski, *Angliyskaya*, p. 17.
100. Ibid., p. 34.
101. G. Troeller, *Birth of Saudi Arabia*, p. 3; G. L. Bondarevski, *Angliyskaya*, pp. 15–45.
102. G. Troeller, *Birth of Saudi Arabia*, p. 3.
103. G. L. Bondarevski, *Angliyskaya*, p. 208; G. Troeller, *Birth of Saudi Arabia*, p. 4.
104. G. Troeller, *Birth of Saudi Arabia*, p. 11.
105. G. de Gaury, *Rulers*, p. 253.
106. Ibid., pp. 254–260.
107. Ibid., p. 260.
108. G. L. Bondarevski, *Angliyskaya*, p. 89. Philby (*Saudi Arabia*, p. 236) erroneously gave 1894.
109. G. L. Bondarevski, *Angliyskaya*, pp. 105–107.
110. Ibid., pp. 109, 114; H. Wahba, *Jazirat*, pp. 85–86; C. U. Aitchison, *A Collection*, vol. 9, p. 262; J. G. Lorimer, *Gazetteer*, vol. 1, pp. 1049–1050.
111. G. L. Bondarevski, *Angliyskaya*, pp. 143–148.
112. H. Philby, *Saudi Arabia*, pp. 237–238.

Chapter 9

1. H. Philby, *Saudi Arabia*, p. 238.
2. G. L. Bondarevski, *Angliyskaya*, p. 217.
3. Ibid., pp. 218–221; *ARFP. The Embassy in Constantinople Section*, 1901, file 1244, pp. 221–224.

Notes

4. H. Philby, *Saudi Arabia*, p. 238.
5. A. Adamov, *Irak*, p. 471.
6. G. L. Bondarevski, *Angliyskaya*, pp. 234–235.
7. Ibn Rashid, *Nubza*, pp. 58–60; H. Wahba, *Jazirat*, p. 86; A. Adamov, *Irak*, p. 471; *ARFP. The Political Archives Section*, 1901, file 364, p. 31; J. G. Lorimer, *Gazetteer*, vol. 1, p. 1029; H. Philby, *Saudi Arabia*, p. 238.
8. H. Philby, *Saudi Arabia*, p. 238; al-Bassam, *Tuhfat*, pp. 358–359.
9. *ARFP. The Embassy in Constantinople Section*, 1902, file 1265, p. 94.
10. H. Philby, *Saudi Arabia*, p. 239.
11. *ARFP. The Political Archives Section*, 1901, file 3195, p. 34; *The Embassy in Constantinople Section*, 1901, file 1245, p. 172.
12. G. L. Bondarevski, *Angliyskaya*, p. 292.
13. *ARFP. The Political Archives Section*, 1901, schedule 482, file 364, p. 7.
14. H. Philby, *Arabia*, pp. 170–171; G. L. Bondarevski, *Angliyskaya*, pp. 357–358.
15. Ibn Hizlul, *Tarikh*, pp. 57–60; A. Rihani, *Tarikh*, p. 110.
16. The capture of Riyadh is described both in the Arab and in the Western literature. We relied on: Ibn Hizlul, *Tarikh*, pp. 57–60; F. Hamza, *al-Bilad*, pp. 12–16; A. Rihani, *Tarikh*, pp. 108–113; al-Zirikli, *Shibh*, pp. 97–102; H. Philby, *Saudi Arabia*, p. 239.
17. Ibn Rashid, *Nubza*, pp. 117–118.
18. Ibn Hizlul, *Tarikh*, pp. 62–63; al-Zirikli, *Shibh*, pp. 129–130; al-Ahsai, *Tuhfat*, p. 199; H. Philby, *Saudi Arabia*, pp. 239–241.
19. G. Bell, *Arab War*, p. 9.
20. G. L. Bondarevski, *Angliyskaya*, pp. 418–419.
21. Ibn Hizlul, *Tarikh*, pp. 62–63; al-Bassam, *Tuhfat*, pp. 361–362.
22. Ibn Hizlul, *Tarikh*, pp. 63–64; al-Bassam, *Tuhfat*, pp. 362–363; A. Rihani, *Tarikh*, pp. 115–118; H. Philby, *Saudi Arabia*, pp. 240–242.
23. Ibn Hizlul, *Tarikh*, pp. 64–65; al-Bassam, *Tuhfat*, p. 363; A. Rihani, *Tarikh*, p. 123; H. Philby, *Saudi Arabia*, p. 242.
24. *ARFP. The Embassy in Constantinople Section*, 1903, file 1266, pp. 36–38.
25. Ibid., *The Political Archives Section*, schedule 482, file 365, pp. 13–14; J. G. Lorimer, *Gazetteer*, vol. 1, part 2, pp. 1145–1146. The latter author claims that it was Ibn Saud who called for the meeting.
26. Al-Ahsai, *Tuhfat*, pp. 200–201; Ibn Hizlul, *Tarikh*, p. 65; *ARFP. The Embassy in Constantinople Section*, 1903, file 1266, pp. 38–39.
27. G. L. Bondarevski, *Angliyskaya*, pp. 393–394.
28. *ARFP. The Political Archives Section*, 1903, schedule 482, file 366, p. 2.
29. Ibn Hizlul, *Tarikh*, pp. 65–66; al-Bassam, *Tuhfat*, pp. 364–368.
30. G. L. Bondarevski, *Angliyskaya*, pp. 427, 495–497.
31. J. G. Lorimer, *Gazetteer*, vol. 1, part 2, p. 1146; H. Philby, *Saudi Arabia*, pp. 243–244.
32. Al-Ahsai, *Tuhfat*, pp. 201–202; al-Bassam, *Tuhfat*, pp. 369–370; H. Philby, *Saudi Arabia*, pp. 244–245.
33. Ibn Hizlul, *Tarikh*, p. 69.
34. H. Philby, *Saudi Arabia*, p. 245; Ibn Hizlul, *Tarikh*, p. 70.
35. H. Philby, *Saudi Arabia*, pp. 244–245; Ibn Hizlul, *Tarikh*, p. 69; al-Bassam, *Tuhfat*, pp. 370–371.
36. D. Howarth, *Desert King*, p. 38.
37. Al-Ahsai, *Tuhfat*, p. 202.
38. Ibn Hizlul, *Tarikh*, p. 69; al-Ahsai, *Tuhfat*, p. 202; al-Bassam, *Tuhfat*, p. 371; H. Philby, *Saudi Arabia*, p. 245.
39. G. L. Bondarevski, *Angliyskaya*, p. 431.
40. H. Philby, *Saudi Arabia*, p. 245; al-Bassam, *Tuhfat*, p. 371.
41. A. Rihani, *Tarikh*, pp. 125–126; al-Bassam, *Tuhfat*, p. 371.

Notes

42. Al-Bassam, *Tuhfat*, pp. 377–379; al-Zirikli, *Shibh*, pp. 155–157.
43. G. Troeller, *Birth of Saudi Arabia*, pp. 28–29.
44. G. L. Bondarevski, *Angliyskaya*, pp. 432–433.
45. Ibn Hizlul, *Tarikh*, pp. 69–70.
46. Ibn Rashid, *Nubza*, p. 120.
47. A. Rihani, *Tarikh*, p. 126; al-Ahsai, *Tuhfat*, p. 203.
48. J. G. Lorimer, *Gazetteer*, vol. 1, part 2, pp. 1147–1148.
49. H. Philby, *Saudi Arabia*, p. 246; Ibn Hizlul, *Tarikh*, p. 71; al-Ahsai, *Tuhfat*, pp. 203–204; A. Rihani, *Tarikh*, pp. 126–131; al-Zirikli, *Shibh*, pp. 150–151.
50. Ibn Hizlul, *Tarikh*, pp. 71–73; al-Ahsai, *Tuhfat*, pp. 203–204; al-Bassam, *Tuhfat*, p. 373.
51. Al-Zirikli, *Shibh*, p. 164.
52. ARFP. *The Political Archives Section*, 1905, schedule 482, file 368, pp. 2–3; J. G. Lorimer, *Gazetteer*, vol. 1, part 2, pp. 1148–1149.
53. ARFP. *The Political Archives Section*, 1905, schedule 482, file 368, p. 4.
54. Ibn Hizlul, *Tarikh*, p. 74; al-Bassam, *Tuhfat*, pp. 374–375; al-Zirikli, *Shibh*, p. 167.
55. ARFP. *The Political Archives Section*, 1905, schedule 482, file 368, p. 10; Ibn Hizlul, *Tarikh*, p. 73; al-Bassam, *Tuhfat*, p. 375; al-Zirikli, *Shibh*, p. 167.
56. Al-Zirikli, *Shibh*, p. 169.
57. J. G. Lorimer, *Gazetteer*, vol. 1, part 2, pp. 1149–1150.
58. Ibid., p. 1150.
59. H. Philby, *Saudi Arabia*, p. 248; Ibn Hizlul, *Tarikh*, pp. 73–74.
60. Ibn Hizlul, *Tarikh*, pp. 73–74; al-Bassam, *Tuhfat*, p. 375.
61. Ibn Hizlul, *Tarikh*, p. 76–77.
62. ARFP. *The Political Archives Section*, 1906, schedule 482, file 369, p. 9; Ibn Rashid, *Nubza*, pp. 121–133; Ibn Hizlul, *Tarikh*, pp. 76–77; A. Rihani, *Tarikh*, pp. 138–142; H. Philby, *Saudi Arabia*, p. 250.
63. J. G. Lorimer, *Gazetteer*, vol. 1, part 2, p. 1152; H. Philby, *Saudi Arabia*, p. 250.
64. Ibn Hizlul, *Tarikh*, p. 80; H. Philby, *Saudi Arabia*, p. 250.
65. J. G. Lorimer, *Gazetteer*, vol. 1, part 2, pp. 1152–1153.
66. Ibn Hizlul, *Tarikh*, pp. 80–81.
67. J. G. Lorimer, *Gazetteer*, vol. 1, part, 2, pp. 1153–1154.
68. Ibid., p. 1154.
69. Ibn Hizlul, *Tarikh*, p. 83.
70. Ibid.
71. J. G. Lorimer, *Gazetteer*, vol. 1, part 2, pp. 1154–1155.
72. Ibn Hizlul, *Tarikh*, p. 83.
73. Al-Bassam, *Tuhfat*, p. 381.
74. J. G. Lorimer, *Gazetteer*, vol. 1, part 2, pp. 1155–1156.
75. Ibn Hizlul, *Tarikh*, p. 83.
76. A. Rihani, *Tarikh*, pp. 143–150.
77. H. Philby, *Saudi Arabia*, pp. 251–253; al-Dakhil, *al-Qawl*, pp. 155–156; A. Rihani, *Tarikh*, p. 160; S. S. Butler and L. Aymler, *Baghdad*, pp. 517–535.
78. Al-Dakhil, *al-Qawl*, pp. 156–157.
79. H. Philby, *Saudi Arabia*, pp. 253–254, 256; al-Dakhil, *al-Qawl*, pp. 156–157; A. Rihani, *Tarikh*, p. 266.
80. Ibn Hizlul, *Tarikh*, pp. 84–85; al-Bassam, *Tuhfat*, p. 384.
81. Ibn Hizlul, *Tarikh*, p. 85; H. Philby, *Saudi Arabia*, p. 252.
82. Ibn Hizlul, *Tarikh*, pp. 86–87; al-Bassam, *Tuhfat*, pp. 384–385.
83. Ibn Hizlul, *Tarikh*, pp. 88–89.
84. Philby (*Saudi Arabia*, p. 251) dates his death to January 1908, while al-Bassam does not specify the month (*Tuhfat*, p. 387).
85. H. Philby, *Saudi Arabia*, p. 254.

Notes

86. Al-Bassam, *Tuhfat*, pp. 385–388.
87. A. Musil, *Northern Hegaz*, pp. 22–31.
88. Ibn Hizlul, *Tarikh*, p. 91; al-Bassam, *Tuhfat*, pp. 386–387.
89. A. Rihani, *Tarikh*, pp. 173–174; al-Zirikli, *Shibh*, p. 195; al-Bassam, *Tuhfat*, p. 389; H. Philby, *Saudi Arabia*, p. 256.
90. Al-Bassam, *Tuhfat*, p. 389; H. Philby, *Saudi Arabia*, p. 255; G. E. Leachman, *A Journey*, pp. 266–267.
91. A. Musil, *Arabia*, pp. 117, 142–143, 159, 285.
92. H. Philby, *Saudi Arabia*, p. 257; Ibn Hizlul, *Tarikh*, pp. 92–94; al-Bassam, *Tuhfat*, p. 389.
93. H. Philby, *Saudi Arabia*, p. 258.
94. Ibn Hizlul, *Tarikh*, p. 94.
95. J. G. Lorimer, *Gazetteer*, vol. 1, part 2, p. 1151.
96. Ibn Hizlul, *Tarikh*, p. 95.
97. Al-Zirikli, *Shibh*, p. 189.
98. G. Troeller, *Birth of Saudi Arabia*, p. 36.
99. G. de Gaury, *Faisal*, p. 13.
100. C. U. Aitchison, *A Collection*, p. 187.
101. P. Graves, *Life of Sir Percy Cox*, p. 92.
102. H. Wahba, *Jazirat*, pp. 254–255; C. U. Aitchison, *A Collection*, pp. 187–188; J. G. Lorimer, *Gazetteer*, vol. 1, part 2, p. 1158.
103. C. U. Aitchison, *A Collection*, p. 188; al-Bassam, *Tuhfat*, p. 392.
104. Nasif, *Madhi*, pp. 18–19.
105. Ibn Hizlul, *Tarikh*, pp. 96–98; al-Zirikli, *Shibh*, p. 197; H. Philby, *Saudi Arabia*, p. 259.
106. ARFP. *The Embassy in Constantinople Section*, 1912, file 1274, part 3, p. 19.
107. Ibn Hizlul, *Tarikh*, p. 98. Philby seems to treat the sharif's first and second campaigns as one and the same.
108. *Lughat al-Arab*, Aug. 1912, p. 74.
109. A. Musil, *Northern Negd*, p. 284.
110. H. Dickson, *Kuwait*, p. 149.
111. Ibid., pp. 153, 156.
112. *Lughat al-Arab*, May 1913, pp. 481–488.
113. *Umm al-Qura*, 1 March 1929.
114. *Lughat al-Arab*, Sept. 1912, p. 120.
115. Ibid., May 1913, pp. 481–488.
116. H. Dickson, *Kuwait*, pp. 155–156. See also C. A. Nallino, *Raccolta*, vol. 1, p. 118.
117. Ibn Hizlul, *Tarikh*, p. 109.
118. H. Dickson, *Kuwait*, p. 250.
119. D. van der Meulen, *Wells of Ibn Saud*, p. 66; P. Leppens, *Expédition*, p. 187.
120. *Umm al-Qura*, 1 March 1929.
121. H. Philby, *Heart of Arabia*, vol. 2, pp. 11–42; *Umm al-Qura*, 20 Sept. 1930.
122. Al-Madani, *Firqat*, p. 41.
123. Al-Zirikli, *Shibh*, pp. 263–264; H. Philby, *Saudi Arabia*, p. 261.
124. A. Rihani, *Ibn Saoud*, p. 191.
125. Ibid., p. 194; H. Dickson, *Arab of the Desert*, p. 109.
126. *Lughat al-Arab*, May 1913, pp. 482–483.
127. C. D. Forde, *The Habitat*, pp. 215–216; A. Musil, *Northern Negd*, pp. 281–282.
128. H. Wahba, *Jazirat*, p. 50; A. Rihani, *Ibn Saoud*, pp. 202–203.
129. H. Philby, *Heart of Arabia*, vol. 1, p. 297; H. Philby, *Arabia of the Wahhabis*, pp. 110–112; H. Philby, *Arabia*, p. 225; A. Rihani, *Ibn Saoud*, pp. 194, 202–203.
130. A. I. Pershits, *Khozyaystvo*, pp. 211–212.
131. H. Wahba, *Jazirat*, p. 126.
132. A. Musil, *Arabia*, p. 427.

Notes

133. H. Dickson, *Kuwait*, p. 156.
134. G. de Gaury, *Faisal*, p. 15.
135. H. Dickson, *Kuwait*, p. 155.
136. Ibid., p. 156.
137. Al-Madani, *Firqat*, pp. 34–35; *Lughat al-Arab*, Nov. 1913, pp. 277–278.
138. Al-Marik, *Lamahat*, pp. 56–60.
139. H. Dickson, *Arab of the Desert*, p. 232.
140. H. Dickson, *Kuwait*, p. 249; al-Madani, *Firqat*, pp. 35–39; H. Wahba, *Jazirat*, p. 153.
141. H. Dickson, *Kuwait*, p. 153.
142. *Lughat al-Arab*, Feb. 1913, p. 360.
143. H. Philby, *Saudi Arabia*, pp. 266–267.
144. ARFP. *The Embassy in Constantinople Section*, 1903, file 1966, p. 87.
145. A. Rihani, *Ibn Saoud*, pp. 207–208.
146. *Lughat al-Arab*, June 1913, pp. 585–586; al-Ahsai, *Tuhfat*, pp. 207–208.
147. ARFP. *The Political Archives Section*, 1912–1914, schedule 482, file 375, pp. 94–95.
148. H. Philby, *Saudi Arabia*, p. 266.
149. Ibn Hizlul, *Tarikh*, pp. 101–102; al-Ahsan, *Tuhfat*, p. 209; H. Philby, *Saudi Arabia*, pp. 267–268.
150. ARFP. *The Political Archives Section*, 1912–1914, schedule 482, file 375, p. 95.
151. A. Rihani, *Tarikh*, pp. 184–190; *Lughat al-Arab*, July 1913, p. 40.
152. ARFP. *The Political Archives Section*, 1911, schedule 482, file 374, p. 15. *Lughat al-Arab* (July 1913, p. 56) estimates the revenues from al-Hasa at 60,000 liras per year.
153. *Lughat al-Arab*, Aug. 1913, p. 112.
154. Ibid., Sept. 1913, p. 156.
155. H. Philby, *Saudi Arabia*, p. 269.
156. [G. P. Gooch and H. Temperley], *British Documents*, p. 193.
157. H. Philby, *Saudi Arabia*, p. 270.
158. ARFP. *The Embassy in Constantinople Section*, Basra, 1914, file 1276, part 3, p. 27.
159. H. Philby, *Saudi Arabia*, p. 269.
160. ARFP. *The Embassy in Constantinople Section*, Basra, 1914, file 1276, part 3, p. 37.
161. G. Troeller, *Birth of Saudi Arabia*, pp. 248ff.
162. See: H. Philby, *Arabian Jubilee*, p. 38.
163. *Memorial*, vol. 1, p. 391.
164. *Lughat al-Arab*, June 1914, p. 672; Nov. 1913, p. 271.

Chapter 10
1. Ibn Hizlul, *Tarikh*, pp. 103–104; al-Zirikli, *Shibh*, pp. 215, 219.
2. Ibn Hizlul, *Tarikh*, pp. 103–104; al-Zirikli, *Shibh*, pp. 216, 286.
3. G. Troeller, *Birth of Saudi Arabia*, p. 83.
4. See: H. Philby, *Saudi Arabia*, p. 271; D. A. Carruthers, 'Captain'.
5. Ibn Hizlul, *Tarikh*, p. 104.
6. G. Troeller, *Birth of Saudi Arabia*, p. 81.
7. H. Philby, *Saudi Arabia*, p. 272.
8. Ibn Hizlul, *Tarikh*, pp. 104–105; al-Zirikli, *Shibh*, p. 222; A. Rihani, *Tarikh*, p. 200.
9. A. Rihani, *Tarikh*, pp. 221–222; al-Zirikli, *Shibh*, p. 222.
10. Ibn Hizlul, *Tarikh*, pp. 104–105; H. Wahba, *Jazirat*, p. 295; al-Ahsai, *Tuhfat*, p. 212.
11. H. Philby, *Saudi Arabia*, p. 272.
12. H. Philby, *Arabian Jubilee*, pp. 40–41.
13. G. Troeller, *Birth of Saudi Arabia*, p. 83.
14. P. Graves, *Life of Sir Percy Cox*, p. 187; A. Musil, *Northern Negd*, pp. 42, 50–52, 179–180, 249; H. Philby, *Arabian Jubilee*, pp. 40–41.
15. H. Philby, *Saudi Arabia*, pp. 272–273.

Notes

16. C. U. Aitchison, *A Collection*, pp. 206–208; H. Wahba, *Jazirat*, pp. 334–335; G. Troeller, *Birth of Saudi Arabia*, pp. 250–256.
17. H. Philby, *Saudi Arabia*, p. 274; al-Zirikli, *Shibh*, p. 286.
18. Al-Ahsai, *Tuhfat*, p. 213; al-Zirikli, *Shibh*, p. 227.
19. Al-Zirikli, *Shibh*, p. 227.
20. Ibn Hizlul, *Tarikh*, pp. 105–108; al-Zirikli, *Shibh*, p. 230.
21. A. Musil, *Northern Negd*, p. 178.
22. Ibn Hizlul, *Tarikh*, pp. 108–109.
23. This section is based on a series of works that will already be familiar to experts in Middle Eastern and Arabian history: G. Antonius, *The Arab Awakening*; E. Bremond, *Le Hedjaz*; G. de Gaury, *Rulers*; E. Jung, *La Révolte*; T. E. Lawrence, *Seven Pillars*; [R. Storrs], *The Memoirs*; G. Troeller, *Birth of Saudi Arabia*; M. S. Lazarev, *Krushenie*; H. Wahba, *Jazirat*.
24. T. E. Lawrence, *Seven Pillars*, p. 283.
25. G. Antonius, *The Arab Awakening*, p. 414.
26. Ibid., pp. 419–420.
27. H. Philby, *Arabian Jubilee*, p. 44; al-Zirikli, *Shibh*, p. 208.
28. Al-Zirikli, *Shibh*, p. 243.
29. A. Musil, *Northern Negd*, pp. 288–289.
30. H. Philby, *Arabian Jubilee*, p. 45.
31. A. Rihani, *Tarikh*, pp. 210–211.
32. H. Philby, *Arabian Jubilee*, p. 46.
33. H. Philby, *Saudi Arabia*, pp. 273–274; G. Troeller, *Birth of Saudi Arabia*, pp. 99–101.
34. P. Graves, *Life of Sir Percy Cox*, p. 214.
35. H. Philby, *Saudi Arabia*, p. 274; A. Rihani, *Tarikh*, pp. 215–216.
36. H. Philby, *Arabian Jubilee*, pp. 46–48.
37. G. Troeller, *Birth of Saudi Arabia*, p. 83.
38. Ibn Hizlul, *Tarikh*, pp. 109–110.
39. H. Wahba, *Jazirat*, pp. 172–174.
40. H. Philby, *Saudi Arabia*, p. 275.
41. Ibid., pp. 275–276.
42. H. Philby, *Arabian Jubilee*, pp. 52–54.
43. H. Philby, *Heart of Arabia*, vol. 1, pp. 284–285.
44. H. Philby, *Arabian Jubilee*, pp. 56–58.
45. H. Philby, *Arabia of the Wahhabis*, pp. 223–224, 296, 100–101, 258, 331–335; H. Philby, *Arabian Jubilee*, p. 59.
46. Ibn Hizlul, *Tarikh*, p. 114.
47. *Al-Qibla*, 24 Sept. 1917.
48. Ibn Hizlul, *Tarikh*, p. 113.
49. H. Philby, *Arabia of the Wahhabis*, p. 19.
50. Ibid., pp. 19–21; Ibn Hizlul, *Tarikh*, pp. 114–115.
51. *Al-Qibla*, 3 Aug. 1918.
52. Al-Zirikli, *Shibh*, p. 317.
53. See: *Noveyshaya*, p. 8.
54. Our description of the developments in Yemen and Asir largely follows G. Antonius' *The Arab Awakening*.
55. H. Philby, *Saudi Arabia*, p. 277.
56. *Al-Qibla*, 3 Aug. 1918; al-Bassam, *Tuhfat*, p. 398; Ibn Hizlul, *Tarikh*, pp. 116–117.
57. H. Philby, *Saudi Arabia*, p. 277.
58. Ibn Hizlul, *Tarikh*, pp. 117–118.
59. Ibid., p. 118; Abdallah, *Muzakkarat*, pp. 150–153.
60. Ibn Hizlul, *Tarikh*, pp. 118–119.
61. Ibid., pp. 119–120.

Notes

62. Abdallah, *Muzakkarat*, pp. 150–151; A. Rihani, *Tarikh*, pp. 219–226.
63. Abdallah, *Muzakkarat*, pp. 153–155.
64. Ibn Hizlul, *Tarikh*, pp. 121–122.
65. *Al-Qibla*, 19 July 1919.
66. H. Philby, *Saudi Arabia*, p. 278; Nasif, *Madhi*, p. 65.
67. H. Philby, *Saudi Arabia*, p. 279.
68. D. Lloyd George, *The Truth*, p. 128.

Chapter 11

1. H. Dickson, *Kuwait*, p. 250.
2. Ibid., pp. 250–251; Ibn Hizlul, *Tarikh*, p. 112.
3. H. Dickson, *Kuwait*, p. 251.
4. C. U. Aitchison, *A Collection*, p. 208.
5. Ibn Hizlul, *Tarikh*, pp. 122–123; H. Dickson, *Kuwait*, p. 251.
6. H. Dickson, *Kuwait*, p. 251.
7. Ibn Hizlul, *Tarikh*, pp. 125–126; H. Dickson, *Kuwait*, p. 253.
8. S. M. al-Shamlan, *Min Tarikh*, p. 186.
9. Al-Zirikli, *Shibh*, pp. 238–239; H. Dickson, *Kuwait*, pp. 253–255; S. M. al-Shamlan, *Min Tarikh*, p. 188; Ibn Hizlul, *Tarikh*, pp. 127–128.
10. H. Dickson, *Kuwait*, p. 257; al-Zirikli, *Shibh*, p. 239.
11. F. Hamza, *Qalb*, pp. 166–167.
12. Al-Bassam, *Tuhfat*, pp. 400–401; H. Philby, *Saudi Arabia*, p. 280; A. Rihani, *Tarikh*, p. 266; F. Hamza, *Qalb*, p. 167.
13. H. Philby, *Saudi Arabia*, p. 280.
14. Al-Bassam, *Tuhfat*, p. 402.
15. Ibn Hizlul, *Tarikh*, pp. 129–131.
16. Al-Bassam, *Tuhfat*, p. 403.
17. H. Philby, *Saudi Arabia*, pp. 281–282; A. Musil, *Northern Negd*, pp. 291–292.
18. Ibn Hizlul, *Tarikh*, pp. 131–133.
19. H. Philby, *Saudi Arabia*, p. 281; Ibn Hizlul, *Tarikh*, pp. 133–136.
20. Al-Bassam, *Tuhfat*, p. 404; A. Rihani, *Tarikh*, pp. 266–267; P. W. Harrison, *The Arab at Home*, pp. 131–132.
21. H. Philby, *Arabia of the Wahhabis*, p. 102.
22. G. Bell, *The Letters*, vol. 2, pp. 534–535.
23. J. B. Glubb, *War in the Desert*, p. 62.
24. H. Wahba, *Jazirat*, p. 262; G. Bell, *The Letters*, vol. 2, pp. 635–636.
25. Wizarat al-Kharijiya, *Majmuat*, pp. 1–3; H. Philby, *Saudi Arabia*, p. 284; G. Bell, *The Letters*, vol. 2, p. 659; A. Musil, *Northern Negd*, p. 293.
26. A. Musil, *Northern Negd*, p. 292.
27. H. Philby, *Saudi Arabia*, p. 283; C. S. Jarvis, *Arab Command*, pp. 101–102.
28. H. Dickson, *Kuwait*, pp. 267–268; H. Philby, *Saudi Arabia*, p. 284.
29. Wizarat al-Kharijiya, *Majmuat*, pp. 5–9.
30. H. Dickson, *Kuwait*, pp. 274–275.
31. Ibid., pp. 272–273.
32. C. S. Jarvis, *Arab Command*, p. 106.
33. J. B. Glubb, *War in the Desert*, pp. 74–78.
34. H. Philby, *Saudi Arabia*, p. 285; A. Musil, *Northern Negd*, p. 295.
35. H. Philby, *Saudi Arabia*, pp. 285–286; Nasif, *Madhi*, pp. 97–98; Saltana Najd, *al-Kitab*, pp. 1–76; J. B. Glubb, *War in the Desert*, pp. 107–111.
36. C. S. Jarvis, *Arab Command*, pp. 115–118; A. Rihani, *Tarikh*, pp. 296–298.
37. H. Wahba, *Jazirat*, pp. 217–219.
38. Ibn Hizlul, *Tarikh*, pp. 144–145.

39. E. Rutter, *The Holy Cities*, vol. 1, p. 63.
40. *Oriente Moderno*, 1920, vol. 4, no. 10, p. 647.
41. F. Hamza, *al-Bilad*, p. 53.
42. Ibn Hizlul, *Tarikh*, pp. 145–150.
43. A. Musil, *Northern Negd*, pp. 294–295; al-Khatib, *al-Imam*, p. 42.
44. H. Wahba, *Jazirat*, p. 270.
45. A. J. Toynbee, *Survey*, pp. 290–293.
46. G. Antonius, *The Arab Awakening*, p. 331.
47. Ibid., pp. 331–335; A. Rihani, *Tarikh*, pp. 292–293.
48. *The Archives of USSR Foreign Policy, Ministry of Foreign Affairs, Russian Federation* (henceforth: *AFP USSR*), 1927, section 127, inventory 1, file 1, dossier 11, p. 20.
49. H. Wahba, *Jazirat*, p. 271; H. Philby, *Saudi Arabia*, p. 285; al-Khatib, *al-Imam*, pp. 43–44.
50. H. Wahba, *Jazirat*, pp. 147–149; H. Wahba, *Khamsuna*, p. 240; al-Khatib, *al-Imam*, p. 41; Ibn Hizlul, *Tarikh*, pp. 150–151.
51. Ibn Hizlul, *Tarikh*, pp. 151–153; A. Rihani, *Tarikh*, pp. 299–303; al-Khatib, *al-Imam*, pp. 45–47; H. Philby, *Saudi Arabia*, p. 287.
52. H. Wahba, *Khamsuna*, pp. 57–60.
53. E. Rutter, *The Holy Cities*, vol. 2, pp. 29–33.
54. H. Philby, *Saudi Arabia*, p. 287.
55. Ibn Hizlul, *Tarikh*, pp. 154–155; al-Khatib, *al-Imam*, pp. 55–65; Nasif, *Madhi*, p. 143; A. Rihani, *Tarikh*, pp. 304–309; H. Philby, *Saudi Arabia*, p. 288.
56. Ibn Hizlul, *Tarikh*, p. 156; al-Khatib, *al-Imam*, p. 69; H. Wahba, *Jazirat*, p. 273.
57. Nasif, *Madhi*, pp. 141–143; al-Khatib, *al-Imam*, pp. 72–79.
58. Nasif, *Madhi*, pp. 156–167; al-Khatib, *al-Imam*, pp. 75–76.
59. Ibn Hizlul, *Tarikh*, pp. 166–167.
60. H. Wahba, *Khamsuna*, p. 61.
61. *Umm al-Qura*, 12 Dec. 1924.
62. Al-Khatib, *al-Imam*, pp. 92–94.
63. Ibn Hizlul, *Tarikh*, pp. 168–169.
64. *Umm al-Qura*, 10 Jan. 1925; Ibn Hizlul, *Tarikh*, p. 166.
65. Al-Khatib, *al-Imam*, p. 101.
66. Al-Zirikli, *Shibh*, p. 344.
67. Al-Khatib, *al-Imam*, p. 106.
68. Ibid., pp. 103–107.
69. Ibid., pp. 98–99; Wizarat al-Kharijiya, *Sahifa*; H. Wahba, *Jazirat*, p. 275.
70. A. Musil, *Northern Negd*, p. 299; H. Wahba, *Jazirat*, p. 275.
71. G. Clayton, *Arabian Diary*, pp. 130–131.
72. H. Dickson, *Kuwait*, p. 284.
73. G. Clayton, *Arabian Diary*, pp. 99–129; Wizarat al-Kharijiya, *Majmuat*, pp. 10–17.
74. A. Rihani, *Tarikh*, pp. 183–187, 392; H. Philby, *Saudi Arabia*, p. 290; Nasif, *Madhi*, pp. 204–213.
75. Ibn Hizlul, *Tarikh*, pp. 173–177; *Umm al-Qura*, 13 Nov. 1925; A. Rihani, *Tarikh*, p. 392; H. Philby, *Saudi Arabia*, pp. 289–290.
76. Ibn Hizlul, *Tarikh*, p. 177; *Umm al-Qura*, 2 Dec. 1925.
77. *Umm al-Qura*, 16 Dec. 1925.
78. E. Rutter, *The Holy Cities*, vol. 1, p. 299.
79. *AFP USSR*, 1926, section 127, inventory 1, file 1, dossier 6, pp. 4–6.
80. Al-Khatib, *al-Imam*, pp. 133–135; *Umm al-Qura*, 15 Jan. 1926.
81. Al-Khatib, *al-Imam*, p. 137.
82. H. Philby, *Saudi Arabia*, p. 301.
83. Al-Khatib, *al-Imam*, p. 143; H. Philby, *Saudi Arabia*, p. 301.
84. *TASS*, 27 Sept. 1926, daytime issue, no. 15.

Notes

85. *AFP USSR*, 1929, section 127, inventory 1, file 2, dossier 18, pp. 3–5, 10.

Chapter 12
1. H. Wahba, *Khamsuna*, pp. 264–271.
2. *Umm al-Qura*, 12 Jan., 25 Sept. 1925.
3. H. Philby, *Arabian Jubilee*, p. 82.
4. H. Philby, *Saudi Arabia*, p. 305.
5. Ibid., pp. 304–305.
6. Ibid.
7. *Umm al-Qura*, 12 Sept. 1926; H. Laoust, *Essai*, pp. 624–630.
8. *Umm al-Qura*, 1 June 1925.
9. H. Wahba, *Arabian Days*, p. 98.
10. H. Wahba, *Jazirat*, p. 22.
11. H. Philby, *Pilgrim in Arabia*, pp. 60–63.
12. H. Wahba, *Arabian Days*, p. 20.
13. H. Wahba, *Khamsuna*, pp. 66–69; H. Wahba, *Arabian Days*, pp. 95–96.
14. *Umm al-Qura*, 25 Sept. 1925.
15. H. Wahba, *Jazirat*, pp. 309–312.
16. Ibn Hizlul, *Tarikh*, pp. 184–185.
17. A. J. Toynbee, *Survey*, pp. 312–319.
18. M. Mustafa, *Fi Qalb*, p. 41.
19. *Umm al-Qura*, 23 April 1926.
20. H. Wahba, *Jazirat*, pp. 309–312.
21. F. Hamza, *al-Bilad*, p. 216; H. Wahba, *Khamsuna*, p. 271.
22. *Umm al-Qura*, 28 Jan., 25 Feb., 4, 11, 18 March 1927; 27 Aug. 1928.
23. *Umm al-Qura*, 2 Aug. 1929.
24. *AFP USSR*, 1929, section 127, inventory 1, file 2, dossier 18, p. 19.
25. H. Dickson, *Kuwait*, pp. 285–287; H. Dickson, *Arab of the Desert*, p. 353; A. Rihani, *Ibn Saoud*, pp. 192–193.
26. H. Dickson, *Kuwait*, p. 281.
27. J. B. Glubb, *War in the Desert*, p. 178; al-Zirikli, *Shibh*, p. 470.
28. Quoted by al-Zirikli, *Shibh*, pp. 464–465.
29. Ibid., pp. 468–469.
30. Ibn Hizlul, *Tarikh*, pp. 185–186; H. Wahba, *Jazirat*, p. 291; H. Armstrong, *Lord*, p. 216.
31. *Umm al-Qura*, 8 April 1927; H. Wahba, *Jazirat*, p. 293.
32. Ibn Hizlul, *Tarikh*, pp. 187–190.
33. *Lughat al-Arab*, Aug. 1927, p. 123; Nov. 1927, pp. 574–575.
34. H. Dickson, *Kuwait*, p. 287. However, according to al-Zirikli (*Shibh*, p. 494), Hamid ibn Muhammad fought against the Ikhwan, though Ibn Saud might have 'forgiven' him, giving him a chance to demonstrate his loyalty.
35. Great Britain, Colonial Office, *Report*, p. 24.
36. J. B. Glubb, *War in the Desert*, p. 193.
37. H. Philby, *Saudi Arabia*, p. 306; H. Dickson, *Kuwait*, p. 294.
38. H. Philby, *Saudi Arabia*, p. 306; H. Wahba, *Khamsuna*, p. 90.
39. H. Philby, *Saudi Arabia*, p. 306; H. Dickson, *Kuwait*, p. 287.
40. H. Dickson, *Kuwait*, pp. 288–289.
41. J. B. Glubb, *War in the Desert*, p. 195.
42. Ibid., p. 200.
43. Ibid., pp. 201–202.
44. *The Daily Telegraph*, 27 March 1928.
45. H. Wahba, *Khamsuna*, pp. 92, 283–286.
46. *Umm al-Qura*, 13 April 1928.

Notes

47. H. Philby, *Saudi Arabia*, p. 307; J. B. Glubb, *War in the Desert*, pp. 209–225.
48. H. Philby, *Saudi Arabia*, pp. 307–308.
49. J. B. Glubb, *War in the Desert*, p. 267.
50. *Umm al-Qura*, 12 Oct., 18 Dec. 1928.
51. Ibn Hizlul, *Tarikh*, p. 191; al-Zirikli, *Shibh*, p. 477.
52. H. Wahba, *Jazirat*, p. 302.
53. Ibn Hizlul, *Tarikh*, p. 192.
54. J. B. Glubb, *War in the Desert*, pp. 236–247, 264–267, 282–284; *Lughat al-Arab*, April 1929, pp. 351–352.
55. Ibn Hizlul, *Tarikh*, p. 192.
56. Ibid., p. 193.
57. J. B. Glubb, *War in the Desert*, pp. 287–289; H. Philby, *Saudi Arabia*, p. 309.
58. H. Dickson, *Kuwait*, pp. 302–303; H. Philby, *Saudi Arabia*, p. 309.
59. Ibn Hizlul, *Tarikh*, pp. 193–194; H. Philby, *Saudi Arabia*, p. 309.
60. H. Wahba, *Jazirat*, p. 304.
61. Al-Ahsai, *Tarikh*, p. 230; H. Philby, *Saudi Arabia*, p. 310.
62. H. Dickson, *Kuwait*, pp. 305–306.
63. H. Wahba, *Khamsuna*, pp. 293–301.
64. Al-Ahsai, *Tarikh*, pp. 230–231; al-Zirikli, *Shibh*, pp. 491–493.
65. Al-Zirikli, *Shibh*, p. 491.
66. H. Philby, *Saudi Arabia*, pp. 309–310.
67. H. Dickson, *Kuwait*, pp. 313–315.
68. Ibn Hizlul, *Tarikh*, pp. 195–196.
69. J. B. Glubb, *War in the Desert*, p. 306.
70. Al-Zirikli, *Shibh*, p. 496.
71. Ibn Hizlul, *Tarikh*, pp. 196–199; al-Zirikli, *Shibh*, pp. 499–501.
72. Ibn Hizlul, *Tarikh*, p. 190; J. B. Glubb, *War in the Desert*, pp. 313–314; H. Dickson, *Kuwait*, pp. 306–318.
73. J. B. Glubb, *War in the Desert*, pp. 320–326; H. Dickson, *Kuwait*, pp. 317–320.
74. Ibn Hizlul, *Tarikh*, p. 199.
75. *Umm al-Qura*, 10 Jan. 1930.
76. H. Dickson, *Kuwait*, pp. 319–320.
77. H. Philby, *Saudi Arabia*, p. 311; H. Dickson, *Kuwait*, pp. 323–324; al-Zirikli, *Shibh*, pp. 504–505.
78. Ibn Hizlul, *Tarikh*, pp. 201–203; al-Zirikli, *Shibh*, p. 507.
79. H. Dickson, *Kuwait*, pp. 326–327.
80. Ibid., p. 328.
81. Al-Zirikli, *Shibh*, p. 507.
82. H. Wahba, *Arabian Days*, p. 145.
83. Pershits considers the Ikhwan's defeat 'a blow at the intrigues of internal and external reaction' (*Khozyaystvo*, p. 218).
84. H. Philby, *Saudi Arabia*, p. 312; Wizarat al-Kharijiya, *Majmuat*, pp. 68–72;
85. *Al-Mamlaka*, p. 258.
86. H. Philby, *Saudi Arabia*, pp. 314–315; al-Mukhtar, *Tarikh*, part 2, p. 453.
87. Al-Khatib, *al-Imam*, pp. 161–163.
88. Ibn Hizlul, *Tarikh*, pp. 204–207.
89. Al-Zirikli, *Shibh*, pp. 557–559.
90. Ibn Hizlul, *Tarikh*, pp. 207–213.
91. *Umm al-Qura*, 5 Aug. 1932; al-Khatib, *al-Imam*, p. 204.
92. *Umm al-Qura*, 5 Aug. 1932; Ibn Hizlul, *Tarikh*, pp. 212–213.
93. See: V. I. Nosenko, *Saudovsko-Yemenskaya*, pp. 294–298; *Lughat al-Arab*, July 1926, p. 54; Aug. 1926, p. 109; Amin Said, *Muluk*, pp. 136–138; H. Philby, *Arabian Jubilee*, pp. 127–128.

Notes

94. *AFP USSR*, 1932, section 127, inventory 1, file 3, dossier 29, pp. 3–4.
95. Al-Khatib, *al-Imam*, p. 207; Ibn Hizlul, *Tarikh*, pp. 213–216.
96. *Konstitutsii*, pp. 437–438.
97. F. Hamza, *al-Bilad*, pp. 84–87; H. Philby, *Saudi Arabia*, p. 325; *Konstitutsii*, pp. 431–437.
98. Al-Khatib, *al-Imam*, pp. 221–223.
99. For details of the Saudi-Yemeni conflict, see: B. I. Nosenko, *Saudovsko-Yemenskaya*; M. W. Wenner, *Modern Yemen*; A. Faroughy, *Introducing Yemen*; G. de Gaury, *Faisal*; S. Mustafa, *Taqwim*.
100. *AFP USSR*, 1934, section 127, inventory 1, file 3, dossier 34, p. 1.

Chapter 13

1. Al-Zirikli, *Shibh*, p. 650.
2. G. Lipsky et al., *Saudi Arabia*, p. 311.
3. *Memorial*, vol. 2, p. 204.
4. Ibid., p. 218.
5. H. Laoust, *Essai*, p. 294.
6. Ibid., p. 310.
7. Ibid., pp. 300–301.
8. H. Laoust, *Le Traité*, pp. 169–170.
9. Al-Madani, *Firqat*, p. 35.
10. H. Wahba, *Jazirat*, pp. 290–292.
11. A. Rihani, *Ibn Saoud*, pp. 204–206.
12. H. Laoust, *Essai*, pp. 316–317.
13. Al-Zirikli, *Shibh*, p. 575.
14. Ibid., pp. 743–744.
15. H. Philby, *Heart of Arabia*, vol. 1, p. 297.
16. A. Rihani, *Ibn Saoud*, pp. 135–136.
17. H. Wahba, *Jazirat*, p. 50.
18. Ibid., pp. 129–132.
19. Aramco, *Royal Family*, pp. 30–31.
20. Al-Zirikli, *al-Alam*, vol. 4, p. 277.
21. H. Philby, *Heart of Arabia*, vol. 1, pp. 76, 300.
22. Ibid., p. 374.
23. F. Hamza, *Qalb*, p. 72.
24. Al-Zirikli, *Shibh*, pp. 355–356.
25. C. Nallino, *Raccolta*, vol. 1, pp. 20–22.
26. F. Hamza, *Qalb*, p. 73.
27. Ibid., p. 74.
28. C. Nallino, *Raccolta*, vol. 1, pp. 66–68, 71–76.
29. A. MacKie Frood, 'Recent Economic and Social Developments', pp. 166–167.
30. M. Sadiq, *Tatawwur*, pp. 25–26.
31. *Konstitutsii*, p. 426.
32. Ibid., pp. 426–427.
33. Ibid., pp. 427, 430.
34. Ibid., pp. 430–435.
35. See: G. Lipsky et al., *Saudi Arabia*, p. 114.
36. Al-Zirikli, *Shibh*, pp. 571–572.
37. Ibid., p. 573.
38. G. Lipsky et al., *Saudi Arabia*, pp. 114–115.
39. Al-Zirikli, *Shibh*, p. 577.
40. Ibid., p. 368.

Notes

41. Ibid., pp. 382–383.
42. Ibid., p. 375.
43. Ibid.
44. Ibid., p. 376.
45. Ibid., p. 377–378.
46. F. Hamza, *Qalb*, p. 78; S. al-Muhammasani, *al-Awdha*, pp. 319–320.
47. F. Hamza, *Qalb*, p. 78.
48. Al-Zirikli, *Shibh*, p. 454.
49. Ibid., p. 358.
50. Ibid., p. 359.
51. Ibid., p. 402.
52. Ibid.
53. Ibid., p. 412.
54. See: N. I. Proshin, *Saudovskaya*, p. 87.
55. A. MacKie Frood, 'Recent Economic and Social Developments', pp. 166–167.
56. *Konstitutsii*, p. 437.
57. H. Philby, *Saudi Arabia*, p. 294.
58. Al-Zirikli, *Shibh*, pp. 909–910.
59. *AFP USSR*, 1929, section 127, inventory 1, file 2, dossier 18, p. 37.
60. Al-Zirikli, *Shibh*, p. 910.
61. Ibid., pp. 910–911.
62. H. Philby, *Saudi Arabia*, pp. 294–295.
63. Ibid., p. 296; al-Zirikli, *Shibh*, p. 367.
64. *Lughat al-Arab*, Jan. 1914, p. 355.
65. Al-Zirikli, *Ma Raaitu*, pp. 27–28.
66. A. Musil, *Manners and Customs*, p. 431.
67. Al-Zirikli, *Ma Raaitu*, pp. 152–153.
68. H. Dickson, *Arab of the Desert*, pp. 118–132; A. Musil, *Manners and Customs*, pp. 438–452; H. Wahba, *Arabian Days*, p. 14.
69. H. Dickson, *Arab of the Desert*, pp. 431–440; J. J. Hess, *Von den Beduinen*, p. 90; A. Musil, *Manners and Customs*, pp. 489–503.
70. *Lughat al-Arab*, Jan. 1914, p. 356; al-Zirikli, *Shibh*, p. 420.
71. *Memorial*, vol. 2, pp. 226–231.
72. P. W. Harrison, *The Arab at Home*, p. 150.
73. F. Hamza, *al-Bilad*, p. 188.
74. F. S. Vidal, *Oasis of al-Hasa*, p. 34.
75. Ibid., p. 209.
76. H. Wahba, *Jazirat*, pp. 71–75.
77. F. S. Vidal, *Oasis of al-Hasa*, p. 34.
78. P. W. Harrison, *The Arab at Home*, pp. 229–230.
79. F. S. Vidal, *Oasis of al-Hasa*, p. 96.
80. Abd al-Jabbar, *al-Tayarat*, pp. 125–126.
81. *Al-Majmua*, pp. 1–15.
82. H. Wahba, *Jazirat*, pp. 300–301.
83. H. Philby, *Heart of Arabia*, vol. 1, pp. 294–295.
84. F. Hamza, *al-Bilad*, p. 189.
85. Ibid., pp. 190–191.
86. *Umm al-Qura*, 19 Aug. 1927; S. al-Muhammasani, *al-Awdha*, pp. 327–329.
87. S. al-Muhammasani, *al-Awdha*, p. 327.
88. Ibid., p. 329.
89. Al-Zirikli, *Shibh*, p. 426.

Notes

90. *Umm al-Qura*, 19 Aug. 1927.
91. Al-Zirikli, *Shibh*, p. 425; S. al-Muhammasani, *al-Awdha*, pp. 328-329.
92. Abd al-Jabbar, *al-Tayarat*, p. 126.
93. *Lughat al-Arab*, Jan. 1914, pp. 355-356; S. al-Muhammasani, *al-Awdha*, pp. 329-332.
94. *Umm al-Qura*, 19 Aug. 1927.
95. S. al-Muhammasani, *al-Awdha*, pp. 330-331.
96. G. M. Baroody, *Crime*, pp. 35-41.
97. P. Hart, *Application*, pp. 165-173; G. Lipsky et al., *Saudi Arabia*, p. 122.
98. G. M. Baroody, *Crime*, pp. 89-101.
99. *Area Handbook*, p. 194.
100. G. Lipsky et al., *Saudi Arabia*, p. 122.
101. G. M. Baroody, *Crime*, pp. 105-107; *Area Handbook*, p. 194.
102. *Memorial*, vol. 2, pp. 291-292.
103. Ibid., p. 328.
104. Ibid., p. 329; *Umm al-Qura*, 18 Sept. 1925.
105. *Memorial*, vol. 2, pp. 292-293.
106. Ibid., pp. 306-308.
107. Ibid., pp. 320-321.
108. A. Rihani, *Ibn Saoud*, pp. 202-204.
109. H. Philby, *Arabia of the Wahhabis*, p. 21.
110. Ibid., pp. 217-218.
111. A. Musil, *Northern Negd*, pp. 253-254.
112. H. Dickson, *Arab of the Desert*, pp. 440-442.
113. Ibid., pp. 442-443.
114. Ibid., p. 440.
115. *Memorial*, vol. 2, p. 318.
116. H. Philby, *Heart of Arabia*, vol. 1, p. 6.
117. Al-Madani, *Firqat*, pp. 42-43.
118. H. Wahba, *Arabian Days*, pp. 67-69.
119. Al-Zirikli, *Shibh*, p. 758.
120. Ibid., p. 1420.
121. Al-Madani, *Firqat*, p. 43.
122. A. Wahba, *Jazirat*, pp. 145-147.
123. Al-Zirikli, *Shibh*, p. 1419.
124. H. Wahba, *Jazirat*, pp. 110-113.
125. Al-Zirikli, *Shibh*, p. 1420.
126. Quoted from: ibid., p. 187.
127. Ibid., pp. 177-178.
128. R. Lebkicher et al., *Arabia of Ibn Saud*, pp. 86-88.
129. Al-Zirikli, *Shibh*, p. 178.
130. Ibid., p. 458.
131. *Umm al-Qura*, 20 July 1950.
132. Al-Zirikli, *Shibh*, p. 991.
133. Ibid., pp. 989-991.
134. Ibid., p. 751.
135. Ibid., p. 412.
136. *Lughat al-Arab*, July 1911, pp. 16-25.
137. A. Rihani, *Ibn Saoud*, p. 207.
138. H. Wahba, *Jazirat*, p. 50.
139. Al-Marik, *Lamahat*, pp. 15-16.
140. A. Rihani, *Ibn Saoud*, pp. 96-99.

Notes

141. H. Wahba, *Arabian Days*, p. 77.
142. Al-Zirikli, *Shibh*, pp. 1023, 1025.
143. Abd al-Jabbar, *al-Tayarat*, pp. 155-156.
144. Nasif, *Madhi*, p. 112.
145. Ibid.
146. Al-Marik, *Lamahat*, pp. 156-157.
147. Al-Zirikli, *Shibh*, p. 1025.
148. *Umm al-Qura*, 18, 25 Jan., 1 Feb. 1929; F. Hamza, *al-Bilad*, pp. 220-223.
149. G. Trial, R. Winder, *Modern Education*, pp. 121-134.
150. H. Wahba, *Arabian Days*, pp. 173, 49-51.
151. F. S. Vidal, *Oasis of al-Hasa*, p. 33.
152. Al-Zirikli, *Shibh*, pp. 1026-1030.
153. Ibid., pp. 635-636.
154. H. Philby, *Saudi Arabia*, p. 327.
155. Ibid.
156. Al-Zirikli, *Shibh*, p. 635.

Chapter 14

1. Al-Zirikli, *Shibh*, p. 1337; H. Wahba, *Jazirat*, p. 146; H. Philby, *Arabian Jubilee*, pp. 170-175; F.-J. Tomiché, *L'Arabie*, p. 56.
2. H. Philby, *Saudi Arabia*, p. 330.
3. H. Philby, *Arabian Jubilee*, p. 177; H. Philby, *Saudi Arabia*, p. 330.
4. S. Klebanoff, *Middle East Oil*, p. 4.
5. Ibid., p. 5.
6. Ibid., p. 7.
7. S. Klebanoff, *Middle East Oil*, p. 7.
8. *Aramco Handbook*, p. 107.
9. H. Philby, *Saudi Arabia*, p. 329; A. Rihani, *Ibn Saoud*, pp. 79-88; R. Knauerhase, *Saudi Arabian Economy*, p. 157; H. Philby, *Arabian Jubilee*, p. 177.
10. H. Philby, *Saudi Arabia*, p. 329.
11. *Aramco Handbook*, pp. 108-109.
12. Ibid., pp. 109-110.
13. K. S. Twitchell, *Saudi Arabia*, pp. 220-224.
14. H. Philby, *Saudi Arabia*, p. 311; H. Philby, *Arabian Jubilee*, pp. 177-178; S. H. Longrigg, *Oil*, pp. 107-108.
15. D. Howarth, *Desert King*, p. 182.
16. *Aramco Handbook*, p. 111.
17. H. Philby, *Saudi Arabia*, p. 331.
18. R. Knauerhase, *Saudi Arabian Economy*, pp. 159-161.
19. *Aramco Handbook*, pp. 113-114.
20. R. Knauerhase, *Saudi Arabian Economy*, pp. 163-164.
21. Ibid., p. 194; J. R. Presley and A. J. Westaway, *A Guide*, p. 51; *Arab Oil & Gas Directory, 1979-80*, p. 252; *Arab Oil & Gas Directory, 1994*, p. 347.

Chapter 15

1. For details, see: N. I. Proshin, *Saudovskaya*, pp. 98-112.
2. H. Wahba, *Khamsuna*, p. 50; see also A. Assah, *Miracle*, pp. 64-65.
3. H. Wahba, *Khamsuna*, p. 121.
4. N. I. Proshin, *Saudovskaya*, p. 100.
5. V. Minaev, *Podryvnaya*, p. 47.
6. H. Wahba, *Khamsuna*, pp. 108-109.

Notes

7. V. Minaev, *Podryvnaya*, p. 48.
8. H. Wahba, *Khamsuna*, p. 111.
9. K. S. Twitchell, *Saudi Arabia*, pp. 167–168; A. Assah, *Miracle*, pp. 64–65.
10. See: N. I. Proshin, *Saudovskaya*, p. 103.
11. V. Minaev, *Podryvnaya*, p. 48.
12. N. I. Proshin, *Saudovskaya*, p. 104.
13. Ibid.
14. V. Minaev, *Podryvnaya*, p. 48.
15. H. Philby, *Saudi Arabia*, p. 337.
16. R. E. Mikesell and H. B. Chenery, *Arabian Oil*, p. 77.
17. N. I. Proshin, *Saudovskaya*, p. 106.
18. B. Shwadran, *Middle East Oil*, pp. 318–319, 324.
19. S. Klebanoff, *Middle East Oil*, p. 14.
20. Ibid., p. 10.
21. Ibid., p. 17.
22. Ibid.
23. Quoted from: V. Perlo, *American Imperialism*, p. 182.
24. B. Shwadran, *Middle East Oil*, p. 319.
25. R. F. Mikesell and H. B. Chenery, *Arabian Oil*, pp. 132–133.
26. R. Knauerhase, *Saudi Arabian Economy*, p. 194.
27. W. Eddy, *F. D. R. Meets*; G. de Gaury, *Faisal*, p. 68; *Area Handbook*, p. 172.
28. G. de Gaury, *Faisal*, p. 68; S. Klebanoff, *Middle East Oil*, p. 21; G. Lenczowsky, *Middle East*, p. 442.
29. S. Klebanoff, *Middle East Oil*, p. 22.
30. Ibid., p. 23; *Aramco Handbook*, p. 86.
31. Ibid.
32. Ibid., p. 113.
33. S. Klebanoff, *Middle East Oil*, p. 23.
34. G. Lenczowsky, *Middle East*, p. 442. N. I. Proshin, *Saudovskaya*, p. 109.
35. For a detailed description of their meeting, see: A. Eddy, *F. D. R. Meets*.
36. Ibid., p. 35.
37. Ibid., p. 42.
38. *Area Handbook*, p. 172.
39. S. Klebanoff, *Middle East Oil*, p. 57.

Chapter 16

1. *Aramco Handbook*, p. 113.
2. B. B. Ozoling, *Ekonomika*, p. 131; R. Knauerhase, *Saudi Arabian Economy*, p. 196.
3. *Aramco Handbook*, p. 77.
4. V. V. Ozoling, *Ekonomika*, p. 111; R. Knauerhase, *Saudi Arabian Economy*, p. 168.
5. *Aramco Handbook*, p. 148.
6. S. H. Longrigg, *Oil*, p. 208.
7. *Aramco Handbook*, p. 111–112; R. Knauerhase, *Saudi Arabian Economy*, p. 193.
8. R. Knauerhase, *Saudi Arabian Economy*, p. 180.
9. Ibid., p. 163.
10. See: A. M. Vassiliev, *Fakely*, pp. 87–91.
11. R. Knauerhase, *Saudi Arabian Economy*, pp. 180–181; *Area Handbook*, p. 246.
12. *Area Handbook*, p. 246.
13. V. V. Ozoling, *Ekonomika*, p. 123; R. Knauerhase, *Saudi Arabian Economy*, p. 181.
14. V. V. Ozoling, *Ekonomika*, pp. 153–154.
15. R. Knauerhase, *Saudi Arabian Economy*, p. 164.

Notes

16. Ibid., pp. 164–165.
17. R. Knauerhase, *Saudi Arabian Economy*, pp. 164–165.
18. N. I. Proshin, *Saudovskaya*, p. 117.
19. R. Knauerhase, *Saudi Arabian Economy*, p. 168.
20. *Keesing's Contemporary Archives*, p. 13655; *Arab World. Political and Diplomatic History, 1900–1967*, 6 July 1954.
21. N. I. Proshin, *Saudovskaya*, p. 113.
22. See: D. Howarth, *Desert King*, p. 214; H. Philby, *Forty Years*, pp. 8, 38–39.
23. A. Said, *Tarikh*, vol. 3, p. 23.
24. G. de Gaury, *Faisal*, p. 77.
25. Al-Zirikli, *Shibh*, p. 986.
26. Ibid., p. 1433.
27. Ibid.; G. de Gaury, *Faisal*, p. 78.
28. A. Said, *Tarikh*, vol. 3, p. 5; H. Philby, *Saudi Arabia*, p. 358; G. de Gaury, *Faisal*, pp. 78–80.
29. G. de Gaury, *Faisal*, p. 80.
30. Al-Zirikli, *Shibh*, p. 1402.
31. Ibid., p. 954.
32. D. Howarth, *Desert King*, p. 231.
33. A. Said, *Tarikh*, vol. 3, pp. 16–17.
34. Ibid., p. 40.
35. Ibid., p. 36.
36. *The World Trade Union Movement*, 1954, no. 1, p. 29.
37. M. Cheney, *Big Oilman*, p. 266; I. P. Belyaev, *Amerikanski*, pp. 178–185; N. I. Proshin, *Saudovskaya*, pp. 284–286.
38. *Jahim*, pp. 32, 106, 309, 319.
39. Ibid., pp. 108, 125; M. Cheney, *Big Oilman*, p. 69; N. I. Proshin, *Saudovskaya*, pp. 277, 289–290.
40. *Jahim*, pp. 82–83, 94–95, 106–111, 118, 125–130, 309, 319; *The World Marxist Review*, 1962, no. 5, p. 92.
41. *Labor Law*, p. 58.
42. D. Howarth, *Desert King*, p. 231.
43. Ibid., pp. 99–100, 179.
44. *Jahim*, p. 12; N. I. Proshin, *Saudovskaya*, p. 144.
45. *Jahim*, pp. 13–14; *The Arab Observer*, 13 Oct. 1961, pp. 7–8.
46. G. Lipsky et al., *Saudi Arabia*, pp. 175–177; H. Philby, *Forty Years*, pp. 168–169; *Newsweek*, 8 July 1963, p. 40; *The Saturday Evening Post*, 30 Nov. 1957; *Jahim*, pp. 48; 255–273.
47. H. Philby, *Forty Years*, p. 171.
48. See: *Jazirat*.
49. Quoted from: N. I. Proshin, *Saudovskaya*, p. 161.
50. Ibid., p. 161.
51. *Jahim*.
52. Ibid., p. 229.
53. Ibid., pp. 6, 65–66, 232.
54. H. Philby, *Forty Years*, p. 34.
55. M. Cheney, *Big Oilman*, p. 282; G. Lipsky et al., *Saudi Arabia*, p. 282.
56. H. Philby, *Forty Years*, p. 34.
57. K. S. Twitchell, *Saudi Arabia*, p. 187; *Umm al-Qura*, 30 Dec. 1962.
58. B. Toy, *A Fool*, p. 134; M. Cheney, *Big Oilman*, p. 284.
59. Quoted from: N. I. Proshin, *Saudovskaya*, p. 155.

Notes

60. Jahim, p. 139; *The Arab Observer*, 13 Nov. 1961, p. 8; M. Cheney, *Big Oilman*, pp. 284-285.
61. Quoted from: N. I. Proshin, *Saudovskaya*, p. 157.
62. Ibid., pp. 143-144; *al-Musawwar*, 13 Oct. 1962, p. 31.
63. *Jahim*, p. 66; N. I. Proshin, *Saudovskaya*, pp. 164-165.
64. Al-Zirikli, *Shibh*, pp. 773-778.
65. M. Madhi, *al-Nahdhat*, pp. 227-253, 259-274.
66. H. Dickson, *Kuwait*, p. 391.
67. H. Philby, *Arabian Jubilee*, pp. 212-214.
68. W. A. Eddy, *F. D. R. Meets*, p. 37; D. Howarth, *Desert King*, p. 253.
69. G. Lipsky et al., *Saudi Arabia*, p. 17; H. Philby, *Forty Years*, p. 202.
70. *Arab World. Political and Diplomatic History, 1900-1967*, 5 Aug. 1946.
71. G. Lipsky et al., *Saudi Arabia*, p. 173; *Area Handbook*, p. 173.
72. *Politika SShA*, pp. 238-239.
73. Al-Zirikli, *Shibh*, p. 1393.
74. Ibid., p. 1394.
75. Ibid., p. 1395.
76. Ibid.
77. J. C. Hurewitz, *Middle East Politics*, p. 251.
78. Al-Zirikli, *Shibh*, p. 1395.
79. Ibid., pp. 1396-1397.
80. Ibid., p. 1398; *Politika SShA*, pp. 244-245.
81. Al-Zirikli, *Shibh*, p. 1399.
82. Ibid.; A. Said, *Tarikh*, vol. 3, p. 107.
83. G. Lipsky et al., *Saudi Arabia*, p. 140.
84. A. Said, *Tarikh*, vol. 3, p. 109; al-Zirikli, *Shibh*, p. 1400.
85. A. Said, *Tarikh*, vol. 3, pp. 120-121; *Politika SShA*, pp. 245-246.
86. A. Said, *Tarikh*, vol. 3, p. 121.
87. *Area Handbook*, p. 169.
88. The situation in Oman at the time is described in: L. Kotlov, *Osvoboditelnoe*, pp. 48-78; *The Arabian Peninsula*, pp. 107-141.
89. Al-Zirikli, *Shibh*, p. 1368; L. N. Kotlov, *Iordaniya*, pp. 74-77, 80-81.
90. M. Madhi, *al-Nahdhat*, p. 207.
91. Al-Zirikli, *Shibh*, p. 1368.
92. L. N. Kotlov, *Iordaniya*, p. 99.
93. Al-Zirikli, *Shibh*, p. 1368; L. N. Kotlov, *Iordaniya*, p. 99.
94. G. Lipsky et al., *Saudi Arabia*, pp. 141-142.
95. A. Said, *Tarikh*, vol. 3, pp. 16-17.
96. Ibid., pp. 123-124.
97. Ibid., p. 127.
98. Ibid., p. 128; G. Lipsky et al., *Saudi Arabia*, p. 143.
99. A. Said, *Tarikh*, vol. 3, pp. 129-134.
100. Ibid., pp. 139-144.
101. Ibid., p. 89.
102. Ibid., pp. 164-169.
103. G. Lipsky et al., *Saudi Arabia*, p. 142.
104. See: A. Kunina, *Doktrina*; *Proval*.
105. O. Tuganova, *Politika*, p. 101.
106. *The New York Herald Tribune*, 2 Sept. 1957; *Area Handbook*, p. 173; F. Halliday, *Arabia without Sultans*, pp. 53-54; G. de Gaury, *Faisal*, p. 83.
107. G. de Gaury, *Faisal*, p. 83.

108. *Pravda*, 2 March 1957.
109. G. de Gaury, *Faisal*, p. 83.
110. *Area Handbook*, p. 165.
111. A. Said, *Tarikh*, vol. 3, pp. 207–208.
112. L. I. Kotlov, *Iordaniya*, pp. 196–220.
113. A. Said, *Tarikh*, vol. 3, p. 211.
114. Ibid., pp. 203–205.
115. *Politika SShA*, p. 247.
116. L. I. Kotlov, *Iordaniya*, p. 229.

Chapter 17
1. G. Lipsky et al., *Saudi Arabia*, pp. 125, 133; G. de Gaury, *Faisal*, p. 90; TASS, 6 Feb. 1958, pp. 106-0, 156-0.
2. G. de Gaury, *Faisal*, p. 92.
3. Nasir al-Said, *al-Risala*, pp. 48–56, 61–62.
4. G. de Gaury, *Faisal*, pp. 91–92.
5. A. Said, *Tarikh*, vol. 3, p. 239.
6. N. I. Proshin, *Saudovskaya*, p. 166.
7. G. de Gaury, *Faisal*, p. 93.
8. A. Said, *Tarikh*, vol. 3, p. 239.
9. *Politika SShA*, p. 253.
10. N. I. Proshin, *Saudovskaya*, p. 169.
11. Ibid.
12. *Umm al-Qura*, 2 May 1958.
13. N. I. Proshin, *Saudovskaya*, pp. 170–171.
14. V. V. Ozoling, *Saudovskaya*, pp. 106–107; V. I. Proshin, *Saudovskaya*, pp. 172–173.
15. *The Middle East Record* (henceforth: *MER*), vol. 1, p. 372.
16. V. V. Ozoling, *Saudovskaya*, pp. 107–108; N. I. Proshin, *Saudovskaya*, pp. 172–173.
17. A. Said, *Tarikh*, vol. 3, p. 235.
18. *MER*, vol. 1, p. 373.
19. Ibid., p. 374.
20. *Al-Gumhuriya*, 25 May 1960.
21. *Area Handbook*, p. 153.
22. *Al-Hayat*, 9 Sept. 1960; *MER*, vol. 1, p. 375.
23. *MER*, vol. 1, pp. 375–376.
24. Ibid., p. 376; *Area Handbook*, p. 153.
25. *MER*, vol. 2, p. 428; F. Halliday, *Arabia without Sultans*, p. 59; *Area Handbook*, p. 173.
26. *Area Handbook*, p. 153.
27. *MER*, vol. 1, p. 377.
28. Ibid., vol. 2, p. 420.
29. Ibid., pp. 417, 420.
30. N. I. Proshin, *Saudovskaya*, p. 175.
31. *MER*, vol. 2, p. 425.
32. Ibid.
33. Ibid., p. 426.
34. N. I. Proshin, *Saudovskaya*, p. 178.
35. Ibid., p. 176.
36. Ibid., p. 177.
37. *MER*, vol. 2, pp. 422–423.
38. Ibid., p. 423.
39. Ibid., p. 424.

Notes

40. N. I. Proshin, *Saudovskaya*, p. 179.
41. G. de Gaury, *Faisal*, pp. 105–107.
42. Ibid.
43. *MER*, vol. 2, p. 424.
44. Ibid., p. 427.
45. A. Said, *Tarikh*, vol. 3, pp. 66–67; *Area Handbook*, p. 166; N. I. Proshin, *Saudovskaya*, p. 180.
46. *Area Handbook*, p. 170.
47. D. A. Schmidt, *Yemen*, p. 52.
48. Ibid., pp. 52–56.
49. *The Times*, 19 Oct. 1962.
50. D. A. Schmidt, *Yemen*, pp. 50–51.
51. Ibid., p. 51; see also N. I. Proshin, *Saudovskaya*, p. 182.
52. A. Said, *Tarikh*, vol. 3, pp. 301–309.
53. *Newsweek*, 8 July 1963, p. 40.
54. Ibid.
55. *Umm al-Qura*, 30 Nov. 1962; V. V. Ozoling, *Saudovskaya*, pp. 68, 98.
56. N. I. Proshin, *Saudovskaya*, p. 186.
57. G. de Gaury, *Faisal*, p. 169.
58. N. I. Proshin, *Saudovskaya*, p. 186.
59. Ibid.
60. *Al-Shaab*, 12 Sept. 1963.
61. *Area Handbook*, p. 154; N. I. Proshin, *Saudovskaya*, p. 188.
62. *The New York Times*, 3 Nov. 1963.
63. *Area Handbook*, p. 155.
64. Ibid., p. 156.
65. Ibid.
66. G. de Gaury, *Faisal*, pp. 130–133.
67. Ibid., pp. 134–135; *Area Handbook*, p. 156; A. Assah, *Miracle*, pp. 75–76.
68. N. I. Proshin, *Saudovskaya*, pp. 190–191.
69. *MER*, vol. 3, p. 452; F. Halliday, *Arabia without Sultans*, p. 67; N. I. Proshin, *Saudovskaya*, p. 191.
70. N. I. Proshin, *Saudovskaya*, p. 191.
71. *Al-Kifah*, 12 May 1963.
72. V. V. Ozoling, *Saudovskaya*, p. 98; L. V. Valkova, *Saudovskaya Araviya v Mezhdunarodnykh Otnosheniyahk*, pp. 77–78, 122–123.
73. *Keesing Contemporary Archives* (henceforth: *KCA*), p. 19965; N. I. Proshin, *Saudovskaya*, p. 194.
74. N. I. Proshin, *Saudovskaya*, p. 195.
75. *Labor Law*, pp. 57–58; *Area Handbook*, p. 264.
76. *Area Handbook*, p. 198.
77. *MER*, vol. 3, pp. 453–454.
78. Ibid., p. 455; F. Halliday, *Arabia without Sultans*, p. 67.
79. V. V. Ozoling, *Saudovskaya*, p. 102.
80. TASS, 19 Dec. 1966, p. 2 SV; 27 April 1967, pp. 5–6 SV.
81. *MER*, vol. 5, pp. 1026–1027.
82. Ibid., p. 456.
83. Ibid., p. 1027.
84. Ibid., pp. 1028–1029; F. Halliday, *Arabia without Sultans*, p. 69.
85. TASS, 8 Aug. 1969, pp. 28–29 SV.
86. TASS, 9 Sept. 1969, pp. 15–16 SV; *Novoe Vremya* (Moscow), 1973, NS, p. 26.

87. F. Halliday, *Arabia without Sultans*, p. 68; *MER*, vol. 5, p. 1030.
88. *Pravda*, 6 Sept. 1969; TASS, 9 Sept. 1969, pp. 6–7 A
89. TASS, 2 Dec. 1979, p. 25 A; 3 Dec. 1979, p. 215 V.
90. *MER*, vol. 5, p. 1031.
91. F. Halliday, *Arabia without Sultans*, p. 69.
92. *MER*, vol. 5, pp. 1033–1036.
93. Ibid., p. 1029.
94. *Umm al-Qura*, 11 Jan. 1963.
95. *The Middle East Journal*, 1963, vol. 17, no. 1–2, pp. 150–151; M. W. Wenner, *Modern Yemen*, p. 198.
96. *The New Times*, 1963, no. 2, p. 22.
97. N. I. Proshin, *Saudovskaya*, pp. 183–184.
98. H. Ingrams, *The Yemen*, pp. 135–137; M. W. Wenner, *Modern Yemen*, p. 198.
99. M. W. Wenner, *Modern Yemen*, pp. 199–201; *al-Ahram*, 29 Nov. 1962.
100. *The Middle East Journal*, 1963, no. 1–2, p. 151; M. W. Wenner, *Modern Yemen*, p. 202.
101. K. Trevaskis, *Shades of Amber*, p. 185.
102. A. Schlesinger, *A Thousand Days*, p. 452.
103. D. A. Schmidt, *Yemen*, pp. 163–164; J. C. Hurewitz, *Middle East Politics*, p. 249.
104. D. A. Schmidt, *Yemen*, p. 163.
105. *The Middle East Journal*, 1975, no. 1, p. 52; M. W. Wenner, *Modern Yemen*, p. 207.
106. For details, see: L. V. Valkova, *Saudovskaya Araviya v*, pp. 129–130.
107. D. A. Schmidt, *Yemen*, pp. 206–207.
108. *Al-Ahram*, 15 Sept. 1964.
109. D. A. Schmidt, *Yemen*, p. 207; O. G. Gerasimov, *Yemenskaya*, pp. 129–130.
110. F. Halliday, *Arabia without Sultans*, p. 111.
111. *The US News and World Report*, 1965, no. 21, pp. 67–69.
112. G. de Gaury, *Faisal*, p. 126; R. R. Sullivan, *Saudi Arabia*, p. 29.
113. See: L. V. Valkova, *Saudovskaya Araviya v*, p. 131.
114. *The Times*, 4 Aug. 1965.
115. F. Halliday, *Arabia without Sultans*, pp. 112–113; O. G. Gerasimov, *Yemenskaya*, pp. 130–132.
116. L. V. Valkova, *Saudovskaya Araviya v*, pp. 131–132.
117. A. Assah, *Miracle*, pp. 88–91; D. A. Schmidt, *Yemen*, pp. 238–239.
118. See: L. V. Valkova, *Saudovskaya Araviya v*, p. 133.
119. *The Times*, 24 Nov. 1965; *The Observer*, 13, 27 Dec. 1965; A. Assah, *Miracle*, pp. 92–95; O. G. Gerasimov, *Yemenskaya*, pp. 135–136.
120. *Area Handbook*, p. 172; F. Halliday, *Arabia without Sultans*, p. 59; UN, General Assembly, 26th session, doc. A/RU, 1966, p. 2.
121. O. G. Gerasimov, *Yemenskaya*, p. 136; *The New York Times*, 25 Feb. 1966; *The Times*, 14 June 1966.
122. *The Egyptian Gazette*, 23 June 1966.
123. *Al-Ahram*, 2 May 1966.
124. *The Daily Telegraph* and *Morning Post*, 18, 27 Aug. 1966; *The Guardian*, 5 Oct. 1966; O. G. Gerasimov, *Yemenskaya*, p. 137.
125. L. V. Valkova, *Saudovskaya Araviya v*, p. 136.
126. *KCA*, p. 22271.
127. Ibid., p. 22276.
128. Ibid.
129. Ibid., p. 22547.
130. See: L. V. Valkova, *Saudovskaya Araviya v*, p. 138.
131. *KCA*, p. 22547; *al-Ahram*, 12 Nov. 1967; O. G. Gerasimov, *Yemenskaya*, p. 124.

Notes

132. *KCA*, p. 22548.
133. Ibid., pp. 22548–22549; *al-Ahram*, 1 March 1968; J. C. Hurewitz, *Middle East Politics*, p. 257; F. Halliday, *Arabia without Sultans*, pp. 118–122.
134. F. Halliday, *Arabia without Sultans*, pp. 122–126; O. G. Gerasimov, *Yemenskaya*, pp. 141–154.
135. L. V. Valkova, *Saudovskaya Araviya v*, p. 142.
136. O. G. Gerasimov, *Yemenskaya*, pp. 156–157.
137. *The International Herald Tribune* (henceforth: *IHT*), 24 July 1970.
138. *The Times*, 30 July 1970.
139. O. G. Gerasimov, *Yemenskaya*, pp. 157–159.
140. L. V. Valkova, *Saudovskaya Araviya v*, pp. 145–146.
141. See: O. G. Gerasimov, *Yemenskaya*, pp. 180–181.
142. *Pravda*, 6, 28 Dec. 1969; O. G. Gerasimov, *Yemenskaya*, pp. 180–182.
143. O. G. Gerasimov, *Yemenskaya*, pp. 182–184; L. V. Valkova, *Saudovskaya Araviya v*, p. 154.
144. *The Economist*, 13 Oct. 1972, pp. 37–38.
145. O. G. Gerasimov, *Yemenskaya*, pp. 186–188.
146. G. de Gaury, *Faisal*, p. 98.
147. *Area Handbook*, p. 172; F. Halliday, *Arabia without Sultans*, pp. 59–60; *The Guardian*, 15 March 1974.
148. *The Guardian*, 15 March 1974; F. Halliday, *Arabia without Sultans*, pp. 59–61.
149. R. R. Sullivan, *Saudi Arabia*, p. 29.
150. *IHT*, 2 March 1971; L. I. Medvedko, *Vetry*, p. 171.
151. *The Economist*, 5 April 1969, p. 24.
152. *KCA*, p. 23072-A.
153. *The Times*, 21 Nov. 1971.
154. *The Times*, 21 Nov., 21 Dec. 1971; *IHT*, 2 Dec. 1971.
155. L. V. Valkova, *Saudovskaya Araviya v*, p. 194.
156. *The Economist*, 2 Jan. 1972, p. 35.
157. L. V. Valkova, *Saudovskaya Araviya v*, p. 195.
158. For details, see: A. M. Vassiliev, *Fakely*, pp. 157–173.
159. *The Economist*, 21 Feb. 1973, pp. 34–35; R. R. Sullivan, *Saudi Arabia*, p. 33.
160. *KCA*, p. 24629.
161. *The Times*, 3, 4, 6 Jan. 1970.
162. *Al-Ahram*, 2 July 1971; see also *Narody Azii i Afriki*, 1975, no. 6, p. 45.
163. *The Times*, 31 Aug., 9 Nov. 1973; *The Economist*, 9 June 1973, pp. 35–36.
164. A. Assah, *Miracle*, pp. 96–98; *The Economist*, 4 April 1966, pp. 1077–1078; *The Egyptian Gazette*, 1 Feb. 1966.
165. *The Times*, 13 April 1966.
166. *Al-Ahram*, 23 Feb. 1966.
167. L. V. Valkova, *Saudovskaya Araviya v*, p. 168.
168. *The Times*, 22 Aug. 1969.
169. *IHT*, 1 Sept. 1969.
170. L. V. Valkova, *Saudovskaya Araviya v Mezhdunarodnykh Otnosheniyakh*, p. 172; *The Times*, 6 Sept. 1969.
171. *MER*, vol. 5, p. 578; *The Times*, 25 Sept. 1969.
172. *MER*, vol. 5, p. 578.
173. *Umm al-Qura*, 27 March 1970.
174. *The Economist*, 11 March 1972, p. 47; *IHT*, 6 March 1972.
175. R. Knauerhase, *Saudi Arabian Economy*, pp. 165–166.
176. Ibid., p. 170.
177. For details, see: A. M. Vassiliev, *Fakely*, pp. 91–94.

178. Ibid., pp. 94-97.
179. R. Knauerhase, *Saudi Arabian Economy*, p. 172.
180. Ibid., p. 174.
181. *The Middle East Economic Survey*, 1972, no. 48, p. 1.
182. R. Knauerhase, *Saudi Arabian Economy*, p. 174.
183. S. Klebanoff, *Middle East Oil*, p. 150.
184. *IHT*, 20 April 1973.
185. Ibid., 7, 8 July 1973.
186. *The Times*, 28, 31 Aug. 1973; *The Economist*, 1 Sept. 1973, pp. 15-16, 34-35; 22 Sept. 1973, p. 64; *IHT*, 31 Aug. 1973.
187. See: A. M. Vassiliev, *Fakely*, pp. 100-102.
188. *The Times*, 8 Oct. 1973.
189. Ibid., 10 Oct. 1973.
190. Ibid., 15 Oct. 1973.

Chapter 18
1. *Pravda*, 19 Oct. 1973; *The Times*, 19, 23 Oct. 1973; *World Oil*, Nov. 1973, vol. 177, no. 6, p. 17.
2. See: A. M. Vassiliev, *Fakely*, pp. 107-108; *al-Hurriya*, 20 Oct. 1973.
3. V. V. Ozoling, *Ekonomika*, pp. 136-137.
4. *IHT*, 25 Dec. 1973; W. Laquer, *Confrontation*, pp. 208-211.
5. *IHT*, 5 Sept., 7, 24 Nov. 1973.
6. See: A. M. Vassiliev, *Fakely*, pp. 107-108; P. Mansfield, *The Arabs*, p. 363; *Izvestiya*, 24 Jan. 1974.
7. *Pravda*, 11 Feb. 1973; *The Times*, 10 Dec. 1973.
8. *Pravda*, 30 Dec. 1973; *IHT*, 26, 27 Dec. 1973; *Washington Post*, 2 Jan. 1974.
9. *Energetichesky Krizis v Kapitalisticheskom Mire*, p. 214.
10. *IHT*, 10 Jan. 1975; *Pravda*, 23 Jan. 1975.
11. L. V. Valkova, *Saudovskaya Araviya v*, pp. 50-51.
12. *Daily Telegraph*, 26 March 1975; *Le Monde*, 27 Jan. 1977; *L'Opinion*, 27 March 1975.
13. *Problemy Mira i Sozializma*, 1985, no. 1, pp. 27-30.
14. *Pravda*, 21 Nov. 1979.
15. The description of events in autumn 1979 and at the beginning of 1980 is based on *Pravda*, 10 Jan. 1980; *Izvestiya*, 10 Jan. 1980; *IHT*, 20 Feb. 1980; *Foreign Report*, 28 Nov. 1979; *Le Monde*, 3-4 April 1980, 3-4 May 1981; *Ahdath Nufambr*.
16. *Foreign Report*, 28 Nov. 1979; *Le Monde*, 3-4 April 1980, 3-4 May 1981.
17. *Pravda*, 10 Jan. 1980; *Le Monde*, 3-4 April 1980, 3-4 May 1981.
18. *Newsweek*, 3 March 1980, pp. 15-18; *Le Monde*, 3-4 May 1981.
19. Ibid.
20. Ibid.
21. Ibid.
22. *Newsweek*, 30 March 1980, pp. 15-18.
23. *Newsweek*, 6 March 1978, pp. 12-19; *Wall Street Journal*, 7 Oct. 1981.
24. *Problemy mira i sozialisma*, 1987, no. 3, p. 67.
25. L. V. Valkova, *Saudovskaya Araviya: Neft, Islam, Politika*, p. 57.
26. *The Middle East*, June 1977, no. 32, pp. 78-80; *The Times*, 24 Sept. 1976.
27. *Pravda*, 26 June 1977.
28. *New York Daily News*, 13 Jan. 1979; *Christian Science Monitor*, 13 Jan. 1979.
29. *MEED*, 18-31 Dec. 1981, vol. 25, no. 51/52, p. 70.
30. *Novoe vremya*, 16 Dec. 1966, no. 51 (1125), p. 7; *Business Week*, 31 March 1980; *Le Monde*, 30 April 1981.

31. *Le Monde*, 29 April 1981.
32. W. B. Quandt, *Saudi Arabia in the 1980s*, p. 41; *Middle East*, March 1983, p. 224; *Christian Science Monitor*, 6 Dec. 1982; *Middle East*, June 1981, p. 305.
33. *Financial Times*, 12 Jan. 1976.
34. *Washington Post*, 20 March 1979.

Chapter 19
1. R. Knauerhase, *Saudi Arabian Economy*, p. 287; *Arab Oil and Gas Directory, 1994*, p. 389.
2. G. Lipsky et al., *Saudi Arabia*, p. 89.
3. H. Philby, *Forty Years*, pp. 38–39.
4. G. Lipsky et al., *Saudi Arabia*, p. 178.
5. Ibid., p. 179.
6. Ibid.
7. V. V. Ozoling, *Saudovskaya*, pp. 105–106; G. Lipsky et al., *Saudi Arabia*, p. 195.
8. *Al-Mamlaka*, pp. 103–104; G. Lipsky et al., *Saudi Arabia*, p. 195; V. V. Ozoling, *Saudovskaya*, pp. 106–107.
9. *Biulleten Inistrannoy Kommercheskoy Informatsii* (henceforth: *BIKI*), 1973, no. 98, p. 8.
10. *OPEC Annual Statistical Bulletin, 1990*; *Financial Times* (Moscow edn), 3–9 Feb., 24–30 March 1994; *Arab Oil and Gas*, p. 339.
11. G. Lipsky et al., *Saudi Arabia*, p. 198.
12. *Umm al-Qura*, 8 Jan. 1960; V. V. Ozoling, *Ekonomika*, p. 164.
13. *Area Handbook*, p. 294; G. Lipsky et al., *Saudi Arabia*, p. 198.
14. V. V. Ozoling, *Ekonomika*, p. 165.
15. G. Lipsky et al., *Saudi Arabia*, p. 198.
16. R. Knauerhase, *Saudi Arabian Economy*, pp. 250–252.
17. G. Lipsky et al., *Saudi Arabia*, pp. 189–190.
18. Al-Zirikli, *Shibh*, p. 758.
19. *Area Handbook*, p. 210.
20. R. Knauerhase, *Saudi Arabian Economy*, pp. 316–320; *Area Handbook*, p. 210.
21. R. Knauerhase, *Saudi Arabian Economy*, p. 301.
22. V. V. Ozoling, *Ekonomika*, p. 174.
23. Ibid.
24. Ibid.
25. R. Knauerhase, *Saudi Arabian Economy*, p. 301.
26. V. V. Ozoling, *Ekonomika*, p. 166.
27. *MER*, 16 July 1977.
28. Ibid.; *Newsweek*, 6 March 1978.
29. See: V. V. Ozoling, *Saudovskaya*, p. 57.
30. G. Lipsky et al., *Saudi Arabia*, pp. 232–233.
31. N. I. Proshin, *Saudovskaya*, pp. 242–243.
32. G. Kheirallah, *Arabia*, pp. 202–204.
33. Ibid.
34. V. V. Ozoling, *Saudovskaya*, p. 59.
35. Ibid., pp. 59–60.
36. *Al-Mamlaka*, p. 122.
37. V. V. Ozoling, *Ekonomika*, pp. 10–11.
38. R. N. Andreasyan was the first to use this term (see his 'Oil Prosperity').
39. V. V. Ozoling, *Ekonomika*, pp. 69–70.
40. *Overseas Business Report*, 1970, no. 38, p. 11.
41. R. Knauerhase, *Saudi Arabian Economy*, p. 136.
42. Ibid., p. 142.

Notes

43. *Jeddah 68/69*, pp. 88–89.
44. R. Knauerhase, *Saudi Arabian Economy*, p. 14.
45. V. V. Ozoling, *Ekonomika*, p. 72.
46. R. Knauerhase, *Saudi Arabian Economy*, p. 132.
47. Ibid., p. 136.
48. G. Lipsky et al., *Saudi Arabia*, p. 235.
49. *The Middle East Economic Digest* (henceforth: *MEED*), 1964, no. 10, p. 117.
50. R. Knauerhase, *Saudi Arabian Economy*, p. 136.
51. Ibid., p. 144; V. V. Ozoling, *Ekonomika*, p. 76.
52. V. V. Ozoling, *Saudovskaya*, pp. 66–67; V. V. Ozoling, *Ekonomika*, p. 74.
53. *Qafilat al-Zait*, 1970, vol. 18, no. 7, p. 39; V. V. Ozoling, *Ekonomika*, p. 74.
54. *Umm al-Qura*, 23 July 1965; *al-Waqai al-Arabiya*, 1965, no. 3, p. 362.
55. *Area Handbook*, p. 238; V. V. Ozoling, *Ekonomika*, pp. 93–94.
56. Al-Ghadiri, *al-Tahaddi*, p. 96.
57. V. V. Ozoling, *Ekonomika*, p. 95.
58. *The Middle East and North Africa, 1964–1965*, p. 171.
59. For details, see: V. V. Ozoling, *Ekonomika*, pp. 97–99.
60. Ibid., pp. 99–105.
61. R. Knauerhase, *Saudi Arabian Economy*, p. 76.
62. V. V. Ozoling, *Ekonomika*, p. 161.
63. *Labor Law*, p. 10; V. V. Ozoling, *Ekonomika*, p. 76.
64. V. V. Ozoling, *Saudovskaya*, p. 117.
65. V. V. Ozoling, *Ekonomika*, pp. 181–183.
66. G. Lipsky et al., *Saudi Arabia*, p. 239.
67. N. I. Proshin, *Saudovskaya*, p. 251; V. V. Ozoling, *Saudovskaya*, p. 127.
68. *IHT*, 2 Feb. 1978.
69. P. Bonnenfant, *Utilisation*, p. 61.
70. Ibid., p. 62.
71. *IHT*, 2 Feb. 1978.
72. F. Shakir, *Dalil*, p. 323.
73. H. Philby, *Forty Years*, p. 33; D. van der Meulen, *Wells of Ibn Saud*, p. 217.
74. P. Bonnenfant, *Utilisation*, p. 62.
75. *Jeddah 68/69*, p. 109.
76. *IHT*, 2 Feb. 1978.
77. P. Hobday, *Saudi Arabia*, pp. 83–84.
78. *MEED*, Saudi Arabia, Special issue, 1978, p. 75.
79. *Area Handbook*, pp. 218–219.
80. Ibid., p. 220.
81. Ibid., pp. 221–222.
82. R. Knauerhase, *Saudi Arabian Economy*, p. 120; G. Lipsky et al., *Saudi Arabia*, pp. 210–211.
83. *Area Handbook*, p. 221.
84. G. Lipsky et al., *Saudi Arabia*, p. 210.
85. V. V. Ozoling, *Ekonomika*, p. 25.
86. *Al-Kitab al-Ikhsai*, vol. 3, p. 137.
87. *Labor Law*, p. 9.
88. *Area Handbook*, p. 222.
89. Ibid.
90. V. V. Ozoling, *Saudovskaya*, p. 41.
91. *Area Handbook*, p. 222.
92. Ibid., p. 223.

93. Ibid.
94. Ibid., p. 224.
95. R. Knauerhase, *Saudi Arabian Economy*, p. 120.
96. *Labor Law*, p. 9.
97. *Area Handbook*, p. 225.
98. Ibid., p. 226.
99. Ibid.
100. Ibid.
101. *Labor Development Abroad*, 1969, no. 8, p. 2.
102. *Al-Kitab al-Ikhsai*, vol. 3, p. 128.
103. Ibid., vol. 2, pp. 110-111.
104. Ibid., vol. 3, pp. 137-138.
105. Ibid.; *Labor Law*, p. 9.
106. See: M. A. Khrustalev, *Sotsialnaya*, p. 31.
107. See: N. I. Proshin, *Saudovskaya*, p. 230.
108. Ibid.
109. *Umm al-Qura*, 19 Sept. 1968; *The Times*, 29 Nov. 1971; *The Economist*, 7-13 Aug. 1971, p. 25.
110. *Umm al-Qura*, 19 Sept. 1968.
111. Al-Sharif, *Mintaqat*, pp. 120-124.
112. See: M. Katakura, *Bedouin Village*.
113. Calculated from: *Area Handbook*, p. 213; E. Y. Asfour, *Saudi Arabia*, p. 15; V. V. Ozoling, *Ekonomika*, p. 4; R. Knauerhase, *Saudi Arabian Economy*, p. 113; K. S. Twitchell, *Saudi Arabia*, p. 21; *Le Monde Diplomatique*, Feb. 1974, pp. 26-27.
114. E. Y. Asfour, *Saudi Arabia*, p. 57; *Geography*, 1970, vol. 55, no. 4, p. 415; V. V. Ozoling, *Ekonomika*, p. 24.
115. R. Knauerhase, *Saudi Arabian Economy*, p. 113.
116. *Area Handbook*, p. 238; G. Lipsky et al., *Saudi Arabia*, p. 214.
117. *Area Handbook*, p. 217.
118. R. Knauerhase, *Saudi Arabian Economy*, p. 126.
119. Ibid., p. 113.
120. *Labor Law*, p. 9.
121. *Area Handbook*, p. 227.
122. P. Bonnenfant, *Utilisation*, p. 64.
123. Ibid.; V. V. Ozoling, *Ekonomika*, pp. 28-29.
124. Ibid., pp. 59-62.
125. Ibid., p. 62.
126. *The Financial Times*, 19 Dec. 1972; *Area Handbook*, p. 227.
127. *The Kingdom*, p. 138.
128. *Jamiat*, pp. 411-412.
129. *Area Handbook*, p. 233.
130. Ibid.; E. Y. Asfour, *Saudi Arabia*, p. 98; *The Middle East and North Africa*, 1965-1966, p. 491; V. V. Ozoling, *Ekonomika*, p. 33.
131. K. S. Twitchell, *Saudi Arabia*, p. 21.
132. *Jamiat*, p. 403.
133. *Area Handbook*, p. 213.
134. *Al-Bilad al-Saudiya*, 11 Aug. 1967.
135. *Labor Law*, p. 39; *Le Monde Diplomatique*, Feb. 1974; *Narody Azii i Afriki*, 1975, no. 6, pp. 42-43.
136. H. Philby, *Forty Years*, p. 57.
137. R. H. Sanger, *Arabian Peninsula*, pp. 111-112.

Notes

138. *Jamiat*, p. 383.
139. F. S. Vidal, *Oasis of al-Hasa*, p. 94.
140. D. P. Cole, *Bedouins*, p. 25.
141. Ibid., p. 25–26.
142. The beginning of this process is described in: M. C. Cheney, *Big Oilman*, p. 300.
143. *Jamiat*, p. 408.
144. *Area Handbook*, p. 60.
145. *Jamiat*, pp. 407–408.
146. *Area Handbook*, p. 86; G. Lipsky et al., *Saudi Arabia*, pp. 186, 211; F.-J. Tomiché, *L'Arabie*, p. 87.
147. F. S. Vidal, *Oasis of al-Hasa*, p. 101; M. S. Cheney, *Big Oilman*, p. 300.
148. M. Katakura, *Bedouin Village*, p. 167.
149. N. I. Proshin, *Saudovskaya*, p. 219.
150. H. Philby, *Forty Years*, p. 57.
151. *Area Handbook*, p. 36; G. Kheirallah, *Arabia*, p. 161; G. Lipsky et al., *Saudi Arabia*, pp. 78, 264.
152. *Labor Law*, p. 14.
153. G. Lipsky et al., *Saudi Arabia*, pp. 79, 91.
154. Ibid., p. 162; M. S. Cheney, *Big Oilman*, p. 293.
155. *Jahim*, p. 148.
156. *The International Labor Review*, March 1957, p. 195.
157. See: N. Hamilton, *Americans*, p. 168.
158. R. Knauerhase, *Saudi Arabian Economy*, p. 207.
159. *Jahim*, p. 308.
160. M. S. Cheney, *Big Oilman*, p. 240; W. Rugh, *Emergence*, p. 16.
161. W. Rugh, *Emergence*, p. 16.
162. *Qafilat al-Zait*, 1971, vol. 19, no. 3, p. 28.
163. *Al-Bitrul wal-Ghaz al-Arabi*, 1969, no. 8, p. 17; *Labor Law*, p. 36.
164. W. Rugh, *Emergence*, p. 16.
165. *Labor Law*, p. 39.
166. *Qafilat al-Zait*, 1971, vol. 19, no. 3, p. 30.
167. *Area Handbook*, p. 258.
168. Ibid.
169. *Al-Kitab al-Ikhsai*, vol. 5, p. 376.
170. *Area Handbook*, p. 258.
171. *Labor Law*, p. 27.
172. M. A. Khrustalev, *Sotsialnaya*, p. 31.
173. *Labor Development Abroad*, 1969, no. 8, p. 10.
174. Al-Sharif, *Mintaqat*, p. 158.
175. *Labor Law*, p. 53.
176. Al-Sharif, *Mintaqat*, pp. 168, 195.
177. Ibid., p. 168.
178. Ibid., pp. 198–199.
179. Ibid., pp. 238–239.
180. Ibid., pp. 239–240.
181. G. Lipsky et al., *Saudi Arabia*, pp. 157–158.
182. Al-Sharif, *Mintaqat*, p. 168.
183. G. Lipsky et al., *Saudi Arabia*, p. 165.
184. Ibid., pp. 166–167.
185. *Area Handbook*, p. 262.
186. Ibid., p. 259.

Notes

187. Calculated from: *Area Handbook*, p. 19; *MEED*, 1971, vol. 15, no. 16, p. 398; *The Overseas Business Report*, 1971, no. 25, p. 4.
188. *Area Handbook*, p. 259.
189. Ibid.
190. R. Knauerhase, *Saudi Arabian Economy*, p. 13.
191. *Labor Law*, pp. 34-36.
192. V. V. Ozoling, *Ekonomika*, p. 6.
193. M. W. Wenner, *Saudi Arabia*, p. 170.
194. *Labor Law*, pp. 63-64.
195. Ibid., p. 64.
196. M. W. Wenner, *Saudi Arabia*, p. 171.
197. D. E. Long, *Saudi Arabia*, p. 50.
198. R. N. Andreasyan, 'Oil Prosperity'.
199. G. Lipsky et al., *Saudi Arabia*, p. 169.
200. P. Bonnenfant, *Utilisation*, pp. 65-66.
201. *The Guardian*, 2 May 1973.
202. Ibid.
203. Al-Zirikli, *Shibh*, pp. 1349-1357.
204. *Area Handbook*, p. 261.
205. Ibid., p. 262.
206. *The Times*, 28 Jan. 1974.
207. G. Lipsky et al., *Saudi Arabia*, p. 168.
208. N. I. Proshin, *Saudovskaya*, p. 272.
209. *Labor Law*, p. 56.
210. Ibid.
211. Ibid., p. 57.
212. Ibid., pp. 65-85.
213. Ibid., pp. 88, 92.
214. Ibid., pp. 60-61.
215. Ibid., p. 82.
216. Ibid., p. 56.
217. Ibid., pp. 55-56.
218. G. Lipsky et al., *Saudi Arabia*, p. 277.
219. Ibid., p. 279.
220. *Labor Law*, p. 14.
221. G. Lipsky et al., *Saudi Arabia*, pp. 280-282.
222. D. E. Long, *Saudi Arabia*, p. 14.
223. W. Rugh, *Emergence*, p. 17.
224. Ibid.
225. *Area Handbook*, p. 102.
226. M. W. Wenner, *Saudi Arabia*, p. 176.
227. *The Times*, 28 Jan. 1974.
228. R. Knauerhase, *Saudi Arabian Economy*, p. 211.
229. Ibid., p. 218.
230. *The Times*, 28 Jan. 1974.
231. R. Knauerhase, *Saudi Arabian Economy*, p. 221; *Labor Law*, p. 25.
232. R. Knauerhase, *Saudi Arabian Economy*, p. 221; *The Times*, 28 Jan. 1974.
233. *Area Handbook*, p. 97.
234. *The Times*, 28 Jan. 1974.
235. G. de Gaury, *Faisal*, pp. 166-167.
236. *The Kingdom*, p. 200.

Notes

Chapter 20

1. *Time*, 19 Nov. 1973, pp. 90–91; *Labor Law*, p. 13.
2. See: G. Lipsky et al., *Saudi Arabia*, p. 116.
3. M. W. Wenner, *Saudi Arabia*, p. 168.
4. *Le Monde Diplomatique*, Feb. 1974, pp. 26–27.
5. *Area Handbook*, p. 157.
6. Ibid.
7. *IHT*, 2 Feb. 1978.
8. Ibid.
9. Ibid.
10. D. E. Long, *Saudi Arabia*, p. 29.
11. *IHT*, 2 Feb. 1978; P. Hobday, *Saudi Arabia*, p. 65.
12. J.-L. Soulié, L. Champenois, *Le Royaume*, p. 59.
13. *IHT*, 2 Feb. 1978.
14. Ibid.
15. D. E. Long, *Saudi Arabia*, pp. 29–30.
16. A. R. Kelidar, *Problem of Succession*, p. 30.
17. *IHT*, 2 Feb. 1978.
18. Ibid.
19. D. E. Long, *Saudi Arabia*, p. 29.
20. *IHT*, 2 Feb. 1978.
21. Ibid.
22. Ibid.
23. Ibid.
24. Ibid.
25. See: *Area Handbook*, p. 143.
26. G. de Gaury, *Faisal*, p. 166.
27. *Area Handbook*, p. 193.
28. J.-L. Soulié, L. Champenois, *Le Royaume*, p. 80.
29. *Middle Eastern Report*, vol. 1, p. 379.
30. P. Bonnenfant, *Utilisation*, p. 69.
31. D. E. Long, *Saudi Arabia*, p. 41.
32. *The Financial Times*, 24 Jan. 1973.
33. D. E. Long, *Saudi Arabia*, pp. 32–34.
34. *The Financial Times*, 24 Jan. 1973.
35. *Area Handbook*, p. 35.
36. Ibid., p. 191; G. Lipsky et al., *Saudi Arabia*, p. 124.
37. *Area Handbook*, p. 191.
38. Al-Zirikli, *Shibh*, pp. 992–993.
39. *Area Handbook*, p. 321.
40. Ibid., pp. 324–325.
41. Ibid., p. 325.
42. Ibid., pp. 326–327.
43. Ibid., pp. 330–331.
44. V. V. Ozoling, *Saudovskaya*, p. 204.
45. Ibid., p. 203.
46. Ibid., p. 204.
47. Ibid.
48. Ibid.
49. *Newsweek*, 6 March 1978, p. 18.
50. L. V. Valkova, *Saudovskaya Araviya: Neft, Islam, Politika*, pp. 15–16; I. P. Senchenko,

Araviya, p. 58; *Pravda*, 30 Oct., 17 Nov. 1981; *Izvestia*, 29 Oct. 1981.
51. *The Kingdom*, p. 127.
52. M. A. Khrustalev, *Sotsialnaya*, pp. 34–35.
53. G. Lipsky et al., *Saudi Arabia*, p. 115.
54. Ibid., p. 110.
55. A. Said, *Tarikh*, vol. 3, pp. 69–72.
56. Ibid., p. 70.
57. Ibid.
58. *Area Handbook*, p. 139.
59. *Al-Kitab al-Ikhsai*, vol. 3, pp. 327–330.
60. M. Sadiq, *Tatawwur*, pp. 197–198.
61. *Umm al-Qura*, 9 April 1971.
62. J.-L. Soulié, L. Champenois, *Le Royaume*, p. 123.
63. Ibid., p. 124; *Area Handbook*, p. 145; R. Knauerhase, *Saudi Arabian Economy*, p. 33.
64. J.-L. Soulié, L. Champenois, *Le Royaume*, p. 123.
65. G. Lipsky et al., *Saudi Arabia*, p. 126.
66. *Area Handbook*, p. 148.
67. G. Lipsky et al., *Saudi Arabia*, p. 126.
68. D. E. Long, *Saudi Arabia*, p. 41.
69. R. Knauerhase, *Saudi Arabian Economy*, p. 33.
70. D. E. Long, *Saudi Arabia*, p. 33.
71. G. Lipsky et al., *Saudi Arabia*, p. 127.
72. Ibid., p. 128.
73. See: M. W. Wenner, *Saudi Arabia*, p. 180.
74. W. Rugh, *Emergence*, pp. 15–17.
75. Ibid., pp. 17–18.
76. D. E. Long, *Saudi Arabia*, p. 16.
77. S. al-Muhammasani, *al-Awdha*, p. 344.
78. See: *The Kingdom*, p. 124.
79. Ibid.
80. R. Knauerhase, *Saudi Arabian Economy*, p. 25.
81. Ibid.
82. Ibid.
83. *Middle Eastern Report*, vol. 2, p. 424.
84. *The Kingdom*, p. 124.
85. S. al-Muhammasani, *al-Awdha*, pp. 325–330.
86. *Area Handbook*, p. 193.
87. *The Kingdom*, p. 125.
88. D. E. Long, *Saudi Arabia*, p. 39; *The Kingdom*, p. 124; *Area Handbook*, p. 194.

Chapter 21
1. *The Financial Times*, 22 April 1985, Suppl.; *The Middle East and North Africa*, p. 729; *MEED*, 1986, no. 13, pp. 37–38.
2. *MEED*, 1986, no. 13, pp. 43–44.
3. *MEED*, 1986, no. 17, p. 56.
4. *MEED*, 1986, no. 16, p. 56.
5. *The Financial Times*, 22 April 1985, Suppl.
6. *MEED*, 1985, no. 29, p. 23.
7. *MEED*, 1988, Special report, April, p. 11.
8. *MEED*, 1986, no. 17, p. 56.
9. *MEED*, 1986, no. 20, p. 24.

Notes

10. For details, see: A. A. Maksimov, *Razvitie*.
11. *MEED*, 1986, no. 14, pp. 28–31.
12. *Quarterly Economic Review of Saudi Arabia*, 1985, no. 3, p. 10.
13. *BIKI*, 20 April 1985.
14. *MEED*, 1986, no. 5, p. 17.
15. *MEED*, 1985, no. 15, p. 36.
16. *Al-Jazira*, 26 March 1985.
17. *MEED*, 1988, Special report, April, p. 16; *The Middle East*, 1988, no. 160, pp. 25–26.
18. *Le Monde*, 12 April 1988.
19. *MEED*, 1988, Special report, April, p. 36.
20. *The Financial Times*, 22 April 1985, Suppl.
21. J. R. Presley, A. J. Westaway, *Guide*, p. 45.
22. *Sixty Years*, p. 112.
23. *MEED*, 1987, no. 13, p. 42; 1992, no. 3, p. 22.
24. *OPEC Bulletin*, 1992, July–Aug., p. 25.
25. *Ekho Planety*, 1992, no. 27, p. 29.
26. *Middle East and North Africa*, p. 732.
27. A. A. Maksimov, *Razvitie*, p. 87.
28. *Ekho Planety*, 1992, no. 27, p. 31.
29. *Sixty Years*, p. 95.
30. Ibid.
31. *Middle East and North Africa*, p. 728; *MEED*, 1989, no. 33, p. 7.
32. *Middle East*, July 1993, p. 26.
33. A. G. Georgiev, V. V. Ozoling, *Neftyanye*, pp. 5–6.
34. *World Resources*, p. 255.
35. *The Middle East and North Africa*, p. 728.
36. *World Development*, pp. 188–189; *The Middle East and North Africa*, p. 728.
37. For details, see: A. I. Yakovlev, *Rabochiy*.
38. R. P. Shan, *Mobilizing*, p. 32.
39. *Ekho Planety*, 1992, no. 27, pp. 28–29.
40. *The Impact of Oil Revenues*, p. 569.
41. *Saudi Economic Survey*, 8 June 1983, p. 10.
42. *Kingdom of Saudi Arabia. Fifth Development Plan (1990–1995)*, p. 125.
43. N. A. Shilling, *Doing Business*.
44. *World Statistics*, p. 36; *World Resources*, p. 271.
45. *World Resources*, p. 271; *This is Our Country*.
46. *Sixty Years*, pp. 115, 121.
47. Ibid., pp. 141–142.
48. *The Middle East Journal*, 1973, vol. 27, no. 1, p. 17.
49. *Social and Economic Development in the Arab Gulf*, pp. 110–111.
50. Ibid., p. 111.
51. M. Katakura, *Bedouin Village*.
52. *Arab News*, 21 March 1985.
53. T. Niblock (ed.), *State, Society and Economy*, p. 204.
54. *MEED*, 1981, Special report 'Saudi Arabia', p. 36.
55. A. Johani, M. Berne, *The Saudi Arabian Economy*, p. 102.
56. Ibid., p. 34.
57. See: A. I. Yakovlev, *Osobennosti*.
58. *Middle East Financial Directory*, pp. 213–214; *Who's Who*, p. 55.
59. J. R. Presley, A. J. Westaway, *A Guide*, p. 7.
60. *International Labour Review*, 1 June 1983, p. 18.

Notes

61. *Orient*, 1980, no. 4, p. 489.
62. R. Cordes, F. Scholz, *Bedouins*, p. 33.
63. *Sixty Years*, p. 39.
64. Ibid., p. 40.
65. Ibid., p. 86.
66. [G. S. McGovern], *Realities*, p. 5.
67. *Sixty Years*, p. 87.
68. *World Resources*, p. 257.
69. *World Statistics*, p. 24.
70. *Sixty Years*, pp. 87–88.
71. *Dawn*, 2 Oct. 1984.
72. *Fortune* (New York), 10 March 1980; *L'Express* (Paris), 3 Feb. 1979; *Le Monde* (Paris), 3–4 April 1980.
73. *La Révolution* (Paris), no. 260, 22 Feb. 1985.
74. *Pravda*, 29 Sept. 1985.
75. *Arab News*, 8–9 May 1980.
76. *The Financial Times*, 23 May 1984.
77. *EIU Regional Review*, p. 206.
78. *Okaz*, 25 and 26 March 1992. For the text in English, see John Bulloch, *Reforms of the Saudi Arabian Constitution*.
79. See: A. M. Vassiliev, *Persidskiy*, ch. 12; A. M. Vassiliev, *Russia's*, ch. 17.
80. L. V. Valkova, *Saudovskaya Araviya: Neft, Islam, Politika*, p. 152.
81. Ibid., pp. 153–155.
82. Ibid., pp. 156–158, 159, 162.
83. V. V. Ozoling, *Saudovskaya Araviya*, p. 109.
84. Ibid., p. 110; *Izvestiya*, 19 April 1977; *Pravda*, 10, 14 April 1977.
85. L. V. Valkova, *Saudovskaya Araviya: Neft, Islam, Politika*, pp. 173–174.
86. *Pravda*, 17 Nov. 1981.
87. L. V. Valkova, *Saudovskaya Araviya: Neft, Islam, Politika*, p. 178.
88. *Krasnaiya Zvezda* (Moscow), 2 Aug. 1987.
89. *Izvestiya*, 1 Aug. 1987; *Pravda*, 3 Aug. 1987.
90. *Pravda*, 20 Sept. 1990; *Izvestiya*, 5 April 1991.
91. *Pravda*, 3, 4 Dec. 1982; 21, 22 Jan. 1987; 29–31 Jan. 1988; 28 Nov. 1990; *Izvestiya*, 18 Sept. 1990; *Nezavissimaiya Gazeta* (Moscow), 31 Jan. 1992.
92. TASS–INO (Foreign Information Bulletin), 078, 28 Jan. 1992; ibid., 060, 26 Feb. 1992.

Conclusion

1. *MEED*, 1964, no. 10, p. 117.
2. *Area Handbook*, p. 5.
3. Ibid., p. 65.
4. Ibid., p. 201.
5. M. W. Wenner, *Saudi Arabia*, p. 167.
6. See, for example: G. Lipsky et al., *Saudi Arabia*, p. 311.
7. *Area Handbook*, p. 201.
8. G. de Gaury, *Faisal*, pp. 107–108.

Bibliography

The bibliography includes all works quoted or mentioned in the present book, together with other important studies on Saudi Arabia. Works in all languages are listed irrespective of the script. Entries in Arabic and Russian are Romanized. The names of Arab authors are placed according to their last component and the definite article *al-* is ignored. English translations are given for titles in Arabic, Turkish and Russian.

The completeness of the bibliographical information varies because of the lack of full information for many entries.

Books and articles

Abd al-Aziz al-Awwal. *Al-Risala* [The Message] (n.p., n.d.).
Abd al-Jabbar, Abdallah. *Al-Tayarat al-Adabiya al-Haditha fi Qalb al-Jazira al-Arabiya* [Current Literary Trends in the Heart of the Arabian Peninsula] (Maahad al-Dirasat al-Aliya, Cairo, 1959).
Abd al-Rahim, Abd al-Rahim Abd al-Rahman. *Al-Dawla al-Saudiya al-Ula, 1745–1818* [The First Saudi State, 1745–1818] (Maahad al-Buhuth wal-Dirasat al-Arabiya, Cairo, 1969).
Abdallah. *Muzakkarat al-Malik Abdallah ibn al-Husain* [Memoirs of King Abdallah ibn Husain] (Amman, 1965).
Abir, M. 'Relations between the Government of India and the Sharif of Mecca during the French Invasion of Egypt, 1798–1801', *Journal of the Royal Asiatic Society*, 1965, parts 1–2.
Abu Aliya, Abd al-Fattah. *Al-Dawla al-Saudiya al-Thaniya, AH 1256–1309/AD 1840–1891* [The Second Saudi State, AH 1256–1309/AD 1840–1891] (Riyadh, 1974).
Aburish, S. K. *The Rise, Corruption and Coming Fall of the House of Saud* (Bloomsbury, London, 1995). X, 326 pp.
Adamov, Aleksandr A. *Irak Arabskiy: Bassorskiy Vilaet v Ego Proshlom i Nastoyashchem* [Arab Iraq: The Wilayat of Basra, Past and Present] (St Petersburg, 1912).
Ahdath Nufambr (Muharram) 1979 [The Events of November (Muharram) 1979] (Manshurat al-Hizb al-Shuyui fi al-Saudiya, n.p., 1980).

Bibliography

al-Ahsai, Muhammad ibn Abdallah. *Tuhfat al-Mustafid bi Tarikh al-Hasa fil-Qadim wal-Jadid* [A Wonder for Those who Derive Use from the Ancient and New History of al-Hasa], vols 1–2 (Matabi al-Riyadh, Riyadh, 1960).
Aitchison C. U. (ed.). *A Collection of Treaties, Engagements and Sanads*, vol. 2 (Manager of Publications, New Delhi, 1933). XXXI, 633, LXXXVI pp.
al-Ajlani, Munir. *Tarikh al-Bilad al-Arabiya al-Saudiya* [The History of Saudi Arabia] (Dar al-Kitab al-Arabi, Beirut, n.d.).
Ali, Ahmad. *Al Saud* [The Saudis] (Dar al-Sayyad lil-Tabaa wal-Nashr, Beirut, 1957).
Ali, S. R. *Oil, Turmoil and Islam in the Middle East* (New York, 1986).
Ali bey. *Travels* (London, 1816). 2 vols.
Ali Sheikh Rustum. *Saudi Arabia and Oil Diplomacy* (Praeger, New York, 1976). XVII, 197 pp.
al-Alusi, Mahmud Shukri. *Tarikh Najd* [The History of Najd] (al-Matbaa al-Salfiya, Cairo, AH 1343).
Amin, Ahmad. *Zuama al-Islah fil-Asr al-Hadith* [The Leaders of the Reforms of the Modern Epoch] (Lajnat al-Talif wal-Tarjama wal-Nashr, Cairo, 1947).
Andreasyan, Ruben N. *Neft i Arabskie Strany v 1973–1983 gg.: Ekonomicheskiy i Sotsialnyy Analiz* [Oil and the Arab Countries in 1973–1983: An Economic and Social Analysis] (Nauka, Moscow, 1990). 255 pp.
——'The "Oil Prosperity" and the Capitalist Transformation of the Arabian Monarchies', *Asia and Africa Today*, 1979, pp. 10–14.
Andreasyan, Ruben N., and Elyanov, E. A. *Blizhni Vostok: Neft i Nezavisimost* [The Near East: Oil and Independence] (Izdatelstvo Vostochnoy Literatury, Moscow, 1961). 319 pp.
Andreasyan, Ruben N., and Kazyukov, A. D. *OPEK v Mire Nefti* [OPEC in the World of Oil] (Nauka, Moscow, 1978). 232 pp.
Andrianov, V. V. *Neosedloe Naselenie Mira* [The Non-Sedentary Population of the World] (Nauka, Moscow, 1985). 230 pp.
Antonius, George. *The Arab Awakening: The Story of the Arab National Movement* (Hamish Hamilton, London, 1945). 470 pp.
al-Aqqad, Abbas Mahmud. *Al-Islam fil-Qarn al-Ishrin* [Islam in the Twentieth Century] (Cairo, 1960).
Arab Oil and Gas Directory, 1994 (Arab Petroleum Research Center, Paris, 1994).
The Arabian Peninsula: A Selected Annotated List of Periodicals, Books and Articles in English (The Library of Congress Reference Department, Washington, 1951). XI, 111 pp.
'L'Arabie Saoudite entre le Moyen-Age et le Vingtième Siècle', *Problèmes Politiques et Sociaux*, 1974, 230, pp. 3–48.
Arabskie Strany: Neft i Differentsiatsiya [The Arab Countries: Oil and Differentiation] (Nauka, Moscow, 1984). 263 pp.
Aramco Handbook: Oil and the Middle East (Dhahran, 1968).
Aramco. *The Royal Family, Officials of the Saudi Arab Government List and Prominent Saudi Arabs* (Dhahran, 1953).
The Archives of Russian Foreign Policy (Ministry of Foreign Affairs, Russian Federation).
Area Handbook for Saudi Arabia (US Government, Washington, 1966).
ARFP: see *The Archives of Russian Foreign Policy*.
Armstrong, H. C. *Lord of Arabia ibn Saud: An Intimate Study of a King* (Leipzig, 1938). 246 pp.
Asfour, E. Y. *Saudi Arabia: Long-Term Projections of Supply and Demand for Agricultural Products* (Beirut, 1965). 180 pp.
Ashraf, Kunwar M. 'Predstaviteli Musulmanskogo Vozrozhdeniya i Sobytiya 1857' [The Representatives of the Muslim Renaissance and the Events of 1957]. In: *Narodnoe Vosstanie v Indii 1857–1859* [The People's Revolt in India, 1857–1859] (Izdatelstvo Vostochnoy Literatury, Moscow, 1957), pp. 121–145.
Assah, Ahmed. *Miracle of the Desert Kingdom* (Johnson, London, 1969). XIII, 330 pp.
Attar, Ahmad Abd al-Ghafur. *Muhammad ibn Abd al-Wahhab* (n.p., 1943).

Bibliography

al-Baghdadi, Ibrahim Fasih al-Haidari. *Unwan al-Majd fi Bayan Ahwal Baghdad wa Basra wa Najd* [The Symbol of Glory in the Events in Baghdad, Basra and Najd] (Dar Manshurat al-Basri, Baghdad, 1962).
Baida, Oleg. *Wahhabite Islam and Power: Asia and Africa Today*, 1993, pp. 32-36.
Balsan, F. *A Travers l'Arabie Inconnue* (Paris, 1954).
Baroody, G. M. *Crime and Punishment Under Hanbali Law* (Dhahran, 1961).
Barthold, Vladimir V. *Istoriya Izucheniya Vostoka v Evrope i Rossii* [The History of the Study of the East in Europe and Russia] (Leningrad, 1925). VIII, 318 pp.
al-Bassam, Abdallah ibn Muhammad ibn Abd al-Aziz. *Tuhfat al-Mushtaq fi Akhbar Najd wal-Hijaz wal-Iraq* [A Curious Extract from the Reports on Najd, Hijaz and Iraq] (microfilm of a manuscript chronicle).
Bazili, K. M. *Siriya i Palestina pod Turetskim Pravitelstvom v Istoricheskom i Politicheskom Otnosheniyakh* [Syria and Palestine under the Turkish Government in the Historical and Political Respects] (Izdatelstvo Vostochnoy Literatury, Moscow, 1962). 326 pp.
Bell, Gertrude. *The Arab War: Confidential Information for General Headquarters from Gertrude Bell* (Golden Cockerel Press, London, 1940). 51 pp.
——*The Letters of Gertrude Bell* (Benn, London, 1927). 328 pp.
Belyaev, Evgeni A. *Araby, Islam i Arabski Khalifat v Rannee Srednevekovye* [The Arabs, Islam and the Arab Caliphate in the Early Middle Ages] (Nauka, Moscow, 1956). 280 pp.
——*Musulmanskoe Sektantstvo* [Muslim Sectarianism] (Izdatelstvo Vostochnoy Literatury, Moscow, 1957). 100 pp.
—— (ed.). *Proiskhozhdenie Islama* [The Origin of Islam] (OGIZ, Moscow/Leningrad, 1931).
Belyaev, Igor P. 'Amerikanski Imperializm v Saudovskoy Aravii' [American Imperialism in Saudi Arabia] *(Izdatelstvo Vostochnoy Literatury*, Moscow, 1957). 227 pp.
A Bibliographical List of Works about the Arabian Peninsula (Cairo, 1963).
Birks, J. S., and Sinclair, C. A. *International Migration and Development in the Arab Region* (ILO, Geneva, 1980). 175 pp.
Blunt, Anne. *A Pilgrimage to Najd, the Cradle of the Arab Race: A Visit to the Court of the Arab Emir, and 'Our Persian Campaign'* (John Murray, London, 1881). 2 vols.
Blunt, W. F. 'A Visit to Jebel Shammar (Nejd)', *Proceedings of the Royal Geographical Society*, 1880, vol. 2, pp. 81-102.
Bodyanski, V. L. *Vostochnaya Araviya: Istoriya, Geografiya, Naselenie, Ekonomika* [Eastern Arabia: History, Geography, Population, Economy] (Nauka, Moscow, 1986). 341 pp.
Bodyanski, V. L., and Lazarev, M. S. *Saudovskaya Araviya posle Sauda* [Saudi Arabia after Saud] (Nauka, Moscow, 1967). 116 pp.
Bondarevski, V. L. *Angliyskaya Politika i Mezhdunarodnye Otnosheniya v Basseyne Persidskogo Zaliva* [British Policy and International Relations in the Persian Gulf Basin] (Nauka, Moscow, 1968). 542 pp.
Bonnenfant, P. 'Utilisation des Recettes Pétrolieres et Stratégie des Groupes Sociaux en Peninsule Arabe', *Maghreb*, 1979, no. 83.
Borisov, Rostislav V. *SSha: Blizhnevostochnaya Politika v 70-e Gody* [The USA: Near Eastern Policy in the 1970s] (Nauka, Moscow, 1982). 216 pp.
Brémond, E. *Le Hejaz dans la Guerre Mondiale* (Payot, Paris, 1931). 351 pp.
Brockelman, Karl. *History of the Islamic Peoples* (Routledge & Kegan-Paul, London, 1949).
Brydges, H. J. *An Account of the Transactions of His Majesty's Mission to the Court of Persia (1807-1811), to which is Appended a Brief History of the Wahauby* (Bohn, London, 1834). 2 vols.
Bulloch, John. *Reforms of the Saudi Arabian Constitution* (Gulf Centre for Strategic Studies, London, 1992). 70 pp.
Burckhardt, John L. *Notes on the Bedouins and Wahabys Collected during his Travels in the East by John Lewis Burckhardt* (Colburn & Bentley, London, 1930). 2 vols.

Bibliography

—— *Travels in Arabia* (Colburn, London, 1829). 478 pp.
Burton, R. F. *Personal Narrative of a Pilgrimage to El-Madinah and Meccah* (Tylston & Edwards, London, 1893-98).
Butler, S. S., and Aymler L. 'Baghdad to Damascus via El Jauf, Northern Arabia', *Geographical Journal*, 1909, vol. 33, May, pp. 517-535.

Carruthers, D. A. *Arabian Adventure: To the Great Nafud in the Quest of the Oryx* (Witherby, London, 1935). XII, 208 pp.
——'Captain Shakespear's Last Journey', *Geographical Journal*, 1922, vol. 59, no. 5, pp. 321-334; no. 6, pp. 400-418.
——'Journey in North-Western Arabia', *Geographical Journal*, 1910, vol. 35, pp. 225-248.
Carter, J. R. L. *Leading Merchant Families of Saudi Arabia* (Scorpion, London, 1979). 190 pp.
Cevdet, Ahmed. *Tarih-i Vekaiya Devlet-i Aliyye*, vols 1-12 (Istanbul, AH 1271-1292). 12 vols.
——*Tezakir* (Ankara, 1953). 12 vols.
Cheesman, Robert E. *In Unknown Arabia* (Macmillan, London, 1926). XX, 447 pp.
Cheney, Michael S. *Big Oilman from Arabia* (Heinemann, London etc., 1958). 320 pp.
Chevalier, Jean-Marie. *The New Oil Stakes* (Lane, London, 1975), 187 pp.
——*Le Nouvel Enjeu Pétrolier* (Calman Lévy, Paris, 1973). 305 pp.
Churakov, Mikhail V. 'Novaya Istoriya Nejda Amina al-Reikhani kak Istochnik po Etnografii Tsentralnoy Aravii' [Amin Rihani's *The Modern History of Najd* as a Source for the Study of the Ethnography of Central Arabia], *Sovetskaya Etnografia*, 1960, no. 1, pp. 83-98.
Clayton, G. 'Arabia and the Arabs', *Journal of the Royal Institute of International Affairs*, 1929, vol. 8, no. 1, pp. 8-20.
Clayton G. F. *An Arabian Diary* (University of California Press, Berkeley & Los Angeles, 1969). XIV, 379 pp.
——'Arabia and the Arabs', *Journal of the Royal Institute of International Affairs*, vol. 8, no. 1, pp. 8-20.
Cole, D. P. 'Bedouins of the Oil Fields', *Problèmes Politiques et Sociaux*, 1974, no. 230.
Cole, Juan R. I., and Keddie, Nikki. *Shiism and Social Protest* (Yale University Press, New Haven/London, 1986). X, 325 pp.
Corancez, L. A. de. *Histoire des Wahabis depuis leur Origine jusqu'à la Fin de 1809* (Prapart, Paris, 1809). VIII, 290 pp. [Published in English as: *The History of the Wahabis from their Origin until the End of 1809*, Garnet, Reading, 1995.]
Cordes, Rainor, and Scholz, F. *Bedouins, Wealth and Change: A Study of Rural Development in the United Arab Emirates and the Sultanate of Oman* (New York University, Tokyo, 1980). 65 pp.
Crane, Robert D. *Planning the Future of Saudi Arabia: A Model for Achieving National Priorities* (Praeger, New York, 1978). XII, 242 pp.

Dahlan, Ahmad ibn Zaini. *Khulasat al-Kalam fi Bayan Umara al-Balad al-Haram* [A Short Statement on the Emirs of the Holy City] (al-Matbaa al-Khairiya, Cairo, 1888).
al-Dakhil, Sulaiman ibn Sabah. *Al-Qawl al-Sadid fi Akhbar Imarat al-Rashid* [A Reasonable Word on Developments in the Rashidis' Emirate] (Riyadh, 1966).
Davletshin. *Otchet Shtabs-Kapitana Davletshina o Komandirovke v Khijaz* [Junior Captain Davletshin's Report on his Business Trip to Hijaz] (St Petersburg, 1899). 145 pp.
Dickson, H. R. P. *The Arab of the Desert: A Glimpse into Badawin Life in Kuwait and Saudi Arabia* (Allen & Unwin, London, 1949). 648 pp.
——*Kuwait and Her Neighbours* (Allen & Unwin, London, 1956). 627 pp.
A Dictionary of Islam (London, 1885).
Didier, C. E. *Séjour chez le Grand-Cherif de la Mekke* (Hachette, Paris, 1857). 310 pp.
Dlin, N. A., and Zverera L. S. *Kuveit* [Kuwait] (Mysl, Moscow, 1968). 148 pp.
Doughty, Charles M. *Travels in Arabia Deserta* (Cambridge University Press, Cambridge, 1888). 2 vols.

Bibliography

Driault, Edouard. *L'Egypte et l'Europe: la Crise de 1839–1841* (Cairo, 1930–33). 5 vols.

Eddy, W. A. *F. D. R. Meets Ibn Saud* (New York, 1954). 45 pp.
EIU Regional Review: The Middle East and North Africa. 1986 (London, 1986).
The Encyclopaedia of Islam. New edn ed. by H. A. R. Gibb (Leiden, Brill; London, Luzac, 1956).
Encyclopédie de l'Islam. New edn ed. by B. Lewis, V. L. Ménage, C. Pellat and J. Schacht (Leiden, Brill; Paris, 1954–79) (vols 1–5).
Energueticheskiy Krizis v Kapitalistichestom Mire [The Energy Crisis in the Capitalist World] (Mysl, Moscow, 1975). 478 pp.
Euting, Julius. *Reise in Innerarabien 1883–84* (Verhändlungen der Gesellschaft für Erkunde zu Berlin, 1886, vol. 13).
——*Tagebuch einer Reise in Inner-Arabien* (Brill, Leiden, 1896–1914). 2 vols.

Falk, André. *Visa pour l'Arabie: l'Air du Temps* (Gallimard, Paris, 1958). 255 pp.
al-Faqi, Muhammad Hamid. *Athr al-Dawa al-Wahhabiya fil-Islah al-Dini wal-Umrani fi Jazirat al-Arab wa Ghairiha* [The Impact of the Wahhabi Call on the Religious and Cultural Reforms in the Arabian Peninsula and Outside] (Matbaa Ansar al-Sunna al-Muhammadiya, Cairo, AH 1354).
Faroughy, Abbas. 'Introducing Yemen', *Orientalia*, New York, 1947. 123 pp.
al-Farsy, Fouad. *Saudi Arabia: A Case Study in Development* (Stacey International, London, 1980). 224 pp.
Feoktistov, A. 'Saudi Arabia in the Arab Life', *International Affairs*, 1977, no. 6, pp. 82–99.
Finati, Giovanni. *Narrative of the Life and Adventures of Giovanni Finati, Native of Ferrara* (John Murray, London, 1830). 2 vols.
Forde, C. D. 'The Habitat and Economy of the North Arabian Badawin', *Geography*, 1933, vol. 17, pp. 205–219.
Fresnel, F. 'L'Arabie', *Revue des Deux Mondes*, 1839, série 4, vol. 17, pp. 241–257.

Gaury, Gerald de. *Faisal, King of Saudi Arabia* (Barker, London, 1966). XIV, 181 pp.
——*Rulers of Mecca* (Harrap, London, 1951). 317 pp.
Georgiev, Aleksandr G., and Ozoling, Vasili V. *Neftyanye Monarkhii Aravii: Problemy Razvitiya* [The Oil Monarchies of Arabia: Development Problems] (Nauka, Moscow, 1983). 224 pp.
Gerasimov, Oleg G. *Saudovskaya Araviya* [Saudi Arabia] (Mysl, Moscow, 1977). 72 pp.
——*Yemenskaya Revolyutsiya 1962–1975 gg.* [The Yemeni Revolution of 1962–1975] (Nauka, Moscow, 1979). 226 pp.
al-Ghadiri, Nahad. *Al-Tahaddi al-Kabir* [The Great Challenge] (Matbaa Alf Laila wa Laila, Beirut, 1965).
Gibb, Hamilton A. R. *Mohammedanism* (London, 1954).
Gibb, Hamilton A. R., and Bowen, Harold. *Islamic Society and the West: A Study of the Impact of Western Civilization on Moslem Culture in the Near East* (Oxford University Press, London, 1950–57). 386 pp.
Glubb, John B. *War in the Desert: An RAF Frontier Campaign* (Hodder & Stoughton, London, 1960). 352 pp.
Goldziher, Ignaz. *Le Dogme et la Loi de l'Islam: Histoire du Développement Dogmatique et Juridique de la Religion Musulmane* (Geuthner, Paris, 1920). VIII, 315 pp.
Golubovskaya, E. K. *Revolyutsiya 1962 g. v Yemene* [The Revolution of 1962 in the Yemen] (Nauka, Moscow, 1971). 207 pp.
Gooch, George P., and Temperley, Harold. *British Documents on the Origin of the War, 1898–1914*, vol. 10, part 2 (London, 1938).
Goodwin, Godfrey. *The Janissaries* (London, 1994).
Graves, Philipp P. *The Life of Sir Percy Cox* (London, 1941).
Great Britain. *Arbitration Concerning Buraimi and the Common Frontier Between Abu Dhabi and*

Bibliography

Saudi Arabia. Memorial Submitted by the Government of the United Kingdom of Great Britain and Northern Ireland (London, 1955). 2 vols.

——Colonial Office. *Report by His Britannic Majesty's Government on the Administration of Iraq for the Period April 23-November 24* (London, 1925).

Grishechkin, K. I. 'Rabochee Dvizhenie v Saudovskoy Aravii' [The Workers' Movement in Saudi Arabia]. In: *Profsoyuzy Stran Blizhnego i Srednego Vostoka* [The Trade Unions of the Countries of the Near and Middle East] (Profizdat, Moscow, 1966), pp. 152-159.

Grunebaum, Gustav E. von. *Modern Islam: The Search for Cultural Identity* (New York, 1964). VII, 408 pp.

Guarmani, C. *Northern Najd: A Journey from Jerusalem to Anaiza in Qasim* (Argonaut Press, London, 1938). XLIV, 134 pp.

Habib, J. S. *Ibn Saud's Warriors of Islam: The Ikhwan of Najd and their Role in the Creation of Saudi Kingdom, 1910-1930* (Brill, Leiden, 1978). XVI, 196 pp.

Hacker B. *Sojourn in Saudi Arabia* (New York, 1963). *Al-Hadiya al-Sunniya wal-Tuhfa al-Wahhabiya al-Najdiya* [A Sunni Present and a Wahhabi Wonder from Najd] (Cairo, AH 1342).

Halliday, Fred. *Arabia without Sultans* (Penguin, London, 1975). 529 pp.

Hamilton, Charles W. *Americans and Oil in the Middle East* (Gulf, Houston, 1962). XI, 307 pp.

Hamza, Fuad. *Al-Bilad al-Arabiya al-Saudiya* [Saudi Arabia] (Matbaa Umm al-Qura, Mecca, AH 1355).

——*Qalb Jazirat al-Arab* [The Heart of the Arabian Peninsula] (Matbaa al-Salfiya al-Kubra wa Maktabatuha, n.p., 1933).

al-Hanbali, Muhammad ibn Afaliq al-Ahsai. *Risala fi Radd Ibn Abd al-Wahhab* [A Message of Objection to Ibn Abd al-Wahhab] (Stiftung Preussischer Kulturbesitz. Depot der Staatsbibliothek. Tübingen).

Haraz, Rajab. *Al-Dawla al-Uthmaniya wa Jazirat al-Arab, 1840-1909* [The Ottoman Empire and the Arabian Peninsula, 1840-1909] (Cairo, 1970).

Harrison, P. W. *The Arab at Home* (Cowell, New York, 1924). XII, 345 pp.

Hart, P. 'Application of Hanbali Law and Decree Law to Foreigners in Saudi Arabia', The George Washington Law Review, 1953, vol. 22, 22 December, pp. 165-175.

Hess, J. J. *Von der Beduinen des Innern Arabiens: Erzählungen, Lieder, Sitten und Gebräuche* (Niehans, Zürich/Leipzig, 1938). 177 pp.

Heyworth-Dunne, James. *Bibliography and Reading Guide to Arabia* (Cairo, 1952). 16 pp.

Hobday, Peter. *Saudi Arabia Today: An Introduction to the Richest Oil Power* (Macmillan, London/Basingstoke, 1978). VIII, 133 pp.

Hogarth, David G. *The Penetration of Arabia* (Lawrence & Bullen, London, 1904). XIII, 359 pp.

Holden, D. *Travels to Arabia* (London, 1966).

Hopwood, D. (ed.). *The Arabian Peninsula: Society and Politics* (Allen & Unwin, London, 1972). 320 pp.

Howarth, D. A. *The Desert King: A Life of Ibn Saud* (Collins, London, 1964). 251 pp.

Huber, C. *Journal d'un Voyage en Arabie (1883-1884)* (Imprimerie Nationale, Paris, 1891). XII, 778 pp.

——'Voyage dans l'Arabie Centrale, Hammade, Sammar, Kacim, Hedjas', *Bulletin de la Société Geographique*, 1884, sér. 7, vol. 5, pp. 304-363; 1885, vol. 6, pp. 92-148.

Hurewitz, Jacob C. *Middle East Politics: The Military Dimension* (Praeger, New York, 1969). XVIII, 553 pp.

Hurgronje, Christian S. *Mekka* (Brill, Leiden, 1931). VI, 309 pp.

Ibn Abd al-Wahhab, Abdallah ibn Muhammad. 'Al-Kalimat al-Nafia fil-Mukaffarat al-Waqia' [Useful Words on the True Unfaithfulness]. In: *Majmuat al-Tawhid al-Najdiya* [The Najdi Collection of Monotheism] (Cairo, AH 1375).

Bibliography

——'Al-Risala' [The Message]. In: *Al-Hadiya al-Sunniya wal-Tuhfa al-Wahhabiya al-Najdiya* [The Sunni Gift and the Wahhabi Masterwork from Najd] (Cairo, AH 1342).

Ibn Abd al-Wahhab, Muhammad. 'Arba Rasail. Tisa Rasail fil-Tawhid. Kitab al-Tawhid. Kitab Kashf Shubuhat fil-Tawhid' [Four Messages. Nine Messages on Monotheism. The Book of Monotheism. The Book of Detection of Doubts in Monotheism]. In: *Majmuat al-Tawhid al-Najdiya* [The Najdi Collection of Monotheism] (Cairo, AH 1375).

——*Masail al-Jahiliya allati Khalafa fiha Rasul Allah Ahl al-Jahiliya* [The Questions of Jahiliya Debated between Allah's Messenger and the People of Jahiliya] (Cairo, AH 1348).

——*Mufid al-Mustafid fi Kufr Tarik al-Tawhid* (Edification for One who Derives Benefit from the Unbelief of One who Deviates from Monotheism] (Cairo, 1954).

——*Mukhtasir Sirat al-Rasul* [A Brief Description of the Messenger's Life] (Cairo, 1956).

——'Usul al-Iman. Fadhl al-Islam. Kitab al-Kabair. Nasihat al-Muslimina bi-Ahadith Khatim al-Murasilina' [The Principles of Faith. The Dignity of Islam. The Book of Mortal Sins. Advice to the Muslims, Based on the Hadith and on the Seal of the Prophets]. In: *Majmuat al-Ahadith al-Najdiya* [The Najdi Collection of Traditions] (Cairo, AH 1375).

——*Al-Usul al-Thalatha wa Adillatuha* [Three Principles and Their Evidence] (Cairo, n.d.).

Ibn Bishr, Uthman. *Unwan al-Majd fi Tarikh Najd* [The Symbol of Glory in the History of Najd] (Mecca, AH 1349). 2 parts.

Ibn Ghannam, Husain. *Tarikh Najd al-Musamma Rawdhat al-Afkar wal-Afham* [The History of Najd, Called the Garden of Ideas and Concepts] (Cairo, 1949). 2 parts.

Ibn Hasan, Abd al-Rahman. *Fath al-Majid, Sharh Kitab al-Tawhid* [Discovery of the Glorious, an Interpretation of 'The Book of Monotheism'] (Cairo, 1957).

Ibn Hashim, Muhammad. *Hadhramawt: Tarikh al-Dawla al-Kathiriya* [Hadhramawt: The History of the Kathiri State] (n.p., 1948).

Ibn Hizlul, Saud. *Tarikh Muluk Al Saud* [The History of the Saudi Kings] (Matbaa al-Riyadh, Riyadh, 1961).

Ibn Isa, Ibrahim ibn Salih. *Tarikh baadhul-Hawadith al-Waqia fi Najd* [The History of Some Events that Occurred in Najd] (Dar al-Yamama, Riyadh, 1966).

Ibn Rashid, Dhari ibn Fuhaid. *Nabza Tarikhiya an Najd* [A Historical Sketch about Najd] (Dar al-Yamama, Riyadh, 1961).

Ibn Sahman, Sulaiman. *Kitab al-Dhiya al-Shariq fi Radd Shubuhat al-Maziq al-Mariq* [The Book of Bright Light with Objections to a Heretic's Doubts] (Matbaat al-Manar, Cairo, AH 1344).

——*Kitab Tanbih Zawi al-Albab al-Salima an al-Wuqu fil-Alfaz al-Wahima* [The Book that Warns People with Unimpaired Reason against Dangerous Expressions] (Matbaa al-Manar, Cairo, AH 1343).

Ibn Sanad al-Basri, Uthman. *Tarikh Baghdad* [The History of Baghdad] (Bombay, AH 1304).

Ibn al-Suwaidi. *Al-Mushkilat al-Mudhiya Raddan alal-Wahhabiya* [Old Questions in Reply to the Wahhabis] (Stiftung Preussischer Kulturbesitz, Depot der Staatsbibliothek, Tübingen).

Ibragimov, D. *Zapad i Araviyskie Strany Persidskogo Zaliva: Kulturno-ideologicheskoe Vozdeistvie* [The West and the Arabian Countries of the Persian Gulf: The Cultural and Ideological Impact] (Nauka, Moscow, 1991). 161 pp.

Ibrahim, Saad Eddin. *The New Arab Social Order: A Study of the Social Impact of the Oil Wealth* (Westview Press, Boulder, 1982). XIV, 208 pp.

Ignatenko, Aleksandr A. *Khalify bez Khalifata: Islamskie Nepravitelstvennye Religiozno-politicheskie Organizatsii na Blizhnem Vostoke. Istoriya, Ideologiya, Deyatelnost* [Caliphs without Caliphates: Islamic non-Government Religious-political Organizations in the Near East. History, Ideology, Activities] (Nauka, Moscow, 1988). 207 pp.

The Impact of Oil Revenues on Arab Gulf Development (London, 1984).

Ingrams, Harold. *The Yemen: Imams, Rulers and Revolutions* (John Murray, London, 1963). XI, 164 pp.

Isaev, Vladimir A. *Ekonomicheskie Otnosheniya Mezhdu Arabskimi i Osvobodivshimisya Stranami,*

Bibliography

1961–1980 gg. [The Economic Relations between the Arab and Newly Liberated Countries, 1961-1980] (Nauka, Moscow, 1983). 151 pp.

Islam: Entsiklopedicheski Slovar [Islam: An Encyclopedic Dictionary] (Nauka, Moscow, 1991). 315 pp.

'Islam v Novoe i Noveyshee Vremya' [Islam in the New and Modern Epochs]. In: *Islam. Entsiklopedicheski Slovar* [Islam: An Encyclopedic Dictionary] (Nauka, Moscow, 1991).

Islam i Problemy Natsionalizma v Stranakh Blizhnego i Srednego Vostoka: Sbornik Statey [Islam and the Problems of Nationalism in the Countries of the Near and Middle East: A Collection of Articles] (Nauka, Moscow, 1986). 237 pp.

Islam v Sovremennoy Politike stran Vostoka (Konets 70-kh–Nachalo 80-kh gg. XX v.) [Islam in the Contemporary Politics of the Countries of the East (the Late 1970s and the early 1980s)] (Nauka, Moscow, 1986). 279 pp.

'Islamski Faktor' v Mezhdunarodnykh Otnosheniyakh v Asii (70-e–Pervaya Polovina 80-kh gg.) [The 'Islamic Factor' in International Relations in Asia (the 1970s and Early 1980s)] (Nauka, Moscow, 1987). 191 pp.

Ivanov, N. A. 'Marokko' [Morocco]. In: *Istoriya Natsionalno-Osvoboditelnoy Borby Narodov Afriki v Novoe Vremya* [The History of the National Liberation Struggle of the Peoples of Africa in the New Epoch] (Nauka, Moscow, 1976).

——'Svobodnye i Podatnye Plemena Severnoy Afriki v XIV v.' [The Free and Tribute-paying Tribes of Northern Africa in the Fourteenth Century]. In: *Arabskie Strany. Istoriya* [The Arab Countries. History] (Izdatelstvo Vostochnoy Literatury, Moscow, 1963), pp. 152–192.

——'O Tipologicheskikh Osobennostyakh Arabo-Osmanskogo Feodalizma' [On the Typological Features of Arab-Ottoman Feudalism], *Narody Azii i Afriki*, 1978, no. 3.

al-Jabarti, Abd al-Rahman. *Egipet pod Vlastyu Muhammada Ali (1806–1821)* [Egypt under the Power of Muhammad Ali (1806–1821)] (Izdatelstvo Vostochnoy Literatury, Moscow, 1963). 792 pp.

Jahim al-Hukm al-Saudi [The Hell of Saudi Rule] (The Front of National Reform in Saudi Arabia, n.p., 1957).

Jamiat al-Duwal al-Arabiya. Idarat al-Shuun al-Ijtimaiya wal-Amal. Riayat al-Badu wa-Tahdhiruhum wa-Tawtinuhum [The Arab League. The Administration for Social Affairs and Labour. The Care of the Bedouins, their Settling and Civilizing] (Cairo, 1965).

Jarvis, C. S. *Arab Command: The Biography of Lieutenant-Colonel F. G. Peake Pasha* (Hutchinson, London, 1942). 158 pp.

Jaussen, A. *Coutumes des Arabes au Pays de Moab* (Paris, 1908).

Jazirat al-Arab Tattahimu Hukkamaha [The Arabian Peninsula Accuses its Rulers] (Matbaa al-Jarida al-Tijariya, Cairo, 1949).

Jeddah 68/69 (University Press of Africa and Arabia, Nairobi, 1968). 174 pp.

Johani, A., and Berne, M. *The Saudi Arabian Economy* (Baltimore, Md., 1986).

Jomard, E. F. *Etudes Géographiques et Historiques sur l'Arabie* (Didot, Paris, 1839).

Jung, Eugène. *La Révolte Arabe* (Paris, 1924–25). 2 vols: vol. I, 199 pp; vol.II, 221 pp.

Kaminski, Sergey A. *Institut monarkhii v stranakh Arabskogo Vostoka* [The Institution of Monarchy in the Countries of the Arab East] (Nauka, Moscow, 1981). 152 pp.

Katakura, Motoko. *Bedouin Village: A Study of a Saudi Arabian People in Transition* (University of Tokyo Press, Tokyo, 1977). XX, 189 pp.

Kelidar, A. R. 'The Problem of Succession in Saudi Arabia', *Asian Affairs*, 1978, vol. 9, part 1, pp. 23–30.

Kelly, J. B. *Arabia, the Gulf and the West* (Wiedenfeld & Nicolson, London, 1980). IX, 530 pp.

——*Eastern Arabian Frontiers* (Faber & Faber, London, 1964). 319 pp.

——'A Prevalence of Furies: Tribes, Politics and Religion in Oman'. In: *The Arabian Peninsula: Society and Politics* (London, 1972).

al-Khatib, Abd al-Hamid. *Al-Imam al-Adil* [The Just Imam] (Cairo, 1951).
Kheirallah, G. *Arabia Reborn* (University of New Mexico Press, Albuquerque, 1952). VIII, 307 pp.
Khrustalev, M. A. *Sotsialnaya Struktura Saudiyskogo Obshchestva* [The Social Structure of Saudi Society] (Narody Azii i Afriki, 1973, no. 4, pp. 27-35).
Kiernan, R. H. *The Unveiling of Arabia: The Story of Arabian Travel and Discovery* (Harrap, London etc., 1937). 360 pp.
King Faisal and the Modernization of Saudi Arabia (Croom Helm, London, 1980). 235 pp.
The Kingdom of Saudi Arabia [ed. Robin Dunipace]. (Stacey International, London, 1978). 256 pp.
Kingdom of Saudi Arabia. Fifth Development Plan (1990-1995) (Ministry of Planning). 406 pp.
al-Kitab al-Akhdar al-Najdi: Mutamar al-Kuwait [The Green Book of Najd: The Kuwait Conference] (n.p., АН 1342).
al-Kitab al-Ikhsai al-Sanawi. Al-Mamlaka al-Arabiya al-Saudiya. Wizarat al-Maliya wal-Iqtisad [Statistical Yearbook. The Kingdom of Saudi Arabia. The Ministry of Finance and Economy] (Riyadh, 1969-).
al-Kiyali, Nazzar Abd al-Rahman. *Al-Wasit fi Sharh Nizam al-Amal al-Saudi* [An Interpretation of the Saudi Labour Code] (al-Dar al-Saudi lil-Nashr wal-Tawzi, Jidda, 1973).
Klebanoff, S. *Middle East Oil and US Foreign Policy* (Praeger, New York, 1974). XIV, 289 pp.
Knauerhase, Ramon. *The Saudi Arabian Economy* (Praeger, New York, 1975). XXV, 361 pp.
Konstitutsii Gosudarstv Blizhnego i Srednego Vostoka [The Constitutions of the States of the Near and Middle East] (Izdatelstvo Inostrannoy Literatury, Moscow, 1956). 591 pp.
Kotlov, L. N. *Iordaniya v Noveyshee Vremya* [Jordan in the Modern Epoch] (Izdatelstvo Vostochnoy Literatury, Moscow, 1962). 262 pp.
——'Osvoboditelnoe Vosstanie v Omane v 1957-1959 gg' [The Liberation Revolt in Oman in 1957-1959]. In: *Arabskie Strany. Istoriya. Ekonomika* [The Arab Countries. History. Economy] (Nauka, Moscow, 1970), pp. 48-79.
——'SSSR i Strany Araviyskogo Poluostrova' [The USSR and the Countries of the Arabian Peninsula]. In: *Sovetsko-Arabskie Druzhestvennye Otnosheniya* [Soviet-Arab Friendly Relations] (Izdatelstvo Vostochnoy Literatury, Moscow, 1961), pp. 106-117.
——Yemenskaya Arabskaya Respublica [*The Yemen Arab Republic*] (Nauka, Moscow, 1971), 287 pp.
Krymski, Aleksandr. *Istoriya Arabov i Arabskoy Literatury* [The History of the Arabs and Arab Literature] (Moscow, 1911-12). 2 parts.
Kudryavtsev, Aleksei V. *Islamski Mir i Palestinskaya Problema* [The Islamic World and the Palestine Problem] (Nauka, Moscow, 1990). 133 pp.
Kunina, A. E. *Doktrina Eyzenkhauera* [The Eisenhower Doctrine] (Gospolitizdat, Moscow, 1957). 80 pp.

Labor Law and Practice in the Kingdom of Saudi Arabia (Government Printing Office, Washington, 1972). VIII, 103 pp.
Lam al-Shihab fi Sira Muhammad ibn Abd al-Wahhab [The Brilliance of the Meteor in Muhammad ibn Abd al-Wahhab's Life] (British Museum, OPB MSS. Catalogue ADD 23346).
Lammens, H. *L'Arabie Occidentale avant l'Hégire* (Beirut, 1928).
Laoust, Henri. *Essai sur les Doctrines Sociales et Politiques de Tak-id-din Ahmad bin Taimiyah* (Cairo, 1939). 755 pp.
——*Le Traité de Droit Public d'Ibn Taimiyah* (Beirut, 1948).
Laquer, Walter. *Confrontation: The Middle East War and World Politics* (Wildwood House, London, 1974). X, 244 pp.
Lawrence, Thomas E. *Seven Pillars of Wisdom* (Jonathan Cape, London, 1942). 672 pp.
Lazarev, M. S. *Krushenie Turetskogo Gospodstva na Arabskom Vostoke* [The Collapse of Turkish Dominance in the Arab East] (Izdatelstvo Vostochnoy Literatury, Moscow, 1960). 246 pp.
Leachman, G. E. 'A Journey in North-Eastern Arabia', *Geographical Journal*, 1911, vol. 37, pp. 265-274.

Bibliography

Lebkicher, R., Rentz, G. and Steineke, M. *The Arabia of Ibn Saud* (Moore, New York, 1952). IX, 179 pp.
Lee, Eve. *The American in Saudi Arabia* (Intercultural Press, Chicago, 1980). 111 pp.
Lenczowsky, George. *The Middle East in World Affairs* (Cornell University Press, Ithaca, 1957). XX, 576 pp.
Leppens, P. *Expedition en Arabie Central* (Paris, 1956).
Levin, I., and Mamaev, V. *Gosudarstvenny Stroy Stran Arabskogo Vostoka* [The State Structure in the Countries of the Arab East] (Izdatelstvo AN SSSR, Moscow, 1957). 312 pp.
Lipsky, G. A., et al. *Saudi Arabia: Its People, its Society, its Culture* (Survey of World Cultures, ed. Thomas Fitzsimmons, HRAF Press, New Haven, 1959). 366 pp.
Lloyd George, David. *The Truth about Reparations and War Debts* (Fertig, New York, 1970).
Long, D. E. *Saudi Arabia* (Beverley Hills, London, 1976). 70 pp.
Longrigg, Stephen H. *Four Centuries of Modern Iraq* (Oxford, 1925).
——*Oil in the Middle East: Its Discovery and Development* (Oxford University Press, New York etc., 1968). XIII, 519 pp.
Looney, Robert E. *Saudi Arabia's Development Potential: Application of an Islamic Growth Model* (Lexington Books, Lexington, 1982). XVII, 358 pp.
Lorimer, J. G. *Gazetteer of the Persian Gulf, Oman, and Central Arabia* (Superintendant Government Printing, Calcutta, 1908–15). 2 vols.
Lutski, Vladimir B. *Liga Arabskikh Gosudarstv* [The Arab League] (Pravda, Moscow, 1946). 28 pp.
——*Novaya Istoriya Arabskikh Stran* [The Modern History of the Arab Countries] (Nauka, Moscow, 1965). 372 pp.

MacKie Frood, A. 'Recent Economic and Social Developments in Saudi Arabia', *Geography*, 1939, vol. 24.
Macro, E. *Bibliography of the Arabian Peninsula* (University of Miami Press, Coral Cables, 1958). XIV, 80 pp.
al-Madani, Muhammad Mughairibi Futaih. *Firqat al-Ikhwan al-Islamiya bi Najd* [The Sect of Islamic Ikhwan in Najd] (Cairo, AH 1342).
Madhi, Muhammad Abdallah. *Al-Nahdhat al-Haditha fi Jazirat al-Arab fil-Mamlaka al-Arabiya al-Saudiya* [The Modern Renaissance in the Arabian Peninsula in the Kingdom of Saudi Arabia] (Dar Ahya al-Kutub al-Arabiya, Cairo, 1952).
al-Majmua al-Ilmiya al-Saudiya [The Saudi Scientific Collection] (Cairo, 1946).
Majmuat al-Tawhid al-Najdiya [The Najdi Collection of Monotheism] (Cairo, AH 1375).
Maksimov, A. A. *Razvitie Otstalykh Obshchestv Pri Neogranichennykh Finansovykh Resursakh* [The Development of Backward Societies with Unlimited Financial Resources] (Nauka, Moscow, 1989). 187 pp.
al-Malik al-Shahid Faisal ibn Abd al-Aziz: Qaima Bibliyugrafiya Mukhtara li-Siratihi wa Amalihi [The Martyr King Faisal ibn Abd al-Aziz: A Short Bibliography Concerning his Life and Deeds] (Riyadh, 1976).
Malysheva, Dina B. *Religiya i Obshchestvenno-politicheskoe Razvitie Arabskikh i Afrikanskikh Stran, 70-e–80-e Gody* [Religion and the Socio-Political Development of the Arab and African Countries in the '70s and '80s] (Nauka, Moscow, 1986). 228 pp.
al-Mamlaka al-Arabiya al-Saudiya fi Ahdiha al-Hadhir [The Kingdom of Saudi Arabia in the Present] (Jidda, 1956).
Mansfield, Peter. *The Arabs* (Allen Lane, London, 1978).
al-Marik, Fahd. *Lamahat an al-Tatawwur al-Fikri fi Jazirat al-Arab fil-Qarn al-Ishrin* [Notes on the Development of Ideas in the Arabian Peninsula in the Twentieth Century] (Matbaa Ibn Zaidun, Damascus, 1926).
Markaryan, Robert V. *Zona Persidskogo Zaliva: Problemy, Perspektivy* [The Persian Gulf Zone: Problems and Prospects] (Nauka, Moscow, 1986). 157 pp.

Bibliography

Markov, Gennadi E. *Kochevniki Azii: Struktura Khozyaystva i Obshchestvennaya Organizatsiya* [The Nomads of Asia: The Structure of the Economy and Social Organization] (Izdatelstvo Moskovskogo Universiteta, Moscow, 1976). 317 pp.
Marlow, J. *The Persian Gulf in the Twentieth Century* (Crescent Press, London, 1962). VIII, 280 pp.
Marston, Thomas E. *Britain's Imperial Role in the Red Sea Area (1800-1878)* (Shoe String Press, Hamden, 1961). XIII, 550 pp.
Mashin, V. V., and Yakovlev, A. I. *Persidski Zaliv v Planakh i Politike Zapada* [The Persian Gulf in the West's Plans and Policy] (Mezhdunarodnye Otnosheniya, Moscow, 1985). 237 pp.
Massé, A. *Islam (Ocherk Istorii)* [Islam, a Sketch of its History] (Izdatelstvo Vostochnoy Literatury, Moscow, 1961). 229 pp.
Mavlyutov, R. R. *Islam* (Politizdat, Moscow, 1971). 168 pp.
[McGovern, George S.] *Realities of the Middle East: A Report by Senator George S. McGovern to the Committee on Foreign Relations, United States Senate* (Washington, 1975).
Medvedko, Leonid I. 'Decolonization of Arab Oil', *Asia and Africa Today*, 1972, no. 11, pp. 32; no. 12, pp. 51.
——*Etot Blizhni Burlyashchi Vostok: Dokumentalnoe Povestvovanie* [This Turbulent Near East: A Documented Narration] (Politizdat, Moscow, 1985). 335 pp.
——*K Vostoku ot Suetsa: Zakat Kolonializma i Manevry Neokolonializma na Arabskom Vostoke* [To the East of Suez: The Decline of Colonialism and the Manoeuvres of Neocolonialism in the Arab East] (Politizdat, Moscow, 1981). 368 pp.
——*Vetry Peremen v Persidskom Zalive* [The Winds of Change in the Persian Gulf] (Nauka, Moscow, 1975). 208 pp.
Memorial of the Government of Saudi Arabia: Arbitration for the Settlement of the Territorial Dispute (Cairo, 1955). 3 vols.
Mengin, Félix. *Histoire de l'Egypte sous le Gouvernement de Mohammed-Aly* (Bertrard, Paris, 1823), vols 1-2.
——*Histoire Sommaire de l'Egypte sous le Gouvernement de Mohammed-Aly, ou Récit des Principaux Evénements qui Eurent Lieu de l'An 1823 à l'An 1838* (Piclot, Paris, 1839). XL, 539 pp.
Meulen, Daniel van der. *The Wells of Ibn Saud* (John Murray, London, 1957). IX, 270 pp.
Mezhdunarodny Neftyanoy Kartel [The International Oil Cartel] (Izdatelstvo Inostrannoy Literatury, Moscow, 1954). 470 pp.
The Middle East Economic Digest. 'Saudi Arabia. Special Report' (London, 1978).
The Middle East Financial Directory 1980 (London, 1980).
The Middle East and North Africa (London, 1988).
Midhat, Ali Haydar. *The Life of Midhat Pasha* (John Murray, London, 1903). XII, 292 pp.
Mikesell, Raymond F., and Chenery, H. B. *Arabian Oil: America's Stake in the Middle East* (The University of North California Press, Chapel Hill, 1949). XI, 201 pp.
Miles, S. B. *The Countries and Tribes of the Persian Gulf* (Harrison, London, 1919). 2 vols.
Miller, A. F. *Mustafa Pasha Bayraktar: Ottomanskaya Imperiya v Nachale XIX v.* [Mustafa Pasha Bayraktar: The Ottoman Empire in the Early 19th Century] (Izdatelstvo AN SSSR, Moscow/Leningrad, 1947). 508 pp.
Miloslavski, Georgi V. *Integratsionnye Protsessy v Musulmanskom Mire: Ocherki Islamskoy Tsivilizatsii* [The Integration Processes in the Muslim World: Essays on Islamic Civilization] (Nauka, Moscow, 1991). 189 pp.
Minaev, V. *Podryvnaya Deyatelnost Germanskogo Fashizma na Blizhnem Vostoke* [The Subversive Activities of German Fascism in the Near East] (Gospolitizdat, Moscow, 1942). 52 pp.
Montagne, R. *La Civilisation du Désert: Nomades d'Orient et d'Afrique* (Hachette, Paris, 1947). 271 pp.
——'Notes sur la Vie Sociale et Politique de l'Arabie du Nord, les Sammar du Negd', *Revue des Etudes Islamiques*, 1932, vol. 6, cah. 1, pp. 61-81.
Mortimer, Edward. *Faith and Power: The Politics of Islam* (Faber & Faber, London, 1982). 432 pp.

Bibliography

al-Muammari, Ahmad ibn Nasir Uthman. *Al-Risala* [The Message] (n.p., n.d.).

al-Muhammasani, Subhi. *Al-Awdha al-Tashriiya fil-Duwal al-Arabiya* [Legislation in the Arab States] (Dar al-Ilm lil-Malayin, Beirut, 1962).

al-Mukhtar, Salah al-Din. *Tarikh al-Mamlaka al-Arabiya al-Saudiya fi Madiha wa Hadiriha* [The History of the Kingdom of Saudi Arabia in the Past and Present] (Maktaba al-Hayat, Beirut, 1957).

Musil, Alois. *Arabia Deserta: A Topographical Itinerary* (New York, 1927). XVII, 651 pp.

——*The Manners and Customs of the Rwala Bedouins* (New York, 1928). XIII, 368 pp.

——*The Northern Hegaz: A Topographical Itinerary* (New York, 1926). XII, 374 pp.

——*Northern Negd: A Topographical Itinerary* (New York, 1928). XIII, 368 pp.

——*Zur Zeitgeschichte von Arabien* (Hirsel, Leipzig/Vienna, 1918). V, 102 pp.

Mustafa, Muhammad Shafiq Afandi. *Fi Qalb Najd wal-Hijaz* [In the Heart of Najd and Hijaz] (Matbaa al-Manar, Cairo, 1927).

Mustafa, Salim Rashid. *Taqwin al-Yaman al-Hadith* [The Making of Modern Yemen] (Cairo, 1963).

Musulmanskoe Pravo: Struktura i Osnovnye Instituty [Muslim Law: The Structure and Principal Institutions] (Nauka, Moscow, 1984). 145 pp.

al-Nabhani, Muhammad ibn Khalifa. *Al-Tuhfa al-Nabhaniya fi Tarikh al-Jazira al-Arabiya* [A Glorious Wonder in the History of the Arabian Peninsula] (Cairo, AH 1342).

Nallino, C. A. *Raccolta di Scritti, Editi e Inediti*, vol. 1: *L'Arabia Saudiana* (Istituto per l'Oriente, Rome, 1939). IV, 472 pp.

Nasif, Husain ibn Muhammad. *Madhi al-Hijaz wa Hadiruhu* [The Past and Present of Hijaz] (Matbaa Khidhir, Cairo, AH 1349).

Neftedollary i Sotsialno-ekonomicheskoe Razvitie Stran Blizhnego i Srednego Vostoka [Petrodollars and the Socio-economic Development of the Countries of the Near and Middle East] (Nauka, Moscow, 1979). 213 pp.

Niblock, T. (ed.). *State, Society and Economy in Saudi Arabia* (Croom Helm, London, 1982). 314 pp.

Niebuhr, C. *Description de l'Arabie d'après les Observations et Recherches Faits dans les Pays Même* (Copenhagen, 1773).

——*Voyage de M. Niehbuhr en Arabie et en d'Autres Pays d'Orient* (n.p., 1780). 2 vols.

Nolde, Eduard. *Reise nach Innerarabien, Kurdistan und Armenien* (Vieweg, Braunschweig, 1895). XV, 272 pp.

Nosenko, V. I. 'Saudovsko-Yemenskaya Borba iz-za Asira' [The Saudi-Yemeni Struggle for Asir]. In: *Istoriya i Ekonomika Stran Arabskogo Vostoka i Severnoy Afriki* [The History and Economy of the Countries of the Arab East and Northern Africa] (Nauka, Moscow, 1975), pp. 292–302.

Noveyshaya Istoriya Arabskikh Stran (1917–1966) [The Modern History of the Arab Countries (1917–1966)] (Nauka, Moscow, 1968). 658 pp.

Noveyshaya Istoriya Arabskikh Stran Azii, 1917–1985 [The Modern History of the Arab Countries of Asia, 1917–1985] (Nauka, Moscow, 1988). 639 pp.

Noveyshaya Istoriya Yemena, 1917–1982 gg. (The Modern History of Yemen, 1917–1982] (Nauka, Moscow, 1984). 230 pp.

'O Sekte Vaabiev, Otpadshikh ot Magometanstva' [On the Wahhabi Sect who Seceded from Muhammadanism], *Zhurnal Razlichnykh Predmetov Slovesnosti*, 1805, vol. 2, no. 1, pp. 18–34; no. 2, pp. 24–44).

Oppenheim, M. F. von. *Die Beduinen* (Harassowitz, Leipzig, 1939–1940). 4 vols.

Orlov, Evgeni A. *Vneshnyaya Politika Irana posle Vtoroy Mirovoy Voyny* [Iran's Foreign Policy after the Second World War] (Nauka, Moscow, 1975). 224 pp.

Osipov, Aleksandr I. *SShA i Arabskie Strany, 70-e–Nachalo 80-kh Godov* [The US and the Arab Countries, the '70s and early '80s] (Nauka, Moscow, 1983). 229 pp.

Ozoling, Vasili V. *Ekonomika Saudovskoy Aravii* [The Economy of Saudi Arabia] (Nauka, Moscow, 1975). 207 pp.

Bibliography

——*Saudovskaya Araviya* [Saudi Arabia] (Mysl, Moscow, 1963). 149 pp.

Palgrave, William G. *Narrative of a Year's Journey through Central and Eastern Arabia (1862–1863)* (Macmillan, London, 1865). 2 vols.

Pelly, Lewis. 'Report on a Journey to the Wahabee Capital of Riyadh in Central Arabia'. In: *Journal of Journey from Persia to India through Herat and Candagar* (Bombay, 1866).

——'Report on the Tribes, Trade and Resources around the Shoreline of the Persian Gulf', *Transactions of the Bombay Geographical Society*, 1865, vol. 17, pp. 32–112.

——'A Visit to the Wahabee Capital, Central Arabia', *Journal of the Royal Geographical Society*, 1865, vol. 35, pp. 169–191.

Penzin, D. 'Saudovskaya Araviya – Neft i Razvitie' [Saudi Arabia – Oil and Development], *Mirovaya Ekonomika i Mezhdunarodnye Otnosheniya*, 1976, no. 11, pp. 114–119.

Perlo, V. *American Imperialism* (International Publishers, New York, 1951). 256 pp.

Pershits, A. I. *Araby Araviyskogo Poluostrova* [The Arabs of the Arabian Peninsula] (Geografgiz, Moscow, 1958). 58 pp.

——*Khozyaystvo i Obshchestvenno-politicheski Stroy Severnoy Aravii v XIX – Pervoy Treti XX v.* [The Economic and Socio-political Situation in Northern Arabia in the 19th and the First Third of the 20th Centuries] (Izdatelstvo Vostochnoy Literatury, Moscow, 1961). 224 pp.

——'Nekotorye Osobennosti Klassoobrazovaniya i Ranneklassovykh Otnosheniy u Kochevnikov-skotovodov' [Some Features of Class Formation and Early Class Relations among the Nomadic Animal-breeders]. In: *Stanovlenie klassov i gosudarstv* [Formation of Classes and States] (Nauka, Moscow, 1976), pp. 280–313.

Philby, Harry St John B. *Arabia* (Benn, London, 1930). XIX, 387 pp.

——*Arabia of the Wahhabis* (Constable, London, 1928). XIV, 422 pp.

——*Arabian Days: An Autobiography* (Hale, London, 1948). XVI, 336 pp.

——*Arabian Highlands* (Cornell University Press, Ithaca/New York, 1952). XVI, 771 pp.

——*Forty Years in the Wilderness* (Hale, London, 1957). XVI, 272 pp.

——*The Heart of Arabia: A Record of Travel and Exploration* (Constable, London, 1922). 2 vols.

——*A Pilgrim in Arabia* (Hale, London, 1946). 198 pp.

——*Saudi Arabia* (Benn, London, 1955). XIX, 393 pp.

Philipp, Hans-Jürgen. *Saudi Arabia. Bibliography on Society. Politics. Economics* (K. G. Saur München, New York/London, Paris, 1984)

——*Saudi Arabia. Bibliography on Society. Politics. Economics* (K. G. Saur München, London/New York/Paris, vol. II, 1989).

Piotrovskaya, Irina L. *Strany Araviyskogo Poluostrova: Neft, Finansy, Razvitie* [The Countries of the Arabian Peninsula: Oil, Finance, Development] (Nauka, Moscow, 1981). 191 pp.

Pirenne, Jaqueline. *A la Découverte de l'Arabie: Cinq Siècles de Science et d'Aventure* (Amiot-Dumont, Paris, 1958). 328 pp.

——*Otkrytie Aravii: Pyatsot let Puteshestviy i Issledovaniy* [The Discovery of Arabia: Five Centuries of Travels and Explorations] (Nauka, Moscow, 1970). 359 pp.

Politika Anglii na Blizhnem i Srednem Vostoke [Britain's Policy in the Near and Middle East] (Nauka, Moscow, 1966). 432 pp.

Politika SShA na Arabskom Vostoke [US Policy in the Arab East] (Izdatelstvo Vostochnoy Literatury, Moscow, 1961). 282 pp.

Presley, John R., and Westaway, A. J. *A Guide to the Arabian Economy* (Macmillan, London etc., 1989). XIX, 233 pp.

Primakov, Aleksandr E. *Persidski Zaliv: Neft i Monopolii* [The Persian Gulf: Oil and Monopolies] (Mysl, Moscow, 1983). 160 pp.

Primakov, Evgeni M. *Anatomiya Blizhnevostochnogo Konflikta* [Anatomy of the Near Eastern Conflict] (Mysl, Moscow, 1973). 374 pp.

——*Istoriya Odnogo Sgovora: Blizhnevostochnaya Politika SSha v 70-e – Nachale 80-kh Godov* [The

Bibliography

Story of a Collusion: The Near Eastern Policy of the US in the '70s and Early '80s] (Politizdat, Moscow, 1985). 319 pp.

——*Vostok Posle Krakha Kolonialnoy Sistemy* [The East after the Collapse of the Colonial System] (Nauka, Moscow, 1982). 208 pp.

——*Voyna, Kotoroy Moglo ne Byt* [The War that Might be Prevented] (Novosti, Moscow, 1991). 151 pp.

Proshin, N. I. *Saudovskaya Araviya: Istoriko-ekonomicheski Ocherk* [Saudi Arabia: A Historical and Economic Sketch] (Nauka, Moscow, 1964). 302 pp.

——*Strany Araviyskogo Poluostrova* [The Countries of the Arabian Peninsula] (Geografgiz, Moscow, 1958). 200 pp.

Proval 'Doktriny Eyzenkhauera': Sbornik Statey [The Failure of the 'Eisenhower Doctrine': A Collection of Articles] (Izdatelstvo Inostrannoy Literatury, Moscow, 1958). 214 pp.

Putintseva, Tamara A. *Sledy Vedut v Peski Aravii* [The Traces Lead to the Arabian Sands] (Nauka, Moscow, 1986). 286 pp.

al-Qahtani, Abdallah Salim, and Saati, Yahya Mahmud. *Muallafat wa Maraji an al-Mamlaka al-Arabiya al-Saudiya* [Literature and Sources on the Kingdom of Saudi Arabia] (Riyadh, 1971).

al-Qasimi, Abdallah Ali. Al-Thaura al-Wahhabiya [The Wahhabi Revolution] (Cairo, 1936).

Quandt, William B. *Saudi Arabia in 1980s: Foreign Policy, Security and Oil* (Brookings Institution, Washington, 1981). XIII, 190 pp.

al-Qutb, Samir Abd al-Razzaq. *Ansab al-Arab* [The Arabs' Genealogies] (Dar Maktaba al-Bayan, Beirut, 1969).

Rachkov, Boris V. *Neft i Mirovaya Politika* [Oil and World Politics] (Mezhdunarodnye Otnosheniya, Moscow, 1972). 272 pp.

Rafiq, Musa. 'V Myateznoy Aravii' [In Rebellious Arabia], *Mezhdunarodnaya Zhizn*, 1928, no. 6.

Ralli, A. *Christians at Mecca* (London, 1909).

——*Mekka v Opisaniyakh Evropeytsev* [Mecca as Described by Europeans] (Kirsner, Tashkent, 1913). 308 pp.

Raswan, C. *The Arab and his Horse* (Oakland, 1955). 148 pp.

——*Im Land der Schwarzen Zelte: Mein Leben unter Beduinen* (Ullstein, Berlin, 1934). 156 pp.

Raunkiaer, Barclay. *Gennem Wahhabiternes Land paa Kamelryg* (Nordisk Forl., Copenhagen, 1913).

Raymond, J. *Les Wahabys: Document Inédit de 1806* (Cairo, 1925). VIII, 40 pp.

Razvivayushchiesya Strany: Zakonomernosti, Tendentsii, Perspektivy [The Developing Countries: Regularities, Trends, Prospects] (Mysl, Moscow, 1974). 474 pp.

Rehatsek, E. 'The History of the Wahhabys in Arabia and India' *The Journal of the Bombay Branch of the Royal Asiatic Society*, 1880, vol. 14, pp. 274–401.

[Reinaud]. 'Auszug aus dem Briefe des Hrn. Reinaud auf Dr. Seetzen, Haleb, 2. Apr. 1805', *Monatliche Correspondenz zur Beförderung der Erd- und Himmelskunde*, 1805, vol. 12, no. 22.

Reisner, Igor M. *Razvitie Feodalizma i Obrazovanie Gosudarstva u Afgantsev* [The Development of Feudalism and the Formation of the State of the Afghans] (Izdatelstvo AN SSSR, Moscow, 1954). 416 pp.

Ridha, Muhammad Rashid. *Al-Wahhabiyun wal-Hijaz* [The Wahhabis and Hijaz] (Matbaa al-Manar, Cairo, AH 1344).

Rihani, Amin. *Ibn Saoud of Arabia: Maker of Modern Arabia* (Houghton & Mifflin, Boston/New York, 1928). XVII, 370 pp.

al-Rihani, Amin. *Tarikh Najd al-Hadith wa Mulhaqatihi* [The History of Modern Najd and its Dependencies] (al-Matbaa al-Muallimiya, Beirut, 1928).

Rodinson, Maxime. *Islam et Capitalisme* (Seuil, Paris, 1966). 303 pp.

Rondot, Pierre. *L'Islam et les Musulmans d'Aujourd'hui* (Ed. de l'Orient, Paris, 1958). 2 vols.

Rouhani, Fuad. *A History of OPEC* (Praeger, New York, 1971). XVI, 281 pp.

Bibliography

[Rousseau, J. B. L. J.] *Description du Pachalik de Bagdad Suivie d'une Notice Historique sur les Wahabis* (Treutel & Würtz, Paris, 1809). VII, 261 pp.

Rugh, W. 'Emergence of a New Middle Class in Saudi Arabia', *Middle East Journal*, 1973, vol. 27, no.1, pp. 7–20.

Rutter, Eldon. *The Holy Cities of Arabia* (Putnam, London/New York, 1928). XV, 593 pp.

Sabry, M. *L'Empire Egyptien sous Mohamed Ali et la Question d'Orient (1811–1849)* (Paris, 1930).

Sadiq, Muhammad Tawfiq. *Tatawwur al-Hukm wal-Idara fil-Mamlaka al-Arabiya al-Saudiya* [The Development of Government and Administration in the Kingdom of Saudi Arabia] (Maahad al-Idara al-Amma, Riyadh, 1965).

Sadlier, G. F. 'Account of a Journey from Katif on the Persian Gulf to Yamboo on the Red Sea', *Transactions of the Literary Society of Bombay*, 1823, vol. 3.

Safran, N. *1985: Saudi Arabia: the Ceaseless Quest for Security* (Bolknap Press of Harvard University Press, Cambridge, Mass./London). XVIII, 524 pp.

Said, Amin. *Al-Muluk al-Muslimun al-Muasirun* [The Contemporary Muslim Kings] (Cairo, n.d.).

—— *Tarikh al-Dawla al-Saudiya* [The History of the Saudi State] (Dar al-Katib al-Arabi, Beirut, 1964). 3 vols.

—— *Vosstaniya Arabov v XX Veke* [The Arab Revolts in the 20th Century] (Progress, Moscow, 1964). 347 pp.

al-Said, Nasir. *Tarikh Al Saud* (Manshurat Ittihad Shab al-Jazira al-Arabiya, n.p., n.d.).

—— *Risala min Nasir al-Said ilal-Malik Saud* [A Message from Nasir al-Said to King Saud] (n.p., 1958).

Salil-ibn-Razik. *History of the Imams and Seyyids of Oman (661–1856)*. (London, 1871).

Saltana Najd. *Al-Kitab al-Akhdar al-Najdi* [The Sultanate of Najd. The Green Book on Najd] (Mecca, 1925).

al-Sammari, Fahd ibn Abdallah. *Bibliugrafiya al-Mamlaka al-Arabiya al-Saudiya fi Ahd al-Malik Abd al-Aziz* [Bibliography of the Kingdom of Saudi Arabia during the Reign of King Abd al-Aziz] (Dar Arakan lil-Nashr wal-Tawzi, Riyadh, 1993). 616 pp.

Sanger, Richard H. *The Arabian Peninsula* (Cornell University Press, Ithaca, 1954). XIV, 295 pp.

'Saudi Arabia. Special Report'. *The Middle East Economic Digest* (London, 1978).

Saudovskaya Araviya: Spravochnik [Saudi Arabia: Reference Book] (Nauka, Moscow, 1980). 271 pp.

Schlesinger, Arthur M. *A Thousand Days: John F. Kennedy in the White House* (Mifflin/Riverside Press, Boston/Cambridge, 1965). XV, 1087 pp.

Schmidt, Dana A. *Yemen: The Unknown War* (Bodley Head, London etc., 1968). 316 pp.

Seabrook, W. B. *The Middle East: Oil and the Great Powers* (New York, 1956).

Seifulmulyukov, I. A. *Strany OPEK v Razvivayushchemsya Mire* [The OPEC Countries in the Developing World] (Moscow, 1985). 24 pp.

Senchenko, I. P. *Araviya: Obshestvo, Traditsiy i Nravy* [Society, Traditions and Mores] (Znaniye, Moscow, 1991). 64 pp.

Shakir, Fuad. *Dalil al-Mamlaka al-Arabiya al-Saudiya* [A Guide to the Kingdom of Saudi Arabia] (n.p., 1948).

al-Shamlan, Saif Marzuq. *Min Tarikh al-Kuwait* [From the History of Kuwait] (Cairo, 1959).

Shan, R. P. *Mobilizing Human Resources in the Arab World* (London, 1983).

al-Sharif, Abd al-Rahman Sadiq. *Mintaqat Anaiza, Dirasa Iqlimiya* [The Area of Anaiza, a Regional Study] (Matbaa al-Nahdha al-Arabiya, Cairo, 1969).

Sharipova, R. M. *Panislamizm Segodnya: Ideologiya i Praktika Ligi Islamskogo Mira* [Panislamism Today: The Ideology and Practice of the League of the Islamic World] (Nauka, Moscow, 1986). 160 pp.

al-Shawkani, Muhammad ibn Ali. *Al-Badr al-Tali* [The Rising Moon] (Cairo, AH 1348). 2 parts.

Shcherbatov, A. G., and Stroganov, S. A. *Kniga ob Arabskoy Loshadi* [A Book about the Arabian

Bibliography

Horse] (St Petersburg, 1900).
Shcherbatova, O. A. *Verkhom na Rodine Beduinov* [Astride in the Bedouins' Homeland] (St Petersburg, 1903).
Shestopalov, Vladimir Y. *Persidski Zaliv: Problemy Kontinentalnogo Shelfa* [The Persian Gulf: The Problems of the Continental Shelf] (Nauka, Moscow, 1982). 327 pp.
Shilling, N. A. *Doing Business in Saudi Arabia and the Arab Gulf States* (North-Holland Publishing Co., Amsterdam/New York, 1976). X, 455 pp.
Shvakov, A. V. *Bibliografiya Stran Yuzhnoy i Vostochnoy Aravii* [Bibliography of the Countries of Southern and Eastern Arabia] (Nauka, Moscow, 1989). 267 pp.
Shwadran, B. *Middle East Oil and the Great Powers* (Israel University Press, Jerusalem, 1959). 630 pp.
Simoniya, N. A. *Strany Vostoka: Puti Razvitiya* [The Countries of the East: The Paths of Development] (Nauka, Moscow, 1975). 348 pp.
Sixty Years of Achievements (Riyadh, n.d.).
Smilyanskaya, I. M. 'Sotsialno-ekonomicheskaya Struktura Stran Blijnego Vostoka na Rubeje Novogo Vremeni' [Social and Economic Structure of the Near Eastern Countries on the Threshold of New Time]. In: *Na Materialah Sirii, Livana i Palestiny* [On the Materials of Syria, Lebanon and Palestine] (Moscow, Nauka, 1979). 252 pp.
Smith, Wilfred C. *Islam in Modern History* (Princeton University Press, Princeton, 1957). IX, 317 pp.
Social and Economic Development in the Arab Gulf (London, 1980).
Soulié, J.-L., and Champenois, L. *Le Royaume d'Arabie Saoudite à l'Epreuve de Temps Modernes; un Homme Providentiel: Faisal* (Michel, Paris, 1978). 248 pp.
Soulié, J.-L., and Champenois, L. *Le Royaume d'Arabie Saoudite face à l'Islam Revolutionnaire, 1953–1964* (Armand Colin, Paris, 1966). 135 pp.
Sparrow, J. G. *Modern Saudi Arabia* (Knightly Vernon, London, 1970). VIII, 124 pp.
Stepanova, Z. N. *Borba Arabov za Obyedinenie Tsentralnoy Aravii i Obrazovanie Saudovskogo Korolevstva* [The Arabs' Struggle for the Unity of Central Arabia and the Formation of the Saudi Kingdom] (Leningrad, 1950). 11 pp.
Stevens, J. H., and King, R. *Bibliography of Saudi Arabia* (Durham, 1983). 81 pp.
Storrs, Ronald. *The Memoirs of Sir Ronald Storrs* (Putnam, New York, 1937). XVII, 563 pp.
Sullivan, R. R. 'Saudi Arabia in International Politics', *Review of Politics*, 1970, vol. 72, no. 4, pp. 436–460.
Syukiyaynen, Leonid R. *Musulmanskoe Pravo: Voprosy Teorii i Praktiki* [Muslim Law: Questions of Theory and Practice] (Nauka, Moscow, 1986). 256 pp.

Tahtinen, Dale R. *National Security Challenges to Saudi Arabia* (American Enterprise Institute for Public Policy Research, Washington, D.C., 1978), 45 pp.
Tamisier, Maurice. *Voyage en Arabie: Séjour dans l'Hejaz, Campagne d'Asir* (Desessart, Paris, 1840). 2 vols.
Thesiger, W. *Arabian Sands* (Dutton, New York, 1959). 353 pp.
This is Our Country (Ministry of Information, Riyadh, 1992).
Thomas, B. *Alarms and Excursions in Arabia* (Allen & Unwin, London, 1931). 296 pp.
——*Arabia Felix: Across the Empty Quarter of Arabia* (Cape, London, 1932). XXIX, 396 pp.
Tomara, M. 'Istoki Vakhkhabizma' [The Sources of Wahhabism] *Ateist*, 1930, no. 53, pp. 71–80.
Tomiche, F.-J. *L'Arabie Séoudite* (Presses Universitaires de France, Paris, 1962). 128 pp.
Toy, B. *A Fool Strikes Oil; Across Saudi Arabia* (John Murray, London, 1957). XII, 207 pp.
Toynbee, Arnold J. 'Survey of International Affairs since the Peace Settlement', vol. 1: *The Islamic World* (Oxford University Press, London, 1927). XVIII, 611 pp.
Trevaskis, Kennedy. *Shades of Amber: A South Arabian Episode* (Hutchinson, London, 1968). XV, 256 pp.
Trial, G., and Winder, R. 'Modern Education in Saudi Arabia', *History of Educational Journal*, 1950,

vol. 1, no. 3, pp. 121-133.
Troeller, Garry. *The Birth of Saudi Arabia: Britain and the Rise of the House of Sa'ud* (Cass, London, 1976). XXII, 287 pp.
Tuganova, Olga. *Politika SShA i Anglii na Blizhnem i Srednem Vostoke* [The Policy of the US and Britain in the Near and Middle East] (IMEMO, Moscow, 1960), 304 pp.
Tursunov, R. M. 'Neftedokhody vo Vnutrenney i Vneshney Politike Saudovskoy Aravii v Seredine 70-kh Godov' [Oil Revenues in Saudi Arabia's Domestic and Foreign Policy in the Mid-'70s]. In: *Vsesoyuznaya Shkola Molodykh Vostokovedov* [The All-Union School of Young Orientalists] (Moscow, 1980), vol. 2, part 1, pp. 139-140.
——'Prikhod k Vlasti Feysala v Saudovskoy Aravii' [Faisal's Advent to Power in Saudi Arabia], *Sbornik Nauchnykh Trudov Tashkentskogo Universiteta*, 1978, no. 564, pp. 80-87.
——*Saudovskaya Araviya v Mezharabskikh Otnosheniyakh v Period 1964-1975 gg.* [Saudi Arabia in Inter-Arab Relations, 1964-1975] (Fan, Tashkent, 1987). 122 pp.
Twitchell, K. S. *Saudi Arabia: With an Account of the Development of its Natural Resources* (Princeton University Press, Princeton, 1958). XIV, 281 pp.

al-Ubaid, Abd al-Rahman Abd al-Karim. *Qabilat al-Awazim* [The Tribe of Awazim] (Riyadh, 1971).
United Nations Organization. The General Assembly. 26th session. Doc. A/RU, 1966.
Uthaimeen, J. A. *The Welfare State in Saudi Arabia: Structure, Dynamics, and Function*. PhD thesis, American University, Washington, 1986, 391 pp.

Valkova, Lidiya V. *Saudovskaya Araviya v Mezhdunarodnykh Otnosheniyakh (1955-1977)* [Saudi Arabia in International Relations, 1955-1977] (Nauka, Moscow, 1979). 224 pp.
——*Saudovskaya Araviya: Neft, Islam, Politika* [Saudi Arabia: Oil, Islam, Politics] (Nauka, Moscow, 1987). 255 pp.
Vassiliev, Aleksei M. *Bibliografiya Saudovskoy Aravii* [A Bibliography of Saudi Arabia] (Nauka, Moscow, 1983). 271 pp.
——*Bitrul al-Khalij wal-Qadhiya al-Arabiya* [Gulf Oil and the Arab Problem] (Dar al-Thaqafa al-Jadida, Cairo, 1979).
——*Fakely Persidskogo Zaliva* [The Torches of the Persian Gulf] (Politizdat, Moscow, 1976). 174 pp.
——'Ideologiya Rannego Vakhkhabizma' [The Ideology of Early Wahhabism], *Narody Azii i Afriki*, Moscow, 1965, no. 6, pp. 113-121.
——*Istoriya Saudovskoy Aravii (1745-1973)*. [The History of Saudi Arabia (1745-1973)]. (Nauka, Moscow, 1982). 613 pp.
——*Neft: Monopolii i Narody* [Oil: Monopolies and Peoples] (Znanie, Moscow, 1964). 40 pp.
——'Nekotorye Osobennosti Sotsialno-politicheskoy Struktury Saudovskoy Aravii (20-e-30-e gg.)' [Some Features of the Socio-political Structure of Saudi Arabia (the '20s and '30s)], *Narody Azii i Afriki*, 1980, no. 5, pp. 52-64.
——*Persidski Zaliv v Epitsentre Buri* [The Persian Gulf in the Epicentre of the Storm] (Politizdat, Moscow, 1983). 288 pp.
——'Pervoe Gosudarstvo Saudov v Aravii' [The First Saudi State in Arabia]. In: *Arabskie Strany. Istoriya. Ekonomika* [The Arab Countries. History. Economy] (Nauka, Moscow, 1966), pp. 146-189.
——*Puritane Islama? Vakhkhabizm i Pervoe Gosudarstvo Saudidov v Aravii (1744/45-1818)* [The Puritans of Islam? Wahhabism and the First Saudi State in Arabia (1744/45-1818)] (Nauka, Moscow, 1967). 263 pp.
——*Russian Policy in the Middle East* (Madbuli, Cairo, 1996).
——*Russian Policy in the Middle East. From Messianism to Pragmatism* (Ithaca, Reading, 1993). XIII, 338 pp.
——'Saudi Arabia between Arkhaism and the Modern Epoch', *Asia and Africa Today*, 1980, no. 8, pp. 19-21; no. 9, pp. 18-21.

Bibliography

Vidal, F. S. *The Oasis of al-Hasa* (Aramco, Dhahran, 1955). 216 pp.
Vneshnyaya Politika Stran Blizhnego i Srednego Vostoka [The Foreign Policy of the Countries of the Near and Middle East] (Mezhdunarodnye Otnosheniya, Moscow, 1984). 287 pp.
Volney, C.-F. *Puteshestvie Volneya v Siriyu i Egipet, Byvshee v 1783, 1784 i 1785 Godakh* [Volney's Trip to Syria and Egypt in 1783, 1784 and 1785] (Moscow, 1791–93). 2 vols.
——*Voyage en Syrie et en Egypte pendant les Années 1783, 1784 et 1785* (Desenne, Paris, 1787). 2 vols.

Wahba, Hafiz. *Arabian Days* (London, 1964). 183 pp.
——*Jazirat al-Arab fil-Qarn al-Ishrin* [The Arabian Peninsula in the Twentieth Century] (Lajna al-Talif wal-Tarjuma wal-Nashr, Cairo, 1961).
——*Khamsuna Amman fi Jazirat al-Arab* [Fifty Years in the Arabian Peninsula] (Cairo, 1960).
Wallin, G. A. 'Narrative of a Journey from Cairo to Medina and Mecca by Syez, Acaba, Tawila, al-Yauf, Hail and Najd in 1845', *Journal of the Royal Geographical Society*, 1854, vol. 24, pp. 115–207.
——'Notes Taken on a Journey through Part of North Arabia in 1848', *Journal of the Royal Geographical Society*, 1850, vol. 20, pp. 293–343.
Wellsted, J. R. *Travels in Arabia* (London, 1838). 2 vols.
——*Travels to the City of the Caliphs* (London, 1840). 2 vols.
Wenner, M. W. *Modern Yemen, 1918–1966* (Baltimore, 1967).
——'Saudi Arabia: Survival of Traditional Elites'. In: *Political Elites and Political Development in the Middle East* (Cambridge, 1975), pp. 157–191.
Weygand, M. *Histoire Militaire de Mohammed Ali et de ses Fils* (Paris, 1936). 2 vols.
Who's Who in Saudi Arabia (Jidda, 1978). XV, 272 pp.
Wilson, A. T. *The Persian Gulf: An Historical Sketch from the Earliest Times to the Beginning of the Twentieth Century* (Oxford, 1928). 327 pp.
Winder, R. B. *Saudi Arabia in the Nineteenth Century* (Macmillan/St Martin's Press, London/New York, 1965). XIV, 312 pp.
Wizarat al-Kharijiya. *Majmuat al-Muahadat min 1341–1370* [Ministry of Foreign Affairs. A Collection of Treaties, AH 1341–1370] (Jidda, AH 1375).
——*Sahifa Tarikhiya an al-Mufawadat al-Akhira* [Ministry of Foreign Affairs. A Historical Bulletin on the Recent Negotiations] (Mecca, 1925).
World Development Report. World Bank (Washington, 1983).
World Resources. 1990–91. A report by the World Resources Institute (New York/Oxford, 1990).
World Statistics in Brief. UN (New York, 1983).

Yakovlev, A. I. 'Osobennosti Razvitiya Krupnoy Burzhuazii v Stranakh Araviyskogo Poluostrova' [The Features of the Development of the Big Bourgeoisie in the Countries of the Arabian Peninsula]. In: *Burzhuaziya i Sotsialnaya Evolutsiya Stran Zarubezhnogo Vostoka* [The Bourgeoisie and Social Evolution of the Countries of the Foreign East] (Nauka, Moscow, 1985). 304 pp.
——*Rabochiy Klass i Sotsialnaya Evolutsiya v Neftyanykh Monarkhiyakh* [The Working Class and Social Evolution in the Oil Monarchies of the East] (Nauka, Moscow, 1983). 200 pp.
——'Reformy i Sotsialnoe Razvitie Neftyanykh Monarkhiy Aravii (60-e–80-e gg.)' [Reforms and Social Development of the Oil Monarchies of Arabia (the '60s to the '80s)], *Narody Azii i Afriki*, 1988, no. 2, pp. 14–25.
——*Saudovskaya Araviya i Zapad* [Saudi Arabia and the West] (Nauka, Moscow, 1982). 208 pp.
——'Zapad i Sotsialno-economicheskoe Razvitie Saudovskoy Aravii' [The West and the Socio-economic Development of Saudi Arabia]. In: *Istoriya i Ekonomika Arabskikh Stran* [The History and Economy of the Arab Countries] (Nauka, Moscow, 1977), pp. 197–223.

Bibliography

Zabirov, B. S., and Shukhin, E. A. *Pod Nebom Aravii (Ocherk)* [Under the Sky of Arabia (an Essay)] (Znanie, Moscow, 1963). 48 pp.
Zehme, A. *Arabien und die Araber Seit Hundert Jahren* (Halle, 1875).
al-Zirikli, Khair al-Din. *Al-Alam* [Directory] (Matbaa al-Thaniya, Cairo, 1954–59).
—— *Ma Raaytu wa-ma Samitu: Rihla min Dimashq ila Makka* [What I Saw and Heard on the Way from Damascus to Mecca] (Matbaa al-Arabiya, Cairo, 1933).
——*Shibh al-Jazira fi Ahd al-Malik Abd al-Aziz* [The Arabian Peninsula in the Era of King Abd al-Aziz] (Beirut, 1970). 4 vols.
Zischka A. *Ibn Saud, Roi de l'Arabie* (Paris, 1934).
Zwemer, S. M. *Arabia, the Cradle of Islam* (New York, 1900).

Newspapers and Periodicals

al-Ahram, Cairo.
Arab News, Riyadh.
The Arab Observer, Cairo.
Asia and Africa Today, Moscow.
al-Bilad al-Saudiya, Jidda.
al-Bitrul wal-Ghaz al-Arabi, Beirut.
Biulleten Inostrannoy Kommercheskoy Informatsii (BIKI), Moscow.
Business Week, New York.
The Christian Science Monitor, Boston, Mass.
The Daily Telegraph, London/Manchester.
The Daily Telegraph and Morning Post, London.
Dawn, Karachi.
The Economist, London.
The Egyptian Gazette, Cairo.
Ekho Planety, Moscow.
The Financial Times, London.
Foreign Report, London.
Geography, London.
The Guardian, Manchester/London.
al-Gumhuriya, Cairo.
al-Hayat, Beirut.
al-Hurriya, Beirut.
International Affairs, Moscow.
The International Herald Tribune, Paris.
The International Labour Review, Geneva.
Izvestiya, Moscow.
al-Jazira, Riyadh.
Keesing's Contemporary Archives, Bristol.
al-Kifah, Beirut.
Krasnaya Zvezda, Moscow.
Labor Development Abroad, Washington, D.C.
Lughat al-Arab, Baghdad.
The Middle East, London.
The Middle East Economic Digest, London.
The Middle East Economic Survey, Beirut.
The Middle East Journal, Washington.
The Middle East and North Africa, London.

Bibliography

The Middle East Record, Jerusalem.
The Middle East Reporter, Washington.
Le Monde, Paris.
Le Monde Diplomatique, Paris.
al-Musawwar, Cairo.
Narody Azii i Afriki, Moscow.
New Times, London.
The New York Daily News, New York.
The New York Herald Tribune, New York.
The New York Times, New York.
Newsweek, New York.
Nezavissimaya Gazeta, Moscow.
Novoe Vremya, Moscow.
The Observer, London.
The OPEC Bulletin, Vienna.
L'Opinion, Rabat.
Orient, Hamburg.
Oriente Moderno, Rome.
The Overseas Business Report, Washington.
Pravda, Moscow.
Problemy Mira i Sozializma, Moscow.
Qafilat al-Zait, Dhahran.
al-Qibla, Mecca.
The Quarterly Economic Review of Saudi Arabia, Riyadh.
The Saturday Evening Post, Indianapolis.
The Saudi Economic Survey, Jidda.
al-Shaab, Beirut.
Sovetskaya Etnografiya, Moscow.
The Times, London.
Umm al-Qura, Mecca.
Uqaz, Jidda.
The US News and World Report, Washington.
Vestnik Evropy, St Petersburg.
Wall Street Journal, New York.
al-Waqai al-Arabiya, Beirut.
Washington Post, Washington, D.C.
The World Marxist Review, Prague.
World Oil, Houston, Texas.
The World Trade Union Movement, Prague.
Zhurnal Razlichnykh Predmetov Slovesnosti, St Petersburg.

Glossary

The glossary includes most of the Arabic and Turkish words used in the book except those in general usage (such as 'Islam').

aawan	(literally, 'assistants'), members of a ruler's entourage
aba	bedouin's cloak-like woollen garment
abd	slave; also freedman
adat	tribal customary law; see also *urf*
agha	(literally, 'venerable man'), an honorary title in the Ottoman empire
ahli	privately run
aib	shameful, despicable
Al al-Shaikh	family of *ulama* who are the descendants of Ibn Abd al-Wahhab
alim	see *ulama*
aman	pardon, mercy
amiri	state-run
aqid	military leader in bedouin and settled tribes
Araif	descendants of Saud ibn Faisal
arif	(literally, 'knowing'), expert in *urf* (q.v.), who conducts court hearings
Ashari	adherent of Asharism
Asharism	one of the main theological schools (founded by Abu al-Hasan al-Ashari, 873–935)
ashira	large kinship group that includes even those families who are distantly related
ashura	the most important date in the Shia religious calendar: the day of mourning in commemoration of the martyrdom of the Shia Imam al-Husain ibn Ali (626–80)
azan	the Muslim call to prayer

Glossary

bait al-mal	state exchequer
bida	in Islamic theology, a reprehensible innovation which contradicts religious norms
Carmathians	adherents of a radical branch of Shiism, participants in a large-scale religious-political movement in the ninth and tenth centuries in southern Iraq, eastern Arabia and Bahrain
daftar	register book
dakhila	bedouin's resort to the protection of a powerful shaikh
damgha	seal
dervish	member of a Sufi order (q.v.), who either wanders from place to place or lives in a dervish convent
dhimmi	non-Muslim subject (Jew, Christian or Zoroastrian) of a Muslim state
dira	pasturelands of a bedouin tribe, considered as the common estate of all its members
dishdasha	long shirt (for men), reaching down to the ankles
diwan	consultative body under a ruler or vicegerent
diwan al-malazim	grievance board
diya	blood money, paid to the kin of a person who has been killed
emir	ruler, a title of the ruler of an oasis (also *rais, wali, sahib, kabir, said*); later, the governor of a province in Saudi Arabia; a member of the ruling house of Al Saud
faqih	expert in *fiqh* (q.v.)
fatwa	official ruling on religious and legal questions, pronounced by a mufti (q.v.) or other religious authority at the request of a *qadhi* (q.v.) or any private person
feddan	unit of land equivalent to approximately 1 acre (4,200.883 sq. m)
fellah	(pl. *fellahin*) peasant farmer; hereditary farmer
fiqh	Islamic jurisprudence
firman	edict
furusiya	courage, daring
ghazu	raid, hostilities against other tribes among the bedouin
hadith	sayings attributed to the Prophet Muhammad; see also Sunna
hajj	pilgrimage to Mecca, one of the main duties of every Muslim
hajji	honorary title of a Muslim who has performed the *hajj*
hakim	governor
haml	bundle; cargo carried by a camel
hamula	see *jamaa*
Hanafi	adherent of Hanafism
Hanafism	the religious-legal school founded by Abu Hanif (d. 767); one of the four main *mazhabs* (q.v.)
Hanbali	adherent of Hanbalism
Hanbalism	the religious-legal school founded by Imam Ahmad ibn Hanbal (ninth century); one of the four main *mazhabs* (q.v.) recognized throughout the Sunni Muslim world

Glossary

hijra	(i) emigration of the Prophet Muhammad from Mecca to Medina, taken as the starting-point of the Muslim calendar; (ii) Ikhwan (q.v.) settlement
hima	reserved pasture, property of a tribal shaikh or ruler
Ibadhi	adherent of Ibadhism
Ibadhism	the most moderate branch of the Kharijites (q.v.) (found chiefly in Oman)
ibtida	see *bida* (syn.)
id	Muslim festival
id al-adha	Muslim sacrificial feast
idara	office, department, directorate
ihram	ritual garment worn during the *hajj*
ijma	consensus opinion of the most authoritative experts in Islamic religious sciences
ijtihad	judgement of a competent Muslim *alim* (q.v.) in solving questions relating to religious and public life on the basis of the Quran and the Sunna
Ikhwan	(literally, 'brethren'), name adopted by the members of a radical Wahhabi (q.v.) movement in the Saudi state in the twentieth century
imam	(i) spiritual leader of a Muslim community; (ii) title of the person who leads the prayers
iqta	conditional land grant in the Muslim countries of the Middle East; feudal estate, feudal possession
jadd	see *jamaa*
jahiliya	(literally, 'ignorance'), the era of paganism, denoting the pre-Islamic era and the religious condition of the people of Arabia before the Prophet Muhammad started his preaching
jamaa	association of several large and small families with a common ancestor (*jadd*) among the settled population of Arabia
janissary	special, privileged detachment in the army of the Ottoman empire, created in the fourteenth century; the janissary corps was disbanded in 1826
jihad	Muslims' holy war for the faith
jinn	good or evil spirit in Islamic mythology
jizya	poll tax collected by an Islamic state from its non-Muslim subjects
jummaa	see *jamaa*
Kaaba	the main sanctuary of Mecca, the Muslim world's most revered sacred object
kabir	ruler of an oasis; see also emir
kadiaskers	two persons second in the hierarchy of the Ottoman Muslim clergy to the *sheikh-ul-islam*; acted as the supreme judges
kafir	('infidel', 'non-believer'), contemptuous sobriquet for all non-Muslims among the Muslims
kahya	(i) business manager of a rich and noble person; (ii) assistant, secretary of a governor

Glossary

kharaj	land-tax
Kharijite	adherent of the earliest religious political party in Islam, which was formed in the course of the struggle for power within the caliphate in the seventh century. On the question of supreme power in a Muslim state, the Kharijites opposed both the Sunnis and the Shia
khatib	preacher who delivers sermons during the Friday prayers in a mosque and on religious holidays
khidma	legal costs
khums	one fifth of the spoils of war, awarded to the chieftain or ruler
khutba	Friday sermon (in a mosque)
khuwa	tribute, or payment for protection, paid by the semi-nomadic and settled population to the bedouin
kiswa	coverlet for the Kaaba
kufiya	traditional headdress of the Arabs, consisting of a shawl held in place by a cord (*uqal*)
madrasa	Islamic religious school or college
Mahdi	messiah, a messenger of Allah whose mission is to restore the purity of the faith and turn his followers on to the right path
mahmal	richly decorated ritual palanquin, sent by rulers of some Muslim states with the pilgrim caravans to Mecca
majlis	(i) tribal council, meeting led by a tribal shaikh; (ii) consultative assembly under a ruler or governor
majlis al-qarya	village council
majlis al-shura	advisory council
majlis al-wukala	council of ministers
Mameluke	armed slave; the Mamelukes formed the ruler's personal guard in some countries of the Middle East both in the medieval and in more recent periods of history; the Mamelukes were the ruling military elite of Egypt in the medieval period
markab	ritual palanquin on camel's back; it replaced the banners carried by the bedouin tribes when riding into battle
markaz	part of a district (see *mintaqa*) in Saudi Arabia
marsum	royal decree
mazhab	religious-legal school in Islamic law
mintaqa	district, or part of a province, in Saudi Arabia
miri	state-owned land and other properties from which the income is transferred to the exchequer
mudir	director
mudiriya	government office or department
mufti	Muslim *alim* (q.v.) and legal expert who issues *fatwas* (q.v.) on religious and legal questions
mugharasa	form of sharecropping
muhafiz	prefect or head of the administration of a district (see *mintaqa*)
muhtasib	official who ensures that standard weights and measures are observed in the markets and controls the quality of handicrafts and the prices of foodstuffs
mujahid	(pl. *mujahidin*) participant in *jihad* (q.v.); warrior for the faith

Glossary

mulk	land and other property owned by private individuals
muqataa	large estate or possession
musabila	nomads' summer migration to trading centres
mushaa	community's land redistributed among the members of a rural community or clan
mutasarrif	head of a *sanjak* (q.v.) in the Ottoman empire
mutawwa	religious instructor among the Ikhwan
muwalid	child of slaves
naib	deputy of an official; regent
nizam	code; regulation
pasha	title of top-ranking military and civil official in the Ottoman empire
pashalik	region administered by a pasha
qabila	tribe
qadhi	Muslim judge who examines criminal and civil cases
qaimmaqam	head of the administration of a *qadha* (q.v.) or *sanjak* (q.v.) in the Ottoman empire
qasida	traditional genre of classical Arabic poetry (usually an ode), with a well-established form
qaza	administrative unit, part of a *sanjak* (q.v.)
qiyas	judgement by analogy, one of the main methods adopted in Islamic theology
rabab	single-stringed violin
rais	(i) ruler of an oasis; see also emir; (ii) attorney
rajail al-shuyukh	(literally, 'men of the chief shaikh'), upper echelon of slaves who occupied posts in the state apparatus of the rulers of Najd
rakab	assembly of the top-ranking officials of the Ottoman empire
Ramadhan	ninth month of the Muslim lunar calendar, the month of fasting (*al-sawm*)
ratib	salary
raya	in the broad sense, the tax-payers of a country; in a narrower sense, the peasantry; can also mean oasis-dwellers
rial	(= the Austrian thaler), the coinage adopted in the Arabian peninsula (1 rial contained 23.387 g of pure silver); it was divided into a nominal 20 piastres
sahaba	Companions of Muhammad, who took part in the creation of the Muslim state during the Prophet's lifetime
sahib	ruler of an oasis; see also emir
saluqs	'poor people' in pre-Islamic poetry
sani	see *sunnaa*
sanjak	administrative-territorial unit, part of a province in the Ottoman empire
sar	blood feud; vengeance
sayid	ruler of an oasis; see also emir
Sayid	honorary name for a descendant of the Prophet Muhammad in the line

Glossary

	of his grandson Husain. Together with the sharifs (q.v.), they form one of the most revered strata in the social structure of Muslim societies
sayl	strong mud stream
Shafii	adherent of Shafiism
Shafiism	the religious-legal school founded by Abu Abdallah al-Shafii (767–820); one of the four main *mazhabs* (q.v.) recognized throughout the Muslim world
shaikh	tribe leader; elder of a village; ruler of a small principality; honorary title of any influential religious leader or learned person
shaikh al-mashaikh	chief shaikh
shaitan	the devil; Satan in Islamic mythology
sharia	complex of prescriptions fixed by the Quran and the Sunna, which form the moral values and religious conscience of the Muslims and are the sources of specific legal norms
sharif	(i) (literally, 'noble'), honorary title of the Prophet Muhammad's descendants in the line of his grandson Hasan; (ii) title of the hereditary rulers of Mecca
shawiya	stock-breeders who breed mainly (or exclusively) sheep and goats
sheikh-ul-islam	supreme religious dignitary in the Ottoman empire and some other Muslim countries; the chief interpreter of religious law; the supreme mufti
Shia	adherent of Shiism
Shiism	one of the two main branches of Islam, whose adherents recognize the Prophet Muhammad's descendants in the line of Ali ibn Abi Talib (the Prophet's cousin and son-in-law) and his sons Hasan and Husain as the only legitimate successors of Muhammad. (See also Sunnism)
shirk	polytheism
Sufi	adherent of Sufism; see also *tariqa*
Sufism	Islamic mysticism
Sunna	(literally, 'tradition'), the body of *hadiths* and accounts of the Prophet Muhammad's deeds and sayings
sunnaa	(sing. *sani*) craftsmen
Sunni	adherent of the Sunni branch of Islam
Sunnism	one of the two main branches of Islam, which recognizes the Quran and the Sunna as the sources of the faith. The majority of Muslims are Sunnis. (See also Shiism)
suq	market
sura	each of the 114 parts of the text of the Quran
tafsir	commentary on the Quran; textual interpretation of the Quran
tariqa	Sufi brotherhood, where a religious teacher initiates his disciples into esoteric religious-mystical practices
tawhid	main thesis of monotheism; the doctrine of Wahhabism (q.v.)
tawila	long metal coin
ulama	(sing. *alim*) theologians, experts in Muslim religious sciences (see also *faqih*, imam, mufti, *qadhi*)

Glossary

uqal — see *kufiya*
urf — customary law, tribal manners, which together with the *sharia* regulated the life of Muslim society
uyun — (literally, 'eyes'), scouts sent to spot the enemy during a *ghazu* (q.v.)

vizier — top-ranking state official or minister; grand vizier: equivalent to prime minister in the Ottoman empire; [for Arabia, see *wazir*]

wadi — valley
Wahhabi — adherent of Wahhabism
Wahhabism — religious-political movement in the Arabian peninsula whose ideological basis was established by Muhammad ibn Abd al-Wahhab (1703/04–1792), who advocated the return to a 'pure, undistorted' Islam
wakil — (pl. *wukala*) [in Arabia] (i) secretary; (ii) (until beginning of 1980s) minister
wali — (i) ruler of an oasis; see also emir; (ii) governor of a province in the Ottoman empire
waqf — land and other property of Muslim religious foundations, donated to them for charitable purposes and enjoying taxation and legal privileges
wazir — (pl. *wuzara*) [in Arabia] secretary of a governor; (recently) minister
wikala — agency, ministry
wisaya — trusteeship of the poor undertaken by a shaikh in return for payment

Zaidi — adherent of Zaidism
Zaidism — moderate branch of Shia Islam (in Yemen)
zakat — (formally) voluntary donation in favour of poor members of the Muslim community; practically a state tax, collected in accordance with the *sharia* (q.v.)
Zemindar — main category of landowners in the Indian state of the Great Mughals
zikr — ecstatic group worship

Index

Arab individuals are indexed under their first name, not their family name (e.g. Hafiz al-Asad will be found under 'H', not 'A'); non-Arabs are indexed under their surname. Note that al- (but not Al) is ignored in the alphabetical ordering of names.

Aba al-Khail 222
Abbas Pasha 175
Abbasids 56
Abd al-Aziz Al Musaid 366
Abd al-Aziz Al Ulayyan 180
Abd al-Aziz ibn Abd al-Rahman ibn Faisal Al Saud (Ibn Saud) 14, 17, 19-20, 22, 201-202, 205, 211-234, 236-239, 244-246, 248-299, 301, 304, 306, 308, 310-311, 315, 321-323, 326-327, 333-338, 343-344, 347, 349, 433, 466
Abd al-Aziz ibn Baz 465
Abd al-Aziz ibn Mitab Al Rashid 204-205, 208, 211-221
Abd al-Aziz ibn Muhammad (ruler of Buraida) 167-168, 181-182
Abd al-Aziz ibn Muhammad ibn Saud 84-86, 88-89, 91-94, 96, 102-103, 114, 116-117, 120, 122-125, 127-129, 133, 142, 162
Abd al-Aziz ibn Musaid 284
Abd al-Karim al-Maghrebi 227
Abd al-Muhsin ibn Abd al-Aziz 359, 361
Abd al-Mutalib 184

Abd al-Rahman ibn Abdallah 158
Abd al-Rahman ibn Faisal Al Saud 187, 199-201, 203-204, 208, 210-214
Abd al-Rahman ibn Hasan 15, 72, 163
Abd al-Rahman ibn Mishari ibn Saud 116
Abd al-Rahman ibn Nasir 14
Abd al-Rahman ibn Rubayin 278
Abd al-Rahman al-Jabarti 14, 138, 144, 151
Abd al-Rahman al-Shamarani 339
Abd al-Rahman al-Sharif 20, 417, 426-427
Abd al-Wahhab Abu Nuqta 55, 103, 109-110
Abd al-Wahhab ibn Sulaiman 64-65
Abdallah Abu Butayyan 180-181
Abdallah al-Bassam 15
Abdallah ibn Abbas 71
Abdallah ibn Abd al-Aziz 154, 395, 398, 437, 441, 466, 473, 480
Abdallah ibn Abd al-Latif 65
Abdallah ibn Abd al-Rahman 359, 437
Abdallah ibn Ahmad Al Khalifa 165
Abdallah ibn Ali Al Rashid 168-169, 171, 172, 176, 178
Abdallah ibn Faisal Al Saud 179-182, 186-187, 192-196, 198-203

Index

Abdallah ibn Hasan 124
Abdallah ibn Husain (emir, later king of Transjordan) 208, 241, 248–249, 263, 330, 348–349
Abdallah ibn Ibrahim ibn Saif 65, 76
Abdallah ibn Jiluwi Al Saud 211–212, 274, 278–279, 438
Abdallah ibn Mitab ibn Abd al-Aziz 254–255
Abdallah ibn Muhammad (Al Saud) 102, 163
Abdallah ibn Muhammad ibn Abd al-Latif Al al-Shaikh 227, 292
Abdallah ibn Muhammad ibn Abd al-Wahhab 15, 76–78, 120
Abdallah ibn Saud 134, 142–143, 145, 149–155
Abdallah ibn Thunayyan 175–176
Abdallah ibn Yahya Al Zamil 181
Abdallah ibn Zamil 178
Abdallah al-Qasimi 20
Abdallah al-Sallal 362–363, 370, 373, 376–377
Abdallah al-Sulaiman 296, 298–299, 316, 430
Abdul Hamid II (Ottoman sultan) 205
Abha 259–260
Abqaiq 329
Abu Arish 109–110, 118
Abu Bakr 269
Abu Dhabi 173, 186, 194, 345–347, 381–383, 385, 388–389
Abu Hadriya 329
Abu Ras al-Nasiri 75
Abu Talib 71
Acca 101, 140
Adamov, A. A. (Russian consul) 210–211
Aden 173, 233, 235, 241, 250, 275, 285, 345, 373
Adib al-Shishakli 330
Afghanistan 321, 469, 472, 473
al-Aflaj 30, 87, 163, 168, 178
Ahmad (imam of Yemen) 362
Ahmad Agha 142
Ahmad Al Sudairi 186, 201
Ahmad Al Thunayyan 438
Ahmad Amin 20
Ahmad Faizi Pasha 219–220
Ahmad ibn Abd al-Rahman 437
Ahmad ibn Jabir Al Sabah 254, 275
Ahmad ibn Nasir ibn Uthman al-Muammari 15
Ahmad ibn Zaini Dahlan 14–15
Ahmad Shukri Yakan Bey (Ahmad Pasha) 160–161, 163, 170, 173

Ahmad Zaki Yamani 450, 453, 455
Ajlan ibn Muhammad 211–212
Ajman 39, 48, 85, 92, 117, 163, 165, 175–178, 181–182, 192–193, 198, 210–211, 214, 228, 239, 253, 273, 279, 294, 381, 383
Akram Uddajah 412
Al Aid 259
Al Ali 169
Al Arayar 159, 161, 164, 335
Al Bassam 181
Al Fidan 117
Al Hazzani 224
Al Humaid 54
Al Jiluwi 294, 438, 446
Al Khalifa 91, 108, 165
Al Marra see Bani Murra
Al Muammar 15
Al Muhanna 215, 222
Al Rashid (the Rashidis) 55–56, 169, 205, 304
Al Sabah 108
Al Saud (the Saudis) 11–13, 15, 19–20, 22, 30, 34, 39, 55, 118, 126, 130, 191, 199, 287, 303, 328, 333, 430, 437, 439, 441, 446–447, 467, 475, 476, 477, 480 and *passim*
Al Shaalan 54
Al al-Shaikh 90, 158, 187, 290–291, 304, 335, 439–440, 448
Al Subhan 221–222, 254
Al Sudairi 175, 446
Al Thunayyan 15, 175, 438
Al Ulayyan 179, 202
Al Zamil 179, 181
Aleppo 16, 35, 66, 108, 111
Alexandria 144, 374
Ali, Imam 71, 97
Ali Al Rashid 169
Ali Bey 91, 141
Ali bey see Badia-y-Leblich
Ali al-Dabbagh 282, 284
Ali ibn Husain (King Ali) 208, 261–263, 309
Ali ibn Muhammad ibn Abd al-Wahhab 90, 154
Ali Kahya 95, 110
Allenby, General 244
Amin al-Rihani 20, 23
Amman 257, 262
Amr ibn Hasan 359
Anaiza 30, 37, 56, 87, 150, 153, 162, 167, 170, 172, 178–183, 202–203, 215–216, 219–220, 310, 340, 419, 426, 430, 459

566

Index

Anatolia 35
Anaza 39, 44, 48-50, 53, 60-61, 110, 113, 116-117, 124, 131, 164, 174, 273, 278
Anwar Sadat 384-385, 399
Aqaba 244, 275, 283, 349
Arabia 12-13, 16-17, 22-24, 29-40, 45, 49, 51, 54, 56, 58, 60, 63, 71-73, 79-80, 96, 112, 127, 137, 141, 172-173, 210, 234, 250, 268, 311
    central 18-19, 35, 55-56, 59-60, 70, 88, 94, 115, 160-161, 168-169, 172, 174, 184, 196, 208, 220, 223, 273, 309
    eastern 20, 40, 59-61, 66, 70, 111, 161
    north-western 18
    northern 18, 35-36
    south-eastern 109
    southern 18
    western 39, 208
Arabian Gulf (the Gulf) 23, 30, 36, 60, 91, 106-108, 165, 172-174, 184, 186, 190-191, 206-209, 211, 213, 215, 225-226, 231-233, 296, 314, 318, 325, 381-383, 389, 469-472 *passim*
Arabian peninsula 111, 287, 368, 469
Arabian Sea 191
Arafat, Yasir *see* Yasir Arafat
Araif 224, 439
Arayar ibn Dujain 84-86, 113
al-Arid 30, 61, 65, 94, 129, 163, 214, 222, 280, 294, 307-308, 442
al-Arish 99
al-Artawiya 227-229, 273, 278
al-Ashari 68
Asir 55, 93, 98, 109, 148-150, 164, 169-170, 172-173, 183-184, 207, 236, 259-260, 281-285, 294, 301-302, 413-415, 419, 446
Ataiba 39, 92, 117, 131, 153, 202, 222, 228, 263, 273, 279-280, 294, 395, 430
Auda 124
Aun al-Rashid 208
Awazim 48, 214, 228, 424
Ayayna 161
Azzan ibn Qais 192, 194

Badia-y-Leblich (Ali bey) 16, 132-133, 135, 137
Badr ibn Abd al-Aziz 359, 361, 368
Baghdad 14, 16, 59, 65-66, 80, 88, 93-96, 101-102, 110, 140, 154, 184, 193, 199-200, 207, 209, 213

Bahhan 430
Bahra 264
Bahrain 14, 17, 35, 71, 91, 106, 108, 117, 129, 131, 142, 149, 165, 167-168, 172-173, 175, 177, 185-186, 188, 190, 194, 206, 232, 238, 314-315, 318, 381-382, 444, 456
Balahita 430
Balfour Declaration 244, 263
Baluchistan 338
Bandar ibn Talal Al Rashid 196
Bani Hajir 177, 214, 228, 294, 430
Bani Hanifa 61
Bani Husain 164
Bani Khalid 40, 54, 60-61, 81, 86-87, 89, 94, 153, 161, 163-164, 177, 214, 228, 294, 335
Bani Murra (Al Murra) 40, 87, 117, 175, 177, 198-200, 211, 214, 294, 422-423
Baqum 39
Baraiq 143
Barrak 60-61, 87
Barrak ibn Abd al-Muhsin 89-90, 94
Basra 14, 16, 30, 59, 65-66, 75, 78, 88, 94, 99, 107-108, 110, 128-129, 170, 181-182, 195, 209-210, 219, 226, 232, 245
al-Batina 30
Beirut 360, 361, 369, 397, 470
Belyaev, E. 78
Berlin 211
Bisha 93, 149-150
Black Sea 100, 146
Blunt, Lady Anne 17, 54, 195, 201
Bombay 107, 190, 209
Britain 38, 60, 107-108, 142, 165, 173, 184-185, 192, 206-209, 213-214, 217, 225, 233, 235, 238-244, 247-250, 253-258, 260-266, 275-276, 279-280, 283, 287, 296, 313, 315, 321-324, 327, 342-343, 345-347, 356, 363, 379-382, 442-443, 456, 480
British India 19, 156, 206, 322
Brockelman, C. 15
Brydges, Sir H. Jones 16, 95
al-Bukairiya 217
Buraida 30, 86-87, 124, 153, 161, 168, 174, 179, 181-182, 202, 216-217, 219-220, 222-223, 310, 340, 415, 419, 459
al-Buraimi 19, 165, 171, 186, 188, 194, 304, 345-347, 356, 380, 382-383
Burckhardt, John Lewis 16, 18, 33-34, 38, 41,

Index

44–45, 47–53, 75, 80, 95–96, 112, 115–116, 118–119, 124, 126, 128, 130, 132–133, 136–137, 145, 149–150
Busaya 275
Bushire 17, 214
Buyuk Sulaiman Pasha 88, 93, 95, 98, 110

Cairo 66, 75, 91, 99–100, 140, 142–143, 146–147, 149–150, 153, 155, 161, 163, 170, 172, 348, 350–353, 357, 361, 368, 370, 376, 385–386
Calcutta 18
Campbell, Colonel (British consul-general) 172
Carruthers, A. D. M. 18
Carter, President Jimmy 397
Chernomyrdin, Victor 473
Chevalier, J. M. 21
China 11, 35
Churchill, Winston 327
Clayton, Sir Gilbert 263–264, 275–276
Corancez, Louis Alexandre Olivier de 16, 18, 75, 96, 118, 120, 135, 148
Cox, Sir Percy 217, 225, 238, 244–246, 254, 257–259
Crane, Charles 312
Crete 173
Curzon, Lord 206–207, 248

Dahham ibn Dawwas 62–63, 84–86
Damascus 35, 48, 65–66, 100–101, 105, 111, 140–141, 241, 244, 253, 384
Dammam 165, 167, 177, 185–186, 329, 403, 405, 408–409, 426, 459
Dari ibn Fuhaid ibn Rashid 218
Darin 225
Davletshin (Russian officer) 17, 73
al-Dawasir 30, 87, 92, 163, 209, 280, 294
Dawqa 326
Delhi 18
Dhahran 312, 318, 326, 337, 351, 356, 370, 372, 380, 405, 408, 426, 442, 459, 463
Dhofar 383
Dickson, H. R. P. 17, 48, 230, 279, 304–305
Didier, Charles 17
Dilam 86–87, 172, 456
al-Diriya 13, 34, 39–40, 55, 61–63, 65, 71, 79, 81–88, 90–93, 96, 100, 102–103, 109–138, 140–142, 149–155, 158–161, 177
Diwaihis 88

Dobbs, Henry 276
Doughty, Charles M. 17, 36, 38, 41, 48, 51–52, 56–57, 178, 198
Driault, Edoard 96
Dubai 173, 381, 383
Dulaim ibn Barrak 278
Dulles, John Foster 356
Durma 84, 124, 153

Eastern Province (al-Hasa) 13, 17, 20, 29–31, 34–35, 38, 54, 58–61, 65, 70, 81, 84–90, 94–95, 98, 113, 117–118, 125, 135, 149–150, 159, 161, 164, 168, 172, 173, 175, 177–178, 182, 186, 190, 198, 211–212, 215, 225–227, 231–233, 238, 253, 268, 273–274, 277, 279, 291, 294, 301, 304–305, 310, 315, 336–338, 341, 345, 354, 369, 396, 405, 408, 410, 411, 413–415, 419, 421, 431, 446, 449, 454, 463, 469, 477
Eddy, W. A. 325
Egypt 13, 20, 29, 35, 38, 48, 56, 71, 91, 96, 100, 105, 107, 123, 131, 137–138, 140–141, 144, 148–149, 152–153, 159, 162, 169, 174, 175, 188, 206–207, 235–236, 241, 288, 292, 296, 327, 337, 340, 343, 347–353, 357, 361–363, 369–370, 372, 374, 376–377, 381, 384–385, 387, 394, 400, 428–430, 433, 469, 476, 479–480
  Lower Egypt 141
  Upper Egypt 99
Eisenhower, General Dwight 351–352, 390
  Eisenhower Doctrine 351–352
Eritrea 469, 470
Ethiopia 338, 469, 470
Euphrates 78, 94, 209

Fahd ibn Abd al-Aziz (King Fahd) 335, 355, 357, 366, 371–372, 395–397, 437, 441, 453–455, 459, 465–466, 468, 469, 470, 471, 473
Fahd ibn Abdallah ibn Jiluwi 279
Faisal Al Dawish 228, 254, 256, 259, 264, 270, 272–275, 277–281
Faisal ibn Abd al-Aziz Al Saud (King Faisal) 250, 269–270, 290, 297, 299, 328, 335, 347, 352, 354–360, 364–369, 371–377, 379, 381–384, 386–387, 391, 394, 433, 437, 439
Faisal ibn Fahd 473

Index

Faisal ibn Hamud Al Rashid 221
Faisal ibn Husain (king of Iraq) 208, 241, 243–244, 254–255, 280–282
Faisal ibn Musaid 394–395
Faisal ibn Turki 163–164, 167–172, 174–191, 192, 195–196
Faisal ibn Watban Al Dawish 124, 152, 158
Falah ibn Hithlain 177–178
Fath Ali 98
Fawwaz ibn Abd al-Aziz 361, 368
Fida 71
Ford, President Gerald 398
France 17, 99, 107–108, 184, 207, 240, 296, 456
Fuad (king of Egypt) 282, 292, 349
Fuad Hamza 19, 167, 293–294, 323, 344
Fujaira 381
Fuyud 430

Gamal Abdel Nasser 350, 352–355, 369, 373–377, 384, 387, 469
Gaza 16, 43, 117
Genj Yusuf *see* Yusuf Pasha
Germany 206, 209, 321–323, 326, 372, 456
al-Ghafiri 106
Ghaith Pharaon 412
Ghalib ibn Musaid (Sharif Ghalib) 92–93, 98–100, 103–104, 109, 145–147
Ghamid 259, 263
al-Ghatghat 228, 249, 278
Ghawar 329
al-Ghazali 68–69, 75
al-Ghosaibi 410, 411
Glubb, John Bagot (Glubb Pasha) 18, 256, 274–275, 350
Goldziher, I. 22, 69
Gorbachev, Mikhail 472
Grey, Sir Edward 233
Grobba, Fritz 322–323
Guarmani, Carlo 17, 190
Gulf *see* Arabian Gulf

al-Hada 261, 264
Hadhramawt 39, 109, 131, 136, 462
Hadm 131
Hafiz al-Asad 384, 399
Hafiz Wahba 19, 75, 269, 276, 296, 299, 305, 322
Hail 55–56, 169, 171, 178–179, 195–198, 202–203, 209–211, 213, 215–225, 236, 246, 254–255, 277, 304, 309–310, 446

Hamad ibn Yahya ibn Ghaihab 168
Hamadan 65–66
Hamid al-Din (dynasty) 362
Hamid ibn Nasir 103
Hamilton, L. 315–316
Hamud Abu Mismar 109–110
Hamud Al Subhan 222
Hamud ibn Samir 88
Hamud ibn Umar 249
al-Hanakiya 150, 152, 170
Hanifa 30
Hannel, Captain (British resident) 173
Harad 373, 376
Harb 33, 39, 103, 131, 150, 153, 183, 217, 228, 273, 278, 280, 418
al-Hariq 49, 114, 168, 171, 175, 223
Harma 86, 114, 123
al-Harq 120
al-Hasa *see* Eastern Province
al-Hasan Al Idrisi 283–284
Hasan Hibbatullah 85
Hasan ibn Ali Al Aid 259–260
Hasan al-Kalay 104
Hasan Nasif 368
Hasan Shukri, Colonel 216
Hashemite (dynasty) 235, 247, 256, 262, 268, 281, 282, 308, 309, 343, 348, 351, 352, 353
Hawazim 294
al-Hawta 114, 163
Hijaz 14, 16–17, 20–21, 29–31, 33, 35–36, 38–39, 49, 55, 58–60, 63, 65, 67, 70, 79–80, 88, 91–93, 98–100, 102–105, 109, 111, 129–131, 136, 138–139, 145–149, 151–152, 159, 162–164, 166, 172, 175, 180, 182–184, 207–208, 218, 224, 236–237, 240–241, 243–250, 259–279, 281–284, 288, 293–299, 301–302, 309–310, 341, 348–349, 395, 402, 406–407, 410, 414, 421, 440, 444, 446–447, 449, 460, 477
al-Hilwa 171
Hitaim 48, 163, 217, 228, 278
Hitler, Adolf 299, 321, 322, 323, 344
Hodeida 109, 173, 184, 283, 286, 377
Holmes, Major Frank 314–315
Huber, Charles 17
Hufuf 49, 90, 164, 166, 168, 170, 178, 188, 198, 231, 294, 317, 406, 408, 419, 430
Hujalain 161
al-Humaid ibn Abdallah ibn Zahal 124

569

Index

Humphrys, Sir Francis 281
Huraimala 84, 115, 122
Hurley, P. 325
Husain, Imam 97
Husain (king of Jordan) 353, 361, 368, 373, 387
Husain Bey 161
Husain ibn Ali (Sharif Husain, King Husain) 208, 223, 235-236, 239, 240-250, 255, 259-263, 266-269, 309
Husain ibn Ghannam (Ibn Ghannam) 13-14, 22, 62-66, 70-71, 75, 81, 85, 88-90, 113, 122-123, 125, 195
Husain ibn Muhammad ibn Abd al-Wahhab 90
Husni al-Zaim 330

Ibn Abd al-Wahhab see Muhammad ibn Abd al-Wahhab
Ibn Isa 195, 199
Ibn Khaldun 48
Ibn al-Qayim 69, 74-75
Ibn Sanad 75, 78, 95, 128, 131-133
Ibn Saud see Abd al-Aziz ibn Abd al-Rahman ibn Faisal Al Saud
Ibn al-Suwaidi 15
Ibn Taimiya see Taqi al-Din ibn Taimiya
Ibn Zaini Dahlan 77, 130
Ibrahim Abu Takiha 368
Ibrahim Al al-Shaikh 440
Ibrahim Al Subhan 255
Ibrahim al-Haidari al-Baghdadi 14
Ibrahim ibn Isa 14
Ibrahim ibn Ufaisan 106
Ibrahim Kuchuk 169, 173
Ibrahim Pasha 151-155, 158-160, 171
Ikhwan 19, 23, 77, 220, 227, 231-237, 246, 247, 249, 253-267 passim, 268-281, 289, 290, 292, 300, 301, 304, 307, 308, 309, 337, 341, 349, 427, 478
Ilitaim 57
India 13, 17-18, 38, 155-156, 206, 321; see also British India
Indian Ocean 108, 173, 206
Iran (Persia) 63, 66, 70, 155, 266, 381-382, 386, 388, 393, 469-471 passim
Iraq 12, 16-17, 30, 33, 35, 63, 66, 70-71, 94-97, 100, 110, 117, 137, 172, 182, 184, 204, 241-242, 256-257, 259, 263-264, 274-276, 278, 280-281, 288, 313, 321-323, 348, 351-353, 385, 389, 427, 469-473 passim

Lower Iraq 93, 96
southern Iraq 175, 182, 208
Isa Al Ali 171
Isfahan 65-66
Ismail Bey 170-171
Israel 340, 377, 386, 388, 398, 469, 470, 472, 476
Istanbul 38, 59, 103, 145-145, 152, 155, 184, 190, 206-207, 208-209, 211, 215, 234
Italinski (Russian ambassador) 99-100, 102-103
Italy 308, 456

Jabal Akdar 106
Jabal Shammar 17-18, 30, 55, 61, 87, 92, 149-150, 158, 163, 169-171, 174, 176, 178, 188, 190-191, 195-198, 201-205, 208-212, 214-216, 218-222, 224-225, 234, 236, 246-247, 250, 253-256, 294, 354, 415
Jabir ibn Mubarak Al Sabah 239
Jabrin 413
al-Jadida 146
Janub 129
Japan 11, 399, 456
Jaussen, A. 18, 73
Jawf 49, 72, 149, 221-222
Jazzar Pasha 101-102
Jerusalem 66, 100, 246, 266, 386, 399, 476
Jidda 18, 21, 36, 38, 55, 59-60, 71, 99-100, 102, 138, 145-148, 169, 182, 184, 208, 248, 249, 262-265, 267, 276, 284, 296, 302, 308-309, 315, 317, 344, 346-347, 351, 367, 369, 375-376, 387, 406, 408-409, 417, 427-430, 434, 442-443, 446-448, 472
Jiluwi ibn Turki Al Saud 179, 181
Jizan 376, 419, 442
Jones, Captain (British resident) 185
Jordan (Transjordan) 17-18, 244, 255, 258, 280, 323, 330, 346, 348-350, 352-353, 363, 377, 384, 386, 408, 429
al-Jubail 71, 81, 310, 317, 408, 456
Juhaiman al-Ataiba 396
Juhaina 117

Karbala 96-98, 102, 110, 136, 141
Katakura, M. 21, 417
Keith, Thomas 145, 150
Kennedy, President John F. 372
Khadija 71, 269

Index

Khaibar 29, 195, 413
Khalid ibn Abd al-Aziz (King Khalid) 366–368, 371, 395, 397–399, 437, 466
Khalid ibn Faisal 438
Khalid ibn Luwai 249, 261, 270, 284
Khalid ibn Salih al-Mahfuz 462
Khalid ibn Saud 170–175, 186
Khalil Pasha 160
Khamis 62
al-Kharj 30, 61, 71, 85–86, 114, 129, 162–163, 213, 406, 419, 428
Khartoum 377, 383
Khashoggi 412
al-Khobar 317, 408–409, 428
Khomeini, Ayatollah Ruhollah 396–397, 471
al-Khurma 93, 145, 246–249
Khurshid Pasha 169, 171–173, 175, 186
Kirram ibn Mani 289
Kissinger, Henry 391, 394
Kitchener, Lord 241
Kozyrev, Andrei V. 473
Krymski, A. 22
Kuchuk Sulaiman 110
Kurdistan 65–66
Kuwait 12, 17, 108, 173, 175, 181, 185, 190, 201, 204, 206–212, 214–215, 219, 221, 223–225, 227, 231–233, 245–246, 253–255, 264, 273, 275–276, 279–280, 304, 316, 321, 330, 377, 381–382, 384, 388, 391, 393–394, 399, 427, 431, 444, 472, 473

Laoust, H. 22
Lawrence, T. E. 17–18
Lebanon 250, 308, 329, 348, 429, 433, 469, 470
Libya 382, 384
Lihyan 418
Lloyd George, David 250
London 19, 273, 299, 313, 315, 346, 348, 438
Longrigg, Stephen 21, 93, 315
Lorimer, J. C. 173, 190
al-Luhaya 117

Maan 240, 349
Maazeh 72
al-Madaifi 55
Maghreb 100
Mahd al-Dhahab 316, 408
al-Mahfuz 462
Mahmut II (Ottoman sultan) 164

Maimuna bint al-Kharis Umm al-Muminin 71
Maitland, Admiral 172
al-Majmaa 65, 86–87, 123, 153, 162, 202
al-Mallaha 181
Manama 108
Manasir 294
Manfuha 61–62, 65, 84, 113, 122, 160, 162–163, 166
Mansur ibn Abd al-Aziz 308
Margoliouth, D. S. 22, 65–66
Marib 127, 373
McMahon, Sir Henry 241–243
Mecca 12, 17, 18, 21, 29, 34, 36, 38, 48–49, 55–56, 59–60, 64–66, 69–71, 79, 91–93, 98–105, 107, 113–114, 130, 135, 138, 140–148, 149, 155–156, 163, 166, 169, 173, 178, 182–183, 208, 224, 240–241, 243, 262–263, 265–266, 270, 274, 278, 281, 284, 286, 296–297, 301–302, 309–310, 395–397, 403, 408, 411, 417, 427–429, 440, 446, 459, 463, 465–466, 471
Medina 12, 29, 30, 36, 59, 65, 68, 70, 79, 99–100, 102–105, 111, 136, 138, 140–141, 143, 145–146, 149–150, 152, 155, 159, 163, 169–170, 182, 195, 207–208, 219, 246, 263–265, 278, 281, 301–302, 308, 310, 334, 395–397, 403, 408–409, 411, 415, 419, 427–429, 440, 446, 459
Mediterranean 329
Mengin, Félix 13–14, 18, 39, 66, 87, 89, 96–97, 102, 130, 134–135, 145–146, 150, 153
Mesopotamia 48, 94, 207, 235–236
Middle East 35, 39, 63, 70, 207, 235, 237, 242, 312, 315, 321, 323–326, 328–329, 334, 341–342, 347–348, 350, 352, 356, 384, 393, 402, 404, 448, 463, 470, 472
Midhat Pasha 198–199
Mishari ibn Abd al-Rahman ibn Mishari ibn Saud 163, 165, 167–168
Mishari ibn Busayis 278
Mishari ibn Ibrahim ibn Muammar 84
Mishari ibn Saud 62
Mishari ibn Saud ibn Abd al-Aziz 161, 165
Mitab ibn Abd al-Aziz 220
Mokha 164, 184
Montagne, R. 18, 72
Morocco 156
Mosul 264, 313

Index

Moulay Sliman 156
Mubarak Al Sabah 208–211, 215, 224–226, 236
Mubarak ibn Adwan 115
Muhammad, Prophet 12, 58, 64, 69, 72, 74, 78, 104, 128
Muhammad Agha (Turkche Bilmez) 164
Muhammad Al Idris 248
Muhammad Al Sabah 204, 208
Muhammad Ali 140–149, 151, 155, 158, 160–164, 169–170, 172–174, 183
Muhammad al-Badr (Imam al-Badr) 362, 373–374, 376
Muhammad Hamid al-Faqih 75
Muhammad ibn Abd al-Muin ibn Aun 164
Muhammad ibn Abd al-Rahman Al Saud 211
Muhammad ibn Abd al-Wahhab (Ibn Abd al-Wahhab) 12–16, 64–67, 71–85, 88–91, 104–106, 118, 120, 123, 125–127, 155, 158, 160–162, 175, 179
Muhammad ibn Abdallah Al Khalifa 185–186
Muhammad ibn Abdallah Al Rashid 196, 198, 201–205
Muhammad ibn Afaliq 84
Muhammad ibn Afaliq al-Hanbali 15
Muhammad ibn Ali al-Shawkani 14
Muhammad ibn Aun 166, 175, 180, 183–184
Muhammad ibn Faisal Al Saud 179, 198
Muhammad ibn Ibrahim Al al-Shaikh 359, 367
Muhammad ibn Ismail 76
Muhammad ibn Khalifa 177, 185
Muhammad ibn Mishari ibn Muamar 154, 161–162
Muhammad ibn Muammar 61
Muhammad ibn Saud (emir of al-Diriya) 62–63, 82–83, 84–85, 126, 132
Muhammad ibn Saud (son of King Saud) 264, 358
Muhammad ibn Talal Al Rashid 255
Muhammad al-Murtadha 76
Muhammad al-Nabhani 14
Muhammad al-Qahtani 396
Muhammad Rashid Rida 20
Muhammad Saud al-Kabir 439
Muhammad Surur al-Sabban 298
Mulaida 203
Munikh 84
Munir al-Ajlani 66
Muntafiq 78, 88, 94–95, 111, 175, 182, 208, 215, 224
Musaid, Sharif 91
Musaid ibn Abd al-Rahman 336, 366, 437
Muscat 49, 100, 106–109, 136, 142, 165, 168, 185–186, 188–190, 192–194, 206–207, 225, 345–346
Musil, Alois 18, 22, 44, 172, 230
Mutair 39, 60, 91, 113, 116, 124, 150, 152–153, 159, 164, 172, 181, 202–203, 210, 214, 217, 220, 222, 227–229, 253–254, 263, 273, 275–276, 278–280, 289, 294
Mutlaq al-Mutairi 106, 109

Nadir Shah 65–66, 97
al-Nafud (Great al-Nafud) 18, 29–30, 41
al-Najaf 98, 110
Najd 14, 16–18, 29–32, 34–36, 38–39, 48–49, 58–61, 63, 65–66, 71, 79–81, 83–86, 91–93, 111, 115, 117–119, 122–123, 129, 142, 149–154, 158–165, 170–173, 175, 177–179, 182, 196, 198, 200, 210–211, 213–220, 223–234, 236–238, 240, 244–250, 253–280, 282, 287–288, 290–291, 293, 297–299, 306–308, 310, 340, 408, 414, 444, 446–447
  central 85, 172, 219
  southern 85, 171, 219
Najim ibn Duhainim 91
Najran 30, 39, 70, 85, 92, 109, 117, 136, 285, 372, 442
Namiq Pasha 184, 193
Napoleon 16, 96
Nasir al-Said 19, 354, 368, 397
Nasser, Gamal Abdel *see* Gamal Abdel Nasser
Nawwaf ibn Abd al-Aziz 357
Negev 117
Neutral Zone 316, 319, 330–331, 347, 369, 431
Niebuhr, Carsten 17, 39, 46, 70
North Africa 236
Northern Frontier Province 446
Nuri Al Shaalan 222

Oman 14, 17, 29, 36, 40, 58, 60, 70, 106–107, 111, 117, 129, 131, 142, 149–150, 165, 168, 172–173, 192, 194, 225, 238, 345, 348, 379, 444, 471; *see also* Trucial Oman
Gulf of Oman 106, 165
Onassis, Aristotle 333
Oppenheimer, M. von 17
Ottoman empire 29, 63, 70, 79–80, 206–208, 235–236, 239–240, 287

572

Index

Pakistan 399, 429
Palestine 16, 111, 260, 263, 266, 288, 344, 349, 387, 469, 476
Palgrave, William 17, 72, 163, 195
Paris 150, 240, 438, 462
Patna 156
PDRY (People's Democratic Republic of Yemen) *see* Yemen, South
Pelly, Colonel Lewis 17, 123, 185, 190
Persia *see* Iran
Peshawar 156
Philby, H. St John 14, 17, 22, 60–61, 85, 96, 159, 170, 199, 246, 248, 269, 276, 291, 304, 312, 315, 402

Qabus (sultan of Oman) 379, 383
Qahtan 39, 87, 116, 163, 166, 168, 181, 198, 222, 259–260, 280, 294
Qasim 17, 30, 35, 49, 56, 60–61, 85–88, 115, 124, 129, 135, 149–150, 152, 161, 163, 166, 171, 174–176, 179–183, 188, 191, 198, 201–203, 210, 214–222, 224–225, 227, 280, 291, 309, 415, 419
Qatar 89, 165, 180, 185, 190, 206, 345, 381–382, 385, 388
al-Qatif 16, 35, 89, 117, 149, 159, 164–165, 168, 173, 190, 198–199, 225, 232, 238, 273, 310, 396–397
Qawasim 106–108
Qom 65–66
Qunfudha 147–150
Quraish 235, 418, 430
Qusai 141
Qusaiba 216
Qut 164

Rajih 147
Ranya 149–150
Ra's al-Hadd 185
Ras al-Khaima 106, 108, 117, 159, 185, 381, 383
Ras Tannura 281, 318, 329, 370, 408, 426
Rashad Pharaon 334–335
Rashaid 48
Rashid (shaikh of Dubai) 383
Rashid Ali al-Gailani 322
Rashid ibn Humaid 165
al-Rass 150, 152–153, 170, 340
Raymond, J. 16, 80, 96, 119–120, 132, 134
Red Sea 48, 141–142, 235, 322, 331, 469, 470
Reilly, Sir Bernard 285

Riyadh 11, 17, 19, 21–22, 30, 49, 56, 61–62, 84–86, 114, 123, 160, 162–166, 168, 175–178, 180–182, 185, 187–189, 193–194, 196, 198, 202–204, 210–234, 237–250, 255–257, 261–262, 268, 273–274, 284, 290–293, 296, 299, 304–308, 310, 334, 341, 349, 351, 353–354, 367, 369, 378, 380–381, 383–384, 390–391, 399–400, 406, 409, 419, 424, 427, 429–430, 433–434, 436, 443, 446, 463–464, 466, 468–473
Roosevelt, President Franklin D. 325–327, 334, 344, 411
Rousseau, J. B. L. J. 96–97
Rub al-Khali 17, 29, 40, 211, 236, 331, 422
Russia 11, 23–24, 207, 244, 250, 473; *see also* Soviet Union
al-Rustaq 192, 194
Rwala 54, 73, 222, 273, 300

Saad ibn Fahd 361, 368
Saad ibn Mutlaq 173, 186
Saadun ibn Arayar 61, 86–88
Saadun Pasha 224
Sadat, *see* Anwar Sadat
Saddam Husain 472
Sadiq 61, 84
Sadlier, George F. 16, 152–153, 158
Said (sultan of Muscat) 165
Said Ahmad Barelwi 156
Said ibn Sultan 108
Salih ibn Abd al-Muhsin Al Ali 169
Salih Isa Bukari 411
Salil-ibn-Razik 14–15
Salim Al Subhan 202
Salim ibn Mubarak Al Sabah 239
Salim ibn Rifada 282–284
Salim ibn Shakban 103
Salim al-Kharq 106
Salonika 147
Samawa 94
Sami al-Hinnawi 330
Sami Pasha al-Faruqi 220–221
San Remo 313
Sanaa 76, 109, 286, 368, 370, 377–378
Saqr 106
al-Sarif 211
Saud ibn Abd al-Aziz (King Saud) 255, 274, 278, 299, 333, 335–338, 340, 342, 350–355, 357–358, 360–361, 366–367, 370, 433, 438

Index

Saud ibn Abd al-Aziz Al Rashid 222
Saud ibn Abd al-Aziz Al Saud 84, 86, 88–93, 95, 99–100, 102–103, 109–111, 117–120, 125–125, 127, 130, 132–134, 142–143, 148
Saud ibn Faisal (son of King Faisal) 438, 471, 473
Saud ibn Faisal Al Saud 179, 187, 192–195, 198–200
Saud ibn Hamud Al Rashid 221
Saud ibn Hizlul 15
Saud ibn Muhammad ibn Miqrin 61
Saud ibn Salih 236, 239
Schlesinger, James 394
Selim III 100
Shakespear, Captain 225–226, 237–238
Shakir ibn Husain al-Dabbagh 282
Shamir 214
Shammar 32, 49, 87, 92, 95, 113, 116, 181, 196–197, 202–203, 209–218, 220, 222–224, 228, 237, 246, 277, 294, 430
Shaqra 13–14, 116, 152–153, 340
Shararat 48, 57, 294, 424, 430
Sharif Husain *see* Husain ibn Ali
Sharif Pasha 102
Sharja 165, 173, 381, 383
Shatt al-Arab 280
al-Shawkani 76
Shcherbatov, A. G. 17, 190
Shiyuf 418
Shukri al-Quwatli 350, 352
Shunana 217
Sibila 278, 279
Sidqi Pasha 219–220
Silmiya 114
Sinai 117, 235
al-Sohar 107, 186
Somalia 217, 338, 470
Soviet Union (USSR) 265–266, 296, 321, 323, 342, 344, 385, 464, 469, 470, 472, 473; *see also* Russia
Sprenger 32
St Petersburg 99–100, 207, 211
Stroganov, S. A. 17, 190
Subai 39, 85–86, 92, 117, 163, 172, 175–176, 178, 181, 198, 211, 214, 222, 228, 280
Sudair 30, 49, 61, 65, 84–85, 114, 124, 129, 149, 153–154, 161, 163, 166, 202, 225
Sudan 156, 384
Suez 98, 141, 144
Suez Canal 207, 235, 329

Suhul 39, 92, 117, 163, 181, 211, 214, 222, 228
Sulaiman ibn Abd al-Wahhab 64, 77, 84, 87
Sulaiman ibn Abdallah 158
Sulaiman ibn Hamad ibn Ghurayar al-Humaidi 81
Sulaiman ibn Ufaisan 87, 89
Sulaiman Ulayyan 411–412
Sultan ibn Abd al-Aziz 335, 366, 371, 466
Sultan ibn Ahmad 106–107
Sultan ibn Hamud Al Rashid 221
Sultan ibn Humaid ibn Bijad 249, 261, 270, 273–274, 276–278
Sultan ibn Saqr 165
Sulubba 48, 57, 430
Sumatra 156
Suq al-Shuyukh 88, 94
Surur, Sharif 92
Sykes-Picot agreement 243, 244
Syria 16, 33, 35, 48, 54, 65–66, 71, 94, 100–101, 105, 107–108, 111, 117, 131, 136–137, 148, 164, 173, 203, 241–242, 250, 257, 308, 322, 325, 327, 329–330, 348, 350, 352, 361, 385–386, 392, 433
Syrian desert 17, 36, 129, 131

Tabuk 31
Taha Husain 75
Tahir al-Dabbagh 282, 284–285
al-Taif 38, 55, 71, 104, 145–146, 163, 249, 261–262, 270, 284, 308, 334, 366, 408–409, 411, 415, 429, 441, 443, 472
Taima 224
Taiz 379
Taj 71
Talal Al Rashid 178–179, 181, 195–196
Talal ibn Abd al-Aziz 357–361, 368–369, 424, 447, 481
Tami ibn Shuaib 148–149
Tamisier, Maurice 17, 169
Taqi al-Din ibn Taimiya 22, 68, 74–76
Tarafiya 222
Tehran 381, 389, 471
Tharmida 85, 162, 215
Thuwaini (sultan of Muscat) 192–193
Thuwaini ibn Abdallah 78, 88, 94
Tigris 94
Tihama 39, 109, 111, 117–118, 129, 131, 136, 283, 286
Tobruk 443
Tokyo 331

Index

Transjordan *see* Jordan
Trucial Oman 173, 185, 190, 206, 233, 345, 381
Truman, President Harry 344
Tuais 78
Turaba 92, 147, 150, 249-250
Turakulov (Soviet consul-general) 298
Turkey 63, 93, 296, 327
Turki Al Sudairi 192, 194
Turki al-Hazzani 171, 175
Turki ibn Abdallah ibn Muhammad ibn Saud 161-168
Turki ibn Utaishan 346
Tusun 141-146, 150
Twitchell, Karl S. 312, 315, 421

UAE *see* United Arab Emirates
UAR *see* United Arab Republic
Ubaid ibn Ali Al Rashid 169, 171, 176, 178-179, 195
Umar ibn Muhammad ibn Ufaisan 165, 168, 170, 175
Umayyads 54, 101
Umm al-Qaiwain 173, 381, 383
United Arab Emirates (UAE) 383, 399, 444
United Arab Republic (UAR) 354, 361, 372, 377
United States (US) 11, 296, 308, 313, 324-327, 329, 342, 344-345, 351, 361, 373, 376, 380, 384, 410, 433, 442-444, 456, 465, 469, 470, 471, 472, 475, 476, 480
Uqail 36
al-Uqair 165, 168, 175, 190, 225, 254, 258, 276
US *see* United States
Ushaiqir 85
USSR *see* Soviet Union
Uthman dan Fodio 156
Uthman ibn Abdallah ibn Bishr (Ibn Bishr) 13-14, 19, 48, 65-66, 85, 95, 97, 102, 104, 115-123, 124-125, 127-130, 135, 143, 149, 152, 155, 161, 167, 178-179
Uthman ibn Hamad ibn Muammar 81, 83-84
Uthman ibn Sanad al-Basri 14
Uthman al-Mudhaifi 93, 99, 103, 145-146
Uthman Pasha 175
Uyaina 38, 61-63, 65, 81, 83-85, 122, 134

Venezuela 331-332
Vidal, F. 20

Volney, Comte Constantin François de 16, 32, 40-45, 52-53, 57, 72

Wadi al-Dawasir 49, 113, 149-150, 168, 178
Wadi Fatima 21, 417-418
Wadi Hanifa 30, 71, 154
Wadi Hawran 198
Wadi al-Rum 30
Wadi al-Safra 143
Wadi Sirhan 198
Waliullah Shah 156
Wallin, G. A. 31-32, 47, 50, 72, 190
Washington 325, 352, 391
Washm 13, 30, 84-85, 114, 129, 149, 161, 163, 176, 214-215, 225
Wellsted, James R. 17, 168
Western Europe 329, 393, 399, 419, 433, 456
Weygand, M. 173
Wilhelm II 206

Yahya ibn Hamid al-Din (Imam Yahya) 220, 224, 266, 283, 285
Yamama 66, 86, 114
Yamani, Ahmad Zaki *see* Ahmad Zaki Yamani
Yanbu 16, 104, 142-144, 149, 170, 266, 408
YAR (Yemen Arab Republic) *see* Yemen, North
Yasir Arafat 399
Yemen 14, 29, 33, 36, 40, 48, 58-60, 70-71, 92, 109, 111, 117, 129, 131, 136, 164, 173, 183, 207, 220, 224, 236, 266, 281-286, 311, 348, 350, 362-363, 370-380
  North Yemen (YAR) 378-379, 470
  South Yemen (PDRY) 235, 373-375, 378-379, 469, 470, 480
Yusuf ibn Saadun 256-257
Yusuf Pasha (Genj Yusuf) 105, 140
Yusuf Yasin 296, 299

Zafir 60, 85-87, 95, 110, 116, 228
Zahran 259
Zaid (shaikh of Abu Dhabi) 383
Zaid (emir of al-Diriya) 61-62
Zaid ibn Arayar 89-90
Zaid ibn Khalifa 194
Zaid ibn al-Khattab 71
Zaid ibn Mughailis ibn Haddad 167
Zaid ibn Musa Abu Zura 62
Zaid ibn Zamil 85-87
Zaidan ibn Hithlain 273, 277, 279

Index

Zaire 470
Zamil Al Subhan 222
Zamil ibn Faris 62
Zia ul-Haq 399
al-Zifli 85–86
al-Zirikli 19, 293–295, 300, 302–305, 310, 334, 343
al-Zubair 14, 65, 88, 108, 110, 170, 181
Zuwaid 167–168